Cambodia Now

Cambodia Now

Life in the Wake of War

KAREN J. COATES

McFarland & Company, Inc., Publishers
Jefferson, North Carolina, and London

LIBRARY OF CONGRESS CATALOGUING-IN-PUBLICATION DATA

Coates, Karen J., 1971–
Cambodia now : life in the wake of war / Karen J. Coates.
p.   cm.
Includes bibliographical references and index.

ISBN 0-7864-2051-0 (softcover : 50# alkaline paper) ∞

1. Cambodia — History —1979–   2. Cambodia — Description and travel.
3.   Cambodia — Social conditions.   I. Title.
DS554.8.C63   2005   959.604'3 — dc22   2005001715

British Library cataloguing data are available

On the cover: (front) An infant in a hammock at the
Chea Sim orphanage, Siem Reap, 2003; *(back)* A recent landmine
victim in the Anlong Veng Health Center. Anlong Veng, 2001
(Photographs by Jerry Redfern)

Manufactured in the United States of America

*McFarland & Company, Inc., Publishers
Box 611, Jefferson, North Carolina 28640
www.mcfarlandpub.com*

For the people of Cambodia

Acknowledgments

This book would not be if it weren't for my husband, Jerry Redfern. My partner, my friend, my editor, my photographer, my cook and housekeeper, my companion and constant source of inspiration — I owe more than words can say to this man. I would like to thank him, also, for agreeing to pick up our lives and move to Phnom Penh in 1998. None of this would have come about had he not trusted and believed in our life together.

I would like to thank my parents, Gary and Helen Coates, for their continued support, both emotionally and financially. I will always treasure the writing space they afforded me in a cottage on Silver Lake. Likewise, I am grateful to Bob and Jenny Redfern for their support and sizable contribution to the Redcoates's work fund, without which this manuscript would not have traveled between countries and continents with such ease on such a tiny laptop.

Special kudos to Kathleen McLaughlin, editor extraordinaire. Kathy, Kate, Kitty — call her what you will, she is a word wizard. Her keen eyes made this book much better.

I am indebted to many, many remarkable people in Cambodia without whom I could not have begun to know or understand Cambodia today. For their insights, wisdom, witty conversation and their help in reporting, translating, guiding and getting around, in no particular order, I sincerely thank: Lor Chandara, Heng Sinith, Saing Soenthrith, Van Roeun, Professor Kang Om, Sok Chea, Ma Anou, Ramlee, Ke Monin, Morn Sor, Kay Kimsong, Hat Saman, Kimsan Chantara, Pin Sisovann, Kim Chan, Kim Thy, Khuy Sokhoeun, Ham Samnang, Touch Rotha, Hing Channarith, Kim Samon and the rest of *The Cambodia Daily* staff who have helped me over the years. I would especially like to thank the members of the Wildlife Conservation Society Cambodia Program, the largest such group in the country. There are many folks doing fine conservation work in Cambodia; I just happened to hook up with WCS in several instances. For their wisdom and help in arranging some fantastic research trips, I thank Heng Sovannara, Tom Evans (doubly so, for his critical editing eye), Phet Phaktra, Hout Piseth and Hang Mary as well as Joe Walston and Colin Poole. I would also like to acknowledge Sebastien Marot, Samnang, Sachak and the rest of *Mith Samlanh* for coordinating a trip with an outreach team.

For their unending encouragement and generosity, I thank Masaru and Yumi

Goto. They are always ready to extend their time and energy (as well as couch and closet space).

There are dozens of people whose insights into Cambodia have helped me form the ideas in this book. For numerous thought-provoking conversations and email exchanges, I thank Elizabeth Wright (who left us way too soon, whose spirit remains in our lives and travels), Chris Decherd, Matt Bording, Seth Mydans and Judy of Wisconsin. I am particularly indebted to the folks at camnews, whose daily email installments of news from Cambodia helped me keep up to date, even while living in the international news vacuum of the American hinterlands.

Some of my research was funded by grants and writing awards. I am grateful to Literary Arts, Inc., of Portland, Oregon; the Council for Wisconsin Writers; and Willamette Writers for their support. A number of sections in this book originally appeared in magazines and newspapers, in slightly different format, including: *The Chattahoochee Review*, *National Wildlife*, *Archaeology*, *Wildlife Conservation*, *Drexel Online Journal*, *NurseWeek*, *BBC Wildlife*, *Overseas Radio & Television*, *Massage*, *San Jose Mercury News*, *Fresno Bee*, *South China Morning Post*, *The News-Review* and, of course, *The Cambodia Daily*.

And lastly, 140 years after his excursion to Cambodia, I thank Henri Mouhot for his prescient comments, many of which sadly remain true today; many of which sadly do not.

Contents

Acknowledgments   vii

Preface   1

Introduction   5

Map of Cambodia   12

PART I: RECONCILING THE PAST

1. War Remnants: Mines and Desperation   15
2. Leaving Cambodia: Passing the Test   34
3. Genocide: Ghosts on the Porch   41
4. Angkor: An Empire in Ruins   50
   Interlude: Siem Reap to Phnom Penh   67
5. Neighbors and Borders: Enemies Through Time   70
   Interlude: The Admiral's House   88
6. Kampuchea Krom: The Land Next Door   90
7. Anlong Veng: Beyond the Khmer Rouge   97
   Interlude: Bond and Than   106

PART II: LIVING NOW

8. Democracy: Rice and Rights   111
   Interlude: Sam and Vic   127
9. Violence and Crime: Blood in the Street   130
   Interlude: A Runner's Course   138
10. Psychology: After the Tragedy   142
11. The Wanderers: A People Uprooted   152
12. Women: The Lesser Sex   165
13. Children: Born Against Odds   175
14. Health: Living Against Odds   199
    Interlude: Dog Bite   214

15. Pollution: Sewage and Waste   218
16. Environment: Threats in the Wild   233
17. The Fringe: People on the Edge   253

PART III: LOOKING AHEAD

18. The Crossroads: Tugged in Two Directions   279
19. Development: Building on Quicksand   291
     Interlude: Cops and Dogs   299
20. Heroes: Doing It Their Way   302
21. Prospects: No Easy Peace   325

Afterword   333
Glossary   337
People, Places and Names   339
Organizations   341
Cambodian Time Line   343
Notes   347
Selected Bibliography   365
Index   377

Preface

Cambodia's war did not end when peace began. And neither has peace fully flourished since war has ended. Peace is a process that takes years, even generations. War is not black; peace is not white; a large swath of gray exists in the life between.

On October 23, 1991, nineteen UN member nations signed the Paris Peace Accords, effectively bringing the country's civil war to an end on paper — yet fighting continued through 1998. While the world spoke of Cambodia's peace, Khmers continued to die in their homes in the west, in the north, in pockets of violence scattered around the country. Their villages were shelled and burned, their children mutilated, their lives ruptured. My friend and colleague, photographer Masaru Goto, covered the war through the 1990s. He photographed a wedding ceremony in Battambang Province in 1994, the bride and groom all pert and pretty, dressed in their finest. They danced and sang and celebrated. In the background: shelling, like deadly rain on their wedding day. The couple told Masaru, "Why wait? Who knows what tomorrow will bring. We might die. We want to marry immediately."

For years, this was Cambodia's peace.

In 1993, the United Nations administered democratic elections through the UN Transitional Authority in Cambodia, the largest UN peacekeeping force to that point. It was declared a major success, but the outcome did not reflect the voters' wishes. Nearly 90 percent of registered voters cast their ballots. It was not an election so much as a "celebration," writes American journalist Elizabeth Becker. "Cambodians were dressed in their best sarongs. Families brought picnics." The people were proud to go to the polls, and they gave Prince Norodom Ranariddh's Funcinpec Party 45 percent of their votes. Hun Sen's ruling Cambodian People's Party won 38 percent. This was a delightful surprise to the foreign experts watching. In the most fundamental way, Cambodians embraced democracy. Instead of perpetuating the status quo, Cambodians voted with their own minds and hearts. Freedom of choice had won.

And then it failed. Hun Sen refused defeat. He and his cronies intimidated the nation and threatened to secede several Cambodian provinces. In the end, he was given a power-sharing post with his rival. Ranariddh was installed as first prime minister, Hun Sen as second prime minister. And the Cambodian vote was betrayed.

More than a decade later, as Cambodia still suffers from a crippled government,

1

notorious corruption, rampant violence, widespread poverty and a lack of basic social services, scholars and analysts are backtracking on their original assessments. Former King Norodom Sihanouk has called his country an "international beggar." Cambodia's opposition leaders tell the World Bank that poverty has grown worse, despite $400 million of investments since 1993. And political violence persists.

How and why does this happen?

The answers, like the country itself, are not black-and-white, nor are they simple and easy to declare. And sadly, the answers become even more obscured through the nature of international reporting. Journalists have always flocked to Phnom Penh for burps of big news—coups, riots, bombings, Pol Pot's death, national elections— but the continuing social aftershocks of genocide, war and isolation that hit Cambodians every single day are largely ignored. This is even more true as the news of Cambodia grows tamer, less deadly, and the country falters toward stability. When stability grows in any small country, papers close their bureaus and wires pull their correspondents. The day-to-day becomes less and less known to the outside. But a country cannot be understood through its major events alone. The name "Cambodia" has become synonymous with genocide, war and mayhem — but life goes on. So often the world remembers tragedies and forgets those left behind. So often people think in terms of war and peace but not the shaded conditions between.

An expatriate reporter I worked with in 1988 at *The Cambodia Daily*, an English-language newspaper in Phnom Penh, looked up from his computer screen one day and told the rest of us in the room, "Isn't it funny how our emails home are always so much more interesting than the stories we write for the paper?" That, to me, said we were missing something. Our reporting was not doing this country or its people justice. So often the articles that end up in a newspaper quote official sources and veil the issues in a lexicon of conservative predictability. They do little to depict the spunk, the verve, the color of a people. They trade the spark of humanity for the banality of bureaucracy. "In the West almost no writers of renown have emerged to make literature of the struggles of ordinary people," writes Australian-born journalist John Pilger.

It is my aim to show the ravines of life between Cambodia's bursts of news, to illustrate the in-between. I did not plan this project, this book, from the start of my work in Cambodia in 1998. It evolved over six years. It unwittingly began when my husband, Jerry, and I lived and worked in Cambodia as journalists for a year. We returned many times after that, and we watched a nation slowly grappling with its sordid past, gingerly pasting itself back together. We learned about this country through the stories of people we met. We came to understand more and more through the conversations we had in markets, on the streets, in schools and villages, in private homes. It is through these stories that I hope to paint a portrait of Cambodian society today.

A few specifics about my methods: I do not hope or attempt to cover Cambodia in its entirety — that is impossible. This book does not focus on Khmer history, politics or the ruling elite. There are many worthy books on these subjects already in print, just as there are numerous insightful and poignant memoirs of life under the Khmer Rouge. I aim instead to complement those books by providing something

A monk sweeps the grounds around the historic 100-pillar temple near Kratie. The original temple was built of wood on the site in about 1900. It was destroyed during the Pol Pot regime and its beams were used to build bridges. The new temple was rebuilt in the 1990s, and Prime Minister Hun Sen contributed sixteen pillars to the construction, effectively making it the Temple of 116 Pillars. Kratie, 2001.

new to reflect on Cambodian life through the stories of individuals, to guide the reader toward informed conclusions about this society.

It is significant timing. The United Nations and the Cambodian government have finally drafted an agreement to put former Khmer Rouge leaders on trial. With luck, proper funding and much planning, those trials may start in 2005. But critics say too much time has passed already. They wonder whether justice will come before the remaining perpetrators die. These leaders are growing old and weary but living in freedom. That freedom is a festering wound in the gut of a nation. The victims wish to be heard and understood.

Most of my sources in this book are named. When they are not, it is for what I believe to be a valid reason: the people have asked me not to name them (though this rarely happens), they fear losing a job or home, they fear violent reprisals for what they say, or, in a few cases, their words and stories tell something significant about Cambodia but they come through chance conversations and encounters in which my role as a journalist was not made clear to them.

The grammatical quality of direct quotes in this book depends on the context in which they were taken. In some cases, Khmers have spoken in fractured English or French. In other cases, I have spoken in fractured Khmer or Vietnamese. Some quotes have been translated by interpreters with years of experience, others by kids who know a bit of English. For the most part, when people have spoken to me in English, I have written their quotes precisely as stated. If the quote is a shaky translation or rough statement in English, I have corrected the grammar for clarity.

Throughout the book, I refer both to the U.S. dollar and the Cambodian *riel* (and sometimes the Thai *baht*). For several years now, the exchange rate has remained consistent, about 4,000 *riel* to the dollar (and about 40 *baht* to the dollar). All three currencies are used in Cambodia. For the most part, if a transaction is made in dollars, I use dollars. If it is made in *riel*, I note the price in *riel* and its equivalent in dollars.

And finally, while much of this book is grim, that is not my sole intent. I do not wish to paint an overly grisly picture of Cambodia, though many of the individual stories are. With expanding tourism in recent years, many accounts of Cambodia depict a beautiful country with charming people. If I did not agree, I would not feel so strongly about showing the other sides to this country that I have also come to see and understand. Just as Cambodia is not all grim, neither is it all glorious. I believe passionately that someone needs to tell these stories, to compile them, to spread them, because it is what the Cambodian people themselves want and deserve.

In late 2001, after working more than three years on this book, I was asked to summarize Cambodia, to tell an acquaintance about the country. My sister-in-law works in a small-town Wisconsin library, and there she met a woman named Judy who was planning to adopt a Cambodian baby. They talked, and later my sister-in-law asked me to send Judy a few notes on the country. The request caught me off-guard. I had no idea what to say.

It took me weeks to formulate an answer. In the end, what I wrote for her was an introduction to this beleaguered country that has equally captivated and perplexed me now for many years.

Introduction

I lie awake in morning fog, wondering what to write. Blank pages, so white they sting my eyes. I scribble, type, delete, searching for words of the perfect hue. How do I tell her about Cambodia? How do I paint the pictures in my mind?

It is nearing the end of 2001, and I gaze through my drizzled window in Oregon. I look upon leaves lacquered in silver mist. Judy, an acquaintance I know only through email, has asked me to describe Cambodia for her. I wonder how best to arrange the pieces, little vignettes of life. Cambodia is a power that fires my work, sculpts my soul, leaves me speechless. My muse, my antagonist, all the same. I can give her chapters on children or democracy or health or environment. But to summarize the country, its people, in an email, to catch its essence in a message — that's an overwhelming task.

Jerry and I moved to Phnom Penh on New Year's Day 1998. He went to work as a freelance photographer, I as a copy editor at *The Cambodia Daily*, an English-language newspaper that trains Cambodian journalists. I took the job because I had studied in Vietnam and I fell in love: the people, the food, the culture, the street sounds that woke me each morning; horns and squeaky bikes and the shuffling feet of women selling rice from baskets slung over bamboo poles. I wanted to feel so alive again. But Cambodia is not Vietnam, and nothing went as we had imagined. Few things in Cambodia do. We left the country thirteen months later, much sooner than planned. We vowed no return, but we eventually did, again and again.

Judy will love and cradle a child borne of a chaos few Americans have known. They will live in a comfortable American burg, just as I did for eighteen years. Judy and I come from the same swatch of Wisconsin land. I grew up amid corn and cheese and beer; well-cropped lawns garnishing small suburban castles; quixotic neighborhoods like Barrington Woods and Glen Kerry. My parents still live on Independence Drive, a name we take lightly, a word no Cambodian does. At the entrance to my parents' subdivision is a stone sign worth more money than a dozen Cambodians earn in an average year.

I aim to sketch Cambodia for Judy, as Georgia O'Keeffe painted the things in her head. She saw shapes—shapes for which she knew no words, shapes that came to her out of the blue. She painted flowers in series, starting with their entirety, their leaves and all the world around them. Each subsequent painting zeroed in, more precisely. She enlarged and cropped, as a photographer would. The final painting showed a simple slice, just a piece of the whole, just the black jacket of a jack-in-the-pulpit. "Nobody sees a flower, really, it is so small. We haven't time…." she said. So she painted them big, in infinite detail, to "surprise" the world into taking time to look at them.

It's difficult to paint with words because they are achromatic, lying flat on the page. I try to give dimension to words, to type shapes on paper, little slices for Judy to assemble into a collage.

I start with the numbers that no Cambodian can escape:

On April 17, 1975, the Khmer Rouge seized Phnom Penh, declared Year 0, emptied cities and enslaved a nation. They taught children to kill elders. Kids were forced to eat weeds and bugs just to survive. They were killed if caught stealing food. The regime lasted nearly four years. At least 1.7 million Cambodians, nearly a quarter of the population, died of disease, torture and starvation in that time. The Vietnamese invaded in late 1978, toppling the Khmer Rouge government and flushing their leaders into the jungle. The Vietnamese left in 1989, but civil war lasted another nine years, in the forests, in the feverish minds of guerrilla soldiers. Jerry and I lived in Phnom Penh during pivotal times— Pol Pot's death, the country's first independent elections, bloody riots and the end of war.

After the last Khmer Rouge soldiers defected, the Cambodian government and the United Nations began discussing how to punish the perpetrators of genocide, how to bring justice to a land with none. When I write to Judy, these negotiations are ongoing. They will continue for another year and a half until finally, in 2003, an agreement is born. And maybe — yes truly maybe — murderers and butchers will be held to account.

Cambodia is colored by numbers. Numbers tell you who lives, who dies, how many people survive — or not — based on little more than karma or luck. They tell you that every year, 13,000 people die of tuberculosis. Land mines kill and maim more than 600. Every child under five suffers up to seven respiratory infections each year. The AIDS infection rate is almost 3 percent, higher than anywhere else in the region, and for years it rises faster in Cambodia than in any other Asian country. Annual income averages $280. Tourism is rising steadily, more than 790,000 people a year, but 22 percent of those tourists come for sex. Every time Cambodia holds an election, local or national, dozens of people die in political violence. These statistics change little in the years I watch Cambodia.

But Judy needs more than numbers. She needs a panoramic view. She should know the country tugs on the heart. Here I am, years later, writing a book about a place I thought I could, and would, leave behind. Yet Jerry and I return time and again; we return for the Cambodian people.

I think about what Paul Theroux says of his first trip to Africa with the Peace Corps in 1963. He writes, years later, that he could not find Africans in any book at that time. Classical authors like Conrad and Hemingway disappointed him because "they ignored Africans or else made them insubstantial figures in a landscape…. As for Africans themselves, they were like a well-kept secret." It's the same with literature on Cambodia today. The politicians, the bosses, the educated elite — their voices are recorded. Survivors who have left for America or France — their words documented. But the rest, the vivid chroma of average Cambodian days— it gets lost in the composition.

I try, for Judy, to paint lives beneath facts, but she must understand my point of view. I left Cambodia the first time bitter and scared. I was trampled by a flood of monks in saffron robes when soldiers broke their protest through the streets. They marched peacefully to mourn a slain friend. I arrived to cover the event, notebook in hand. I watched, through layers of flesh, as batons smashed skulls on pavement. I can still hear the thuds.

Another night, I watched a thief put a gun to Jerry's head and demand the gold wedding band on his finger. Three times we were robbed in front of our house. We were shot at; we saw many dead bodies. It was a harrowing year for us, but we had the luxury of leaving.

Yet agony enhances beauty, like the black backdrop for a painted rose. There is good, there is progress in Cambodia too. I tell Judy about a former coworker who built a school in his rural village, using his own hands and money. And another friend who opened a library in his own community. I write to Judy that I am continually amazed by Cambodians who plaster old walls of hardship with dazzling new life. But then, luster is one thing never lacking. I have never sensed life — through eyes and ears, through nose, tongue, hands and heart — more fully than I have in Cambodia. Sounds and colors, tastes and smells explode: purple bougainvillea cascading

Sambo the elephant trundles down a Phnom Penh street heading home to a field on the outskirts of town after a day of work carrying tourists around Wat Phnom. Phnom Penh, 2003.

over balconies, monks in orange strolling beneath parasols of gold, sweet jasmine caking a room, the clanking of aluminum spatulas against woks of bubbling oil, shrill cicadas marking the night or roosters rupturing a dawn. When Jerry and I returned to the States, to Wisconsin, in 1999, the sterility jolted us. Stark quiet woke us in the night. Our noses curdled in the absence of smell.

There is history, too, in Cambodia that rouses a mind to life. You can wander for days, even weeks, through the ancient Angkor temples, every nook and nodule carved with dancing nymphs and powerful gods. When we lived there, the ruins were crawling with eager kids waiting to lead you by hand to headless Buddhas and faceless nymphs, looted long ago, sent worlds away to museums and shops in London, Paris, New York. Cambodia's children are a bridge to the past. They are the country's future.

Yet, as I write all this to Judy, I'm not sure how to convey the complexity of a Cambodian childhood. How do I explain that some orphans have parents, some kids are stolen, some children are sold for a small sum? Sometimes a broker from Phnom Penh will appear in a village and tell a young mother: "Give me the kid. I'll give you $50, and you'll get pictures of the child's happy new life overseas." And the broker will go away, with the kid in her arms, and the mother will think it's all for the best. But she starts to wonder when the letters don't come — they never arrive — and she never hears another word of her child.

Eventually the U.S. government gets involved. It tries to stop such breaches of human dignity. As I write to Judy, her adoption is up in the air. Adoption proceedings are stopped and started, stopped and started, with everyone — kids, parents-to-be, adoption agencies— in limbo until an OK arrives. For some, it eventually does (for Judy it will), but others continue to wait years.

Just as Cambodia's orphans always do.

For our last story in 1999, Jerry and I visited an orphanage where some of the babies had AIDS. Those children never had a shot at foreign adoption; foreign embassies wouldn't allow it. That old yellow building was the only home they would ever know. We visited the orphanage again two years later, but the rules had changed. Journalists now needed government permission to enter and observe. We didn't have time for the red tape; it could have taken the entire month we had in Cambodia that year. I still wonder what we would have found. Who's inside that orphanage today?

In reality, most orphans never get the option of leaving their land. Those kids live on the streets, they work for their food. They shine shoes or peddle flowers or sell their bodies. Jerry and I get to know many street kids over the years. They own nothing except the will to survive. I have tried to envision that sort of life, a life with nothing. Just a body, a being, no possessions. I recall when I was nine years old, we moved to the outskirts of Milwaukee, and my parents said we'd be "poor" for a while, until our previous house sold and the recession receded. That was 1981, during the thin years, but none of us understood "thin" as Cambodians do.

Twenty years later, I draw an image for Judy, of walking through the far northeast corner of Cambodia along a sandy trail through overhanging crops and scattered huts. We met an old man with ripples of veins on skinny, wrinkled legs. He came up from behind and passed us on the path. He had walked ten hours from his home. He sought a small village ahead with his teenaged daughter and young thigh-high son, who dangled a roll-your-own cigarette from his lips. Another long day on a sunburnt path that kept going and going behind us, all the way to Laos if the inclination arose. Jerry took the man's photo, then the three continued on. The girl changed clothes in two steps and a twirl; off with one sarong, into another, a flash of undies, a peek at the bra, on with a bright green shirt, the color of rice in an incandescent afternoon. Presto. She was dressed for town.

When we reached the village, I plopped my dirty self on a snack stand and bought neon-colored sodas, each 2,000 *riel*, 50 cents. Corn chips, 400 *riel*, 10 cents. A triangular pouch of candy, 200 *riel*, 5 cents. We ate and drank our goodies, then spotted the old man again. Father and daughter were cleaning the yard across the road, trimming trees, dragging branches to a pile. They worked for food. They had walked the ten hours to town because they had nothing to eat.

We asked if they had any money.

No.

Jerry extended the man 1,000 *riel* as payment for the photo he had taken. The man examined the tattered note and handed it to his daughter in confusion. He asked what it was.

One thousand *riel*, Jerry said. Twenty-five cents.

That pleased the father and daughter immensely, and they bowed in gratitude.

Buy rice, we told them. One thousand *riel*, it would buy two pounds. Then we said goodbye. We crossed a river by boat, 1,000 *riel* for both of us, 25 cents. We bought coffee, 1,000 *riel* a glass, 25 cents. We purchased water, 1,000 *riel*, 25 cents.

One thousand *riel*, 25 cents. The man hadn't known.

I tell Judy more. I tell Judy that Cambodians survive today amid the death that haunts their past. I try to impress that notion upon her. Everyone had, everyone has, stories of murder. I know a woman who, at age seven, crawled to safety from the Khmer Rouge through a field of human bones. Another woman watched soldiers rip the liver from her father's body and eat it while he bled to death. She has a divot in her head where her father's murderers whacked her with a hoe, trying to kill her, too. They left her in agony with her parents' bodies.

How do thirteen million people live after so much pain?

I tell Judy that Jerry and I have visited the Killing Fields of Choeung Ek a few times. It is an eerily peaceful place — more than 100 mass graves amid tranquil village landscapes. More than 8,000 human skulls displayed in a memorial that towers over pastoral grounds. And amid all that death at Choeung Ek, I found beauty. A brilliant monarch butterfly fluttered over a green hole, a grave. An intricate banyan stretched branches and dug roots among human leg and arm bones. Bright red dragonflies with wispy wings flitted among baby trees. So bright, so brisk, so stunning. Those dragonflies, the color of fresh blood.

I must remember that, I tell Judy. I must remember life persists.

I must remember Professor Om, our Khmer teacher, who has told us about his surprising marriage, forced by the Khmer Rouge. He and his appointed wife lucked

Women sit with their fresh produce for sale at the Old Market. Siem Reap, 2003.

out and liked each other, though they were kept in camps six miles apart. Three days each month, the Khmer Rouge permitted Om to walk that distance, trudging through stifling heat to meet his bride for short moments before returning to work in the fields. Decades later, he still calls her his sweetheart. They still love each other immensely.

Sometimes I need reminding of the splashes of light, the bold strokes of color I cherish so much in Cambodia. Being in Cambodia makes me feel sharply aware. I adore the taste of ripe mango in March, the breeze felt on the back of a motorbike, the swirl of incense in a *wat*, the fact that my feet are never cold when I'm there. I cling to the stories of hope, to people like Professor Om, who now has three bright, enterprising college-age sons. It's not all bad; it's not all dead. The Khmer people are a clever, witty bunch, and they tend to find joy in the smallest moments of life. I need to heed that. We can all learn from those who love to laugh as much as they have reason to grieve.

I tell all these things to Judy. I type up my comments and send them to her through the mail. The words are out of my hands but not my mind. I continue to wonder. I'm never finished with Cambodia.

Many people ask me, "Why on earth do you go there?" It's more of an exclamation than a question. They can't understand. Perhaps I go to Cambodia for the same reasons Judy finds a child there — to challenge, awaken, expand the soul. To give. To receive. I am not alone in this thinking, I learn. "Fascination, beauty, stimulation, empathy, compassion. It's a strange place that many people love despite the fact that just about anything you would describe there is awful," Seth Mydans writes to me. He covered this country for *The New York Times* for several years, from his base in Bangkok, and he was also in Vietnam during the American war there. He was stationed in Russia awhile, but returned to Southeast Asia. Cambodia remains in his head, too. "Kierkegaard said, more or less: What is a poet? A poet is a person whose cries of pain come out as beautiful music. Maybe that's a reason to love Cambodia."

A reason to love it, a reason to keep going back. It's a land steeped in poetry, both tragic and terrific.

Map of Cambodia. ©2005 Jerry Redfern.

PART I

RECONCILING THE PAST

1. War Remnants: Mines and Desperation

He hobbles in the dark, an elusive shadow of one leg and one crutch, the whispery glow of a cigarette held in his mouth. A yellow-and-red checkered scarf shrouds half his face. He limps from table to table, slowly, through a sea of customers dining patioside at an Indian restaurant. He says nothing, doesn't see our eyes, just makes his way.

"That's the guy with the face," Jerry says.

He is Bun Na, a man with no right leg and no left eye. A vast, fleshy scar traces the line where a cheekbone should be. We have seen this veiled man before, along the riverfront, near our hotel. He is working now. He works every night. He moves toward the street, plops a cap atop his scarf and heads into the blackness.

His is the face of an everlasting war.

Everlasting. Although the last battles ended in 1998 and the last Khmer Rouge soldiers retired from their jobs that year and Cambodia has lived in "peace" ever since, post-war tremors still joggle this nation. The country has shed its wartime past for "the everyday misery of a land of poverty, injustice and continuing brutality," *The New York Times* reports.

That assessment comes more than twenty years after the genocidal Khmer Rouge regime of 1975–1979, when 1.7 million people died — a quarter of the Cambodian population. Thousands died in a civil war that lasted twenty more years. Everything in this country was destroyed: schools, hospitals, homes, temples, banks, roads, the human mind and human trust. All in shambles. The nation is slowly awakening now. "Step by step," my Khmer friends love to say. Bit by bit, peace is assembled.

But for some, war still wages on. It is indiscriminate. It is evil.

Land mines and unexploded ordnance (UXO) still dot this country, killing and maiming innocent victims every day. These unjust weapons were sprinkled like pepper across the landscape through decades of war. It is impossible to know precisely how many land mines remain in Cambodian soil, but most estimates put the number between 4 million and 6 million. Half of all Cambodian villages have mines in and around them. More than 313,000 mines were destroyed in the decade following UN intervention, but so many are left. Villagers can't wait forever, so they clear the

15

land by hand, readying fields for planting and plots for new homes. The International Campaign to Ban Landmines calls this "spontaneous" de-mining, and it is not unique to Cambodia. A February 2003 Rand Corporation report predicts, at the rate of current technology, it will take half a century to vanquish the world's land mines, responsible for 15,000 to 20,000 casualties a year in 90 countries. In Cambodia, land mines and UXO still kill and disfigure more than sixty Cambodians every month.

In July 2003, a primary school cook in Kompong Thom Province finds an unexploded 81-mm mortar shell while cleaning the school's kitchen. Two months later, four young brothers and a friend retrieve an old shell from a river. It detonates, and they all die. In January 2004, again: Four brothers find an old bomb. They take it home; it explodes. The blast destroys their house and kills all four brothers. Two months later, two brothers and a friend find a war-era mortar and try to extract the explosives to use for fishing. It bursts; they all die.

These examples appear in the papers because several people die at once. Mines, by contrast, kill individually. One casualty does not merit a story—but it should. The tally mounts. It is not just one casualty, but two every day, every week, every month, every year. This is six years after all battles have stopped. That should warrant something.

Jerry and I first meet Bun Na camped in a cart beside the national museum. It is summer 2002, and we have started work on a story about the adult beggars who wend their way through the city. We find Bun Na in his home here on the street, where he lives with his wife, Poeun, and a dog named Leak who is chained to the cart and wears a jingle bell around his neck. We have seen Bun Na here many times, our functional feet passing his body, napping beneath a mat in the cart. Today we stop with Sok Chea, our translator. Bun Na is startled that we want to talk. No one talks to him, he says.

We ask his story, and with a little prodding, it tumbles from his lips. He is in his early thirties. He's from Takeo Province but worked in the west as a soldier for Hun Sen. He stepped on a mine in Pailin just a few years ago. "The government brought me to the hospital, I-79," he says. He stayed in that Phnom Penh military hospital five months until they kicked him out. He had nowhere to go; the mine ended his soldierly life. He had sold his Takeo home years ago to help his ailing mother. She is gone now. So here he is, with Poeun and their dog.

The government did nothing after Bun Na's hospital stay, and he expects that won't change. He hasn't had a job since; he says he'll never get enough money to start fixing *motos* and bikes, a job he can do. "I want very much but no one can help me," he says. He has the know-how, but it costs a few hundred dollars for tools. He doesn't have a few hundred dollars and has no expectation of ever having it. "I feel it's very difficult to work or do anything," he says. "I will ask money from the people forever."

Begging is what Cambodians with no options do. He earns 1,000 or 2,000 *riel* a day, 25 or 50 cents. He and Poeun never thought this would happen to them.

When we first start talking, Bun Na seems to accept this lot in life. But we talk a little longer, and his anger escapes. He's mad at the government for not helping him find a job and at the people who refuse to look at him—although that makes him sad, too. "The people who pass me say the person with no leg, no eye — there's no need to look at him," he explains. He says nothing has really changed in Cambodia. War has ended, but he will live with its legacy forever.

Poeun squats on the sidewalk beside him. "I'm very sad," she says. "My husband has no leg. And sometimes the people don't let us stay here." She means: The police shoo them. Cops round up the beggars, herding them out, threatening force. It's an endless cycle among Cambodia's homeless and the men in uniforms commissioned with "cleaning up" the streets. And so the homeless wander. "We have no limits," Bun Na says. "We walk forever."

I try to ask how he feels, what he would like people to know about him, the person inside this scarred body. I am not sure he fully understands my question, translated from English to Khmer, from one culture to another, but this is essentially what he says: "I am not the same person. Now, I have no eye or leg. I am not whole. I am different." He picks a cigarette from his pack and looks at me with one brown eye and one red socket, glassy and empty. "I want the government to help me. I would like the government to find an easy job for me." Bun Na says he goes to the *wat* regularly to pray. He answers my questions quietly, in sparse words. But five words is all he needs to explain what he wants in life, in the future: "I want to be happy."

When our discussion ends, we walk with Sok Chea, and he tells us he did a school project interviewing amputee beggars and tourists. He wanted to find out what foreigners think, and many told him they did not like to see beggars because beggars make them feel sad, and that sadness interrupts their pleasant vacation. They want a tidy experience, and beggars are not. Sok Chea also learned from the beggars that they don't believe in themselves and they think they have no options — which is largely true. The government does not help its own people, even former soldiers like Bun Na. Corruption is everywhere, Sok Chea says. Poor people are trapped.

The afternoon grows late, and it is time for Sok Chea to leave. We try to pay him, but he refuses. "You try to help my country; I help you," he says. We agree to meet again soon.

We realize our project is only beginning, and I have trouble framing this story. Are we documenting the plight of the homeless? The disabled? These two adjectives invariably converge, describing veterans. And so the story transforms. It is about disgrace, about the egregious discarding of a population. Cambodia is full of veterans, but few people want to deal with them or hire or feed or acknowledge them. So they slink through the streets, hoping for obscurity, for it is better to go unnoticed than to be crucified by cruelty.

We meet Sok Chea again and again, strolling from street to street, asking and hearing more and more stories like Bun Na's. Missing an arm or leg or an eye is more than an amputation of the body, it is a severing of social harmony. A Cambodian who cannot work the fields cannot partake of Khmer tradition. "And a person who is physically disabled can become a burden," says a 1991 report by AsiaWatch and Physicians for Human Rights. It's called *Land Mines in Cambodia: The Coward's War*, published more than a decade before we meet Bun Na. "Many amputees drift to Phnom Penh and become beggars...." So it was in 1991. So it remains.

There is Samnang, thirty-five. His name means "luck," but his ran out in 1990 when he, too, stepped on a mine in Pailin while fighting for Hun Sen. He spent six months in the hospital, then came to Phnom Penh. He heard there was money to be made on this street corner, below the popular FCC restaurant and bar. Here, he earns 4,000 to 5,000 *riel* a day, much more than elsewhere.

Samnang is actually marginally lucky. The government pays him about $12.50 each month, but that's not enough for every day. Not enough to feed a wife and seven kids, so he begs. He has a home, a "cottage" he calls it, but not in the American sense. It's a very small house, and although I don't see it, I imagine many I have seen: shacks with tin roofs, no running water, no electricity, situated beside plains of garbage in slovenly neighborhoods of hundreds like them with barking dogs and kids galore.

A Westerner leaves the foreign correspondents club and heads to his dirt bike. Samnang hobbles over on his crutch and catches 100 *riel*, then returns to our conversation — to which he has agreed if we pay him 2,000 or 3,000 *riel*. He smokes a cigarette in his right hand and drapes his body over his left stump, resting on his crutch. He wants the government to do more, he says.

What would make him happy? The chance to start his own business fixing *motos*. "I know how to fix tires." Sok Chea tells us this is a popular dream for the disabled because it requires little movement, which is painful and difficult for amputees. But it would cost $200 to $300 just to start, and Samnang doesn't have it.

We pay him 3,000 *riel* and wish him luck. We wish him truth in his name.

Phon Pheap cruises the river walkway, his left leg lost to a land mine in Pailin fifteen years ago. He's dressed in army pants, a khaki shirt and one combat boot. Phon Pheap doesn't have a house. He and his seven kids sleep on the street. He was a fisherman before the war, but he didn't like that job and has no wish to fish again. "I cannot find the fish because I have no leg." Many disabled Cambodians answer this way. Whether it's physically true or they're conditioned to think so, they sometimes believe their disabilities make them less than human, invariably incapable.

Phon Pheap never wanted to fight. "Hun Sen arrested me and made me become a soldier," he says. "I got angry but they forced me. I've stopped being angry now."

Sok Chea verifies this story. Many Cambodian men were conscripted, forced into the military. That happened to his cousin, and Sok Chea feared it would happen to him. But he's lucky now because war has ended, and he can don the crisp white shirt of a college student, never having worn a soldier's fatigues.

One morning, we meet nineteen-year-old Sok Chamran inside Wat Ounalom, one of the city's most famous temples. Sok Chamran was never a soldier, but he suffers the curse of his nation's past.

The young man crouches on the red-checkered floor, head down, demure. He wears a towel, covering his stump. We explain why we want to talk.

Sok Chamran has lived in this temple two years. He stepped on a mine in Battambang, his home, while taking his cows to the field. His mother died soon after the accident, and given the circumstances— motherless and missing a leg — this seemed to him a logical place of refuge. "I came to study," he says, which is why many

A monk studies in the evening light at Wat Langka. Phnom Penh, 1998.

young Cambodian males enter a *wat* with shaved head and new orange robes. But Sok Chamran is not here as a novice monk, just a student with no better options. He's not sure how long he'll stay.

I ask what he'll do in the future, and he takes a very long time to answer. He looks away, he doesn't want to answer. There's an uncomfortable silence. And after several vacant minutes he says, "I want to fix *motos*."

I want to know how he feels, what he thinks about the accident. How did he think it would affect his life? His eyes drift again. Monks crowd around and prod him. He says his parents took care of him. For three months, he was in pain. People used to warn him, "Be careful when you go to the mined areas." But he never thought much of it, never thought it would happen to him, "because people used to walk there." He'd seen it over and over in the same area, footprints through the same field. "Before this happened, I didn't care about land mines. Relatives told me to be careful. But the people who told me to be careful also didn't know where they were."

The land mine took Sok Chamran's happiness. "I'm sad in my mind." It also took his innocence. He is an angry young man, mad at the deadly bombs beneath his feet, hidden, speckling his country's terrain. "I want the government to take out all the mines in my homeland, and, especially, I want the government to make a school for all the handicapped children." He doesn't know if that will ever happen.

He's also angry because he comes from a family of farmers, not soldiers. His family did not instigate war, they never fought, they never wanted to. His dad grows corn and plows the fields. "I'm angry at the people who make war."

I ask what he thinks of beggars, street denizens with missing legs. "I feel frightened because I'm afraid in the future I will be begging," he says. "I hope I will find a job, same as anyone else."

Before leaving, we ask Sok Chamran what he would like, what would help him most. He wants a small bag for his schoolbooks, so Jerry and I go to the market across the street and buy a bag for a few dollars. We fill it with notebooks and pens, and we give it to Sok Chamran.

Down an alley behind Wat Ounalom, we find forty-one-year-old Nhat Pon sitting in a patch of shade against a wall. He was a Hun Sen soldier, from Phnom Srong in Kompong Speu Province. He lost his left leg to a mine. He has a two-seater wheelchair for him and his seven-year-old daughter, who has a leg deformity and can't walk. He is a wanderer, looking for solace. "I stay all over the place. Sometimes I stay in Battambang; sometimes I stay in Kampot. I have no place. I'm a beggar. I go anywhere to ask for money. I'm very poor. I have no money, no food. If I had money, I would make a business, such as selling chickens or rice at a little shop."

Nhat Pon says he didn't mind soldiering as a job, but that's no longer an option. His disability precludes it. During the war, he explains, the government took care of its soldiers. But not now.

He's tried to ask for help. "The government doesn't want to see me. I want to see them, but they don't want to see me." He once went to a public ceremony in which swarms of Cambodians gathered in the presence of Prime Minister Hun Sen, who commemorated a new pagoda and school, built with his money. Nhat Pon tried to speak to the prime minister, but Hun Sen's bodyguards blocked the way. Nhat Pon's wife, Pong Sieng, is sitting nearby, and she inserts: The bodyguards kicked her husband.

Nhat Pon hugs his naked baby to his lap. "The people of Cambodia, we have two parts," he explains. "My people are the low part. The prime minister is the high part. So I don't know what to do."

The Khmer Rouge used to tell the Cambodian people, "You are of no value to us, to the system. To destroy you is no loss, to keep you is no gain." When a Cambodian soldier loses a leg or the ability to walk, he, too, is worthless to the system.

In late August 2003, about forty hospitalized soldiers from the Royal Cambodian Armed Forces gather their strength and their chutzpah and march to the Ministry of Defense to complain. Their grievances: The hospital feeds unclean food, and a new proposal would dock their salaries 1,500 *riel* a day to pay for better food and sanitation. The protesters say they cannot afford to lose 1,500 *riel* a day when they make only 40,000 to 70,000 a month. That's about $10 to $17.50. Most of the soldiers are HIV-positive and unlikely to work again. A military official says the issue will be "discussed and resolved." But such issues rarely are.

Once disabled soldiers are discharged from the hospital — those who are — they have little to do. They can't return to their fields. They can't get jobs in the city. They become, as that 1991 AsiaWatch report notes, "a burden." Cambodians live by nature's cadence, by the rain, the floods, the paddies, the harvests of rice. When a man, woman or child can't work through those rhythms of the field, that person's worth has withered.

But there is a place where the disabled can go, a place that inspires some hope. The Kien Khleang Physical Rehabilitation Center sits across the river from Phnom Penh, off National Road Number 6a, down a dirt path that turns to mud in the slightest rain. Inside is a place where anyone in the country can go to be fitted with a free prosthetic arm or leg, or get a free wheelchair or free cane. A free arm or leg — a free chance at a new life.

Jerry and I enter a boisterous foyer and a woman asks us to sign in: name, organization, purpose of visit. The air shrieks and rumbles with the background noise of welding, sawing, drilling, sanding.

This organization is run by Veterans International, a program of the Vietnam Veterans of America Foundation. We meet Rithy Keo, the administrative supervisor, who tells me the center provides only artificial limbs, not job and life skills; those things must be found elsewhere. Most clients have stories like the ones we meet on the street. "Mostly from war by land mines. Eighty percent," he says. Their workload is consistently full, even now, years after war has ended. Some people come with old stumps that were never fitted with new limbs. Others come for new prostheses to replace those worn and used. And sometimes they get new amputees, fresh stumps from fresh calamities. "The war is stopped but the people are still affected by land mines," Rithy Keo says.

I tell him I want to know about the social ramifications of missing a limb. I tell him we've heard people say amputees are thought to be crazy. "That's not true," he assures me. This society is well versed in the dangers that lead to amputation. They understand. "Cambodian people ... they know about this." But some amputees turn to begging. Some are lazy. Some don't want to work. Some think they can earn more money by holding out a hat than getting a job. "If we provide prostheses to them or some nongovernment organization (NGO) provides vocational training to them, they don't want to do work," he says, though he emphasizes: "That's not everybody."

He admits it's harder for the disabled to find jobs. *The Cambodia Daily* reports that government schools refuse to employ disabled teachers. "Sometimes candidates have a mark on their face, and it frightens children in class. Or a teacher with a disabled hand ... or crooked back makes the students feel bad," the Ministry of Education's undersecretary of state tells the paper. Just after the Khmer Rouge regime ended, the government allowed the disabled to teach amid a shortage of qualified candidates. That's all over now. The need is gone, and the disabled are expendable.

Rithy Keo takes us through the center, through the steps to crafting an arm or leg. All clients are interviewed about their history. For each person, the staff makes a mold from which a prosthesis will be formed, each one custom fit. "Every patient has a different stump," he says, and every patient has different needs.

We stroll through the center's shop, passing white plaster in carts and bits of it strewn across the floor. And all around us: replacement body parts. A garbage bin full of feet and legs. Diagrams of human extremities. There's a female leg in a spiked-heel shoe with sandal straps, its toenails painted white. There are two fake hands, one with long, manicured nails on fingers holding a pen and fork. There's an upside-down cast on a stand. It's a foot that will fit a three-year-old child.

A man scrapes and sands and rubs limbs into shape. He's surrounded by brushes, graters, rulers, chisels, palettes and workbenches with tool boards. The room is loud with airbrushes and torches. The next room over, they're making wheelchairs. This is a lively place with welding, sewing, torching, metal being pounded into shape, sparks flying over leather aprons. The sparks are blindingly white, but many Kien Khleang workers cannot see them. Thirty percent of the workers here are disabled themselves.

Outside, rehabilitation begins. There's a playground for adults, jungle gyms and rock beds, a trail of feet painted on the floor where clients practice walking and moving again. One woman traces the path, slowly, on her new left leg, following that blue-foot road. Her name is Moheap, and she comes from Memot, a small town in the east near the Vietnam border. Back and forth, slowly limping on the left. She stepped on a mine a long time ago, in Pol Pot time, she says, but she has come here for a new leg. What she had before is broken. She wobbles back and forth along the rocky path, which is strikingly similar to most national highways in this country.

Not all the clients here are land mine victims. Some have injuries from *moto* accidents or polio. One woman has fallen off her roof; one man's leg was crushed by a tree. On this day, May 20, 2002, a sign in the center's dorm room notes daily attendance at twenty-one amputees, seven polio patients, twenty-eight others and twenty-five family members for a total of eighty-one.

The only patient we see that day who owes his injury to direct combat is twenty-eight–year-old Sok Soreun. He is here to have a broken prosthesis fixed. He has no right leg, but you can barely tell the leg is gone, the prosthesis hidden beneath black pants and blue tennis shoes. Sok Soreun was a Hun Sen soldier and stepped on a mine in Koh Kong Province in 1997. "The government is not interested in me," he says clearly. The government paid him for three months after the accident, and that was it. "It's a long time without a salary." Now he works as a farmer in Takeo, growing corn and potatoes, doing what many amputees say is impossible or impractical. "When I farm, it's very difficult. Not the same as it is for a normal person. I can work like a normal person ... but my work is so slow."

Sok Soreun has stark recollections of his accident. "I remember well. There was fighting, then I lost the battle and I ran back and I stepped on the mine. When I stepped on it, the other soldiers carried me and walked me to Thailand." The mine shattered only his big toe and the ball of his foot, but it took three days to get to Thailand. And for three days, worms ate his foot and gangrene set in, moving up his leg. "The first thing I felt was not fear. I just wanted to die because I lost my leg," he says. "I thought, how can I live?" He worried about his future. "I was born in a farmer's family." It's in his blood. "When I grew up, the government forced me to be a soldier." He lost the battle, he lost the leg, and for a while, he lost his hope.

That changed in 1998, when a doctor at a Phnom Penh military hospital suggested he come here to get a prosthesis. This is a common, recurring government response to most problems: Why should we fix it when a foreign group will do it for free? But the new leg — and people talk about prostheses as "new legs" and "new feet" — improved Sok Soreun's prospects. "I wanted to live because I thought I can do many things, like planting." And that is exactly what he does now, living on his parents' farm. He insists he will not end up on the streets of Phnom Penh. "I will not be a beggar." He is emphatic. "I will not be like other amputees because I have the power to do many things, like other people. If I plant one year, I can eat five years." If this doesn't work, he will make do.

Sok Soreun hurls stark and beautiful words of determination into an atmosphere of weak hope. We chat a bit more, then I hear a commotion and head to the yard.

There is an intense game of volleyball going on. Most players are wearing prostheses and tennis shoes. One man hops and balances on a huge, muscled left leg, his only leg. The right stump hangs just below his red satin shorts. Between the two teams, there's a missing right hand and a lower right arm, a small left arm that doesn't move like the right, and another right arm gone, leaving a limp jersey sleeve to hang from its wearer.

The human eye plays tricks, the subconscious fills the blanks. At a glance, the eyes see nothing unusual about these teams. But in focus, the handicaps become clear. The players do pushups, one-armed and one-legged. Many prostheses are not shaped like real legs; they are more like mechanical sticks, with pins and screws for maneuvering. You can see how they bend, how they work like a human leg would. These players wear muscles of a different kind, for whatever the reason that prompted these limbs, their owners have each endured a brutal exercise of not just legs and arms — but also of the mind.

A year passes, and Jerry and I return to Phnom Penh. We see Bun Na again. We looked for him beside the museum, but his cart was gone, the hedge swallowing the fence, no beggars in sight. Where did they all go? Now in the midday heat, he asks for money outside the FCC. He wears the same yellow-and-red *krama* across his face. Jerry gives him some *riel*, and he thanks us in English — something new.

Jerry and I rent an apartment around the corner from the FCC, and our front porch has a perfect view of the street below, of the beggars we see every year. For months we watch their routines.

We see Bun Na approach a couple of grizzled *barangs*, fresh off a *tuk-tuk*. He hobbles up and brushes his hat against their bellies, the woman first, then the man. But they look instead up the street, for something or someone who perhaps does not exist. They move along as though Bun Na weren't there, nonexistent, invisible to their eyes. He limps off around the corner, with empty hat in his clutches. I can see all this from our apartment balcony with its rattan chairs and purple bougainvillea. Inside, we have air conditioning, hot water, cable TV and a fridge full of food and beer and bottled water and gin and tonic. It's a basic but pleasant place, unremarkable in the hierarchy of expatriate accommodation in Phnom Penh, but a place to which the beggars below could never aspire. Bun Na cannot see us up here on the third floor, but I can spot him. He masks his face and proceeds with his evening's work.

In May 2003, *The New York Times* runs a story about a place called Veal Thom, a place where hundreds of disabled veterans have gone to clear fields, build huts, plant rice and make new lives. We want to go.

Veal Thom is a project entirely conceived and run by the veterans themselves, led by a former Khmer Rouge soldier named Touch Soeur Ly. Veterans International has become involved, almost by default, because people in America read the *Times* story, and they call up; they ask how to help, how to donate, how to get rice and cows to these people. And so, every month or two VI make a trip to Veal Thom with a truck bed full of items: plants, fish, rice, stump socks, crutches, cows.

It is mid–July, shortly before the 2003 national elections, when Jerry and I hitch a ride to this new village with Veterans International. We meet early at the group's office in Phnom Penh as people load a 4 × 4 pickup with a generator and metal rods that will be sawed to height and made into crutches. Our companion and guide is Kim Samon, who speaks English well. We chat along the two-hour ride down National Road 4, heading toward the sea. When we reach a blip in the road called Prek Nul, we turn left down a dirt track, and the trek turns daring.

Kim briefs us on Veal Thom. There are now 1,000 residents, 200 disabled with their families. The village name means "big field," and the residents share almost 5,000 acres of fertile land. It is no easy life. They are surrounded by sparse forest; they have no farming equipment, and most come empty-handed. They must carve a living with nothing but the land they are given and the things they can carry with them.

Many of Veal Thom's residents are former soldiers of all stripes, coming from all over the country. The village sits an hour and a half by oxcart from the highway. When money and food run out, the residents must pay for an oxcart to take them to that highway or walk that distance — often on crutches — to sell a few bunches of vegetables, homemade charcoal, whatever they have to offer.

Khin Reth gives his son Khin Sroah, age three, a ride to a town meeting in Veal Thom, a village created for limbless former soldiers. Cambodians sometimes treat disabled people as less than human, so the village is an attempt for the families there to lead normal lives. Veal Thom, 2003.

Veal Thom has no school, no paved road, no doctor. Malaria is a problem. People treat themselves when they get sick. "They know some Khmer traditional medicine," Kim says, using trees and plants for fevers and pains. Every two months, a Japanese aid group visits Veal Thom with medicines and supplies.

This is Kim's third visit to the village in a month. He has delivered cows and grain on previous trips. He laughs: Maybe he'll live in Veal Thom someday "to make a farm, to plant trees, to plant rice," he says. "Because I am also disabled." In 1975, he stepped on a mine near the Thai border. He was sixteen at the time. One foot was amputated, the other was scarred. Pants and shoes conceal him, and only a slightly rolling gait hints at the injuries.

There is not much to see in Veal Thom. It's an expansive village, with huts scattered here and there across undulating patches of scrub and trees. At the village entrance sits a large golden Buddha beneath a thatch rooftop, an opulent welcome, donated by King Sihanouk. The landscape is hot and green and clean. Blue mountains line the horizon. Trees in the distance, flowers all around. When voices stop, the air is stingingly silent, the homes swept and cared for, no garbage, no smells but the land around them. It simply feels fresh — a word which, when spoken in Khmer, is equated with beauty, cleanliness, newness and most everything good.

The residents of Veal Thom are missing hands, legs, arms, feet, fingers and eyes. They walk on crutches or on their hands; they crawl on boards; they wheel around in chairs. They do all they can to proceed in life. They are happy to have made it here to stay because out there, out in Cambodian society, people look at them in that certain degrading way.

But here they're all the same. Some fought for Pol Pot, some for the Vietnamese, others for Hun Sen. Some were conscripted; others fought by choice, but now it doesn't matter. "We love each other like brother and sister," one man tells me. In Cambodia, "brother" and "sister" are terms for close friends and confidants as well as siblings.

Touch Sour Ly, the former Khmer Rouge soldier who started this village, has a slight limp beneath his dress slacks, shoes and socks. "I know about the problems of the disabled," he says. He felt compelled to do something for his comrades and his former enemies because no one else did. They regret their past, the things that made them disabled, but they will make the best of what remains. They have nothing more to lose. "We spent a lot of time working for the nation," he says. "Before I worked as a soldier, and I didn't have the economic capital to start a small business. I needed to make an association, so we could help each other." He created a commune to show that disabled people could make their own way and build a dignified life.

He gathered about thirty veterans. They formed a committee, drafted a law. They found this land, fertile and unused, perfect for their needs. "The first time I came here by foot. There was nothing," he says. The land belonged to high-ranking military officials nearby. Touch Sour Ly and his men set up camp and refused to leave, and eventually the officials said OK, stay. The land was parceled into plots 164 by 328 feet. They planted rice and vegetables and started anew. The *Phnom Penh Post* wrote an article, then *The New York Times*. The king donated the twenty-foot Buddha statue at the village entrance, as well as 400 sheets of metal for roofing. And the people started coming.

Among them are people like Huong Rim, who keeps a small shop among bananas, cassava, moss roses, and brilliant marigolds lining the walkway to her house behind. She is not disabled, but her husband, San Son, is missing his right eye and left leg. They lived in a nearby village until Touch Sour Ly asked them to come here. "Touch Sour Ly is a good man," she says. She would like to stay forever, despite the difficulties. Her kids have no school. "They went to school in our old village, but when they came here, they stopped going. It's very far." And people don't have money to pay for their purchases. People take things— small bags of peanuts or crackers—and they don't have money today, so she tells them, "Pay me tomorrow." But tomorrow the people still have no money, and that's just the way it is. She understands their quandary, though it's a hard way to profit.

Just up the dirt path, No San and his family run another little shop. He has no arms and relies on his eight children to help him eat. He was a Khmer Rouge soldier. He lost his arms to a land mine near the Thai border. When the Khmer Rouge were integrated into the government, he was left with nothing to do. He says living here is good for his son and daughters. They grow a wide tropical spread of coconut, papaya, mango, cassava, potato and rice. He feels at home. Outside Veal Thom, people don't talk to him. Here, "people don't look down on me."

His neighbor, Say Bon, knows just what he means. The people here share tools and build homes together. "It is different in our home village ... we have to hire someone to help us build a house." In Veal Thom, they share cows. They share wells. They share an understanding of how and why they're here. "We help each other by heart," Say Bon says.

Kim takes us up the path, talking with villagers as we go. But we don't go all the way, we haven't the time. The track continues two miles, with more huts and families spread all along. We return to the village entrance instead, where a crowd gathers around the Veterans International truck. Kim and our driver measure new crutches and saw them to length, topping each one with a new green plastic armrest. People trade their old, rusty pegs for shiny new supports.

On the drive out, we stop briefly at a highway restaurant for lunch. Over plates of fried beef and pork with tomato, Kim tells us few people visit Veal Thom. Many local authorities see the village as a nuisance, a headache. They know the people there need food, roads, health care. They prefer to ignore the village entirely, he says.

But that — to be left alone — is perhaps more peace than the people have had in a long time. No one is telling them to leave, to get a job, to fade away. No one is giving them the look. No one is looking at all.

Not yet.

It is August, and we finally untangle Bun Na's story with help from a translator. He and Poeun no longer live near the museum. "The police don't allow me to stay there." They have moved across town to the railroad tracks behind a technological school. And his dog, Leak? "The dog died." The money he makes each day? "Last year I got 2,000 or 3,000 *riel* a day. Now I get 5,000 *riel*." That's about $1.25 a day, but he's no better off. Now he has to pay rent, $10 a month. He has to take *motos* between his room and the river. The riverfront, the epicenter of street life, its pull is magnetic. Bun Na hates it, but it's his lifeline.

I ask Bun Na if he has heard of Veal Thom, and he doesn't know anything about it. He wants to know more.

A few mornings later, we meet again. Bun Na wears a camouflaged jacket, one of two tattered outfits he owns. The three of us pile into a *tuk-tuk* and cross the river to Kien Khleang. He rests his stump on the cushion, facing his body toward the street, watching it bounce by as we move through the city.

We meet the Kien Khleang site manager, Hing Channarith, who goes by Rith for short. He tells Bun Na all about Veal Thom. Bun Na is nervous. His left hand trembles. It has smooth skin and long, healthy nails, the sort a woman envies. Rith tells him it's hard. He asks Bun Na many questions— his name, his age, a wife? any kids? any job? And there, Bun Na smiles nervously, sniggers and says he's a beggar.

Rith shows him pictures of Veal Thom, printed from his computer. There is land but no road, no school, no doctor. He repeats: Life is hard, very hard. Do you want to go? If you want to go, you must commit. You must stay and work the land. You cannot leave and return, leave and return, like many in Cambodia, wandering, forever seeking something better.

To all of this, Bun Na smiles and says firmly he wants to go; he is not afraid of farm work.

Rith tells him he must abide by the rules of Veal Thom, creating no problems for the chief or his neighbors.

Again, Bun Na smiles and agrees wholeheartedly. He really, truly wants to leave Phnom Penh. Rith says he will help.

When we return to Bun Na's corner, he resumes his habit and asks us for 2,000 *riel*. When we see him later that afternoon, he's still on that corner, his old crutch a dogged ally. He gambles with the other street dwellers and finishes this day like any other. But tomorrow, he may change his life.

Later in the week: another meeting. Pen Mony of Disability Action Services explains everything again to Bun Na: the hardship, the work, the lack of amenities. He must build a house. He must plant his food. He can cut wood from the forest, but he must make or buy a roof.

Bun Na smiles and nods, still certain of his intentions. He has talked to Poeun; they are not afraid. But he wants two weeks before he commits because he has no money, and Poeun will go to another town to sell his pension.

This is common, Pen Mony says. The government, in theory, owes veterans a pension. They must travel to the towns from where the pension is issued, often many hours or several days away, across an array of provinces. And when they arrive, the money is not there. They go again, and it still isn't there. They spend all their money on transportation and rarely receive the pension due. So they sell the rights to that pension, at cut rate, to brokers willing to pay in cash right now. Oddly, the brokers always manage to collect the pension money on time. It's a racket — and it's the only way Bun Na and Poeun figure they can find the $20 needed to pay off two months of back rent.

We ask Bun Na if he thinks they will be happy in Veal Thom.

He says yes.

We ask if he has any problem leaving Phnom Penh, where we see him every day, the heart of his life, amid a chorus of other beggars.

He answers ardently: No! No problem leaving!

We tell Bun Na: Don't sell your pension. We will try to help.

We write a letter to friends and family. We tell them about Bun Na and Poeun, their cart by the museum, their dog, their life on the street. We tell them about Veal Thom, about this rare chance to change two lives in a resolute way. We hope for $50 to get them started. And we receive in return an outpouring of aid. Over several months a flood of $617 comes in, for Bun Na, Poeun and the villagers of Veal Thom.

Back to Pen Mony. We sit in a circle around a glass-top table, this time with Poeun as well. It is September 4. Poeun tells Pen Mony she wants to wait six more days.

Why? What's the delay? We worry they're hedging.

She wants to wait because she has a paycheck coming. She used to work for the local garbage company, sweeping the city's streets. She quit that job weeks ago; it made her sick. The company owes her money. It's supposed to pay by the tenth. She doesn't want to leave Phnom Penh without cash in hand. The company owes her $30. That money will pay their rent and fuel their move.

For that, they are ready. "The security here is not good," Poeun says, tugging at

Bun Na's scarf, peeling it away from his face. He flinches. Five months ago, a gang beat him up near the FCC. They wanted money; he had none to relinquish. They punched him in the scarred half of his face. His nose bled, and he needed a doctor's attention. That cost more money they didn't have.

She tells us this as we sit here with a brick of *riel*, worth $50, intended for them. That's 200,000 *riel* in notes of 10,000, 1,000 and 500. We hand Bun Na the thick pile and his eye bulges. He doesn't know where to put it. He hands Poeun a wad of 10,000s and tries to stuff the rest into his shirt pocket, but it doesn't fit. He crams money into his pants, the same blue pants he wears every day, pants with hand-stitched seams. His ragged camouflaged jacket covers the lump in his pocket. They make plans to visit the market, to buy rice and dried fish and all the appurtenances required of a new hut in the sticks. And tomorrow, we will all go to Veal Thom. Three days later, Poeun will return to Phnom Penh alone, to retrieve her money.

When we leave Pen Mony's office, the two turn to us, eyes big and sincere, smiles heavy and happy, *sompiahs* profuse and repeated. We can feel their gratitude.

At times during our different stays in Phnom Penh, we have met Bun Na on the street and he's been drunk. He hides his mouth behind his hat, but I can tell. He sweats, his eye goes glassy. Other times, he doesn't recognize us as we step toward him. He begins to extend his hat, as though we're two anonymous foreigners—then he sees, he smiles and offers his hand. A year ago, he hesitated to shake our hands; now he does all the time. Jerry has taken to slipping him 2,000 *riel* in that handshake, and if he doesn't, Bun Na is sure to ask beneath his breath, two fingers extended. I'm still not sure he knows we have an apartment here, that we look down upon his street every day, that we watch him stagger to the same shop where we buy our water and beer. That we see him all the time.

And I'm still not sure Veal Thom will work, not sure he will leave these streets forever, not sure that he can kick the easy oblivion in a bottle of Cambodian rice wine. We have seen too many failed plans in this country; we have seen enough of Cambodia to know not to hope too much. But we are not jaded enough not to try.

Here we are, 500 yards from the dirt turnoff to Veal Thom. We're spending the night with a friend of Touch Sour Ly's, waiting for an oxcart in the morning. We're in a wooden house twenty-five yards from the highway, from all the trucks and vans and buses and *motos* and cars passing by, between Phnom Penh and Sihanoukville, on Cambodia's best and busiest highway. We have that twenty-five-yard stretch to roam, and nothing more. Behind this house are rice paddies and bogs and sopping fields. It is raining; we have nowhere to go.

Bun Na ambles from here to the highway and back, glancing anxiously up the road. Poeun looks at my notebook and says, "You write beautifully," though she can't read a word I've written. Touch Sour Ly lazes in a hammock; he does little to acknowledge Bun Na and Poeun, and this disturbs us. Touch Sour Ly is a bit angry with them, and this is the way Khmers deal with ire between a higher rank and a lower one—even between two former soldiers, two disabled men, two men fighting the same social stigmas.

This is why he's angry.

We all agreed to meet at a gas station early this morning. We sat in the truck, in a light drizzle, and waited. There was no Bun Na and there was no Poeun. We spent hours looking for them, for the house, driving up and down roads and dirt paths parallel to the railroad tracks. The path kept going and going, a long spread of shanties bunched upon it, a medley of brick and wood and metal. People everywhere and tiny muddy corridors shooting off from this one: a slum, a maze of humanity, hundreds poking out from huts, a whole population beyond sight of the university behind this mess. We asked everyone along the way, but no one knew where Bun Na and Poeun lived. There were literally a thousand possibilities, tiny rooms in ominous places. Dogs, chickens, eggs, shops, laundry, kids, bikes, houses, *motos*, teakettles on stoves. A mass of life. A growing knot of worry rose in our stomachs: They took the money and ran. They got cold feet over the thought of so much work. They were robbed. Bun Na got drunk and lost the money gambling.

Finally, a little shirtless kid scampered in front of the truck, guiding us.

And finally, we stopped beside a wooden walkway that led over a mound of sludge and garbage, between wooden homes, down a rickety flight of stairs, through a narrow corridor to a concrete cell in a dark corner. Bun Na was there, on their bed with big sacks of rice and dried fish and a kettle. He was tying a bag of blankets and pillows. There was one window on the far wall, a radio and an old sardine can full of cigarette butts. There was just enough room for one bed and one cistern for water.

Bun Na had gotten a haircut, shaved short along the neckline. He wore a white shirt and blue pants and no hat or scarf when I first arrived. He looked fresh. From the back, he looked like a clean, handsome young man. He scooted around on his bed, packing. Then he turned around, his whole face showing just half a smile with every muscle that still works. He exuded a look of hope I had never seen on him, a certain gravitas, as if this potential wiped clean the slate of his troubled mind. He explained why they didn't show up: Poeun went to get her money. The company called her that morning on a borrowed phone. They told her, come now and get it. That's why they couldn't meet us at the gas station.

All around that room, outside, were piles of wet stinking garbage, the grime of a neighborhood, everything imaginable. Those homes were built on filth. The floor was wet and musty. The only toilet was communal, outside their room, through a narrow wedge in the walls.

Bun Na turned on a fluorescent light, his only light, and it hummed as he stuffed a mosquito net into a sack. He began to roll up their sleeping mat, and he draped a Buddha medallion around his neck. Obviously, they were ready, perfectly willing, to go. We realized we had given them no way to get in touch with us. We felt awful for thinking the worst.

Poeun returned with her money, and the neighbors crowded around to watch the moving. The truck was piled high with their things, with everything they owned — just enough to survive in the woods for a few months, plus a few extras, a few niceties recently bought: a rusty old Chinese bike, a small radio, a cheap pair of sunglasses that promptly broke. As we drove off, Bun Na covered his face, put on those sunglasses, and twiddled a cigarette in his mouth. It was 11:15 A.M.; we had planned to leave at 9. We end up missing the last oxcart to Veal Thom. And that is why Touch Sour Ly is mad.

After dinner that evening, in the house on the highway, Jerry and I are given bedding upstairs inside; Bun Na and Poeun are left below outside. I descend the ladder to find them sitting in the dark. I offer a candle and flashlight and sit with them. I learn they've been married fifteen years. She had a child, but the child didn't live. She asks when we'll return to Phnom Penh, and I say two days more, and she thanks me for accompanying them. She is happy we've come along.

The next morning, everyone rises early with the karaoke machine next door, which starts before the sun emerges. There is little sleep all night, with trucks rumbling down the road, dogs barking, people whispering, an old man snoring, chickens crowing, a radio playing for many hours. The Cambodian countryside is not quiet when people are involved.

But Bun Na is ready. He has fetched his bike from the truck, and he rides little circles up the road. He itches to get there. The others pile onto an oxcart, with Poeun huddled against a blue tarp over everything they own — which fills the oxcart only half way.

All the way there, Bun Na alternates, on the bike, off the bike, on the cart, on the bike, flat on his rump in the mud. He pedals ahead with a big grin, smoking while he rides. It's misting in patches around us; a full rainbow spreads itself over the southern hills. The air smells of indigo, and crickets chirp. Bun Na stops and points to papaya trees. He likes them, he says.

He falls many times on this journey, always picking himself up, always laughing at his misstep. When he meets a dubious bridge, with a hole three feet wide, Bun Na scoots himself across on a log.

When we reach the village entrance, after an hour and a half of trekking, Bun Na and Poeun set up in a small shelter, with tarps for walls. They have neighbors, another family that arrived just two weeks before. Saroeun, the man of that family, stepped on a mine and blew off half his foot. That was decades ago. It has taken him years to carve a niche.

That afternoon, an oxcart arrives in the village with fifteen sacks of clothes. No one knows where they came from, except to say Phnom Penh. Children jump in the piles, they do backflips and somersaults, they screech and run and scamper about. They try on the clothes, they throw it all about them. Little boys wear jackets and shirts made for girls, but no one cares. Everyone loves the bright colors best. Then another cart comes, and another. Suits, shirts, jackets, pants. All used. All needed and appreciated here. A mountain of clothes, with a bevy of people digging, flinging, donning the attire.

We explore the village, now heavy with mud. We introduce Bun Na to people we met before, people whose gardens have grown in six weeks, whose homes are bigger, whose fields are looking more mature. It is a Saturday afternoon, and villagers go about their business. An old woman chops wood; a man stirs a pot of rice.

We pass a villager with a chainsaw, cutting wood to make charcoal. He works above a pit eight feet in diameter with dozens of logs standing upright, packed in tight. These logs will smolder for fifteen days, then he will haul them up the road to the highway to sell them. By the next morning, this pit will be covered and smoking, like a hot earthen igloo.

Then we find the village TV. There is one hut here with an antenna sprouting from its roof. On Saturday afternoons, most every man in Cambodia, if he has the chance, sits down to a boxing match. Today, there are sixteen people gathered in this one room on stilts, eight feet above ground. They are huddled around a fourteen-inch black-and-white "Sunny" TV. They are mostly men. They erupt with oohs and ahhs as the boxers punch. Downstairs, at the base of the ladder, are an uneven number of flip-flops and sandals. Up here, there are many legs resting beside their owners, numerous crutches and more legs stashed against the wall.

Bun Na hesitates, but I invite him up. Up here, there's a fine view over a green sea: cassava and papaya and rolling fields, iridescent in their rainy season hues. Bun Na sits by the door and looks toward the horizon, away from the TV. He tells us later, "I don't like to watch boxing." It is the first time I have ever heard a Cambodian man say such a thing. I don't know why.

Somehow, along this walk with Bun Na, the subject of reading comes up. I ask if he can read Khmer and he says, "No, I can't read so much ... I went to school just a little."

How many years? I ask.

"One month."

One month?

"One month."

Not so much, Jerry says. And Bun Na agrees.

A storm arrives, and its breezes sift through the trees around us. Bun Na sits in a red chair under an awning, looking out on his new home. He spent half his life as a soldier—fifteen years, starting at age fifteen — he lost a quarter of his body to the job. And then he had the streets of Phnom Penh and a run of bad luck and utter squalor in which to place his head at night. I hope this is better for him.

That night before dinner, Bun Na and Poeun call us to their shelter. He wants to give us a gift. The only thing he has to offer are two pictures, two photos taken by a foreigner on the street in Phnom Penh. Then she, too, rifles through her things and pulls out a photo of herself, passport-size. Take this, she says. She looks better in the picture than she does in life right now, she insists, but I see no difference. I tell her both are beautiful — the picture and reality.

Bun Na and Poeun bought all they needed for this trip, this move. A hundred pounds of rice, a few gallons of rock salt, a new bed mat, a new plaid shirt and orange sarong, chilies in a jar. They were set to go, their word meant everything, and I was wrong to doubt.

But I couldn't have known it until I saw it.

I saw it in his face, on his bed, packing their last things. A face uncovered, all scars bared, hair cut and clean. I saw it in his smile, a half-smile that says more than all the words of Khmer I know, more than most full faces I've met in this land.

But I doubted. I thought, as we plied the railroad line, asking every other neighbor for the house of the beggar, that he has stood us up; they have taken the money, and now they're gone. For all the reasons those thoughts didn't reconcile with what we had already seen and heard, I still thought them. Nobody trusts anybody outright in Cambodia.

When I walked the planks between two shacks, over the sludge and down the ladder to the narrow corridor; when I peered then into their room, I saw their desperation. No one deserves a life like that. But Bun Na and Poeun are burdened three and four times over, with lives that cast them out. He is disabled — but also disfigured. They have no parents, nor any kids, no security for their older years. Nothing to say when other mothers coo over their *coen,* their precious children. Until the move, they had no land, no job. They cannot read. He was known to their Phnom Penh neighbors as "the beggar," nothing more. I cannot think of an unluckier lot — except they have each other; they don't have AIDS, and they aren't addicted to drugs. And they seem to get along.

Sometimes, every now and then, I close one eye just to see the world as he might — but I can't. I can't because I can always open that eye. I can't, also, because I don't know the language in his head. I can't fathom the way he sees life, or Cambodia, or me, or us, or this move. I have so many questions that will never be answered, and I must simply accept that.

I would like to somehow check, in a week or month or year, how they're doing — but I can't do that either, unless I go there. I can't send a letter, even in Khmer; they couldn't read it. I can't show them a story I write, even in Khmer, because they couldn't read it. I can only think and hope.

A few days after our trip to Veal Thom, I peer over our nighttime balcony in Phnom Penh. I notice an absence. His shrouded face, his leaning figure, no longer dances through the shadows of Street 178. I hope they are happy, listening to the frogs of a Veal Thom night.

2. Leaving Cambodia:
Passing the Test

She has unkempt hair, a splotched white shirt, coarse hands, an ex-husband and thirty-five-day-old Chea. She comes from Prey Veng, the province east of Phnom Penh, a morning's ride away. A *moto* driver shuttles the woman to her destination. She sits behind him, clutching the boy to her lap. They ride through billowing dust to the gate of a yellow orphanage, where she leaves her son.

It takes moments, no more. Time lost in the Sunday morning sun, shining hot and bright, causing pearls of perspiration on her skin, our skin, everybody's skin. The mother is divorced; she can't make a living; she has two other children. The baby must go. She hands Chea to a caretaker, entrusting him to a stranger.

We're at a place called the Nutrition Center, an orphanage popular among foreigners who whisk bedraggled Cambodian babies to enriching new lives. This is 1999. In the next few years, adoptions will come to a halt amid a scandal involving brokers who buy and sell babies to agencies and parents abroad. But for now, the babies come and go with relative ease.

The staff takes the mother's name and pertinent information. She signs blank pages by thumbprint, the only way she knows how. A French woman, clutching her newly adopted baby near her breast, offers $10 to the poor mother; she accepts. Jerry empties the wad of *riel* from his pocket — spare change. She clasps her hands in gratitude, the Buddhist way.

Then she is gone.

"It is every day like this," the French woman says. She sees mothers leaving their kids all the time, simple as this.

Every day, but Jerry and I will escape it soon, for this is our last assignment in Cambodia, the last story of our thirteen-month tango with heartbreaking news. When I accepted this job in Phnom Penh, I hadn't imagined the mental monsoon we would face.

The mother from Prey Veng leaves through the gate with a bundle of clothes in her arms. From behind, it looks like she carries a baby — but she doesn't anymore. Those clothes are hollow.

Inside, Chea gets a new home and the new name Sachon. He's cleaned, fed, coddled. He's pricked with a needle, probed for HIV, destiny sealed in a drop of his blood. It will take three days before the test results will return. During and thereafter, regardless of HIV status, Sachon gets love, compassion, lots of food and soft arms to cradle him. But everyone wonders. "Everyone waits for the HIV test," says Chan Si Vun, who works here. She sleeps each night with fourteen-month-old Nearadey, HIV-positive. She devotes such attention because the girl's father asked her to, when he left his baby in her arms. "If the test comes back negative, the babies go away. If it comes back positive..." her voice trails.

This orphanage, it's a final refuge for many. "Some families want to adopt HIV-positive babies, but the embassies don't allow," explains Director Youn Sovanna.

Jerry and I spend some time with the other children, then gather our emotions and go for lunch. A few dusty blocks through screeching, beeping traffic is a French-Khmer restaurant. It's an upscale place that caters to Westerners with a set menu in English. Conversation is difficult. My eyes cloud. I look away and force back tears. I snap at the waiter because my soup comes with egg when I ask that it not. I complain of prices too high and service too slow. Jerry and I wonder about our future, away from Cambodia. No clue what to do. What do you do after a place like this?

After the meal, Jerry returns to the orphanage for a few more shots because he doesn't have quite enough, he hasn't spent quite enough time. There's never enough time to tell these stories.

Right around then, amid packing and preparing to leave, I arrange an interview I mulled for several months. I want to know about psychology, about the minds of this country that pierces me so. I head to the Transcultural Psychosocial Organization. It's a non-profit Dutch group, founded in 1995, aimed at mending the mental wounds of refugees and victims of war, trauma, human-rights abuses and organized violence. It's one of those paradoxical organizations whose goal is to eliminate itself, but the world steadily spits up an interminable supply of clients. So the group has inundated offices in Algeria, Bosnia, Congo, Ethiopia, Gaza, India, Mozambique, Namibia, Nepal, Sri Lanka, Uganda and, of course, Cambodia. The Phnom Penh branch works from a house much like ours, in a neighborhood two blocks away. Inside are explanations for much of what goes on in this country.

Program Assistant Kang San, who is now the program coordinator, works in a cool, comfortable office with the organization's posters and leaflets dotting the room. He explains that the program helps people cope with their psychological problems through counseling, group sessions and clinical treatment. It operates in several provinces.

He need not remind me of why this country suffers so—I have been here long enough to know. It doesn't take much time for a resident to see how genocide eats at the heart of a society, how the ramifications of a thirty-year war linger long after the guns stop. How dire poverty compounds the pain; how ill health, poor sanitation, high unemployment, ubiquitous corruption—how all these things combine to abrade the functionality of a nation.

Kang San digs into his mind and deeper into the heads of Cambodia. "Some people say OK, stop thinking about the past but consider national reconciliation."

It's not an uncommon sentiment: That perhaps national reconciliation with the Khmer Rouge is more important than punishing former Khmer Rouge leaders. That perhaps the Tuol Sleng Genocide Museum should be closed, shrouding torture rooms from public view, burying the atrocity. Kang San disagrees staunchly. "We have to condemn them in a lawful manner … we cannot just forget, because the people suffer a lot." The "them" of whom he speaks are the Khmer Rouge, themselves Cambodian people.

This conversation takes place shortly after Khieu Samphan, former Khmer Rouge head of state, and Nuon Chea, Brother Number Two behind Pol Pot, defected to the government. They stayed in swank style, at a Phnom Penh hotel, and issued smoke-screen apologies. Their words rang around the world: "Naturally, we are sorry — not only for the lives of the people, but also for the animals," Nuon Chea said. Followed with Khieu Samphan's, "Let bygones be bygones." Then they flitted away to western Cambodia to join other former Khmer Rouge colleagues in freedom.

That same week, Agence France-Presse tabulated the myriad reactions, through headlines and sound bites from a plethora of Khmer papers, many politically aligned. "Cambodia should throw away sentiments of vengeance: even if we killed Khieu Samphan or Nuon Chea the lives of those who died will not come back…. All Cambodians must come together and love each other so we can find real peace," the daily *Rasmei Angkor*, the Light of Angkor, proclaimed. According to *Stabna Cheat*, or National Reconstruction, the defections signaled an end of hope. "They can only try the wind, because Pol Pot is already dead and the other criminals have defected to the government already." And *Neak Prayuth*, the Fighter, wrote that such defections only prolong Cambodia's "cycle of impunity," that hackneyed but accurate tag hung on a country with no justice.

Kang San remembers the Khmer Rouge years well. Soldiers separated families. "Once or twice a year, I could see my mother." His little brother was kept elsewhere. "During that time people lost touch with each other. We could not trust each other." They learned to look out for their own lives, but no one else's. The Khmer people have a saying for that. They refer to the "hair on your head." If a friend is accused of something he didn't do, and you defend the friend, then you also will be accused. "Mind your own business. Mind your hair on your head," Kang San says. And little else. He gives an example: In Kang San's village, soldiers had come regularly to chat with the leader. For two years, they had come for "a good meal together, and good talk." Then one day, the soldiers came and the leader was arrested. So much for friendship.

Kang San need not illustrate further how such events, day after day, rupture all social trust. It is evident everywhere.

He takes me to his colleague, Kann Kall, TPO vice director. The thirty-five-year-old man sits on a red-checkered pad on a rattan love seat, legs crossed, hands folded, eyes cast downward as he says a large percentage of his country's population suffers some form of mental illness. Trauma typically occurs among a small group within a larger population, he explains. A fire destroys one home. A flood disrupts one neighborhood. But genocide is different. "This happened to the whole country. So people don't identify it because it's too big." When everyone suffers, that anguish seems normal. "That is a big problem because if people are not aware of their psychological problems, they can project that to the younger generation. That is dangerous to Cambodia."

These mental troubles don't always bob on the surface. It takes some diving. Reality is exposed layer by layer. "It's hard to see," he says, but watch for the signs. "You expect people to be working eight hours a day." But they don't. They say, "I have this problem, that problem." They squat on the sidewalk, laze atop *motos*, stare into viscous air, sleep the day away. He estimates up to forty-five percent of Cambodians have psychosomatic illnesses, physical problems rooted in the mind. "When you go a little bit deeper," he says, "people complain, 'Oh I can't sleep — exhausted.' And we go a bit deeper. 'Yes, I lost my child in Pol Pot time.'" The traumatized mind controls the body. "This is a mental problem. You can find it everywhere."

He continues: "I am sure that the violence in our society is also psychological from that time."

What can be done?

"Big question. It's a really big question."

He thinks as he speaks.

"The whole structure of this country has to be restored." That will take generations. Societies are built like homes, with steps and foundations. When you destroy the foundation, as the Khmer Rouge did, everything collapses. As Khmer Rouge leaders gently roll into the government folds, the problem festers. People have snuffed their pain in public, but an inferno rages within them. "It is burning again."

Kann Kall is admittedly morose. "Even friends of mine say, Kann, you are too pessimistic. But I say let's see the facts. If you do not see the facts, how can we improve?" Cambodians will think of nothing but guns, nothing but revenge, nothing but their visceral pain, "until they understand the taste of peace," he says. "If you've been eating with the war for twenty years, you don't know the taste of peace. So let them taste peace."

I exit his office and enter a city full of change. Western change, economic change, change often equated with peace. Nike, Coke and Tommy Hilfiger clothe the bodies and quench the capitalist thirsts of many young Cambodians. Giant billboards in tropical Phnom Penh advertise Japanese smokers on snowboards in mountains nowhere near here. Face-whitening cream occupies aisles of shelves in city supermarkets, calling to self-conscious young women. There is Lucky Burger, KFC Chicken Burger and Pizza Hot. There is a new business atmosphere, and some say that's a mark of progress.

But peace and democracy aren't made-to-order. They take time, and they take an exceptionally long time in a place where genocide and thirty years of war have left a country without education, law, medicine, human rights. It is still a crippled peace.

It's Wednesday afternoon, my last day of work in Cambodia. I return to the Nutrition Center orphanage to learn of Sachon's fate. The gates lead to another world, a world where the pace doesn't change much; nothing much changes except the names and faces on different days. New arrivals replace the departed. Many of the kids here will never leave for another country, never know a parent's kiss, never see the temples of Angkor, never climb a mountain, never play in the snow or shiver in winter, perhaps never reach another birthday or two or three.

The room is noisy with the afternoon hubbub of kids at play. They tell me Sachon's test has come back negative. Everyone smiles. I do too, but then I must leave quickly to finish the story, because all stories end in print even when they live on and die in reality.

Chea's story, Sachon's story, happens every day and every week and every month in that old French colonial building on those dusty grounds off a Phnom Penh thoroughfare. Bedrooms stem from an octagonal play area. Murals in primary colors shroud the walls. They show white boys and girls flying kites on the beach, sailboats and bunny rabbits, kids frolicking, butterflies flitting and other happy scenes that some kids will see someday. But most will not.

Blonde parents speaking French and English sit on the veranda, rocking and cooing and bouncing the lucky ones. This, too, happens every day in much the same manner. Those rocked and cooed babies don't have HIV. They might suffer diarrhea or respiratory infections; their remedies exist. But not for HIV.

And so the HIV-positive children stay until they grow sick and weak, until they go to the hospital, and they die.

On my first visit to the orphanage, I make a list. A worker leads me through the wards—an introductory look. There is Sony, born July 26, 1998, entered here October 24, 1998. And Seila, born January 20, 1998, brought here May 13, 1998. Noupheap entered the world November 19, 1998, and came here December 28, 1998. The list goes on and on, and I name them all because they don't get much more than that in life — if they still have that. A name. Two dates. And the big "+" sign beside that name and those dates in the book, from which I copy their details:

Samedi, born October 5, 1998; entered 75 days later

Sopeah, born June 23, 1998; entered 70 days later

Santhy, born October 5, 1998; entered 21 days later

Bunna, born October 20, 1998; entered 14 days later

Neardey, born September 16, 1998; entered 10 days later

Dany, born November 3, 1998; entered 13 days later

Angkea, born December 18, 1996; entered 1 year, 355 days later

Ros, born July 8, 1996; entered 2 years, 23 days later

Duongchet, born April 14, 1998; entered 20 days later

Morakad, born July 27, 1998; entered 14 days later

Samrath, born November 15, 1996; entered 2 years later

Rasmei, born September 10, 1995; entered 3 years, 68 days later

Bunheng, born April 16, 1995; entered 214 days later

Sok Tang, born June 7, 1996; entered 70 days later

And there are two others I fail. There's Meanletah, or Meanyetch, or Meanleah — a four-year-old boy born July 15, 1994, and entered February 21, 1998. And there's Sros, another boy, born either April 11, 1996, and entered on his second birthday; or perhaps born September 11, 1996, and entered nineteen months later. I fail to write their names and dates precisely, legibly, in my notes.

I am careless with two names and two dates. I do not actually spend time with those particular boys; I simply copy their information, insufficiently, from ledger to notebook. Then I move to another corner of the room where I find more notes to take on other babies. I return to the orphanage, but I don't return to those entries in my notebook because those two boys never fit largely, individually, into my story. I unconsciously see them as notes, not people. They are two of many names and dates.

But not just names and dates—a life, two lives. Two little Cambodian boys who have names and birthdays and some very generous women who take care of them, and little else. I don't realize my error until much later. And when I do, I reach a humbled reporter's dilemma: I could skip this part and report no more, no one the wiser. Or I could vow to do better and offer what I do know about Cambodia.

I opt for the latter.

I opt to write about Samrath, a two-year-old boy, with a body full of sores, complications from AIDS. He sits and picks at himself. "He doesn't have a friend to apply medicine to his sores," a worker says. And Sok Tang, who can't walk, who spends a lot of time in a crib, in a separate building where other physically impaired children play on the floor. They are fed and pampered and dealt with gingerly, for what do you do with a limbless, sightless, wordless or motionless orphan in Cambodia? A young girl lives here as well. She doesn't have AIDS, but she has just a stump of a leg and two partial twigs of arms.

Angkea is a special case, for he is Vietnamese. He is two years old but looks barely one. He sits on the floor by himself. The workers clean him and feed him like any other child. One woman teaches another youngster to call Angkea *yuon*, the common Khmer word for Vietnamese people. Some say its meaning is the equivalent of "nigger," although Cambodians have used the word for ages, and many insist no harm is meant in the name.

"The kids who come here are not in good health," Youn Sovanna says. She and coworker Heng Sarin rattle off a list of afflictions that plague 95 percent of their children—tuberculosis, malnutrition, low birth weight, encephalitis. "It is sad to work here. Every day," Heng Sarin says.

Youn Sovanna pulls out a notebook displaying the math. At the end of 1996, the center had eight HIV-positive children. The next year, twenty-three more arrived, for a total of thirty-one. Ten later tested negative—several false positives, not so uncommon among the very young. Five died. That left sixteen. In 1998, there were thirty-six new arrivals, twelve new negatives and eighteen deaths, leaving twenty-two. This month, there are two newcomers, making twenty-four. Twenty-four HIV-positive children in all. When they get sick, she says, they go to the children's hospital up the road, "and there they die." *Slahp.* Dead. It's a common word here, like *baay*, meaning rice, or *tuk*, meaning water.

That week, Dany, barely three months old and brought here at thirteen days, goes to the hospital up the road.

The problems only swell. For years, Cambodia has the highest rising AIDS rate in Asia, which eventually steadies as the death toll rises. Officials estimate 200,000 people have HIV, and up to 100 new people are infected each day, in a country where AIDS was unknown until the early 1990s. For that new affliction, some blame UNTAC, the United Nations Transitional Authority in Cambodia, which brought about democratic elections and spawned a volatile industry in sex for foreigners.

The aftermath is here.

Day after day, lives blend into one another at the Nutrition Center. One baby makes a puddle of diarrhea that seeps through his cloth diaper, onto his legs, under his buttocks and atop the vinyl floor mat. A caretaker maneuvers him, disrobes him, shimmies to the sink, and gags on the stench. She lifts his tiny body to the basin and bathes him with bare hands. She caresses his skin; it sags like an old elephant's. She wipes the mess and swaddles him in clean clothes. His limbs jiggle in the air. He lies, almost indistinguishable, in a bevy of babies. I ask his name. The workers don't know; they tell me to ask at the front desk. But they know he is HIV-positive. I find out later he is Seila, one year old but looking much younger.

Another worker passes through, holding Noupheap, urging a bottle through her frail, underdeveloped lips. Born November 19, 1998, entered here December 28, 1998. She falls asleep, wearing a faded blue shirt, the color of her body.

Sometimes foreigners pluck a lucky baby from the bunch and plop the child in a pastel-colored bassinet, offering crackers to eat and crisp new frocks to wear. The foreigners come every day, pampering the child and cooing over the preciousness of infancy until one day, they leave together on a plane. One Frenchman, who adopted a boy a few years earlier and has come back for a daughter, tells us his girl was found in a garden near the river.

Inside the orphanage, snapshots deck the hallway walls. Some kids have new homes in other countries. A proud white couple holds a baby. The photo says, "Viruth (Louis) June 98." A toddler dressed in bright pink and yellow lies on her belly. The photo says, "Alexandria Kalliyan (formerly, Veacha)." Those babies had no "+" mark.

Other photos show kids still in Cambodia at orphanages linked to this one, eating, playing and smiling for the camera. They look happy, well-fed, well-loved.

In those photos, you cannot tell who passed the test.

You cannot tell who did not.

3. Genocide: Ghosts on the Porch

In June 2000, a man digs up his yard in Phnom Penh, hoping to extend his house. He unearths several skeletons, the remnants of genocide, right there in his front yard, just a few steps out the door.

Cambodians live with the dead, with the hauntings of the past. The spirits of 1.7 million people wander restlessly through an air that has never cleared. Their killers have never been punished, and their descendants have not reconciled their history.

Cambodians are famous for their friendly nature. But they live in a shroud. "When we meet an affable, smiling Cambodian, it is easy to forget that quite often he or she has suffered incalculably under the Khmer Rouge regime and that inside, he or she may be a broken person," writes Youk Chhang. He is head of an institution called the Documentation Center of Cambodia, which exists to better explain the Khmer Rouge regime, to aid victims in pursuing legal redress, and to quash any possibility of a return to the Killing Fields.

A broken people — it's easy to see why, when injustice still rubs salt in victims' wounds. In December 2003, Khieu Samphan, the former Khmer Rouge head of state, admits the regime committed genocide, but he denies any involvement in the killings. Less than a month later, Nuon Chea, the infamous Brother Number Two behind Pol Pot, admits he made "mistakes" during the Khmer Rouge regime. He will willingly face trial, though he denies there was a genocide. The newswires, the international papers, pick up this story. They print his words around the world. "People died, but there were many causes of their deaths," the *Los Angeles Times* quotes him. Nuon Chea speaks from his home in Pailin, that safe enclave in western Cambodia.

Pailin: It is the fiefdom of Ieng Sary, former foreign minister of Democratic Kampuchea, the Khmer Rouge government. (That they called it "Democratic" was an abomination of the word.) He quit the Khmer Rouge in 1996 and brokered a deal with Hun Sen that secured freedom for him and his personal army in this wild west town.

Pailin: It is where many former Khmer Rouge live today with no shackles, where they are allowed to speak their minds, where they are permitted retreat from public view, should they desire. It is where Nuon Chea rests his head. His announcement about "mistakes" comes two years after he gathers with friends and family for his daughter's wedding. The stalwart comrades of his past celebrate with him. There is

41

a party. There are white gowns and gold shirts. There is merriment among murderers.

And as always, Nuon Chea goes home a free man. Former Khmer Rouge leaders have lived freely for years.

For years, the Cambodian government and the United Nations negotiate how best to bring these criminals to justice. Back and forth, playing ping-pong with the Cambodian psyche. Opinions vary; allegations fly. Some accuse the Cambodian government of stalling, of stymieing a tribunal because it could do the ruling party harm. Some say the government hopes the guilty will die before they face justice, thereby avoiding the whole messy affair. Why? Let us not forget many current leaders once ranked highly in the Khmer Rouge, including Prime Minister Hun Sen. He was a deputy commander of a special regiment in the eastern region before escaping to Vietnam in 1977 and organizing the overthrow of Pol Pot. He has political ties to the accused. He granted amnesty to former Khmer Rouge leaders in the last days of war. "These commanders still retain the loyalty of some former troops, and they bolster Hun Sen's own power as long as he serves as their protector," writes *The Asian Wall Street Journal.* Hun Sen "has sabotaged the trial at every opportunity." Plus, he wants to please China, a big Cambodia donor and the number-one backer of the Khmer Rouge, in their day.

Meanwhile, time slips by. Pol Pot dies in 1998. Ke Pauk, a former leader of the Khmer Rouge northern zone, follows in 2002. He dies as a general in the Cambodian Army, the plum of his defection deal. By early 2004, only two high-profile Khmer Rouge criminals are in custody: Ta Mok, "The Butcher," and Kaing Kek Ieu, known as "Duch," the infamous boss of Tuol Sleng.

In February 2002, in a low point of negotiations, the UN pulls out, saying it cannot work with Cambodia anymore because the country is not cooperating. The UN cannot guarantee a tribunal's "independence, impartiality and objectivity." Hopes deflate, blame is cast, more accusations made. And then a year later, the tide changes again. The Cambodian cabinet and the UN sign a draft agreement for a tribunal. Finally, in March 2003. Finally, more than twenty-four years after the collapse of the Khmer Rouge regime, a plan is made. There will be a court of two chambers: a trial chamber with three Cambodian and two international judges and a supreme court chamber with four Cambodian and three international judges. Decisions will be made by a majority of four and five judges, respectively. The court will examine crimes committed between April 17, 1975, and January 6, 1979. The maximum penalty will be life in prison. Costs will be covered by the UN, the Cambodian government and international donors. The total bill is expected to reach about $50 million. And finally, the Khmer people may rest.

While this doesn't please everyone, it is better than nothing. It is better than the septic wounds of a nation with no justice at all. Many Cambodians still don't believe it will happen. They have waited too long already, and their minds reel. "Every time I hear about the tribunal, I am very sick," says our good friend, photographer Heng Sinith. "I don't want to hear."

The dead crumble beneath the earth in piles, in anonymous pits, in a quarter century of injustice. And still, the Cambodian people wait.

"There was not a single child, not one living creature," writes François Bizot, French author of *The Gate*, an account of his experiences in a Khmer Rouge prison. "This sudden suspension of life in the heart of what had been the great commercial center of the Mekong Delta — this city famed for its many and varied activities, its colorful population, and its cosmopolitan lifestyle." Phnom Penh was an extinguished city after the Khmer Rouge swept through in 1975. A city abandoned. The Paris of the Orient, silenced and shamed.

They were soldiers, young men with guns, blindly following the orders of the *angka*, an organization they never saw and never met. They were told to amass the people and ship them out. They emptied hospitals, forcing the feeble to trudge hours out of the city. They made families flee in an instant. They raised their guns and lied to the people, saying America would bomb the city. They insisted this forced migration was for everyone's good. They shot recklessly through the streets. People died along the way. Children stumbled, the old toppled, the weak perished. It was called the "death march." The soldiers kept pushing. So it was for nearly four years.

Scholars and journalists since have expounded on this era, in volumes — the people, the perpetrators, the victims, the psychology, the trauma. Survivors have spilled their memories in beautiful renditions, in tragic narratives, in horrific dreams. Artists have painted and sketched and spread their hearts across canvasses splattered with the blood of their nightmares. There are a thousand ways to remember this tragedy, a thousand ways to live on. There are a thousand explanations for how it happened, and a thousand more academic dissections of the Khmer Rouge mind. "Everyone I met had a different explanation for how the Khmer Rouge could have happened there, but none of these explanations made sense, just as none of the explanations for the Cultural Revolution or for Stalinism or for Nazism makes sense," writes Andrew Solomon in *The Noonday Demon*, a book that examines depression. He chose Cambodia as a focus because of its demonstrable suffering. "These things happen to societies, and in retrospect it is possible to understand why a nation was especially vulnerable to them; but where in the human imagination such behaviors originate is unknowable. The social fabric is always very thin, but it is impossible to know how it gets vaporized entirely as it did in these societies."

Scholars have tried to deconstruct the circumstances, the reasons for an emergence of Khmer Rouge power. The Khmer Rouge offered hope to peasants. They painted their fight as one against historical adversaries, the Vietnamese, and the modern foes, the Americans. It was a struggle of the classes. They preyed upon a society betrayed in their neighbor's war. Most Cambodians had no idea what was happening as the Khmer Rouge tsunami swept them up and into its fold. Most Cambodians knew only to fear, to obey, to expect the worst.

The Khmer Rouge recruited young, unmarried men, easily malleable and lacking attachments. They also took advantage of Cambodia's traditional class structure and the expectation that the commonfolk bow to the powerful. "This culture of exploitation, protection, obedience, and dependency had deep roots in Cambodian social practice and strengthened the grip of those in power," writes historian David Chandler. What happened, he chillingly concludes, follows human nature. "Most of us, I suspect, could become accustomed to doing something (such as torturing or killing people) when people we respected told us to do it and when there were no institutional constraints on doing what we were told."

The line between victim and persecutor is maddeningly gray.

Yet in this shaded reality, it seems some black-and-white truths should prevail. The murders of nearly 2 million people should be, must be, wrong. The guilty should be, must be, punished. But it still hasn't happened.

The Killing Fields of Choeung Ek sit outside Phnom Penh amid pastoral vistas and quiet village life. It just happens that people's homes exist on the fringe of buried atrocity.

This is a place of 129 mass graves, a place where 8,985 bodies were unearthed in one year alone. Human bones lie scattered about, jutting from the dirt paths that meander between graves. Pigs feed nearby; cows graze the pits of death. And people come to see the remains. Jerry and I first visit Choeung Ek in 1998. It is a somber encounter with sorrow. I pluck a femur from the ground, pricking my hand on the jagged human shard as I dust it off.

A large glass memorial towers above the ground where the Khmer Rouge bludgeoned some 40,000 people. The daily tally varied from a few dozen to several hundred. Death by hammer, sickle or scythe came cheaper than death by bullet, so many victims were hacked, not shot. About 8,000 skulls now rest within this memorial in

Stacks of human skulls sit in a memorial to the dead at the Killing Fields of Choeung Ek, just outside Phnom Penh. About 40,000 people were killed here and buried in mass graves during the Khmer Rouge regime. Phnom Penh, 1998.

tiers, divided by age and gender and ethnicity—the only certain identity these remains will ever have. They are categorized: "senile" female Kampuchean over sixty years old, mature male Kampuchean forty to sixty years old, adult female Kampuchean twenty to forty years old, juvenile male Kampuchean fifteen to twenty years old, European.

We return to Choeung Ek in 2001. There once was a picture of Ieng Sary, former Khmer Rouge foreign minister, hanging on a wall here—but now, no picture. Now there is a long vertical sign with a statement: "The Most Tragic: They massacred the population with atrocity in a large scale; it was more cruel than the genocide act committed by the Hitler fascists."

Holes like bomb craters dot this landscape. I find more human pieces. The paths are beds of bones, white and worn beneath visitors' treads. More bones, more shirts, more pants, two teeth. More death unearthed, poking from walkways through the fields. It's the rainy season now and water pools beyond a dike that separates graves from fields. I touch bones, I examine molars, and I can't erase the feeling on my hand. Is it irreverent to touch the bones of the dead? Is it disrespectful to step on them, hear them crunch in the path?

I walk outside the fields, into the surrounding village, into life running its usual course. There is a school here, donated to the village by a Japanese man in 1998. I am surrounded by kids asking me for pens, for money, for the chance to have their picture taken, anything I have to give. I walk past pigs and dogs and a new home in the making—cement and wood, the marks of a wealthy family. Buddhist monks drone in the distance. Birds tweet, frogs and insects croak, a weed whacker buzzes, a *moto* zooms. This is an ordinary rural tempo.

This is not the only killing field in Cambodia. There are others. Villagers find them, little mounds of bones in their fields. There is one near Battambang, the country's second-largest city, in a cave where the Khmer Rouge tossed their victims through a hole, hurling them a hundred feet to their deaths. There is another in Siem Reap, inside a *wat* with a pink *stupa*, where skulls are locked behind glass doors. The bones press against that glass; they were taken from a nearby field. A sign states: "We do not have enough money to build a dignified and proper memorial to honor these innocent people the world once stood by and let another demented dictator murder 1000000 in four years. Now we can help provide comfort to these dear departed soul with a donation."

Tuol Sleng, Security Office 21, is close to our home in 1998, just a few blocks. We can walk to the chamber of evil. Tuol Sleng was a center where the Khmer Rouge questioned and tortured some 14,000 "enemies," thousands of ordinary people the Khmer Rouge leaders insisted had betrayed them in some way. The Khmer Rouge deemed most everyone an enemy. The prisoners were shackled in tiny rooms. They were starved and beaten. They were brutalized and driven insane. Some were used as medical dummies, bled to death or sliced open on the operating table. The prisoners were never let out, never, until the Vietnamese invaded in early 1979 and discovered this place reeking of death. They found fourteen bodies. They found corpses still chained to their beds and just a few prisoners nearly dead.

In 1998, the government tries to turn the museum into a polling station during national elections. A table is set and preparations begun on the eve of voting day. But the idea fails, the station is dismantled and moved when people complain.

Jerry and I tour Tuol Sleng a few months before this happens. A sharp quiet envelops the walled grounds of this museum. A young woman named Sok Chi Vee guides us through the morbid halls. With practiced formality, she ushers visitors through Building A, Building B, and room after room of murder. She explains the paintings, memoirs of a Tuol Sleng survivor, one of seven — seven of 14,000. He lives in Phnom Penh now. Our guide points to photos of torture devices used during months of interrogation. "And after that, they killed them, even those who confessed," she says. Room Number Four contains a photo of a dead prisoner, as the Vietnamese found him when they discovered the place. "It was a bad smell because the body was rotting," Sok Chi Vee says. "The corpse could not be identified."

She takes us through a room lined entirely with little black-and-white portraits of prisoners before they were killed. The Khmer Rouge kept meticulous records. The Tuol Sleng archives contain 6,000 photos of prisoners and 20,000 documents detailing the horrors that happened in the prison.

We look at the eyes in these photos. In one picture, dated May 14, 1978, a woman holds a sleeping baby. Her eyes droop sadly. In another photo, a man smiles. In this nation known for its curved lips and bright faces, his is the only smile we see among the Tuol Sleng photos. "The interrogator made him smile by tickling," our guide says.

She leads us through tiny brick cells where prisoners remained except for their infrequent bathroom excursions. She takes us past glass cases of machetes, probes, bamboo poles and yokes. Torture tools. In one method the interrogators yanked fingernails from the prisoner's hands and poured alcohol over the raw nubs.

Finally, our guide leads us to a map of Cambodia made of human skulls. It hangs on the wall. She points to the bones of men and women and children. She stands quietly as we and several other visitors contemplate the map. "It's real," she says. "All real."

I touch a skull. It is dark brown with four top molars and no teeth between, its cranium dusty in the rear but smooth and shiny up front. The skull to the right has two perceptible eye sockets and the beginnings of a nose; the skull to the left has just one complete eye socket. A femur is draped above them all. A tooth has fallen on the tile floor. That curved brown bone, twenty years dead by brutality, complete and utter anonymity stifling the answers to any questions about it, hangs among 300 others just like it. When my finger, a live finger, touches that skull, the profundity of what it is burns for hours.

This map is the last thing visitors see before exiting the museum, before entering an ordinary Phnom Penh neighborhood where kids play soccer in the dirt, *motos* zip around, streetside stalls sell sticky buns, and stagnant sewer waters rest beneath small wooden bridges leading to average homes.

Four years later, Cambodian authorities say they want a new image for Tuol Sleng. The map is dismantled, the skulls are removed, and a new map is hung in its stead. Monks hold a ceremony for the victims, and the remains are sealed in a case. A bit of the macabre is closeted.

It is not unusual for survivors to mourn their losses and celebrate their lives through art. A man named Svay Ken picks up a brush at sixty years old. He paints 128 pictures of his life, of his family's life. They are images of unremarkable events, and the introduction to his exhibit in a Phnom Penh gallery says the paintings are "neither pretty nor decorative and thus these pictures function in a different register than the vast majority of paintings in Cambodia today." What is different about Svay Ken's work is that he paints the everyday of life in hell. He paints his family fleeing Phnom Penh and working in the fields, shoveling manure with no gloves or shoes. He paints scenes of a Khmer Rouge hospital, and his family watching the invading Vietnamese in early 1979. He titles his collection, "The History of My Family."

In 1998, Vann Nath publishes his memoirs, *A Cambodian Prison Portrait: One Year in the Khmer Rouge's S 21.* He survives. He survives through his art because his captors commanded him to paint portraits of Pol Pot. In 1980, Nath and the other survivors returned to make the prison into a museum. Nath wanted to leave, but a friend told him, "I believe that the spirits of the dead would be very glad about this." So Nath stayed. He painted painful pictures of torture and death, and as he painted, he became adamant that the world must see these images. "I believe that the spirits of the people who died must have applauded our work."

Many writers have reconstructed their memories of that ghastly time. The written word is catharsis for a troubled psyche. "As a survivor, I want to be worthy of the suffering that I endured as a child. I don't want to let that pain count for nothing, nor do I want others to endure it," writes Chanrithy Him, author of the memoir *When Broken Glass Floats.* She was just a girl when the Khmer Rouge ravaged her country. History envelops her life as an adult.

Every survivor enlists a different coping mechanism, a personal method of release. If he or she doesn't, that rancor stays bottled inside. Some find their serenity in a fight for change. "I'm doing this for my mother," says Youk Chhang, director of the Documentation Center of Cambodia. "I see this as a family issue.... I want my mother to be happy."

Perhaps more than any other Cambodian, Youk Chhang's life and career are immersed in the pursuit of a just Khmer Rouge trial. He has studied the Khmer Rouge; he has gathered the evidence and has chronicled the victims, and he has dedicated his life to making things right.

When Youk Chhang was fourteen, during the Khmer Rouge years, his older sister had nothing to eat. "I went out to the rice field, and I picked water grass and mushrooms for her." He was caught and tortured by the Khmer Rouge. They tied him up, hit him with an ax. They made his mother watch. "They tortured me in front of my mother, and they forced her not to cry." And ever after, the relationship between son and mother remains tarnished. Seeing him — even now as an adult, a survivor who escaped to the United States and returned again to help his people — reminds his mother of the little boy disgraced before her eyes. "I blamed the Khmer Rouge for doing that," he says. But he doesn't let that anger destroy him. "Instead, I use it as a way to make myself better." His nation's scars give him strength. "No one can destroy your soul. No one can destroy your love."

Youk Chhang, director of the Documentation Center of Cambodia, has dedicated his life to collecting information about and tracking down those responsible for the crimes committed by the Khmer Rouge, so they can eventually stand trial. Behind him are photographs of guards from the notorious Tuol Sleng torture center in Phnom Penh. That building is now a museum to Cambodia's genocide. Phnom Penh, 2003.

Youk Chhang's work today is all about remembering. Remembering the Khmer Rouge, remembering their crimes, remembering their victims in precise detail, so that the future is different and the past never recurs. But what about those who want to forget? What of those who say the past is best left to rest?

"I support it if they can do that," he says. "Who wants to remember the horrible things in their lives?" But the human mind does not block the past, and it is important to question those who say they have forgotten. Peer into their eyes, he says. "You realize they are human beings and humans cannot live without memories." Especially when the pain is personal.

This tribunal will happen "one way or another," he says. He doesn't believe the former Khmer Rouge leaders will escape justice by death. There are six criminals in the fore, and even the two in jail are receiving good care. "Six of them will not die at the same time."

The trial won't solve everything but it will allow the country to progress. It will be a symbol of justice — what it looks like, how it works—for a country with a notoriously corrupt judicial system.

"Will the tribunal bring back my sister? Will the tribunal bring back 2 million lives?"

No.

"Who can compensate for what we have lost?"

No one can.

But that is not the point, he says. This is not about revenge; it's about remembering, about dredging the pain so it is never forgotten and never endured again.

There is one more reason Youk Chhang so desires this trial: He believes it will bring the Cambodian people to a critical reckoning. "Cambodians like to blame someone else," he says, but the Khmer Rouge were themselves Khmer. "So I hope with a tribunal they realize it was them. It was you."

4. Angkor: An Empire in Ruins

Eleven-year-old Hui plays with four-leaf clovers. He stands knee-deep in a murky pool beside a monument built to twelfth-century gods. He is surrounded by piles of stone near a terrace where ancient elephants paraded before divine kings. He twirls two clovers; thousands more grow in the muck around his feet. In this little nook of Cambodia, four-leaf clovers sprout like weeds. Hui has no idea of the irony.

He wears a tattered yellow polo shirt, his only shirt, buttoned to the top. His frail body is covered in dirty smudges. The dirt is where he plays, where he runs, where he makes his living. Hui is an Angkor child. This is early 1999, when hundreds of these kids lead visitors to pretty carvings and big trees straddling old walls. The kids come from villages scattered through this historical park. The people of the temples are living icons of Angkor, the tangible memory of a glorious past.

The children take you through back doors, dodging soldiers who guard the temples and harass the youngsters for hanging around. These children know Angkor's feel, its rhythm, its legends. They know the touch of stone, fallen from an empire. They know where to find carvings of heavenly creatures called *apsaras*, deep inside dank caverns. They know where monkeys roam and which snakes can kill. They grab your hand and guide you to headless statues and faceless nymphs. They'll tell you, "Khmer Rouge cut head." And where people have since rebuilt bright replicas of Buddhas draped in robes and adoration, the kids proclaim, "But new Buddha now, new Buddha now."

Mothers sell drinks from handheld coolers; sisters pawn hand-woven scarves and imported sarongs. Their sing-song calls resonate in your head: "Sir, you-buy-cold-drink-from-me, two-for-one-dollar! Two-for-one-dollar!"

The children of Angkor live in a land of deities, though their thatch homes, bare feet, cracked skin and torn clothes don't show it. They till parched lands with bony cows. They bribe underpaid and underworked soldiers to allow them in the temples. These kids are some of Cambodia's most prescient entrepreneurs. They probe the past to sculpt their own futures. They learn textbook histories from tourists who read books and tell them. They study English, French and Japanese with help from their newfound foreign friends. Then they ask for 500 *riel*, maybe a dollar, explaining that they either eat or go to school, but seldom both.

The youngsters who study go to dilapidated classrooms around the ruins, such as a one-room school we visit on the flanks of the Bakong temple. The classroom has hard wooden desks; its walls are scarred by bullets and rockets. A boy with thick black hair and bushy eyebrows stares attentively at the teacher, jotting notes with a blue Bic pen. Sunlight streams through a rocket hole, lighting his work.

But most kids swarm the tourists instead. A topless little girl in a blue skirt, hair shaved short, grasps my hand. She ties a green grass ring around my finger. Then another. She follows me through a set of ninth-century ruins called the Roluos Group, swinging my arm. She uses hands and feet to clamber up steep stairs to the top where stone lions guard an old temple that smells of guano.

Angkor Wat is known the world over, but the temple complex is much grander than one building. It extends deep into the Cambodian countryside, covering 120 square miles with 1,000 temples, pools, gates, *barays* and the spirit of an empire that once covered much of Southeast Asia as it is known today. At its peak, some 50 million rice paddies stretched through 12.3 million acres of land. Ancient Angkor was huge.

Angkor Wat is the largest religious structure ever built. It contains a moat, three levels reaching almost 700 feet tall, five main towers on the top level and almost 13,000 square feet of tremendously intricate bas-reliefs depicting ancient Indian epics and Angkor-era battles. The mere sight of the temple enraptures a traveler, "making

A photographer gathers his costumes and horses before heading home for the evening. During the day, he sells souvenir photos of people dressed up in western cowboy garb sitting on his horses in front of Angkor Wat. Siem Reap, 2001.

him forget all the fatigues of the journey, filling him with admiration and delight. Suddenly, and as if by enchantment, he seems to be transported from barbarism to civilization, from profound darkness to light," the French explorer Henri Mouhot waxed poetic in his diaries 140 years ago.

Today, Angkor is the pride of a people. These temples are in ruins, but assuredly alive with a nation's aplomb. They remind Cambodians of their own mighty past, seeding hopes that they may someday attain such grandeur again. "Greatness flows in our veins," proclaims a Web site posted by Khmer Americans. Greatness of the Angkor legacy.

At this time in early 1999, when we meet Hui, Khmer Rouge bandits still creep through the jungles around Angkor. Though war has ended, former soldiers take to thievery. The month before our visit, Khmer Rouge rebels kidnapped three aid workers from the NGO CARE but released them unharmed a week later. That same week, more rebels took forty villagers hostage deeper into the northwest, demanding ransom money. They freed the villagers after collecting $2,000 from their captives' friends and neighbors. These bandits turned to kidnapping because they didn't have food, the provincial police chief said. That's that. That's the way of life.

Many tourists visit the temples on a well-trod route, skittering among the famous ruins, perhaps indulging in some favorites—Angkor Wat, the Bayon, Ta Prohm, Preah Khan. But temples are sprinkled through this land like ancient jimmies on a giant cake. They are everywhere, and some of the most unassuming sites are the choicest finds.

Jerry and I hire a *moto* driver one afternoon, and he takes us off the tourist map. We pass a dusty, empty market with tarps flapping in the breeze and sand all around. We scoot deeper into rural culture. Half-naked kids wade through dense paddies up to their thighs, scrounging for fish. Three men pass through the grass on a *moto*, the middle one clutching a rifle aimed at the sky. Everyone points and grins as we pass. We are only five miles from Siem Reap and closer to town than anyone visiting Preah Khan. But that's just it: We've left the expected course, and villagers are pleasantly surprised. The sky blackens in the distance and rolls over a radiant paddy. Up a sandy hill ahead, we encounter a reclining Buddha rarely visited by outsiders.

The monks here keep him locked and chained in the dark. They offer us a peek, but we must wait for the man with the keys. He opens a tomb to a concrete cavern and reveals a statue with gold face, red lips, burnt candles and spent incense at its base. They say this Buddha is a thousand years old. They say it is lucky because its head was not hacked, it survived the Khmer Rouge. They speak of karma. If you cut a Buddha head, our driver tells us, you will die. (Of course, the Khmer Rouge paid no attention to such superstitions. They were more interested in money to fuel their cause.) We offer a donation, and the young monks kindly accept. Then we race off to beat the rain, returning this ignored corner of the old empire back to the locals.

Many Cambodians never make it to Angkor. For some, it's a lifelong dream. When I return from that trip to the ruins in early 1999, a Cambodian reporter at my paper asks me how many times I have seen the great temples, 190 miles from Phnom Penh.

I tell him three.

"Really. I have never been," he says. "But finally, next month I will take my family there. Do you think one week is long enough?"

One could walk forever among the ruins, some cleared and primped for visitors, others still deep within the jungle. My colleague explains he actually did see Angkor Wat once — for two hours, right after the Vietnamese invaded and drove the Khmer Rouge into the surrounding jungles. The circumstances were hazy; it was a time when all the nation moved, hoping to escape. Now he has a week among the temples, and he wants to see them "properly."

He remembers one thing from those two hours at Angkor Wat: thousands of bats fleeing the temples at dusk, scoping the skies for dinner. "Are they still there?" he asks.

Indeed, they are.

People have lived at Angkor for centuries. In its heyday, vast waterways kept the region fertile and assured plentiful rice harvests that perpetuated the regime's power for centuries. But it didn't last. Neighbors invaded. The ruling class exchanged land for weapons. Some scholars speculate Cambodians themselves — the commonfolk builders of Angkor who were never allowed inside the grandiose palaces of kings — welcomed outside forces who promised them a better life under a different regime.

The majestic temples fell and crumbled beneath giant trees stretching their roots. Thieves stole diamonds and sapphires from statues and walls. They chopped Shiva and Vishnu heads from their bodies and left an ancient empire to the jungle's encroaching tentacles. But village life continued around the temples, largely unchanged. Time erased the Angkor narrative, and locals grew to know the tumbling city as a mysterious, ghostly place where gods once lived. They knew little else. "There have been so many hiatuses in the history of this poor country that one can no longer find any trace of conscious memory," writes François Bizot. "The thousands of temples scattered throughout the country had no other history besides that of the earth spirits that have haunted them for centuries."

The history of Angkor lapsed into an archaeological black hole. And so it remained until Henri Mouhot happened upon it in the late 1850s and early 1860s. He told the world what he found. More Europeans followed. L'École Française d'Extrême Orient funded the first Occidental expedition to the site in the early 1900s, later embarking on a massive project to clear and restore the area. The first wave of tourists arrived in 1907, and the Angkor Conservation Authority, the headquarters for French archaeologists, opened that year. The world was eager to preserve this magical site. In the late 1920s, Dutch scientists tried to reconstruct the monuments, applying a technique called anastylosis — literally piecing together the dismembered parts of broken buildings. By the 1960s, cranes, earthmovers and surveyors dotted the landscape.

But war silenced the commotion. Soldiers of the Khmer Rouge, the Vietnamese, the Cambodian Army all sprayed the temple walls with gunfire, littered the grounds with land mines, blasted rockets through stone. They scoured the bas-reliefs and statues for antiquities to sell and fuel their war. The pilfered prizes have surfaced in museums and homes around the world. Today, about 5,000 treasures-in-waiting sit behind locked fences and doors in a war-patched building in Siem Reap. Here, Cambodia's finest remaining statuary is numbered, catalogued and stored. Many items cannot safely be returned to their origins. Others cannot be traced to their roots. There is only one national museum, in Phnom Penh, and it cannot possibly hold all of Cambodia's homeless loot.

Jerry and I don't see Angkor again for more than two years, and in that time things change. In 2000, the Cambodian government announces a $3 million plan to upgrade the temples for tourism. That same year, a military general opens a karaoke hall, flamboyantly painted blue, and it throbs through the ruins until the government orders it closed. Each quarter, the government releases new figures on tourists, new predictions and hopes for the following year. Always the same hope, year after year: one million, that's the number. One million tourists by next year.

And then there is Siem Reap, a ragged little sometime colonial town when we see it in 1998. When we return in 2001, it's hot, sticky, wet and loud. The town pounds, rumbles, clinks, clanks, revs with construction. They're paving the road to the airport. There are guesthouses everywhere and Western-style restaurants with pizza and espresso near the old market. The building doesn't stop. Between 2000 and 2003, the number of guesthouses in Siem Reap skyrockets 60 percent, hotels 34 percent, restaurants 50 percent. Glorious multistarred international establishments pave the road to Angkor. The Sofitel, the Pansea, the Raffles—where guests pay up to $1,900 a night.

On the streets of Siem Reap there are more and more tourists, both foreign and Khmer. This is a welcome change. Many more Cambodians are coming to view their own heritage. They can now. There are more Khmers with money. There's a growing middle class that can scrimp and save for a weekend at the temples, a family excursion, a sacred event. They stay in hotels and guesthouses, beside the foreigners. They dine at Khmer and Western restaurants, with foreigners seated at the next table.

This is good to see.

But also on the streets of Siem Reap there are more squatters, more street kids, more glue-sniffers with ripening addictions to amphetamines, known locally as *yama*. More disabled and homeless veterans, camping their lives away. New markets open, but the old one remains soiled and flooded by rain. The river is dredged, a walkway is made, footbridges built, lamps placed along the way. They make these things new, yet they are not maintained, and much of it grows shabby in short time.

And though thousands of high-end tourists come each day, renting cozy and comfortable rooms, many more Cambodians set up shanties wherever they can until the police shoo them away. There is not nearly enough work to satisfy a saturated labor pool, and workers are easily exploited.

This continues over time. In April 2004, more than 2,000 luxury hotel workers go on strike, demanding at least part of the "service charges" that customers pay, typically an extra 10 percent added to their overall hotel bills. In early 2004, the government declared that "service charge" money belongs to the workers. In response, hotels promptly dropped those fees altogether, prompting workers to demand a reinstatement of the charges.

During one of our visits to Siem Reap, a former Sofitel employee complains he made only $30 a month because he wasn't considered "staff," though he worked full time. When guests ran off with towels or ashtrays, his salary was docked by whatever price his boss thought sufficient to cover the costs. So he went to work instead for a low-key guesthouse, where he gets no time off but a monthly income of $40. Jerry and I see this young man year after year, and he's a reliable source of information. But he asks me not to name him, for fear his current boss will fire him for speaking out. He is expendable: Siem Reap is crawling with eager young men, thirsting for a job at a guesthouse.

There is a drastic gap between rich and poor in this city, between the glorious wonder of Angkor and the reality in its shadows. I sit at a breezy riverside cafe, drinking a Beer Lao as I write, as I witness how that gap fits into people's lives. The wind rains dry, crackled leaves onto the streets. From here I can see across the river, over banks where cows graze in the grass, where squatters relieve themselves, where men stand waist-deep in the murky water, casting their nets. The cafe itself is lovely, but in another six weeks it is gone, another business turned belly-up. This place is dismantled, piece by piece, until only its framework remains with a few benches on the river. In another year, it will look abandoned and worn, and the sidewalks around it will smell of human excrement.

Another day, I sit and write at the balcony of a guesthouse across the river. From there, I watch a crazy soldier dancing in the street. I have seen him many times, year after year. He wears green pants, a green hat and a red shirt draped around his left shoulder. He buys an ear of corn from a woman's grill and stumbles about the road. *Motos* honk and swerve around him as he raises and swings his metal crutch. He shouts and taunts his neighbors. He is an addled, drunken amputee. He talks to himself, and people laugh at him.

They're all missing limbs, the soldiers who ply the streets by day and sleep at river's edge. Their world is this sidewalk, near a series of fruit stands along the river. These people live among garbage heaps behind big shady trees, in a plot of grass twenty feet wide that emerges only in the dry season. They spread mats on the sidewalk, and they trample the dirty earth barefoot. For the most part, they are ignored, sometimes tossed a few scraps to eat, like the stray dogs that live among them.

Another man, with his left leg hanging, hobbles on two metal crutches toward a pair of Western tourists passing by. They avoid his eyes fixed in their direction, and he fails to hobble fast enough. They are gone, and he turns back toward the river. Opportunity has passed, so he awaits whatever is next to amble by.

Up the road a few blocks is a man named Ian Kerr, a British expatriate. He used to run a guesthouse, but the building boom ate his profit. "It became unpleasant, and it also became impossible to make money." So he opened a butterfly garden instead.

His life passion is gardening, and he's always liked butterflies. His garden now has 1,000 specimens of almost forty varieties, all from the Siem Reap area, all caught by kids living nearby. He hires them. It's a job. "They're actually paying their way through school." He posted notes in Khmer around town, announcing he'd pay chil-

dren a small sum to catch the flitting insects. There was a deluge in response. They
came with sacks of broken butterflies, and he had to teach them care. He won't pay
for the dead, and he doesn't pay a lot for the living—about 2.5 cents for small ones
and 7.5 cents for big ones. Still, a steady contingent of kids comes to deliver their
catch and retrieve their pay two mornings a week.

At 7:50 A.M. one Sunday, fourteen children gather at his gate, each holding a
basket wrapped in a fishing net with scores of butterflies inside, twitching their wings.
The kids swarm when Ian approaches, raising their hands. He picks them one by one
and takes them inside. He goes through each child's basket, pulling the big ones first.
The baskets teem with brilliant colors, wings of orange and yellow, brown and
turquoise, stripes and dots, intricate patterns.

Outside the gate, the children discuss how many butterflies they have, how many
he chooses, how much money they earn. They know the numbers. They keep careful track; it is their job. They already have business savvy.

A fourteen-year-old girl named Chan Tla is the "chief catcher." She has 146 butterflies, but Ian hasn't chosen them all, and she is dismayed. "The money goes to my
mother and to school," she says. She sets the remaining catch free, outside Ian's gate.

The children still come and wait. They play flip-flop games in the street. They
buy ice cream from a man on a bike. The street is littered with little wings, thirteen
dead butterflies on the ground. "Every day, many die," says a girl named Lek.

In an hour or so, Ian has purchased 560 butterflies, and he sends the other kids
on their way. They will go out to the temples on a new quest while Ian steps back
inside his garden. It flourishes with life: orchids, bananas, palms, mangos, longans,
water custard, hibiscus, bougainvillea, a large pond full of koi. And 1,000 shades of
flutter.

At the temples, too, things change little by little, year by year. The ruins feel
millions of footsteps upon them, feet from all over the world, more and more people, until scientists wonder how many are too many. A sign at the entrance of Angkor
Wat now says no sitting on the balustrade. Inside, new wooden steps stand over old
worn stone. Metal nets are hung from the ceilings to catch falling rocks. Signs warn
tourists not to touch the reliefs and not to climb the towers. Instead of children these
days, the guides are adults speaking English and French, Chinese and Japanese. They
wear official tags and pressed, button-down shirts as they guide busloads of tourists
through the ancient halls. The temple opens at sunrise and closes just after sunset.
The visiting hours are set; all this is new.

Gone, too, are the children. They, like their mothers, are cordoned off from visitors by a string placed in the soil near the temple boundaries. They are kept in line
by sentries with sticks as they teeter, bounce, anticipate the exiting visitors and their
chance for a sale.

One day, Jerry and I visit an ancient pool in the dead heat of afternoon. We are
lulled by the sun and sounds of traditional music, and we follow our ears. We find
five men playing violins, cymbals, xylophones and drums. Most of them cannot see
us.

The drummer holds a snakeskin instrument, beating it with the stub of his left arm. He has no eyes. He has a bullet scar on his right arm, and a body full of burns and lucky tattoos. The violinist is also blind. They have a pile of tapes, with their music for sale, $5 apiece. We ask the band's name, and they say they have none. We ask again, and they decide that, logically, they should be called "The Samroang Group," since that is where they're from. Samroang is a village in the far northwest, one of the last and most brutal fronts of the Khmer Rouge war.

Among the handsome sights of Angkor are many scarred bodies. The most popular sunset perch is atop Phnom Bakheng, where tourists clamber up steep, rocky steps—or pay a fee to ride an elephant up instead. At the top, the crowds watch the day fade in a panorama over rice fields and ruins. There is a Khmer man up here. He is dressed in a beautiful purplish, bluish, *krama*. He has a chunk missing from the bottom of one foot, a bashed-in nose, a sharp bony rib cage. He prostrates himself and sings for a long time as tourists meander about, pointing cameras and attention elsewhere. He flings his body on stone before an incense bucket and a few small Buddhas. Then a flicker of pink illuminates the sky. With a whoosh, the crowd shuttles past his bent body, their eyes on that sky. Then back again, the people sway, to see the moon rise higher over Angkor Wat. All the while, the crowd has its back to the man. All the while, he prays.

A few miles away is Choun Nhiem, eighty-three years old. He is known to thousands of tourists as the sweeper at Ta Prohm temple. He has spent thirteen years at that temple, every day, sweeping the leaves that fall from the silvery trees that swaddle this ruin in snaky roots. In late afternoon, he goes home, up a dirt path, to a one-room shack on stilts. His wife died several years ago, and he lives alone. His walls are metal, full of holes, with sunlight pouring through. The house grows stifling in Cambodia's cumbersome heat. He sleeps on the floor and lights his home by a small candle lamp. "I would like a nice house, but I have no money," he says.

Choun Nhiem is dirt poor, but he is famous. He is famous because *Lonely Planet* has put his picture on the cover of its 2002 Cambodia guidebook. *The New York Times* features him in a story the following year. Many a tourist leaves Ta Prohm temple with a few shots of the sweeper, whose furrowed countenance and simple routines lend a quaint magnificence to the scene.

Thousands know the face, the hunched figure; yet few people know about Nhiem's life. Few even know his name.

Jerry and I first meet Nhiem in 1998. We talk to him every time we visit Ta Prohm — nearly a dozen times in half as many years. In 2003, we decide to acquaint ourselves a little better. We hire a translator and learn his story.

"There's a famous picture of you with a tree," two foreign tourists tell Nhiem one morning in August, as he takes a rest on a temple stoop. They ask him the usual questions—his age, his name, where he lives. Then they ask to have their picture taken with him.

"I don't know how many people I meet in one day, I don't count," Nhiem says. "When photographers take a picture of me, I don't know when or where. But I have seen my picture in *Lonely Planet*. I don't think anything about it."

Nhiem speaks in a gruff, gravelly voice, and he is delightfully blunt. His back

hunches severely when he stands, so that he is no more than four feet high. He wears
blue flip-flops, a blue cotton shirt and green shorts that reveal skinny, veined legs.
His head is shaved. "Someone does it for me. My hair takes a long time to care for if
it gets too long."

Nhiem sits among little bronze elephants and a snakeskin instrument. He fiddles
with a carved wooden bird, which he tries to sell for a few dollars. Beyond the 25
cents he earns for a day of sweeping, these little trinkets are his only income. "Sometimes I have no rice to eat, so I can sell these and get some money," he says.

His schedule has grown flexible with his age. "Now I'm too old, so it's not so
regular." Some days he starts at 6 A.M., other days at 8. He always leaves by 5:30 P.M.
"I never take a day off. I can, but I don't want to." Sweeping is not difficult, he says.
In fact, it's rather productive. He uses handmade brooms of twigs tied with twine.
"I bought this one from someone who sold them from the back of a bicycle," he says.
But they don't last long, which frustrates him. "Ugh, ten days, it's broken already."
When he was younger, he made his own brooms, but his eyes have failed of late.
"Some German people came here and saw my eyes and bought me some glasses.... I
wore them for two years, but no better. So I gave the glasses to a monk."

As Nhiem sits on the stoop talking about his life, people filter through. "In the
Khmer Rouge regime, two of my sons were killed by Pol Pot," he says. Soldiers knocked
on his door one day. They told Nhiem he could stay, but they wanted his sons, both
teenagers at the time. "The soldiers 'invited' my sons to work," he says, "but actually
they killed them. I didn't know the meaning of 'invite.'" Now he knows its curse.

This has haunted Nhiem for decades, but time slowly assuages his pain. "I used
to think about it a lot, but now I'm too old." He doesn't know how to adequately
describe his feelings, so he doesn't try. "It's very difficult for me to talk about." Instead,
he talks of his surviving family, two sons and a daughter now grown. And he talks
about this temple.

Nhiem chose Ta Prohm as his worksite for practical reasons. "It's next to my
house, over there," he says, nodding toward a village two miles in the distance. He
finds sanctuary in this place. "Ta Prohm temple is Cambodian heritage," he says. "I
like everything about this temple. More than a thousand yards by 650 yards and
thirty-nine towers. I like it all." Yet he knows nothing of the texts and guides tucked
beneath tourists' arms. "I don't know at all about Angkor history. I never went to
school at all. I don't know how to read or write. When I was born, there was no school,
only the pagoda."

He breaks his story for a moment to pose for a photo with a pretty woman who
sits beside him. A few moments later, a young man standing nearby drops a bag at
Nhiem's feet, then scampers off. Inside the bag is a miniature wooden oxcart, another
tchotcke for him to sell. Nhiem says he doesn't know the young man. "The people
around here take care of me." His neighbors bring him lunch at the temple and dinner at home. "If you don't believe me, at the nighttime, you can come and see."

At 12:10, it's nearing Nhiem's lunchtime and the start of a daily routine. One of
his sons is sitting nearby, here to bring Nhiem some food. At twenty-seven, Son Ta
has his old man's face, minus many decades of hardship and lines. He chuckles at his
dad's fame. "Many people take pictures of my father."

Nhiem slowly rises, sweeps a little, then hunches his way to an inner corridor of the temple, to a small Buddha statue. He squats to pray, lips moving briskly, no sound. Light flickers on his bald head. He keeps his flip-flops by his side. Every minute or so he leans over, pressing his hands to the packed earthen floor. "I pray every day before lunch. I only come to this spot," he says. It is one of the few statues that didn't perish during decades of war. "In the Pol Pot time I had no Buddha, so I just prayed by myself around here. If I had prayed openly, I would have been killed like my two sons."

When he's done, he ambles to an open area by a tree. A shirtless Western man snaps photos as he moves along. Then another, and another. It's something of a camera parade, trailing the old man's feet. There are more comments among the visitors: "He is very famous, no?"

Nhiem reaches his favorite spot again, in a courtyard near a large tree. He prepares for lunch in the corner of the temple wall. He peels off his shirt and hangs it from a nail in the tree. He mumbles an adage to himself, "Earn a little, eat a little," then fills a plastic bottle with water from a jug, squirting his mouth, spitting it out, washing his legs and feet.

There's a large pile of leaves beside a nearby tree. "I've swept all this," he says. "Every day, every year. I always put them here." Four years worth of leaves beneath an orange tree he planted. He closes his eyes and grimaces, dousing his head in water.

A golden dog with a gouged eye sits near him as he eats a simple lunch with rice. Another tourist takes pictures from a distance, then approaches to offer Nhiem some money. The dog snaps at the tourist, protecting the old man and his food.

When Nhiem has finished his meal in silence, he offers to show us his home. "Before, I walked. But now my son has a motorbike and comes to pick me up."

It's a shady village shrouded by palms, bananas and papayas. Nhiem directs the way. There are three wooden steps to his door and inside, a mattress on the floor. He knows his house is small, "but it's fine for my purposes." He also knows he is unlikely ever to have more. His mosquito net is tied to the ceiling, and he sleeps on a pink sheet below it. Mats are spread across the floor, some clothes piled in the corners, empty perfume bottles stashed against a wall, a package of incense, and that's it. It's excruciatingly hot now, but he insists it cools at night.

Nhiem's village is adjacent the settlement where French author and ethnologist François Bizot lived in the 1970s. Bizot's recently published account of his time in a Khmer Rouge prison sells around the world. Nhiem remembers the Frenchman clearly. "Ah, Bizot! He had a Khmer wife," Nhiem says. "I don't know the history of Bizot except that he married a Khmer woman, and she has gone to Paris. Before, he worked at Angkor Conservation. In the Pol Pot regime, Mr. Bizot was already gone but his wife was here.... She was a good farmer," he says. "Later, someone took her to France. If Mr. Bizot had stayed here, he would have been killed by Pol Pot." That's what Nhiem remembers of the man.

Nhiem is surrounded by larger wooden homes and shops. Sometimes at night, he watches TV at the neighbor's house — but he never listens to karaoke, he assures us. He likes this home of a lifetime. "I like everyone here," he says. "The people who live near my house never quarrel."

And after many years of pain, Nhiem has found a peace in the dusk of his life. "Now I'm happy." He wouldn't mind going on, sweeping, meeting tourists, spending his days at Ta Prohm for years to come. "I want to live a long time, but it is up to the Buddha how many years he gives me," he says, pointing out, "My mother lived to ninety-nine."

Jerry and I spend that night, after speaking with Nhiem, at Preah Khan up the road. This is not an ordinary event. The Angkor Park closes after sunset, and all the tourists go home. But we are here in the interests of journalism.

We are here because of a guard named Keuen. Jerry and I met him the previous year, off duty as an officer, but guiding tourists for money. That is not unusual. With a salary of less than $25 a month, Cambodian cops find other means. Keuen had no watch and wished he did. On his wrist, Jerry had a new $5 ticker from a market in Phnom Penh. He plucked it off and handed it over. Keuen gladly traded a story: He said he carries an AK-47 at night, fending off looters, shooting first, asking questions later. He had our attention. Shoot-outs? Chases? Bullets bouncing off temple walls? I imagined a thriller of a night. Why not camp with the guards? Everyone savors these temples by day — but what of the night?

It's a fine idea, but getting permission is a harried affair. It requires several meetings with Preah Khan's top cop Prum Saroeun, numerous visits to a government office, a few minor altercations with government workers, a multitude of phone calls and faxes to Phnom Penh, several rounds of beer, and a $60 bribe. It all comes down to power.

Our mission puts us face-to-face with modern Khmer social order — not so different from that of Angkor times when Jayavarman VII reigned over Preah Khan and the elite paraded beneath golden parasols while the peasants worked like slaves. Cambodian society has always been structured by class, with wide gaps between rich and poor, powerful and powerless. And today, a rift remains. Some have Land Cruisers, others have bare feet. Some live in palatial villas, others in shacks next door. Wealth and power are social yardsticks. And the power to grant or deny permission — to anyone, for whatever reason — is largely how social rank is defined.

Today, the Angkor Archaeological Park is equally striated, with managerial powers divided among several entities. UNESCO oversees the park's upkeep as a World Heritage site, the government-run Apsara Authority manages the park, the World Monuments Fund spearheads conservation projects, and several police forces protect different areas at different times. That's a lot of hands and egos in one place.

Our quest begins with a search for Keuen, which is quickly thwarted by an unexpected meeting with his boss, Saroeun. The chief comes to our guesthouse with officer So Sambath as his translator. Saroeun is large, round and stoic; Sambath is not. Saroeun wears a patch on his sleeve that says "POLICE." He doesn't look at us when he speaks. Sambath wears a smile and brings a respectfully jovial demeanor.

Saroeun explains that he and his men protect the temple at night, that tourists buy passes for the daytime, but at 6 P.M. they must leave. Defining his turf, Saroeun tells us, "The Apsara Authority has no authority at night." The dark is his domain alone. As chief officer, he has the power to "open the way" for us. He has ten men; they will protect us. For that service, how much will we pay?

We have no idea of the expected answer. We weren't really expecting this conversation. We ask how much he wants. Sambath translates again. Perhaps we don't understand, he says. And that's all.

There's an uncomfortable pause.

Asian communication is different from that of the West. "It is the hearer's responsibility to understand what is being said," writes American psychologist Richard E. Nisbett in his psychological examination of Western and Asian thought. So, while it seems as though nothing is said, perhaps a great deal is being communicated. With Saroeun, we're not really sure.

It is, perhaps, why these negotiations take nearly a week. It is, perhaps, why Saroeun becomes distressed when Jerry and I, in our quest for permission, also visit the Apsara Authority, the government entity created to protect and manage the Angkor Archaeological Park. It is, perhaps, why the worker in the Apsara office immediately and repeatedly denies our request. And it is, perhaps, why that worker becomes quiet when we call his boss in Phnom Penh, and the boss faxes us permission to spend a night at Preah Khan.

Power is a precious commodity in Cambodia; people wield it in the biggest and smallest ways. This is not a critique but essential to understanding how things work. But navigating the proper channels is never a clear-cut path.

Luckily, in all this negotiating, one rule is universal: Beer is a powerful palliative.

During one of our meetings with Saroeun and Sambath, Jerry orders cans of Tiger beer — the tiger being Asia's preeminent symbol of power, the brand being a top choice in tipple. Saroeun gulps, then burps in mid-sentence. He becomes calm and talkative and even smiles. We discuss snakes — he's seen many. We ask about the last time he tussled with thieves — it was 1994. People still steal from the ground outside the temple walls, he says, but they run if spotted. Saroeun has worked at Preah Khan for nine years. Before that, he was an officer in town, handling statistics and IDs. He likes this job better. "Because I am the boss and I don't have to think too much."

Then he asks if we need anything else.

No, that pretty much answers everything. We shake hands and thank him for his time. We still haven't settled on a price, but that's OK. Morn, our trusty translator who has politely attended our negotiations, tells us we're doing very well.

We arrive at the Preah Khan entrance as the day's last tourists exit and incense clouds the temple arteries. A yellow twilight bathes us all. Thunder calls and trees squeak — big trees, growing through the temple, their roots like octopus tentacles, straddling stone, smothering rooftops. They shimmer by day, but look menacing now.

Dusk falls upon sprightly nymphs and intricate lintels, and the carvings seem to dance in the gloaming. A small wind rustles through trees as day melds with night. "Maybe the ghosts will come," Morn teases. When he was a boy, his mother would tell him about the ghosts in the countryside. One evil spirit, dressed in white, would appear to her in the nighttime forest. But Morn doesn't believe in ghosts, and he isn't afraid to spend the night here.

This temple was built in 1191, commissioned by King Jayavarman VII and dedicated to his father. It is vast, covering 140 acres in all. It is possible to lose oneself for hours in its mossy nooks and private corners. When the World Monuments Fund started work here in 1989, it was a precarious structure; visitors could hike to the roof, climbing upon piles of stones. I like to sit at the far reaches of its southern hallway, where the lower half of a giant Buddha rests against a wall and serpentine vines slither through windows. From this spot I can see all the way to the center, through a shrinking tunnel of walls and doorways.

Jerry and I walk with Morn outside the temple, 180 degrees opposite the Buddha, across the stone blocks of an ancient bridge. There's a scurry of nocturnal jungle life as diurnal critters retire. Cicadas whistle, and a faintly pink sky glosses over lily pads nearby. Things fall from their perches in the trees—what things, we have no idea.

In darkness, the temple ripples in flashlight. Shadows prance across walls; spires and towers grow mystical. Cambodians have never trusted the night; there is much to fear in the jungle. If not an evil spirit or enemy soldier, then a dangerous beast or vermin. This has always been so. "You cannot be too much on your guard; going to bed or getting up, you are ever in peril of putting hand or foot on some venomous snake," explorer Mouhot writes of the Cambodian jungle 140 years ago. And: "I have had to wage war with savage foes, from whom I never before suffered so much. Nothing avails against them; they let themselves be massacred, with a courage worthy of nobler beings. I speak of mosquitoes."

Such was the Cambodian forest in the 1860s, and so it is now for the officers who guard the nation's treasures at night.

After viewing the bridge, we find guard Sambath eating dinner with his wife and two kids in a small hut on the temple's outskirts. Sambath doesn't remember, but Jerry and I met him two years before, in the afternoon. We sat on the temple's south side that day, and I found a bullet shell near my feet. I picked it up and kept it, all dusty and worn. Sambath said it was left from one of the frequent battles here. "Poom, poom, poom," he pantomimed pulling a trigger.

Now, he is eager to show us a safe night. He tells us ten officers are on duty, four inside the temple and six outside, though we never see more than three. "We work in shifts," he says, "and every hour or two we change. Two people sleep, two awake." But not tonight. "I got the information that you were coming, so I slept already today."

It ends up a peaceful night, the reality less dramatic than our visions and Keuen's tales. In truth, the guns aren't fired so often, and most nights pass in tranquility. "I've had this two years already, but I've never used it," Sambath says, gazing at his AK-47. "In the four years I've worked here, I haven't caught anyone stealing anything."

He and chief Saroeun take us on patrol. Sambath carries his gun all the while, but Saroeun has only a flashlight, a walkie-talkie and a watermelon tucked under his

Police officer So Sambath strikes a pose in the middle of the night in a passageway in the empty Preah Khan temple. The two lit carvings depict mythical Hindu guardian monsters.

arm for a late-night snack. He has a gun like Sambath's, but "I'm the boss, so I let him use his."

As we stroll through the temple, Sambath points to phallic *lingas* and Buddhist bas-reliefs. He takes us to an inner sanctum. "I read in the inscriptions it was painted gold on the wall and had holes with diamonds," he says, though other reports indicate the holes held plaster covering the walls. Sambath points to a relief that once was a Buddha but later changed to an *apsara*, a celestial dancer, the epitome of Khmer beauty and charm. "I studied at a private school about the history of this temple," he says.

Saroeun shines his light on something in the corner: no worries, just a toad.

The jungle grows black, and blacker still as the moon rises higher and smaller, then disappears beneath a thick seal of clouds. There is no natural light, and the human eye adjusts poorly to the glaring tunnel of a flashlight. This is disconcerting, as vines and roots turn to arms in our path, grabbing at us as we pass. A line of red ants crosses our trail, and Morn jumps at the thought of a snake. There is venom in these forests, and it kills with efficiency.

Toward the east side, we find another guard standing alone, quiet and still, in pitch darkness. His name is Reth, and he's worked here for four years. I ask him questions, but boss Saroeun answers for Reth, in Reth's words. "Before, I was a policeman in Ta Prohm temple. Here it is better. When I was at Ta Prohm, there was still war. When I moved here, there was no more war." At Ta Prohm, Reth says, he caught people cutting trees and stealing statues. In such cases, he says, "I protected." And that's the only description he gives.

All these Angkor ruins recall a brutal and violent past. Like other temples, Preah Khan spent several centuries obscured by jungle after the Angkor empire's fall, until French explorers "rediscovered" it in the 1860s. A hundred years later, these buildings sheltered warring soldiers. The Viet Cong tromped about. The Vietnamese fought the Khmer Rouge and the Khmer Rouge fought the Cambodian Army. Sambath says a friend was stationed here in the late 1980s. "The guards who stayed awake were fine. Those who slept always died."

Even since the last Khmer Rouge defected in 1998, the ruins still face threats from a deluge of tourists and from thieves plundering the last riches. Poverty and greed are cited as predominant motivators. The largest and most popular temples are guarded, but ruins in the countryside — and there are hundreds— are pillaged with little recourse. When Jerry and I visited Angkor in 2001, we took motorbikes to Banteay Samre, an outlying temple surrounded by rice paddies. We found new holes where carved heads had been stolen from the walls. There was powdered stone on the ground below, still white from recent chiseling.

Chief Saroeun bristles at such thievery. "Cambodian people come to the temple and dig things and steal things, and I regret that very much," he says, "because it is their own. They steal their soul." It is precisely why he's here now.

That — and the money.

As we continue on patrol, Saroeun flashes his light and bats skitter overhead.

"I never studied in school about the history of the temples," he tells us, "but I used to know from the old people. When I was in school they didn't teach Angkor history yet. But now they do."

We chat a bit, and I ask about Keuen, the guard with Jerry's watch. We learn that Keuen now works in the Apsara office. "They have some problems with customers who don't pay for the tickets," Saroeun says. But he also works in a hotel at night, where he makes an extra $30 a month. This is an enviable sum to every officer here, and it is obvious they think Keuen has done something right in this life.

We head to a grassy heap of stones and climb its crumbling steps. It once served as the King's arsenal, Sambath says, though scholars aren't entirely sure. Before the king sent his soldiers to fight, "They came here and sat together and talked about their plans for war." Only the king and high commanders were allowed this high; common soldiers remained below. Sambath illuminates an altar of burnt incense. "Even now many general commanders come here to pray." They pray for good luck and a better life.

We're sitting on 1,000 years of history, and no one else is around to share it. All the tourists have retired in their rented beds; it's just us and the onyx night. Jerry sets up a tripod, hoping to capture images the eyes can't see. The moon long gone, we sit in a blanket of darkness. Jerry opens up the camera and takes exposures thirty minutes long; he has done this before, many times in many places. But when his film is developed weeks later, he's shocked to see opaque frames, little rectangles of unexpected black. It's that dark that night.

And hot. We're swaddled in heat, our clothes sticky cocoons around us, but we can't bare skin. "Many people get malaria here," Sambath says. So we immerse ourselves in sweat. As we sit here, steaming, Sambath talks of his favorite spot. It's the "Perfect Woman," a carving of Jayavarman VII's wife. When we first saw her in 2001, she was difficult to find: over piles of stones, under a falling roof, through a low doorway, into a trapped alcove. Restoration since has made her slightly more accessible. Long ago, she had diamonds in her forehead and eyebrows. She represents all the characteristics of a good Khmer woman, including the stretch marks of a mother many times over.

"Before my daughter was born," Sambath says, "I went to pray there and gave some fruit and said if I had a daughter, I would stop smoking and stop drinking and buy a motorbike for that daughter and build a new home. And now my dream is coming true." His girl was born, he's building a house, he bought a *moto* for the family to use until his daughter can, and he stopped smoking. "But I can't stop drinking because it's social. If friends ask me out, I can't refuse."

I ask Sambath if he wonders what it was like here in Angkor times, if he wishes he had witnessed the heyday of Preah Khan. The question confuses him, and he answers matter-of-factly. "In Angkor times I was not yet born." He thinks more about his immediate concerns, about feeding his family. It's hard. His salary nets him just over $20 a month, not including tips from tourists. "In the rainy season, I'm a farmer also." But he wouldn't give up this job. "I want to stay here for a long time to protect this temple, to protect the Khmer soul, especially for my son and daughter. All of the policemen here think like this."

As the night deepens, Saroeun prepares a cot for us in an open-air building near the temple's entrance. Sambath ties a hammock between two trees. Reth has vanished as mysteriously as he appeared. Geckos cluck in the forest; a single frog barks through the night. And every few hours, we go for a walk.

On one of these sorties Jerry follows Saroeun, who shines his light on a scorpion, adjacent their feet. *Crunch.* Enemy down. Death by combat boot.

On another patrol, Reth magically returns. Saroeun goes his own way as the rest of us head through the southern corridor, past the Buddha legs, my favorite spot. But it's different now at night. We follow the long corridor to its end, where the rock meets jungle. Turning around and facing north, we meet two giant headless statues, looming like ogres. Our sight is funneled into flashlight beams, and everything seems to attack from the periphery — vines, leaves, bugs, rocks. When Reth decides to leave, we follow at a brisk trot, making our way back to the cot.

Eventually, everyone snoozes among puffing mosquito coils. I get the cot; Morn and Jerry sleep on hard wood. Light breaks around 5:20 A.M., and we all pop up. We admire the temple in a muted sunrise, its stone pillars gracing a pastel sky.

Then nature calls, and I head off to find the facilities, without announcing where I'm going. The only facilities, I discover, lie outside the temple's main entrance. So I walk all the way through, across the street to an empty food stall, to a broken bathroom.

I head back. But now I meet an Apsara Authority guard who wants to see my ticket. I show him the sweat-drenched remnants of yesterday's $20 pass. He tells me it has expired. I explain, in Khmer, why we are here. He says I cannot return to retrieve my backpack, my translator or my husband.

Just then, Saroeun approaches by *moto*, to see where I am. He shows the guard my permission letter from the Apsara Authority, but the guard insists it has expired, too. It was good for one night; anyone can see the sun has risen. I must go. "Mr. Saroeun has authority in the nighttime, but not in the daytime," the guard tells me.

Saroeun concedes, "I have no authority in the daytime."

I head inside anyway, with the Apsara sentry snipping at my heels. He leaves his post at the entrance, where tourists now pass unnoticed. The guard trails me all the way, telling me I am a scofflaw. He follows until Jerry, Morn and I exit the temple boundaries with our belongings. It takes all of fifteen minutes.

We sit then with Saroeun at a snack stand near the broken bathroom, and we square away our deal. We hand him $60, and he is eminently pleased. He grins as he relates the morning's adventures to Morn. As we drive away, Morn tells me Saroeun is impressed with my fortitude. "He says you have a lot of power."

A few weeks later, back in Phnom Penh, I decide to visit the Apsara Authority headquarters, hoping to interview the director general, wanting his input on the state of Preah Khan.

That does not happen.

The Apsara Authority works from a large, hulking pink building with little inside. I enter its bowels, a cavernous place of stone and concrete and high ceilings. There is no one around. I find my way upstairs to a hallway of closed doors. I knock on one, open the door and find three people sitting quietly at their desks in a chillingly air-conditioned room. Mao Vibol, an assistant to the director general, asks if he can help. He tells me there is only one person for me to talk to—his boss—and it would behoove me to write a letter. I ask if I can make an appointment, but he thinks that would be very difficult because his boss is the big boss, a very busy boss, and appointments with him are not easily made.

So I offer to hand-write a letter right here, right now, and this makes the young man smile. "I think that would be administratively correct," he says. I write it, and he tells me he will call "if I get the information from him."

But he never does. In the following weeks, I call the assistant several times, but he doesn't answer the phone. I hoped to ask the "big boss" about looting at the temples and whether officers still do, occasionally, encounter thieves in the night. My answer comes a few months later in an article published by *The Cambodia Daily*. Early in 2004, authorities spot a car of suspicious men entering Angkor Thom one evening. Two hundred provincial police officers and another fifty military police are deployed; they arrest a thirty-four-year-old man with an ancient vase. The others get away.

Our experiences with the Preah Khan story—the negotiations, the morning departure, my attempts to talk with the Apsara director—aptly reflect the dichotomy of Cambodia today. On the one hand, it is a land endowed with beauty and wonder; on the other, a country crippled by corruption and myopia. That system is kept in place by a power structure unlikely to change. It was, after all, a similar rigid hierarchy that enabled Angkor kings to have these temples built for them, centuries ago.

Preah Khan, like all the Angkor temples, is mired in the tumbled culture around it. Something so sanctified, bogged down in dirty little deals. Yet most visitors can slip right into the charm of Angkor and leave again, never noticing the troubles that Cambodians face every day, never discerning the muddle beneath an alluring veneer. And that's the unfortunate trouble with tourism, anywhere. It lulls people into the comfort of a quick glance, a rosy view. There's nothing wrong with a pleasant vacation. But it becomes dangerous when those blinded observations turn to conclusions about what a place really is. Many keen travelers visit Cambodia with lots of questions, and they leave understanding the country's complexity. Others don't. Others leave believing their two-week vacation gave them answers and showed them truth.

But truth doesn't often parade in the open. Truth lurks in Cambodia's deepest shadows.

Interlude: Siem Reap to Phnom Penh

Getting from point *A* to point *B* in Cambodia is always brutalizing, dehumanizing, asinine and interesting—all of that, all together, and it makes one feel utterly blessed for having survived the excursion.

In this case, point *A* is Siem Reap, point *B* is Phnom Penh, and modus operandi is National Route 6 by minivan. While these sorts of jaunts often make for exhilarating travelers' tales, what many a travel tale often emits is the sad fact that *this* is it: This is all Cambodia has in the way of transportation and infrastructure. This is what all Cambodians must endure, every time they want or need to get from point *A* to point *B*, wherever those points may be. The experience is inevitably a hot, sticky, painful, smelly ride, be it on a minivan, oxcart, motorboat or motorbike. It's too fast, too long, too cramped. It's downright dangerous and often senseless. Yet most Cambodians take it in stride as the hours pass by. No books, no papers, no travel games to occupy the mind. Only the ride itself.

While it is, perhaps, "an experience" to the traveler who can go home, it's simply life to a Cambodian whose home is here.

That said:

Every tire is bald, worn to a smooth sheen. Jerry and I inspect each one and it's obvious, not a single minivan in Siem Reap is effectively equipped for the 195 bone-pulping miles to Phnom Penh. But if it isn't a minivan, it's the back of a pickup truck piled high with boxes and rice sacks, at least a dozen people and possibly a motorcycle strapped to the bumper. We choose the van, pay the $20 and reserve two seats for the next morning. The ticket sellers tell us the trip will take six hours, so we assume at least nine.

The van arrives at our hotel at 6:30, with half a dozen Khmers already scrunched in back. It then meanders through town, fetching a few foreigners here, a few Khmers there. Our group numbers twenty-two on a vehicle made for twenty. But we're not done. We stop at a guesthouse to retrieve two more passengers. They're not here, so we sit and wait. The back row begins to grumble. A well-dressed Khmer woman announces that she must be in Phnom Penh by 3 P.M. She has an appointment. After more than an hour, two young Khmer women leisurely saunter aboard. They were eating breakfast. They lost track of time. Now they're cranky because the seats they wanted are taken, so they squeeze in next to us, all four of us nuzzled together on a seat near the motor, heat pouring into our feet. The mood is acrid.

This is no way to start a road trip through Cambodia.

We begin the long hobble through town, toward the highway. It's a mellifluous swirl of *motos*, cars, trucks, bikes, dogs, cows, and two smooth lanes of pavement — for 300 yards. Serenity quickly ends when the road turns to dust. If you peer very closely at the red dust, you can almost detect an ancient strip of pavement about ten feet wide. That's it, National Road 6, beneath our bald tires. Pick-up–truck taxis ride our tail then honk up our side and scoot by in a breeze. One passing pickup truck passenger, riding in back, has tethered his leg to the truck so he won't fall off as he sleeps.

A race begins. A white minivan wants to pass us, so it announces its presence by horn. The Asian horn is not a warning signal: It's a codpiece. He — and Cambodian drivers are always he — with the biggest horn has the right of way. So this van wants to pass, but another truck comes our way. They miss each other, but only just.

There is an odor among us. It seems someone has a digestive problem, not uncommon in Cambodia. It stems from either our driver, the Grandma and Grandpa beside him, or their grandkid wedged between. All four share the front seat. Grandma fans her nose and wrinkles her face, signaling another waft. It comes every fifteen minutes; the whole van suffers in waves. Women rub their nostrils with menthol, the Asian traveler's panacea. Someone in back lights a cigarette and waves it around.

After sixty miles, we approach a one-lane bridge, a mishmash of rotting boards spread crosswise over a few rotting beams with wide gaps and clear views of doom. As all drivers hope to cross as quickly as possible, everyone tailgates, and several vehicles approach the bridge at once. This particular bridge comes with a bonus. It's plastered with red signs sporting white skulls and crossbones, the international warning for land mines. On the bridge? Beside the bridge? In the fields around the bridge? Who knows! Our driver plows through with his hand on the horn.

Along the way, we pass many dusty children the color of sandalwood. They stand at the roadside, then pounce into traffic, demanding money. They're day laborers. Their job is to fill potholes, then ask for payment. They're remarkably unsuccessful on both accounts. One throng of boys latches onto the window of an oncoming minivan, pulling arms and *riel* from the front seat as the driver tries to shake them loose. One boy falls to the road, nearly filling a pothole with his scrawny body.

Buddhist monks also sit beside the road, asking for donations to their nearby temples. They are inevitably accompanied by a man beneath an umbrella who blares screeching music through a megaphone. Noise never seems to bother Cambodians. Even French explorer Mouhot noticed this, when he wrote in his diaries about a musical performed for the King 140 years ago. "The play was simply a phantasmagoria tolerably well managed, and accompanied by music more noisy than harmonious; but which appeared perfectly to satisfy the public." A British expatriate once told me: "There's only one thing noisier than a bunch of Khmers — another bunch of Khmers."

We bump along as Grandpa in the front seat chews on a snack of fried beetles. He plucks them one by one from a bag, cracks them open, sucks out the innards and pitches the shells in a plastic bag on his wife's lap.

We've been traveling eight hours now. The road is still full of potholes that could swallow small buffalo— of which there are several on these highways; an elephant, too, under the rump of its *mahout*. Dusk draws near. The woman in back has long since missed her appointment. The driver grows weary of our trip and takes to the left side of the road. He races the vehicle in front, passing in a rush. We reach the Udong area, twenty-five miles from Phnom Penh, where the landscape changes, the road curves and small hills sprout from the earth. It's not a good place to pass blindly on the left.

Suddenly, the front seat erupts in gasps and groans and a collective "Tsk, tsk, tsk!" A wreck. A flipped white Toyota Camry, and another smashed and turned around, with most of the nearby village looking on. Everyone sighs, "What a terrible thing!" All the more reason to drive faster.

Right around this time, Grandpa (now identified as the mystery farter) rolls down his window. The driver swivels his hand beneath the air vents. He fiddles with the controls and a sad wheezing sound burbles through the van. No air conditioning. And then: tragedy. Our driver realizes his horn — his lifeline — has quit. We face the road without one of Cambodia's essential driving tools. Now the vehicles ahead, which inevitably have no mirrors, or mirrors turned on the driver so he can watch himself sing karaoke, can't hear our maniacal approach.

Grandpa clears his throat and spits out the window, nearly striking a *moto* driver on the head.

"Gross!" exclaims a tourist among us. But in Cambodia, there is nothing socially wrong with picking one's nose, burping or spitting in public. Just don't pick your teeth without covering your mouth, don't point the bottoms of your feet at someone else and don't rub a child on the head. Crucial lessons in social grace.

Our driver is really antsy now. He pulls left, peering around vehicles, wiggling his way around and through. Left, right, forward, left, right (but never entirely on the right). There's a small break, he races beside the vehicle in front, farther, faster, straight into a swarm of *motos*, trucks and cars. Slam! on the brakes. We miss an oncoming *moto* by inches, and its driver slaps our driver's window in contempt.

So it is all the way into Phnom Penh, light dimming, smog thickening. Finally, the city. We go all the way through town, way beyond our destination because the driver is paid to take us to a particular guesthouse and none other. When we emerge from the bowels of our minivan, we hail two *motos* and retrace our route, back toward the river. My driver is very excited to learn we have just come from Siem Reap, home of the famed Angkor temples. He has never been there because he doesn't have the money.

"You are very lucky!" he tells me.

5. Neighbors and Borders: Enemies Through Time

How many victims, how much blood and suffering, are connected with this business of borders! There is no end to the cemeteries of those who have been killed the world over in the defense of borders.
— Ryszard Kapuscinski, *Imperium*

They douse them with gasoline and splatter them with red paint — the blood of their angry hearts. They shout and hack with a sledgehammer. They burn. They taunt. They feel a proud solidarity.

It is just a sculpture, the Vietnam-Cambodia Liberation Monument, built in 1979 to honor the Vietnamese invasion that ousted the Khmer Rouge. They are not real people, not real Vietnamese, only three whitewashed soldiers with chiseled faces, wearing carved uniforms, carrying guns of stone. But they are symbolic and easy to lash. The real deaths, real people shedding real blood, those will come later.

It is bright and sunny this Sunday in early September 1998, with pillowy clouds floating in the sky. The kids are riled and ready to pounce. This is Democracy Square, a tent city erected in protest of dubious national election results, with Prime Minister Hun Sen claiming widespread victory and the opposition crying foul. The camp sits in a park across from the National Assembly building. In the center of the park is this memorial.

Democracy Square has bloomed into a village over the past few weeks. Rattan mats spread beneath bright blue tarps, shirtless kids and their mothers sprawl across the ground for afternoon naps, crowds huddle beneath umbrellas in the nighttime rain, thieves work through a bulge of people with so many satchels and pockets. Women carry babies on their hips, begging for handouts. Vendors sell snacks from baskets. Kids pee in the grass: the makings of a Cambodian community. More than an ongoing protest with political inclinations, this demonstration has become life.

But some students remember precisely why they are here, or at least why they say they are here. They are here for democracy. For freedom. For fighting the Vietnamese invaders they believe to be ruling their country, still. They are here to show the ruling party just how they feel. And they don't feel good. They feel rage. They burn Hun Sen in effigy. They carry signs with caricatures of the prime minister wearing Vietnamese conical hats, with Ho Chi Minh pulling his strings like a puppet, and of his head sitting on a dog's body with a bubble saying "I am a *yuon.*"

"*Yuon,*" that word of fierce debate. Toddlers learn from parents who point, there, that person is a *yuon.* Vietnamese pineapple-and-tomato soup, a staple, is "*samlar meechou yuon.*" *Samlar meechou* is all that's necessary to describe the soup, but the added *yuon* denotes its origin. The *yuon* are everywhere. Kids grow up identifying Vietnam as an enemy, not a savior. Centuries of *yuon* have tried to kill the Cambodian race. The *yuon* steal Cambodian land. Every day, the *yuon* push their border markers west, ever so slightly, encroaching on Khmer rice paddies, seizing Cambodia inch by inch. These rumors saturate the streets, the bars, the restaurants, the minds.

And within them lies a lot of truth.

This fearsome, bitter animosity dates back centuries; it has had that long to evolve. In Angkor times, southern Vietnam belonged to the Khmers. Ho Chi Minh City, or Saigon, was then called "Prey Nokor," and it was a small Cambodian fishing village in the heart of what is called "Kampuchea Krom" today. Cambodians still claim that land as theirs, stolen by ruthless invaders.

Centuries ago, as Vietnam's population grew and population pressure mounted from China, the Vietnamese spread from their center in the Red River Delta around Hanoi in the north. They moved south, in search of new land. They conquered the Chams, a Muslim population that rivaled the Angkorean Khmers and still lives in small pockets in Cambodia today. They met the people of the ailing Angkor empire and began to move west. They swallowed the Khmers, bite by bite. In 100 years, Vietnam gobbled up the whole of the Mekong Delta.

There were uprisings. The hostilities lasted through the French colonial period, for the French gave Cambodians little reason to like the Vietnamese. They favored their Vietnamese subjects and thought the Cambodians troublesome. "The French had decided that the Vietnamese were the industrious race of the future and the Khmer a lazy doomed people grown decadent on Buddhism and the rule of their opulent monarchs," writes journalist Elizabeth Becker. "Cambodia would support France and Vietnam but would receive nothing in return."

When Lon Nol presided over Cambodia in the 1970s, he thought himself a holy man commissioned to wage war against the infidels next door. Ethnic Vietnamese had been living on Cambodian lands and fishing its waters for generations. He put Vietnamese citizens in detention camps. Thousands were arrested, and many killed. In April 1970, the Cambodian Army attacked a large ethnic Vietnamese settlement on the Chruoy Changvar peninsula, in the river across from Phnom Penh. Becker describes that attack: "The soldiers came at night and took the men away, some 800 Vietnamese laborers. They tied their victims' hands behind their backs and shoved them onto waiting boats." The men were killed, their bodies dumped. "For days these bloody, bloated corpses floated on the waters, an open, hideous warning to all Vietnamese living in Cambodia."

The Khmer Rouge enacted likewise pogroms against the Vietnamese in their efforts to exterminate all enemies and build a Khmer agrarian utopia. They orchestrated mass slaughters. Pol Pot surmised his war could be won if every Khmer combatant personally killed thirty Vietnamese. Many tried their best. They killed entire villages in one swoop.

This ire did not end with the Khmer Rouge regime. In 1994, Vietnamese were attacked at Piem So village in Kandal Province; thirteen died. In 1996 again, in Koh Keo village, Pursat Province, thirteen died. In April 1998, Jerry and I are in Cambodia. We hear the news in Phnom Penh. Khmer Rouge bandits attack the fishing village of Chhnouk Trou in the night. They fire rockets, torch homes, swing a boy against a boat like a baseball bat against a wall. They destroy twenty houses and force forty-five families to flee. They kill twenty-three in all. They are Khmer Rouge outlaws looking for Vietnamese enemies, but eight of their victims are Khmer and two are Cham, the minority Muslims long persecuted by the Khmer Rouge. The villagers know these bandits. They know their voices and faces from the market. They are no strangers; they are neighbors.

Jerry goes to Chhnouk Trou to photograph the wreckage. I see his pictures. I see a man jabbing at an ash pile as the residents of Chhnouk Trou sift through the dead. I see a boy teetering on the burnt logs of a home on water, his legs and hands blackened in ash — the dust of his people. Sheet-metal roofing drifts in the background. Two men wade waist-deep in water, chaining logs together into a raft. I see others in physical agony. A man lies on a mat, right shoulder taped and bandaged. A woman waves a fan over a small child huddled in her lap. A grandmother prays over a five-year-old boy whose gut is ripped by metal shreds. The villagers have nowhere, no way, to bury the dead. Their bodies burn and cover the village in soot. Jerry returns that night from Chhnouk Trou, and we fight — I don't know what about. And then he breaks. He sobs, as I have never seen him do. He curls on our bed and sobs and tells me he needs me and says he cannot comprehend such awful humanity. And then he gets drunk.

Today, when Cambodian politics turns ugly, when people are not satisfied with the status quo, they still condemn the Vietnamese. Many Cambodians think the current government *is* Vietnamese because they see no difference from the 1980s. Prime Minister Hun Sen fled to Vietnam when he escaped the Khmer Rouge and organized forces to overthrow that brutal regime. He was appointed deputy prime minister in 1981 and prime minister in 1985. To his enemies, his political connections make him Vietnamese. And when Cambodians rise against their oppressors, when they want to fight the system, their national unity is couched in anti–Vietnamese sentiments.

Such incendiary rhetoric colors the campaigns of opposition candidates in 1998 and again in 2003. It is an open wound and a political tool. Sam Rainsy, the country's most vociferous opposition politician, strikes at the Cambodian People's Party by saying the party allows the Vietnamese — the *yuon* — to steal jobs and pilfer Cambodian land. Sam Rainsy's voice carries clout. He is the country's leading democracy spokesman, and when he speaks, people hear. If he derides the Vietnamese, people take his words to heart. Every election season sends Vietnamese fleeing Cambodia in droves before the polls open.

But it is not only the Vietnamese who field such rancor. The Thais to the west have another long and hostile history with the Khmers. The power of the Angkor empire could not last forever. "The extravagant building program and foreign policy of the God-kings led to the destruction of Angkor. No society could sustain such enormous undertakings indefinitely," according to British historian William Shawcross. As the empire imploded, much of it fell into Thai hands. In 1431, the country "became a vassal of Siam, unnoticed and almost unmentioned." Over the next several centuries, Cambodia slimmed to "a sliver" between its neighbors. The Angkor temples vacillated between Thailand and Cambodia. As late as World War II, Thailand controlled the ruins until the French took them back for Cambodia.

These are wounds to Cambodia's national and ethnic psyche. To many minds, both neighbors pose tangible threats to sovereignty, identity, to everything that makes the people Khmer. Sometimes those fears explode.

And so, back to this sunny Sunday in September 1998, when student protesters gather for the slinging of a statue. The three monumental Vietnamese crack. The slurs continue. By week's end, four real Vietnamese are dead.

All due to a rumor.

Ang Snoul is a small, dusty village on the outskirts of Phnom Penh, past the airport, heading west as bustling streets turn empty. Wooden houses stand on stilts. The village looks like many others. But in September 1998, this is a village of poison and death. Skulls and crossbones and scarecrows drape the doors and walls in fear. People are superstitious. Nearly 60 have died, and another 400 head to the hospital.

The real explanation is simple, but Vietnamese get the blame. Ang Snoul villagers drink rice wine tainted with methanol, and they die, one after the other. Hysteria breaks out. Rumors fly: The Vietnamese are trying to kill the Khmers. Word spreads through Phnom Penh: It's in the water. It's in the fruit. It's in the soup, their stories go. The maids at the house where we live with other foreign journalists won't serve tap water to the house cats. A colleague's maid doesn't want him to take a shower. Pineapples, bananas, mangos, tomatoes: like time bombs sitting in their market baskets.

The sick stumble into emergency rooms citywide. Their pale, listless forms crumple on cots and floors. Doctors and nurses pump glucose into their veins. Spouses cradle the patients, wrapping them in blankets while standing guard.

It's in the meat, it's in the spinach, it's in the juice, the talk of the town goes. But in truth, it's in the mind.

Daniel Perez, municipal health adviser for the World Health Organization, visits the Calmette Hospital in Phnom Penh after some fifty-five workers fall ill at a garment factory just down the road from Ang Snoul. Friends rush them to town, claiming poison but, "It's just hysteria," Perez says. "I've seen them. They have absolutely nothing. They are perfectly healthy."

He emails my newspaper, angry at the stories racing through the city. Dozens are admitted to hospitals, all released within hours. No deaths, no illness. Everyone fears "this plague ... this sudden death," he tells me over the phone. "It's not uncommon." He tells me to ask a psychologist.

I call Dr. Ka Sunbaunat, chairman of the Health Ministry's Mental Health Subcommittee. He tells me about a long tradition of blaming Vietnam for Cambodia's ills—physical, mental, geographical. In the early 1980s, a similar case of tainted wine generated the same talk of Vietnamese malevolence. To dispel such apocryphal beliefs, he says, someone must prove them wrong. He suggests this: Submerge a small fish in tap water. "If the fish dies, there is something in the water. If the fish is still alive, it is not true that there is poison in the water." He does this at home. The fish lives. "The rumor will go away if you can prove it is not true."

Jerry and I visit Calmette Hospital that week. We enter a hot, sticky emergency room where people cluster on beds, others sprawl across the floor, men and women in white coats shuffling from person to person to file folder. I meet Stephen Borron, an American toxicologist flown in from Texas to save the genuinely sick and mitigate the mania. His company, Orphan Medical, is donating $400,000 of medicine for the real poisonings caused by methanol-tainted wine. "We've seen a number of patients claim to be ill from anything—from the food, the water, the meat," he says. "We haven't seen any evidence whatsoever of food-product or water poisoning.... It seems to be a kind of collective fear." It is a common reaction amid a genuine scare. "It happens frequently when there's any type of mass intoxication." People watch their friends and neighbors languish and fear prevails. "To them the illness is very real. They let their emotions completely overcome their state of health." They suffer real headaches, upset stomachs, dizziness and shortness of breath. "These are all symptoms that can be brought on by fear."

This has happened before. "A rumor startles Phnom Penh. Food is being poisoned! It's the oranges from Battambang. Yes, and bananas and cucumbers—they use syringes to inject the poison. No, fingernails. Even money can be contaminated. Four have died. No, fifty," *National Geographic* reports in May 1982. Who is the culprit then? Perhaps Pol Pot, or if not him, the non–Communist Khmer People's National Liberation Front. Or maybe even Sihanouk's Funcinpec Party. Those were the guesses in 1982.

But sixteen years later, people are certain it's the Vietnamese.

Borron and I chat in an office adjacent the animated emergency room. He leads me outside, across a grassy courtyard, to another office where he digs up numbers and answers to my questions. We again cross the courtyard. How hot it is, we agree. How different from Texas, Wisconsin, Oregon, the places we've lived in the United States. While we talk, a man dies.

We return to a different scene. Police drag in two men, their heads bashed, their limbs bleeding. One man is dead, the other almost so. Dr. Taing Sovanna says a crowd attacked them near a drink shop on a city street. They're Vietnamese, everyone says. The doctors, nurses and patients all agree. Yet these men are not conscious, they are not clothed, they can't talk and cannot speak for their own identities. But the story circulates: They're Vietnamese. They went to buy wine at a drink shop. A crowd charged, beating them until both were nearly dead. "No name, no family, no one has come for them," Sovanna says.

The patients are laid on a tile floor in an empty hallway. Workers give the live man a sugar drip. The dead man lies on his back, left leg on a rattan mat, his shirt open, skin missing below his right breast, a purple welt beneath his left eye, blood on his forehead and left leg. They wrap him in a white sheet and carry him off on a green stretcher.

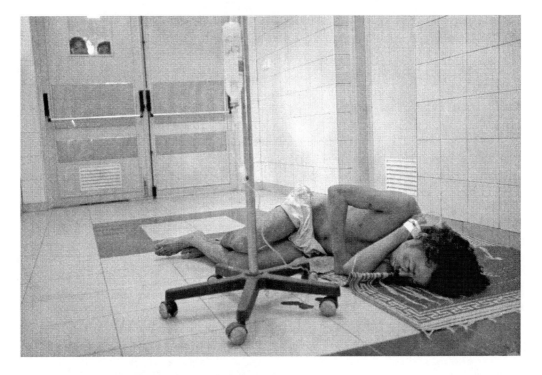

A Vietnamese man lies near death in a hallway at Calmette Hospital as nurses look on. In the grip of food- and water-poisoning hysteria, a Khmer crowd beat the man and killed his friend, imagining that Vietnamese people had poisoned the city's food and water supplies. Hospital staff were reluctant to treat the man because he was Vietnamese. Meanwhile, the emergency room filled with people claiming to have been poisoned by their food or water. None were. Phnom Penh, 1998.

The live man, naked to his underwear, curls on his left side, blood pooling beneath the glucose stand, urine dripping, stench growing, muffled murmurs escaping his bruised body. The hall is quiet. Two women workers peek through the window. I count the time. Ten minutes, twenty minutes. No one comes. Meanwhile, a steady flow of new arrivals fills the mats lining the emergency-room floor next door. I hail doctors and nurses, they say the beaten man "is being treated." I ask and ask someone to help this man, but no one comes. More than half an hour passes before a French doctor enters the hallway, instructs orderlies to clean up the mess, and takes a closer look at the man.

Later, the district police chief says: "I don't know what nationality the two were."

They were Vietnamese. The beaten man lives, but barely.

After the man is finally attended to, Jerry and I survey some of the patients in the emergency room. Borron tells me the hospital treats the rice-wine patients accordingly, the others get glucose drips and go home a few hours later. "We just reassure them that there's no evidence they've been poisoned."

We pace through the crowded room, and my colleague translates the patients' answers to my questions. Ouk Saroeurn lies on a mat covered with a blanket. "This morning I ate hog plum. After half an hour, I was feeling dizzy, vomiting, exhausted with diarrhea. My eyes could not see very well. My feet and hands were cold. Before I ate hog plum, I was afraid of the poisoning. But I don't think my fear made me poisoned."

Pha Sokea dozes on a mat; her friend tells us the story. The young woman works at the Thakral garment factory. She ate fruit near the factory. In half an hour, she felt dizzy, her breath short, her body fatigued. She lies still, her eyes misty.

Som Virak talks about his wife, Chin Nem, unconscious for two days. She drinks rice wine every day. Tuesday, she drank one cup and felt dizzy. "She could not see me, even though I was in front of her. She said that she could not see anything." She was hospitalized that afternoon. "I have warned her not to drink rice wine any more, but she refused."

Moun Tha is from Ang Snoul. She lies in bed near the door. "Last week I got a cup of rice wine, and since then I have not felt very well. I had a very bad headache before I was sent here this morning. I have problems breathing, and my eyes could not see things very well. My neck is still tired right now. I believe that I was poisoned by rice wine."

After everything we've seen, my article shifts focus. No longer is it a story of poisonings alone. It is an obscenity, an indictment of cultural fears run astray. The beating death runs high. A photo of the bleeding man in the hallway accompanies the story. Borron calls my paper and scolds me for tarnishing the hospital's reputation. Calmette does all it can to help all patients, he assures. Calmette will not, in the future, talk to my paper, he asserts. When we return to Calmette for another story in 2003, the emergency room is plastered with signs saying no cameras allowed.

In the next four days, the furor continues. The Khmer newspaper *Moneseaka* runs a story under the headline "*Yuon* start to kill Khmer again." The story reports that "*yuon*" are finishing off Khmer people "by putting poison drugs into water, food and especially in wine imported from Vietnam." The story recounts a confession from an unnamed "*yuon*" who says, "they are ordered to do this from above." The article refers to enemies among the people, those "with Vietnamese heads but Khmer bodies." The only way to stop the poisonings and ensure Khmer happiness, the story attests, "is to get rid of all *yuon* in Khmer country and then eliminate the *yuon* from power."

Another diatribe runs in *The Voice of Khmer Youth*, in an account of another beating. A shop owner purportedly witnessed a girl putting poison into porridge. The girl ran away but a *moto* driver caught her. A crowd beat her to death. Two Vietnamese men tried to protect her; the crowd beat them. One died; the other lived. The story blames the "*yuon*" and Hun Sen for organizing these mass poisonings. The doctors who deny it are merely scared.

In all of this, it is hard to discern roots of truth from pure rubbish. But this is known: At least four Vietnamese are beaten to death that week.

The Cambodians at my paper type and translate these reports. They type and type and talk and talk. I enter their room one afternoon as they discuss the situation. They say, as children, they learned of domineering Vietnamese. And now their people are dying. They are horrified and sad and they don't know what to do.

Just over the Monivong Bridge, in a place the locals don't call Phnom Penh, ethnic Vietnamese lead a tight-knit life between two worlds. They have come from Vietnam, yet most insist Cambodia is their home. That dual identity blankets them in a quiet but ever-present fear.

"We are worried that this society is not safe, and we will have to escape again," says Nginh Soeur, a sixty-five-year-old man who has endured much uprooting in his life. He came here many years ago from Vietnam, then returned to his homeland during the Pol Pot regime. In 1980, he and his family came back to Cambodia to open this restaurant on the Bassac riverfront, in business ever since. "We pray for peace in order to make a living," he says, then grows quiet. The panic that has swept Cambodians in the past week leaves ethnic Vietnamese fearing reprisals.

"Honestly, the innocent people are worried," says Chay Bun Hom, the man's 33-year-old son. He recalls other times of ethnic tension. "It's usually when something happens, like the recent democracy demonstrations."

But this, Nginh Soeur says on his veranda with a clear view of Phnom Penh proper, is where he'll stay. "I feel that my home is here." His wife, Ngouv Goi, nods in agreement. "It's difficult to go back to Vietnam." Their house, their livelihood, their neighborhood compel them to remain in Cambodia. Everything they need and know is here. As for the family's Vietnamese heritage, "We feel nothing," Nginh Soeur says with an air of indifference.

Surrounded by Vietnamese and Cambodians, they have carved a niche in this enclave seemingly far from "the capital over there." The restaurant doesn't need a name; familiar faces know where it is, and they know the people who run it. This is a place where friends look after friends, and families don't venture far from home.

But Phung Thi Thuy Nga sees what is happening. She sold cakes in the local market until a week ago, when an ambulance came for customers who fell ill after eating fruit. "Since then, I haven't gone to the market to sell because I am afraid." Since 1979, she has divided her life between Cambodia and Vietnam. She came here for business but frequently visits family in the homeland. She doesn't want to talk about intra-country relations. "I dare not say." Meanwhile, a curious neighbor listens intently outside, clinging to the bars on her windows.

But 18-year-old At Son Tin is not afraid to speak. He was born here, although his name and ethnicity are Vietnamese. He speaks in clear English: "After the elections, Vietnamese people have had a lot of problems with Cambodian people. Especially when you buy something in the market. They always say we poison people. I am very afraid of this problem." It weighs heavily on his mind. "My life is in Cambodia forever," he says. "Because now I think I am Cambodian. Now I think I am not Vietnamese."

I report this story with the help of a Cambodian colleague. We drive up and down the dusty riverside streets, searching for Vietnamese people. Some we find by signs, written in their language. Others we find at karaoke bars and coffee shops with short tables and chairs like those popular in Vietnam. And sometimes, we make mistakes.

My colleague says Cambodians can tell a Vietnamese from a Khmer. They look different. Khmer noses are flatter, their hair curlier, their skin darker. He approaches a woman in a narrow alleyway. They exchange a few words, then he returns and says we should go. I ask what happened. He says he thought she was Vietnamese. "But she is not."

Four Vietnamese killed. Eleven attacked. The streets grow bloody that week, human beings ripped apart by human hands. The Royal Cambodian Government issues a televised statement, decrying "this barbarous and inhumanitarian act." And it warns the opposition to "stop immediately their anarchic acts, criminal acts and aggressive violations of law, which are destroying the achievement of democracy."

Two days later, grenades explode in Hun Sen's compound, shootings begin, Democracy Square is dismantled, and the poisonings fade into history as a new social current rides in. Riot police are firing guns and cracking skulls. All thoughts of poisonings pass.

Five years later, ethnic animosity rides high again, but this time it's aimed at the Thais.

This fracas starts when a popular Thai actress known as Kob is quoted in Khmer papers as saying Cambodians are "like worms," and Angkor Wat should be returned to Thailand. She apparently never said these things, but the words burn through Phnom Penh. Since Thailand actually has controlled Angkor several times, the rumor jeopardizes national honor. More than land, it is Khmer culture at stake. Thai travel companies promote trips to Angkor, part of their "Amazing Thailand" campaigns. Cambodian markets brim with goods from Thailand. Music, videos, movies— most come from next door. Cambodians see this, and they seethe.

But their anger stems from memory, too. Cambodians have plenty of reasons to despise the Thais. Hundreds of thousands of Khmers lived in vile camps along the Thai border in the 1980s and early 1990s. They were treated more as prisoners than refugees. "The entire camp was surrounded by barbed wire and if someone walked outside the wire, they were shot," Sarah Streed relates in stories told to her by Cambodian refugees in the American Midwest.

What's more, Thailand acted as a conduit for Chinese guns heading to the Khmer Rouge. The Thais allowed Pol Pot's forces, scattered throughout remote enclaves along the border, to use roads in Thailand. And the Thai government gave the Khmer Rouge much of the foreign food aid intended for refugees. That's because Cambodia served as a buffer between Thailand and Vietnam. If the Khmer Rouge weren't fed and kept intact, Thailand would be but a hop and skip away from the feared Communists of Vietnam.

And so, sparked by a rumor of an unpalatable quote by a Thai actress, on January 29, 2003, mobs of Cambodians torch seventeen Thai businesses and storm the new Thai embassy building. Slum dwellers behind the embassy help diplomats to safety as they escape through the back door. Seven hundred Thai nationals flee the city in fear for their lives. The Thai government sends in two C-130 military aircraft, on guard and ready to fly people out. The land border between the two countries is closed.

Through all this, the Cambodian police stand watch, doing nothing. The U.S. government calls the Cambodian government "irresponsible," "incompetent" and guilty of "nationalistic rhetoric." The bill for damages totals $50 million. The violence and subsequent criticism prompt Hun Sen to reassign popular Phnom Penh mayor Chea Sophara as ambassador to Myanmar, an unsubtle demotion. The prime minister's critics claim he does this to stop a rising star before his power grows too strong. Regardless, the damage of these few hours in January is mortifying.

Fifty-eight suspects are arrested. Many months later, King Sihanouk questions their involvement, and eventually all fifty-eight are freed. And in those months after the riots, a new nationalism emerges. A new resentment lingers against Thai movies, Thai food, Thai people, Thai products. "Many Cambodians feel that Thailand has looked down on them for too long," the *Far Eastern Economic Review* reports.

The rest quickly fades into memory. The Thai embassy is reconstructed. Politicians and scholars promote talk of friendship and reconciliation and the burial of old feuds. Life in Phnom Penh goes on much the same. Another tragedy blown aside by prevailing winds.

But the borders—the borders are a different place.

Jerry and I travel the roads between Thailand and Cambodia many times. In April 2002, we cross through Poipet, on our way to Siem Reap. It is but a dance of steps and stamps. No problems, no hitches, but we come with a busload of tourists, and four in our group get stuck for a couple of hours. So we wait at the tour operator's office on a typically Cambodian, typically dusty street awash in the haze of no rain. Kids are begging, women are selling, and trucks are hauling so much bric-a-brac all around us.

The trucks go to Thailand empty; everything enters Cambodia full. Three-length semis full of cement sacks. Men and women hauling overloaded carts bulging at the sides. That hasn't changed over the years. When our bus finally moves, we find the road is paved fifty yards from the Angkor stylized concrete gate; then it's not. Miles toward Siem Reap it's paved again; then it's not. I read a bit, lift my head, gaze through our dusty blue-tinted window and see flashbacks of anywhere, any moment, in 1998. It all looks the same—the huts, the naked kids running, women slouched over tables full of snacks for sale, piles of refuse along the road, air choked with heat and dust and humidity, dogs trotting along with mouths agape. We are on this horrible, bumpy road so long, it eventually disappears in the crepuscular hours. It sinks into a sky busting with orange sunset and red earth awhirl before us.

Jerry and I never stay in Poipet, but we walk through, several times over the years, and we see the same scenes of tragic filth: diseased and homeless kids scrounging beneath the bridge that separates country from country, a swirl of humanity straining to make it through another day. The scenes we don't see, which we know from interviews and personal testimonies, are even worse: girls locked in brothels as slaves; kids stolen from parents and trucked across the border; the rampant spread of AIDS in back rooms. A microcosm of horror that people can't elude.

There is another border crossing south of Poipet, on the Gulf of Thailand. It is where Koh Kong on the Cambodian side meets Hat Lek on the Thai side. We first make this crossing in 1998, within a month of its opening. It is a contrast of two worlds. Thailand's asphalt river of Volvos, Mercedes and BMWs stops abruptly, the land becomes Cambodia and ramshackle huts, mudslides and one-legged beggars appear.

On the Cambodian side, ten miles of rutted mud leads to Koh Kong, the only town around. On the Thai side, a mere sliver of land wends its way between the sea and the Cardamom Mountains, which belong to Cambodia. Those mountains, impenetrable malarial forests, were home to Khmer Rouge rebels through 1998.

But one thing on Cambodia's stricken causeway jingles and shines: The Koh Kong International Casino, opened four months earlier by Cambodian-born Thai businessman Ly Yung Phat. It's a monstrous concoction of concrete, knot-free hardwood, red carpets, chandeliers, flush toilets and soap dispensers, brass railings and card dealers dressed in silk vests with bow ties. There is a chamber with blackjack, roulette and six baccarat tables and a downstairs room with traditional Thai and Khmer card games and a luxury hotel, bungalows for rent, a restaurant, a duty-free shop, a staff housing complex. There are earthmovers, cranes and graders readying the land for more to come.

Between 300 and 400 Thais cross this border each weekday, up to 1,000 on weekends. But the small trickle of Cambodians heading west rarely tops fifty. Gambling is illegal in Thailand. Gambling in Cambodia is illegal for Cambodians. But gambling for Thais in Cambodia is a growing pastime.

In Koh Kong town, I ask Governor Rong Plamkesan about the law against Cambodians gambling. He says it "comes down from Phnom Penh." He doesn't know why. "How can I tell? But it is very good because the Cambodian people are very poor," he says as his driver cleans his Mercedes with a feather duster.

Strangely, this Mercedes cannot easily leave town. There is not yet a bridge across the waters between Koh Kong and the border; there are no useable roads connecting Koh Kong with the rest of Cambodia. This town is an island.

Officials from both sides insist the border opened with everyone's best interests in mind. "We opened it just for the person-to-person contact," says Pisanu Suvanajata, first secretary of the Royal Thai Embassy in Phnom Penh. It's meant to stimulate trade. "We have thousands of people crossing the border to do business in Koh Kong." He says the two governments signed an agreement that gives Thais and Cambodians equal chances to prosper. It costs $20 for a border pass, Thai or Cambodian. No passport or visa is necessary.

"Before opening, the people could pass the border, but not officially," says Rong Plamkesan. There was no immigration office on the Cambodian side. He says the new $20 border fees go straight to the Ministry of Interior in Phnom Penh, which distributes the money throughout the nation.

I ask him, "Why open the border now? Who benefits?"

The governor chuckles. "It's for the daily life of the people," he says. Simple as that.

Not surprisingly, some local officials dispute his words. Tun Mean Bun, Koh Kong director for the Ministry of Economics and Finance, says the $20 fees go directly to Governor Rong Plamkesan's office.

Prach Chan, deputy director of administration for the Interior Ministry in

Phnom Penh, flatly denies that people pay anything for a border pass. He says it's free.

Keo Sokha, who works in the Koh Kong Social Affairs Department, says before the border officially opened, Cambodians paid 10 *baht*, or 25 cents, for provincial permission to cross. The new $20 fee is an abominable price, he says. "I think it is not good because it is bad for the poor people. This is a problem with the government I cannot explain to you."

This is a problem that never dissolves, as more people cross, as Western tourists begin to trickle through, as visitors report scams on the border, and as border officials demand payment when none is legally due.

But such is the way of a Southeast Asian border crossing.

Koh Kong is small by nature but oddly international by necessity. The *baht* pays for anything on the Cambodian side, the U.S. dollar is also used, and the *riel* trails far behind. Most people on the edge of Cambodia speak both Khmer and Thai. Many also speak English. But ten steps across the border, Thai is the main language.

On the Thai side, you will find a host of Cambodians, most working there illegally, trying to make more than they can in their homeland. The village of Khlong Yai, ten miles from the border, is home to several Khmer fishermen. "I love Cambodia, but the Khmer Rouge cause violence," says Rotha, who has spent the last five of his twenty-five years fishing the waters of Thailand. He repeatedly mimes a gunshot and death. There are still Khmer Rouge in the jungles around Koh Kong when we talk to him in early 1998.

Closer to the border, we meet Heng, who comes from Phnom Penh. He runs a stall in Hat Lek, selling jade, wood and ivory curios. "Thailand has work and money. Cambodia doesn't have. Phnom Penh doesn't have."

But his biggest business involves a motor boat, shuttling passengers back and forth across the border, for 500 *baht* a head. "I take ten, maybe twenty people a day." He doesn't have a passport, nor do his customers.

His life is far from that of those found seated in a red BMW at the border, just before closing. Inside is Birth, a Thai economics student at Chulalongkorn University in Bangkok, and her father, who runs a logging operation in Trat, fifty miles northwest of the border crossing. They have spent the day tooling about southeastern Thailand and enjoying the casino in Cambodia. "When it rains, we have nothing to do, so we go to the casino," Birth says.

They offer us a ride to Trat, where we all catch a bus to Bangkok. Along the way, Birth's father tells us he would like to do more business in Cambodia — legally — but he tires of the bribes and corruption. He's been trading in prime Cambodian timber for years, and it dawns on Jerry and me that he's been dealing with the Khmer Rouge. Despite years of interaction with Cambodia, both he and his daughter have many questions. They fire off a volley: Is it safe in Phnom Penh? Are there constant coups and gun battles? What's it like living in a war zone? How are Cambodia's roads? Does Phnom Penh look like Bangkok? Indeed, they know very little about the world beyond the border, except for the new development sandwiched in limbo between Thailand and the real Cambodia. And that's about as far as most Thais seem to get, in 1998.

Five years later, this spit of land between two countries resembles a different world. A steady flow of tourists passes through. The road is paved on the Cambodian side, a straight two-lane shot through dirt and greenery, as though unrolled like a strip of hard black sod. Where there had been mudslides there are new buildings, hotels, an exotic animal park, cars, cultivated plants, a sculpted median with red flowering bushes, no beggars and plenty of young men speaking English, hoping to take us to town.

We choose a taxi and soon reach a bridge that looks nothing of Cambodia five years previous. It's a grandiose new $7.2 million architectural marvel, more than 2,000 yards long, built by the man who runs the Koh Kong International Resort. From a distance, that bridge spanning blue water between green hillocks under a patchy sky almost looks nice.

But then we enter Koh Kong.

All that seems to have changed here is the added noise of cars, for there are many now. The market still smells of fish and rot, its floor soupy with seawater and muck. Kids still bombard us with hellos. *Motodops* still pester, putt-putting beside us, looking to take us for a ride. People still smile an enormous lot, and I suppose, if you didn't look at their environs, you might think people were happy.

A circle of young men play cards in an open area on the second floor of our hotel. They were there before we arrived; they will play through the afternoon. They while the day away at the prime of their lives. They sit on the hotel's only chairs—which annoys Jerry.

This is not a clean hotel, but it's the only one we see upon entry into town. I open the drawer to the vanity in our room and find a treasure trove: two condom packets, one opened, one not; a #1 Condoms box and a rolled-up poster in Khmer promoting the benefits of birth control.

When Jerry talks to the young man behind the desk, he says five years ago, things were very bad — but better now: No more Khmer Rouge; no more bandits. Another Khmer fellow soon enters the lobby with soccer on his mind. Turkey just beat the United States, two to one, but the United States is improving, he tells us. He changes into a red satin jersey. He plays the game every day. Each player plunks 10 *baht* down. "If we don't pay money, we don't run fast." It's an interesting psychological admission. The money is incentive. Playing for free would be useless, he says. Then he races off to his game.

Koh Kong still seems a place where people come looking for change, hoping for more; or a place people leave, going elsewhere for similar reasons. Wandering through here is depressing — to see what's changed, to see more that hasn't. Thick black sewage still flows through town, toward the aqua sea with its distant sun and hills. I look up to patchy gunmetal clouds sweeping in, blowing through the street. When I frame that view, just palms and coconuts and sky, it's strikingly idyllic.

I write about these things in my journal. I write about the wind and palms and handsome sky above the stench below, and a young man interrupts me. He has the face of a carved Buddha. If that face were gold, it would display the elegant, stylized arcs of Buddha's eyes and the precise lines of his nose. Sometimes you find this in Cambodia, as though the people have jumped straight from legend to life.

This young man speaks English well and says he's learned it from his father, who teaches Army generals and businessmen and other Koh Kong elite. But that's his afternoon job. In the morning, he's an immigration cop. "Good job, but the pay is very bad. In the States, I think if you have this job, you have good pay." His father makes about 1,300 *baht* per month, about $32.50 (most transactions in Koh Kong occur in *baht*, a more solid currency than *riel*). That's not even enough to buy two sacks of rice. So he supplements with teaching.

When I ask where his father learned English, he says Vietnam, during the American war. "We are Cambodian people," he rants, "but we live under the authority of fucking Vietnam." His opprobrium is clear. He lived in Vietnam until he was two, when his family moved here. He's twenty-three now, "but I look older because I drink a lot and smoke a lot."

Jerry and I go for a walk through town and return to our hotel four hours later. The same five guys still play cards, now beneath glaring fluorescent lights.

At the base of the bridge, we find a park, courtesy of the Thais. It's clean, the air smells fresh and fragrant with flowers, the waters are clear except for a few plastic bags and shirts and toys that have washed up on shore. But the rest is sand. It's tranquil here. Jerry goes off to take pictures while I sit on the wall overlooking the water and begin to write in my journal.

"What do you write about?" a young man asks. Two approach me on their *moto*; others come later. My instinct, here alone as sunlight dips into evening, is to clasp my bag and hope they don't have a gun because my passport, my checks, my U.S. dollars, my new laptop are all inside this bag.

But they just want to practice English.

Din Sokhan is twenty-one. He's finishing grade twelve this year, which means he'll take an exam that will determine whether he can go to university, and if he does, he'll perhaps live with his mother's cousin in Phnom Penh. But college is expensive, and he doesn't know what he would study. Right now, his mind is on the exam.

He moved to Koh Kong four or five years ago with his parents, from Takeo Province. They were poor and came looking for work. When they first arrived, his father was a porter, lugging bags from boats. Now his dad has a better job, and his mother sells fish and meat in the market. They make more money now than they ever have. In leaner times, Din's dad picked the leftovers from fishermen's nets for his family to eat.

Din has never been to Thailand, but he sometimes visits the casino's safari park, which he recommends for its many animals and peaceful nature. It costs 200 *baht* for Khmers to visit, and only occasionally can he scrounge the money. Din says Khmers and Thais both work at the casino, but the Thais have management and computer jobs while Khmers do the cleaning. "Many people in this town want to work at the casino. It is very difficult to find a job."

I ask about the anti–Thai riots in Phnom Penh, five months before. He says there were problems in Phnom Penh, but not here. "Because our governor is Thai. He speaks Thai, and he has very good relations with Thailand."

What does he think of Thai people and the country across that bridge?

He says many people want to claim Angkor, but it belongs to Cambodia. He says the Siem Reap people are Khmer, they are Cambodian, not Thai. He says this sitting in a Thai-made park, gazing upon a bridge that leads to a country that brings his parents work.

I ask about next month's election. "Yes, we must vote." I don't ask for whom he will vote, that's not the point. But I ask what he thinks, Will it be a good election? Not so good? "I don't know because I never think about it." What he thinks about is finishing school, leaving Koh Kong for Phnom Penh, going to university — all those things and the poverty his family left in Takeo when their harvests reaped little. These are the things he mentions of his own accord; the things he's learned to discuss in English. Politics? It's like the other side of that bridge he's never seen, the other side of the gate. What good does it do him if he can't go through? Why think about politics when his immediate concerns are much more visceral?

We look at that bridge. He says it has brought a few more people, but not many. There are tourists, but not many. Most stay a day or two, then move on.

The bridge is amazingly empty. It's almost like stepping into a propaganda photo from North Korea — barren, silent streets, empty as though no people existed. Just before sundown, photographers gather here, waiting for Khmers who want their photos taken atop the bridge with the smoky backdrop of Koh Kong's hills. We find a family of takers, a young couple with a one-year-old girl named Ta Chen. They place her, in new shoes and hat, on the center yellow line. No one comes; it's safe to leave a one-year-old standing mid-bridge while the photographer snaps her shot.

As we leave, the photographer tells us the lights will come on in half an hour, and it will be lovely. Indeed they do, just as the sun peeks from behind a cloud, igniting the sky in pinks, purples and blues. It's truly beautiful. There's no end to irony in Cambodia. We watch from below as one truck and a few straggling pedestrians walk across this monstrous bridge linking two vastly different milieux. And that's it. The concrete stands almost empty beneath that glorious sunset over those calm lapping waters, beside this fetid town.

A few weeks later we head cross-country, to the border with Vietnam. We go with our good friend and colleague, photographer Heng Sinith. He is taking us in his car — *his car* — which is an amazing development in Sinith's life. We have known this man since 1998, and he has always been a struggling photographer. But every time we see him, he's gained a little bit more, a little more work, a new lens, a company-bought computer, a regular gig with a foreign news service and now — this gray Toyota Camry. "Step by step," he says. This is the way of the Cambodian middle class, a slow but steady ascent toward better life.

Sinith tells us little about this trip. He tells us only that he will poke around the controversial border before the election and see a friend who works at the crossing.

He picks us up at our Phnom Penh apartment at 6 A.M., and we scoot past the Thai embassy, in repair, and over the Vietnam bridge on a highway that hasn't changed in five years. Actually, it has. Sinith says the government repairs the road all the time. "They build every two years. Already it's becoming bad." Our drive is a weave from side to side along potholes, around *motos* and carts hauling whole families.

Along the way, we ask questions. Jerry wonders whether Cambodians regret the American bombings in the 1970s, during the secret air war against Cambodia when U.S. forces tried to route out Vietnamese Communist bases. Those bombs wreaked havoc across the country, killing and maiming and displacing millions of people. Do the Cambodians harbor hard feelings? No, never, Sinith says.

Then he recounts the anti–Thai riots. "Thailand doesn't really kill people, not like U.S. bombs. But the Thais always steal everything, like the culture, like the land. You understand?" But that is no excuse for what happened. Demonstrators threw rocks, and the police didn't stop them. He asks over and over again: "Why couldn't they stop the violence?" The impotence, the ineptitude confounds him.

Sinith keeps weaving up the road. In an hour or so, we reach Kompong Cham-lang on the west side of the river from Neak Luong — Neak Luong, famous for the American bombs that ripped it apart in 1973, in a wartime accident that killed 137 people and wounded 268. This is the only Mekong crossing around; no bridge, only ferries. It is filthy here. Sinith hasn't seen this place in years, but he says it looks the same. Garbage and flies and tiny bawling kids and dirt and the daily refuse of cars and trucks moving through each hour.

Sinith parks his car at an indoor garage, and we catch a boat downriver, heading toward Vietnam. A black-and-white kingfisher hovers in the air twenty-five feet above the water, then swoops to the river and plucks out a small fish.

We reach a checkpoint in an hour, and the border lies just ahead. This is where we disembark. The station is tidy with neatly planted grass and flowers and toilets and offices with new desks. Foreigners come through here. It's obvious, because it's so clean and well-groomed.

Sinith figures his friend is near the border line, so we catch *motos*. Our drivers take us over the rippled, gutted dirt road to a guardhouse on the edge of a 100-yard strip of no-man's land between Cambodia and Vietnam. The guard does not want to let us through; he worries we'll skip to Vietnam. We do not have our passports or proper papers to leave the country. Sinith bargains with the man, saying he's a jour-nalist, he doesn't do bad things; we're all journalists, and the man can trust us. The guard lets us through.

But Sinith soon learns his friend is back where we started, so off we go.

Sinith's friend is a childhood buddy. He works for the chief of the border patrol, who invites us to sit. Immediately, a minion fills the cooler with cans of ABC Stout beer. Many cans. Sinith explains we, too, are journalists, and he elicits a conversa-tion with the boss.

His name is Tep Pudara, and he controls the international border crossings in two provinces. He has seventy-seven people on staff and four departments under him: immigration police, customs, gun control and health. He is by all accounts a Cambodian official, not exactly high-ranking, but on the way up. Sinith impresses the point of this man's eminence, a strongman of the provinces.

Tep tells us about his job here, the border, his responsibilities, the increase in tourists, and certain tasks he's been granted recently, to comply with new "interna-tional procedures." But those things are said off the record.

He says security here is fine. "The border is quiet. No problems." If there is a problem, they schedule a special meeting with the Vietnam side, in addition to their regular monthly tête-à-têtes. When his office cannot decide how to solve a case, he goes to the governor. When the governor can't handle it, it goes to the government in Phnom Penh.

I ask more complicated questions about trafficking; he says there is none, only prostitutes who come a short time. I ask about Vietnam; he says they have good relations with the bordering province. When I ask about his personal feelings toward Vietnam, he chuckles and says he doesn't know how to explain it. Then the ABC is poured and our host raises his glass in toast, insisting we drink. The bitter dark beer is tempered with ice.

A young man serves a plate of ginger fried chicken, as per Tep's request. But this isn't lunch. This is just drinking food. We talk some more until a plate of fried fish is served with a bowl of spicy lime vinegar and garlic. And now Tep, with some beer in his belly, asks us questions on running his border estate. He asks Sinith, "Do they have any advice for me, for running this checkpoint?" Tep wants to know what we see with foreign eyes.

We tell him we don't have much advice on running international border crossings, but we appreciate his asking. Then I ask more of him in his uninhibited state. Sometimes he crosses to Vietnam. "There is much better electricity, roads and health centers. And also agriculture," he says. "This is my personal opinion," he is careful to point out. He tells us cargo sometimes slips through the border, that is possible. But not people. That never happens because others always know. Eyes are always watching.

We eat and drink more, and it becomes a sloppy mess of beer and chicken and greasy fried fish. It is finally time for lunch, and rice is served with fish soup. Sinith drinks more beer — we all do at Tep's repeated clinks of the glasses. Sinith apologizes and declares he will do no work today. Instead, he will stay here and drink beer. "I checked with the *moto* driver, and nothing is going on." This is not as preposterous as it may sound. In Cambodia, *moto* drivers are the telltales of a town's temper. They know the latest news and gossip.

We'd like to see the village, so the strongman — a title that makes Tep smile — arranges two *motos* with two drivers. But we must assure the boss we will not slip into Vietnam. If we lose our way we will have a big problem, he says, suddenly very serious.

Our guides take us up the road, away from the border to a local *wat*. We're the pinpoint of town. Kids latch onto us, big and small, clinging to us as we tour the *wat*. We look around, then tell our drivers we would like to walk back. This confuses and bores them, especially the younger, who speeds ahead then rests with chin in palms until we catch up. But they never let us out of their sight. It's an order, come down from above.

This is not a poor village, but it's not a rich village. It's spectacularly pastoral and clean by most Cambodian comparisons. The dirt road is lined with shady trees. Dogs laze beneath two-story homes, and the air smells clean, not fecal. Closer to the border, shops sell all manner of necessities. The local currency is the Vietnamese *dong*.

When we return, Sinith is sloshed. It's almost 4 P.M., and the men discuss our route home. We discover as we step into the boat, that Tep has arranged a ride. He and Sinith's friend will accompany us all the way to Phnom Penh.

We leave behind a table littered with chicken scraps, cold soup, stale rice and some twenty-five empty cans of ABC. Tep is remarkably unconcerned, considering that beer is worth about seventy percent of his monthly salary of 160,000 *riel*, about $40.

We mosey to the boat and slip inside. Tep sits in back, in sunglasses, with a stoic look shielding his face. He doesn't talk. He is somber as we head upriver, past villages along the way. In public, he is not the jovial comedian of the afternoon. He is a man of formidable power, and now he acts the part.

We stop briefly at a landing shortly after 5 P.M., the kindest hour in Cambodia, when the heat breaks and the sun nears its nadir. Families are preparing their homes for the evening, and men are fishing for dinner. We stay in the boat, and someone serves us coconuts, holes drilled through the top, straws plopped inside, lime drizzled into the sweet juice. Another kingfisher swoops to the water, then up again where it hovers until the next dive. There are spiderwebs hanging, magically drifting in the river air. Three feet off the surface, large white threads glom together in a plexus of silk for us to motor through. They seem to have no attachments, no borders—*awt prum daign*, as the Khmers would say.

We continue on and reach Neak Luong just as the sun dims. This town, if possible, looks even shabbier at dusk when cooking fires smoke the air and the day's rotten garbage lies everywhere, with dogs and kids and flies wallowing in the squalor. There is talk now of building a $100-million bridge here, with Japanese funding. What if, instead, they built a $90 million bridge and put $10 million into garbage bins, garbage service, gardens and a trust fund to hire the people to keep the city clean? Just an idea, but I guess I'm dreaming.

We retrieve Sinith's car, and he pulls it around. Tep kicks Sinith out of the front seat in a politic way, saying he wants to drive the Camry. Sinith worries Tep isn't familiar with the car. Jerry tells Sinith, don't fret. He'll get the hang of it.

Tep starts the drive in the dark, taking extreme care for potholes and sinkholes lurking in the road. He drives at snail speed, all the way to Phnom Penh, as cars and motos and Land Cruisers race up from behind and pass. We stop for several visits to the bushes, as various bladders require. And eventually we reach Phnom Penh. All through that ride, all is dark but the dim headlights, a few fluorescent-lit homes along the roadside and the blue face of Tep's top-of-the-line Nokia phone. Everything else is black.

About two weeks later, a story in *The Cambodia Daily* gives credence to what we have heard through the years. A seven-mile stretch of disputed rice paddies lies between Vietnam and Cambodia, east of our visit with Tep. Villagers report the land was theirs, but now Vietnam claims it and is evicting families from their farms. This story runs eleven days before the 2003 national election. Villagers say they will support any political candidate who vows to tackle the most volatile issue in their lives— the Vietnamese.

Interlude: The Admiral's House

Late one Sunday afternoon in April 2002, Professor Kang Om and his wife, Top Kiel, show up at our hotel unannounced. They are nicely dressed for an outing. They want to take us to their friend's house in Takhmau, about twenty miles away. Their friend is an admiral in the Navy.

Jerry and I have known Professor Om since 1998, when he came to our house for weekly lessons in Khmer. He is a professor of psychology at the university, and he also teaches Khmer to foreign aid workers, journalists like ourselves and an impressive coterie of diplomats. Professor Om is always full of news and new adventure to relate — a research trip to Vietnam, an academic stint in France, a long-awaited invitation to the East-West Center in Hawaii, a new car.

His new car: He's thrilled about it. It's not actually new, it's almost two decades old. It's a rickety Toyota, a gift from a foreigner who has since left. When we first see it, Jerry, Om and I joke about what to name it. I take to calling it the Brown Beast. It has a semifunctional air-conditioner, a well-worn interior and seats low to the ground. This is Professor Om's first car. Before, he had only a *moto*. Kang Om may be a university professor, but he is not rich. He is one of many middle-class Khmers, working diligently to make his honest way up in the world.

And now we all pile into that Beast, heading toward Takhmau, to the house of his friend the admiral — who is a *very* rich man.

We weave for several miles through Phnom Penh traffic through the garment-factory district, over a bridge, into another dusty strip of city. It looks more like urban sprawl than another town entirely. But this is it; this is Takhmau.

The admiral's house is set back from the highway behind a large green gate. He has an exquisite yard with a pond and a miniature naval ship and a swinging picnic table (the latest rage) off to the side. His driveway is brick and his grass is very green, presently being watered by a young man.

Strangely, the admiral himself is not here, but his house is aflutter with his underlings. Admiral Ong Sam Kann is attending a wedding in another province, but his family and attendants are here to greet us. Jerry and I are a bit confused, but we go with the flow. We can tell this is going to be one of those interesting, inexplicable experiences familiar to anyone who has spent time in Asia.

It's hard to tell who is who or what everyone's connection is to this house and its absent owner, but everyone is cheerful and welcoming. We meet the admiral's son-in-law, who speaks English well and is eager to practice. He shows us around the air-conditioned receiving room at the front of the house. The room is dressed in Khmer frippery, replete with gold chandeliers, Indian rugs, red hardwood and trinkets of great stature. There is a larger-than-life bronze Buddha head and a fan of red coral, a foot tall and a foot wide. The family doesn't know what it is, and they ask if we can explain it. Is it an animal? A tree? We tell them it's alive (was alive) in the sea.

There are framed photos on the shelves: one of the admiral with the king, another taken in 1994 when he traveled to the United States. "He went to the pen-TAAH-goon," his family tells us.

The what? We're confused.

"The pen-TAAH-goon. Don't you know?"

It takes us several minutes to realize they're saying "Pentagon," which explains the photo of the admiral with former U.S. Defense Secretary William Perry.

Everyone sits in big sticky leatherette chairs, and a maid serves tea. We talk. The son-in-law tells us he studied in Japan for seven years and returned to Cambodia, to a predetermined wife. Professor Om steps in and continues the story: The young man is actually a relative of Professor Om's. Om had been teaching the admiral English for several years, and he knew the admiral had a daughter of marriageable age. He also knew the young man would be needing a wife soon. So he and the admiral arranged for the two to meet. When the young man returned from Japan, he was invited to the admiral's house and led to a room. Lo and behold, the girl was there too. She was shy. But not too shy — they soon married.

We poke around some more, and the young man leads us out back. We pass a multiple-car garage that houses a late-model Mercedes sedan and an immaculate U.S. Army Jeep with all the original accoutrements. The house staff is large; larger yet is the population of Khmers living in huts in the backyard, which extends to the horizon, through fields of fruits and vegetables and a personal pond, where a man tosses food to the fish. The admiral has his own farm and his own farmers to work it. In the distance is the palatial compound of neighbor *Samdech* Prime Minister Hun Sen.

The sun is setting, casting a lovely light over the peasants who live behind the admiral's house, fishing and planting his land, catching and harvesting his food. Jerry, of course, has a camera, and everyone, of course, is eager for a photo. We spend several minutes posing for shots, all standing in a line on this aristocratic stage.

Then we pile back into the Brown Beast, making our way toward Phnom Penh. Professor Om tells us he wishes we could have met the admiral himself, but perhaps another day.

A few weeks later, Om calls us. He has another invitation, but we are busy with a story in the provinces. It's too bad: The admiral wanted to take us on a helicopter to the sea.

6. Kampuchea Krom: The Land Next Door

There is a land in southern Vietnam where people speak and think in Khmer, where monks wear fire-colored robes and live in *wats* like those found 100 miles to the west in Cambodia. Three hundred years ago, Saigon was a small village of Khmer fishermen and today, an enclave remains in this place Cambodians call Kampuchea Krom.

It's an ironic twist of history: Pol Pot and his men originally set out to recapture this land for the Khmers in the 1970s. But in the following decade, the Khmer Rouge attacks against the Vietnamese prompted an invasion that would instead put all Khmer land, for a time, under the control of Vietnam.

Now, it is 1998, just after four Vietnamese are beaten to death on Phnom Penh's streets, just as post-election riots rupture the peace and the Vietnamese are blamed for everything wrong. Jerry and I decide to visit Kampuchea Krom, this slice of Cambodia now tucked away in another country. It was stolen centuries ago, Khmers believe. It remains dear to the heart of Khmer memory and legend.

But first we must wait for the guns to stop.

There is a woman who runs a small Vietnamese tourism shop around the corner and up the block from our house. I pass her every day on my way to the *Daily* office. She works beside a Vietnamese karaoke bar, where I interview customers during the apex of racial furies. In these tense times, shopkeepers pull their gates to a screeching close. Her gate is a sign of the city's mood. Is it shut? Is it open a smidgen? When she flings the gate wide and invites people in and the air feels washed of anxiety, we go to her with passports, photos and money. In a few days, we have Vietnam visas and tickets on a minivan, departing for Saigon around 5 A.M. the following Friday.

That hour comes when Phnom Penh's streets are dark and bare. No *motos*, no noise, no people. We warily walk the three blocks up our dark street and around the corner to the woman's office, where she has told us the van will be. It's not there, so we take strong Vietnamese coffee and milk from the bar next door, where a man sweeps up after a long night.

And we wait. A pig trots down the street, then a man. The morning light begins

90

to peek around the buildings, and other passengers come with sacks of groceries and clothing and mementos to take with them. When the van arrives a tall Vietnamese man flails his arms wildly, yammers loudly and directs passengers in, out, around the vehicle. He is not the driver, but he is definitely in charge. He shoves five people, ten people, a whole lot of people, into this tiny van. A weak young man on crutches boards with us. He's going to Saigon for treatment. He's been shot.

And the journey begins. We're moving quickly, horn blaring, weaving erratically through cyclos and *motos* and other vans and women with breakfast baskets. We cross the river, over the bridge, past the Vietnamese neighborhood where I interviewed several residents. The bad driving is nonstop. The horn blasts constantly, cows lumber awkwardly out of the way, and we bounce down the road over giant pits. It's a road that connects two major cities, Phnom Penh and Saigon, and will be just as bad five years later. I fret about crashing. We've heard stories of boys on buffaloes blown to bits by land mines five feet from the road. I gaze over a sea of green rice and wonder about toppling, head over lap over head over lap, with so many others in this metal trap.

At Neak Luong we cross the Mekong by ferry. Women and children poke their arms and heads through our windows and door, selling fruits and sweets. The ferry carries us and dozens of other cars across this small stretch of water, then we're off again, apace.

At the border, we must walk across separately. Guards inspect cars brimming with food sacks, VCRs and boxes full of merchandise. On the other side, we are told to take a different van, and we continue on to Saigon. The roads are paved, and the drivers are better, too. We arrive intact, find a guesthouse with a bed and shower and start our quest for the Khmer in Kampuchea Krom.

Our search leads us south to a town called Tra Vinh.

Thach Ket, dressed in saffron robes, opens a wooden window full of cobwebs that hasn't been touched in ages. Light streams inside, swaddling a gilded Buddha thirty feet tall, surrounded by twenty-four small statues. This temple is built on a thousand years of sacred soil at a place called Chua Phuong. Outside, the remains of an even older ancient structure poke through a thicket of greens. Its ceiling has collapsed, and patches of light penetrate the chamber. Mold smudges the walls.

The map calls this place Vietnam, but chief monk Thach Ket asserts otherwise. "This is not Vietnam," he says later, standing in his living room, surrounded by century-old portraits of monks and banners written in Khmer. "This is Kampuchea Krom."

Tra Vinh is five and a half hours by rickety bus—125 miles as the egret flies—southeast of Ho Chi Minh City. This town of a few hundred thousand, not far from the South China Sea, is central to that parcel of land once belonging to the Angkor empire. It's still noticeably Khmer.

The gates to Tra Vinh say "Welcome, all visitors," in Vietnamese. They stretch across a highway on an archway topped by snakelike spires and scaly roof tiles, like those found throughout Cambodia. The Tra Vinh Tourist Company puts out a brochure that welcomes outsiders to traditional Khmer festivals and ethnic customs that make this town diverse, thirty percent Khmer, thirty percent Chinese.

Despite their geographical proximity, Cambodia and Vietnam practice two different styles of Buddhism, two of numerous takes on this same religion. In Cambodia, Theravada Buddhism thrives. It is known as the "southern school," having spread from Sri Lanka and India through Myanmar, Thailand, Laos and Cambodia. Its goal is the end of all suffering and desire in a state called nirvana — the last reincarnation. In Vietnam, Mahayana Buddhism prevails. It is called the "northern school," predominating in Nepal, Tibet, China, Korea, Mongolia, Vietnam and Japan. It is, according to Theravada Buddhists, a corrupted form of the religion. While Theravada Buddhism shuns all sensual and aesthetic pleasures and desires, the Mahayana sect takes a less rigid stance. Its followers claim the sect expanded to better fit the needs of common people.

The two types of Buddhism look different: Vietnamese monks often wear drab colors; Cambodians are always brightly cloaked. Vietnamese temples have Chinese characteristics; Cambodian temples reflect influences from Thailand and India.

So here is this town Tra Vinh, where monks dressed in radiant robes walk among those wearing traditional Vietnamese brown; where fanciful, painted *wats* have stood for centuries. Indeed, Khmer culture is alive and well in this pocket of Vietnam — in some sense, more so. The Khmers of Kampuchea Krom say they are at peace, at home, retaining their ethnic identity while living among the Vietnamese. The Khmer *wats* here are lively, painted, intact. If you want to see elegant, historic Khmer *wats*, you won't find them in Cambodia.

Go instead to southern Vietnam, where hand-built centuries-old temples dot the Mekong flood plain. They were not bombed and destroyed in war, as those in Cambodia were during decades of civil conflict. The United States specifically avoided bombing the sacred sites of Vietnam.

The history of this land is something many Vietnamese people know well — not only in Tra Vinh but throughout Kampuchea Krom. Random conversations with Vietnamese businessmen, drink sellers, shop owners, teachers, students, monks, tour guides and taxi drivers reveal similar sentiments: They know Cambodians deeply resent the Vietnamese, although they don't return that feeling so intensely. They may think Khmers uneducated, naïve, silly or troubled. They don't think Vietnamese people in Cambodia are safe (for that matter, they don't think anyone in Cambodia is safe).

And perhaps more than anything, they want peace inside and outside Vietnam after so many years of war.

Thach Ket has a Vietnamese name but a Khmer heart. He uses his hand to draw pictures on the slat platform where he sits. He outlines Vietnam and Cambodia, with a shared space between. "There are two places, but one people," he says. "Vietnamese and Khmer people here are friends." He raises his two index fingers and brings them together, the same fingers but different hands.

For him, the melding of two places began in childhood. Home for Thach Ket was Battambang. He was ten years old when the Khmer Rouge turmoil started in 1975. He remembers through his scars: red and purplish slits at the base of his right pinky finger and on both sides of his rib cage. He doesn't elaborate on their origins, except to say they are from the Khmer Rouge.

In 1983, soldiers plucked him from what is officially called Cambodia and plopped him in what is officially called Vietnam. This happened after Vietnam invaded Cambodia in late 1978 and continued to govern the country. Today, home is here. "I don't want to go to Cambodia because this is my *wat*," he says. To him, borders are delineated by governments, not people. And to him, there is no difference between here and Cambodia.

When we finish our conversation, we wander around the *wat*'s shady grounds. There is a man wearing a *krama*—very Khmer—and a woman raking rice, wearing a conical hat—very Vietnamese. A woman named Tieng, standing nearby, speaks fondly of her brother who lives near Olympic Stadium in Phnom Penh. She has never been to the Cambodian capital, but she is intrigued when we say we come from there.

There is more cultural mingling up the road half a mile. The Museum of Indigenous Khmer occupies a new building done in modern, stylized architecture with spires snaking from the rooftop. The museum is sparsely decorated with traditional Khmer clothes, silks, jewelry, tools and baskets. Around the bend, another *wat* peeks through the trees. This is known as Chua Ang in Vietnamese and Wat Angkorechabori in Khmer. Its welcome sign and name are written in Khmer, but Vietnamese lettering marks the monks' classroom, the park benches studding the gardens and the donation boxes inside.

Head monk Sok San stands in his doorway, welcoming guests. Inside is a mesh of Cambodia and Vietnam: a portrait of Ho Chi Minh, an academic certificate written in Vietnamese, a photo of Sok San with a police officer at Angkor Wat, a portrait of King Norodom Sihanouk. On his ceremonial altar, adjacent his living quarters is another portrait of Ho Chi Minh, a Vietnamese flag and about three dozen Khmer Buddha statues. Sok San is Khmer by blood but born in Vietnam. He speaks, reads and writes fluent Khmer and Vietnamese. He is a living example of this cultural amalgam.

At noon, about fifty faithful followers gather in the *wat* with incense sticks and candles to pray while the monks eat. Their rhythmic chanting fills the dark room while a thunderstorm beats down from above. When the clinks and clanks of plates and chopsticks have stopped, the monks leave, and the congregation consume their leftovers, chattering away in Khmer. It is an ancient Buddhist custom for monks to eat first, and everyone else to dine on what remains.

Far from there, in Saigon, many folks fear their Cambodian neighbors. They know protesters vandalized the Vietnamese monument in Phnom Penh. They know Vietnamese people were beaten to death. They know the Vietnamese government has told the Cambodian government these things are unacceptable. They know because they read Vietnamese papers, they watch the news and people talk.

They also know their land once belonged to Cambodia. But that was ages ago, and Kampuchea Krom has long since amassed its own Vietnamese history, they say. It's a view most Cambodians have not accepted.

The year we visit Kampuchea Krom, Saigon celebrates its 300th anniversary. Banners and billboards festoon the streets, proclaiming three proud centuries of progress, development and Vietnamese culture. A photo exhibit depicts remarkably peaceful scenes from a place that hasn't always been. There are no war shots here — just women in traditional *ao dais*, a monk using a laptop, the Catholic cathedral lit for Christmas. There are no scenes depicting Prey Nokor, the Khmer fishing village that Saigon once was. That history is displayed in another museum.

The Vietnam History Museum contains an outdoor exhibit with dozens of replica Khmer figures and carvings, a *singha* lion statue from Angkor Wat, a *linga* stone, cracked *apsaras*, lifesize *Vishnus* and armless *Laksmis*. A sign explains the many strands of Buddhism that have criss-crossed the Asian continent. Starting in the first century, Indian Buddhist monks took their message abroad. Each society — the Khmers, the Vietnamese, the Japanese, the Chinese — braided the new ideas into the filaments of their existing cultures, creating their own styles of Buddhism.

In another room, a map of modern-day Vietnam depicts the country's fifty-four indigenous groups. Nationwide, schoolchildren learn these groups collectively form the diversified culture of Vietnam. Number fourteen on that list are the "*dan toc Khmer*," the ethnic Khmers of Vietnam's southern coastal region. And just across from the floor-to-ceiling map stands a glass case full of Khmer baskets and cages, labeled as ethnic fishing artifacts.

In another room of the "Primitive Period," there are displays of Neanderthal heads, humanity's earliest tools, and a theme that runs throughout the museum: Vietnam sprang from many pasts and many peoples. Khmers are part of that motley framework supporting a modern-day Vietnam. And through all the histories enveloped in this pagoda-like building, every map, be it ancient or modern, shows Vietnam's current boundaries. There is nothing to depict Kampuchea Krom as a one-time slice of Cambodia.

On the street, we meet a man named Lu Thanh Hai, who spends his days and nights thinking about work. He's a banker, an educated and energetic go-getter, one of Vietnam's rising entrepreneurs. He wants to make a better life for himself.

He speaks of business, business, business — he wants to make money, and his plan includes Cambodia. "Vietnam has many people. Cambodia has much land," he says with a twinkle in his eye. "Cambodian rice is better than Vietnamese rice. Cambodian land is better than Vietnamese land."

Many Vietnamese talk and think this way, he says, and numerous are the rumors about Vietnam pushing its border farther west. "Yes, I have heard that story." He heard it from his father, who said it was true when he fought near the border from 1965 to 1968. "Even today," Lu Thanh Hai says his country encroaches on its neighbor. He thinks Cambodia should harvest more rice and sell it to the Vietnamese. Instead, Cambodia has created problems for itself. Its political crises have consumed the country's energy and stymied its economy. It's hard to argue with him.

Then Lu Thanh Hai professes what Cambodians hate and fear most: He thinks Cambodia would be better off under Vietnamese control because the country can't govern itself.

The thought of returning ancient lands to Cambodia is unfathomable to Lu

Thanh Hai. Ridiculous, as are people who think such thoughts. "Cambodians are silly," he says with pity in his voice.

Sixty-two-year-old Ngoc, proprietor of a popular draft-beer house on the edge of Saigon's tourist district, spent 1982 to 1986 as a soldier in Cambodia and harbors hard memories. He still wears army green. He speaks in Vietnamese with an occasional word or two of Khmer. "I don't like Cambodia. Vietnam is better," he says. "Vietnam sent soldiers to Cambodia to fight against Pol Pot. But the Cambodians didn't do anything." He is bitter about what happened during war and everything since. The anger, the beatings, the animosity toward Vietnamese people living in Cambodia today. "Many Vietnamese people died for Cambodia, but they don't treat us well, and they want us to leave."

Across the table is a well-dressed 28-year-old Vietnamese businessman who isn't as enamored of Vietnam. He talks, in rapid and nearly perfect English, of becoming a tour guide. "I don't want to become a translator because in my country, you have to translate according to the government," he says. The government censors its people. He talks of joint ventures, of Vietnamese money swelling the pockets of foreigners and politicians but never the ordinary Vietnamese. He, a firebrand with the idealism of youth, is frustrated. He says foreigners don't see the real Vietnam. He doesn't want to be named, but he wants his sentiments known.

Meanwhile, Ngoc sits quietly watching the street and talking of the good, decent life in Vietnam.

We return to Ngoc's place the next night, and a fifty-two-year-old Vietnamese man sits where the younger man did the night before. The older man teaches English by day and frequents this shop at night to practice what he teaches. He, too, was a soldier, for five years during the war with the United States, a deskman who avoided the frontline. "I was too scared to fight. It was very dangerous." This evening, war dominates the conversation — not just one war but many: those against the French, the Americans, the Chinese, Cambodia.

The teacher knows much about modern-day Cambodia and its affairs. But tonight he learns — "I like to learn" — that Cambodia had thirty-nine parties in the 1998 elections. "That's too many," he says. "Too much fighting in Cambodia.... They don't trust each other." In Vietnam, it's different. "We don't have any protests because we have only one party. We are not allowed to say anything against the government." It's a freedom many Vietnamese are willing to sacrifice after so many wars. "We want peace," he says. "People just want to think about their rice fields."

The teacher doesn't understand the acrid feelings that Cambodians have toward Vietnamese. He sees his country as somewhat a savior. "They killed many people, a million people. Many Vietnamese died too, especially from land mines." He can't comprehend the recent beating deaths in Phnom Penh.

Through all this, a younger English student in wire-framed glasses sits and listens intently. He says very little except that he comes here to practice listening. He nods and absorbs accounts of Khmer monks and glorious *wats* in Tra Vinh, of Phnom Penh politics, of everyday life in Cambodia. He adds little to the conversation except a few "umms" and "ahhs" when his listening teaches him something he didn't know.

At midnight, the circle breaks, the young man pays for his Coke and says he enjoyed listening. He leaves, having learned his home sits in the heart of Kampuchea Krom.

Jerry and I soon return to Phnom Penh, and I write my story. After it's printed, I get a call from a Western diplomat who thanks me for the article. He has lived in Phnom Penh several years; he has friends and colleagues both Khmer and Vietnamese, and he struggles to work through deep-seated misunderstandings.

I'm also approached by a Khmer journalist whose friend is a monk in Kampuchea Krom. He was sent there many years ago, and my colleague fears for his safety. Many Cambodians say the Vietnamese government is cruel to Khmers there. My colleague is certain Thach Ket is his friend, and he is sure this article could do him harm. The Vietnamese might kill him, he says.

I explain that Thach Ket wanted to talk to me. He was not afraid to speak, and he knew my story would be published. I also determine, based on age, that Thach Ket could not possibly be my colleague's friend. He is much too young.

But still, my colleague is scared.

7. Anlong Veng:
Beyond the Khmer Rouge

If you look at a NASA map of the world at night, a dark blotch covers Cambodia. In the blackest edge of that void is Anlong Veng. The village sits seventy miles north of Angkor, its antithesis in splendor. A dirt road connects the two. Skull-and-crossbones signs mark minefields along the way. Soldiers with assault rifles occasionally extort money from passersby.

For decades, Pol Pot and Ta Mok kept this remote village, their stronghold and political headquarters, in a cultural black hole. The residents of Anlong Veng never saw monks, never went to a *wat*. Children learned to hunt the enemy, and families were sent to the jungle for years.

In 1998 it is too dangerous to visit Anlong Veng. It is isolated by a cordon of mines, its people equally impenetrable. But all that changes as the war ends. Pol Pot dies in April, and Ta Mok — the bloodthirsty Khmer Rouge military chief known as "The Butcher" — is captured near the Thai border in 1999. The shutters of Anlong Veng begin to open. Clean air is let in, and the people begin to breathe in freedom. There are murmurs within the Cambodian government, even, about making this an atypical tourist haven: Come and see the homestead of our ruinous past!

Jerry and I travel to Anlong Veng in 2001. The people look disturbed. They do not smile like Khmers everywhere else do. Many here are missing legs and arms. Faces are hardened, their eyes like granite. That night at our hotel, the electricity shuts off, the fan stops, the glint of fluorescence ceases through the door. Frogs chirp and crickets sing a chorus from the wet earth. The heat hangs heavily upon us in the darkness; the sort of darkness that looks the same with eyes open or closed. I can't sleep. I wonder what the people here think when they see our faces, white faces they were taught to hate. Our driver from Siem Reap tells us people lived by fear for years. Betrayal meant death. They couldn't escape their Khmer Rouge masters. Now, after switching sides, they have a new leader to follow — the Royal Government of Cambodia — and a new set of rules. But most of the people in Anlong Veng remain the same. Old commanders have shed their Khmer Rouge uniforms, adopted new government-issued attire and acquired posts in the ruling regime. Same people, new agenda: old boss, new wardrobe. And still, the masses obey, they follow suit, they do

Dead trees loom over a large reservoir on the outskirts of Anlong Veng. Anlong Veng, 2003.

what they're told because they're told to fear the repercussions. That, and everyone is sick of war and danger. Everyone welcomes liberation, such as it is.

My journal from this trip to Anlong Veng is rife with nerves because no one knows what to expect, because the past is still too close, too raw. This will smooth over time.

Anlong Veng circa 2001 is a muddy little affair, everything doused in russet waters. There is no sewage system, no paved roads, no mail service, no cell phones, a new market and all its accompanying filth. It is "where the losers live," Cambodia scholar Craig Etcheson tells the *Wall Street Journal*, explaining that the more successful Khmer Rouge faction was led by Ieng Sary. He and his people defected to the government in 1996 and assembled an enclave farther south in Pailin, rich with gems. But the rest of the Khmer Rouge got Anlong Veng, rich in despair.

There is a bridge in town, near a dam. Men cast fishing nets into the roiling water, and amputees sit near the roadside. The dam has created a brilliant lake, with silvery trees standing tall and dead in its center. And on this lake are the remains of Ta Mok's house — an eerie reminder of what was.

And who was, who is, Ta Mok? The embodiment of his moniker. He was the Khmer Rouge military chief of operations, a commander of brutal forces. In 1978, his men helped Pol Pot and Brigadier General Ke Pauk slaughter more than 100,000 people in the east, in the largest mass murder in Cambodian history.

Ta Mok — the Butcher.

His house isn't much of a home anymore — nothing is left. Just a few pillars, made from uncut tree trunks, just a few amateur paintings of Angkor temples on the walls, and two toilets. The house is open to the air, and everything has been looted from it. The windows, the doors, the screens, the fixtures, the switches, anything that could be lifted and taken is gone. A couple of cops "guard" the place, eating and sleeping and working here, in the vestiges of malice.

Behind the house the lake is serene, reflecting blue-gray sky and vibrant greens, casting an aqua pall over Anlong Veng. A small neighborhood surrounds the house. Some homes have no windows, just planks the people can remove from their walls. Men stare icily from darkened doorways as we walk by. Children smile and yell hello. Women look away, then steal a glimpse, then smile demurely after we smile first. It's as though they don't know what they're supposed to do, seeing strangers.

Not far from Ta Mok's house is the Anlong Veng Health Center. Upstairs, in a room full of patients, a thirty-five-year-old woman named Kim sits on a woven mat atop a metal bed, gazing out the window toward the lake. She has lived all her life under war. "If you compare before and now, now is better. We have the hospital, the bathroom and water supply," she says. "And at nighttime, we have lights as well."

Kim suffers heart palpitations, numbness, headaches and nighttime pains. Exams show nothing. Lab tests say she's clean. The doctors determine her problems are mental, manifested in the physical. An example of the psychosomatic illness that permeates this society, as it often does in countries after war.

Médecins Sans Frontières began work here in 1999, after raising a ruckus with the military. As government troops fought off the last Khmer Rouge, soldiers occupied these buildings. MSF pleaded: Please go. Let this place be used as it was intended. Eventually, the request was granted, and MSF started its work.

The plan was to train locals in medicine, with hopes they could run the center on their own one day. MSF started with the basics — a reception area for admitting patients and recording blood pressure, weight, temperature and height; a standardized filing system; a lab with a microscope; drugs to stock a pharmacy that didn't exist during Khmer Rouge times. Since then, the group has taught employees to work as nurses and sent staff to training sessions at other Cambodian hospitals. It's also started a program for sex workers and twice a month, three dozen prostitutes gather here to learn about AIDS, condoms and STDs.

The center employs forty-six people, including a Dutch doctor, three foreign-educated medical assistants and several workers trained under the Khmer Rouge. MSF pays Cambodian employees $15 a month, consistent with national rates. It supplies drugs when the government doesn't. Patients pay small fees for regular visits and up to 10,000 *riel*, about $2.50, for an emergency-room procedure. Exempt from all costs are monks, health-center employees, the severely poor and the elderly.

Every day the center sees up to 100 people. The maladies here are common to impoverished war-torn countries of the tropical belt: tuberculosis, typhoid, dengue fever, childbirth complications, respiratory infections, parasites, gunshot wounds. And sometimes injuries from land mines and war-era bombs. Kids find the old ordnance and think it's a toy. "They like to play," says MSF project coordinator Raden Srihawong.

But something is different about this health center. It's not like others in the region. Anlong Veng employees have no formal education, and the Cambodian government does not recognize this center as a hospital. Titles are nebulous.

Ta Mok originally built this place and workers were trained to deal with the atrocities at hand. They learned to amputate limbs, pry bullets from flesh, and treat recurrent tropical fevers. Some studied under a Khmer Rouge doctor near the border, while some were educated in China. Sometimes health workers crossed into Thailand for supplies. Others simply learned on the job.

Now, some of those same workers in white gowns tend to exam rooms and patient beds, loosely calling themselves "nurses," but that designation is unofficial. "This is not a hospital, said Oung Saroeung, an MSF medical assistant. "This is a health center with beds."

Ong Phan works in a dim room with a metal table, where he examines children. He trained under a Khmer Rouge physician from 1980 to 1986, but no document verifies that. "During the Democratic Kampuchea, we had no certification."

Chin Pharin examines a pregnant woman, four months along, behind a pink screen. She sees ten to fifteen pregnant woman a day now, but under the Khmer Rouge no one sought prenatal care, and women gave birth at home. She worked as a midwife for twenty years; there were no drugs, no check-ups, no doctors. "Before I didn't know so much, and now I know a lot because I always go for training," she says.

When we visit, MSF is scheduled to leave ten months later, its program nearing an end. From there, the Ministry of Health is supposed to take over. This has workers scared. They wonder how they will survive. With a little Western medicine in their repertoire, they're afraid they will be left alone with no one to guide the way.

The patients here are thankful for this center — and for their awakening. They attest to a discernable difference between everything that existed "then," and everything that is "now."

Upstairs, we meet Ram, a seventy-three-year-old woman with hookworm, here for her first visit — ever — with a doctor. She lived in the jungle for years. Most Anlong Veng residents never had any formal medical care until MSF came along and introduced a new awareness of health. In the past, locals collected their medicines from the forests and made tinctures with ingredients that grew around them. Ram laughs at the notion of formal health care in Khmer Rouge times. She can't imagine it. And I wonder: How does this shape her view of the world?

Among the patients is a young man who points to his leg. When he presses his finger into his calf it leaves a lasting depression in the skin, like silly putty. He wants someone to fix it. He looks to me for help, but I have nothing to offer, nothing that could heal him.

Downstairs, Jerry and I wait to speak with the Dutch doctor, but we never do. She is too busy with patients. Instead, we sit in the hallway watching people pass by. A toddler with a bump above her nose, and eyes coated in a creamy film, waddles across the floor. Her mother teaches her to clasp hands the Buddhist way, begging us for help.

A man's metal-tipped crutch *thunks, thunks, thunks* as he hops along the tile. He approaches a corner, where sunlight silhouettes his body and illuminates the dark stump of his right leg, resting on the crutch. Jerry takes a photo of that man, a picture of sadness caught in a bright chink of light.

This place is full of contrasts like that. The center's second-floor balcony overlooks an outdoor kitchen where patients' families cook on open stoves and women bathe in brightly colored sarongs. So much color and flair. But behind all that: the lake with its dark, spindly trees, and the house of a madman.

All around this town: the numb faces of survivors. The visages of ravaged people. "Expressionless faces imprint themselves on your mind and it did not matter what bad news you had, these people took it as though they were not surprised," writes an Australian nurse, Lyndall Moore. "Here was a country where nobody was immune from harm in those stormy, blood-soaked days. But life went on, people died, babies were born, herds were managed, crops planted, work was done and the fabric of society was re-sewn."

She could have been writing about Anlong Veng but instead, her words describe Rwanda during its own emergence from war and genocide.

As Jerry and I prepare to leave, a "nurse" named Pich Sokha enters the hallway. He doesn't know what the center will do after MSF leaves. He hopes another aid group will take over. Otherwise the clinic will have no money. And neither will the staff. So please, he asks, can't someone help?

It is not just health care that needs a new foundation, a structure. It is everything. It is education and family and government and social trust. It is religion and business and a perception of the outside world. Anlong Veng, like much of this country, needs a rebirth.

Tim Sangvat and Kong Vanny understand these things. They work for UNICEF, sharing an office and mission of immense proportions. Take education, for example. Under the Khmer Rouge, Vanny says, children learned how to make snares, how to fight the enemy. Students went to school, then went off to fight, then returned to school, then fled again to the jungle. This was no way to educate a child. One of his biggest challenges is teaching people the mere idea, the concept, of education. Imagine that! He has to teach a whole community what it is to learn before the people even begin to understand how and what to teach each other. Moreover, the community is not cohesive, it is spread through tracts of jungle, past land mine fields, in forests thick with malaria. How does one teach like that? Sangvat asks.

Now, Vanny adds, the people are moving. They're shuffling around, looking for work, leaving their jungle posts. "They do not stay in one place. For education, I think it's very bad." For how does one teach to a rootless wave of humanity?

But there's hope. Some people understand. Some send their kids to school. Some realize the new opportunities that have come on the tail of war. Those people determine to do better for themselves. "This is a strong point of the community," Vanny says.

And something else is clear. "The people here hate war." They lived it every day, all their lives, and they want no more. Ta Mok? "They don't care," Vanny says. Let him go to trial, let him go to prison, let him face his demons. The people don't care; they want to move on.

Sangvat agrees. This is his assessment, he says, but ask the people. Ask, and they will talk.

Over time I find he's right about that — to a certain degree.

In 2003, Jerry and I return to Anlong Veng for the national elections. We come with our translator, that decorous young man named Morn, quiet, smart, polite. He asks to switch guesthouses after we realize our original choice sits next to a house that will morph into a noisy karaoke bar with prostitutes at the onset of dark.

Morn normally earns money by guiding tourists around Angkor, and he's acquired a vast knowledge of both English and Japanese. He's never been to Anlong Veng, and he's eager to see it. He does not have a car, so we take a packed taxi truck. When we arrive, we find a town that has grown. It has spread tentacles through the mud. The market goes way back and way out, though it remains uniformly foul. There are half a dozen guesthouses now and restaurants to feed their customers. Half the population, it seems, comes from somewhere else. They're here to work. Trading on the border, selling chicken or plastics or clothes in the market, serving coffee and beer, making new starts and leaving other impoverished lives behind.

But the old contingent of Anlong Veng remains as well. The men wear green fatigues, some new and starched from the Army, others ripped and rumpled from years of wear. It's almost as though they're two nationalities, the original inhabitants of Anlong Veng and the imports. The former Khmer Rouge and the others. But they're all Khmers, all Cambodians, all of the same ethnic blood, all of the same hot land.

There is a woman who runs a lunch spot across from the market. She's from Kompong Cham, three large provinces away. Business is better here than there. On weekends tourists, mostly Khmer, come to see Ta Mok's house and climb the nearby mountain where Pol Pot perished.

She says the former Khmer Rouge are her neighbors and customers, and she has no problem with them. They "never fight anyone here. We all get along." But she's not so fond of this town. She lives here out of desperation, divorced and staying with her sister. "I don't know what to do."

Up the road, on the bridge by the lake, is Moak Kakada. He was born in Anlong Veng, and he has witnessed the changing guard. "It's different here now. Before we had no freedom, and I could not study."

Moak Kakada is twenty years old and in eighth grade at the local school, built by Hun Sen. His previous education was sporadic. "I went before, but sometimes I didn't because we had war." Despite what others have said, he insists he studied language, math and geography — not the techniques of war. Yet this interrupted education left him lagging and wanting more. He wants to be a doctor, but he's not sure how. "There's no high school here, so I'm waiting for the government to build a high school for me."

Moak Kakada eagerly awaits tomorrow's polls. It's his first national election. He does not say who will get his vote, just that the candidate stands for independence and peace. "I understand democracy," he says. He thinks the future looks good.

And then we meet Oun Khemara.

Oun Khemara doesn't think of his adoptive father as a human butcher. He thinks instead of a loving man, a ruler who strolled the streets and chatted with the masses, an affectionate figure with a heart for small children and animals. He recalls Ta Mok as a hero from better times. "I think he's a good man."

Oun Khemara steps from the shady sanctuary of a thatch hut to talk about the man who adopted him, an infamous man remembered widely across Cambodia for nothing good and everything evil. Ta Mok is in jail in Phnom Penh, and Oun Khemara hasn't seen him for four years, but his dark eyes brighten when he recalls the past. Besides "the Butcher," Ta Mok is known as Brother Number Four, three steps behind Pol Pot in the Khmer Rouge hierarchy. Yet Oun Khemara simply calls him "father," with the conviction of a compassionate son.

"He loved me. He wanted me to live with him." Ta Mok had four daughters but no sons, and he chose Oun Khemara as a surrogate child. He saw the young boy and liked him, simple as that. Oun Khemara's parents agreed to the "adoption." They thought it an honor that Ta Mok loved him so. "He regards me the same as his son," Oun Khemara beams.

He grew up in Anlong Veng. His real parents were doctors in the hospital under the Khmer Rouge, and his father fetched fame for performing expert amputations. They hoped Oun Khemara would follow their lead, but he refused. "I was afraid of blood."

Ta Mok is seventy-seven now, and Oun Khemara worries about his health. "I miss him." He recalls dreams of his adoptive father, so vivid they make him cry.

The young man makes a living by selling tourist tickets to Ta Mok's abandoned home and by teaching English and Thai to a new generation of youngsters. I ask what Ta Mok would think of his teachings, and he says the old man would approve. "Now when you want to have a good job, when you want to have a bright future, you have to study English," he says, "because it is the international language." True, the Khmer Rouge killed people for studying foreign languages between 1975 and 1979. But there were no more killings after 1979, Oun Khemara insists.

A few weeks later in Phnom Penh, my Khmer teacher, Kang Om, will balk at Oun Khemara's outright lie. "That is wrong. They killed all the time."

Om tells me, "I met Ta Mok." In 1977, while working in a labor camp alongside a highway. The Butcher pulled up in a Chinese military truck, stopping briefly to address his minions. "Ta Mok said, 'Everybody has to be a hard worker. Anyone who is lazy, we take to kill.'" That was it, then he left. "So we thought Ta Mok was very bad, but nobody said so. Everybody said Ta Mok is very good." No one wanted to die.

Om has spent time in Anlong Veng, studying the people emerging from a social shroud. He has encountered others who share Oun Khemara's ideas. "I met many people who thought like this. They love Ta Mok." He doesn't understand them.

Om has a friend, a soldier, who participated in a reintegration ceremony of former Khmer Rouge soldiers defecting to the government in 1998. Ta Mok spoke to the people: The only thing on my head is a hat. The only thing above the hat is the sky. There is no one, there is nothing, above me. I am the top.

"And so the adopted child of Ta Mok, I don't know," Om says to me. "Maybe he is the same as Ta Mok."

This frightens him.

But Oun Khemara reminisces about the Anlong Veng of his youth. "I think it was good at that time." He got to drive Ta Mok in a car, an astonishing rarity in that "agrarian utopia." He poked around Thailand's hinterlands on the sly, as he translated for the Butcher. These were little perks reserved for Ta Mok's closest allies.

Sure, new life has come to Anlong Veng. But with the opening of Anlong Veng, so too have come thieves and petty crimes. Of all Oun Khemara's pleasant memories from years past, he chooses to note this: It was possible to get drunk at night, leave your motorbike by the roadside and pick it up in the morning. Not now, he says, someone might steal it. Anlong Veng is different, he says.

There are no jobs, this government is corrupt, and it takes money to buy employment. His mother studied medicine in China for seven years, yet she cannot find work under this regime. She has no money to pay "the big man." And this angers him.

Oun Khemara takes us on his motorbike across town as he switches from ticket-seller to teacher. In a simple hut on stilts, about twenty bright young girls and boys gather for their Headstart English lesson. Oun Khemara disappears behind the school briefly, then reemerges in clean gray slacks and a checkered black-and-white shirt.

The children sit at hard wooden desks, lined in rows, squashed into a crowded room. Oun Khemara begins a lesson titled, "In the Street," and two kids stand to recite a conversation as written in their books.

"Excuse me, can you tell me where the Ta Mok house?"

"I don't know very much English. Speak slowly please."

"Can you tell me where the Ta Mok house please?"

"Of course.... You can go street this way."

Several pairs of students, the sons and daughters of former Khmer Rouge soldiers, attempt the discussion. Oun Khemara sits in front, evaluating their pronunciation, correcting their faults—though he doesn't catch them all. His own English is fledgling.

When the kids finish, he lectures the group on the importance of English and the value of hard work and study. In this stuffy little room, Oun Khemara is a powerful figure — this man at the front of the class, Ta Mok's chosen son, who speaks big truths, talks to foreigners and holds the key to a promising future. These kids know nothing outside Anlong Veng, but their teacher assures them possibility lies ahead. The world will be coming soon to see this historic Khmer Rouge homeland.

As the stifling afternoon fades to night, the students sit patiently and upright, ogling their teacher with eager eyes.

That evening, monks gather in the Anlong Veng Pagoda at dusk, for their routine prayers. Theirs is a new *wat*, established in 2000, though still under construction. It is the first *wat* for a people denied religion most of their lives. They live and pray half a mile up a sandy path, surrounded by shimmering rice fields in the epitome of Cambodian idyllic wonder. Of the fourteen monks here, twenty-three-year-old Roan is the only native to Anlong Veng. He heads this *wat*. He has only recently become acquainted with Buddhism. "In the Ta Mok regime, there was no pagoda or school. So I didn't know about Buddhism then." He has learned from others, and now he spreads his knowledge. "Fifty percent of the people in Anlong Veng know about Buddhism, the rest I have to teach."

The monks all laugh when I ask his feelings because in Cambodia, people naturally say they are tired — which he is, which is what he says. But he also says he likes this position. "I'm very happy, and when we have celebrations, the people from Anlong Veng come here."

Roan's father is here, too, to pray. He squats by the temple. This is a new privilege for him, for everyone. "I wasn't a soldier, but I lived here in the Ta Mok time, so if he said something I had to do it." That included not praying, which he did on the sly.

The monks ring their bell, a big spent cannon shell found in nearby fields. Then they invite us inside. Their sounds, their soothing chants, transport me to a sanguine realm. But all around them is rubble. It's an unfinished temple, just a skeleton but no connective tissue. The floor is rocks, the cement is not yet poured. Bricks and stones lie everywhere. The monks joke: We should bring more cement when we return. But none of this chaos around them hinders their melodious prayers.

This setting is striking, out in these paddies, with trees enveloping the horizon. Morn likes the serenity. He wants to return, to take in a picnic and fill his lungs with fresh air. This surprises him, he didn't expect to like it here. "Actually, I was scared to come here." He thought perhaps it wasn't safe. His parents told him not to come, and they don't know he did. He couldn't shelve the innate curiosity about this once-sinister place in his midst.

The following morning voters rise with the sun and cast their ballots in the national election, the event that brought us here. What happens in the course of two days is a blatant display of undemocratic principles (which appears in the following chapter). But Anlong Veng survives the day in peace, and the next afternoon an overwhelming victory is tallied. As we wait for those final numbers, we return to the Anlong Veng Health Center for the first time since 2001.

I recognize a few Khmer staff faces, flitting in and out of patient rooms, busy. But MSF is gone. The workers' once-lively house stands boarded and abandoned. The group has left as it said it would.

The center's floors are filthy, full of dust and peanut shells and mud and food scraps. The patients welcome us with desperate eyes. A mother displays her ill son, a girl leads us to her ailing father. There is another man with a rail of a body, white wavy hair and an unnaturally black face, much blacker than his torso. The patients and their families look at us, as though our white faces can offer some cure. But we have nothing to offer, and they have little to hope for. A doctor leads us through the rooms, bed by bed, so many people sick with malaria: an eighteen-year-old boy with goosebumps, brought by malaria's feverish chills; a family, all infected; a woman four months pregnant, in a coma, bloody urine, signs of deadly cerebral malaria. The rooms smell of bodily fluids and sweat and that tropical hospital smell when nothing is clean and everyone suffers.

Everything the nurses feared two years ago has come true. "Please, can't someone help?" Pich Sokha asked in 2001. And now, no one has come to fill MSF's shoes—not another aid group. Definitely not the Cambodian government.

In 2001, Jerry and I sat on a bench in a clean hallway, waiting to speak with the busy Dutch doctor. That hallway is now streaked with mud; that doctor is now gone. Empty shelves stand amid the floor; nearby, a pile of garbage. The path to the old MSF house is overgrown. Besides a few old MSF stickers stuck to doors and windows, it almost looks as though the group were never here.

Still, Ta Mok's lake gleams beautifully — an incongruous backdrop, askew to the execrable social surroundings. It is so sickly within that center, yet so healthy in the vacant lands all around.

The hospital staff have fingers stained with indelible ink, proof that they've voted. They have had their say on the future of this country, this province. The district has spoken loudly for Hun Sen and the ruling CPP.

Those inside the health center of course do not get that chance to choose. They lie in fever while their neighbors vote for another five years of the government that liberated them from the jungle.

Interlude: Bond and Than

Anlong Veng in 2001 is not a usual destination, not a prominent pick for tourists. We circulate the idea at our Siem Reap guesthouse, looking for a driver. Than, the guesthouse manager, says he has a friend named Bond who can fill the bill. This is Cambodia, and anything is possible for a price, and the price will be hefty because the road is atrocious. We arrange the trip nonetheless, and in the morning Than appears at the car as well. He wants to join us. He has never seen this enigmatic town, and he is equally curious as we — but a little nervous.

Than is twenty-one and recently introduced to the responsibilities of adulthood. He has been given control of the family nest egg, this guesthouse. A few years back, Than's parents sold their rice field — a bold step — and invested $4,000 in a parcel of land in Siem Reap, where they have plunked down their dreams. The duty now rests with Than, a typical twenty-one-year-old, typically jaded, typically interested in the diversions of young men and typically uninterested in any saddles of responsibility.

So Than escapes with us to Anlong Veng. He tells his mother he will return by nightfall, distinctly contradictory to our stated plans. Than is still under the thumb of a mother who pays his way in life. When she doesn't pay enough, he takes it. He takes it while she sleeps, $10 or so, to loan his friends when they're broke or to buy a night of drinking. Like last night when he went out with the guys, other guesthouse managers like himself. Or like the night a busload of Japanese tourists arrived, and, as guesthouse proprietor, he was obliged to entertain. That night cost him $30 in drinks, the price of schmoozing. But it's important for an entrepreneur like Than to maintain an image of fiscal nonchalance. It's a critical facade for any cool, young Cambodian male. It's a matter of saving face, just as important as haircut, strut or physique.

As Bond drives, the two young men discuss the escapades of the previous night. Bond asks how much he paid for a cover charge.

"Only $5." (Again, an astronomical amount to most Cambodians.)

"Oh, that's very good," Bond says.

As we pass through the Angkor temples, Bond tells us: "Angkor Wat is my mother because I can get money from Angkor Wat. If there is no Angkor Wat, then the tourists don't come and I have no job."

Both young men are of the marrying age, but Than is clear: He's not ready "because now I save money. But every night I go drinking. I save for drink, not marriage."

Farther up the road, Than and Bond throw two Coke cans out the window. "For children," they say. A poor child will come along, grab the can and turn it in for money. "Three cans, 200 *riel*." At that price, it would take 300 cans to pay for the previous night's cover charge.

Pavement stops beyond Banteay Srei temple, about eighteen miles from Siem Reap. Just a few years back this temple was secluded, still lost to the dangers of an ongoing guerrilla war, the jungle thick around it. Now the soldiers are gone, and tourists arrive by the busload. Locals have erected bathrooms and restaurants and trinket stalls. But beyond here there is little for the tourist. Our journey slows with bumps and potholes and broken bridges. It's all pits and mud, and farther ahead, land mine signs line the road. This is better than before, our companions assure us. The government fixed the road seven months ago. But as Than says, good roads in Cambodia don't last long.

And he's right.

We arrive in Anlong Veng in early afternoon, and our two companions are ready to leave shortly thereafter. They sigh and pout in a puerile pique. We have told them repeatedly we may spend the night. They don't like that idea at all.

And when darkness falls in Anlong Veng, and we're still there, Than calls home on a radio phone at 5,000 *riel*, about $1.25 a minute. But that's all the communication available. Cell-phone service has not yet arrived in Anlong Veng.

Later that night, Than decides to drown his frustrations in alcohol, and he invites us to join him. We eat dinner and drink beer at a restaurant run by a military general's wife, and Than flashes big wads of *riel* when the bill arrives. (We pay our own way.) But Than jokes: It's his mother's money, stolen in the night. He's soon tipsy and singing, and in this crapulous fun he forgets how desperately he wanted to get back to Siem Reap tonight.

On the drive back the next morning, we stop behind a taxi with oodles of people and stuff, piled higgledy-piggledy fifteen feet high. They're stuck in mud six inches deep. The men jack up a hind wheel and accomplish nothing in the ten minutes we're here. Another path heads to the right, rutted but better. Bond is scared to proceed, afraid of consequences to the car. It's not his car, it belongs to his boss.

Then a round-bellied military general drives up from behind, stopping beside us. The man hops out of his truck —full of soldiers in back with big guns— and asks the matter. Jerry, equipped with thousands of dollars of camera gear, is rightfully nervous. So he decides to befriend the general before he and his army have a chance to raise a ruckus.

It works. Even big generals in Cambodia are eminently polite and friendly if you reach them before their guns are drawn.

The general barks at Bond, instructing him to do exactly what we have tried to tell him: Don't wait for the stuck truck. Go around. Drive fast. Gun it. Keep it in first. Then the general nods goodbye and passes through with little ado, off with his men.

The general's fiery mouth has Bond petrified but convinced. After a few moments of spinning wheels, we're back on course, and Bond exhales in relief.

Bond curses these roads and the government that allows them to exist in such a perilous state. "I don't like this government," he declares. Politicians are corrupt. Every election is the same. The politicians promise new roads, new development; they vow to redeem the countryside. Then they win and don't do a thing. Every year Bond pays $30 in road taxes, but look at this! he exclaims. "If I were prime minister I would build the roads." He would link Cambodia to its neighbors; he would make trade easy. But the ruling elite? "They don't care."

Along the drive, Bond and Than also inform us news overheard at an Anlong Veng car wash (the young men insisted on cleaning the Camry for our grimy return): Earlier this week, soldiers at a checkpoint stopped a van heading into Anlong Veng, demanding money from the passengers. But we shouldn't worry, Bond and Than say. It probably won't happen to us.

And they're right. All the way back, we pass soldiers with automatic rifles. Though they never stop our car, they stop many others.

PART II

LIVING NOW

8. Democracy: Rice and Rights

"I don't know exactly what democracy is," says Pao Sitha. "We just think about whether we have rice to eat."

Pao Sitha is a twenty-eight-year-old farmer in Kompong Speu Province, just outside Phnom Penh. She gazes across her emerald paddies, the fields that have fed her family since 1979, and muses over the results of the 1998 election. Forty minutes away by car, gunfire shakes the streets and riots set the capital on fire. Protesters are calling the election a farce; they don't want Hun Sen in power anymore. They want change, and this election is not the democracy they had in mind. But here in this sun-parched garden, the air is quiet, and Pao Sitha thinks about food, not politics. "Because I am a farmer, we never hope for anything other than the rice field."

What is democracy? Everyone has an answer, a slightly different vision in mind, like the subtle variations in grains of rice. Some, like Pao Sitha, say they don't know democracy at all. And yet, they do. They know what they need to survive. They know their own struggles to feed their children; they know their country's brutal crimes and the culprits who have never been brought to task. They have begun to learn the concept of human rights, ideas brought from afar from learned people who first came before the 1993 UN-sponsored elections. And they know, all Cambodians know, the noose of corruption around their country's throat. They know it's wrong; they know they don't like it; they believe they can do little to fight it.

Many Cambodians, understandably, have lost their faith in democracy — lost it before it ever had a chance to flower. They believed in democracy in 1993. They had high hopes the UN would bring them peace and a stable future. Peace, after all, was a goal of the Paris Peace Agreements, which also set up UNTAC and aspired to bring Cambodia free-and-fair elections. But neither happened. Fighting against the Khmer Rouge continued through 1998, and the election's outcome betrayed the voters' will. The UN failed, and "it did not acknowledge that they had abandoned the main objectives of the Paris Agreement," writes journalist Henry Kamm. In May 1993, the Cambodian people voted with gusto for Prince Norodom Ranariddh of the Funcinpec Party. They did not elect Hun Sen, but Hun Sen and his CPP allies threatened to break away with six eastern provinces, forming an "autonomous zone," where "People's party hoods went on a rampage against UNTAC and Funcinpec offices and assaulted opposition party workers. The secession ended five days later," writes

Kamm. The result? Ranariddh was installed as first prime minister, Hun Sen as second prime minister. More than a decade later, Hun Sen still rules the country. And many Cambodians say they don't trust elections.

What's more, every Cambodian election is marked by brutal violence — twenty-one killed before the 1998 vote, fifteen before commune elections in 2002, thirty-one killed before the vote in 2003. "Many Cambodians have been made acutely aware that active involvement in politics, particularly on behalf of the opposition, could result in death," Human Rights Watch notes in 2003. "They know that little or nothing is done to bring the perpetrators to justice, especially if the perpetrators are local officials or members of the ruling Cambodian People's Party."

The tally is long.

In November 2001, five men are paid $10 each to kill a Sam Rainsy Party candidate in the commune election campaign. The chief prosecutor later denies the murder had political implications.

In January 2002, three female opposition candidates are shot to death — two in their homes and one in her rice field.

In February 2003, prominent democracy supporter and member of the Royalist Funcinpec Party, Om Radsady, is shot to death after eating lunch at a restaurant.

In October 2003, three months into the post-election stalemate, journalist Chou Chetharith of the Funcinpec Party radio station is shot to death in front of his office.

Three days later, singer Touch Srey Nich, "the voice of Funcinpec," is shot and her mother killed while leaving a flower shop in mid-morning. As of April 2004, the singer remains hospitalized.

And in January 2004, Chea Vichea, leader of the country's largest trade union, is shot to death while reading a newspaper near Wat Langka in Phnom Penh.

What is democracy? By definition, it is "a government in which the people have a say in who should hold power and how it should be used; a government in which the majority rules." This is taken straight from the *Oxford English Dictionary*— a straightforward, clear explanation. Even if Cambodians don't say these things in so many words, they know the void that exists in democracy's stead.

The 1998 elections go like this: The ruling Cambodian People's Party wins sixty-four seats, the Funcinpec Party wins forty-three seats and the Sam Rainsy Party wins fifteen. The CPP lacks the two-thirds majority required to rule alone, so it must form a coalition government. But the opposition parties protest, claiming widespread election violations. Protestors erect the tent city known as "Democracy Square." For weeks, thousands of people camp in the square until early September when two grenades mysteriously explode in Hun Sen's house in central Phnom Penh. Using that as a pretext, the government cracks down on protests, demolishing the square, shooting at demonstrators in the streets. A coalition government is formed in November, making Hun Sen the prime minister and dividing key government posts between CPP and Funcinpec.

The opposition determines the results of this election an affront to democracy. International observers deem it free and fair, if not perfect. Many foreign journalists find the election a letdown — not enough blood, too little buzz, lacking the titil-

Soldiers loyal to Prime Minister Hun Sen dismantle a protest camp across from the National Assembly Building following the 1998 elections. Phnom Penh, 1998.

lation typical of Cambodia. "I think it's pretty fair to say the rest of the world doesn't give a damn," says Rob Elliott, an Australian freelance photographer shooting for Agence France-Presse and regional newspapers at the time. The calm of 1998 pales against the drama of 1993, when elections were primed with $1.6 billion and 20,000 foreigners, courtesy of the UN.

To long-term Cambodia-watchers, the whole affair is troubling. "Cambodia teetered between democracy and authoritarianism, and the international community showed little interest," Glenys Kinnock, the European Union's special representative to the elections, writes in a 2002 analysis of Cambodia's recent electoral history. "The European Union needs to accept that democracy is not synonymous with holding elections."

And to Cambodians, the answers surface in the streets, in the markets, in the rice paddies.

The protestors set up camp in August 1998, a few weeks after the elections, in the park across the street from the National Assembly. This is the same park where grenades shattered a Sam Rainsy gathering the year before. They erect blue tarps, a medical corner, and all the trappings of a mini-city. They hoist banners and signs and placards in English, mocking Hun Sen, espousing freedom, calling for help in a language not their own, but a language the world may understand. They post a sign naming this new enclave: Democracy Square.

And so it goes for weeks, and the people come. First hundreds, then thousands; first students and educated demonstrators, then peasants and pickpockets and hangers-on. Everyone wonders: How long will it last? How long can this country go without a government? How long can these people sleep in the park?

They do until September 7, a Monday, the day two grenades explode in Hun Sen's compound. That evening, he summons his troops. Sam Rainsy, fearing for his life, takes refuge in the Cambodiana Hotel, and his supporters congregate in the street outside. The cops stand ready with weapons poised; monks parade through as an homage to peace, and the city breathes cautiously until the gunfire starts. Protesters hurl rocks at the cops. I am at *The Cambodia Daily* that night. The office is a few blocks from the square, and gunshots rumble through our concrete building. Jerry is on the scene. Each shot pierces my worried gut.

It starts at 7:30 P.M. Police fire hundreds of rounds into the air, on the ground, bullets scattering, people scrambling. At least one man is killed. Jerry sees it. He photographs the body, dripping in blood, still lying astride a *moto*. An officer shoves a hot gun in Jerry's face and tells him to leave.

The next day, soldiers and police scour the city. They yank the Democracy Square sign from the ground, pummel the tent city with hoses, threaten to shoot if people don't leave. It takes five minutes to dismantle the camp. "It is not a crackdown," government spokesman Khieu Kanharith tells the *Daily*. "We just moved them out. This demonstration was starting to get out of control."

All day, the "noncrackdown" continues. Police fire into the air, into crowds. Protesters hurl Molotov cocktails. There are chases all across the city. At least one person is killed, although rumors claim many more. Casualties mount at local hospitals.

Riot police chase demonstrators who hurl Molotov cocktails and rocks near the Royal Palace following the destruction of Democracy Square by army troops. The encampment had been a protest against the outcome of the national elections, and its location across the street from the National Assembly building had held up the government for weeks. Phnom Penh, 1998.

I'm in the newsroom when I hear of "something" happening near the Central Market: a procession of monks, peacefully marching for another monk they say was killed the night before. I arrive at the market amid calm and quiet, 600 men in saffron striding neatly in single-file lines. I head to the front for a better view. Someone, a monk, is shouting through a loudspeaker. I can't understand. It's a "mistake, mistake." I rush forward.

"Mistake. Problem."

A soldier with a stick sends traffic south on Monivong, the city's busiest street. The road clears. A gap appears. Soldiers come running, waving sticks and guns. I see half a dozen, then truckloads. A mob of monks turn around and sprint toward the market. Some fall to the street and kneel in prayer. Others run faster. There's a telephone pole ahead. The guy beside me hurdles a motorbike. Soldiers aim their guns. They're behind me. They're beside me. A soldier whacks a monk with a stick. I run.

I can't move faster. I'm pushed to the sidewalk. I trip over robes. I shove, people shove me. There are *motos* in the way. Why are all the stores closed? Not one is open. Locked. Iron gates closed. I could hide. I can't. I'm wedged between monks and concrete walls. There's a car parked on the sidewalk. A woman fusses with a bike in the way. She can't move it. She gives up. The soldiers are here now.

Everyone falls. Three layers of monks pile atop me. I can hear the electric batons. I can hear them whacking skulls. It's closer now. I'm surrounded. Panting. Sweating. I'm pinned against a wall.

A monk dumps a water bottle on my foot. They're all on top of me. It stinks of sweat. I'm caught in a yellow parasol. I'm covered, smothered, except the tip of my head. I'll be shot in the head. I'll die with strangers. Can bullets penetrate three layers of flesh? Am I selfish for thinking these thoughts?

I turn my head. Screaming. This is it. No, I really don't want to die. I didn't come here to die. I never wanted to be a war reporter. I haven't been nice enough to my husband.

Breathing, panting, dripping sweat. A hole between bodies opens to my right. A soldier clobbers someone with a stick again and again. I can't see the person, only the stick and each heavy crack. I can't see again. All that flesh.

Another hole. They run past, dozens, guns pointed ahead, sticks held high, people falling to the ground in submission, others running on. Crack.

Then a clearing in the mob. I see sunlight. Monks fall to my sides, praying. And there he is, AK-47 in my face. His mouth is open, baring gaps between his teeth. He stares, I look at him in panic. It's up to him.

"Go," he motions with his gun.

I stumble to Monivong, my sandals unstrapped, falling off my feet. I turn my back on them. I turn away from the monks, the beatings, the story. I got out. They didn't, but I go anyway.

I turn south on a barren street and for the first time notice the monk's yellow parasol caught on my arm. A hundred yards ahead, in a safe place: the photographers, the bystanders, the jeering crowd waits. They look at me, laughing. Some offer me a ride. They didn't see any of it.

I keep walking.

They say the lead monk was killed that afternoon, although no one finds a body.

I return to the *Daily* in a stupor. I relate my story to colleagues. One young expatriate reporter tells me, "C'mon, you know you loved it." The adrenaline, he means. Another foreign reporter tells me: "No story is worth your life. Dead reporters can't report."

I try to call Jerry, looking for support, worried about his safety. He's several blocks away, in another bloody scene. In front of him are protesters throwing rocks, chunks of concrete, more Molotov cocktails. Behind him are the police, the targets. They fire randomly at the crowd, over Jerry's head. He's stuck in the middle, hiding in a doorway after racing out to help a friend, another photographer who was felled by a hunk of concrete.

Months later, that photographer will clean out his photo bag and find a bullet lodged into a roll of film. That film literally saved his ass.

The week continues with these scuffles. People congregate in the alleys and streets, the cops sweep through, and everyone scatters. Then everyone regroups, and it all happens again. Schools and businesses close, and life is put on hold. "Our students, they keep trying to come to school, but we told our students, 'Please go home,' because we cannot protect them," says Kep Chanto, then a deputy director of the Cambodia Academy of Business Studies, which sits a block from the U.S. embassy, epicenter of these chases through a gridwork of streets.

Police and soldiers guard all the major street corners, the parks, the palace, Hun Sen's house and all the city's prominent buildings. But even the enforcers grow weary. "In the past two weeks, I've had no time to rest. Sometimes I have no rice to eat — too busy," says Seng Bunthon. He is forty-four years old, a police officer stationed on a stone bench near the Independence Monument, watching for protesters. With a two-way radio in his left hand and a pistol on his right hip, he says breaking up demonstrations is his public duty. "I sometimes get angry with demonstrators," he says, but "this is my job." He works as he was trained, giving little thought to the weapons he has and sometimes uses: the pistol, an electric stick, a police baton. "I carry the gun for defense. Sometimes the demonstrators throw stones…. I feel worried, too."

It's remarkable we don't see more deaths, though no count is ever confirmed. One person one day, another the next, a boy shot in the leg. Students take shelter at *wats*, monks at a human-rights group. The CPP hires its own rabble-rousers; they carry sticks and pipes and other rudimentary weapons. They come to town by the truckload, meeting the opposition with force. Some say they are paid in bread and rice for their services.

There are rumors about bodies in the river. Protesters are missing. I visit Ta Cheng hospital to see who is there and why. I meet Pen Tin, thirty-two, a demonstrator who scuffled with police near the National Assembly building. One cop hit him upside the head with a gun barrel, and now he has three stitches. Another cop kicked him in the ribs. A UN car picked him up and whisked him to the hospital. "I feel very upset with the police, to see the police use violence on the demonstrators."

Son Sawath, twenty-two, was in the same spot at the same time, also swept out by a UN car. He was shot in the shoulder. "Many people were beaten by the police. I just attended the demonstration because I wanted to help the Cambodian people. We want to have peace."

San Sitha, twenty-nine, is a soldier from Pailin. He is here with a large welt on the right side of his face. "I was severely beaten by an electric club and also kicked. The police said to me, 'You are a stubbornhead.'" He twitches as a nurse sticks a needle in his arm. Police took his bag, his wallet, clothes, ID card. They took other people's *motos*. "Everything was looted."

Ieu Mony is beside his fifteen-year-old brother, Ieu Pou, who was shot in the neck outside the Cambodiana Hotel the night before. The boy is in critical condition. Doctors show him the bullet they retrieved from the boy's neck. In the next bed over is a thirty-six-year-old woman, shot in the arm and back. Same time, same place. "I think it's very fierce and brutal," says Ieu Mony.

The week goes on.

Jerry and I wait in simmering heat outside the U.S. embassy, waiting, waiting for something everyone says will happen, although no one knows what or when. We're among a crowd of 200 on the corner of two narrow streets, several parachute journalists among us as well as scores of Cambodians. Many come to the streets, looking for action. Riots are a thrill. While some truly march for democracy, others seek a break in routine.

A drunken soldier slowly approaches. No one pays much attention. No one really notices until he takes aim through blurry eyes. He fires his AK-47 into the crowd, straight up the narrow street as innocent feet flee the scene in a stampede. Hot shells tumble to the ground, bullets dripping through air. Jerry is pinned to the ground with a terrified Cambodian man half on top of him, half hiding behind him. They are in clear view of the soldier, open to his gun. I crouch behind a post around the corner. A cameraman for a wire service kneels behind the soldier and films the scene. "Don't! Don't! Don't!—turn it off," everyone shouts. The soldier spots him and turns our way.

But the soldier runs out of bullets and pauses to reload. People scramble, trying to pick themselves up. The cameraman races off with a dagger of voices nailing his back, "You stupid shit!" But no one gets far before more shots. My knees tremble beneath me. Red *motos* are strewn about the street. A drink cart is abandoned. Somehow, miraculously, no one dies, and the drunken soldier is led away by another man in fatigues.

The reporter who earlier said I really, truly loved the adrenaline rush as I was trapped with the monks is here on this day. He is scared shitless, as we all are. I overhear him on the phone later in the afternoon, recounting the scene to a UN source. He is still jittery, and he smokes like a fiend.

About a week after these incidents we visit Pao Sitha in her field, twenty-five miles out of town, asking questions about democracy. She, like many Cambodians, has much clearer thoughts on politics than she acknowledges. She, like many of her neighbors who echo her words, knows the essence of democracy, even if she doesn't articulate it. Democracy, in its barest terms, means being afforded the basic right to survive and work and live in peace. And people tend to define democracy in terms of the work they do and the lives they lead.

Democracy for Pao Sitha's family is food on the table, the rice itself, the right to own and work the land and the responsibility of cultivating it.

A few miles from there, in the tiny home of Nai Sokhoeun and Ty Khan, democracy means peace. Their home isn't much — just a one-room thatch hut for themselves and six children (five now, since one died a few months before). They have no floor but the earth, two slat beds, a few hammocks and that's about it.

They have no rice field, just a small swath of ground surrounding the home. Ty Khan once worked as a security guard in Phnom Penh until the company moved and left him jobless in 1984. He suffers a recurring illness, probably malaria, from working in the jungle during the Vietnamese rule. Nai Sokhoeun sells eggs in the local market, but business has dwindled since the poisoning scare left customers wary of market foods. "I don't know exactly what democracy is," Ty Khan says. "But I just want peace in the country. I don't want to see both sides fighting each other. If there is peace, maybe we can start a business and make a little money."

They do have a small radio, dangling from their wall. He knows vaguely of Phnom Penh's demonstrations and political paralysis. "I just want the government to talk, to form a new one and work together nicely," he says, with a grin that never leaves his face. "If the three big parties can talk together and work together forever, then this country will be OK."

By expert definitions, democracy is an equation of rights and freedoms. It includes free speech, a free press, the right to form political parties, elections that are regular and credible and free and fair, a transfer of power after those elections, a separation of power within the government, tolerance and, perhaps most important: rule of law. And that, Cambodia lacks. "Civil society cannot develop in a legal vacuum," says Kao Kim Hourn, executive director of the Cambodian Institute for Cooperation and Peace. "Rule of law, not rule of man. What we have in Cambodia is more a rule of man. That is a setback to democracy."

But these things do not develop quickly. "Cambodians should understand that democracy is a long process. People have high expectations. They're frustrated. But the thing is, it's normal in society. No one expects the road to democracy is going to be easy, is going to be speedy, is going to be smooth, is going to be less painful. People forgot that democratic countries took years, they took centuries to be where they are today."

Part of that process is building a foundation of human rights. Equal rights for all. But that is a foreign concept to much of Asia.

All across this continent are cultures with no innate ideas of human rights. Many Asian societies flourish and founder on systems of hierarchy, on views of humanity as inherently unequal. Rich man on top, poor woman at bottom. If a man is rich and powerful, then he must have done something right in a previous life to make him so. His power is deserved — as are the misfortunes of those he treads upon.

If a woman is poor and ugly, she was born into those confines, based on bad behavior in some other realm.

Asian societies do not think in Western ways. "Westerners seem inclined to believe there is only one kind of relation between the individual and the state that is appropriate," writes American psychologist Richard E. Nisbett. In theory, the Western world views a person as an individual entitled to certain rights, freedoms and duties. But this is not in the Asian way. "Most peoples, including East Asians, view societies not as aggregates of individuals but as molecules, or organisms. As a consequence, there is little or no conception of rights that inhere in the individual." To change that thinking would require "not just a different moral code, but a different conception of the nature of the individual."

Yet there may be no other Asian society so ripe for that shift. Cambodia: purged, stripped to nothing, murdered to its barest bones, and then slowly rebuilt, the saplings of democracy planted with seeds imported wholesale from abroad. The West has introduced democracy and human rights here. Mere seeds but planted nonetheless, and planted deeply. Cambodian culture was so uprooted that perhaps, now, there is room for new ideas to grow. "I will say, the UN did leave one very positive legacy that offers hope for change ... the concept, at least, of human rights," *New York Times* correspondent Seth Mydans tells me. He reiterates the words of Kek Galabru, a prominent human rights activist. "Now at least when someone steals your land or rapes your daughter you realize that you have a right to complain. And at the other end

Opposition party leader Sam Rainsy kicks off his national campaign at the start of the 2003 election season from the back of a truck in Phnom Penh. Phmon Penh, 2003.

of the power scale, when Hun Sen wants to kick ass, he has to take at least a little glance over his shoulder and make sure he bamboozles the human rights busybodies."

But these seeds face a long, harsh winter, tropical as the air may be.

The 2002 commune elections go like this: The CPP wins control of 1,598 communes nationwide; the Sam Rainsy Party wins control of thirteen, and Funcinpec wins control of ten. It's another sweeping victory for the CPP.

A year and a half later, the 2003 national elections go like this: The CPP wins seventy-three seats; Funcinpec wins twenty-six seats, and the Sam Rainsy Party wins twenty-four seats. Hun Sen again does not have the two-thirds majority required to rule alone. The opposition refuses to join a coalition. Funcinpec and the SRP create the Alliance of Democrats. There is a stalemate; no functional government well into 2004.

The February 2002 commune election is the first since independence, and it's business as usual. Fifteen mysterious political deaths, alleged vote-buying, threats, bullying, more of the same. And as usual, the analyses contradict. "The 2002 election was anything but free and fair," according to opposition candidate Sam Rainsy. The election is "free and fair enough," from Hun Sen. A declaration: "Cambodian elections neither free nor fair," says the International Republican Institute, dedicated to spreading American-style democracy around the world. But "a little democracy is better than no democracy at all," from the *Far Eastern Economic Review*.

For years reporters, scholars, analysts, human-rights workers, activists, senators, travelers—everyone has picked apart the state of Cambodian politics. It's good; it's bad; it's getting better; it's sliding into the abyss, all at the same time. Everyone couches reality in their own terms. Cambodia is a land "steeped in blood" states the *Washington Post*. It is ruled by a "culture of impunity." (Ubiquitous, but also in the *Review of Contemporary Asian Affairs*.) It is a "lawless country with the thin veneer of democracy," says Republican U.S. Senator Mitch McConnell of Kentucky. The 2003 elections were true, acceptable, transparent and conducted in a meticulous manner "that one would like to see everywhere," says the francophone delegation of election observers. The 2003 elections were so successful that Cambodia "could easily shame most of its regional neighbors," states Inter Press Service. The elections were "well conducted," but there is "still some way to go to full democracy," according to the European Union.

Confusing?

Yes—but these statements also reflect the complexity of judging and defining democracy. In some cases, they cause critics to wonder whether personal agendas are intertwined in these assessments.

McConnell and colleagues work hard to increase U.S. government support for Cambodia's opposition, painting the ruling CPP as undemocratic and the Cambodian people as needy. The U.S. pumps $11 million into NGOs working on the 2003 elections, and experts begin to question how far and in what direction the United States should step into Cambodian politics—particularly when potential future aid is tied to the election outcome. "If the conduct of these 2003 national elections provides a safe environment for all participants to compete," the U.S. State Department announces two months before the election, it might "explore" the option of increasing aid to Cambodia.

But the biggest accusations of over-stepping the lines come against the International Republican Institute, a nonpartisan, nonprofit organization that started in 1983 after former U.S. President Ronald Reagan called for Americans to help build democracy around the world. The IRI has a heavy hand in the 2003 election, right down to the booklets election workers use as procedure manuals on setting up polling stations, conducting the elections and counting the votes.

But critics say the IRI's goal of spreading democracy is merely a front for the group's ulterior mission to get Sam Rainsy elected. "IRI's support for Sam Rainsy is accompanied by its visceral hatred of Prime Minister Hun Sen," writes Andrew Wells-Dang, a two-time Cambodian election observer for another nonprofit group. "IRI's vendetta is supported by key Republican leaders in the U.S. Congress, most vehemently by Mitch McConnell of Kentucky." Wells-Dang claims the IRI funneled $450,000 from USAID to start the Cambodian Center for Human Rights, which works in concert with IRI. "When CCHR allegations of pre-election violence differed from that of other organizations," Wells-Dang writes, "IRI routinely quoted CCHR's reports. Conveniently, the CCHR expatriate adviser is married to the IRI country director." His conclusions: "A not-so-fine line exists between foreign support to foster democratization and the direct funding of a single political party."

When things do not go as planned in Cambodia's pre-election period, the IRI recommends Congress "increase its pressure on Cambodia to hold free and fair elections...." Free and fair, meaning no sweep by the CPP.

What does all this mean? At the very least, it means rumors and misconceptions trickle down to the Cambodian people. There is confusion and misunderstanding, false hope and unnecessary fear. And so, right around election time, Jerry and I are hard-pressed to answer our translator, Morn, when he says he fears for Cambodia's future because Hun Sen will likely win, and he thinks the United States will become an enemy of his country. And everyone knows, the United States has a habit of invading its enemies.

Morn is not the only Cambodian thinking this.

Morn accompanies us to Anlong Veng to observe the 2003 elections that trouble him. We choose this town again, out of curiosity, to see how the old bastion of the Khmer Rouge interprets democracy.

We're out the door early on election morning, but we can't find anyone who knows where the nearest polling station is. We're told it's near the market, we ask along the way, but no one knows. We ask all around and finally find polling station Number Five, a small wooden building. On the front wall are tacked eighteen pages of names, about 700 in all. Eight people loiter in the doorway.

There are six observers inside, in the cramped quarters of this tiny room, all wearing yellow tags around their necks. They line the walls, scribbling notes. A big metal box, like a tin safe, takes center stage. Two aluminum voting booths stand behind it.

An hour later, the doorway is thick with people, a dozen heads peering through an opening in the slat walls, giving a bird's eye view inside. Each voter must squeeze through the doorway past the others waiting and watching, to the front table where he shows an ID and the election worker checks off his name, then to another worker who distributes a ballot ripped neatly from a stack. The voter heads to the booth, marks a vote, pushes the ballot through the slot in the box, then dips the right index finger into purple indelible ink to show he's done his duty.

It's a steady stream of people one by one through the slat doorway. People dress in pajamas, in embroidered shirts and festive sarongs, work shirts, pants suits, every-day clothes. There are many CPP T-shirts but few of the opposition. There are preg-nant women, young guys in shorts and flip-flops, mothers with children. Outside the door, there are chickens and ducks waddling through sugarcane.

One woman enters the room and hands over a family record book instead of a proper ID. Another man offers a tattered slip of paper. These are questionable vot-ing documents. The people are turned away.

As I watch voters sidle through the door, I think of what Morn has said about this election. The CPP has power and money; the opposition doesn't, so no matter who wins, he thinks there will be corruption. "I don't think it will ever stop." Improve, perhaps, but not cease.

A European Union Land Cruiser pulls up with a Khmer man and two West-erners wearing stone white vests branded with the EU flag. One of them is Glyn Ford, a British member of the European Parliament. This is the third station they've seen this morning; they're roving throughout the day. Yesterday, they found a polling sta-tion that forgot to seal the election box. Today, they've witnessed voters with no photo IDs. They have spotted a man in a tan Camel brand shirt delivering a carload of people with no IDs to a polling station. It is the same man who has been hanging around this station for hours, watching everything with raptor eyes. An election observer here tells us the Camel man has lived here a long time, since the Ta Mok years. He seems to have adopted the CPP trademark swagger and round face with full belly.

Ford says only one thing is certain: The ink works—he tested it himself.

Across the street is a man on a bike poring over papers with photos, handing out IDs as people approach with slips of paper. An observer tells us he's a village chief. This is a problem. Village chiefs are not supposed to come near voting stations on election day, except to vote. These people should have had IDs weeks ago. And some of them are at the wrong polling station. "This I will note in my report," the observer says.

Whatever happens today—if people vote at the wrong station, if the man in the Camel shirt stuffs the stations with voters, if the ballot box isn't sealed—the valid-ity of these elections is questionable because people think these things will happen. Even if the vote is fair, it has the appearance that it's not, and people think it isn't. People don't believe it's democratic. People fear the ruling party. People don't think Cambodia has democracy. And that must factor heavily in any credible assessment of Cambodia's reality.

The CPP has a strong hold on things here, from the radios slung on election workers' hips to the streets where men wear their hats and assert their presence. Everyone says the CPP is "famous" here, and even if they're holding no guns or waving no carrots, they ensured their votes in the months of Anlong Veng's transition.

Perhaps Cambodians will never see democracy through the Western eye of law. For a thousand years, this culture has had *bong thoms* and *praw tiens, samdechs* and *ai-u-doms* — and then all the rest, the masses. Angkor was built by slaves; the CPP sends its goons to far-flung polling stations to rally the votes. In either case, those with money garner the power and build their temples to themselves.

At 3 P.M., the stations close. A few stragglers without IDs are turned away, and that's it. The cap is screwed on the ink jar, the jar is placed in its box. Clasps are snapped on the ballot box, the extra ballots are tied away. The door is still open, and the Camel man returns with a couple of women, peering inside. An observer happily shutters the door in his face.

The ballot box is wrapped in plastic, then hoisted on the back of a *moto*, whose driver is randomly hailed from the street. An election worker rides behind the box, arms clasped around it. Two cops follow on another *moto*, and a caravan parades through town, to the Hun Sen school, where the counting will occur.

Hun Sen schools like this one dot the Cambodian countryside. The prime minister grew up a poor farm boy in a Kompong Cham village that had no high school. At the age of thirteen, his family sent him off to study in the capital with a few *riel*, a packet of rice and the clothes on his back. "They could barely afford to pay his school entrance fees in Phnom Penh. They could not rent a small room for him, or pay for his meals," Harish and Julie Mehta write in their biography of Hun Sen. "They were forced to entrust their bright little boy to the care of Buddhist monks." Hun Sen tells the Mehtas, "I am now determined to build more schools—more than any other Cambodian because I do not want our children to share the same fate as I." Problem is, there is often little money to pay the teachers or maintain the buildings in his name.

This one, where the ballots go, has cows grazing in the yard and a chicken scurrying through classrooms. Each of the district's boxes arrives in awkward fashion, on carts and *motos*. All but one. By the time we leave, one box remains out there, in the great rural yonder.

The 7 A.M. scheduled counting begins the next day, after 7:30, with all observers and workers crowded around school doors where many slept the night before. Hammocks are strung on the porch and belongings are stuffed in sacks. The Camel man's driver parks his Toyota outside the gate; the cops don't let the Camel man in.

The ballot boxes, seven in all (the last finally arrived), are distributed throughout the schoolrooms, and their observer teams follow. Everyone sits at simple wooden desks, as though students in class. Cops lounge in a hut behind the school. We're watching Box Number Five. The observers carry it to the floor and check and double-check and triple-check the numbers on tags. There is meticulous attention paid to the step-by-step instructions in the IRI manual — which everyone consults routinely. "This teaches me," a nineteen-year-old observer tells me.

Coming from an outlying polling station, a man with a ballot box on his bicycle rolls into a school where ballots will be counted for the 2003 national election. For years, until mid–1998, Anlong Veng had been the last stronghold of the Khmer Rouge. Anlong Veng, 2003.

By 8:10, the team still sits, yawning, poring over manuals, staring at the still-wrapped, still-locked Box Number Five. Jerry and I leave to eat breakfast.

We return after 10, and they still haven't tallied a single vote. Everyone here is learning, as though building a skyscraper from an instruction manual. A heap of materials, a stack of directions and a pool of people to get started. The tasks we as Westerners take for granted — running an election, counting ballots (except, of course, in Florida), knowing when not to count a vote — they must learn.

Finally: Two boxes are opened, flipped, all the ballots dumped into a bag, shuffled and shaken, then read by the man in charge, one by one. Each party has a number, and votes are indicated by a check next to the party of choice. The CPP is number 17. The readings are overwhelming: 17, 17, 17, 17, 20, 20, 17, 17, 17, 17, 17, 17…. An election worker stands at a chalkboard, ticking each vote beneath its corresponding number.

Outside the schoolroom window is a man with a walkie-talkie, relaying counts to someone on the other end. He is an unofficial and illegal election observer. When Jerry takes his picture, he runs.

When a questionable vote appears, the whole team pauses to analyze. One voter has failed to mark the standard check inside the #17 box. Instead, said voter has sketched a chicken. After some discussion, the vote is dismissed.

This goes on for hours, and we break again at a restaurant. A Hong Kong gangster movie plays on TV. Two large men in dress slacks slurp tea and soup while monitoring ICOM radios, gathering numbers from the counting station as their buddies call them with results. They chuckle with the latest word. The man on the left grins, picks his teeth and settles back against the hardwood chair. He wears a large ring with a red gem. His companion's rotund body spills off the seat.

Another dispatch, another smug smile, more scribbles onto small notepad pages. A final call sends the men up the road, lickety-split. A waitress sweeps greasy tissues and chicken bones from beneath their seats.

When we return to the school late that afternoon, the rooms are empty but the boards are full of 17s. It's an overwhelming victory for the CPP.

Overwhelming, but nationwide Hun Sen does not garner the votes needed to rule alone. In the days following, the opposition cries foul (again). A stalemate follows (again). The government prepares for riots (again). The people brace for the worst. And everyone wonders, what next? Unfolding events sound strikingly like 1998. But the riots don't happen, and the stalemate continues almost a year. For almost a year, Cambodia has no functional government.

The week before the election, Police Chief Hok Lundy warned that riots would be met with force. He has thirty trained dogs, and there were jokes about buying elephants to stomp out protests. That — and the officers would need two tons of sugar to boost their energy.

After the election, Funcinpec and Sam Rainsy join forces, calling themselves the Alliance of Democrats. The king is frustrated. He calls upon his people to cooperate. The rival parties negotiate well into April, time ticking. Eight months. No government. And only a scintilla of progress among the custodians of a nation.

Eight months. No government. No end in sight. We leave, we return to Thailand. Time slips into the hot season again, hedging toward a year since the election. A year of rains and droughts and seasonal rotations since that day in Anlong Veng.

There are some who wonder whether democracy is right for Cambodia right now. "Sometimes I think the importation of Western-style democracy is not suitable for Cambodian society," says Dr. Sorn Samnang, president of the Royal Academy of Cambodia. He thinks the ideas may have surfaced too soon. After World War II, the French allowed Cambodians to establish political parties and a National Assembly. The country's first constitution, adopted in 1947, was a copy of France's constitution. But there's a key difference between the two societies: "French people have more than 150 years of experience with democracy," he says. Cambodia is only beginning. Full-fledged democracy was attempted too soon, in a country with its own age-old systems. "This was not suitable for the national reality of Cambodia," he says.

Then war came, and genocide and a communist regime. Now, in the childhood of peace, Samnang sees a country of people who don't yet understand the duties tied to a working democracy. "Most Cambodians are living in Cambodian society only as human beings, not citizens. They say they have no duty, no obligations. They do what they like, no responsibility." The country must be taught. "I think that we should educate citizenship to them. They should not live in society simply as human beings."

Is the country ready?

"That is a question," he says. "That is a question for scholars."

Interlude: Sam and Vic

When the UN set up Cambodia's 1993 elections, Vic, as he calls himself — no more, no less — figured he would sign on, do some work, make some money, help out the country, then return to his itinerant British lifestyle. He got a little more than he anticipated: a home here for five years and running, avowed love and companionship and daily home-cooked meals by the self-proclaimed preeminent chef of Sihanoukville. He got it all when he married Sam.

She runs Sam's Guesthouse and accompanying restaurant in the Victory Beach sector on the north end of Sihanoukville, Cambodia's only port. It is 1998, and she does all the cooking, she pours all the beer and she wears the famous Cambodian smile most all the time.

Sam's place is a sturdy wood-and-concrete structure with a single dining room and three tables that empty onto the street and soak up the sunshine. In the back, a single darkened chamber just a few feet wide emits grilled, boiled, chopped, fried and stewed aromas of curry, rice, chicken, ginger, coconut, peanuts and an all-around well-cured kitchen. Also in the back is a wooden door to a restroom with standing-room-only toilet, shared by customer and proprietor alike. A wooden ladder leads through the ceiling to the single sparse guestroom upstairs, to which Sam and Vic occasionally retreat for a siesta at the scorching height of afternoon.

Sam's place overlooks a bumpy, gravelly street on the hill above Victory Beach, with views of blue in the distance. "Five-minute walk," she repeats three times. Chickens, cows and pigs roam freely. At night, the avenue assumes a romantic air as vendors illuminate their wares by candlelight in small wooden shacks on stilts. This will change in a few years, when Southeast Asia's buzz of tourists wends its way to Sihanoukville and this avenue pulses with Internet shops, backpackers, mountain bikes and middle-aged men repairing over beers, leering over girls. But this is 1998, and that tide has yet to come. Like the sea it sits on, this town still ebbs and flows to slower rhythms of time and change.

Jerry and I order a Khmer delight called amok—fish in coconut, steamed in banana leaf—a bowl of curry, two servings of rice and two sweetened coffees. Sam sends her assistant up the street to buy a pouch of peanuts for the curry. The woman soon returns, heads for the kitchen, and the room trembles with vigorous pounding. At the table beside us, Vic issues advice to an Australian adventurer about hopping through the dollops of land in the Gulf of Thailand. The two men meet at the wall, pointing hither and yon at a map, deliberating the appropriate responses to finding oneself alone and in trouble on Cambodia's treacherous seas. Vic warns, "There's a lot of malaria in that area." The Australian clarifies his sole intentions to just "look around."

The Australian asks Sam for orange juice. She squeezes the pulpy fruits, green on the outside, orange inside, into a glass, one by one. She brings the drink to his table. Fifty cents. Sam and Vic playfully exchange words, she in Khmer, he in English. "Five years in Cambodia and he doesn't speak Khmer," she says to us. "So I say I finish speaking English with you. I speak Khmer."

Then she brings our food. Some of the world's best fish is found in Cambodia. Some of Cambodia's best fish is found just like this, bathing in an autumn-colored cornucopia of curried soup with green beans, carrots, potatoes and spice. In another bowl, another fish crumbles into a mouth-tingling mix of coconut and ginger. Amid the flavors, we listen as Sam explains the evolution of her place.

She was once a chef at a prominent Phnom Penh restaurant. Before moving here, she had a bustling beachside business. "Every day it was full. Fifteen rooms. Hired cooks." But in an instant, it changed. Second Minister Hun Sen ousted First Prime Minister, Prince Norodom Ranariddh, in a bloody putsch in July 1997. Tourism stopped cold. The town went silent. Roadblocks, both real and imagined, kept visitors at bay. Sam could no longer afford her rent, so she moved here, up the hill and down on the scale of prosperity.

Now she tries to rent her upstairs room for $5 a night, which includes a fan and streetside view. "People know my good cooking from before," she says, "so people come to eat, but not to sleep."

Some people do like the ambiance of Sam's place. A Canadian artist recently booked the room for a week so he could paint the life outside his window. Fascinated, he parroted the woman across the way who ekes out a difficult living raising and selling pigs. The animals mill about her hut all day and mingle with the neighbors.

Sam brings our bill. Four dollars for all that taste. She tells us most tourists these days bypass Cambodia and head for Thailand instead. This will change in a few years, but now, Sam's menu is testimony to tough times. A white sign lists the fifty-four meals on offer, ranging in price from 20 cents to $4, half what they used to be. The cheeseburger, the hamburger, the fishburger, the meat and veggie pie are crossed off the sign.

Two dollars is pasted over the previous $4 for amok; $1.50 is pasted over the previous $3 for fish curry. And so it goes across the board.

But Sam still offers big fluffy banana pancakes with maple syrup in the morning, which we wisely select the next day before taking a longboat cruise to a nearby island. Sam arranges the outing through her fisherman friend, and she rents us snorkeling masks and fins.

At night, after most restaurants close, Sam's fluorescent light still beckons the occasional caller, and the well-lubricated laughter of a few beer-drinking vagabonds wafts through her open door. We stop in to tank up on gossip, as Vic has plenty. He's full of tales. There's one about his close call with a Cambodian cop, who sat in the street one day as Vic sped up in a UN vehicle of the Land Cruiser sort. The guy didn't move, and, well, the guy lived, although his face suffered some damage, Vic says. And then there's the time he snoozed on the beach briefly while a few wily kids emerged from the bushes to remove the short-wave radio from his clutches. He delves into stories of pickpockets and passports. The pickpockets take the money; the passports inevitably surface at the cop shop. Give the cop a small tithe, and you'll get your passport back, he says. Vic assures us Sihanoukville is safe and comforting like a small town. It has its quirky crimes, but nothing to try the mind. "They'll hurt each other," he says of locals, "but they won't hurt you."

Of course, those tides will change too. In another five years, Sihanoukville will become a hotbed of crime against foreigners—*moto* drivers pulling guns on tourists, axing them in the head, stealing their money. Rapists attacking women on the beach. But in 1998, Vic laments the lack of people here. "This is the last place people come because they've got beaches in Thailand, too." He thinks the perpetrators of the 1997 coup picked the wrong time to do it, with the rest of Asia suffering a dire economic crisis. Cambodia could have emerged prosperous and triumphant. Instead, people are too scared to come here.

Yet, Vic and Sam seem well-suited to their way of living. If you ask either one about the future, they shrug it off. Though this place isn't what it used to be, Sam says it's hers, and that makes her happy for now.

But as Cambodians know quite well, the tides are always changing.

9. Violence and Crime:
Blood in the Street

The people living here are also characterized by a startling and incomprehensible emotional seesaw, unpredictable, sudden changes of mood. In general they are friendly, hospitable.... And then suddenly, suddenly, something happens.... They just ... rush at the enemy and do not rest until they see blood. But each one of them, on his own, is pleasant, well-behaved, kind. The only explanation is that somewhere, a devil must lurk, fomenting strife.

— Ryszard Kapuscinski, *Imperium*

I brush past my editor's desk one afternoon in early 1998, and I see the photos. They're strewn among faxes and journalistic litter, surrounded by piles of paper and books. There is commotion all around this desk, all across the room, but I stand in silent contemplation. The photos are raw: blood and splintered bodies, singed tissue, pink holes, skin peeled back like a deer hide. I ogle them, and I know. I know how it looks when shrapnel gouges a leg, when a bomb bursts and rips through human flesh, scraping away fat, exposing muscle to air. When men and women turn to meat, their limbs like freshly butchered beef. Moments between life and death.

I stand at the desk, seeing the viscera, the veins, the humans frozen in photo time, and I wonder how so many people can pass this desk, day after day, never flinching. I wonder how a society lives among so much mutilation — how it remembers, how it forgets, how it moves on. One minute the heart beats, eyes blink, skin holds innards intact. The next minute they don't. These photos spark questions I will spend years trying to answer, never fully succeeding.

The photos are a record of March 30, 1997. It was hot Sunday in the park, with 200 people gathered for a Sam Rainsy speech. A car passed and BAM! A grenade exploded. Then another and another and another; four blasts shattered the day. At least sixteen people died, and more than 100 were injured. I read the news in Oregon, where I lived at the time, nine months before moving to Phnom Penh.

It happened in a park across from the National Assembly building, adjacent to the Royal Palace, where I go running nearly every day in 1998. Jerry and I attend a memorial ceremony a year after the attack. Saffron robes, clicking cameras, women

130

with tears and flowers, sputtering motorbikes and Rainsy's entourage, all clogging the same park beneath another relentless sun. Mothers, brothers and sisters mourn the dead. Throngs of journalists move with the flow of flower wreaths, burning incense and prayers for justice. The heat pounds our faces, backs, arms, legs. Sweat gushes in saline streaks down our bodies.

A few years later, there's a statue in the park honoring the dead. Every year there's a ceremony. Every year the attackers remain unknown and unpunished, but many people cast blame. Time passes, lives change, but survivors remember. And the scene lives on in pictures, with every jagged detail exposed.

Human rights groups have a phrase to describe a society like Cambodia's. They call it a "culture of impunity." They call it a place where violent crimes—political, personal, random—disrupt life in the most egregious ways, then lapse into history with no recourse. There are thousands, perhaps millions, of unsolved crimes in Cambodia. Thousands of criminals living freely; thousands of victims mourning their losses. The victims are opposition candidates, judges, actresses, mistresses, a labor leader, a democracy advocate, monks and neighbors, fathers and brothers, mothers, sisters and friends, high-profile, anonymous. Murders happen all the time in Cambodia, the embroidered patterns on a violent fabric of life.

Is it angst among the new generations? Did it come from the Khmer Rouge? Does it stem from ancient times? It is all these things combined. In Cambodia, violence is but one string in a weave of social ills. Cambodia is "plagued by four basic evils—poverty, violence, corruption and lawlessness," notes Peter Leuprecht, the UN human rights representative for Cambodia. These conditions feed each other, strengthening that fabric, making it taut. They are all attached to the country's tortured history. It's as though that thread were pulled and twisted, dyed and spread, through the entire tapestry so that it's no longer a distinguishable strand. It is a piece of the whole, inseparable from the other threads. They are tied to the past, present and future.

"This country," Kann Kall of TPO tells me in early 1999, just after the last Khmer Rouge soldiers defected to the government, "has fallen into a vicious circle." People don't trust each other, they suffer psychologically without realizing it, they project anger on the wrong people, and they pass their grievances to the next generation. "You have to do everything for survival," he says. Kill, steal, whatever it takes. That's the mentality.

More than two years later, when I interview him again, he tells me he worries about people snapping, about extreme reactions to mundane situations. "Today, when I read the newspaper, it scares me a lot." Dead bodies plastered on the front page; violence permeating the news. Youth seem especially vulnerable. "They're dancing in a club; they step on each other; they shoot people dead," Kann Kall says. "Everyone's pulling guns, shooting, all these things…. It should not happen, and the whole society is complaining of the loss of social morality."

Many Cambodians say their society will change little by little through a long while. That recognition itself is a sign of improvement. But the country's streets remain troubled ground. More beggars, more drugs, more villagers cramming Phnom

Penh to look for jobs that don't exist. Gangs and turf wars. A population of street kids that grows each year. According to Sebastien Marot, coordinator of the aid group *Mith Samlanh*, "The kids have nothing to look forward to."

Jerry and I return to the States in 1999 and spend more than two years away from Cambodia. But I still write about the country; I still read the news; I still keep in touch with friends there. And I use his photos to prompt my memory, poring over boxes of slides and envelopes full of images I have witnessed: There is a young man in flip-flops poking at a grenade lying by the curb. He tickles it. I see the green legs and black boots of a uniformed man beside him and the rear end, white pants, black belt of another man bent over. That day in January, one of our first in the country, we walk through the park, the same park where the grenades shattered Rainsy's parade. We stop for a beer at the bar across the street, wondering about a hubbub. People gather; police arrive, and the grenade just lies there. Live? Could be. Curious onlookers sidle by. People peek, careful not to get too close, as if ten feet between flesh and grenade is enough to keep a body from scattering to bits. It's apparently a dud, but it's a grenade in the park on a weekend afternoon, nonetheless.

Another photo: A man in a light blue shirt sits on a green plastic chair. He points to blood seeping from a rag tied around his left arm. Five minutes earlier, Jerry and I are eating lunch at a restaurant on the corner of Sihanouk Boulevard and Street 63. We're seated on the patio. I face west. I see two teenagers on a motorbike approach another motorbike with wife seated behind husband seated behind a small child in front. The teenagers try to steal something. They don't succeed. Or maybe they do— I don't recall. But I see this clearly: They speed up, racing toward us. Noon-hour traffic chokes the road. The husband chases them, reaches into his pants and pulls a pistol. Jerry only sees the look on my face. The man fires into the air. He fires over his son. Again. And again and again. The man shoots randomly up the road into traffic coming our way. We fall to the floor, ducking behind leafy potted plants. A *moto* driver rounds the corner and catches a bullet in the arm. It's the man in the light blue shirt. He is hit less than ten feet from our table. The family, the teenaged thieves, they all disappear into the swarm of the street. The *moto* driver takes a seat, wobbling. People gather from all sides. The corner cops approach slowly; there's a great deal of jabbering and gesturing, and then the wounded man disappears. He vanishes with the cops. We later search the local hospitals but find no trace of the victim. No trace of him, no record of the shooting, no report with the authorities. Just another incident in Phnom Penh. No death, no news, nothing to dwell on.

In another photo: Chubby cops wield batons and automatic rifles, exploring a room riddled with broken tile. Brown pants, black boots, green helmets, white gloves.

Jerry and I walk our normal route to work up Street 63, in a heat stupor. We're drowned in the clutter of everyday sounds: squeaky *cyclos*, tinking tools, hissing arc welders. And then a boom. We're curious: Jerry speculates something fell at a nearby construction site. I guess a grenade.

But we have little time to think before a man races up the cross street firing an AK-47 into the air. Shopfronts close, and we duck inside a restaurant, waddling low across the floor, under the windows. Everyone takes turns peeking through a tiny window in the kitchen door. A crowd swells at the intersection. A few people brave the street, then disperse as police approach. After ten calm minutes, the journalist clan arrives, and people inch closer to a cluster of uniforms gathered outside a quiet house. The officers carry guns and cell phones; one cop stuffs a grenade into his pocket. I avoid him. The story circulates quickly: Kidnapped man overcame captors, stole gun and grenade, tossed grenade, fired into house, escaped and ran to nearest intersection. Traffic cops arrest him and confiscate the gun.

There are so many guns in Cambodia the year we live there — everywhere, nonchalantly. Another photo: A soldier naps on the street, slung up in a hammock in afternoon haze. His boots rest beneath him, his big toe exposed, his gun propped against the wall beneath a green Army jacket. In another image: Kids smile and pause for the camera, for their portraits with guns. Three schoolboys play with a rifle on the sidewalk. Three pairs of flip-flops, six vibrant eyes, three infectious smiles. Four hands on one gun.

More photos: A swirl of black smoke sputters into the sky, rising far beyond the chanting and sniffling below. It hovers briefly above napping *cyclo* drivers, honking Toyotas, women selling fried fritters from their sidewalk grills. Then the smoke disappears. It is the funeral of a murdered man, a night guard at my paper. Eighteen hours from life to ash. He is shot dead, six AK-47 bullets in his body. He and a friend, a bodyguard, attended a wedding across the river from Phnom Penh. His friend fought with another man; our guard stepped between the two. The other man retreated, frustrated; our guard and friend returned to Phnom Penh. The other man rounded up cohorts and guns; our guard and his buddy filled up at a gas station. The others appeared and blew them away. A colleague at the *Daily* went to see our guard's body when they moved it. He says it spilled blood and stank already of tropical decay. The man died at 9 P.M. Friday (the thirteenth with a full moon). He burns at 3 P.M. Saturday.

I see images of three robberies, but of those I have no photos. I have only the pictures in my mind. Each robbery happens in the same manner. They come at night. They trail us as we ride home on *motos*, after dinner. They pull guns as we stop at our gate. They rob us two feet from safety. The first time, they take whatever we have in our wallets, just a few dollars. The second time, one robber sticks a gun to Jerry's head and demands his wedding ring. The third time, the thieves tug on Jerry's pants and photos spill from his pockets. Something scares them off before they have a chance to take anything. We are lucky.

And so when Jerry and I return to Cambodia in 2001, we tremble a bit because we don't know what to expect. We find the guns are fewer — thanks to a government push to disarm civilians — and everyone tells tourists this country is safer now. Our nerves relax a bit.

Then one morning we ride *motos* to the airport, weaving through busy sections of town, past shops and schools and markets. We jounce through the unpaved streets near *Psar Thmei*, dodging potholes and bumps, when the sharp crack of a rifle explodes a block behind us. It happens twice. My knees go weak; my heart pounds; my head feels open and vulnerable to the world. I remember. I hate this feeling. A cop chases up the street on a *moto*. I tell my driver to hurry, but he's stuck in a mud puddle, and we can't move. He assures me, "No problem, it's no problem for you, you are tourist." But I am not a tourist; I've seen too much of Cambodia to believe there's no problem.

In all the commotion we lose Jerry and his driver, far ahead. But we meet again at the airport, and Jerry tells me he saw the whole scene. A kid on a *moto* plowed through an intersection, cutting off two drivers. The cop fired twice, into the air, to warn him. It's not as dramatic as I feared, but still, the bang of rifle fire on a neighborhood street is disconcerting. That same trip in 2001, an expatriate reporter tells us his barometer for judging Cambodian safety. "It all depends on what happens to you." We extrapolate that into our own Cambodia motto: "Cambodia is perfectly safe — until it isn't."

Dreadful violence harks back centuries. The halls of Angkor are adorned with bas-reliefs depicting ghastly battle scenes. Visit a modern temple and view ancient Buddhist lore, enacted on the walls: humans pecked by birds; people gouged on spears; wild dogs gnashing at torsos; human guts spilling open. For all the outward peace that Buddhism proclaims, it exhibits the macabre in its parables. Listen, too, to folktales as Khmer children do, stories of lust, murder and deceit. "Obviously a culture that produces such stories is not as single-mindedly gentle as its reputation," writes journalist Elizabeth Becker.

Centuries ago, the Angkorean society was not kind to the guilty or down-and-out. "Criminals were sometimes punished by having their toes cut off and they were subsequently banished to live outside the walls of the city," Robert Philpotts writes in his book on life in the Angkor era. Serious crimes were punished by "amputation of fingers, a hand, a foot or their nose," and the worst offenses warranted execution, which occurred outside Angkor Thom. "There a pit was dug and the person about to die made to get into it before being buried alive."

Reality mirrored the legends chiseled into Angkor walls. The ancient bas-reliefs depict an elite class enjoying Paradise while the condemned suffer fiercely. "Some are being pounded in mortars, while others hold them by the feet and hands; some are being sawn asunder; others are led along, like buffaloes, with ropes through their noses," Henri Mouhot describes in his diaries. There are scenes of executioners "cutting men to pieces with sabres." And others of the guilty "roasted on spits, tied to trees and pierced with arrows, suspended with heavy weights attached to their hands and feet, devoured by dogs or vultures, or crucified with nails through their bodies."

Angkor, in all its glory.

In a thousand years of history and legend, the Khmer Rouge installed the quintessential violent state. They brought everyone's nightmares to life. They executed the ancient punishments inscribed on Angkor walls. They killed without thought; they maimed without flinching. The resultant terror still punctuates this society. This is a country on edge. "Visitors are often struck by the apparent normality of Phnom Penh, the spectacle of people trading, building and repairing, thronging at a cinema, waiting for a bus," writes journalist John Pilger. "But this, too, is part of the dream-state. Watch the eddies of panic when masonry falls from a building … or people immobilized when a burst of automatic fire is heard in the distance." Today it is still easy to monitor a loud noise of unknown origin. Watch the locals. Do they stop what they're doing? Do they close their gates? Does the air grow quiet? Or does life continue, uninterrupted? Cambodians know when to fear. Calm skies may blanket recent times, but Cambodians harbor the memory of precarious days. "Danger," writes François Bizot, "is like a wind that blows, disappears, and returns again."

If one wants documentation of such violence, of the form it takes, of the pitiful forms it takes today, one needs only read the news. Read the Khmer-language papers because they post the bloodiest atrocities upfront, pictures and all. Read the wires because they cover trends—street beatings, acid attacks, assassinations. And read the English-language *Phnom Penh Post* police blotter, published in each bi-weekly issue, culling from all the above and tallying the most tragic events of two weeks' time. One will find selections such as these:

On June 23, 2003, police arrest a fisherman named Sim Mao for stabbing his neighbor to death when the man refuses to drink more wine with him.

On June 26, 2003, a deputy village chief in Pursat Province is hacked three times and set on fire by the village chief, who escapes. The apparent motive is jealousy because the deputy chief was working harder for the ruling party during the election campaign.

On September 5, 2003, a man demands $10 from a brothel owner and threatens her with a grenade. The grenade accidentally explodes, blowing up the man.

On September 14, 2003, a monk allegedly stabs a twenty-three-year-old villager in the gut after he and three companions try to steal coconuts from the monk's temple. The monk is not arrested.

On December 22, 2003, twenty-year-old Heng Pesith of Phnom Penh is stabbed in the head by a friend who is angry Pesith did not invite him for a drink after they stole a hand phone and sold it.

On January 8, 2004, a man is shot in the leg and robbed of his *moto* as he drives his wife to a relative's funeral.

Every two weeks, there is more. Murders, axings, beatings, rapes. Death over bananas, gunshots and gambling tiffs, stabbings and suicides over jilted love, and run-of-the-mill robberies that leave scores of people dead.

Disturbing, it is, that word of these crimes rarely leaves Phnom Penh. They are often left unsolved, and justice is not met. Only occasionally, due to the curious nature of Cambodia, do snippets of Cambodian misdeeds make the international news. And then, they are written in a sadly sardonic style. But there is nothing funny about Cambodian crime.

In 2000, the *San Jose Mercury News* runs a "News of the Weird" piece about a chess player who clubs his opponent to death. The opponent violated game etiquette by moving a knight to a new square, then moving it back without lifting his hand. Around this same time, the *Times* of London reports that the Cambodian government has banned water pistols from the country's New Year festivities because jealous lovers often use them to squirt acid at their intended prey. And in February 2004, The Associated Press reports on a "monks' war" in Battambang, where two sects of robed men skirmish over their *wat's* future leadership. They fire metal balls from slingshots. They launch burning petrol bottles. They damage their temple with fire. Seven monks and one civilian are injured.

Strange? Perhaps. Funny? No.

Crime only mimics what the system does to the Cambodian people. This "culture of impunity" is perpetuated by the authorities themselves. "In fact, the police and military are often involved in crimes and human rights violations," notes the UN Commission on Human Rights in 2001. Authorities are not punished for their crimes and the people view police as "a threat to their safety and security, they are mistrusted and regarded as criminals."

Five months before that report, the *Phnom Penh Post* publishes the results of an investigation of torture, as widespread today as in years past. The story is an indictment. "People are regularly and routinely beaten black and blue with punches and kicks. They are hit with batons, iron bars, gun butts, pieces of wood or other objects, subjected to electric shocks, whipped with wire, bamboo, rope or belts. Some are nearly suffocated with pieces of plastic, or have their feet crushed under wooden or iron bars." And they are raped.

According to the report, 36 percent of prison victims say they have been beaten with solid objects, 14 percent with firearms, 7 percent have had their limbs crushed, 5 percent have been whipped and 5 percent have suffered electric shocks. "While Cambodian and international law may prohibit torture, the reality is that many police see nothing wrong with it."

Grim as these reports may be, slow change creeps through the door. Cambodians understand more and more when their rights are denied. When Jerry and I return to Cambodia in 2003, I meet with Kay Kimsong, a Khmer reporter I've known for years. He talks at length about problems that never cease — poverty, bad roads, corruption. And then he asks me what I think: Has Cambodia changed since 1998? He thinks it has in one critical way. People have expanded their minds. They have a wider view of the world. They are learning. "We used to be, you say, 'a big frog in a small jar.'" But now, people see the vast world around them. They embrace the ideas of far-away nations.

There is a dark side to those new ideas. When justice doesn't come and crimes continue unabated and the people want change, they take charge. They step in for ever-truant police; they mete punishment as they see fit. They chase their grievances in the street:

We see it one day from our balcony. It's lunchtime on a Wednesday in September 2003. Mid-way through a bowl of fried noodles, we hear the shouts outside.

A soft-bellied man in a pale shirt, one shoe on, one shoe off, sprints up the street with his cell phone in hand. A mob quickly gains ground; he's caught by the back of his neck and shoved to the ground. His head hits pavement. They're all over him, a dozen gawkers, half a dozen others, kicking and grabbing and clobbering the young man until his blood streams.

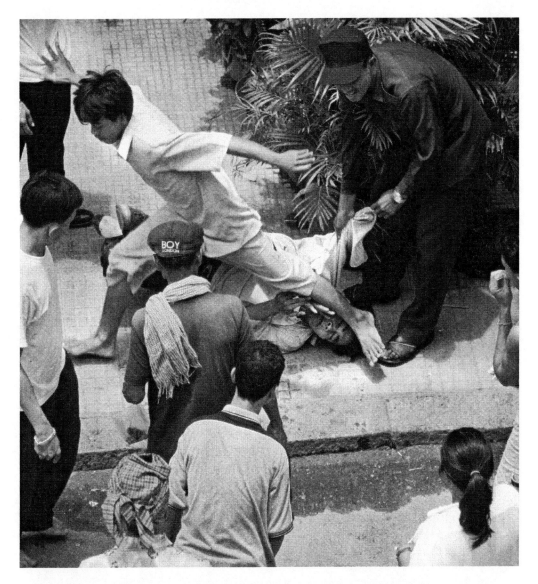

A teenager stomps a man's head to the pavement after he was caught by a vigilante mob on a street in Phnom Penh in the middle of the day. The beaten man and a friend (not shown) were trying to rob a woman on a motorcycle when they were stopped by bystanders and attacked. The man here managed to escape from the mob briefly before he was caught again and severely beaten. Mob violence, or "people's courts" as they are frequently called in Cambodia, are increasingly common as Cambodians see the police and government as unwilling and unable to deal with day-to-day crime. Phnom Penh, 2003.

He's a thief, and this is how Cambodians dole out justice. He and a partner tried to snatch a purse from a woman riding on a motorbike around the corner on the riverfront. People see the attempted robbery; they spring to action and smother the perpetrators with fists and feet. The soft-bellied man gets away briefly. We watch him run up our street.

He is collared in front of an Internet shop, and customers leave their keyboards to view the mayhem outside. The crowd kicks and punches the man. A teenager stomps his skull. A man in a white T-shirt takes his cell phone. They trip over his bleeding body, sprawled across the sidewalk. He lies still a moment, then slowly sits up, hand against forehead, half his face swollen and raw. A man from the Internet shop offers him water. He pulls himself up, stumbles, and pleads for mercy, with the crowd still ready to pounce. He agrees to turn himself in to the police around the corner (who do nothing while this happens). The mob trails him until he's arrested and taken away. Then life resumes its usual pace.

The Internet shopkeeper douses blood and sweat from her walkway, flushing the evidence into the gutter. Gone before the lunch hour ends. Our neighbor, an Australian advisor to the Cambodian government, asks what happened. She is disturbed but not surprised by the story. "Last year, they just beat a guy to death," she says.

This is not new. It has happened for years in Cambodia, on average twice a month. A March 2003 U.S. State Department report documents sixty-five cases of mob assaults and killings in Cambodia from mid–1999 through May 2002. Many mob victims are caught in robberies, stealing motorbikes or necklaces, and the police often stand by as crowds beat the accused to death. In August 2000, villagers in Battambang pulled an accused rapist from his police cell and beat him to death with sticks, knives and axes. Angry women chopped off his penis and cut it into pieces.

Lynchings, or "people's courts" as they are frequently called, occur in countries where violence is rampant, crime goes unpunished and few people trust the courts or cops. It's the result of "a legal system that has proved itself incapable of dispensing justice objectively," according to the Asian Human Rights Commission. Street violence offers an "instant remedy to appease the appetites of people made insecure."

The United Nations Commission for Human Rights lays it out plainly in 2001. Cambodia lacks a functioning legal system because it has no penal code, no basic criminal procedure code and no professionally competent judiciary. Many drafts codes have been sitting around for years. In November 2003, the UN General Assembly again urges the Cambodian government to make legal and judicial reform a priority. But no: The Cambodian government remains in limbo, and there will be no new legislation until a government is formed.

And violence continues.

That same month, Ouch Borith, Cambodia's ambassador to the UN, informs the UN General Assembly that mob killings have ceased. All is OK now, he assures. He says the government has established a Council for Legal and Judicial Reform.

Two weeks later, three thieves are caught stealing a motorbike in Phnom Penh, according to a local newspaper. The police arrest them, then turn them over to a waiting crowd. The mob beats two of them to death.

Interlude: A Runner's Course

I am a runner, going on twenty years now, and I do not stop running in Cambodia. I am not fazed by the stares, the catcalls, the children racing alongside me. I endure

100-degree heat and sweat that laces my legs in salty streams. For a year I take notes of my runs, and if I were to assemble a collage of those journeys, it would look something like this:

It starts with the flattened rear end of a rat. My right foot finds the brittle remains just outside our gate. Our street isn't paved. It's prone to potholes; it's full of old tires, broken bricks, plastic bags, banana peels, *moto* drivers awaiting work, sand piles and sugarcane bits sucked dry. A work crew with *krama* scarves and bare backs erects a new villa, in one week, behind a tall gate directly across from a squatter family. The workers watch me trot along, up, down, around and over the gouges in the road. A boy pushing a cart of pineapple chunks and papaya boats calls to the neighborhood in a singsong voice, then fades into the distance behind my tread.

I wear my Walkman, though I know it brands me an easy target. I wonder when, where, with whom around, a man with a gun will pry those earphones from me. I begin to leave my jewelry behind—first my silver bracelet, then my antique engagement ring, then my austere white-gold wedding band.

Before 8 A.M., which I don't see often, the corner of our street bustles with break-fast eaters at a temporary restaurant of folding tables and chairs. It lasts a few hours, then a metamorphosis occurs. By late morning, the corner stands bare except for one armed guard with a walkie-talkie. Later still, *moto* drivers congregate here beneath a wide shade tree that shields them from a piercing sun. They perch over handlebars, eyes shrouded in Ray Ban imitations, stickers still in place—a fashion statement among the *moto* crowd. One month, it's gold-rimmed glasses, everywhere, big or small, round or square, new spec-tacles framing the eyes of *moto* drivers all over town. Many of these men squint for days, then remove the glasses with little ado. Apparently an aid group donated them, and the street crowds eagerly took them, only to learn not all prescriptions suit all eyes.

They're a friendly bunch. They smile as I totter by. One says to me, "Hello, why do you run?"

It's a good question.

I turn right on Street 63, dodging *motos*, Mercedes, *cyclos* and cycles, the rubber sole of a sandal, nebulous piles of dirt. I turn left on the next block up, across the street from a welding outfit where young men crouch with blow torch in one hand, metal scraps in the other and nothing to protect the eyes as sparks shoot against their dark and dirty skin. They're making gates for the villas that cleave our neighborhood into two distinct crowds: people with guards and people without.

I veer east on Street 352, past NGO abodes and more armed guards, past another construction site where men lay bricks one by one and clutter the street with refuse. I dance through broken bricks and pipelines until a car forces me to the roadside where grass shavings ferment in the sun.

Now four blocks into my run, I greet the corner of Norodom Boulevard which, once a year, undergoes a great sewer cleanup. Workers jump right in, sullying their britches as they shovel a year's worth of muck onto the sidewalks. And there it stays until it dries in the sun and blows in the wind and lands where it may.

I turn left here, and the shrill whirr of sirens salutes me in return. Speeding past are two military police trucks with a long bench running the length of their truck beds. Men suited in army green squash together, sitting erect, gripping AK-47s in their laps.

I head north and duck around a drooping tree that shelters a tire repairman, sleeping soundly in a patio chair, surrounded by tubes and tools and grease. A shoeshine boy asks if I want my leather and mesh sparkled, but I decline. I continue around a Mercedes, back on the sidewalk, past a little girl selling cigarettes, through a sand pile, over orange peels, past a citadel of foreign apartments for rent by day or week or month. The road bends slightly, and the towering Victory Monument, the highest point in the sky, dominates my view. Built in 1958 to mark the end of French colonialism, it survived the Khmer Rouge and now honors Cambodia's war dead.

I scamper past a French wine bar, under a tarp string tied to a tree, to a place where I attempt to cross the street. I calculate my chances. I latch onto a local's lead, and together we jostle through a persistent sea of traffic. A staccato rhythm, we assume: run, walk, skip, halt for a beeping BMW, jog, run in place until four lanes pass, sprint, dodge a rock, sidestep a woman with clams on her head, eye the other side, reach the curb, jump to the road, around a parked car, past a lottery-ticket stand, into a driveway, around the corner of Norodom and Sihanouk to yet another crossing, darting into traffic, turning head to the left, beating a barreling car, reaching the other curb, and finally the dirt path of a park. I am alone. I gaze: one open, empty football-field stretch of running space. Just me, the heat and mental anguish, in a pattern of green grass and red dirt paths, a sanctuary of squares.

I plod along the ground, the color of sunkissed skin. I look up to a blindingly white horizon. So close we are to that ring around the Earth where the sun beats straight upon it. Farther into the white I go, crossing streets, leaving trees behind, heading for grass-studded pastures that lead to the Tonle Sap and Mekong rivers. Goosebumps form on my legs, born of heat not cold. Eight lanky oxen mosey down the road with two herders bringing up their rears. Their bovine humps are as tall as my head.

I round the corner, cross another road and enter a park with the Vietnamese monument at center. I watch this land change over a year, from parched soil where men and children defecate in public, to the trampled ground beneath Democracy Square, to healthy green grass and lampposts erected to bury the memory of deadly riots. I continue through the park. I see the Royal Palace from here, its gilt spires flirting with the treetops. The squiggly figures never cease to remind me how far from home I am. And then, as though on cue, the Talking Heads sing to me through my earphones: "You may ask yourself: Well, how did I get here?"

I wonder all the time.

I'm back in Hun Sen Park, the northern side now. I skip electrical cords stretched fifty yards along the sidewalk between outlets hanging in the trees and blenders perched atop fruit carts. I choose the same route back, thinking only about my moment of return. In my home stretch, kids swarm a fruit cart, and I think of the succulence inside that glass case. My feet stop. My hands reach squeamishly for the hot metal gate latch. "*Sua s'dey*," I say to the guards and maids, and I trudge up one flight of stairs. I see our door and know the air-conditioned air that awaits me. If only our shower would run cold.

Many days are like this, all at once or separately. I see the same sights, encounter the same pitfalls, ponder the same questions about this country whose ground I pound into my soles. I think of the saffron monks I see in the park, their bald shiny heads. I run behind them; they part ways and let me pass through their chasm of orange. I think about those monks, their philosophies, their seemingly peaceful ways of living. I think about their country, its brutal politics and its hard-core ways of surviving. I think about both, and how they intertwine, all the time, on Phnom Penh streets and distant battlefields. If I look with blinders, I see those saffron robes swooshing through an air of peace. Gentle, with ease.

And then one day, I turn on Norodom and soldiers with rocket launchers and machine guns line every corner. Some days, I can't run at all because the streets are hissing with gunfire and riots, and my heart already pounds from fear.

Other times, I choke back tears, gulping and panting in unison, when I think a little too hard about the kids who race me near the Tonle Sap, sprinting and smiling, as smoke billows from garbage heaps around their flimsy riverside shanties. They don't know it yet, but their houses will burn and their families will be moved to a camp outside Phnom Penh, where their homes will again perish in monsoon storms. And the people will return, again, to these streets, with no work or money or food. The mayor will build new parks and walkways where their old homes once stood, and they will move farther upstream or down, or deeper into the heart of Phnom Penh, where thousands just like them wander through life, forever looking, but rarely finding, a stability that simply lets them stay in one place.

And it is on my most difficult runs that I think of this egregious irony: My runs are by pure, free choice; theirs by the chance cruelty of life.

10. Psychology: After the Tragedy

Po Kith Ly spent three years and eight months shackled and tortured inside a Khmer Rouge prison. "There were thirty-five people at that time they planned to kill, but only I survived." That took a lot of luck and a lot of lying. He learned to tell the Khmer Rouge exactly what they wanted to hear. His wits saved him. When he was finally free of his captors and thought his past a distant nightmare, he rode a train that hit a land mine planted by the Khmer Rouge. The explosion shattered his arm, leaving a wrist bone nearly poking through skin and an elbow puffy and scarred. Now, almost twenty-five years later, Po Kith Ly shakes and stammers and nearly passes out as he openly tells his story in his psychiatrist's office.

"I come here to get some treatment from the doctor because at night I cannot sleep," he says. "I have a lot of nightmares about mine explosions and I run, run, run…. I have dreams that many people are killed, and they are tied up." He saw all these things as a prisoner. When he finishes his story he lies on a bed, holding his head, eyes closed.

Jerry and I meet Po Kith Ly in July 2003. Millions of Cambodians still suffer psychological damage from decades of civil war, and their sons and daughters follow. Many don't recognize this. Cambodians traditionally don't have a concept of mental health like that of the West. And there aren't enough trained specialists to meet the need. There are only twenty psychiatrists in Cambodia, says Dr. Ang Sody at the Preah Bath Norodom Sihanouk Hospital. She is one of those twenty. That number is not enough to nurture a very troubled nation of thirteen million.

Cambodians appear jovial and engaging, but a smile can be humanity's most convincing facade. Beneath is a "tone of melancholy and compensation for deeply experienced sadness," writes Cambodian psychology expert Seanglim Bit.

In the summer of 2003, the Ministry of Health outlines a twenty-year plan for dealing with mental illness across Cambodia. The chairman of the Ministry's Mental Health Subcommittee estimates 60 percent of Khmer Rouge survivors suffer from mental illness. The estimated cost of this twenty-year plan is $500,000 a year. That's the same amount the Pentagon spent in a single minute, every minute — before the United States went to war in Iraq in March 2003. It's the same amount the U.S. Congress earmarks in 2003 for a bike path in Florida. It is one-hundredth the amount Congress slates for a $50 million indoor rainforest in Iowa. Meanwhile, in the real rainforests of Cambodia, there is no money to fix the population's broken hearts.

Po Kith Ly talks with his psychiatrist, Ang Sody, in a new examination room at the Preah Bath Norodom Sihanouk Hospital in Phnom Penh. Po Kith Ly was imprisoned and tortured by the Khmer Rouge between 1975 and 1979. He now has a hard time sleeping and is always nervous. He came from his home in Kandal Province for his monthly appointment and psychiatric presciptions. Phnom Penh, 2003.

"The people of Cambodia live in the compass of immemorial tragedy," writes Andrew Solomon, author of *The Noonday Demon*, perhaps the definitive book on depression. "What happens to your emotions when you have seen a quarter of your compatriots murdered, when you have lived yourself in the hardship of a brutal regime, when you are fighting against the odds to rebuild a devastated nation?"

There is no simple answer, and Cambodia is not even equipped to deal with the question.

Jerry and I meet Ang Sody one morning, a typical morning, when the aisles of the Sihanouk Hospital psychiatric ward bulge with people who wait hours for help. She leads us to a cramped hallway with seven cabinets, each with four drawers. This is where she stores patient files, marked by number, placed in the cabinets by year. She grabs a file, then takes us to a white-tiled room with a white bed, white sheet, white fans. It feels unnaturally institutional. Everything is white except her desk and a few chairs, which are brazenly red and blue. Through the windows, we can see the waiting lines outside; they have spilled into courtyards and parking lots.

Po Kith Ly enters. He is animated when he speaks, and he carries a packet of pills. Jerry and I watch quietly from across the room until Ang Sody calls us over to hear his story.

It's amazing: You step into a consultation room, a foreign stranger interrupting a meeting between patient and doctor, and the patient tells you everything. This sort of outpouring happens to us often, in Cambodia, in East Timor, in Myanmar. The people want their stories known: their travesties, their humiliations, how much money they make, the deaths they've seen, their thoughts on suicide. This is common, writes Stevan M. Weine, co-director of the Project on Genocide, Psychiatry, and Witnessing at the University of Illinois, Chicago. Refugees and torture survivors often want someone to chronicle their stories. He calls this "testimony psychotherapy," and he uses it with victims of Bosnia's genocide. "The survivor tells the witness the story of what happened when violence shattered his or her life. Together they make a document of the story, and then look for appropriate ways to make that story known to others."

Po Kith Ly, like others, sees a witness in us.

He has post-traumatic stress disorder (PTSD) from his time in prison. He was another doctor's patient, but that doctor left to take a higher-paying job at an NGO, says Ang Sody. So she squeezes Po Kith Ly into her already cramped schedule.

He rolls up his shirtsleeve to show us scars from the train accident. Then he talks about his prison days, when he was chained like a beast, an iron rod pinning him in place. "My name was on the list of people they planned to kill," he says. He describes the torture mechanisms of Pol Pot's prisons. They yanked out his fingernails. "It was very painful." They threw scorpions on prisoners. They fed people banana trunk, dried and boiled, and nothing more. "None of the prisoners had energy," he says. He couldn't stand upright. "I saw one prisoner who was chained by his legs, his waist, his arms, his neck. I pitied him." He saw a teenager who was forced to do hard labor, digging holes. The boy took a rest, and the soldiers asked why he stopped. He lunged at a soldier in retaliation, but they nabbed him first.

The guards interrogated each prisoner, one by one. Po Kith Ly was last in line, number thirty-five in a row of shackles. He saw one man beaten on the head, his blood dripping down his back. He tried to ask the others what was in store, what the questions were. The interrogators asked everyone the same things. What did you do before 1975? Were you a soldier? A teacher? Government staff? "All the people answered no, no, no. All the people who answered no were killed," he says. "I tried to think what answer I could give." When the interrogators told him a woman had identified him as a high-ranking military commander, he lied. He was never a high commander, but he told them he had been a quartermaster behind the scenes. He said he supported the Khmer Rouge takeover. It worked, and he is here today because of those lies.

"He is very smart," Ang Sody says. He tried to outthink the soldiers for his own life.

But for Po Kith Ly, the aftermath still smarts like a raw wound. "I have a lot of bad history."

Today, he lives in Kandal Province and runs a small shop. It's the only job he's been able to hold since his accident. "After the liberation of the country, I wanted to be a soldier," he says. But he was sick and couldn't work.

I ask Po Kith Ly whether he thinks putting the former Khmer Rouge leaders on trial will help him recover, perhaps ease his pain. This is the only time he speaks in English, and his answer is emphatic. "No, no, no, no." Then he goes to the bed and lies with his hand across his forehead. He wants us to know his whole story, every filthy detail, but he's not up to it, not now. "I want to tell you all of my history, but now I feel tired."

Ang Sody talks a bit more, then we leave. Outside the door is a cloud of patients, still waiting. She calls out a name, a single name in a nest of thousands.

Ang Sody sees four types of mental illness: psychosis, depression, anxiety and PTSD. Although Khmer Rouge atrocities certainly factor, it is impossible to name one cause, or two or three, for the poor state of the nation's mental health. It's a web. Environment is one facet, as are history and family. Some patients can't sleep; they don't eat; they suffer nightmares; they can't work. Some patients were malnourished; some witnessed killings; others suffered torture. Sometimes the symptoms of PTSD don't surface for many years, and sometimes people can't put a name to their condition. But they pass the repercussions on to family and friends.

"The younger people have a lot of problems," Ang Sody says. The war left hordes of orphans. Some grew up in orphanages with not enough food or money. Now grown, these sons and daughters of Pol Pot's legacy try to make their own living, but they can't scrape by. Some take drugs to diminish their hunger. At 500 *riel*, about 12 cents a can, it's cheaper to buy glue to sniff than a meal to eat. "This is a big problem," she says dryly.

We meet a woman in the hallway, a volunteer from Kompong Speu Province. She has a silvery head of hair and a big plug of betelnut spilling from her scarlet mouth. She comes here once a week, chaperoning rural patients to the city for psychological help. "Depression is the most common," she says. And poverty exacerbates everything. It matters critically whether patients have families who care, reasons to hope and people helping them through.

Many don't.

And war continues to gouge the heart of a society long after the battles cease.

Cambodia is perhaps doubly cursed because there is no certain line between guilty and innocent. The Khmer Rouge were Cambodian. Many soldiers were conscripted, many robbed of their childhoods. Guards and gatekeepers, survivors and their children, the whole of society suffers— including former Khmer Rouge. "They carried the corpses," says Dr. Sotheara Chhim of TPO in Phnom Penh. And in later years when the Khmer Rouge split into several factions, many soldiers themselves were tortured and brutalized. "We feel they are all victims," he says.

That's why his group has joined forces with Youk Chhang's Documentation Center to treat the mental health problems of former Khmer Rouge soldiers whose lives are indelibly scarred. This program is still new, and the patients are not yet ready to divulge their stories to outsiders. "They are afraid when they reveal problems, their past memories, past history, something will happen to them," Sotheara Chhim says. That's changing gradually. "They seem to talk more openly now.... They are able to go out alone."

Sotheara Chhim says that while an upcoming tribunal may prove cathartic, it could equally exacerbate Cambodians' pain. "The tribunal can be a trigger," a spark of memory that burns the psyche, particularly so if the process doesn't go well, if the leaders aren't convicted, if Cambodians aren't happy with the outcome. Then their sorrow will last, unabated.

Sotheara Chhim tells me he became a psychiatrist, in large part, because so few people examine Cambodia's mental health. He was a junior surgeon in 1993. "I met some psychiatric patients, and I did not know how to treat them, and I was curious, I wondered, 'Why didn't I learn this at medical school?'" He asked around about a subject to study to help these people. He was told about psychiatry — but it wasn't an option in Cambodia then. There were two psychiatrists before the Khmer Rouge came to power in 1975. There were none when Cambodia's medical school was resurrected in 1980. There was still no one to teach psychiatry in 1993, when Sotheara Chhim started asking around.

Then, early in 1994, the University of Oslo advertised an opportunity to study psychiatry in Norway, and he snatched it up. He stayed four years, then received an additional scholarship to study in Australia. When he returned to Cambodia, he worked at the Sihanouk Hospital, but he saw the environment as institutional. And he saw it as the tip of a Cambodian iceberg. A doctor sees patients in a clinic or hospital, "but there are a lot more in the community," he says. He wanted to broaden his scope. Thus his move to TPO.

Sotheara Chhim opens his laptop and shows me a diagram of the country's mental health problems. It's a triangle with arrows running here, there, inside, up, down, around. The arrows point to all the factors causing societal, familial and individual problems: violence, alcoholism, lack of productivity, lack of trust, exploitation, vulnerability to disease. In the center is poverty. And all around is the undeniable realization that most every Cambodian social problem is tethered to every other.

To all of that, add education — or its absence.

Kang Om is my Khmer teacher, my trusted friend, the father of my translator and a psychology professor. He is a natural to ask about mental health.

He agrees that war is a major factor in Cambodia's psychological ills. He agrees many elements combine to erode the mental health of his nation. He agrees with the triangle and arrows in Sotheara Chhim's diagram. But Kang Om also believes one of the most devastating blights on Cambodian society is the nation's lack of basic education. Children who grew up under the Khmer Rouge had no education, and hence education is not a priority for their own children, he says.

Without proper schooling, Kang Om says, people haven't the mechanisms to deal with the other branches in that diagram. Nor do they think critically beyond daily survival. They are burdened with a difficult present and little thought of what lies ahead. The few educated, the few who do ponder and plan for the future — those people are susceptible to mental illness, too, because their minds are full of worry. "They have stress," Om says. They bear the load of a nation.

He sees this in his students, but few Cambodian teachers know enough about psychology to help their troubled classes. He wants kids to know he's there to help. "I always tell students about my background in psychology, even if I'm teaching

English." It's often a student's first exposure to the concept of mental health. "They don't know how to talk. They don't know what a mental health problem is. They just say 'I'm very sad,'" Om tells me.

Indeed, a 2002 study of college, university and technical-school students finds that many young Cambodians are wrapped in a continuous cycle of worry. They agonize over everything from civil unrest to a poor national economy to pollution and border disputes. Constant fretting leads to a destructive state of "catastrophic worry."

Kang Om thinks mental health should be a higher priority for international donors who aim to develop Cambodia. Development should focus not just on buildings, roads, schools and technology but on the mind.

TPO has a branch in Battambang, home to some of the nation's most traumatized war victims. "The problem in Battambang is worse than in other provinces," says program manager Kim Sophornn. The war lasted longer here, forty years of battles that waged through the late 1990s. Now whole villages suffer psychosocial disorders. "They try to cope with this by drinking, smoking or violence."

And they are so poor — eating only tamarind, salt and rice — that diet stymies their mental capacity. It stunts their children's growth, mentally and physically. Nutrition is crucial for the mind, "especially pregnant women, they need to have plenty of food; not just plenty, but many types," Kim Sophornn says. "It's still a big problem."

Jerry and I arrange to visit a TPO session among women, with a staff member named O Ran. She takes us several miles outside the city, down a dirt road and into a rural settlement, stopping at a bamboo gate. She drops us at a house and asks us to wait while she summons the people. Women begin to straggle in, gathering beneath a thatch awning, sheltered from alternating sun and rain.

O Ran returns and begins asking many questions. Do the women have any problems? The villagers chirp back and forth, mostly about the difficulties of health, finding money and going to the doctor. Most agree: They don't have enough money for food.

O Ran emphasizes nutrition, that eating well and eating a variety will boost their overall health. She points to the garden, where bananas and cassava grow — but more could be planted. They could harvest mangos. They could fill their gardens with fruits and vegetables. They could plant their way to better health.

Illness, children, money, food — these are the overwhelming concerns for everyone here. These topics are icebreakers, O Ran explains. Women talk about their kids before they talk about their sadness. So she asks each woman about her children, a topic they willingly discuss. It's a good window to the mother. When the meeting ends, she hands out tiny plastic packets of bright red pills. "Multivitamins," she later explains. Nourishment for mind and body.

Then we're off to another village, through a needling rain over mucky terrain. Here, we meet TPO worker Savie, who has gathered the village women for their first meeting. The thatch house is packed with a circle of women and babes at their laps. The floor looks like desert earth, mud cracked and caked into flat boulders. They sit on rice sacks while Savie takes each woman's name and age, and the number and names of their children. Then she explains the TPO mission, the importance of talking about problems and listening to others.

The meeting is full of interruptions. One mother after another leaves to wash her baby. One poops a green mess onto a young woman's sarong. The woman and baby are cleaned, the child's soiled clothes tossed out the window. All this, as Savie continues to talk.

When the meeting ends, Savie divvies up a large sack of rambutans among the crowd. Each woman gets a handful, but there is great effort to ensure each handful is the appropriate size. But what's equal? Some families are bigger than others—should they get more? Some think so. Some don't. Khmer people are constantly wary of being cheated—a legacy of the Khmer Rouge. Savie wants to start this program right.

Afterward, Jerry and I ask if our presence has created a problem, if it deterred the women from speaking. O Ran says not for the women, but the babies were afraid when they saw our faces. She says the first meeting is always difficult because the babies are distractions, but the women have no one to leave them with. If TPO wants a session to work for the women, it must contend with the kids.

Despite years of despondency and buried memories of tragic times, many Cambodians have never talked to a counselor. They don't even know what one is. When Cambodians feel the need to talk, they go instead to a fortuneteller, a sorcerer or a monk. "Cambodian people believe in the monks to pray for them to be better from mental health problems," Kang Om says. Prayer is catharsis, and the monks act as substitute counselors. "But they didn't study about psychology," he says. They just listen and pray.

Although sanctuary can be found in a *wat,* or comfort in a monk's words, the Buddhist religion itself does not necessarily help matters of the mind. It is not structured in a way that would. "Theravada Buddhism offers rational explanations for previous life and any future lives, but is largely silent on how to resolve the dilemmas of this existence," writes Seanglim Bit in his psychological study of Cambodia. The religion teaches people to take what comes, that they are not responsible for their lot in life, that outside forces control their fate. The act of living becomes passive because so much lies beyond a person's grasp. This is true of Buddhism in many places, but particularly now in Cambodia. The entire Khmer social system, writes Seanglim Bit, makes for complacent sufferers. Social mores emphasize "serenity, acceptance of injustice, conformity to a higher authority and Buddhist principles of accepting suffering as the expected order in life."

And within this structure breeds a culture of superstition. Take a walk through a rural village, and you'll find scarecrows at the foot of a house, or skulls and crossbones painted on walls to ward off evil. Pass three times beneath an elephant's trunk, and you'll have good luck. Wear a hair from an elephant's tail in your ring, and you'll find fortune. Khmer culture is riddled with superstition. You can see it in the daily paper, in stories of neighbors killing neighbors they deem to be sorcerers bringing bad luck. Or you can read about beasts and babies endowed with special powers. In 1998, villagers in Sihanoukville take to drinking the urine of two oxen they believe are charmed. Also that year, a "Dragon Baby" is born with scaly skin. It's a disease, but villagers think she can bestow good luck. Pilgrims flock to see her and touch her. In 2003, it's the three-year-old "Python Boy" who garners such attention. His best friend is a twelve-foot snake. A fortune teller says the boy must have been a dragon in a previous life. He will likely use his "special powers" as a traditional Khmer healer.

Superstition lends answers to the inexplicable; it makes sense of the nonsensical. And it gives hope where there is little.

For a short time, in 1998, Cambodians find hope on a small island off Phnom Penh. It is a little more than two months past an election that angers thousands. People want peace. People want change. They find inspiration in a tuft of weeds. They build their aspirations tall and shiny.

A small patch of land emerges that year, where the Tonle Sap, Bassac and Mekong rivers meet. And with it springs an expanse of prospects. People come. They spread the word, collect money and pool their resources. They build three small temples to look like gold, silver and diamonds, in homage to the legendary three-tiered Buddha who will spring forth from this place called Yukuntor Island. That Buddha will appear in silver from the waist down, gold up to the neck and topped with a diamond-like head, explains Prum Lay, an eighty-three-year-old man who maintains the new shrines.

This legend of a three-tiered Buddha is an old religious teaching. "In Buddhist history, we were taught that the palaces existed here already. But we didn't see any so we wanted to build the palaces as a symbol," says monk Sin Say.

Visitors confide they are not certain the Buddha will appear, but the place is magically soothing, nonetheless. From this island, Phnom Penh is clearly visible across the Tonle Sap. But all that's heard is lapping water and occasional Buddhist chants. "We built it in order to pray for peace and nonviolence and to pray for happiness for all people," says fifty-four-year-old Yek Kim who has come from her Phnom Penh home to offer food.

The temple is hope in troubled times.

In two years, that island is gone, washed away in monsoon floods, its temples swept into the river. The island comes and goes, comes and goes; it's here one season, gone the next. In early 2004, Yukuntur is back, minus the shrines. There is no one on the island, but the land is there. It is six months after another national election, and people are weary again. The people's hopes and dreams come and go, as the island does, never rising enough to stay afloat for long.

Just before those 2003 elections, Ouk Yom brings his wife, Em Nhor, for their first consultation in the psychiatric ward of Sihanouk Hospital. The meeting is for her, although it's hard to tell just by listening.

He wears a green military uniform with a badge. His wife is sick because of family problems. Her grandfather just died; her brother suffers severe injuries from a land mine accident; one of their daughters just separated from her husband and is now "the burden of the family," and she feels pity for her children. A fan swirls above as she talks to the psychiatrist, a young woman named Chea Dany. This is the same hospital, the same day, that Po Kith Ly tells us of his torture and maiming by the Khmer Rouge. His room is white; this one is tinted blue. Blue bed, blue tile, blue curtains.

Ouk Yom has his own history. During the Pol Pot time, "I was arrested and imprisoned. They accused me of betrayal." For more than a month he was scrunched in a tiny chamber with many others. Insects crawled on his skin, and he had nowhere to wash. "One small room, they put thirty people. They tied me up. There was only room to sit." Meanwhile, his family perished. "Fifteen siblings—all died." But time has helped ease his grief.

His wife, however, has suffered for a long time, and their poverty only compounds the trouble. He works for the Ministry of Interior and makes little money, about $32.50 a month. "It's not enough."

Their problems spill from their lips like grains of salt, this here, that there, another thing here, another trauma there, and soon enough it's a mountain of strife.

And here's another problem: The couple's son wanted to marry a woman whose parents disapproved. The young lovers tried to run away. Her parents caught them and beat them in public. Their son killed himself. This happened five years ago, and Em Nhor has been depressed ever since. They have paid many dollars on treatment at private clinics, and that has eaten up the family's funds.

While Ouk Yom talks his wife cowers in the seat next to him, as though she's afraid of the day itself. "I never go out of the home," she says when I ask whether she talks to her friends about her problems. She doesn't. "I have no close friends."

He has taken her to *kru Khmer*, to no avail. "I have seen nearly 100 traditional healers." She would improve for a week or so, then return to her old, disconsolate self. "The traditional healers say some spirit possesses her." At first, she trusted the healers and thought they knew best. "I expected some improvement." But after 100 failed attempts: "I don't believe anymore." She no longer thinks she's possessed. If she were, she'd be speaking in Pali or Sanskrit, the ancient languages of spirits. That hasn't happened.

Through all this, psychiatrist Chea Dany takes notes and assesses the situation. Em Nhor suffers from a multitude of problems. "At home she sleeps, sleeps, sleeps." She's also suicidal. "She feels if she can die, it's better," Chea Dany says. "She has lost interest, does not want to contact anyone." Her diagnosis is clinical depression, and the doctor will prescribe an anti-depressant. If necessary, she will combine it with other drugs to stop Em Nhor's heart palpitations.

"Everyday, my wife is sick like this. I take responsibility, even the housework," Ouk Yom says. He carries her hat under his arm. He says one *kru Khmer* told him: Feed her dog penis. The room erupts in laughter, even Em Nhor. "I tried to find dog meat for her to eat," her husband says, "because I thought the meat of the dog could chase the spirit out of her."

Now, they hope a scientific diagnosis and modern medicine will do the trick.

What comes next in a country with all these traumas and superstitions, dog-penis prescriptions and a scarcity of licensed doctors? Cambodians are living in a state of lawlessness, disaffectedness, lacking the usual standards of good behavior. "No single traumatic episode, not even the barbaric extremes of the most recent period, fully account for the state of anomie which characterizes Cambodian society today," Seanglim Bit writes. Decades, centuries of societal history must be faced, examined and "expunged from the collective memory."

It is no light diagnosis for a nation. The weight of this assessment is what Seanglim Bit, Sotheara Chhim, Kang Om, Kann Kall, Ang Sody and their colleagues fear, for Cambodia's future. They see some problems improving slowly, very slowly, but they also see things growing worse. Children today are violent. They act recklessly—racing *motos*, taking drugs, gambling, stealing, fighting. Parents don't fight for their rights when they should. Their kids see this, and they fight for everything. In late 1998, when the final curtains of the Khmer Rouge war draw closed and the leaders leave stage for their enclave in Pailin, Kann Kall hears the news from afar. He is furious that these murderers are getting off. "I was in Thailand and I said, Fuck! ... Ooohh! ... Grrrr! why isn't anyone organizing a demonstration?" Apathy is another hallmark of all that's wrong.

Four and a half years later, when I ask Sotheara Chhim at TPO whether he has hope for the future of his country, he answers cautiously. "I still cannot say because things are still unpredictable in Cambodia."

By 7:45 A.M., the inner courtyard of the Sihanouk Hospital psychiatric ward is stuffed with people, about forty in all. Sunlight silhouettes faces against walls. There are people of all ages, all types. City and country folk, old men, little kids, monks and mothers. A jittery man hugs his legs upon the bench, shaking, a big bloody gash above his right eye. He can't sit still. A woman hunches herself over, with head buried in arms. An elderly one-eyed monk wrapped in vivid robes asks Jerry if we're here in Cambodia for the upcoming elections. "Kampuchea has a lot of *yuon*," he says in English, apropos of nothing. Then in French: "Les Vietnamienes sont pas bon." Vietnamese aren't good.

By 8:10, there are nearly eighty people here. This is routine. Every day, this place swells with patients waiting for help.

By 8:15, it's standing room only. People pack the corners, and when they fill, the crowd oozes through the aisles. The hallway is stuffy with human smells. Twenty more patients line the stoop at the back door. They keep coming and coming. The ward's director, Y Tuon Seang, is flummoxed. "We don't have enough rooms, really, to take care of them all."

It is an astonishing understatement.

11. The Wanderers: A People Uprooted

I sit on a man's back, choking him and making him carry me, and yet assure myself and others that I am very sorry for him and wish to ease his lot by all possible means — except by getting off his back.
— Leo Tolstoy, *Writings on Civil Disobedience and Nonviolence*, 1886

Seth Mydans cultivates the image in a story for *The New York Times*. Cambodia is a land largely populated by "wanderers"—people with nowhere to go, so they move all the time. Land ownership was destroyed during the Khmer Rouge, all titles and deeds abolished, and in 1979, it became a free-for-all. Some people chose new plots and stayed for decades and secured rights to that land. Many others never found a place to settle — or a place where they were allowed to stay.

Today the rich and mighty grab the land they want, evicting those beneath them on the social scale. Before the 1993 elections, Cambodia's privileged politicians quickly sucked up the once-stunning villas of pre–Khmer Rouge times and renovated them for an influx of foreigners. "This outrageous plunder found general acceptance; questions about ownership were never raised," writes journalist Henry Kamm. Perhaps that's because everyone knows this longstanding Cambodian truth: The elite own this country. They are stationed, while the majority roam.

When the Seth Mydans article runs in 2000, only 14 percent of land in Cambodia is registered, and many of those registrations are fraudulent. Evictions are forceful, evoking grenades and rockets, machetes and fire. Even the most dreadful land is disputed. In August 2003, a hundred military police armed with AK-47s force hundreds of scavengers from the Stung Meanchey dump outside Phnom Penh. Families have built shanties and tarp homes atop the rot of garbage, but they don't have permission. It's not their land. The police order a youth gang to destroy the homes. Kicked off the rubbish heap. What refuge remains?

And what does this mean?

This means that in times of flood or famine or general strife, people crowd the cities. They flock to Phnom Penh and camp in the streets. They cling to the Royal Palace gates. This happens in September 2001, in several waves. More than 1,200 farmers beseech the king and queen. A few days later, 1,506 country folk appear at Sam Rainsy's stoop, begging the opposition leader for help. "Most of these destitute people are women, babies and children," Rainsy announces. "They survive in very precarious conditions: lack of food and clean water, shortage of tents, mats and mosquito nets, inadequate sanitary facilities, risk of epidemics."

It means others move, in the hands of traffickers, to neighboring countries, where they beg, scavenge, pilfer and sell small goods. And then eventually, they are forced to return to Cambodia, still with no home or job. In June 2003, Thai police arrest Cambodians illegally scavenging at a dump and eating stray dogs. Two months later, Vietnam deports 206 Cambodians found begging in the streets. They have come from Svay Rieng Province, bordering Vietnam, and the governor there says this has happened fourteen times in his memory.

Thousands of Cambodians are forever roving the country, roaming through life, never at ease or peace.

One Sunday in August 2001, Jerry and I take the train from Phnom Penh to Battambang, fourteen hours over warped tracks built before World War II. Only the poorest travelers go by train; it costs a dollar.

We leave our hotel at 5:30 A.M. An ad in a local magazine says the train leaves at 6. A sign at the station says 6:20. Our guidebook says 6:40. The train begins its crawl around 7.

We sit three per wooden seat. The glass is missing from our window, as it is from most. Sky peeks through the sagging wooden roof. We can see tracks through the floor. Weeds swamp the rails and branches slap us from the side. People pack the roof and cargo cars, scattered across a soiled floor, swinging in hammocks from side to side. The train chugs past farmers planting rice, ankles and calves buried, a radio crooning in the field. We see a man swimming up to his neck in a lotus pond. It is beautiful and bucolic, but the train pitches like a boat in a storm. We can't travel faster than about twenty miles an hour, or we'll be tossed from the tracks. I watch the bobbing car ahead, an indicator of jolts to come. But this is no better than Cambodia's highways. "Same like car down the road," a man says. I am nauseous, bruised and cranky.

We stop for an hour in a small village, waiting for another train to pass. Everyone sits in suffocating heat. A man named Khim shuffles through, singing for *riel*. He has no right eye, half a right arm, face scarred by shrapnel. A little dog chained to his arm holds a yellow plastic pail by mouth. Khim sings a ditty about his problems, and people chuckle, tossing *riel* they can't really afford to spare. "From war," says a man in our row. "I feel pity but I cannot do everything."

A child pees on the floor, and the urine flows our way. The bathroom is the next car up, a standard squat style with a basin of water and a plastic bottle to rinse directly to the tracks. Parents often don't bother; they point their children's rears to the center aisle instead.

The rain starts in the afternoon. People shift to the other side of the train. They pull out *kramas* and ponchos; water seeps through the roof and dribbles down my right side. It mixes with the urine on the floor.

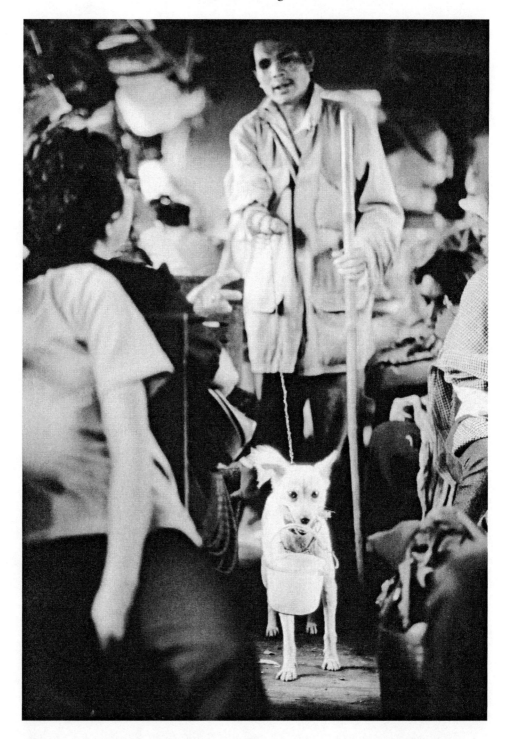

Khim lost his sight and his right hand to a bomb during the civil war. Now, with the help of his dog, he sings for money from passengers on the trip between Phnom Penh and Battambang. Near Pursat, 2001.

We stop again, and men shove wooden beams atop the roof. It sounds like thunder and rain, with the heavy thunk of logs and pitter-pattering feet whispering above us. One beam falls off and nearly knocks a man in the head. Vendors pass through with drinks and snacks, offering goodies from small coolers and baskets. One woman carries a tray of meat. People around us snicker and say it's dog. They scrunch their noses.

We pass so many remote little village stations, shot-up buildings, just the frames remaining, yellow paint abraded and pockmarked by war. We pass dirt roads that taper to the horizon with nothing else around. And the train bobs on, into dusk.

Darkness draws slowly, a thousand shades of pink and orange and yellow in the dimming sky. We trundle through miles of fields with skinny paths, an occasional dirt road, a few cows and buffalo, nothing more. For all they don't have, Cambodians possess a staggering diorama. That costs nothing. Cambodia's landscape is a masterpiece, traded for the price of living there.

This train is full of people moving, here to there, seeking family, seeking work, seeking a new life. They move with nothing but the clothes on their backs; for some, that is all they own. Ten months later Jerry and I spot Khim in Poipet, on the Thai border, sitting on the ground with his bucket and his dog. He is an itinerant man. This train, from east to west, is the picture of a migratory nation, a nation on the move.

Thousands of people live in squatter camps across Cambodian cities. Not infrequently those camps burn to the ground. Everyone has his or her own theory, but many say it's the government's way of cleaning house, razing the eyesores, so it can create new parks or buildings, anything that looks better.

In December 2001, two fires roar through a squatter camp on the Bassac River in Phnom Penh. Ten thousand people are left homeless. Officials do not let them rebuild in town. Instead, they are taken by truck to the rice paddies, to the flood plains, several miles outside the city. Each family is given a plot of paddy, twenty-three feet by forty-nine feet, on which to live. Phnom Penh governor Chea Sophara tells the *Financial Times* this is a good deal for the homeless victims. "They are happy, very happy because they have a bright future," he says. "In the old place, they are very poor, never making any use of their life."

Their new home is called Anlong Kong Thmei. Their old home is turned into a riverfront walkway, and soon a towering casino sprouts nearby, and a market is raised. There is no sign of the shabby, squalid homes that once were.

Jerry and I visit Anlong Kong Thmei the summer of 2003. Our friend and colleague, Saing Soenthrith, known as Rith, takes us on his *moto*. He has been here before, on a story for *The Cambodia Daily*, and he is eager to show us his findings.

Anlong Kong Thmei sits in flooded rice fields, nine miles outside town. Take the road out of Phnom Penh leading to Choeung Ek, the Killing Fields, and when you come to a crossroad, turn right. Keep going past the market, through rural fields dotted with palms, into the countryside quietude. Turn left near a small cement factory and keep going.

We venture here in the middle of monsoon season, and the settlement springs from wet muck. It's surrounded by a square dirt dike with a road atop that circles the shacks. Outside the dike, it's all drenched fields. Those paddies don't belong to anyone in Anlong Kong Thmei — they belong to neighboring villagers. They belong to people with money.

Inside the square, some 450 families live on those rectangular twenty-three-by-forty-nine-foot plots in thatch homes low to the ground. They have wells with water pumped from a nearby *baray* and a school funded by foreign NGOs. There is no electricity, no running water. The residents have enough land to raise a few chickens and pigs, grow some papayas and sugarcane and squash. They have one toilet for every ten families, if someone hasn't fenced it off as sometimes happens. Even squatters dispute their territory.

Most residents do not have jobs. But they do have Christians coming frequently to gather kids in a truck and take them outside the settlement to a church where they learn the word of God. If residents want to pray at a Buddhist *wat*, they must find their own transportation to the closest temple near a coconut farm on the horizon. The Christian group is building a small church on site and funding other community projects. They also console villagers when they run out of money.

Many of the people in Anlong Kong Thmei lived along the Bassac for a decade. They came from other provinces when jobs fell through or their land was confiscated in the countryside. Though they didn't own the land on the Bassac, they had convenience. They could work — construction, selling meat in the market, begging and scavenging on the streets. But here, so many dusty, bumpy miles from anything, they have no work. No one comes to do business in Anlong Kong Thmei, save for a few neighbors selling vegetables. Even the children have nothing to scavenge. "They now have to go to Phnom Penh for work. But they spend their own money," Rith tells us. They must arrange their own transportation. They must pay for lunch and incidentals in the city. They must return home again, using more money. And by sunset, their 7,000-*riel*-a-day wage is whittled down to 2,000 *riel* take-home pay. Fifty cents, if they're lucky.

So the people of Anlong Kong Thmei borrow $100 or so from rich landowners nearby, just to make ends meet, and they're forced to pay exorbitant interest — whatever the landowner demands. When they fall behind in payments, the landowner confiscates their little plot in Anlong Kong Thmei and rents it out to another family of squatters. The first family returns to Phnom Penh to live on the streets again.

And if Cambodia's social and political systems aren't enough to break the spirits of those in Anlong Kong Thmei, the weather will. The road floods and heavy winds and rains regularly smash huts to the ground. Pools of storm water still stand, hot and muddy, around these homes. Houses collapse like sodden tents. Neighbors move in with neighbors next door. Men pound and piece together new homes with corrugated metal and thatch and supplies, all of which cost more money.

But it is quiet here. Dragonflies buzz through the breathable air. Stunning moss roses surround homes that pale in every comparison. It's icing on a bitter cake.

We stop to talk with Sok Samath, a forty-five-year-old neighborhood leader, a member of the commune council. She spends most of her efforts fighting the Phnom Penh government, which she thinks has disgraced her people. "When the government moved us from the squatter village in Phnom Penh, they gave us only land. No job, no food supplies."

She lived in the Bassac camp for ten years; before that, in Svay Rieng Province, which she left for lack of money and work. "On the Bassac, we had a house but no land, and it was easy to find a job to do." She bought meat from a middleman and sold it for a small profit. "But here no businessmen come to do business."

She asks me many times if I will help her send her message to the government. "They promised to train our children and women to do sewing." If women had the know-how, they could in theory get jobs in garment factories. But the government hasn't followed through with its vow.

Sok Samath's house is stuffed with all she owns: an old Honda *moto*, a bike, a small table, two wooden slat beds, a few plastic chairs, clothes hung from the walls, dishes, a small radio, a flashlight. The dirt floor is wet and crawling with ants. Pigs snort and sniffle out the back door. She sells the piglets, ten or eleven at a time, and earns $140 for six months of feeding and raising them.

It's less than twenty days to the national election, and Sok Samath will be an official observer. "But I'm afraid to speak the truth." She says many people here haven't registered to vote. They haven't been allowed. The registration committee came and went, while several residents were working menial jobs in Phnom Penh. She says if the government doesn't change, if the system doesn't improve, the problems will never retreat. People will return to Phnom Penh with no options, and then what will the government do?

We take a walk, following the laterite roads that trace the camp. All around us is the sound of pounding as people build and rebuild, one step forward, two steps behind.

DanChurch Aid of Copenhagen has pumped money into this village, and the Christian influence is evident. A small church is one of a few solid buildings here. It's surrounded by a metal gate, enclosing a submerged yard. Every house, every hut, in the vicinity is thatch.

Not far from here is the home of Teap Im and her husband, Yok Y, who is deaf and sits quietly through our conversation. Their place is an airy hut, not so cramped. There's a spot for a barbecue in the corner near the door, and a place for chopping food. There is one large wooden table, which serves as a chair, a bed, a dining spot. Teap Im says they came from Prey Veng Province. They lived on a farm with their kids until some of the children grew ill. "I borrowed money from rich people to treat them, but all of them died. So the lenders confiscated our land, and we went to live in the squatter village." They spent eight years on the Bassac until its burning in 2001. Two months later, she turned to the Christian God.

"I like some chapters of this book, like the symbol of the cross, when Jesus died," she says, flipping through her Bible, written in Khmer. "I believe in Christianity. I saw that God died on the cross and that he died for my crisis, my security, my sickness." This knowledge gives her strength. "I offer God my soul."

Teap Im begins to read the creation story. There was darkness, and God asked for light. The Earth was under water, so God asked the water to recede for the human race. Land emerged, and plants grew when the Earth was born. "I couldn't read and write," she says, "but when I became a Christian, I could. Before, my eyes were bad, but then suddenly I could read. It's very strange to me. Maybe God offered that ability to me."

Religion helps her through troubling times, and she has many. Her daughter, who recently had a baby, borrowed $100 from a rich man. It's a twelve-month loan, on which she must pay $20 a month, for a total of $240. She has thus far paid $190, but her daughter and son-in-law have no steady work, and they haven't made a payment in three months. The owners are mad. "They still want to confiscate our land."

It is this sort of doing that leads her to say: "Our country nowadays is not a free democracy because we have a difficult life and we are intimidated."

But she keeps her faith. "I believe God will help me. The priest gives offerings to God, and I hope God will solve the problem for me."

A few weeks later, two days after national elections, I sit in a Siem Reap restaurant drinking tonic. A little boy squats behind potted plants surrounding the tables here. He calls me, "Madame, madame." He wants money. A man without feet wheels by, and another with a missing leg hobbles on crutches. He wears a CPP shirt, and I wonder what the ruling regime has done for him.

Jerry and I read in a French-language newspaper, here in Siem Reap, that Anlong Kong Thmei no longer exists. A storm spawned by a passing typhoon sweeps it under, drilling holes into the dike, flushing homes into the surrounding fields. Villagers climb atop the school and wait until they no longer can, and they leave. They float their belongings on tables, through the flood, seeking refuge at the nearest *wat*.

Eight months later, some of the people return to the flooded paddies, hoping to try again.

When Kim Sophornn tells foreigners about his country, he doesn't croon about the splendors of Angkor. He shares this reality instead: Seventy percent of Cambodians worry about what they will eat tomorrow, 25 percent worry about food the following day or week and only 5 percent never worry at all. At TPO in Battambang, Kim Sophornn sees, every day, how poverty cripples the people around him. He tries to convince tourists of that, but they respond, "Oh, I don't believe you." They don't see past the sheen of tourism, a fine shellac that covers the bare realities beneath. He says, "They just visit the happy places."

The "happy places" are the ancient Angkor temples, where 700,000 tourists in one year revel in the beauty, indulge in the mystique. It is possible to fly to Siem Reap directly from Bangkok, Saigon, Singapore, Tokyo, Vientiane. It is possible to retire at a five-star hotel, to savor world-class food and sip the finest wines, to visit the ruins by private air-conditioned limo, to soak up the wonders in the most conceivable comfort. And it's possible to never encounter a visibly poor Cambodian — save, perhaps, for a nice smiling woman selling *kramas* at the Bayon or a beautiful young girl with bracelets at Angkor Wat.

It is possible to vacation at Angkor and never know the misfortunes of Cambodia.

That's possible even in Phnom Penh these days. Parts of the city are looking spunky. The riverfront area has a new coat of paint, some new hotels, grass plots along the quay. A cursory glance looks pretty good. But: "Everything you see, the new buildings, it's not by the government," says Sam Piseth, who runs a coffee shop just around the corner from a large new riverfront hotel in the capital. The government isn't sprucing things up — business owners are. And they're not doing it for the people of Cambodia. They're doing it for foreigners. For the people who live here, little has changed. "Phnom Penh still has no safety. People still live in fear," he says.

Sam Piseth is Khmer but lived in Kampuchea Krom for years. He says he fled the Big Brother Vietnamese Communism there ten years ago and opened this tiny streetside cafe. His customers are *moto* and *cyclo* drivers and many men with no work at all. Some linger all day. "When the foreigners come to visit Phnom Penh, they say Cambodia has improved," he says. They see the buildings and think things have improved. But if they live here a month, they will know."

Those who come for a quick little jaunt often see the country through blinders. Those who visit Cambodia and find a sanguine view are missing a significant lot:

They're missing Me Kaem, a thirty-year-old beggar who sleeps behind Siem Reap's old market, who has no family, who owns nothing but his shirt and pants and a prosthetic leg, who has bad memories of 1975 and who graciously accepts a seat at a restaurant table to gobble leftover rice and ginger fish.

They're missing all the other beggars congregated along the murky trickle of a river through town, spreading their mats on the banks, sleeping where they can, with the cows and the dogs.

They're missing Sao Chun, a forty-two-year-old man who lives across the alley from the Pansea resort, beneath a tarp on a narrow dirt road, with his TV and mosquito net full of holes, surviving on the dribbles of income he gets repairing bicycle tires.

They're missing nineteen-year-old Chhret and his twenty-nine-year-old wife, Mao, who came from Kompong Thom Province, hoping to find work and money but finding nothing instead and ending up on the street, where they will stay for the foreseeable future because they have no money to go home; they have no money to go anywhere.

They're missing the woman sitting next to Chhret and Mao, who holds up her small bug-bitten child saying, "We don't have a mosquito net."

And they're missing the sixty-four families evicted from lands around Angkor Wat, forced out by Angkor police authorities, their fenced-in huts destroyed in an effort to clean up for thousands of foreign visitors.

They're missing the people who trudge through life in the shadows of Angkor. These people are missed, invisible to those who arrive with a rosy veil across their eyes. It's easy to do. No one wants a sad vacation.

"The days of begging children at Angkor are over," Donald Richie writes in *The Japan Times* in 2002. "The children now sell guidebooks and postcards and act as guides; they behave with dignity and self-respect. Likewise, adult beggars are no more. I saw just one and that was in Siem Reap." Perhaps he doesn't see more of them because the cleaning crew has already swept through this tourist hub. Perhaps he just isn't looking.

A few miles up the road from Siem Reap town, between the Raffles, the Sofitel and the Angkor temples, is another squatter camp of thirty-seven families on a red dirt road in little thatch houses on short stilts over opaque yellow pools. "When it rains, this area fills with water. It's difficult to get to our house," says twenty-five-year-old Sambo Sok, a resident who carves wooden puppets to sell in Siem Reap. He and his neighbors came from other provinces years ago, looking for work, same story over and over. They lived for five years in another spot until they were forced to move. "The government wanted to make that road, so the people moved here," he says. "I don't know if the government will move us again." It's always a worry. "The people are angry with the government, but we don't know what to do."

Some of the residents work in nearby hotels and restaurants, although those jobs are scarce. Even so, the work is not lucrative. "In one day we earn only 5,000 *riel*," says Chom Ny, clutching her six-month-old baby girl by the rump. Her husband works in one of those hotels.

The people here are surrounded by private land. They live in a divot fifteen yards wide, where the water collects when monsoons sweep through. "Before, we lived on flat land. It was better," Chom Ny says. As we talk, her neighbor digs for a missing spoon below her home, up to her calves in goop.

Sitting by the roadside is thirteen-year-old Kroh Ngaing, with a red tub of rambutans and a pile of watermelons by her side. She sells them. She makes 10,000 *riel*, about $2.50, if she sells them all, but that's a dream because few people come down this gravelly road; there's little reason to. She starts at 6 A.M. and works until 5 or 5:30, yet she insists she fits school into that schedule as well. All the money goes to her parents. When I ask if she likes this job she exclaims: "*Awt te*! No way!"

And then we meet seventy-year-old Preung, a widow with a stubbly bald head. We take refuge under her thatch roof when a storm pounds down, adding to the yellow mess below these homes. Preung stirs a steaming cauldron of rice and smokes a cigarette. I can see the water roiling beneath her, through the slats of her raised porch. She says she has no hard feelings about this place, where she's stationed at the end of her life. Her neighbors give her money, little that they have, and they're kind to her. "I'm not angry," she says. "I'm old so I can't find a job."

The rain passes and black clouds bank against a sallow sky. A few more feet, and these houses will be flooded. A kid pushes a bike through water. A man digs a small canal parallel to the road, attempting to control the water flow, but it caves in.

Two women and a boy come trudging up from a distant woods. They have hiked all the way from Angkor Wat with a load of wood. How far? "Far, far." They have taken a circuitous route, avoiding authorities. "We have a problem with the police. We cannot go by this road, we go by another path through the woods so the police will not find us," one of the women tells us.

And this is life, every day, in the shadows of Angkor, the blind spot of Cambodia.

If a Cambodian woman needs a job, chances are she'll aim for a garment factory. She'll leave her home province; she'll bid family and friends farewell; she'll move to Phnom Penh; she'll scrounge together money for sewing lessons; she'll rent a little room for $10 a month; she'll apply for the job, and if she's very lucky, she'll get it.

Cambodia exports more than $730 million worth of garments to the United States each year, and another $220 million to Europe. The industry accounts for more than 90 percent of the country's export earnings. Some 220 factories across the country employ more than 230,000 people, mostly young women.

It's not an easy job. Cambodia's garment factories actually have a reputation for treating their workers well compared with those in other nations. But still, conditions are not fantastic. The pay is lousy—often not enough for women to support their children, so they send their children to their home villages to live. Employees still complain they are forced to work overtime, sometimes without extra pay. Workers still report physical and emotional abuse on the job. And many say they get sick from fumes, fainting through the factories, dozens at a time. "People fall down and have convulsions," one woman tells me. In April 2004, the International Labor Organization reports "solid progress" in improved working conditions at Cambodian factories, but it notes this problem of forced overtime. Sometimes workers strike, and sometimes those turn deadly.

In June 2003, garment workers demonstrate peacefully in front of a factory for five days, demanding better conditions and higher pay. The police block them from marching into the city. Protesters pelt the officers with stones; the cops open fire; one worker is killed and so is an officer.

There are many such incidents through the years. In 1998 an Agence France-Presse photographer returns to the office after covering a riot. He is covered in red, shirt splattered, bright crimson stains. What happened? Was he shot?

It's chili sauce. Little packets of chili sauce, the weapon of the day, sprayed on cops, launched at the eyes, raining down upon the crowd, spicing up the demonstration.

The wife of our friend Hat Saman works in a garment factory. They both live on the western edge of Phnom Penh, in a small wooden room, dorm style, with dozens more factory workers. Saman takes us there on a hot Saturday afternoon in 2003 and introduces us to his neighbors.

Sar Rann is a thirty-year-old widow with a young son. Her husband died of malaria a few years back, and she came here "because my family is poor." She lives in one of these identical wooden rooms, but she can't keep her child here. "I sent my son to live at home in the province." It is this way for many parents, eking out a city living while relatives in the countryside raise their children. She worked construction for four months when she first arrived, but that proved too strenuous. So she tried to find work at a factory—no easy feat. She paid factory managers $20 to train her. And after she finished successfully, they handed her an application. It's the same in all the factories, she says. Prospective employees wait for an opening that might or might not come.

For her, it eventually came at Build Chheang Factory, run by Chinese managers, and she says they aren't nice. "When I sew the clothes, sometimes I make a mistake, and the Chinese always speak cruelly to me." They threaten to fire her, and then she doesn't know what she would do without her $60 a month salary. Her normal day is eight hours, but she sometimes works overtime and earns an extra $10 or $20 a month. This is not by choice. The bosses force her to work overtime, and they don't pay her on time. Her higher-ups tell her the money is late coming from the bank. She commiserates with coworkers, but no one dares complain. "We are afraid they will fire us."

This boarding house contains twenty rooms, each about ten feet by ten feet, with renters who work at different factories. Most everyone comes from another place; few laborers are native to Phnom Penh. This hot, dusty, noisy, smelly city life is not by choice.

Nineteen-year-old Hour Sreyneang came here from Kompong Cham Province with her brother. She, too, paid for her own training, $10 for a private course in the market. Two weeks later she found a job at Lucky Zone Apparel, alongside 2,000 other workers. She doesn't particularly like it. "It's hard for me to work at the garment factory. I would like to ask permission to rest, but they don't like to give it to me. Sometimes they force me to work overtime. Sometimes I get a little sick, and they still force me to work." The factory's chemicals make her dizzy, and she informs the bosses, to no avail. "They're always mean to the workers, especially when they need the clothes quickly to export overseas."

If Hour Sreyneang had her choice, she would not be here. She would return to her village. "I want to raise pigs…. I think it's better in the village, but there's nothing to do there. We have no money." For now, perhaps forever, this is the only job she can afford.

Her brother, Hour Chinsong, is in the minority of garment workers, being a man. Factory owners don't hire many men "because men always make complaints," he says. "They provoke demonstrations." But those demonstrations have helped improve life for employees. "Before, they used to beat the workers, but now they have a law, and they don't do it anymore."

I tell the people here there is a divide in Western thinking about garment work. People call it "sweatshop" labor. They hear the hours are long and the conditions hard. Some say the factories should be closed; that it's better to have no factory, on principle, than one that violates workers' rights. Yet others argue a dubious job is better than no job at all. I ask them what they think.

Twenty-three-year-old Moeun Pao, another Lucky Zone employee, answers from a tired worker's perspective. She would rather have a manager who respects her rights. "I want to have the factory temporarily close. It's better for me to have a new investor." A new boss. She makes $45 a month, up to $70 with overtime pay. Lots of people — NGOs, human rights workers, government officials—come to check up on the factory, but the youngest, most persuasive employees are paid to keep quiet. "The Chinese owners always pay them $5 each and tell them, 'Don't say what's happening in the factory.'"

Like most people, Moeun Pao would rather do something else, "but we don't have other experience so we just keep on at the factory."

Just keeping on — it's what millions of Cambodians do.

It's late August 2003, and the bougainvillea on our Phnom Penh porch has burst into fuscia, brighter each day. I once thought it nearing death, but the plant has revived, and it burgeons with color. Some days I need that. I need to look at something stunning when all around me is staggering.

I talk today with our regular *moto* driver, Monin, who has become one of our translators. His English improves each time we visit. But this conversation is an interview, and it's one of the saddest yet.

Ke Monin is thirty-one and he has no hope. "Other people, if they have money, they have hope." He comes from a village twenty-five miles from Phnom Penh. He moved here ten years ago after finishing high school. It's a classic tale: no work in the village, harder yet in the city. He did what most men like him do, offering his *moto* as a taxi, driving customers around town, accepting whatever customers choose to pay when the ride is over. "When I came to Phnom Penh, I wanted to find a job, and I wanted to save some money to take care of my family, my grandmother, my aunt." He can't do that.

He used to study English, but he doubts he will ever have the $40 a month again. Three years ago, he married a woman named Sy Yom, and they soon had a son. Now, he can barely afford his $10 a month apartment, just a hovel, "very small bed, you know." It's no place for a little boy, no yard to play in, no friends to make, no security. So they sent their boy away. "My son lives in my hometown with my parents." He sees his boy only when he gathers enough money to make the trip — and take a day or two off from work. "Sometimes two times a month."

Monin's wife works at the National Library, and her monthly salary should amount to 30,000 *riel,* about $7.50. Even so, they pay her only one month's wages in three months' time. "Every day I'm worried. When I go home, I cannot sleep. I always think about my life." The same is true of his wife.

I ask about the changes he's seen in Phnom Penh. His answer has nothing to do with the decade since the UN planted the seeds of democracy, nothing about social improvement that can reasonably be expected. His answer: "Before, there were a lot of old buildings and a lot of land." Now, there are new factories and new buildings. That's it, except the gap that has widened between top and bottom. "The rich people are very rich. The poor people are even poorer."

He thinks there is only one solution for Cambodia: a colonial power, another country to take it over. Britain, Australia, America — it doesn't matter, so long as a better-off nation comes to teach the people, foster business and offer new life. Western countries have the power to change Cambodia. "They are democracies. They have higher knowledge."

He, like many Khmers, thinks Vietnam holds sway over the country today, and the country will never improve like that. "I think if they change the government from communist to democratic, it will be easy to find a job," he says. But now his country is pulled by communist roots. This is not just a crackpot theory. Hun Sen's ruling CPP evolved from the Khmer People's Revolutionary Party, an offshoot of the Indochinese Communist Party.

Monin is morose, but he does not beg for help, he does not extend his empty hat. Instead he offers his potential. "I am capable." He just doesn't have an opportunity. He wants to study; he wants the chance. "I can change my life. You know, when I go to be a *moto* driver, a lot of people look down on me." Even his landlady, who threatens to kick them out. She doesn't like people who don't work, and she doesn't consider driving a *moto* a job.

Monin spends most of his days on the street near the river. He sits atop his *moto*, waiting, waiting, waiting for a possible fare. He waits among a dozen others, other men on *motos*, other men with no work. And after all that time together on the same streets hour after hour, these men are "not really friends." They tolerate each other. They don't trust each other. This is common. People talk behind each others' backs. "Good friends? Yeah, I have," Monin says. "But outside Phnom Penh."

Talking to him, absorbing his hopelessness, ingesting his glances—the downward smirks, the shake of his head when he speaks of the gulf between rich and poor or the people who scorn him because he drives a *moto*, it's so sad. Our conversation lulls at times, and he sips his coffee, and we sit short moments in silence. He confirms and summarizes what I have feared about this country through the years. It is not a happy appraisal. I have looked for good news from the grassroots and it's hard to find. Not impossible, but rare. We mourn together, the loss of hope and the utter uncertainty of it all. For where does a country go from here?

I ask one more question. Is his country a democracy? "No," he says. "Never. Never democracy."

12. Women: The Lesser Sex

I see the portrait of a fourteen-year-old girl.

She drapes a tattered black-and-white *krama* across her face. She wears a yellow headband with a red plastic flower atop her head. Her eyes are deep brown, her skin is young. She is veiled by her own tragic story. Her mother sold her to a pimp, who sold her virginity and her innocence for several years. But now she has made her way to a safehouse.

You cannot name this girl from the picture; her identity is concealed. But she is one of hundreds, thousands, sold into this dismal trade in human life, day after day, in Phnom Penh's sex shacks. Parents come to town with daughters to sell. Men come to buy them. Sometimes government officials do too. The wealthy, the upper class, the "sexpats," the tourists on the prowl — they visit these brothels; they buy their way and take it from the girls, then leave. Sometimes they beat them, tie them up or set fire to the buildings. Sometimes they give the girls HIV or get it from them.

And sometimes they kill.

As with most violence in Cambodia, you can find crimes against girls and women in the papers. There is Ny, a twenty-five-year-old prostitute at a village brothel whose boyfriend shoots her in the head, dead, with an M-16 before shooting and wounding himself. There is a four-year-old girl raped while her parents go off to collect firewood. There is an eight-year-old girl lured to the forest, raped and left. There is Mon Chinda, raped and killed, her ten-year-old body dumped into a pond. And there are little girls in Preah Vihear, raped by two men who think the virgins could cure them of AIDS.

Some of the country's most atrocious crimes are inflicted on sex workers. The human rights group Licadho finds, through interviews, that thirty-eight percent of prostitutes have been physically abused. The group accuses Cambodia's police and military of condoning that behavior. Licadho condemns the all-too-frequent tendency of "viewing humans as possessions."

Viewing humans as possessions. That's the way it often is with women in Cambodia. It is deeply entwined with Khmer culture and life. It is deeply sown in the expectations men historically have. Wives, mothers, prostitutes, workers: Most every woman has a role, an expected persona, at the foot of a man.

It is culture, and many Cambodians see nothing wrong with it. "There is *joie de vivre* again. Nightclubs have reopened with taxi dancers. I am sure soon there will be massage parlours. It is our way of life: it is a good life," the journalist John Pilger quotes Norodom Sihanouk, then prince and later king, who said this upon his return to Phnom Penh in 1991 after years of absence.

To get a feel for this country's attitudes about sex and the place of men and women, one need only watch. Sit for a while at a cafe or bar or Internet shop. Listen to the conversations. Pay attention to the men in the street, and the women. Visit a market and think about the scenes. It's easy to stereotype, and it's easy to find generalizations in print. But look long enough and ask whether the stereotypes are true. Women sell themselves to men for a few dollars. Men — Khmer and foreign — obligingly buy them. Mothers sell daughters to brothels; madams enslave young girls to rich men. Rich men pay more for virgins.

There are prostitutes who leave, then return again and again because their villages shun them or they have nothing else to do. There are men who take mistresses, and there are jealous wives who hire men to throw acid in said mistresses' faces. There are all these things and, of course, the antitheses: Men who love and cherish their wives and remain faithful. Women who hold vital positions with big companies or aid groups or the government. Girls who determine to avoid the traps that so many don't. But those few men and women and girls face staggering odds and a culture that prefers the *joie de vivre*.

The sex in Cambodia is legend — the clubs, the karaoke bars, the cathouses (and there is a place in Phnom Penh with precisely that name). Travelers arrive wondering, is it really true? Can I really buy a virgin or take a dancer home to bed?

Yes, it really is true, and yes, people really do come here for that alone. Twenty-two percent of all tourists to Cambodia come for sex, according to the Cambodia Development Resource Institute and reported by the Singapore *Straits Times*. That number is rising as other countries in the region discourage such cavorting.

"Shy boys on motorbikes will ferry you from bar to bar, waiting outside while you drink yourself into a stupor. You can eat dinner, then penetrate indentured underaged prostitutes, buy a kilo of not very good weed, drink yourself stuttering drunk, and be driven safely home to your spacious apartment — all for under thirty dollars," chef-writer Anthony Bourdain proclaims in *A Cook's Tour*. He travels the world for this book, trying exotic foods. But when he visits Cambodia he cannot ignore the omnipresent perversion. "Cambodia is a dream come true for international losers — a beautiful but badly beaten woman, staked out on an anthill for every predator in the world to do with what he wishes."

I see it for myself every time I go there, as does anybody else who isn't willfully blind. And I never have to go out of my way to find it. I sit in a restaurant on the coast. Two hoary Western men eat large plates of meat and mashed potatoes at the table beside me. With them sits a very petite, very pretty young Khmer girl wearing four-inch heels and a loose tank top. She drinks her coffee. She does not talk. There may be a perfectly innocent explanation for this, but it's unlikely.

And then across the street, I check email at an Internet shop. Inside is a large

American man with a southern accent, downloading pornography. I sit at another computer, and the customers before me have left several links open, one to a page called "Pussy," another marked "XXXX," with photos to match.

A few days later, Jerry and I rent a hotel room in Phnom Penh. The bathroom wall ends a foot below the ceiling, leaving a gap, a direct link to the bathroom in the adjacent room. We can't help but listen to the conversation next door. At first we think it's a movie playing in the background, it sounds so ridiculous. A Western man rants at a woman, but there is no response. He goes on and on, spewing words, virulent words at some woman presumably in the room. We go to breakfast and return an hour later to more of the same. "Money, money, money. Asian women, American women, they're all the same," the man snarls. "No, I don't know any good Asian women. I thought you were one." He threatens to leave, to cross the border. He mentions a sum of 4,000 *baht*, about $100, which the woman apparently, somehow, lost. He tells her she must get it back. He'll go to South America, he says. He'll tell everyone he's been there for years. He'll make no mention, ever, of having lived here with this woman. "No one will ever know I ever went to Asia.... Like I never met you."

And then a few days later, I read a lengthy report in the *Phnom Penh Post* that starts like this: "Cambodia's women thought they were at the start of an equal future in 1958, when the first female parliamentarian, Mrs. Tong Siv Eng, was elected to the National Assembly." But the following decades of war and civil strife have left the Cambodian women's movement seemingly "stuck in the Sixties," and only 10 to 12 percent of the candidates in upcoming 2003 national elections are women. I read in that same edition that a woman, four months pregnant, is raped on the job at a rubber plantation.

And later that week, I meet with a photographer, Nicolas Lainez, who works with an aid group that fights AIDS and helps prostitutes. His is a massive project to document prostitution and sexual slavery throughout Asia. He has seen much of the worst in the Philippines, China, Vietnam, Myanmar, Thailand and Cambodia. He spends several weeks on the Thai border. He says there are thousands of prostitutes in the town of Poipet alone and more than a dozen NGOs working there, trying to help them. When I ask how he goes about his work, how he takes his photos, he says in some ways it's easier here in Cambodia than in other countries. There are many reasons: Prostitution is part of the culture. It's a lucrative business, and the government tolerates it. Cambodians are used to foreigners among them. They're used to answering questions and opening their lives to social workers. If Nicolas spends enough time with Khmer prostitutes and gains their trust, he can stay in the rooms while they work.

Another day, another month, another year, Jerry and I drink Beer Lao and eat popcorn at a Phnom Penh bar near the river. An obese American man wearing a tattered green cut-off T-shirt, full of holes and falling off his immense body, sits with a few *barangs* at the next table. He's drunk and speaks loudly about the pleasures of a young woman, who is also seated at the table. She sits quietly while he speaks boisterously.

"Pure bliss," he says. "BLISS," when a woman trusts you, and you trust her implicitly. She has given him such pleasure by shaving his back. He speaks proudly of said event and smacks her on the lips. Then he gets up, teeters on his feet, carries an unlit cigarette and searches his wallet for change he doesn't have. So he goes next door to find change while she remains at the table, silent, head turned downward. He returns and insists on changing seats, "because I have to see the street," giving us the pleasure of viewing his unsightly sagging torso in that wretched tank top. The woman sits beside him, smacking on green mango. He ignores her.

Instead, he speaks to his foreign friends about the Middle East, about suicide bombings and life in Phnom Penh. His friend reads the sports page and ignores the drunkard. The drunkard fidgets and lifts his top, baring his belly. "I lived in Israel during the cease fire," he continues on a worldly diatribe while his woman of pleasure pours herself Angkor beer. She plays with her cell phone and smokes a cigarette. She is bored. He keeps talking. The whole bar smells of marijuana, even though a sign on the wall says "No spliffing."

The drunkard yaps some more, waving his cigarette while his friend progresses from the *Bangkok Post* to the local *Bayon Pearnik*, reading a selection titled "Notes of an Idle Life." He finishes the article, announces it is "ah, time for a wash," and exits. The mouthy man begins again about the pleasure of being shaved. "When you do that, you find your erogenous zones," he tells his remaining companions, who are thoroughly unimpressed. One of them stares at him point-blank and says, "You missed your arms."

Through all this, the woman says nothing.

There is silence, and silence is what's expected. There are a hundred expectations of Khmer women, at home, in sex, at work, in the market. The parameters of a woman's life are largely based on tradition. And perhaps above all else, she is expected to be silent around her man.

It is not surprising women carve their own niches among each other.

Her foot goes up and down, silver-pink toes flashing to the rhythm of her machine. Her brow sweats, hair drips, eyes sparkle. She covers her face with a mask as she sews a sheet for my bed. She is deep inside a maze of market aisles, smothered in heat, buried beneath racks of cloth and clothes stacked twelve feet high. She is surrounded by women who spend their days in this market, hour after hour, an enclave hidden from the life outside.

The women invite me to sit. They smile and howl and ask me lots of questions, in Khmer and English. They give me a fan, to cool my face, as I wait for the work to be done. They are squeezed on metal tables, clustered with shirts and pants and dresses and cloth beneath whirring fans and spider webs a decade old. The seamstress attaches three large *kramas* together, then hems them beautifully. It takes at least half an hour and a reliable foot with a steady drizzle of sweat. But she charges me only $1. The women around here talk about the upcoming national election, about what number the ruling CPP will be on the ballot (17). They giggle and joke and have fun. When my sheet is finished and I rise to leave, they invite me back anytime. Anytime — to share this other life of Khmer markets and women, scrunched in stuffy corridors. There is a pulse in here, the pulse of women away from home, away from men, sweating and making money and doing the menial tasks they have always done.

It is a woman's role.

It is woman's job to be in the market. It is her job to be at home, to have and raise children, to clean the house and cook the food and greet her husband with enthusiasm. And if she is not doing these things—there is another assumption. She must look beautiful and young and give herself to men.

It is custom.

Just as it is custom for men to rule the house and tell their wives what to do. Just as it is custom for men, on occasion or with regularity, to beat their wives when they're angry or drunk or confused. Domestic violence, "It's like a tradition in Cambodia," says Nop Sarin Srey Roth, monitoring coordinator of the Cambodian Women's Crisis Center (CWCC), which runs shelters for victimized women. It's tradition, and people don't feel it's their business to intervene. It's tradition, and there is no law prohibiting a man from beating his wife.

It's tradition, just as it is for men to keep women of pleasure.

That, too, is rooted in Angkor times. The monarchs, legend has it, would meet each night with a beautiful woman in a chamber atop a mountain. "It was believed if he did not go, trouble would befall his kingdom," writes Robert Philpotts. "If he went and found the woman absent his own death was foreshadowed. Not until they had made love was the king allowed to leave the tower at which point the woman turned herself back into a naga, a seven-headed cobra."

At that time, young girls under the age of twelve reportedly underwent a coming-of-age ceremony performed by a priest. No one knows precisely what that ceremony entailed, but the two spent hours together, alone in a pavilion while village musicians grew louder and louder until they reached a crescendo just as the ceremony also did.

Fast forward 800 or a thousand years: Recently, women's advocates say gang rape has burgeoned into a popular form of entertainment for young Khmer men. It is "now one of the most popular after-dark pastimes among the affluent, unmarried twenty-to-thirty-something males of the country's larger towns," according to a London *Observer* story that runs on the day of the 2003 national elections. The rapists "see it as a bonding experience with their friends." They call it *bauk*. It's a game, a night on the town. The culprits often target prostitutes. They corner the women and attack as though it's their right. A survey of 580 Phnom Penh youth indicates that 34 percent of male respondents say they know other young men involved in this sort of gang rape. Among university students, that percentage rises to 60.

Bauk is symptomatic of the country's larger mental-health crisis, says Leakhena Nou, dean of the College of Social Sciences at the University of Cambodia. It's an epidemic. This is especially true for youth "who have yet to constructively deal or are currently struggling with the uncertainty surrounding the country's transitional state," she writes in the *Phnom Penh Post*.

It's one of many disturbing trends in rising violence against women.

In the first quarter of 2003, the small Phnom Penh office of the CWCC deals with 63 sex trafficking cases, 130 domestic violence cases and 35 rapes. In 2002, there are 141 trafficking cases, 635 domestic violence incidents and 98 rapes. The year before: 120 trafficking, 443 domestic violence and 44 rape cases. All in Phnom Penh. Only in Phnom Penh, with a population of 1.3 million, one-tenth of the country as a whole.

But these numbers do little to reflect the actual number of rape, trafficking and domestic violence incidents. That's because people have never trusted the cops— nor had reason to. People haven't always known these crimes are wrong, and they haven't known about places like CWCC. So the crimes haven't been reported. When numbers go up, Srey Roth says, it means more people are seeking help, more people realize their rights have been violated. The crimes are just as bad as they've always been.

But one thing is certain: "Rape cases continue to go up, and the victims are younger and younger," Srey Roth says.

And prostitution? It leaves an indelible stain. "In some cases, at first the women are forced," Srey Roth says, but many voluntarily continue because they are barred from their villages or they have no money or they've racked up debt at the brothel.

Many women want to leave the job, but they can't overcome the blemish it leaves on their names, says Nanda Pok, head of Women for Prosperity, an NGO that promotes women's leadership. "We live with that scar for the rest of our lives," she says. "Society punishes us even though we didn't do wrong. It's not our fault."

She says: "Ask the women, 'Why? Why are you doing this?' If you ask prostitutes where they take the money to, they give the money to their family." That takes courage. Her group questions current prostitutes as well as those who have left. "When they try to get out, society still looks down on them and condemns them." When they try to get a job, they can't. When they go home, neighbors snicker. Even when chosen freely, prostitution makes them slaves with its stigma.

So she has a message to the world: "Think about how the women of Cambodia are being used as sex objects, are being sold as animals, and it is not we who want to do that," she says. "Look at us as the women who have courage to struggle."

Yet many struggles fall flat, when it comes to helping women in trouble. Police condone the flesh trade. They make money off crimes against women. They take bribes from criminals. And the brothel owners, the people making the most money: they're elusive, never seen. "Usually we cannot arrest the real brothel owner, the real one who is behind this business," says Srey Roth at CWCC.

When arrests are made, the guilty often get off for a price, or the victims lose for lack of money. The court bows. The whole system is corrupt. "The reality is quite different from what the law says."

Moreover, the legal definition of rape is narrow. The law defines sex as penetration by the male sex organ. But sometimes, Srey Roth says, "the male doesn't use sex organs, he just uses tools." By law, that's only sexual assault. But it's clearly rape in Srey Roth's mind, as is forced marital sex, which also escapes the law. Custom precludes women from discussing unwanted sex with a husband, she says. "There is no way to inform the local authorities because people will laugh at them."

Besides the abuse they face, education — lack of it — is perhaps the greatest impediment to Cambodian women. Most women are poor, they suffer greater health problems, and they do not hold positions of authority as their counterparts in other countries do. Without education, there is little chance for these things to change, says Koy Veth, of the Khmer Women's Voice Centre.

Girls account for only 35 percent of secondary high-school students, although they make up more than half the overall population. At the university level, the number is even lower — 20 to 25 percent. Many young women drop out. Their families are too poor to send them, so they stay home and work in the fields. Or they marry young. Or their parents think they have no need to learn. "The culture is the cause of this," Koy Veth says. Society does not value men and women the same.

But that is custom, not law. Legally, girls are entitled to the same education as boys. And some women are willing to buck the status quo.

Women like Nanda Pok. "We still struggle to get women to go into higher education," she says. "The country is now developing, and the world is developing." And something else has happened: Women now head 20 percent of Cambodian homes since war has left their husbands dead, missing, disabled or simply not around. This statistic to her is a pleasant, unintended consequence.

Nanda Pok's group trained 5,000 women to run in the 2002 commune elections, and 954 were elected. It was the first commune election since the country gained independence from France. In the past, commune leaders were appointed by the government, and there were only ten females. "That's the improvement; that's the progress we see."

Taking such a stand requires fortitude of infinite measure. "In Cambodia you have to do it yourself. There is no system to help you. So you have to be brave enough to make a decision and stick to your decision," she says. "The women of Cambodia are very courageous."

Mu Sochua is another example of pure gumption. She is, when I speak with her, the minister of Women's and Veterans' Affairs. She is a member of the opposition Funcinpec Party, known for speaking up, for honoring the poor, the outcasts, the people others ignore. "Every day is a battle. I am just so much out of the norm."

I interview Mu Sochua shortly after the 2003 elections, and she knows she is most likely on her way out the door when a new coalition government is formed. But she is not finished with politics. She will run again. "The only regret I have when I leave here is who's going to be speaking for the women? I don't think the next minister, no matter who she is, is going to feel confident that way," the way Mu Sochua does.

I have a forty-five-minute slot in her busy schedule, and we sit at a big table in a quiet conference room. It starts out formal, but Mu Sochua cannot hide who she is. She cannot hide her emotions; she does not speak in political rhetoric, and she cannot stop her tears.

Her tears start when she begins to talk of the future for Cambodia's youth. She talks of her own children, three girls, ages twelve, sixteen and eighteen. Her oldest is leaving soon for college in Canada. "It's going to be a very difficult part of my life, letting her go.... But at the same time I have to say that's her life." She does not cry over her daughter's impending departure — that's not it. It's the fact that few Cambodians have the life she and her daughters do. Few Cambodian women have it so good: "the best education, the best family, the best opportunities." She thinks all of Cambodia's youth deserve this "because the country depends on them."

But she doesn't see those opportunities coming anytime soon.

Mu Sochua grew up in Phnom Penh. "My mother was half Chinese, very beautiful, very business-oriented. She didn't have more than three years of education." But she ran an airline company for her father. Her mother was the staff of her childhood, the one who held it all together, the "foundation, the soul of the family." Her influence on Mu Sochua is enduring.

But so much was ruined. Even her childhood neighborhood no longer looks like the place in her memories. "The city is no longer the same. Cambodia is just not the same," she says. "The war has destroyed it all, and that is so sad, so painful, so painful not to have the things you grew up with…. I cannot imagine putting those things back together. There is no way."

And now her tears are flowing. She says she can't fix everything for all women, all kids; that task is too big. But she tries, nonetheless. "That is why I cannot go and live anywhere else but Cambodia…. We are here to face the fact that Cambodia has changed."

As we exit the building, she points to the ministry's logo on the wall. "Do you know this?" she asks me. It shows women as precious gems. The logo used to depict men as gold and women as cloth, "and I said no way." When cloth is dropped in the mud, it is stained forever. The first thing she did as minister was change that emblem. Now it portrays women hard as rock and shining forever.

Around this time, I return to CWCC to interview three women from the shelter. I arranged these meetings with Srey Roth, but she has the day off, and when I arrive the women on staff don't know my purpose there. My translator, Sok Chea, and I wait in the lobby. I begin to think these interviews won't happen. I think what else Sok Chea and I could do. We wait forty minutes until the crisis center staff brings three women to meet us. I see them enter, and I hope it's not them, not the ones for me, because one is so very small, just a little girl.

But it's them. The staff leads me to Srey Roth's desk, and I sit at her cushioned gray swivel chair. They ask if I want to do this one by one or all at once, and I opt for one by one.

The first woman enters. Her name is Ket Seu Leun, and she is thirty-eight. She sits across the desk from me but looks at Sok Chea the whole time because he's the one talking. And it's just as well because talking to her directly — I don't know how I could keep my composure as she describes the husband who has beaten her since 1987, nearly killing her several times, threatening to kill her and their kids and anyone who helps her.

She starts systematically, as though outlining the details of an architectural plan. It's her life she maps for me. A few times, she stops to say her whole life is agony. She fingers a small pink towel; she will use it later to wipe her eyes.

"My husband, my husband likes to gamble, and my mother didn't allow him to gamble," she says. "But he still played." He played for a lot of money that he lost. When he ran out of money, he took hers. "When I didn't have money, he beat me." She used to hide cash. "My husband found money under the bed, then he left."

But he never left for good. He always returned, and he always beat her more. They divorced in 1987, for five years, but he returned again. By then she had a son, their son, and she feared for his life. "I tried to get away. I rode a bicycle carrying my son and rice, trying to leave him. But he tried to cut me off the road." Then the husband spoke and "said the sweet words," and she believed he might be better. They got back together, and he took her to a village in the far northwest. "There I met my husband's second wife."

The second wife made her a servant. "I did a lot of hard work. I brought water for the second wife and made their bed." The three had an arrangement. "When my husband was angry with his second wife, he came to me. When he had problems with me, he went to her."

After she became pregnant with her second child, her husband started beating her and their son; he "kicked him and beat him until blood flowed from his skin. And he beat me until I was unconscious…. He put me on the bed and lit a fire beneath it." But that wasn't all. "He also cut my stomach, my neck and my nose. Maybe he wanted to see if I was dead or not."

This goes on and on. She talks nearly two hours. People come and go, the phone rings, a woman brings tea. She keeps talking, and her story spills from her — her gut, her head, her arms, her legs. She begins to act out the beatings, the way her husband hit her with sticks. She starts to cry and wipes her face with the pink towel. She says she has a lot more to her story, but she doesn't know how to tell it all. "My life, it's full of suffering," she says. "He called me a crazy woman. 'Why do you run away from me?' He said he gave me an easy life. But it wasn't an easy life, it was suffering."

By the end of this interview, she is gone. She's in another world, living the memories in her head. She talks and talks and cries and cries and doesn't hear or see anything around her. Sok Chea and I look at each other. Neither of us knows how to stop her, what to say, what to do. She turns her back to the desk but keeps on going. Eventually, after much consolation, we thank her and tell her we don't want to push anymore, and Sok Chea stands. She disappears out the door, down the stairs, alone in tears. It is a sloppy ending, and I feel sick and embarrassed, but there is no graceful way to finish this.

I go to the bathroom and wipe my eyes. I breathe a few moments, then return to the room. There she is, the very tiny, very pretty girl with bright black eyes and a wide, wide smile. She greets me warmly. She's actually seventeen but looks much younger. She's here because her father wanted to sell her to another man. She tells me the story, and although she is strong, the details are utterly crushing, like an ant trying to carry a sack of rice. I go through this interview, then another one like it, absorbing their weight.

I open each interview by telling the women my purpose, this book, this chapter on women. I say I will not use their names if they prefer, but all three offer readily. There is Ket Seu Leun the first woman; and the two younger girls, Sok Ly and Som Tith Minea. The girls' stories are heroic, and they will come later in this book.

I take down these women's words, and they depart. I see them again in the lobby when I leave, as though I didn't just learn the most intimate details of their histories, as though they had told me about their sewing classes or what they ate for breakfast.

Sok Chea and I ride back to the riverside, and our morning is complete. I have all this information, all these notes, and not an inkling of what their lives, their tragedies, must be like. How do they get through? What pushes a society to this? These stories can be found everywhere in the world. Are they any different here? What do these women do right now as I write? What will they do tonight? Tomorrow? Next year?

The first woman says she wants to find an organization to help her kids; then she wants to die. I don't even get the chance to ask her things: How does she feel about her husband? What does she know about human rights? What does she think about the status of Cambodian women? She breaks before I can ask more.

But her answers lie in her story. The look on her face when she demonstrates the beatings, her husband swinging a log at her, the blood trickling down her head. The way he tries to strangle her and she begs him to think of their children. The way her children kneel before him; the way she clasps her hands and begs him to spare her life.

She need not tell me in words what I can see in her eyes.

13. Children: Born Against Odds

Six-year-old Mo Da ambles up to us one evening as we stroll along the river in Phnom Penh. He wears a bright orange vest that gleams in waning light. He trails our heels, extends his hands, opens his lips and softly begs for money.

We ask him about his head wounds. He has three: a scabby bump beside a droopy eyelid, a protrusion in the back, a fine scar across the crown of his shaved scalp.

"Where did they come from?" we ask.

"Cut head," he says.

"Who cut your head?"

He mumbles an imperceptible answer.

"Father cut head?"

"No."

"Friend cut head?"

"No."

"*Bong thom* cut head?"

"Yes."

The *bong thom* are Cambodia's "big brothers," roaming the streets, ensnaring little kids in circles of crime and violence. They force boys like Mo Da to beg; they sell girls and drugs. They take the money, beat the kids, feed them addictions. They start young, with boys and girls whose parents are dead or don't want them or can't afford to keep them anymore. The kids move to the city, looking for work, looking for food. They find a trap they can't escape.

Mo Da says his father has died, and now he's here. His *bong thom* waits behind him beside the river. We give him 200 *riel*, worth 5 cents, and watch him fade into the quickening dusk. The next day, farther upriver, Mo Da appears again — with a puffy new welt over his left eye.

Most every city corner has its Mo Da.

The humanitarian organization *Mith Samlanh*, or Friends, explains there are three types of street kids: those who work on the street day and night but return home on a regular basis; those who have run away and live alone in the city; and those who live with their families on the pavement. Of this latter group, there are an estimated 500 to 1,500 kids. Another 1,200 live alone, and 10,000 to 20,000 children work on

Phnom Penh's streets. Ten to twenty thousand: a striking range, an astonishing number, either one. But the numbers change with the wind and rain. Kids and families come and go as the seasons do. They work in villages when there is rice to be planted or harvested, crops to sell, a way to make a living. When there isn't, when their hopes shrivel in the hot, dry air, they come to Phnom Penh. And the problems rarely solve themselves. "We have an increase of about 20 percent in the number of street kids per year," says Friends coordinator Sebastien Marot.

A child born in Cambodia is born against odds. Cambodia is one of the world's worst countries for children. Ninety-seven of every 1,000 babies die before their first birthdays; 138 perish before turning five. Each year, in a country with a population of only 13 million, 66,000 Cambodian children under age five die. Fifty-six percent of all child deaths are associated with malnutrition. Fifty-one percent of kids are moderately or severely malnourished. Thirty-five percent are not immunized against polio, measles or diphtheria.

Even the luckiest kids live challenging lives. Those children might grow up in households with parents who come home each night. They might go to school. They might have friends and neighbors they trust. They might have enough food to eat, clothes to wear and people who love them. And they still melt under perpetual worries about money, the country's political future, a lack of decent health care, substandard education and the rampant crime on their streets and the cops who extort money from all the neighborhood shop owners. Their parents worry about these things. The kids themselves worry. All of these stresses make the prospect of being just a kid nearly impossible.

When Jerry and I return to Oregon in 1999, I hang a portrait on my bulletin board. It reminds me that some kids have mothers and fathers who love them immensely, and they will never end up on the street. It shows a girl, about six years old, about the age of Mo Da when we meet him. This girl stands beside her younger brother, their mother and us. They are the wife, the son and daughter of a dear friend, a photographer, Heng Sinith.

The girl is the best student in her class. She excels in every subject and makes Sinith gleefully proud. One day, he comes to the *Daily* and boasts of a ceremony he must attend in her honor. He hopes to buy her a gift, but he's worried about the money. He's always worried about money. He makes $10 for each photo that runs in the paper, and he struggles to pay his bills. He hopes his daughter will study in America someday, but he wonders how. He wishes that for himself, too—to become a better photographer, to improve his English. He loves his country; he hates its problems. He hates the way his country embarrasses him. He wants to learn; he wants to grow; he wants his son and daughter to get good jobs so Cambodia will change.

And each time we return to Cambodia, he says the same things, like a record spun round and round. And each time we see him, he is a bit more sullen about his country because these changes haven't come at all. His life and work improve steadily, but he never has enough money to relax. By 2003, he has a new job for a wire service, but he still worries about his country and his future.

That summer, Sinith picks us up in his car and takes us to retrieve his son from class. We pass his daughter's school around the corner, and he mentions she was hit by a *moto* while crossing the street just a few days before. We are horrified. What happened?

She was crossing from one school to another, between her English school and her primary school. The driver didn't stop. He knocked her to the ground; he knocked her unconscious for fifteen minutes. She'll be OK, Sinith says, but she is small, and it was a close call, and the driver will never be punished; he won't even be found. "Because no one cares," he says with the exasperation we know well in his voice.

I remember one time when we met with Sinith and asked how his wife and kids were doing. As usual, he answered with exhaustion. "Now, I am not so close to them." He hasn't the time. He spends it all at work, for the whole family's benefit, pedaling through a sea of sand. If he stops for a moment to rest, the family stumbles.

These are the things he hates so much about his country, the things that make him far from proud. And when he rants about the status quo, he vents an anger riled on behalf of his son and daughter.

Yet Sinith's son and daughter live an opulent life compared with tens of thousands of others. Many of the unluckiest Cambodian kids are orphans.

But before we look at the problem of orphans, we must study the concept. What makes an orphan? For many, it's simple: An orphan is a child whose parents are dead. A tight, neat definition. But how, then, do we have American women facing federal charges for allegedly making orphans out of children born to poor Cambodian mothers and sending those babies to couples overseas? And how do we get mothers selling their children for $20, $50 or $100 to Cambodian adoption brokers because they believe their babies will have better lives in another person's hands? And what of the children who are trafficked to Thailand, forever cut from their families, forever wondering what happened to their parents? Or the girls plucked from the street at eight years old, put in a brothel, sold to sex tourists and never reunited with family and friends? Or the boy who runs away because his father beats him and steals his money? Or the child who leaves home because the father married another woman and the new wife had a child and neither parent likes the father's firstborn?

It is no easy task to define an orphan in Cambodia. And when rigid Western concepts are applied to quagmires like this, we're left with a sticky legal mess.

Many loving couples abroad see the suffering of Cambodian kids, and they want to take them away. They want to give them new homes, comfortable lives, fresh hope. There are people to help these couples, adoption brokers who arrange the deals. The brokers tackle the red tape and charge a fee. That fee often ranges between $12,000 and $20,000 for their services. The parents sign the papers, sign the checks and believe they are doing a good deed.

For several years, wire reports from Cambodia note mothers selling their kids for as little as $12 to people who shuffle the children through a system that eventually ends with the child living in a new home abroad. The United States suspends adoptions from Cambodia in December 2001, in light of such concerns. In the next two years, France and the Netherlands follow suit. This dismays many prospective parents overseas. They see it as "a cruel interruption of the journey to parenthood," according to the *Boston Globe*. They write op-ed pieces and converse in Internet chat rooms about the death sentences being handed to Cambodian kids. "Key people in the U.S. government think it's better for a child to die in Cambodia than be raised in Akron," writes John Ringo in a *New York Post* column. "They condemn the kids to a life that is short, brutal and hellish. To be whores in Phnom Penh brothels. To be child-soldier minesweepers for the Khmer Rouge. To die in a thousand miserable ways." (Never mind that the Khmer Rouge are defunct, and have been for four years, by the time this column appears.) These kids are, Ringo concludes, "better dead than American," in the eyes of U.S. lawmakers.

Ringo's fury is blatant. But many couples are less enraged and more enamored of the child they have in mind. Amid this whole fiasco, Judy, the woman in Wisconsin for whom I wrote an essay about Cambodia, waits for her child. She is caught in the middle, as are dozens of other Americans. Her adoption was nearly settled in December 2001 when the U.S. government suspended adoptions. "We were strongly encouraged by the U.S. government to choose a different country," she later tells me through email. But she couldn't do that, not in her heart. "Once we chose Cambodia as the adoption country, we really felt that at that moment there was a particular child meant for us," she says. "Had we turned our backs on the Cambodian program, we would have spent the rest of our lives wondering what had happened to the girl who would have been matched to us."

The outcome of her story will come later in this book, but in the meantime, the adoption scandal grows worse. Critics call the system "a lucrative business" that encourages trafficking. According to a 2003 study by the Netherlands embassy in Bangkok, most of the money Westerners pay in adoption fees is unaccounted for and untraceable. "The biggest chunk" is thought to go to adoption facilitators, not ministry officials or orphanages. Only 22 percent of Cambodian children are registered at birth yet, "amazingly" all kids up for adoption have birth certificates, the report points out.

In response to this whole adoption mess, UNICEF proposes a law for Cambodia that recommends international adoption as a last resort. The message is clear: First, try foster homes, extended families, neighbors, friends. Adopt the kids locally. Don't look outside the country unless it's the only option. This law would require that international adoption agencies be accredited, and that those agencies be non-profit.

This proposal is released just a few weeks before the 2003 elections. Eight months later, the government remains in a stalemate, and there can be no new legislation on anything until a coalition government is formed.

And then: More stories of baby selling and baby buying brew. Lauryn Galindo is famous for her humanitarian work and now infamous for her alleged crimes. She and her sister, Lynn Devin of Seattle International Adoptions Inc., have arranged hundreds of adoptions, even high-profile adoptions for people such as Angelina Jolie. Then, in December 2003, a U.S. government investigation named "Operation Broken Heart" alleges many things: That the sisters have falsified documents, claiming children have no parents when in fact they do; they have paid mothers small fees to relinquish their babies; they have made a business of expediting adoptions and misleading immigration authorities so as to secure visas for the children. These accusations come from findings by the U.S. Bureau of Immigration and Customs Enforcement and the Internal Revenue Service's Criminal Investigation Division. That month, Devin pleads guilty to visa fraud and money laundering. The next month, Galindo turns herself in to federal agents. Lauryn Galindo is sentenced in late November 2004 to 18 months in prison and ordered to perform 300 hours of community service, forfeit her $1.4 million home and pay more than $60,000 to couples who used her adoption agency.

When I ask Judy what she thinks of the whole situation, she acknowledges severe problems. But stopping all adoptions, she says, is not the answer. "The children of Cambodia deserve to have families in which to place their love and trust forever. It would be a sad, sad turn of events if the suspension is never lifted. There are many U.S. families that want to adopt, and the orphanages in Cambodia are full. Rather than punish both of those sides, the governments need to work harder at finding adoption procedures that screen out the fraud and ensure the children that are adopted are truly orphans."

What happens in a Cambodian orphanage? They are all different. Some sparkle, others stink. Some are new, some are old. Some feed and clothe and treat the children well; others provide the barest of care. Some function on the whims of rich donors or the fiscal schedules of foreign governments or the threadbare strings of the owner's fortune. Some are full of babies waiting for adoption; others teem with older kids who will never leave their homeland.

Jerry and I first visit the Chea Sim Orphanage in Siem Reap in 2002, just a few months after American adoptions are banned. We walk right in, no questions asked. We come here because a friend, a medical staffer at a local hospital, tells us the orphanage hangs its kids in nets strung from the ceiling, tied up and out of the way. He is appalled.

And it's true.

There they are, a dozen toddlers swinging from the rafters, dangling a few feet off the ground in hammocks strung up like fishnets. Some sleep, some suck bottles, some squirm with the hammock taut against their skin. They spend several hours at a time like this. It's an easy way for the workers to keep track of the kids. It's a sure way for the children's minds to dull and their bodies to not properly develop.

There are no diapers; their bottoms hang open. Sometimes they piddle on the floor. When that happens, sometimes staff workers clean up the mess, sometimes they don't. One child urinates, a worker arrives with mop in hand, then a shaggy white dog plops where the piddle was. A while later, another boy pees, and a new puddle forms on the floor. His net is wet, his clothes are soaked, and it's all plastered to his body.

One young boy, a year and a half old, barely fits his net. He watches us, fidgeting and staring. Another child, a year old, lifts his chin up to the net's edge and smiles. Some nets are torn and stitched back together with plastic twine. A mangy, one-eyed dog naps nearby.

The woman who runs this orphanage is Thou Rem. She is plump; she looks tired, but she smiles a lot; our friend has told us this about her. She is pleasant to us, if ultimately out of her depth in fiscal and social responsibility. We chat with her and

Bun Chah, age one, peers out from his hammock at the Chea Sim Orphanage. There are about 55 small children and so few caretakers that the infants are kept out of harm's way hanging like this. In 2002, an international scandal halted all adoptions between Cambodia and the United States, France, and many other Western countries. It was found that many so-called orphans had been taken from unwitting parents by unscrupulous adoption brokers and sold to foreign parents for exorbitant fees. Siem Reap, 2002.

Ryla, a twenty-seven-year-old man who grew up in this orphanage. He doesn't have a home of his own now, so he stays here when he needs to.

Thou Rem tells us there are fifty-five kids here. I ask about adoptions, and she says no, the children are not for sale — an odd answer, I think. There are no more adoptions. That stopped when the visa trouble started. "I just take care of all the kids so when they grow up they will take care of me when I'm old," she says.

Ryla explains, "It's very difficult to take a baby to another country." But he has seen, in his years here, about twenty kids go away. He shows me their pictures on the wall. There's a girl bundled in a snowsuit, and alternately on a beach, somewhere in the United States. She was adopted five years ago. But the kids here today will stay.

I enter a playroom, and a young girl with cropped hair immediately pulls my hand. She wants me to help her and a group of boys assemble a colorful jigsaw puzzle, a map of the world, each country and its wild animals. Tigers and elephants and monkeys and creatures they know from legends.

The kids sit on a gritty floor, full of broken balloons, used straws, milk cartons, paper scraps. The girl's name is Kun Thy; she's ten. She's been here three months, since her mother died. When I ask why, she says, "I don't know." She says she goes to school every day at 10:30, although it's eleven now and she's here, playing this puzzle. She says she likes it here, but she wants a new mom and dad.

One young boy has a sore on his head and scabs across his body. When he peels off his clothes in preparation for a bath, he reveals a sadly distended stomach. He has ant bites, the workers say. Thou Rem kisses the child's head, full of more scabs. Most kids here have skin diseases. They cling to us as we shuffle through, gripping our shirts and shorts and legs, silently shadowing us.

It's lunchtime now, and most of the toddlers are out of their nets, waiting to be spoon-fed rice porridge. Older kids eat rice and bitter-melon soup. Ryla invites me to sit with them on the floor while they eat. He says he moved here many years ago with two younger brothers. His parents were shot with a "big gun."

"I don't know why because I was very young." Ryla says to me, "Ask me anything you want." So I ask him why children come here.

"Sometimes the families are very poor and sometimes the children's parents died so they come here."

Are most parents dead?

"Yes."

But some are still alive and too poor to care for their kids?

"Yes. But ... I don't know how to say ... sometimes very poor ... it's the same, it's the same."

I reiterate my question. Do you mean that kids come here for two reasons: either their parents have died or their parents cannot afford to care for them?

"Yeah, yeah. Thank you, because I don't know how to say in English."

When lunch is over, the kids nap. The younger ones go to their nets or cribs. Older kids line the walls, sleeping in the kitchen like sardines on the floor. A radio blares. The workers nap too, and a baby sucks on a sleeping woman's breast. Jerry and I say goodbye and exit, simple as that, as easy as our entrance. We have seen two hours of their world.

We return to the orphanage the following year. The youngest still hang in nets, but they are different kids. Some of the babies have left, some even to the United States. It's possible now, with the right documents, Thou Rem says. The U.S. government is allowing some adoptions again.

A one-year-old boy named Sras has diarrhea, and grayish feces press through his hammock like cranberries through a sieve. It covers his lower body and flip-flops. Thou Rem unties the net from its ceiling hold and carries Sras to the kitchen, like a sack of potatoes. She plops him on the floor, peeling off the net. She removes his shirt and douses his rump with water from the kitchen pump. Then she drenches his body and shampoos his head. He gets clean clothes. She carries him back to the other room, leaving the soiled net behind near the lunch dishes.

Several months later when an Italian aid worker sees a photo Jerry took of Sras and his bath, she exclaims over the child's large head, hands and feet compared to the rest of his body. She says it's a sign of a baby who rarely moves, plays or exercises.

The older children in the orphanage take turns pushing a mop across the floor, seemingly cleaning the morning's messes but accomplishing little beyond the transfer of dirt from one spot to another. Everyone has wet, sticky, grimy feet. The tiles beneath these nets are stained — blemishes that weren't here a year ago — from a ceaseless cycle of expulsions. To the eye, nothing here has improved in a year.

We stay only a short time; Thou Rem is not nearly as friendly as the year before. After leaving the orphanage, we walk to a Japanese restaurant on the river. It's a quaint spot with bookshelves and jazz music, mood lighting and thick wooden barstools, a spotless bathroom and lemon-honey shakes that aren't too sweet. Outside is a riverfront as decrepit as I first remember, with broken sidewalk tiles and garbage fires and urine stains. In the past five years, these sidewalks have been built anew, then left to rot and crumble and soak the stains of dogs and humans and cows. Jerry wonders whether there is hope for this country to change in another five years, or even twenty.

We have many discussions like this one after days like these. What to do? I have no idea anymore. I wonder, how can I conclude a book that way?

It is August 2001. It is the rainy season, when the Mekong swells, when the river swallows homes and yards, gardens and fields, as it does every year. When rice grows luminescent in thick wet paddies; when villages float and people move on water where, before, there had been land.

Jerry and I are in Kratie, a small town, ninety miles upriver from Phnom Penh. We have come to do a story on Cambodia's endangered Irrawaddy dolphins, sleek shy things that once danced through these waters, hundreds at a time. Now only small pools of these snub-nosed creatures remain. But they still show their noses nearby and swoosh around fishermen's boats.

We sit one afternoon in the doorway of a Chinese restaurant, drinking Angkor beer and eating salted peanuts. We gaze onto the sidewalk, watching the world scatter as rain comes, watching sheets unfurl from an endless bolt of wet fabric. Street kids gather, and Jerry offers candy. One boy bawls and snorts and moans. What's wrong with him? I ask, and Jerry responds with the obvious, "Well, he's homeless, he has no food, he's wet and his knee's all fucked up."

Cheth has no shoes, no parents, no hair on his head and a bloody, festering knee. He has a sister named Khet; we will later learn they live in a field. He is ten, she is twelve. Her hair is wild and stringy. She bandages Cheth's owie, but he hugs his knee and cries, "I want to go home."

We take him to the hospital. We coax the boy onto a *moto*, and he looks at us with wide eyes. The seat is wet. He is scared. He looks at Khet, and we tell them she can come, too. The kids ride on one *moto*, we take another, motoring through Kratie's flooded terrain.

It's 6:30 P.M., and we enter an empty hallway. Where is everyone? This is the provincial hospital, the only one, but it's eerily quiet. We see a man with a white coat and nametag clipped to his breast pocket. He's not a doctor. There is no doctor in sight. The man in the coat tells us to go right, to another building with a red cross on the wall. We do, and the kids follow with ginger steps behind us.

There are patients on slat beds with metal frames, no mattresses, only the rattan mats they bring from home. It is customary in Cambodia for families to nurse their own sick, at home or at the hospital. Blankets, toiletries, food — they come from home. The hospital provides only a bare bed frame upon which to lay one's mat and the patient's weary body. That bed becomes a camping ground, with entire families huddled together, fanning and feeding and tending the sick one. But of course, there are always patients alone — no one to help, no food to eat, no fan to deter the pestering flies.

The patients tell us the doctor has gone to eat dinner, maybe he'll return at 7. We sit on an empty bed, and Cheth hops aboard. Khet stands in the doorway, shaking her head. The adults ask questions: Where did the kids come from? What do they do? The kids are scared, they tell us. We know.

It grows dark, and we wait. Evening evolves to night. Finally, the doctor arrives, and we explain the situation. He tells us Cheth needs to stay, perhaps five days. We tell him Cheth has no family, no home. The doctor says: Hmm, that is difficult. And who will pay for the treatment? He gets the point across that medicine is not free. Payment is always a problem in these cases of poor people with no homes, no families, no means.

Jerry and I look at each other and exchange a few sentences, wondering how much the bill could possibly be. We tell the doctor: We will pay.

The doctor says it will not be cheap, maybe 3,000 *riel*, 75 cents.

No problem, we say.

A nurse dons stark clean gloves and douses Cheth's knee with alcohol from a plastic bottle. Then he pours iodine solution on the knee. The russet liquid stains his wounds. Next, the nurse pads pure-white gauze on open flesh. Cheth winces all the way, but never says much. Pigs squeal outside, in the hospital yard. We ask how this happened, and the nurse surmises Cheth has bug bites, scratched to infection.

When the cleaning is done and his knee is bandaged, the doctor tells Cheth he must return the next day, to the clinic across the street. We promise to help get him there. The doctor writes a prescription, and we head through the aisles, Cheth hop-

Cheth, ten, leaves the local hospital through a dirty puddle left by a monsoon storm. It took $1.75 to treat his infected insect wounds, which had bled and bothered his knee for months. Cheth and his older sister and brother were orphaned six years earlier and have begged in town ever since. Kratie, 2001.

ping on his newly wrapped leg. We reach the door and it's wet outside, still drizzling. Jerry plops the boy onto his shoulder, carrying him across the flooded way.

We find a man in a closet of drugs, pouring pills into a bottle. I pay the 3,000 *riel* and hand the medicine to sister Khet, to distribute appropriately, one pill in the morning, one in the evening, and only to Cheth — no one else. She nods in quiet agreement.

Then we take them to the market, in the center of town, where they ask to go. They say they are not hungry. They both look shell-shocked. We tell them to find us the next day. But we wonder: Does our message get through? What's in their minds? What is it like to be scared, with a hurt knee, no food, no money, no parents, no bed, and two foreigners who drag you to the hospital? So many questions — it's that way in Cambodia. So many questions are never answered, only imagined.

The next morning, hot sun steams the town. We set out to find our friends. We pass a man roasting coffee beans until they smoke and burn. We pass teak homes on stilts as we walk toward the low tones of monks chanting midday prayers. We turn toward a field where cows graze and tin roofs flank the far side. Cheth is relieving himself in the weeds when he spots us, then he and Khet and all their friends come dashing. We follow them toward bleachers cast in concrete, stairs ending in sludge mixed with plastic bags and rot. We climb steps to a crowd of homeless squatters, living in the stands of this abandoned athletic field, surrounded by all they own: a pet monkey chained in the corner, some clothes, some *krama* scarves, rattan mats, rice pots, a few quilts, some stuff — but not much. Khet hurdles the bleachers with pills in hand. She has given Cheth two, precisely as told.

One young man speaks English. We tell him we want to take Cheth to the doctor; he asks when we will return, will we return? The adults want to know. "They worry about the children," he says. They think we'll steal the kids and sell them; we insist we will not.

Everyone has heard these rumors of baby-stealing and child trafficking; in the next two years, we will know the stories are rooted in truth.

We find *motos* and head across town, just as the rain arrives with a vengeance. We reach the clinic, but it's noon, that hour when all of Southeast Asia bobs to sleep. We sit outside and two teenaged girls ask questions. Cheth remains silent, but Khet tells them she and Cheth are brother and sister. They have no parents. They come from a town called Chhlong. She says their parents died ten days ago, which doesn't seem right, but that's what she says. Cheth naps briefly while she talks. Then he wakes and counts his sores, stopping at eleven.

A man comes along and tells us the doctor works no more today, he "relaxes" until tomorrow. So we aim for the hospital again, hoping someone can help. The kids walk barefoot through the sodden streets and climb the hospital fence before we have a chance to open the gate. They're so used to doing it — life — the hard way.

Inside, we meet a nurse wearing a white smock and hat, shiny gold bangles and high-heeled glittery sandals. She leads us to the same room we visited the previous night. Another nurse wakes from a nap, dresses and starts the same procedure. I notice this time, we are surrounded by posters with wide-ranging messages: Eat well, breast-feed your baby, cover your water pot, wear a condom, go to the doctor.

It rains again, and birds fly through the room. Pigs, chickens and dogs galumph through the mud, while patients trundle outside to shower in the downpour.

When the nurse is done, Jerry pays, and we wait for the rain to stop. We slush through puddles at the gate. We cross the street, wait for *motos*, hoist Cheth on the seat and return again to the market. The streets have sunk beneath the rain. We offer them lunch, and along the walk, Cheth steps in cow dung with his naked foot.

At the restaurant, we order pork fried rice, pickled vegetables and tea. The kids gobble, inhaling the food like little vacuum cleaners, and Cheth serves himself seconds. He doesn't quite eat the plate. The bill comes to 10,000 *riel*, about $2.50. So much! Cheth exclaims.

Then we take the kids "home."

Later that evening, we head to the riverfront and find the kids there. We have changed and cleaned, but the kids have not. Cheth wears his bandage, a little damp, a little soiled, but still clinging to his spindly leg.

Nine months later, Jerry and I return to Kratie. I spot a gaggle of ragged kids, four youngsters and two toddlers in tow, near the riverfront *tuk-a-luk* stands. We go searching for familiar faces. I don't recognize Khet immediately, but I ask a girl her name and whether she knows Cheth. She knows. She knows immediately: "I'm Khet! You took our picture last year!" she says. She points to Cheth, taller and thinner now, with new scars on the left side of his forehead and the right side of his jaw — a bike accident, he tells us. He smiles, and all the kids around us know we are the foreigners who took Cheth to the doctor. He lifts his pantleg and reveals a fully healed knee.

The looks of fear are gone. The kids see us with familiarity. Khet points proudly to her wild hair cut short, thick bangs she designed with her own scissors to make herself pretty, she says. We ask if they're hungry, and all six kids categorically nod yes. We buy each child a boiled egg from a nearby stall. The woman plucks them from a steaming pot and plops them into separate plastic bags. One boy thanks us in English; then they all thank us and transform before our eyes: rambunctious hunters melting into innocent kids. They grow quiet after eating their eggs, hunger pangs tempered with a nosh. They thank us again and leave us for the night.

So we have found them, but what comes next? What do we do tomorrow? What do we do with six hungry kids? What do we do with Cheth and Khet? We didn't think about that. We thought: Let's look for them and see their lives after nine months, a full gestation period. We didn't think: What next?

The next afternoon, Jerry and I stroll to the bleachers where men laze in hammocks. We go from shanty to shanty, asking about Cheth and Khet, and the adults keep pointing to the fields behind the stadium, through a gate and into a maze of squalid huts. A drunken (or mentally ill) man leads us down a path into that maze, as the kids gallop toward us. Cheth smiles big today, and Khet invites us to their home.

The one-room shack stands on stilts about two and a half feet high, over chickens and weeds. Cardboard beer boxes and old pants line walls of thatch, plugging up holes bigger than Cheth is. We find they have an older brother, Mao, who sleeps on the floor. He is eighteen and has no job, but that is not unusual, especially not here.

Khet invites us inside, and we squash near the door. It stinks of unbathed humans. The hut is about eight feet wide and eight feet long, full of dirty clothes, mosquito nets, two mats, a charcoal grill, a blackened wok, two cucumbers on the floor, a pot of rice, a plastic mirror and matching comb and a pack of Crown cigarettes. But they insist neither Cheth nor Mao smokes.

Khet grabs the mirror, combs her hair and smiles. We ask about Cheth's scars, and they show us a lump on his left leg, another injury that we didn't know he had. They don't know what it is, but he's had it ten years. It hurts and makes him limp.

We ask about their parents, and they say they were sick before they died. It's unclear precisely when that was. The family comes from a village across the river, and they point to the southwest.

The three siblings say they have never gone to school. Have we? We tell them yes, for many years, and that we finished long ago.

Jerry takes pictures. He tells the threesome to gather outside, but soon there are shrieks of excitement as flocks of kids appear. They all crave attention. They love to touch. They grab our legs and arms, tug our shorts. There's a boy with a scaly scab across his upper mouth. There's a toddler with red sores in circles and curlycues across his arms and legs. We can buy them each a boiled egg, we can leave a few thousand *riel*. But there is no cure for this deprivation that runs so deep, so far.

When we start to leave, Cheth, Khet and a friend named Ping follow. They show us the way to market, along dirt paths that skirt the backsides of neighborhoods. The kids leap over muddy patches, making games of their trek.

In town, they head into a dingy building, with two TVs and six rows of small chairs facing the shows: Khmer music videos on one, and a *National Geographic* special on baseball. Among the chairs are small tables with men drinking tea from tiny cups. The beggar kids take the floor. Cheth plays with a chunk of Styrofoam he has found on the street, tearing it to pieces in loud cracks. He pounds it with his elbows and gnaws with his teeth. The object occupies his mind for quite some time. Then, apropos of nothing but her wishes, Khet leaves. Cheth looks about, gathers his pieces and follows. We're next, with Ping trailing behind.

We meander through the market, where the kids stop at the electronics stalls, listening to raucous music and watching boxing on TV. We mention food again and suddenly they've lost all shyness. Yes, they want to eat. A sullen woman behind a long metallic counter seems dazed when we ask for three plates of food. She looks around.

"Do you have money?" she asks the kids.

"They buy," Khet says, nodding to us.

The woman scoops up three small plates of rice, topped with a dollop of green beans and chicken. Jerry tells her not to be stingy. The kids fill their mouths; the woman pours glasses of tea. The kids grab pieces of meat and chomp to the bone. They take beans and sauce and eat it all. We ask for more: beef curry with boiled eggs and bamboo shoots in a red sauce. They sup and slurp, and they talk with mouths open, hurling rice into hungry jaws. Khet and Cheth finish, and Ping takes the last piece of meat. He's not modest. He says his mother's dead and his father is sick. He takes food when he can get it.

A woman at a nearby stall watches the scene. I ask if she knows them, and she says yes. "If they beg, and they have money, they eat. But if they don't have money, they don't."

We pay the 3,500 *riel*, about 87 cents, and Khet whispers something to us—but she's coy. She tells Cheth to tell us. We're standing by a shoe stall. They want shoes. OK, we say. They dig through flip-flops, trying on for size. Cheth chooses red, Ping chooses green, but Khet has her eye on something else: high-heeled tan canvas with embroidered little flowers. They're all happy, and we pay the $2 for three pairs of shoes. We wander through the market some more, buy them a thick bar of soap and tell them to wash before eating. Then Jerry drops off a roll of film to be developed.

The photos are ready that evening, and we take them to the riverfront, with good intentions. I hand Khet the Konika pack, each picture bound in a plastic sleeve. There is instant mayhem. Screaming, crying, flailing arms, more crying, baby falling, barking, bedlam. We tell them not to fight, but the kids grab and cheer. Each child wants a photo of his or her own, to hold, to keep. "Listen, listen, listen!" Jerry instructs. You must be careful. Don't hit, don't shove. The photos can't get wet. Water will break them. They nod in understanding, then continue with their fracas. Jerry has tried hard to take individual shots of each child, but they always want to pose together in a group. Now, they all want their own photos.

And soon we're bombarded: The other kids want shoes too. One child has no shirt, only overalls and, Oh how nice a shirt would be! They want photos; they want food; they want money; they want love. We tell them we'll do what we can but in truth, we have no idea what to do now. We exit the scene at an opportune moment, when no one notices amid the screeching and hollering.

I do not think it will be my last chat with them before leaving Kratie, but it is. Things happen that way. The rain has its way with Kratie, and life scatters for a few hours. When it calms to a drizzle, we head out in a quickening dusk, searching the *tuk-a-luk* stands and the nighttime food market. I see a boy, shirtless, with dark pants. I see him from behind, browsing the food stalls, heading toward the path that leads "home." I follow quickly, never catching up. But I know it isn't him. This child wears black sandals, not new red flip-flops.

And that's it. No more Cheth or Khet or Ping or crying babies. I hunt for small dark shadows on dim streets—but theirs aren't there.

We must return to Phnom Penh by boat early the next morning. Jerry and I agree that next time we should think more about how to approach these situations, how to help people in need. I continue to think about them, long after we've left Kratie. Will they trust us? Will they trust foreigners? Have we done more harm than good? I feel as though we've failed.

But I don't know what could succeed.

Cambodian children must be saved, writes Laurence Gray in 2000. He directs Cambodia's child protection programs for the humanitarian group World Vision, and he writes that sex slavery is one of the biggest threats to Cambodian kids today. "When developing countries like Thailand make progress in reducing sex tourism, opportunistic men simply travel to poorer, less-developed neighbors. Cambodia is ripe for such exploitation." He estimates a third of the country's sex workers are children. "Their 'careers' on the streets of Phnom Penh will lead from HIV infection to AIDS to premature death."

The next year, The Future Group, a Canadian organization that scrutinizes international issues, reports that Cambodia, a country of 13 million, has 80,000 to 100,000 sex slaves and prostitutes. A third of Phnom Penh's sex slaves are children and 4,000 boys are the victims of foreign pedophiles, according to the group. The report also notes that prostitution is an industry worth $500 million a year. By comparison, the Cambodian government's total expenditures in 2001 came to $544 million.

These are staggering numbers, and critics question their veracity. But what no one seems to deny is that depravity exists on Cambodia's streets. It is indisputable. And it often involves children.

Cambodia starts to crack down on the child sex industry in 2003. The government begins to deport foreign pedophiles. This comes with help from the U.S. government. A new law allows Americans charged with sexually molesting children overseas to face trial in U.S. federal court. The first person ever charged under this law is Michael Lewis Clark, a Seattle resident deported from Cambodia in September 2003 for alleged illegal sexual conduct with young boys. Two months later: another Seattle man deported, more accusations of illegal sex with boys. In March 2004, Clark pleads guilty in the United States to having sexual contact with boys in Cambodia. He faces up to thirty years in prison and a $250,000 fine.

It's a crusade against pedophiles. "How can we turn away?" then–U.S. Secretary of State Colin Powell tells an NBC *Dateline* reporter. He says a "moral nation" such as the United States is duty-bound to fight pedophilia. "We wouldn't be living up to our values if we didn't do something about it." These comments come in a *Dateline* episode examining the infamous village of Svay Pak, just outside Phnom Penh, where $600 buys a virgin for three days, where girls as young as eight are up for sale and where young teenaged boys handle the transactions, giving their mothers a slice of the profit.

The U.S. State Department is giving World Vision $500,000 to fight these crimes in Thailand, Costa Rica and Cambodia. The group is issuing warnings on Internet websites that advertise child sex tourism, telling travelers they can be arrested for exploiting a minor. World Vision calls these sorts of potential criminals "situational offenders," people who are not necessarily born as pedophiles but perhaps swayed when conditions are right.

And perhaps a little pop-up message will deter a man from harming a child. That is good. But what of the culture that remains? What of the curiosity that prompted the man to look at the website in the first place? What of the madams who run child brothels? And the pimps who broker the deals? And the police who happily extort money from all of them? And the children who are ensnared? Unfortunately, for those children, the answer is simple: They are commodities; they are chattel. They are things to be bought and sold. They are not treated as human.

They are not treated as children deserve to be.

Life on Cambodia's streets is not only dangerous, it's deadly. It's a fight to find food and make money. It's a battle to keep the body whole. Jerry and I meet many street kids through the years. Some work, some beg, some have families, some answer to the *bong thom.*

We meet a boy in 1998 named Cheth — another Cheth, in Phnom Penh. He is barefoot and wears a dark blue shirt. He hops on his right leg with his left foot bound in white and dangling. He's eleven years old, and he's safe in a shelter for street kids now, after a sordid history. He has no parents, no means to survive. He was alone in the streets. His foot was scrunched in a train ride at an amusement park, and the injury opened doors. For months after the accident, Cheth and a friend worked the New Market, *Psar Thmei,* begging for handouts, using his mangled foot as bait. They dragged the gangrenous, bulbous appendage around town. It grew worse, and Cheth refused help. After all, a foot chopped off could garner more money, they surmised.

But when we meet Cheth, he is staying in a shelter. He's fed; he's rested; he's bandaged. A doctor visits him every day. He likes his new home, the regular meals, the others kids with whom he can play. His street friend stops by now and then, but Cheth stays behind. He says he wants to go to school and learn to become a mechanic. He says he wants to keep the foot and doctors say it will heal.

Hong Vicheth is a shoeshine boy in Phnom Penh. He is seventeen. He comes from Kompong Cham, and he has only one full leg. The other, he lost in an accident when he was eight. He has lived in Phnom Penh for several years. "I don't have a family. They died." He leans against a pole on the street. "My father was drunk, and he got in a car accident. My mother got an illness. They died when I was young."

We talk in front of a popular tourist restaurant, where foreigners eat pizza and drink beer. "I sleep here on the sidewalk," anywhere along this stretch of pavement. He moves as he must.

"Before I cleaned shoes, I begged for money." He saved his earnings until he had enough to buy a brush, some polish and a bag. With those tools, he earns about 10,000 *riel* a day, about $2.50. "I use it to buy food. But sometimes when I don't have money, I ask the foreigners here. Sometimes they scold me."

I ask if he's ever gone to the Friends shelter, and he says he has, but there's a problem. "The bigger kids fight me, so I cannot stay there. It's always like that. When the staff goes home, the bigger people always fight the smaller kids. It happens on the street, too." He doesn't feel safe here. "I stay in a dangerous place." The ground is divided; different gangs claim different turf.

Does he have friends? He points to the handful of kids around him. They're all friends, from children who are nearly adults down to youngsters barely reaching my knees. "I also have enemies," he says.

Someone hands him a papaya in a bag, and he slurps the juicy fruit. "I don't go to school now." For a couple years, he studied at Friends. But he quit when he left the shelter, and he doesn't want to return. "I forgot how to read."

What does he want in the future? He hasn't thought that through.

Nop Penh is twelve, and his job is to be pushed around Phnom Penh in a wheelchair by his sister. He says the work is "*tourmada.*" It's normal. *C'est la vie.* He has done this for two years now. His arms and legs never developed properly; his body is little more than a torso and head, and these disabilities fetch him sympathy money. His body feeds his family.

But it's not what Penh wants to be doing. "I really want to go to school. I want to study English. I want to be a translator." Yet he has never attended class.

Neither has his sister, Pou, who is thirteen. "I don't want to follow my brother. The job I want is to be a waitress in any of these restaurants around here," she waves at the multitude of tourist havens along the riverfront.

That is unlikely to happen. Their father, Vann, explains the family situation. He has ten kids and seven grandchildren. They come from Kompong Speu Province. "I'm a farmer. We always come and go, come and go, every year." When he can't make money in his fields, he brings the kids to Phnom Penh. "We live in front of the Royal Palace." They sleep on the ground at a small pagoda.

Vann says five of his daughters are married, and to each one he has given a field. "So now I have no fields." He visits them each month, and they are likewise poor. "They can only feed their families." So he returns to Phnom Penh, to the streets where he watches his daughter pushing his son, to the foreigners who occasionally stoop to Penh's level, stuffing a few *riel* between his stumped arms.

"I don't want to do this," Vann says. "I wish I did not have to do this."

Nonetheless, we also watch Vann from our balcony perch, day after day, as he plays cards among the homeless crowd on the street below. It's obvious where his money comes from. It's obvious where Penh's and Pou's labor goes.

Sovann is our paper boy. He's eleven years old, and we've known him for a few years. He lives with his family near a Phnom Penh market, and every morning he hits the streets with the English-language papers, which he gets from his grandfather. "My grandfather takes *The Cambodia Daily* to the shops, and then he brings some to me."

When we live in Phnom Penh during the summer of 2003, Jerry lowers a rope from our third-floor balcony down to the street. It has a little loop at the end, wrapped around 1,500 *riel*, about 38 cents. Sovann takes the rope, grabs the money and inserts our morning paper. Then Jerry brings it on up. People on the street think it's a fantastic arrangement, and they always stop to watch.

Sovann earns about a dollar a day. "Some I use for school, and some I share with my mother," he says. "I buy books and a school bag and shoes." His father is a *moto* driver, his mother is a housewife, and his job supplements the family income.

On some mornings we don't see Sovann if we're not to our balcony by 7:30. He goes to public school those mornings, so he sells his papers early, goes to class, then returns to the street in the afternoon. On these days we must wait for Sovann's return to buy our paper or else purchase a second copy because Sovann grows deeply sullen when we buy one from another seller. Such is the nature of a Cambodian business relationship.

Sovann can't yet read the papers he sells, but he would like to. "The newspaper can show me how to read and talk, and how to do many things."

In late afternoon, Sovann heads to English class, a lesson at a private school. It costs $6 a month, and he pays the bill himself. "I decided to go there to get good knowledge."

Pros is fourteen. He lives on the street near the Lotus Market in Siem Reap, where foreigners go to buy chocolate and beer and newspapers printed in English and French. He comes from a village named Angkor, next to the Preah Khan ruins. But he's lived here on the street for six years "because I was angry with my parents." Years ago he worked at the temple, peddling things, until one day a foreigner in a car hit him on the roadside, injuring his head and arm. "The car owner gave me $400, but my father took the money for drinking or gambling." So he left home.

"My parents know I'm here," Pros says, and sometimes his mother comes to visit. "Two or three times she took me home, but I still came back here. My father wanted to fight me."

He sleeps among other boys and girls, a few families and several lone veterans who lay their mats on shit-stained sidewalks in the heart of the city's colonial old town. "The people around here help me and take care of me," Pros says. "Sleeping at home is better, but I'm angry with my father. I ask customers for money — they give me food and money, sometimes $1 or $2."

With his earnings, he buys dinner and glue. It's what most street kids do. When their stomachs burn with hunger, they sniff glue, and it eases the pangs. "I start at 6 in the morning and I stop at 8 at night," he says. "I do it every day. I started to do this when I left home and came to live here. I was upset. It makes me happy."

Glue-sniffing street kids in Siem Reap share a fresh can they pooled their money to buy. Siem Reap, 2003.

Glue is, according to a recent study, the drug of choice for poor, young Cambodian males. When they get older, they might combine it with other drugs, such as heroin or amphetamines, which are known as *yama*. The study, conducted by the aid group Friends, has found that almost 48 percent of Phnom Penh's street kids habitually sniff glue. In Siem Reap, the old-town markets don't sell glue to kids anymore, so the youngsters walk a few miles to find it at another market where vendors sell it for 1,400 *riel*, about 35 cents, a can.

Pros tried to quit, once. He was staying at a shelter run by Friends. "The Cambodian people at Friends told me not to sniff glue. When they told me that, I stopped maybe two or three months. Then I started again because I was angry with kids at the center, hitting me and fighting me." That's why he eventually left Friends. "There's a big kid there, and he wants to fight me. I'm afraid."

Pros used to take classes at Friends, too. Now he doesn't go to school, but he would like to. When I ask him about his future, he says, "I would like to do construction work," and he gazes across the street where men pound at the skeleton of a building-in-progress. Jerry asks them later, and those men make 5,000 *riel* a day, no more than Pros can make from begging. Pros looks at those workers across the street on a framework of crossbeams. He has no idea how to get from this cracked and soiled sidewalk to that bottom-rung opportunity over there. He can't envision a life beyond the one he has. "I don't know how long I'll be here," he says. "I don't think I'll make up with my father."

Don't feed the street kids, says Sebastien Marot. Don't give them money; don't buy their flowers; don't pay them to shine your shoes. "The more you help them, the less we can help them in the long term."

This contradicts the hearts of many well-meaning foreigners. But Sebastien Marot knows what he's saying. The best way to help a street kid is to direct him to a shelter. He has worked with Cambodian street kids since traveling here with two Americans in 1994. They found kids everywhere, and their hearts spilled. They did as many others and bought food for them. But they learned the harm it brought "because you were actually maintaining the lifestyle," he says. They figured they had two options: forget the kids and move on, or do something.

They did something. They created *Mith Samlanh*, or Friends, now one of the longest-standing and best-known aid groups in the country. Everyone on the street knows *Mith Samlanh*. Its volunteers scout the streets, day and night, looking for kids to help. They bandage minor wounds, feed growling stomachs, play games and engage needy minds. Friends runs a shelter, a restaurant and shop, and training workshops in welding, electrics, hairdressing, beauty, sewing, cooking. It reaches about 1,800 kids each day.

Nearly a decade since the group started, its work continues to grow and shift with the country's demographics. "It doesn't look like it's going to get any better in the near future," Marot says. There are more street kids now, and the reasons are myriad. War, civil unrest and land mines are no longer the primary factors; family dysfunction, divorce, remarriage and poverty are. The city offers the only spray of hope. "If you want to make it, you have to come to the city," he admits.

And the city will continue to bulge. AIDS will leave a devastating trail of children in its wake. "There will be 140,000 orphans by 2005," Marot says. And if you assume half will die — not an unreasonable assumption — that leaves 70,000. Where will they go? They will go to the street. "Probably, we will be overwhelmed," he says. "Eventually the money will run out." Donors don't like projects that have no end in sight.

Marot says the group has tried to bring the government to task. "It's important the government takes some responsibility." But it's not interested. Why should the government fix a problem with its own money when foreigners will throw their money at it? And in the end, street kids are a problem of poverty. Why should the rich and powerful spend money on the poor and destitute?

"In general, there's no real future for people in Cambodia — not just street kids," Marot says. The future looks bleak, drug use is rising, so are prostitution and violence. "And if I were fifteen, I'd be doing all the same bullshit."

This all sounds frighteningly grim, but a few successes outweigh the overall gloom. "If you look at the wider picture, it's depressing. If you look at individual stories," Marot says, "that's what gives you the fuel to move on."

This interview with Marot takes place a month before the 2003 election. I ask whether he thinks the situation will change after the vote. He looks me in the eye. Why should it? "Either it stays the same or it gets worse." It will stay the same because the government will be the same. Or it will be a new government facing the same problems with less money, less experience and less political clout in a country where the same party has ruled for decades.

These are the pictures in mind in June 2003. But a year later, neither scenario has proved true because a government has not emerged from the election.

It's a Friday morning and Jerry and I accompany Samnang and Sachak, two members of a Friends outreach team, to a small *wat* in Phnom Penh. A handful of teenagers are smoking *yama* when we arrive. "If they are smoking or injecting, we don't disturb them," says Samnang. It's against Friends policy to interfere — with good reason. People on amphetamines have notoriously short fuses, prone to attacking those around them.

The kids slouch around a *stupa*, surrounded in garbage and syringe wrappers. Most are boys; one girl left to sell drugs. "And sometimes she sells sex," Samnang says. About eighteen kids hang out here by day and a handful linger through the night. The monks don't like it, "But they have no solution," Samnang says. "They have no authority." As long as the kids cause no problems here, they can stay.

The Friends team tries to counsel the kids and teach them about reproductive health and hygiene. "Sometimes their girlfriends are pregnant." But it's hard to get the kids to listen when they're high on *yama*.

A tall, dark-skinned young man named Chan, whose nickname is Buffalo, sits beneath a tree. He carries a packet of glue in his back pocket. He has a wound on his head, which Sachak addresses, tenderly cutting the hair around the bloody gouge and pressing gauze to the injury. "Someone hit him," Sachak says. A hard hit, most likely with a rock. Buffalo has tussled with another group of youths.

The team's second stop is another *wat* across town. This one bursts with life. We arrive and forty kids immerse us in their arms. They hug and squeeze, and we cannot get off our *motos*— so many kids hounding us. They ask for money, they ask for food, but mostly they want love and attention. Another woman on the Friends team is already here, playing games and reading books to the kids. It's always like this, Samnang says. "They miss me so much."

These kids are younger, and some are with parents. The monks don't allow them to sleep here, but they congregate by day. "We teach them about literature and mathematics," Samnang says, although a few of the kids go to public school. "Sometimes they don't stay a long time in school because they have to work for their family."

These youngsters are loving but sickly. There's a girl with red burn marks on her chest. There are sores and scabs, drippy noses, mud-crusted feet, rotten teeth and one little boy with a dog bite several weeks old. Many kids recently arrived from Kandal Province. They are here to work; they will return home to their parents, with some money in hand, in a few weeks. "They always do like this," Samnang says.

Sachak grabs the medical kit. One mother holds a baby with a large cut all the way down the spine, all the way down to his butt, and another gash over the eye. The mother says he fell — obviously not the case. There's a lot of wailing, screaming, crying and bleeding, children tumbling and bruising their bodies. One by one, Sachak treats the wounds he sees, but he can never reach them all. He can never clear all the noses, wipe all the eyes, stanch the flow of all the blood and mend the wounds of worry.

It is the week of a Buddhist holiday, and outside the gates of this area, visitors stream in and out of the *wat*. The women wear their finest silk sarongs and white embroidered shirts. They tuck flowers in their arms and stroll beneath Buddhist flags. Several people stand just outside the throng of kids and stare before going inside the temple. There, they make personal offerings to Buddha, the great disciple of compassion. One woman comes to the gate, peeks inside at all the grubby kids, then turns her back and leaves.

The third stop takes us to the back side of Phnom Penh's Olympic Stadium, down a small path adjacent a gas station, to a cluster of tarps and tiny shanties. Inside one is a twenty-year-old man named Poll, who used to stay at the Friends shelter. He left a month ago, but Samnang doesn't know why. "He nearly finished his training." He studied to be a cook but returned to his life of drugs.

The young man is passed out beneath a custard-apple tree, surrounded by plastic mats with peacocks painted on them. He has a bandage on his arm, a silver chain on his wrist, and a large tattoo of a flower beside several self-inflicted gashes. "He cut his arm himself because he says he's heartbroken," Sachak says. It's common for lovelorn street boys.

Around the corner is a water hose and buckets where two kids wash themselves, standing in a pile of garbage. They have jerry-rigged a shower from the water tower looming above. A family lives back here too. They sell coconuts, pushing a cart all over Phnom Penh, returning to their tarps at night.

The movement, the fluidity of Cambodian society makes for a pool of prey, exploited in the sale of humanity. It is, according to a 2001 BBC World report, "the perfect hunting ground for child traffickers."

If Cambodian street kids don't meet their devils in Phnom Penh, they find them on the border with Thailand, in the seedy stretches linking Poipet and Sisophon and Battambang. Kids are prime property, and they fetch a pretty price when traded. A neighbor eyes the boy next door, and soon enough he's on the street in Bangkok, selling flowers and gum, sleeping in a boarding house with a boss who beats him. Or if he's lucky, she doesn't hurt the boy, she just doesn't let him go.

If it's a girl in question, her odds are worse.

In August 2001, Thai authorities round up 142 Cambodian beggars for deportation. Most are kids and elderly folks brought to Thailand by a gangster who forced them to beg. In September 2003, the Thai government transports more than 600 Cambodian beggars via C-130 military aircraft back to Cambodia in an effort to clean up Bangkok's streets before an upcoming Asia-Pacific Economic Cooperation summit. In February 2004, Thai police intercept a busload of gangsters trying to smuggle Cambodian kids to Bangkok, where they are either sold or forced to beg. A baby sells for about $25; an older child for $50.

The Homeland Shelter works out of an ordinary-looking house in Battambang. It sits on one of the city's main roads behind a gate in a large yard, and nothing much looks unusual. But step inside, and you will find boys racing through a longhouse playing tag, girls painting each other's nails, kids plucking ancient instruments, and a classroom of English students. Every child here has a history that shouldn't be.

Director Mao Lang says this place opened in 1997 as a halfway home for children who have been trafficked, kids whose parents have died of AIDS, and who end up homeless for any number of other reasons. When another group rescues children on the Thai border, they call Mao Lang, and she takes them in. About sixty children live here, but her ultimate hope "is to send them back to live with their families." When found, she asks the kids' parents what they want to do. "Some families are very bad with children," she says. They don't take care of their kids, or they have no money, or they don't want the responsibility, or they don't understand their duties as parents. If Mao Lang finds a child's parents unsuitable, after much discussion, she will find a foster family for that child.

Some mothers and fathers find themselves in insurmountable debt to their neighbors. They see only one option: "They must send their kids to Thailand." A trafficker offers money to take the children to Bangkok, where they will work. The trafficker promises to send the child's earnings to the parents, though that rarely happens. The parents don't know this beforehand, and they agree without thinking. Then the money doesn't come, and the child is gone. For the trafficker, the child is gold.

Mao Lang has a network through the province, connecting three districts, twenty-one villages and 672 kids. They work with extended families to ensure each child is treated properly, once returned. They help women find jobs. They teach parents sewing and mechanics and motor repair so they can support a family. "We provide skills training; we provide school materials." And they deal with the psychological effects of a child's forced and unwanted, sometimes brutal, always damaging trip to Thailand.

It is common for these kids to have spent a year or two in Thailand. Some don't even know how long it's been. The years have slipped into obscurity. The time in Thailand is a shackled routine. They sleep by day and sell flowers and candy by night.

Some kids know no alternative, and when they are first rescued, they want to go back. They say Thailand is happy, and it's easy to earn money; here in Cambodia, things are bad. "They want to earn the money to take care of their parents," Mao Lang says. When the parents hear this, they often tell their kids to run away from Homeland.

Mao Lang is not sure how many children are trafficked to Thailand. No one is certain. "I worry about the future," she says, about girls sold for sex and AIDS rates rising. Also increasing are drug use, mental problems and torture. Many masters electrocute the children if they don't earn enough money. She tells us about a thirteen-year-old girl named Mao Sokha, who endured just that. The girl doesn't know all the details of her journey to Thailand, because "she was very, very young."

I ask to interview Mao Sokha and Mao Lang heads off to find her.

The young girl sits quietly, shyly, at our table. She wears a yellow braided strip of yarn around her wrist. She begins to tell her story: Her mother sent her to a neighbor who took her to some older people who sent her to Bangkok to sell flowers on the streets. "The master took me every night to get money. If I didn't get money, the master beat me." The method was a metal clamp fastened to her wrists, with electricity fired through — not enough to kill her, just enough to get the point across.

Mao Sokha was first taken to Thailand when she was five. "I went and came back many times," she says. She lived in house with a dozen other kids, Vietnamese and Cambodian, somewhere in Bangkok, but she doesn't know where. The boss was Vietnamese. "I think she's very, very bad," Mao Sokha says. She had to earn at least 1,000 *baht*, $25 a day, a goal she often failed because the master allowed her only one hour of sleep each night. So instead of selling flowers, she fell asleep on the street.

Mao Sokha was rescued the year before, and she is happy to be free of Thailand. But the girl no longer knows where her mother is. "I heard my mother had problems with her husband." And that's all she knows. Her happiness here is tarnished by the void in her life. "I want to find my parents," she says. But that is unlikely. She has been gone so long, she doesn't remember her parents' names. She doesn't remember the name of her home village.

Mao Sokha grows weary of talking, so she scampers off to another room. Next, twelve-year-old Tree Wan enters. He, too, has been trafficked. "When I stayed in Thailand, I begged money, and I sold flowers," he says. "A Vietnamese trafficker took me to Pattaya." He lived there on the sea for two years.

Before that, Tree Wan had a home in Poipet. His mother was very sick and wanted her son to find money in Bangkok. Now twelve years old, not even a teenager, Tree Wan knows his mother condoned his slavery.

Mao Lang interrupts and says she thinks it is difficult for a child to comprehend the truth about his parents, but it's important. "I explained to him about his mother," she says. "He should know about his life."

Tree Wan no longer wants to go home. "My mother doesn't take care of me. She wants only to send me to Thailand." He didn't like his captor either, although she didn't beat him. He lived in a home with two other kids just like him, forced to work on the streets.

He says he was "very, very afraid" on that first trip overland, to the country next door. He didn't know what was going on. He's happy to be here now, and he's studying in grade three, which he likes eminently. He never had this chance in Thailand.

Tree Wan already has plans for the future: He has decided to become a teacher of traditional Cambodian music.

14. Health: Living Against Odds

I have two telltale ways of assessing Cambodian health. I read the numbers, and I watch the people. Combined, the portrait is distinct: It is the undeniable depiction of a tainted nation, of people wasting in sickness that doesn't have to be. Cambodia is inflicted with "a growing burden of disease," according to Médecins Sans Frontières. The numbers, the faces, the daily lives show you precisely why.

The numbers are found in annual reports, through organizations such as MSF, such as the World Bank and the World Health Organization, such as the lengthy installments by the UN Commission on Human Rights. There is always a section on health, and it always enumerates crushing raw facts such as these:

Life expectancy in Cambodia is 54 years, but 27 percent of the population won't live past 40. The maternal mortality rate, at 470 per 100,000 live births, is one of the world's highest. Forty-five percent of children under five are underweight. Sixty-four percent of Cambodians have no access to good water, and 47 percent are nowhere near a doctor or clinic. The infant mortality rate, between 90 and 100 per 1,000 live births, is 14 times that of the United States and 24 times that of Japan. Aside from a baby in Laos, a Cambodian child is more likely to die before the age of one than in any other Asian country. One in eight Cambodian kids dies before his fifth birthday — that's the highest rate in the region.

Read a bit more, and you'll find that there are 0.3 physicians for every 1,000 people, compared with 2.7 in the United States. AIDS, for years, spreads more quickly through Cambodia than in any other country outside Africa. For a while the rate surpasses even that of Africa, some experts say. And then the picture brightens a bit when the rate stabilizes. Some say this is due to more prostitutes forcing their clients to use condoms. Others say it's even more simple: The sick are no longer passing on the disease. They are dead.

Then look to the streets.

Look to the streets, and see the face of health. See it in a disabled beggar, crawling along on two hands, one limp leg and a stump, making his way down an unpaved road full of garbage and flies and excrement and the stench of urine. Follow that image to the market two blocks away, on the same obscene street, where women rest their bananas and papayas, where a fresh load of fish unleashes more hot smells, where other women hang their fresh meats dripping ichor beside vegetables and shaved coconut, where flies attack everything edible, where the afternoon rains turn all the market drippings to muck, where all that muck attaches itself to shoes and feet, and where it's absolutely no wonder how disease breeds and spreads with abandon.

The beggar in that scene is thirty-four-year-old San Dara. He was in a car accident in 1989 near the Thai border. His right leg is gone, and his left is useless. He places a pillow beneath his chest and two flip-flops beneath his chin, and he crawls like that, on a board, through the filthy streets. He lives across town at the railroad station, where he rents a small place with his father. His father is too old to work, and begging provides their only income. He is one of millions who can never afford to see a doctor, who will survive on their own luck and skills, who will survive until they simply don't anymore.

Look again, and see Kiev Vin. He is thirty-eight, and he's in a wheelchair. He can't use his legs, and he's not certain why, but he probably had polio as a child. He's been in this chair since 1979. He has a house, but he's never worked. "I have no education, so I can't find a job." This is not just a statement about education and labor, it's also a statement about health. For in Cambodia, many diseases and injuries go untreated, and they result in disabilities that could have been prevented. And then, the disability becomes a lifelong burden. There are jobs the disabled simply cannot perform; there are employers who simply will not hire the disabled.

So, Kiev Vin, with his mangled legs, earns his living as a beggar, fetching 2,000 to 3,000 *riel* a day, less than a dollar. On that, he tries to feed two kids. I ask how people treat him, and he says, "Nobody treats me." They ignore him. And by doing so, they dump more toxins into the murky morass of Cambodian health.

"The health situation in Cambodia is still a catastrophe," says Beat Richner.

Dr. Beat Richner's name is posted and plastered all over Siem Reap, all over Cambodia. He is a Swiss doctor. He runs three free pediatric hospitals—Kantha Bopha I and II in Phnom Penh and Jayavarman VII in Siem Reap. By his numbers, his hospitals treat 600,000 children each year and deliver 450 babies a month. By his numbers, 2,800 children would die each month if it weren't for Kantha Bopha and Jayavarman.

His facilities are not open to foreigners, only Khmers, but every Saturday evening Richner plays cello at his new, modern, spacious auditorium in Siem Reap, and he tells his audience everything he wants them to know about his hospitals and health care in Cambodia. His opinions are vitriolic, and he doesn't hide them. He offers no chance to rebut. And he allows no one in the audience to snoop around after the performance — his guards are there, in corners and hallways, ready to pounce on anyone heading toward the hospital itself.

Nonetheless, Richner has some interesting things to say.

To his thinking — and this must be emphasized: these are his personal opinions, announced at his weekly public concert — there are two reasons for Cambodia's health crisis. The first is long-running war, starting with former U.S. National Security Adviser and later Secretary of State Henry Kissinger's secret bombing campaign, which started in 1969. Richner says that provoked the whole Khmer Rouge revolution. Without Kissinger's intervention, there would have been no Khmer Rouge, he tells the audience between renditions of Bach. And from those bombings, Cambodia still suffers. Tuberculosis, which Richner claims was once nearly eradicated in Cambodia, is the biggest child-killer in Cambodia today. He says it blossomed in the 1970s, in refugee camps in Phnom Penh, where 2.5 million people clustered together in unsanitary conditions. After that, tuberculosis spread through the malnourished and weakened masses during the four-year Khmer Rouge regime. Then the Vietnamese intervened, but health did not improve. "Only the communists had a chance to be treated by proper medical care," he says. The rest languished. And now TB is everywhere. If a child gets malaria, dengue, Japanese encephalitis, typhus—these maladies are only complicated by TB. In the West, we know of TB as a coughing disease. But left untreated, it attacks the body. It settles in the bones. "The hips are destroyed, the spines are destroyed." Mothers give TB to their nursing children. For all of this, he says there is a clear culprit to blame. "Tuberculosis is a direct consequence of the war, and the war was brought by the Western world."

The second reason for Cambodia's health straits, Richner believes, is arrogance, particularly in the West. Richner says the Western medical world typically looks upon developing nations as undeserving of high-tech medical advances. But Richner has managed to bring first-world health care to Cambodia's children through private donations. His annual operating costs total $13 million, half of which goes toward medicine, 30 percent toward salaries for a staff of 1,100 and 15 percent for medical supplies.

But this is not the norm. When donors come to examine poor countries, he says, the common attitude is: Let's get the locals to wash their hands first, then we'll talk about expensive machines. He says drugs that are banned in the West, for dangerous side effects and unacceptable risks, are showered upon the poor because they're cheaper. And this is true: For example, many countries have banned the antibiotic chloramphenicol, which can cause aplastic anemia, a potentially fatal disease when bone marrow stops making enough healthy blood cells. Yet the drug is still sold in Southeast Asia, and it's on the WHO's Model List of Essential Medicines, updated in April 2003. That list outlines the bare minimum supplies that the organization thinks a developing country should have.

There is a third component to Richner's thoughts on Cambodian health: There is a lack of justice. A system of justice "is the most important contribution to a peace process," he says. "Without justice, there's no peace." And without health, there is no justice. Many Cambodian doctors can't even afford to give proper care, earning $20 a month through the Ministry of Health. "The doctor is forced to do corruption," he says. That's why Richner's hospitals are sanctuaries. Everything is free. "We have a system without corruption, where everybody has the right to be treated." And in his mind, that's well on the way to justice — and peace.

As Richner sits on an empty stage, just he and his cello, he implores the audience: One life. Save one child's life. It is "not a drop on a hot stone," he says. "Every child has only one life, and life is all we have."

Just a few miles from there is another hospital, the Angkor Hospital for Children. It's 3 P.M. Thursday; the rain has stopped; the air steams; faces glisten with beads of sweat. Fluorescent light shines on rows of beds; mosquito nets await unfurling at dusk. A wave of workers in blue and green scrubs moves from child to child, checking charts on daily rounds.

It's been six days since Matt Bording, a critical-care nurse from California, finished his year here. He volunteered for $350 a month plus room and board. He gleaned a wealth of introspection. He bestowed his knowledge on a fledgling Khmer staff. He helped save hundreds of lives. "Would I do it again? Yes, but differently," he says. "Of course we can say that about anything in our lives. There were both personal and professional gains from this."

The AHC workload never ends. Day after day, a steady stream of need flows through its doors. In Bording's last week, a newborn arrived. Dad dropped off a tiny child, less than three pounds, born at thirty weeks gestation, a month and a half too soon. A tiny body with blue-gray skin and blistering lips, bundled in an incubator. Father left and never returned. This is not unusual, Bording says. He doubted the child would live when she arrived.

But six days later, on Thursday's rounds, the baby still sleeps soundly, and the staff is hopeful.

In bed 10: a thirteen-year-old boy, fluid in the knee. His water buffalo gored him.

In bed 15: a malnourished girl. The father holds her twin in his arms. "Are we feeding both children?" asks Dr. Eugene Tragus, director of surgery and critical care. He's asking the crowd of doctors and nurses following his lead on rounds. There's discussion in the crowd. "Please see that the mother has money so she can buy food so she can eat so she can have breast milk to feed the babies," Tragus instructs. The mother has eight kids.

In the ICU, a girl with rheumatic heart failure sits in bed. She has a file inches thick from many visits. She came the first day the hospital opened, in 1999. She will die soon. Although the staff has not told her this, she knows they can do nothing for her. If she lived in Malaysia or France or the United States, she could have an operation. But she doesn't. She lives in Cambodia. "We've run out of money to send congenital heart patients to Malaysia, and they're going to die," Tragus says wearily. They're going to die because there's no money to send them to a nearby country with top-rate medical facilities. That — the inability to do a thing — is the most stinging reality of his job.

Cambodians see death everywhere. They're used to it. Survivors saw it in horrendous ways, from 1975 to 1979. They still see it in daily life, from diarrhea, from AIDS, from *moto* wrecks, from malaria, from grenade accidents, from political killings, from stabbings over seemingly petty disputes. Life is tenuous. Health is fragile.

This hospital opened in 1999 through the nonprofit Friends Without a Border, founded by Japanese photographer Kenro Izu. The hospital sits on a dirt road smack in the middle of town, just a few miles from the Angkor temples. It sees 135 patients a day. Its staff averages more than sixty nurses, thirteen physicians and more than a dozen expatriate professionals. For those who can afford it, a visit here costs about 25 cents. For those who can't, it's free.

Each morning, hordes of parents and children crowd the wooden benches of an open-air waiting room, watching cartoons in Khmer, awaiting help. They come for every imaginable reason. "My God, every day brought bizarre and unusual things," Bording says. "I saw a couple of kids die of rabies, severe malnutrition, heart failure from rheumatic fever, traumas from hand grenades, worms climbing out of colostomies...."

The expatriates here routinely see cases they only read about in school — land mine injuries, typhoid, tuberculosis, malaria, dengue fever and hemorrhagic shock. "There was almost always at least one case of meningitis in the hospital, including TB meningitis, which I had only heard of," Bording says. Neither had he seen children with empyema, a pneumonia complication of pus surrounding the lung. When Bording came here, most of his Western critical-care training fell to the wayside. It simply didn't apply. "There wasn't much in the way of technology." The ICU had a few heart monitors and an ECG machine, but that's about it. "So it was clear that reinforcing good basic nursing care was a priority."

Consequently, many diagnoses are made through a process of elimination rather than expensive, definitive tests. "We're a very poor hospital financially," Tragus says. "It would be nice if we could afford an X-ray. A lot of the time we just can't." I interview him amid a fundraising campaign for a ventilator so nurses don't have to manually "bag" the patients, forcing air into their lungs with a bag for as long as it takes.

There are tough decisions in the face of such funding shortages. "Many of our long-term ICU patients in the U.S. have hospital bills higher than the AHC's annual budget," Bording says. "Using maximum resources to try — often unsuccessfully — to save a few people while others are dying of easily treatable conditions is just not part of my value system."

Before coming here, nurse Prak Manila worked at a government hospital that paid her $10 a month. "We cannot provide good nursing care like that." As the AHC nursing education coordinator, she now makes $200 a month. "This hospital is very special in Cambodia," she says. Implicit in her job is learning. Although the Khmer staff graduated from Cambodian medical and nursing schools, that education wasn't enough. Everyone here agrees. Language is an obstacle. "They learned their curriculum in French," Bording says. "I taught about heart failure, and no one understood the word 'pump,' so I'd have to think of ways to describe the action of the heart, in simple terms. It was usually a matter of finding the right analogies."

Most Cambodian medical students can't afford textbooks, "so the teacher just lectures and the students just listen and take notes," Bording says. They don't ask questions; it's not in the Khmer culture for students to do so, or to admit they don't know something. "Nurses are just doctors' extra hands and legs — that's all," says Nursing Director Mieko Morgan.

These are all barriers to the expatriates trying to teach the locals. So, too, is culture. Bording couldn't fathom the Khmer people's nonchalance over death. Upon hearing the news of their child's death, "They'd just say, 'OK,' and walk off." This is a country where families are big for a reason. "It was almost expected they'd lose one or two." And this is a country where death is "in their face all the time," he says. "It's not some sanitized and far-away thing like it is for us in the West."

Some foreigners simply aren't prepared to deal with these realities. They simply aren't prepared for such a stint abroad. Initially, the hospital administration thought any short-term surge of foreign skills would be good. But Morgan estimates it takes three months for an expatriate to get used to Cambodia and the living conditions. "And then they can function." It takes six months to understand Cambodia and how to work with Cambodians.

"I had traveled to many countries in Asia before," Bording says, "and that definitely helped, but living in a place like Cambodia is much different than being a traveler, where you can just pick up and go when you want."

By the end of his stint, it's the cultural incongruities that have worn him down. It's trying to break old customs that maim and kill. It's trying to persuade a people to live differently, to act and think in ways they never have. It's trying to shift a culture from superstition to science, from custom to what we see as common sense.

And it rarely works.

Spin through a Cambodian market, and you'll find stacks of Alaska brand sweetened condensed milk, full of fat and flavor but short on nutrition. On the can's label is a round-faced light-haired white-skinned boy. He looks healthy. He looks happy. Why shouldn't a Cambodian mother feed her child that milk? How can you tell her that a diet of such milk, and only that milk, will malnourish her baby? Why would she believe you, when her baby grows fatter with every can served? After all, fat is prized. It shows you can afford to eat. But she fails to realize those chubby babies are often listless and sleepy and glassy-eyed because they don't get the vitamins needed to play and grow.

Spin through that same market, and you'll find stall after stall selling barrel after barrel of white rice — but no brown. People were forced to eat rough brown rice during the Khmer Rouge regime, and now they want nothing but white. "They're all malnourished," Tragus says of his patients. "So they all go home with vitamins. In fact, that's part of their routine."

It's a taxing battle, trying to fight deep-seated superstitions, some of which are deadly.

Kru Khmer, while meaning well, often issue treatments that make things worse. Umbilical cords cut with rusty blades, wounds smeared with unclean ointments. "So many infections," Bording says. One hospital patient fell from a tree and sustained an open fracture in his arm. He went to a traditional healer, who "made some sort of goobery poultice and waited two weeks before coming to the hospital with the bone still sticking out," Bording says. "We tried unsuccessfully to save the limb."

Tragus says they try to dispel these ideas and practices but, "I don't know if they listen to us."

To most Khmers, tradition and medicine go hand in hand. Everywhere, there are people covered in red circles the size of a silver dollar. They are "cupped." They are given hickeys across their backs and foreheads and chests, blood pulled to the surface through a cup, heated over a fire and pressed into skin. The treatment is believed to suck pain and disease from the body. And all across Cambodia are people with burnt red lines over arms and bellies. They are "coined," scraped hard with metal until the flesh bruises and scorches and the evil energies supposedly depart.

A man with health problems submits to the ancient healing method of cupping. Heated glass cups are placed on the skin. As they cool, they stick to the body, and aches and pains and evil spirits are thought to be sucked out in the vacuum. Phnom Penh, 2003.

There are women with white patches of "medicine" stuck to their temples to ease headaches, and children with cigarette burns on their bellies to stop stomachaches. There are soldiers with intricate tattoos across chests and arms and fingers to stop bullets in their path — we see them on nearly every disabled veteran we interview. There are those scarecrows planted at the foot of people's yards, warding off evil when it comes knocking.

These notions of health and luck and the whims of the gods are little different from ancient times.

Dr. Puth Yeang practices medicine from his Phnom Penh home, a small electronics shop with a medley of paraphernalia: a computer, scores of dusty bottles filled with black brews, a basket of seashells, stacks of dried leaves on plastic-wrapped paper and the ancient secrets of Khmer healing.

Puth Yeang is deputy secretary of the Cambodian Traditional Medicine Association, whose sixty-some members once traipsed through the forest searching for medicinal plants. They perused medical dictionaries in French, English, Vietnamese and Khmer. They compiled booklets on the natural remedies their ancestors knew.

But the group's official status collapsed during the July 1997 factional fighting that clogged Phnom Penh streets with tanks and blood and mayhem and subsequently disrupted most doings in the country. When we visit Puth Yeang in late 1998, his association awaits a new permit from the new government. Still, a fluctuating flow of patients, sometimes ten a week or ten a month, still seek his help. He treats them in his shop. He says Khmer medicine is faster and cheaper than Western techniques. "According to the people who know how to use it, it has similar effectiveness."

Puth Yeang got his start as a Western medical doctor. About that, he says simply, "I retired in 1975." Starting that year, most every educated Cambodian either fled or died or lived a life of lies and retired under the Khmer Rouge. Ever since, Puth Yeang has practiced traditional medicine, using a motley mix of local plant and animal parts pounded and ground into stews and potions. He hauls out 200-year-old Khmer scripts, written in Pali on thin sheets of bamboo. He flips through the books, pointing to tiny sketches of plants and animals, pointing to his head, to his stomach, indicating which remedy fixes which ailment.

In walks nine-year-old Roeung Sei. He fell off his roof. His father talks with Puth Yeang while the boy lies on a wooden bed in a swoon. This is where Puth Yeang does his trick. He yanks on the boy's broken left arm, taps it all around, Roeung Sei howling in pain. Then he slathers a viscous goo on the arm, wraps it in cotton, attaches bamboo slits to keep the bones in place, and wraps the arm in gauze.

Ong Thy, a technician who shares this office, gazes fondly upon his father-in-law, the doctor. "Better than a Western doctor," he says. "Faster, too. Western doctors take a long time."

He says Roeung Sei will return in three days, then once every five days for a few weeks, until the arm heals. Each visit costs less than $5, less than a Western doctor would charge, he assures. Still, Ong Thy says many Cambodians don't trust non–Western medicine. Though popular in the countryside, many people don't trust *Kru Khmer*. "Cambodian people look down on traditional medicine. They don't know how to use it," Ong Thy says. He was once skeptical, but then he studied his father-in-law's ways and the old tattered books that fill the room. He used the treatments for his own minor ailments, and they worked. "So now I believe."

Several weeks later, we return and Puth Yeang says he has since treated ten more broken limbs. And Roeung Sei's arm has healed. "That boy has been cured already, completely," he announces proudly.

There are some vectors in Cambodia that no one can quash, no pill can rid, no magic brew can absolve.

There is the mosquito. More than a pesky insect, its bite more than an itchy bump. It's a killer. It comes in many varieties. The *Aedes aegypti* mosquito carries dengue fever, which infects more than 10,000 Cambodians each year, and that number is rising. Dengue is debilitating, lasting for weeks, sometimes months. It zaps the energy and sends sharp pain through the bones. Sometimes it turns hemorrhagic, causing serious breathing difficulty and bleeding from the nose, mouth and gums. It's fatal in 5 percent of cases.

Malaria is even worse. Three *Anopholes* mosquitoes carry the disease. They generally fly at night or early morning. Though the numbers are falling, still more than 110,000 cases of malaria are reported each year. Dr. Nong Sao Kry, program manager of the National Malaria Center in Phnom Penh, has come to a sobering conclusion: "Malaria in Cambodia can be reduced, but not eradicated." Spraying the city never works completely, he says. You can never catch all the mosquitoes.

A young girl lies sweating with dengue in a small village. Her father keeps watch nearby. Takeo Province, 2003.

Money is his main hurdle. I speak with him just before the 2003 election; the rains are here; mosquitoes are out, and he's waiting for the money to fight these diseases. The funds are in the budget — $6,800 from the Ministry of Health; $16,552 from the World Bank; $7,160 from the WHO and $169,559.41 from the Global Fund. But the money isn't in his hands. It's stuck in the Ministry of Health, which has spent less than 10 percent of its $50 million allocated budget, according to *The Cambodia Daily*. Some say the money is going to election campaigns instead.

"This is the rainy season, and malaria is increasing," Kry says. "Maybe this month or next month we can receive the funds." Meanwhile, he has stacks of mosquito nets waiting to be dispersed, for free, in rural villages. "We distribute free to the population." But not this year, not yet.

Malaria is worst in poor areas, where illiteracy is high and people don't understand those little pests can threaten a life. Sometimes people don't sleep under nets because it's too hot, Kry says. "People believe malaria is not caused by mosquitoes. They think it's caused by the gods." This is particularly true among hill tribes in the far east, although they are learning. Before, "If we gave them nets, they used the nets for fishing," he says. "It takes a long time to change their behavior."

And so the center is taking a new approach. It's teaching school kids to spread the word, to tell their parents about mosquitoes and disease and the importance of always sleeping beneath a net. Sometimes the kids understand better than the parents, Kry says. "It depends on the literacy level."

Kry is optimistic but realistic. "There is no vaccine," he points out. Further complicating problems, up to 25 percent of malaria drugs sold in pharmacies are fake. But they're cheaper, so people buy them. It's Kry's mission to steer people toward medicines distributed through the center. "All free of charge," he notes. But there remains that problem of money for distribution.

Ignorance is the main cause of malarial death, although people have learned more about the disease in the last decade. "Now people have come to believe modern medicine is very good," Kry says. But that's if Cambodians live near a doctor or hospital or place to find packaged pills. Thousands, even millions, don't. They get sick alone at home, miles from help. "The people cannot go to the hospital, cannot go to the health center because it's very far and the road is very far. People have to walk."

It's a grueling haul to recovery.

It's a hot Sunday afternoon in the dry season, in the spring of 2002, and the streets of Phnom Penh bustle as usual: cars honking, trucks growling, *cyclos* creaking, people pushing carts. Motorbikes zip in and out and through the chaos. Teenaged drivers tease their karma, racing at ludicrous speeds. There is no structure to Cambodian traffic. Sometimes it works, but more and more it doesn't.

There is, on this particular Sunday, a commotion south of the city on a main drag near several garment factories. Cars creep along, and people crowd in the street, peering downward. They're looking at a man on his back, hips and legs twisted, head turned to his side. There is a puddle of blood beside him and more on his head. He is not moving. Nearby is a black car with airbags deflated and a man talking on a cell phone. Between him and the corpse is a piece of the car's front bumper and another man sitting in the street with blood on his head, legs and feet. In the distance, an ambulance whirrs.

As more people move to Phnom Penh, as more people buy cars and fewer ride bikes, these scenes are all the more common. By January 2004, there are 22 percent more vehicles on the road than the previous year, according to a *Cambodia Daily* story. Road accidents account for 80 percent of Phnom Penh's medical emergencies. Fatalities are rising. They keep hospitals in a flurry of activity.

It is August 2003, and Cambodia's only free, twenty-four-hour public ambulance service is busy with these accidents. It is called SAMU, a French acronym for Emergency Medical Aid Service. SAMU works in teams, sent from two public hospitals in Phnom Penh. Each team constitutes a driver, a medical assistant and a doctor, as well as a dispatcher who relays calls to both teams. Everyone works a twenty-four-hour shift, followed by two days off. They do not get holidays. Their work never ends.

With SAMU, Phnom Penh has the only public ambulance service in this country of thirteen million people — nothing in Siem Reap, nothing in Battambang, nothing in Sihanoukville. Director Dr. Svay Kamol estimates Phnom Penh alone needs five or six stations. "It's very, very difficult," he shakes his head. Private ambulance companies run by private clinics and hospitals charge a fee, generally about $10 per trip, well beyond most Cambodians' means. And those ambulance services, according to SAMU workers, often bribe the cops $5 or $10 to call them first when there's an accident. Some Cambodians "when they see a private clinic ambulance, they don't go with them," says SAMU dispatcher Sun Chan Dina. They can't afford to pay so they make their own arrangements—such as a *cyclo* or *moto*.

The French Red Cross has funded SAMU since 1997, in concert with the Cambodian Red Cross, but each year the French cut back a little more. This is common among donors: decreasing the money bit by bit, with belief that local groups and governments will pick up the slack.

But the Cambodian government has not picked up the slack. Neither has anyone else. This worries Kamol. His is the only emergency service most people in Phnom Penh can afford. Without SAMU, people would resort to *motos*, *cyclos* or something else too slow. For an emergency patient, time is danger. "In five minutes, if the brain has no oxygen, the brain dies," he says.

It's 7:45 A.M. on a drizzly Wednesday at Calmette Hospital. One SAMU team is just getting off its shift while another is coming on. The office sits adjacent an open garage in the hospital's rear, where transfer vans, dirty cars and old *motos* are stored. A young boy swings a fishing pole in a rain puddle next door. Hospital employees play chess on a homemade board of shredded cork, hand-drawn squares and hand-carved teak figures. Nearby is the SAMU sleeping room, with clothes hung from its windows, and a sheet and towel rumpled atop a cot.

The team readies the ambulance for a new day. In the rear window is a sticker with a red line through a picture of an AK-47. No guns allowed. Kamol says drunks are a problem, so are guns, and drunks with guns are the absolute worst. "Three years ago, if the drunkard was a soldier or policeman—ooh, very mean." But the government's weapons eradication program has surprisingly worked, and there aren't as many guns these days. Even so, when I ask if he can call the police for help, his answer is clear: "Noooooo."

The first few hours pass with no emergencies. In the lulls between calls, Dina is eager to talk. She is twenty-two and has a good grasp of English. She wears pink and purple nail polish, gold earrings, pink eye shadow, blue mascara and fuscia lipstick. She has worked here since 1998, and on her days off, she sells drugs at a pharmacy. "I like this job because I can help so many people in the city." Saturday and Sunday nights are the busiest times. "Sometimes we don't eat dinner until 10 or 11 o'clock." The victims are generally Khmer and often drunk. "Most of the foreigners know the traffic rules." They wear helmets but few Khmers do. She implores: Wear a helmet.

Dina smiles and says there's a slight issue with the ambulance today: Its windshield wipers don't work. "If it rains, we cannot see." It's the middle of the rainy season so, "Yeah—it's a problem." It will have to be fixed.

The phone calls come every few minutes, but they aren't emergencies. They're pranks, hang-ups, little kids looking for their mothers, wives who accuse Dina of dating their husbands. This is ridiculous, she says, but it happens all the time. "Every day, every night, every hour." It's exercise, lifting the receiver up and down, up and down. "Sometimes they call and ask me about their parents—the street children."

Sometimes callers "lie" about emergencies. They might report an accident in front of the Royal Palace, "but when we arrive, there is no victim." Dina says she gets about 100 pranks a day, but counts at random thirty-minute intervals pin the number at nearly one every two minutes— or 720 pranks a day. "I say please don't disturb me anymore. Please give me the time to contact with the ambulance."

The drizzle continues. There's boxing on TV. There's breakfast in the other room: hot bowls of noodles on the floor. At 9:30: an accident. Dina dispatches the ambulance from the other hospital across town.

At 9:45, the team takes the ambulance in for repairs. The windshield wipers are fixed, and an estimate is made on faulty rear springs. That will take half a day to fix; it will have to wait. The crew returns to port at 10:45, just in time for a call.

"There is a victim in front of the Cambodiana Hotel," Dina shouts. Driver Set Thet turns on the sirens as he hits the road. Through open windows the noise blares, constant and screeching. The ambulance reaches the hotel in a few minutes, but no one is there. "We haven't seen anyone," Dr. Ser Hong calls Dina on his cell phone. Thet drives back and forth until he spots a man waving across the street. There, on the sidewalk, is a man crumpled beneath a tarp. His mouth is moving, and he emits little puffs of breath. He has a wound on his head. Within seconds, a crowd congeals on the sidewalk, and the team jostles its way through. Hong lifts the man's eyelids; he's not awake. He dabs the man's wound with gauze, and the team lifts his limp body to a stretcher, toting him around a puddle to the ambulance doors. In a few minutes, he's convulsing on a bed in the Calmette emergency room, nestled beside other patients.

Thet has kept the motor running; there's another call. Back on the street, sirens blaring again, heading to *Psar Chas* just a few blocks away from Calmette. A young man sits in the grass with eyes closed and head swaying. The crowd is thick, and the team can barely squeeze through. People snap quick pictures of the guy in the grass. They get him into the ambulance, then into Calmette, *con brio*. The older man, the first call, is still convulsing. Doctors and nurses work to intubate him.

Back in the office, Dina fills us in. A human-rights group has called about the first man, who has no family. They think he was in an accident the previous night. The second man was poisoned by a thief who drugged his water.

The beat slows, and the workers wait again. They toss out used gloves, wash their hands, record the events in a log book and watch cartoons on TV.

Next call: an elderly woman, fallen off a *moto*. At the scene, a thin gray-haired woman lies on her back with eyes open, staring straight to the sky, a splotch of blood beside her. A younger woman arrives, spots her and begins to wail. She clasps the old woman's hands, her own face riddled with fear. The victim moves her eyes. The team wraps her head in gauze and lifts her from the shoulders, onto a stretcher. She goes hand-in-hand to the hospital with the younger woman.

The vehicle meets the lunch-hour traffic now, and no one stops. People drive as usual, giving way only when the ambulance is right upon them. Otherwise, the lights and sirens mean nothing to the passing crowds, except to draw stares and pointing fingers.

Back at SAMU, everyone breaks for lunch together, and everyone talks about life. Dina is not married, she says, for practical reasons. "You know many young

Cambodian women want to live in the United States or somewhere else abroad. They don't want to live here." Here, work is hard, and money is slim. She is one of five daughters born to a soldier. "But you know in Cambodia the soldiers have small salaries," about $15 a month. "So I can help support with my salary." It's what many bright, young, middle-class Cambodian women do: They send their paychecks home to parents who earn less than they do. Feeding the family is a potluck job. Each member tosses in what he or she can. For Dina, that's $60 a month from SAMU and another $60 at her second job. "I give all of it to my mother. If we depend on my father's salary, it is not enough."

After a few more calls, Jerry and I head home. Along the way, we pass the young poisoning victim on the street. He rides in a *cyclo*, hooked to an intravenous drip. A relative sits beside him as traffic zooms past in clouds of exhaust. The young man and his companion mosey along at the pace of two pedals and three wheels.

It is the picture of emergency health in Cambodia's near future.

Other days come and go, other emergencies beckon SAMU's help. A choppy cycle of hurry-up-and-wait takes the team through year's end. SAMU faces more of the usual and some of the extraordinary. They gather an unconscious man with stomach problems from a rural neighborhood clinic, a twenty-minute ride through dark villages, radio rasping, tires whining, siren shouting, hazards clicking.

Another time, SAMU finds silence, a day without calls. It rains hard that week, killing the phone line. "When the rain is coming, we always have a problem," Dina says. It takes nearly twenty-four hours to fix.

Another night, there is tragedy, an accident that kills five. "The driver was drunk," Dina says. The group leaves a bar at midnight; their car rams into a tree. Three Koreans and two Khmers die. Kamol works that night, midnight to 2 A.M. "He is a very good director because whenever we have a serious accident, he always goes," Dina says.

He goes to the accidents to help. He goes to the office to manage. He goes to firefighter training at the airport, taking his staff with him. And he goes to donors, pleading for money. He asks the Japanese embassy for help, and it offers to pay for a new ambulance and equipment. "But for the salary, noooo," Kamol says. He tells the embassy "the government never supports us." But the Japanese can offer only equipment.

SAMU workers fear the worst. They sense an impending doom. "Every day we worry that next year this service will finish because we don't have the funds," Dina says. "You know, when the ambulance is busy and there's an accident, they transfer by *cyclo* or by *moto*. It's not good for the victims."

Three months later, there is no SAMU. Poof—just like that. It's all gone. No more free ambulance for Phnom Penh, or for Cambodia.

The SAMU office is empty, the glass panel in its door is shattered. There is nothing inside, just a few chairs, a plastic bag, some medical supplies. It is quiet—no phones.

The vehicles sit in storage, awaiting word from the Japanese embassy, the donor, about what to do. The employees have gone home, a few have found posts in Phnom Penh hospitals. "The majority, they become jobless," says Dr. Uy Sam Ath, director of the Disaster Management Department for the Cambodian Red Cross. Doctors and aides, Cambodia's only trained emergency medical staff, now unemployed.

With years of warning, the French Red Cross has ended its funding, the Cambodian Red Cross has run out of money, and its central committee has voted to cease service. Sam Ath says three Phnom Penh hospitals are now running their own ambulance service, through the Ministry of Health. But it's starting from scratch. Its vehicles are old; some do not run; the hospitals have not yet coordinated their routes; the ministry's budget has not increased; the vehicles run on gas— more expensive than diesel — and it's unlikely the service will ever be free again. The ministry has not hired SAMU employees. In fact, he says, there is no communication between the ministry and the Red Cross at all. No communication between Cambodia's only trained emergency health-care workers of the past six years and those who are newly charged with this task.

This is all very distressing to Kamol. "We are sorry, sorry," he says. "I worry. For our staff." And for the public.

Kamol is learning English, and he keeps an English-Khmer dictionary on his laptop computer. He refers to it several times in our discussion. The first time, he types a word in Khmer and it bounces back in English: "defeat." The second translation: "suffer."

Just a few months before this conversation, Kamol sat in the SAMU office watching news from Iraq, more ghastly scenes of emergencies. "I want to work in Iraq or Afghanistan, in emergency services," he said. He wanted to get better. He wanted to learn and improve his skills. But even then, in September, he knew his job was in peril.

"If I were a millionaire, if I were like Bill Gates," Kamol said, "I would organize an ambulance service in my country."

And then there is AIDS.

It is again a story of numbers and faces. The numbers lay bare a human scourge. AIDS has killed about 90,000 Cambodians since 1991. Another 200,000 people are expected to develop the disease in the coming ten years. Only 6.5 percent of Cambodia's AIDS patients receive antiretroviral drugs.

The faces of AIDS in Cambodia: They are like you and me, him and her; like anyone we know on our street or in our school. They are everywhere. Everywhere, until they start to fade, drowning like a whisper in a clamorous world where a silent death goes unnoticed amid the hum of life all around.

Dr. Sutthep Mak arrives at our hotel in a clunky blue 1982 Toyota Corolla, rusty outside, bare wheel wells inside and worn gold velvet seats. He apologizes for his car and drives us through a thrashing rainstorm to the flooded grounds of Battambang Provincial Hospital. He is embarrassed by this hospital. It is grimy, his office cramped, his salary a pittance at $45 a month; the buildings neglected, it seems, since their French colonial days. "Very small, very bad, very old," he says.

This hospital was built by the French, and it suffered under the Khmer Rouge.

"In April 1975, when Pol Pot came to power, Battambang Hospital was abandoned, its equipment and research files destroyed and most of its staff murdered," writes journalist John Pilger. It has never been restored properly.

This is Sutthep's day off. We have contacted him about AIDS because our friend, Masaru, a photographer who follows this new Cambodian tragedy, suggested we meet him. For years, Battambang hugged the front line of the old war against the Khmer Rouge, until the end in 1998. But now many call Battambang, on the thoroughfare connecting Bangkok, Phnom Penh and Saigon, the front line of a new war. Cambodia has the highest AIDS rate in Asia, and the disease travels this route.

The soft-spoken doctor leads us from one ward to another, sloshing through pools of rainwater. We're all drenched, skin and clothes. Inside, we meander through hallways and cubbyholes, past windowsills lined with patients' food, past a man burning a plastic bottle on a charcoal grill to cook his dinner. Sutthep discovers a woman in shock, alone and unattended in a dark room, and he rushes off to fetch a nurse.

He tells us there are not so many patients with AIDS right now because many have died. He works in the respiratory ward, where patients are screened for tuberculosis. We pass through the aisles and see an old woman, bones and skin, on her third visit here for TB treatments. She still tests positive, and Sutthep thinks she's drug resistant, an alarming thought.

We see a thin man wrapped in a *krama* scarf, his body awash in a sickly pallor. He has water in his lungs. He has AIDS.

We see another man with his back to the aisle, sitting on the wooden slats of a rusty metal bedframe, swatting flies with a fan. They swarm around him and the food on his bed. He is TB-positive and HIV-positive, a common combination. He has come with his wife, and they've been here forty days. He coughs into his checkered *krama*, his head bowed down.

In another room, we find the same: another man with TB and AIDS. His wife is here too, she also has AIDS. The man is emphatic and astonished: He went to the brothel only two times.

These men are lucky, Sutthep says, because their wives have come and stayed. "Some persons, they come alone. They have no family." Or they come with several relatives and on the second day a few will leave, and the third day a few more, and by the fourth or fifth day, the patient is the only one left. For TB patients without AIDS, "The family will stay," he says. But AIDS patients die alone. And when no one comes to claim the corpse, the government pays 50,000 *riel*, about $12.50, for cremation. The bones are kept at a nearby pagoda, just in case someone eventually comes to pay their respects.

We gaze outside as more rain buries the path between this musty room and the outdoor toilet. Sutthep asks that we take no photos of him in this ward. He apologizes again for the state of his hospital.

Then he takes us into his office, and I sit on a spare bed squeezed beside his desk. He pulls out a photo album full of patients from 2000 to 2001, every one with AIDS, every one dead now, about ninety in all. Page after page of skeletal people, all gone. "Yes, every one, all in my service." There were many more, but only these people wanted their pictures taken before they died.

In the end, many AIDS patients die of chronic diarrhea. "We have no medicine," he says. "We see the patients, but we don't know what to do." Sometimes he uses his own money to help them. "They come alone. They have nothing to eat. They have no money.... They wake up, they have excrement on the bed. They have no family to take care of them."

I tell him many people say AIDS is Cambodia's new war, and I wonder what he thinks. "Yes, I think the same as war."

The primary problem, as health workers know well, is unsafe sex. Men go to brothels; they buy sex from beer girls; they buy sex at roadside drink stalls; they buy sex from karaoke girls, and then they go home to their wives. Sutthep says most brothel workers now insist on condoms since they've learned about AIDS through educational programs aimed precisely at them. But many other commercial sex workers haven't learned about condoms and AIDS.

Villagers don't know either, he says. "The knowledge in rural areas is very low, so they don't use condoms." When city prostitutes with AIDS get sick and lose their jobs, they return to the village to work again. " In the future, we will have so many HIV cases in the rural areas."

I ask what I hear few people asking in this country: Will the brothel culture itself ever change? Will men stop going to sex workers? Sutthep looks me clearly in the eye and answers, "I don't think so."

The room grows quiet. There is nothing we can do; there is little Sutthep can do. Nearly 3 percent of the Cambodian population is HIV-positive, and social workers estimate there will be 140,000 children orphaned by AIDS in the next few years. A torrent is coming.

Outside, the rain eases a bit, and we pile again into Sutthep's old blue Corolla. He takes us on a detour, on a side street, past wooden hovels and fenced-in cement-block buildings. This is the local brothel district. These places look no different from the homes around them, except for bigger barbed-wire fences and young women congregating on benches outside, peering into hand-held mirrors, dusting their faces with fresh coats of powder and shadow.

Past the primping women, Sutthep has a mango field, and he'd like to show us. We drive a bit farther, and he points to rows upon rows of luminous green, off to the side. It's a mesmerizing spot along a very bad road, not really a road at all but a broken track caked in thick red mud. We bump along, and a giant pothole catches the car, jolting our innards. We hit another hole, and the muffler dislodges. This has happened before.

Sutthep parks the car, jumps to action, examines the muffler, yanks it off and tosses it in the trunk. He smiles, and apologizes again for his car.

The rain has stopped now, and twilight approaches. The air is damp as we move along, leaving in our wake miles of green mango trees and, beyond them, dozens of well-coifed women awaiting the night's work.

Interlude: Dog Bite

I have time enough to think only this: Two dogs sleeping, small sidewalk, uh-oh.

I am returning from an interview about psychology at the Transcultural Psychosocial Organization in Battambang. There is a parked car up against the walkway, and I maneuver around it. There they are, one small tan dog and one large black-and-brown beast, not an Asian dog, not a street dog. It's much more brawny. Both dogs are chained to a gate. They're somebody's guards. In a split second, the big dog wakes, spots me and latches onto my arm. His head is the height of my elbow. It happens fast, and I twist my arm to set it free, and the dog's jaws rip flesh from the inside of my elbow. Blood trickles to the street.

I hold my arm straight, cursing the dog, racing back to the hotel, where Jerry has stayed behind to do laundry — my laundry, he's a good husband (and he thinks this statement should be made far earlier in this book). I pound on the door; he comes; he sees the blood. I explain. He rinses me off and inspects the wound. Is that a flap of skin? No, it's fat poking through. He douses me in surgical cleanser and Betadine, then plucks from our REI first-aid kit the medical guide that comes with it. The book is written for North American backpacking injuries. It says for animal bites, to fill a plastic syringe with water and squirt it directly into the wound to prevent infection. That stings, and I stomp my foot. Then Jerry tapes me up, and we try to call the TPO office, where we know people, people who speak English. But the phone isn't working. Cambodian phones never work when they need to.

This is Battambang, where health care is rustic at best. I remember hearing about an Emergency Hospital for War Victims, an Italian-run facility. It's 5:15 P.M. when we find the place. We squeeze through gray doors to a spacious room with a lab technician and a patient. The doctor is finishing in another room.

While we wait, the men ask what happened. When I say dog bite, they shake their heads, crinkle their noses and scowl. "Ooooooh." What does that mean? What do they know? One of them asks how long ago it happened, and I say about forty minutes. He shakes his head again, muttering.

The doctor enters. I tell him a dog has bitten me, and he asks who dressed it. I say Jerry did. "Why don't you trust our doctors to do it?" he asks me. He is stern, and we say we did not know where to go immediately after the incident. He asks me what I did to provoke the dog.

The doctor is Polish, here eight months through a collaborative program with the Italians. We learned about this hospital the year before, talking with a local at the boat dock. That man is proud to have in his city one of the few emergency hospitals in the world. There are others in Iraq and Afghanistan. These hospitals exist to amputate legs and repair war wounds. Hence, my doctor is accustomed to sawing off limbs and stanching the spread of gangrene. To him, I imagine, my dog bite is a fussy little matter. I'm right.

He takes me to a corner, and I sit on a table as he removes the bandage and pours more Betadine. He squeezes the wound and pulls a string of fat from my arm. I look away. "That's gonna hurt," Jerry says, but the doctor corrects him. It's only fat, and he's right, because I don't feel a thing. He pulls that fat like a tapeworm, snips it with surgical scissors and tosses the tissue in the garbage can. Jerry tells me later I have just had about eight inches of unplanned liposuction. Then the doctor pinches my skin together and tapes it shut with a bandage, so it begins to heal. That's it.

What about rabies? we ask.

He says he has never seen it here. I'm the first dog bite victim he has encountered. Cambodians take care of their dogs, and I should have no problem.

I ask what the symptoms are, anyway. (I've heard the worst.)

He cackles and says, eyeing Jerry, "He'll know." But seriously, it shouldn't be a problem and even so, he has no vaccine. He finishes our conversation quickly, then scoots out of the room.

Three Khmer workers stick around as we fill out paperwork, and they tell us politely it would behoove me to get the rabies vaccine pronto. A private clinic near the market has it. I should get it today. They write the name of the clinic in Khmer on a paper so a *motodop* can take us there. I ask if they've seen rabies here, and they say rarely, but yes. We thank them very much.

A man who speaks passable English greets us at that clinic. On the wall is a sign listing vaccines on offer: hepatitis, typhoid, the usual options. By far the most expensive is anti-rabies, a six-shot treatment for $30. The doctor asks how long we'll stay in Battambang; we plan to leave for Siem Reap the next morning. That's fine, he says. I can get the first shot here and finish the others in Siem Reap. He writes a schedule on a card, indicating six shots to get every other day.

He leads us into a small room, and a woman in white enters. She has the syringe, capped, on a silver tray. She tells me to roll up my sleeve, and she pushes it in my left arm, simple as that, it's over before Jerry even notices. We pay $5. The following year we will visit this clinic again, when Jerry comes down with a 104-degree fever and bone-rattling aches. The doctor runs a few tests, determines it's not malaria or dengue, and sends Jerry up the road to a pharmacy for some drugs. There, the man says, "You're American! You're strong!" Perhaps he just needs some vitamins. He should return to fine health in no time. Remarkably, Jerry sleeps it off in two days.

I get two more shots in Siem Reap and then, a few days later, we travel to Bangkok where the vaccine is different. The very knowledgeable doctor there tells me, to be safe, I must start the regimen again from day one. This whole affair has me addled, and I keep checking my mouth, certain it's starting to foam.

When I email a couple of nursing friends about the dog bite, they respond promptly, with great concern. So, so glad you got the shots! they tell me. Around this same time, I also happen to be writing an article about Matt Bording, the American nurse who has spent the past year working in Siem Reap. I email him questions about his work there, about the cases he saw that differed from anything he'd find in the United States. He tells me it's probably not what I want to hear — but he watched a couple of kids die of rabies.

It's not a peaceful death. The mouth foams, an insufferable fear of water sets in, and sometimes a fear of air. And the mind loses control.

Several people later ask me what I did about the dogs. Did I tell their owner? No. I wasn't about to go anywhere near that sidewalk again. And a Cambodian with two guard dogs chained to the outside of a gate is not the sort of someone I want to tangle with.

However, a few months later in Thailand, Jerry buys me my own personal dog whacker: telescoping chromed steel springs with a sharply-knurled brass dongle on the end, all of which collapses in a compact steel and rubber handle and easily extends with a flick of the wrist. High-tech chop-socky stuff. Used properly, I'm assured it's utterly effective, although that opportunity hasn't come up.

Yet.

15. Pollution: Sewage and Waste

A woman rifles through pig fat in a yellow plastic bag, sorting saggy white lumps, sniffing them, fondling them, tossing them behind her. A man wheels his cart through thick muck, selling frozen yogurt on sticks with flies buzzing all around. On the ground, little black and yellow chicks eat among mounds of blue shredded denim. A few miles southwest of Phnom Penh, afternoon light filtered through smoke casts a foreboding glow over the Stung Meanchey dump, a sprawling tableau of life among filth.

This is 1998, but little changes over the years.

The hulking four-star InterContinental Hotel, where Coke sells for $3 a can, gleams in the sun directly north. My publisher stays in that hotel when he comes to town. He holds staff meetings on the fourteenth floor where I sit, nibble a croissant and gaze out the window. I can't see the faces of Stung Meanchey, but they are down there. To some, there are riches in the refuse, and so, day after day, 200 families stab at the chance to make a small living.

They keep the best of what they find. They find the worst of human waste. A maxi pad, syringe wrapper, medical needle, school bag, the constant drone of flies. Stagnant lotus ponds, moldy Styrofoam jutting from a pool of green blobs. A bobbing coconut shell, meat trays, egg trays, thousands of insects and larvae taking refuge. A pile of short, black, curly human hair.

The dump spills into surrounding rice paddies, trickles into nearby ponds, courses through all the life in and around it. It is the epitome of pollution. And pollution, in the broadest sense of the word — that which makes our environment unclean or impure — lurks as a fatal danger in Cambodia, more than land mines or AIDS.

It wafts through the air breathed, the food eaten, the water drunk, the people loved. It kills and sickens people every day. It harms in hundreds of ways. We know what it is; we know how to stop it, and still countless Cambodians die because of it each year. Countless, because it is often invisible, microscopic, and nearly impossible to link for certain to individual deaths.

The problem is another lasting legacy of the Khmer Rouge. Phnom Penh once thrived, full of art and music and education. The Paris of the Orient, some said. But then the Khmer Rouge evacuated the city and let it stand empty for almost four years.

When the horror ended, people returned, and newcomers arrived in droves, taking up residence anywhere they could. Building records were lost. The first to arrive secured ownership rights. Country folk came not knowing how to live in a city. "In their overwhelming majority the rural settlers in Phnom Penh never became urbanized," writes journalist Henry Kamm. Even today, they don't have the education, the experience or the jobs to do so. "What they can do, wherever they are, is raise household animals. Pigs, chickens, or ducks were as uncommon in pre-war Phnom Penh as they are in New York. Today they are part of city life, along with an occasional lumbering water buffalo for good measure."

Squatters still come by the thousands, every year. Their shacks along the river have no bathrooms; they go where they must. Many Cambodians have never learned the germ theory, the path to illness, the reasons why people shouldn't urinate in the water they drink or eat among swarms of flies. So these things go on, largely unchanged, year after year. The scene is similar in Siem Reap, Battambang and other Cambodian towns, though less pronounced.

It's like this: Imagine a rural village of fifty people scattered across several miles of rich, bountiful land. They are poor. They live in thatch homes. They wrap their food in banana leaves, and they eat from handmade bowls of coconut and wood. Their bathroom is a wide, flowing stream of clear water. The air is pure. And almost all their garbage is biodegradable, so it doesn't matter if they pitch it below their homes. It doesn't matter if they toss their fruit rinds and sugarcane stalks on the ground. It all goes away.

Then: Imagine those same fifty people moving to Phnom Penh with a million others. They cram into one city block, living in tiny apartments stacked atop each other. They bring their cats, dogs, chickens, pigs. They share a few indoor toilets that flow into a faulty drainage system that floods in the rain and reeks in the dry season. Everything they buy comes in a plastic wrapper and a plastic bag. The can't afford a stove or clean-burning gas, so they still cook over smoky charcoal grills in the narrow alleys between apartments, on their balconies or in their living rooms. They still toss their garbage next to their homes, but it doesn't go away. They still don't clean their bathrooms, but here those bathrooms collect flies and rats. The waste doesn't disappear in a sparkling stream. These people are living as they did in a spacious jungle or open plain when everything they owned came from nature, and nature could clean itself. But it doesn't work that way in a city.

And when the city starts to spread to the countryside — new *motos*, candy in plastic wrappers, plastic bags for every papaya or watermelon sold in the market — the village changes too. The garbage mounts beneath homes on stilts. The air smells of exhaust. Mother Nature can no longer clean these foreign influences from her land.

Strangely enough, whenever we visit Cambodians in the countryside, I have a hard time tossing my dragonfruit rinds and lychee pits into the yard. It seems so unnatural to me. But for Khmers it is perfectly natural, and when they move to the city, it is equally natural for them to chuck a candy wrapper like they would rambutan peel. In the city, they continue to live as they always have.

Jerry and I decide to do a project on pollution in fall 1998. But the impetus for this reporting endeavor really begins our first days in Phnom Penh. We arrive during

A dry-season cloud of dinner-fire smoke and wind-whipped dust blows up around a *cyclo* driver near the riverfront. Respiratory ailment caused and exacerbated by smoke and dust are common among urban Cambodians. Phnom Penh, 1998.

the dry season when workers tunnel into wastelands beneath city streets, unclogging the arteries of a colonial drainage system. They hoist tons of muck onto the sidewalks, and there it stays. For days, for weeks, for human feet, dog paws and chicken toes to tangle with. Until the dung parches, the wind whisks it, and tiny particles settle on people's clothes, skin, lungs. We breathe through scarves and exfoliate our faces. For four months, all of Phnom Penh inhales excrement until the rains wash it into the river or back into the old colonial drains.

And when it rains, it floods. All that crud flows through this city of a million people, to the rivers and rice paddies around Phnom Penh. I try to run one day, amid a monsoon that swamps everything around our house: the street, the main thoroughfares a block west and six blocks north, the avenue a block east, who knows how far south, and all points between. My shoes soak up a warm, wan goo. I am wet to my knees. A lost pig trots beside me.

Another day, a similar deluge. A downpour traps the western half of the city. People loiter at a newsstand, snagging tea at a cafe, watching naked kids splashing and thrashing in an overflowing sewer that geysers brown water up to their heads.

When I start this story on pollution, my expatriate colleagues are indifferent, but several Cambodians on staff thank me and agree it's a good idea. They tell me they hate the dust, they cough too much, their families get sick, they want better health, they want the government to clean up the city.

Phnom Penh's old drainage system continually breaks down, leaks and pollutes the groundwater through cast-iron pipes. Sewage has never been treated. Wastewater flows directly from sink and toilet to street drains to the Tonle Sap, Mekong and Bassac rivers or a number of overfilled sludge ponds around town. Eighty percent of Cambodia's pollution comes from people.

And that pollution is dangerous, in part, because people often don't recognize it as such. Smog and toxic waste are largely absent from Cambodia, but the problem prevails in other forms: the raw sewage and flood waters entering rivers, the spoiled meats and vegetables sold in markets, the garbage on the street that draws flies and rodents, the stagnant roadside puddles that breed life-threatening mosquitoes. And everything else that indeed makes the environment "unclean or impure."

Stung Meanchey is a hotbed of unclean, impure life. So are the sewer pipes that empty into the Tonle Sap and Mekong rivers. So are the layers of sludge that ring Boeung Kak Lake in city central, surrounded by homes and brothels, where plastic bottles and edible greens and little boys and human urine mingle in one all-purpose pool.

Unlike land mines, AIDS or other diseases that rack Cambodia, pollution's toll on life is hard to quantify, though no less staggering. Every year, 13,000 Cambodians die of tuberculosis; a polluted, unsanitary environment factors into that number. Every year, every Cambodian child under five suffers up to seven respiratory infections; air pollution is a major factor. Every year, diarrheal diseases kill Cambodian kids more than any other ailment; water and food-borne pollution are the leading factors.

When I begin research for this story, I visit the local World Health Organization office. Joel Vanderburg, project management officer, readily pries himself from his computer and rattles off a wealth of information. He exhibits the WHO library; he scans his literature and plucks a few books from his shelf for me to borrow. He offers his card and extends his services in any way.

"There is a curious irony that is so blatantly evident that at times we miss it: That we are the source of so many of our dilemmas," he says. "Pollution is the classic example of this." He explains, "A garbage dump, in and of itself, just because it has a bad smell, doesn't necessarily have to be a health problem." But if that trash attracts rodents (it does) and if it leaches into the ground and water (it does), the dump turns threatening. And with it ride the pathogens that cause itchy eyes, skin rashes, food poisoning, cholera, tuberculosis, pulmonary diseases, dysentery, typhoid fever, acute respiratory ailments and literally hundreds of other illnesses.

International experts agree on an indisputable tie between our health and our environment. I want a Cambodian opinion. Dr. Phoeng Chhy Leang treats children at the Municipal Hospital adjacent the Sihanouk Center of Hope, a free clinic started by my publisher. The Center of Hope doles out time and medicine in a clean, shiny building where hundreds of patients line up each morning to see foreign and Cambodian doctors. Next door, across an expanse of puddles, is the much more ragged, dingy, paint-chipped Municipal Hospital.

There, Phoeng Chhy Leang sits upright and answers questions formally in his office. "The environment is the biggest factor in health." The trouble starts at home and spreads from there. "We try to be clean among our family members, but we cannot separate ourselves from outside the family," he says. We all live in the same world, we all breathe the same air. "We cannot separate ourselves from the environment." If one person is sick in a clean place, the illness likely won't spread. "But if you live in a society without sanitation, it is easy for disease to spread."

And of sanitation — flush toilets, sewage treatment plants, clean water supplies — Cambodia has precious little. What's worse, many Cambodians don't understand sanitation or why it is necessary or why their sons and daughters cough and itch. They often attribute illness to evil spirits or bad karma. "They don't know," says Dr. Kaing Sor of Preah Bath Norodom Sihanouk Hospital. "The patients don't know about dirt, feces." His hospital tries to teach cause and effect. "We tell them to keep their houses clean, to try to keep sick people away from other people. We try to tell them to be healthy because they lose money if they're sick. They can't work if they're sick. They understand that, but of course we still have sick people." Precisely, there are 114 patients, many with pollution-related diseases, on that particular December day when Jerry and I visit. "We have a lot of work to turn around the thinking of the population. They have many old ideas."

The biggest boost to Cambodia's health would be "to give them clean water and a place to dispose their waste," says the WHO's Vanderburg. But as with all other societal troubles, pollution is tied to an endless cycle of politics, poor education, money shortfalls, corruption, government instability and the constant presence of some other obstacle that demands more immediate attention.

It doesn't help that hard numbers and studies are rare. "There haven't been a lot of good epidemiological studies here on the sources of diseases," Vanderburg says. The Environment Ministry and the European Commission start a lab to study water quality; just as it gets up and running, the EC pulls the plug on funding. Other studies do indicate just 31 percent of Cambodians have access to clean water and 15 percent have sanitary toilets. Many Khmer facilities today are little different from those of 700 years ago. "Ordinary toilets in Angkor were simple pits used until they were full and then covered over," writes Robert Philpotts in his book on Angkor-era life. "A visit to the toilet was followed by a visit to the pond where the left hand was washed, the right hand always being left completely clean for eating rice." Even now, the typical Khmer bathroom consists of a squat hole, a pail of water and a scoop. Nothing more for one's hygiene needs.

I want to know how Phnom Penh compares with the rest of the world. I ask my dad, a civil engineer who has long worked on sewer and sanitation projects. (While my husband vacationed in France as a child and visited the Louvre, I got to visit waste-water treatment plants in the Midwest.) My dad puts me in touch with Al Zanoni, a professor at Marquette University in Milwaukee. Through email, I describe for him what life is like in Phnom Penh. He tells me the Western world faced the same problem a century ago. "By the start of the twentieth century, conditions became so intolerable around major cities that it became necessary to 'intercept' these storm sewers and direct the total waste flow to central treatment plants."

That hasn't yet happened in Cambodia.

In addition to water, there is rubbish. I call PSBK, the company in charge of Phnom Penh's garbage collection as well as the dump, for an interview with the president. Her name is Sieng Pich. After several phone calls, translations and explanations of what I want, her staff arranges a formal interview. Someone will pick me up; I'm not sure who. I'm not sure where we will go or what will transpire. But clearly, Sieng Pich's door is not regularly open to the public.

Early the designated morning, Sieng Pich's official translator arrives at the *Daily* in a chauffeured vehicle with window curtains. Together, we ride through a boisterous morning market. We stop at an old concrete building near the Olympic Stadium and wait in a dank room for further instructions. A man talks briskly on the phone. Sieng Pich is not yet ready.

When it is time, we are escorted upstairs to the room where we meet the boss. A cloud of helpers surrounds the woman, who faces us from a long table. Her staff fetches her tea while I ask questions, a translator translates, she answers, the translator translates again.

Sieng Pich is a large round woman, stern but polite. She runs through a series of numbers, saying PSBK has 692 employees who sweep and load the city's trash onto 40 PSBK trucks every day. The studies vary, but Phnom Penh generates between 400 tons and 700 tons of garbage a day.

But she laments, the job isn't smooth or easy. Only 40 percent of garbage left for collection is bagged. Cambodians have little education, "so they don't understand," she says. People don't know that putting garbage in a bag, then leaving it at the corner for pick-up, is better than throwing it loosely on the ground. Trash "soaks up the rain and blows in the wind. The remains are spread all over." She hands a report to one of her underlings to hand to me. It says PSBK collected 11.63 million cubic feet of trash in the previous nine months. It also reported people's tendency to "anarchically throw garbage"—a phrase I love for its eminent truth. Furthermore, the report indicates only 60 percent of clients pay their collection fees. PSBK has asked city officials to educate the public through radio and television commercials "so that they understand about the cleaning process in Phnom Penh, the heart of the Kingdom of Cambodia."

Sieng Pich asks me to reiterate those things in my story. She asks me to tell people they should bag their garbage, not dump it on the ground. They should pay their bills and respect PSBK employees doing their jobs.

I tell her I want to ride on a garbage truck and interview workers. She misunderstands. She thinks I want to watch a truck drive around or perhaps interview a supervisor or perhaps drive by the dump. I explain again. I want to ride on the truck, talk to the workers while they sweep, walk through the dump. She doesn't understand, but she tries to arrange another meeting. I explain again, and she exclaims at the shocking request. You want to get on the truck? And get dirty? And talk to peasant workers? And spend a day doing it? You, a foreigner?

Yes, I say.

She rumples her nose, says that is no problem, but she's never heard of such a thing.

And that leads to Thanksgiving morning 1998. Jerry and I rise in the dark, sometime after 4, and catch a prearranged *moto* ride through the quiet, empty streets. Workers and homeless families sleep beneath mosquito nets on the sidewalks, *cyclo* drivers stretch beneath their awnings, and masked workers in conical hats sweep the street with brooms and a steady swish, swish.

The trucks sit overnight at a dark and empty parking lot on the north side of town. This is also where the garbage collectors meet. A small light dangles from a corner soup stall. It is quiet and eerie as we trudge through the muddy lot and peek around big tires. People begin to gather.

A well-dressed man in clean oxford shirt, khaki pants and brown leather dress shoes arrives. The sweepers begin to load onto trucks and slowly they pull out of the lot and rumble up the street. Our guide shuffles from truck to truck. It quickly becomes clear he wants to find the newest, cleanest, biggest, strongest truck for us to follow. We tell him no, we want to ride on an average truck. He fires up a big, powerful turbo vehicle from France. Then he motions for us to hop on his motorbike, trailing the truck as it stops two blocks ahead. We tell him no again, we'd like to walk with the workers or ride in the cab. He looks confused.

The day's rays rise slowly under faint rain. It is 5:32 A.M. The truck with its whirling yellow light is stopped between streets 106 and 108 in downtown Phnom Penh. The truck's mighty mechanical arm pushes and crunches, mauling the rubbish, shoving it deep into its maw. Three men and a woman work silently, diligently heaving then refilling three baskets of refuse: grass clippings, a pizza box, plastic bags, soap boxes. Their boss stands back in the grass observing. I realize I must ignore him if I want to see how the collectors work; he keeps getting in the way, making the others self-conscious. As I guessed he would, he soon putters off on his *moto*— bored.

Truck driver Lan crumples a cigarette pack and throws it out the window, onto the ground. Then he hops out, looks around, looks to the ground, picks it up and throws it into the rear of the truck. Lan is forty years old and has driven a garbage truck for thirteen years. He makes about $50 a month. He sits in the cab and listens to the radio while the others work on the ground. When they are through, he drives ahead a few yards, then waits again. He keeps the engine running.

Forty-year-old Ya is hard to talk to because she works swiftly and doesn't stop moving. She has four kids, from ten to seventeen years old, who study at the Stung Meanchey school beside the dump. Her husband is dead. She makes 3,300 *riel* a day, less than a dollar. "I like this work. Why? Why? Because I need to make money." After we talk, she runs off to her coworkers and repeats our conversation verbatim.

In the next batch of garbage they find shirts, a burned mat, an incense can, cockroaches scuttling between their feet. Up a block, they sweep up a box of flower perfume and a 10,000 Vietnamese *dong* note. Forty-two-year-old Ret promptly picks up the money and shoves it in his pocket, nearly doubling his daily wage.

Next stop: a broken pot for traditional, home-brewed syphilis remedies, a pile of shells, a dirty syringe, an empty penicillin bottle, a pineapple head, a fish spine, a page from a Vietnamese newspaper wrapped around human excrement and a used maxi pad.

A kid runs up to the workers and throws a black plastic bag onto the street at

Ny's feet. Ny usually doesn't say much, but he tells this kid to throw the bag onto the truck. The boy scampers off, disobeying.

Psar Chas, a nearby market, yields charcoal and a pile of snail shells. Mo Vanna breaks for a moment to buy bananas and a baggie of food. There is a mound of human hair on the ground. The crew starts work on a pile the size of a Mercedes just west of the river at 7:10. They find more dirty needles. The guys pick up three empty Mild Seven cigarette packs. Collect twenty, they say, and they'll get a free shirt. The last basket's contents fall into the truck at 7:39, just as the mist turns to droplets. "We work in the rain," Ya says. "The rain stinks."

Asked about hazards, Ya says she's never stepped on a needle. "But," she says, pointing to her index finger, "twice I pricked myself a few months ago." Then she turns her head and shovels some more. The truck lumbers on, slowly, until it fills up and heads for Stung Meanchey.

We know what to expect. We have visited this place already, one overcast afternoon two weeks before. On that trip our regular *moto* driver, Sovann, chortled and pinched his nose as we drew closer to the dump. He dropped us at the foot of billowing debris, then drove in the other direction to wait as we explored the bedlam before us.

Coming to the dump to examine pollution may seem a bit too easy, but it's not. People live on the dump. Hundreds more work there every day. Hundreds more have their homes backed right up to the mountain of filth, and it seeps into their rooms and fields. It's an ugly, creeping, cancerous growth, and people live in it.

That first day, we met Mai, thirty, in her home — the space under a ragged, torn tarp. She hardly flinched at the pestering flies. Her floor was garbage twenty feet deep. Her two kids and husband all worked at the dump, scavenging. Little black spots flecked her skin.

On the southern hillside, a woman wrapped in a purple *krama* sold ice slushes from red and blue baskets. Switchback trails descended from the top of a mountain of refuse to the squishy garbage floor. Away from the trucks' pulsating rumbles, swallows chirped and dive-bombed the hills. Flies collected around dense green pools of excrement. The stench of fire stifled the air. A wrinkled woman passed through, carrying a bundle of firewood atop her head. The ice-cream man clanged his bell as he snaked, barefoot, along the trail. He strained to pull his cart over lumps and ruts; flies clinging to his ice-cream sticks. A pig waddled along an earthen ridge and sniffed the ground. A black dog with dragging nipples rolled in a pile on the hillside, then shook flies from her matted, muddy fur. Two schoolgirls took a short cut through the dump.

The trail diverged. Straight ahead, two boys, one naked, emerged from the weeds. Boils, scars and lesions covered the naked boy's skin. He scratched at the ground with his toes. Orange flowers grew beyond. A calm lagoon sat to the left, a long dirt road to the right. A cow plodded through a distant field. Beyond that: homes.

Meanwhile, each new load drew flocks of human scavengers, pouncing with pokers in hand. The bulldozers came and went, razing the earth, clearing paths, churning the piles, the ground trembling below. Green scum and bright plastics shone amid decay. A cadre of boys gripped a truck and giggled as the rear door swung them to the top.

It is much the same on Thanksgiving (we don't realize the irony of the date until that night, while discussing what to eat for dinner). The landfill constantly grows. In the two weeks since our first visit, it has inundated fifty more feet of the entrance road and claimed the swath beside a house, now for sale behind a new concrete wall erected to stem the trash tide.

Among the scavengers is Kut Vundy, seventeen. He is not working too hard this morning and, dressed in a white windbreaker, looks fresher than his colleagues. He has worked at the dump for two years. He studies at a nearby school. He has parents, but: "They don't work. They are old," he says. His job here earns money for his family. "I don't like it. It smells. I get sick, I get headaches and stomach aches, bad health." He studies English, tries hard to practice it here with me but knows very little. He doesn't want to stay at the dump. "I want to be a teacher."

All around, the dump lives. A dog gnaws on a pile of entrails and hair. Black sludge rolls around the tanklike treads of earthmovers. A new road has parted the garbage mountains so tractors can blaze through, missing people by inches in their frenzied runs. The top of the pile — wet, barren and smoldering — offers panoramic views of surrounding ponds, rice fields, homes and life. A pig walks up from the scree of garbage that links the heaps to surrounding fields. Pond waters ruffle in the breeze. A woman walks toward homes across the pond. A man picks greens from another pool.

And on the dump, up close, the ground is remarkable. No grass, no earth, nothing natural, just mounds of tiny particles crushed to bits, plastic and paper and glass and food, forming a spongy floor scores of feet deep. Across it all, hats bob up and down amid this maze of hills and valleys, pitchforks flinging and pokers stabbing debris.

When we decide to leave, we see a smartly dressed man fussing over his shiny shoes in all the muck. He follows a newly hewn rut and studies the trucks. He spots us and knows exactly who we were. He is a PSBK official, and he insists on giving us a ride to town in his Toyota Camry. We gladly accept. We get inside the car and find a dangling air freshener on the mirror, which is good.

We reek.

Stung Meanchey is not our only encounter with polluted life on the edge of garbage. Thirty-eight-year-old Bun Pheng sells grilled bananas from a roadside stand across a wooden bridge from her home of eight years. Beneath that bridge bubbles a dark brew of raw sewage, water, garbage and, as she puts it, "everything from the residents of Phnom Penh." The open sewer meanders through her neighborhood and dozens of others. Residents recall the same dark sludge, lined by riverbanks of trash, ten or more years earlier. They've all heard the city talk of cleaning it up, but answer unanimously: "I've never seen it."

Indeed, Mom Sandap, chief of the Phnom Penh Municipal Office of Planning, rattles off a litany of reasons the original clean-up plans have failed. They selected an American company for the job; the company's technician left, and his replacement had to "re-study" the situation. And then the July 1997 political fighting got in the way. Such things take time here, he says.

Meanwhile, another rainy season dumps its load inside the wooden homes lining the canal. "When the rain falls down, it floods. In less than half an hour, it's on the street and into the house," Bun Pheng says while roasting bananas over coals. She slides a few onto a stick. She motions to her mid-calf, where the water sometimes reaches. "We have to bring everything into the house to put on the bed. After the rain, we wash the house."

My Cambodian colleague, who has come to help translate, gets antsy because his *moto* sits on an unsafe street while we talk. He wants to leave. He stays outside while Bun Pheng heads into two dark, cavernous rooms with walls painted blue. A green moldy smudge near the door, two feet high, shows where water comes and goes. "I don't have money, so we have to stay here," she says. Her youngest child has come down with dengue fever, bitten by the mosquitoes that breed in the water. "No one likes to live like this. Everyone would like to live in a good house." But she makes less than a dollar a day.

Down a block, the same black water flows steadily through the neighborhood. The detritus of urban life lines the banks and bobs in the water. Twenty-four-year-old Sok Chantheoun sits outside on a slat platform with his seventy-six-year-old father and a few other relatives. The family has lived here since 1979. He says the canal has become ordinary, mundane, the bend in the road we no longer notice, the spot on the wall we've seen so often our eyes forget, those things of habit that stop being right or wrong and just become normal. "We have lived here a long time, and we're used to it. We don't feel anything about it," Sok Chantheoun says.

Down the road farther and across the street, Kim Tech, twenty-five, and his mother Em Siem, fifty, sit outside their white-tiled home. They, too, suffer the sewage floods. "The smell is bad, and also it's a source of disease," Kim Tech says. The government sprays for mosquitoes but still, people get sick. "Especially the little kids always have a problem." He wears a long-sleeved pink-and-gray dress shirt over new blue jeans; he drives a rugged Honda *moto*, and he admittedly flaunts greater wealth than his neighbors across the street. Regardless, the swamps still invade life on his side. He's lived here ten years. "It's the same. It never changes. Every year when the rainy season comes, the floods start here." He calls it muck, a thick mixture of land and water and human waste. "The people here want to have a proper system, but we know the government is facing a political crisis" and doesn't have time to pay attention to them. It's a remarkably forgiving comment about a government that pays little attention to them even when there is no political crisis.

He says this is the worst section of Phnom Penh. "If we see the sky looks like rain, we are afraid."

In five years, the canal changes. When Jerry and I return for a look in 2003, a Japanese-funded project — not the Cambodian government — has poured concrete, graded roads, built pumping stations. The sewage waters now flow quickly through the city in a deep, solid trench. The neighborhoods no longer flood, and the people say they are happier. "Even the hard rain cannot flood our homes anymore," says resident Lao Mang Hour, a *cyclo* driver. "Now there are no mosquitoes because the water flows."

But one complaint persists: the smell. The canal remains uncovered, and the horrible stench of sewage ferments in the sun; it still permeates homes.

It's been a long time since we've seen this neighborhood, and it takes a while to find the spot. I look for Bun Pheng. I ask around, and there's some confusion about the name. But I find a woman, Cheng Hong, who says her neighbor used to sell grilled bananas, but she thinks her name is Bun Keng, not Bun Pheng. But then she says: "The people around here don't know each other's names; they just know their business." They call each other by occupation — agriculture person, rice man, sticky-bun woman, things like that. It's common in Cambodia to have longtime relations with friends and neighbors but never learn their names. Cheng Hong tells me the banana seller now has a job outside the neighborhood. She leaves each morning at 6 and returns each night at 9. And I realize I will not be able to find her because I would never find her place in the dark, and I would have difficulty finding a translator to take me to that part of town at that hour.

But Cheng Hong is happy to talk. When she learns I'm a journalist, she asks me to write her words so perhaps the government will listen. "The government will hear, but whether they do anything or not, I don't know," she says. Cheng Hong moved here in 1992 because she had little money. Before that, she lived in an upstairs floor of a multilevel house with no spot to open a shop. But here in her living room, she sells an eclectic array: clay pots, brooms, coils of wire, incense, electrical outlets, scouring pads, shampoo, milk, soda and Tide detergent. Most anything a neighbor could need or want in a quick buy.

Cheng Hong bought this house not knowing it would reek so horribly for so long. "When I came here, the government promised they would fix this canal, but the promise took ten years." Even then, it was the Japanese who paid for the changes, not her own government. She's glad for the improvements, but they're not good enough. "I want to sell this home because of the smell," though she doubts anyone will buy it.

As we talk, a black cloudy stream trickles by. It pours through concrete pipes into the concrete trench. There are railings along the trench separating it from the streets. There is a distinguishable dirt road between the houses and the canal; five years previous: just a murky path. It's better, but not great. Step by step, as Cambodians say.

A few miles downstream, the canal dumps into fields on the outskirts of Phnom Penh. It flows all the way to Choeung Ek, the Killing Fields, through rice paddies and ponds of *trow kooen* spinach. At the point where the canal dumps through massive pipes into those fields, there is a horrid sulphurous stench and mountains of suds. Bubbles swirling and floating, growing and drifting, like icebergs on black water. Massive white sheets, all the detergent of Phnom Penh, swimming straight out to the vegetable fields.

The people who live along Phnom Penh's canal have good reason to wonder about what flows through their neighborhood. "There are literally hundreds of water-borne diseases," says Zanoni, the Marquette University professor. He teaches his students about "the big seven": typhoid fever, bacillary dysentery, cholera, amoebic dysentery, giardiasis, cryptosporidiosis and infectious hepatitis. Though rare in the West, those diseases threaten the developing world and are common in Cambodia.

I talk with a woman named Som Sokhoeuthy in 1998. She lives with her husband and two kids in Tuol Kok, one of Phnom Penh's poorest sections, known for its miles of brothels. The family's home is surrounded by garbage and a polluted pond where flies and mosquitoes breed.

The day we meet her, the thirty-three-year-old mother sits on a bed at the National Pediatric Hospital with ten-year-old So Samnang, who has intestinal problems, and his two-year-old sister, So Srei Pek, asleep in the throes of dengue. The boy eats only porridge; his stomach can't tolerate other foods. "Near the house, it's like a pool with water," Som Sokhoeuthy describes their home. "People throw garbage in there." She doesn't know what to do because people build houses on the pool. "The pool is too deep." It would take a lot of money to fill it up. The garbage is everyone's problem, everyone's responsibility. She tosses garbage in there too. Her neighborhood doesn't have a designated pick-up spot, so people throw where they always have. "The Phnom Penh Municipality should take action," she says.

By 2004, it is still like this, all over Phnom Penh.

Aid workers and health officials say sanitation is not something humans know instinctively.

"The household environment is a dangerous environment," says Jamie Meiklejohn, project officer for UNICEF. The group has helped Cambodians build some 12,000 latrines. "If you consider that nine million people are defecating on the land or near the rivers, I'd say that's a large pollution problem." But people don't understand the danger. "I think for most people it's habit. Not having sanitation facilities, they go where they need to go. But that's in the absence of understanding that defecating wherever can be dangerous." At any moment, he says, about 50 percent of Cambodian kids have diarrhea. Education makes progress, but it's not quick or simple.

Across Cambodia, mothers wipe babies in the same waters where they fish, in the same waters where toilets empty, where kids swim, where people take drinks. This, too, is reminiscent of Angkor times. Philpotts, in his book on Angkor life, describes an ancient type of cistern where people bathed, grew their vegetables and raised their ducks in the same pool of water. "Peelings, stalks and skins were thrown back into the water to feed the ducks and fish. Such was the life-cycle of the cistern."

It's hard to break habits, which makes it hard for health workers to teach sanitation. "It depends on the family," says Dr. Phoeng Chhy Leang at Phnom Penh's Municipal Hospital. "Some families teach kids, but other parents don't take care much. So the children also do not take care.... We need to remind them, to educate them."

Perhaps people don't instinctively understand because they can't see the connections. "I think people are probably very aware when they don't have good water — up to a point," says the WHO's Vanderburg. They know when they don't have toilets, but they don't always understand the consequences. In 1992, aid workers who conducted a sanitation study in Pursat Province found among villagers "a near-total lack of awareness of the relationship between human waste disposal and excreta-related diseases." Those same workers reported difficulty in motivating people to build latrines. Another study, conducted by the aid group Overseas Development Administration in Battambang, found Cambodians' thoughts on sanitation "were closely associated with tidiness, order and beauty, rather than the germ theory or concepts of invisible contamination of pollution. There are several Khmer words used to translate the word dirty; most seem to relate in some way to the concept of disorder or matter out of place."

People appreciate the chance to live clean lives, Vanderburg explains, but they don't associate cause and effect. "That's where superstitions arise." People blame demons or magic or gods for their ills. "What it says is that people do have a certain logic because they're looking for a cause," even though the cause they determine might not be right.

He pulls me into different mindsets: of having to choose between eating dinner or wearing clean clothes, of cooking rice over a smoky fire or not at all. "Given the options, most animals, including human beings, will choose to do things most hygienically," he says. But more often than not, people can't afford to change their lives.

But there's hope in that, Vanderburg says. "With water pollution and communicable disease transmission, we know how to prevent that." It just takes money. And in a happenstance world of illness, accident and death, money isn't such a daunting dilemma. "If you look out the window directly at the moment, you might not be optimistic." But look again, he tells me. "Even as things at times look desperate, there are examples of improvements taking place."

So I find people who have learned and places that have changed.

In 1992, the aid group CARE began a project that would change the way families living along a small alleyway of Phnom Penh would think about their environment. It was dubbed HELP for "Health, Environment and Livelihood Project."

The project involved the people living on a little trail off Street 221 in a busy section of the city. From each family, CARE collected $7 for every meter their homes fronted the alleyway. With that money and some of its own, CARE hired a contractor, used volunteer labor and cleaned up the neighborhood. Perhaps most importantly, CARE workers taught residents about sanitation — why and how to keep their habitat clean.

I read a report on this project in 1998, and I want to know if the project met with any lasting success. Even after less than a year in the country, I see many aid workers come and go, and their projects lost in the short-term memories of an itinerant expatriate posse. Many such projects meet with early success, but then the workers are gone and no one follows up.

So I contact CARE, and the group is predictably on to different projects by now. Most of the officers who ran HELP have since left Phnom Penh. The venture only vaguely tweaks the memories of current volunteers. It takes several phone calls juggled among half a dozen people and a visit to the CARE office to find anyone who knows anything about HELP. I indeed jog the memory of one woman, who invites me to peruse the CARE library. But she can't understand why, now, a reporter wants to know about a project six years old, a career lifetime for many foreign aid workers in Cambodia. But she tells me where to find the tiny street, and I go.

And there, I find that HELP has left a lasting mark in the people's minds and lives.

Deep in the maze of Phnom Penh, where homes and shops spring from back alleys and side streets, one narrow footpath looks a little different from all the filthy others. It's paved, drained and swept clean.

"Today the living is very good," says forty-six-year-old Kim Ly. She has lived here since 1979, and she remembers when it wasn't always so pleasant. This slender little alleyway, just a few feet wide with scarcely room for a car, was a sludge-filled gully until CARE came through. "It was very dirty before the construction," she says. "We had very bad hygiene, and some of the families were sick." Every day, some fifty families trudged through the dregs en route to their homes, dotting the path. "I learned," Kim Ly says. "Everyone, all the residents living along this way, were trained in sanitation and hygiene."

Her neighbors echo those thoughts. "The NGO educated us," says thirty-five year-old Chan Bora. "Now my neighbors and I put garbage in plastic bags.... Everyone follows the explanation from CARE." Indeed, a white plastic bag, tied tightly, sits on her curb. Across the street, green plastic bags sit beside potted plants. An underground drainage pipe lies below.

This afternoon, in a light drizzle, water trickles off the ground and disappears. Bright red and blue umbrellas gleam in the rain. A man sells sandwiches from a pushcart, and a woman sells steaming soup from a corner stall. That woman is forty-year-old Try Saing Khong, who lives up the road on another alley that isn't paved. She started her business here when the pavement went in, and she's made a tidy profit ever since. "These were the worst roads in the area," she says, sweeping her arms widely.

Kim Ly, standing nearby, smiles when she talks of the past three years. She paid $35 for her five meters on the walkway. She smiles even more when contemplating the expense. "I was glad to pay this money because we have such a good road to walk on now."

I find another place of change — and in that place, change means life over death.

Forty-nine-year-old Peng Thon sits in room T.09 in Preah Bath Norodom Sihanouk Hospital's tuberculosis ward. He's been here a few months. After a strict treatment regimen, his TB is in remission. "I was tired and lethargic at the beginning for three months before coming to the hospital," he says. He was in great pain; the pharmacies didn't help him, so he came here.

He sits at the edge of his slat bed, bony arms poking through a white tank top, a red-and-white *krama* draped over his left shoulder. A guitar sits on the adjacent bed. He plays occasionally, to lift his spirits.

Peng Thon lives over the Monivong Bridge, across the Tonle Sap River from Phnom Penh. "My village is not too clean, it's regularly flooded." He also has stomach problems when he eats. "There are five people in my village in the same state I'm in." Three others went to the hospital but didn't follow their TB treatments. They died. "I can now see why they died. They neglected their TB treatment. They tried to drink wine, to pray to God.... For a while, I thought God could save me." But now he knows it takes more than prayer.

What is pollution? He talks about what it is not, about living in a clean place where the people around him aren't sick, about a beautiful home and clear water on fertile land. "That is a clean life," he says. "That is good health."

16. Environment:
Threats in the Wild

We are surrounded by forests, which are infested with elephants, buffaloes, rhinoceros, tigers, and wild boars, and the ground all about the pools is covered with their footprints. We live almost as in a besieged place, every moment dreading some attack of the enemy, and keeping our guns constantly loaded.

— The diaries of Henri Mouhot

Just a couple years after the last Khmer Rouge soldiers emerge from Cambodia's jungles, conservationists and scientists start going in. For decades, the Khmer Rouge hid in the country's westernmost mountains; few settlers or developers would think of venturing there. But all that changes with the end of war. For the first time in decades, the nation's wildlands are open for study as well as logging, poaching, road-building and development.

In 2000, reports start to trickle out of the Cardamom Mountains, near the Thai border, that a biological treasure trove has been found. The group Fauna & Flora International dubs it a "lost world of wildlife." *Time* calls the area "the largest, most pristine wilderness" in the "mountains that time forgot." A plethora of species new to science is found—frogs, moths, birds. Also found are the wolf snake and the Siamese crocodile, long thought extinct in the wild.

It's an irony of Cambodia's civil war that large tracts of jungle remained undisturbed and wildlife endured while humans were slaughtered by the millions. While the countries around Cambodia—Thailand, Laos, Vietnam—hacked their forests and choked their ecosystems, Cambodia's lands endured through a strange twist of ecological fate. Today, conservationists tout the new findings and appeal for help in saving Cambodia's, perhaps Southeast Asia's, last great wildlife frontier.

True, some scientists take issue with these "discoveries." The Cardamoms aren't as biologically diverse as other places in Cambodia. And the species "new to science" have shown themselves to locals for ages—they just weren't known to foreigners. Even so, Cambodia has a lot to save. It has more than its neighbors. It also has hope, where other countries have little.

This is a country where tigers and elephants still roam, where old-growth trees still stand tall in dense forests, where fish swim the waters and feed the nation's bellies. Cambodians are a people born of land and water. They are farmers and fishermen; their landscape gives them life. Eighty percent of the population lives in the countryside, and most who live in Phnom Penh now didn't come from there. It's a nation of people who grow their own rice and vegetables, raise their own chickens, pluck their own fruit from the trees. Cambodians live and die by the cycles of nature, by the wind and rain, by the flooding and drying of their paddies. And when the cycles lilt off-kilter, too much rain or too little, people go jobless and homeless. When the fish stocks dwindle, children go hungry. When the forests are cut, the critters within scatter. And when that happens, the ecosystem collapses. When an ecosystem collapses, when the riches vanish, the people perish. Without its natural treasures— fields, forests, rivers and lakes—much of what makes Cambodia Cambodia is lost.

This danger exists.

"One has to expect that on the whole the overall conditions are going to get worse," says Joe Walston of the New York-based Wildlife Conservation Society Cambodia Program. "To expect the environment in Cambodia to remain as it is, static, is unrealistic." Logging will not stop. Development will continue. Wildlife will die. These things will not change. "We're going to lose more habitat." What fires his hope is that pockets of Cambodian lands will survive, diverse and intact. And so, his group's goal is not to save all of Cambodia but to redeem key parcels of the environment. "You're seeing direct immediate success in some areas," he says. "And I think that's what we're about."

He points to a place called Prek Toal, a biosphere reserve around the Tonle Sap lake in the heart of the country. "A few years ago, the situation was desperate." Birds were killed; eggs were collected, and populations were disappearing. Today, conservationists are hiring villagers to sit on platforms and protect the birds' nests. Some used to collect eggs themselves. Endangered bird colonies "have literally blossomed."

It's not just Prek Toal. "The same thing's happening in different parts of the country," Walston says. He deems himself "conservatively optimistic."

"There are a lot of reasons to be negative about the future for Cambodia but there are certainly enough reasons to be positive — well, to keep me engaged in Cambodia," he says. "I genuinely wouldn't be here if I didn't think I could achieve something here." When he feels he is no longer useful, it's time to go.

That hasn't happened yet.

> *The entrance to the great lake of Cambodia is grand and beautiful. The river becomes wider and wider, until at last it is four or five miles in breadth; and then you enter the immense sheet of water called Touli-Sap, as large and full of motion as a sea.*
>
> — Henri Mouhot

Cambodia's great Tonle Sap is its lifeblood. It is a massive body: 1,100 square miles at its smallest in the dry season and more than triple that in the rainy season. Its river of the same name does a magical thing with the turn of seasons: It changes direction. When the waters of the Mekong farther south swell with monsoon rains, that mighty river pushes the Tonle Sap northwest, back toward the lake, filling it.

When the monsoons cease and the Mekong recedes, the Tonle Sap flows once again south, toward Vietnam. It is the rocking of a cradle that holds the country's bounty.

Fish.

With rice, they are the sustenance of a people. Cambodians capture the world's fourth-highest number of freshwater fish each year, at 300,000 to 400,000 tons. Khmers ferment fish and turn it into sauce, drizzled on everything. They pound it into paste, the *prahok* that defines Cambodian villages by scent, watering the mouths of most every Khmer (and turning the noses of many *barangs*). The lake and river spur legends of giant eels, and they give birth to humongous 300-pound catfish.

These waters fed an empire, so many centuries ago. Angkor could not have existed without this lake. "Certainly a riverside city at this position could never have reached the size and splendor that the Cambodian capital had," Robert Philpotts writes. Not without the Tonle Sap, not without its fish and the rice it engendered.

But something is happening up north, and the bounty is in peril. The waters of Cambodia may never flow again as they have for centuries. China already has built two dams on the Mekong, and it has plans for six more. Everything downstream bears the consequences. Both the Mekong and the Tonle Sap could drastically wane or, just as drastically, lose their annual floods. Some 1,700 fish species are thought to live in the Mekong, whose annual floods enrich lands that feed some sixty million people in the six countries along its banks. That could come to a sudden, shattering halt. China may very well extinguish the lifeblood of a region. It may already be happening. In March 2004, the Mekong River Commission reports the lowest water level in a decade. Farmers' fields are shriveling. Most everybody but the Chinese government blames it on Chinese dams holding back water farther upstream.

What's more, in 2001, China, Laos, Burma and Thailand agree to expand commercial navigation on the Mekong, to make it a major shipping route. The four countries—without consulting Cambodia and Vietnam—plan to blast through eleven sets of Mekong rapids to clear the way.

Something else is happening off water. The Mekong's periphery is expanding with village growth. The population of the Lower Mekong has doubled in nearly thirty years and likely will exceed 100 million by 2025. Trees are falling, and development is decimating the fish supply—not just in Cambodia but all the bordering countries as well. "The pressure on natural resources will increase dramatically, as will the demand for additional food, water and energy," according to an article in the *International Herald Tribune*.

Fishermen have sensed this coming for years. Like a bad fish, they can smell it in the air. Ply the waters outside Phnom Penh, ask around, and they'll tell you: They aren't catching what they used to. They have more neighbors. They aren't selling enough to survive. "But except from the fishermen and a few environmentalists, there is no cry of alarm along the Mekong about the decline of fish in the river. No organization or country has gone so far as to study the Mekong's progressive decline of fish stocks, its causes, or ways to stop it," the *Bangkok Post* reports.

It's a political issue, and complex at that, says Bruce McKenney of the Cambodia Development Resource Institute. Fishing, for one, is a difficult practice to manage. The law frowns on fishing with explosives and nets too big or with a weave too small. But what's big? What's small? How do you enforce the rules? Borders are blurry, and boundaries are as clear as a line traced through water. So how do you determine one man's fish pool from another's? The very nature of what's at stake lies beneath the surface. "Trees at least you know when they're gone — you can look," McKenney says. But fish? Not so easy.

And time is slipping.

In spring of 1998 Jerry and I head to Prek Toal, on the edge of the Tonle Sap. It sits on the boat route between Battambang and Siem Reap, near a maze of swampy forests and narrow canals that attract magnificent populations of birds. A small village of the same name floats on these waters, and this is the site of a new research station. It is still a "desperate" time for this ecosystem, as Walston of WCS says. In five years, this will change. But during our visit, we see what he means.

We go there for the birds, for Prek Toal is home to numerous rare and endangered species. We find, too, a portrait of Cambodian life on water, and all that encompasses — the birds, the fish, the food, the people, the poverty, the clash between rich and poor, the interaction between owners and workers. But all around is beauty.

Just after 4 P.M., another day retires, and Cambodia's wetlands turn cool and calm. Creatures — human, avian, aquatic and other — respond in kind, going about their evening routines. Flocks of cormorants cackle as they scope the river for dinner. A monkey family picks and preens each other, then scuttles along the riverbank. Our rowboat's paddle swishes through the water, while Buddhist chants from a distant *wat* imbue the air.

All is peaceful at 4:54 P.M.

Then a rapid spree of gunfire shatters the calm.

This is Cambodia 1998, and gunshots are common. Everywhere. They could be hunters, or they could be fishermen scaring off birds. They could be soldiers. They could be drunken men firing into the air.

The birds know what to do. Their instinctive flutter mars the quiet as they hurry to flee. They abandon their hunt, leaving their nesting trees alone to shimmer in waning light. Such is the punctuated life of Prek Toal in the Tonle Sap Biosphere Reserve.

It is part of a UNESCO Man and Biosphere project, one of more than 300 worldwide. The goal here is not easy to attain: to strike harmony among all native creatures, their activities and environment so each can continue in perpetuity. The reserve started in November 1997, and the country's first research station has just opened in Prek Toal a couple months before our arrival. In the following years, conservationists will scatter their programs across the country, saving everything from royal turtles to resin trees to vultures and tigers. But this, in 1998, is one of the first. It is meant to be a model project in Cambodia. "It's showing the way forward for future work," says Lincoln Young, project director for the European Commission Support Program to the Environmental Sector.

Biosphere reserves, like this one, usually contain three parts, "like three concentric circles," Young explains. The first, a core area, is managed purely for conservation and not for economic gain. "Normally we should not have any human activity in the core area, which is not the case now," says wetlands specialist Etienne Baijot, Young's project partner.

Cambodia's reserve contains three core areas: Prek Toal's 77,266 acres on the north end of the lake, a place called Moat Khla or Boeung Chhmar on the north-central side and a third spot, Stoeng Sen, on the south end. The second part is a buffer zone around each core, in which economic activities such as commercial fishing are allowed as long as they don't seriously harm the core. This zone surrounds the entire Tonle Sap. The third zone is a transition area of "sustainable development," where there might be organic farming or controlled logging. The aim is sustainability, but "it might take twenty years," Young says.

Obstacles crop up everywhere. Locals trap the waterbirds and gather their eggs. Fishermen complain of diminishing fish stocks and colleagues who use explosives and giant nets. Workers claim their daily wages aren't enough to feed their families. And Prek Toal village is awash with grumbles about the way the government auctions off large tracts of fishing grounds to the highest bidders every two years. The system hands power and prosperity to the man with the most money, leaving his neighbors dry and hungry.

Meanwhile, gunshots faze few people with their regularity.

Fisherman working a fishing lot concession for a distant boss haul in their morning's catch. The people here each earn a little over a dollar a day. Prek Toal, 1998.

Where there are fish, waterfowl flitter not too far behind. Prek Toal contains Southeast Asia's only colony of spot-billed pelicans. It has the largest-known flocks of oriental darter, painted stork and black-headed ibis in Southeast Asia. Twenty percent of the world's greater adjutants live here. It is the only known breeding area in Indochina for the milky stork. And significant populations of white-winged duck and gray-headed fish eagle live here as well. It's no wonder this area is christened "an area of environmental importance to the world."

Ly Sun is a forty-six-year-old village elder whose crow's-foot eyes and saggy skin look far more weathered than his age accounts for. He is a lifelong Prek Toal resident, and he knows the cyclical patterns of Prek Toal's birds. They flee during the rainy season when flooding immerses Prek Toal's patches of aquatic forest, leaving the village to float on a vast sea. In December, the water begins to recede. "In January, the birds migrate from the mountainous areas and the forest area to the biosphere reserve, and they try to make nests," Ly Sun says. In February, they lay their eggs; in March the young ones hatch.

The only feasible means of birdwatching is by boat. The reserve, when not submerged, bares a dense thicket of forest that few bipeds dare attempt on foot. "Mud," Ly Sun says, slicing his thigh with his hand. "It's up to the knee, sometimes the waist." But that's good for the birds. "This is the best place for birds to live, to inhabit, because there is a lot of food, a lot of fish."

The Prek Toal research center, a simple wooden building in the heart of the village, is just getting started when we visit. The center houses a handful of male employees whose bedrooms turn to guest rooms when visitors arrive. They've had about forty guests so far, half on business, half for pleasure. The living/dining/working room opens onto a small deck that receives all callers as they motor in. A television, the late-night village attraction, sits in the right rear corner of the room. There are plans to conduct monthly waterbird surveys, but they haven't gotten to that yet. "It's just a start. There are so many things to do. But the first thing is to get better protection for the birds," Baijot says.

The village and the research center share something of a symbiotic relationship: The center relies on villagers' anecdotes and personal knowledge to find, classify and count the birds. And in return, villagers look to the center's potential for preserving their homeland. "If all the hunters were prohibited from killing the birds, the people around here would be happy," Ly Sun says.

Current bird populations reflect nothing of bygone decades. "When I was young, there were many, many kinds of birds," Ly Sun says. "But right now there are a lot of species of birds extinct from the area. There's no crane. But I used to see vulture." That was in the 1960s. "After that, no more vultures." During the 1980s, when Vietnam controlled the country, most villagers raised waterfowl chicks they plucked from the wild. And the Vietnamese, in a typical story told frequently, poisoned the birds to kill them but not the humans who ate them. The bird population quickly plummeted.

Studies show that people collected 26,000 eggs and 2,600 chicks in the area in 1996. "That's too much," Baijot says. "The problem is, yes, we have some people who are very poor." Eggs fetch up to 200 *riel*, about 5 cents, apiece; small chicks go for 2,000 *riel*, 50 cents; and big ones for up to 10,000 *riel*, $2.50. Although the law controls hunting and gathering in the reserve, its interpretation differs. Ly Sun says the Fisheries Department "long ago" banned people from poaching birds, "but no one complied." Only recently, through the European Commission's efforts, have people stopped, he says. And yet bird traps still line the riverbanks in Prek Toal.

When asked about the law, Young dons a puzzled face and rifles through a file cabinet in his Phnom Penh office. "I don't think there's anything that I've come across in law that specifically relates to waterbirds," he says. "There are a lack of legal tools in Cambodia which can be used to protect wildlife." This sort of confusion over laws— whether they exist, what they mean precisely — is common in Cambodia, especially in 1998. Few things in Cambodia go by the book, in a Western sense of the phrase. And a law alone does not suffice. "The enforcement side has to be developed." Yet Young does not aim to prohibit catching altogether. "If it's a traditional activity, there's no reason it should be banned outright."

Environment Minister Mok Mareth agrees. He says the law does prohibit hunting and catching wildlife in the reserve, but people need food, and he won't punish them for that. "We only educate them. We have to consider the poor farmer, the poor fisherman."

There is at least an appearance of law enforcement in Prek Toal — of some sort.

Dusk approaches the Tonle Sap and a Cambodian man wearing a flowered Hawaiian shirt pilots through Prek Toal on a fishing boat equipped with a 50-caliber machine gun mounted on its bow and four uniformed soldiers holding AK-47s in their laps. They point their guns at Jerry when he tries to take their photo as they motor past.

The next morning, two Fisheries Department officials park their boat beside the research center and disembark, leaving an array of rocket-launchers and an AK-47 lying on the deck. It is still an era in Cambodia when officials openly wield their weapons.

This is how Prek Toal waters are patrolled.

And many locals say they are afraid to hunt.

If the reserve is to succeed, Cambodia's fishing system must change. This is general consensus. The government auctions off fishing rights to the highest bidders, who become two-year "owners" of those domains. Most pertinent to Prek Toal is fishing lot 2, which extends roughly a mile within the reserve. The year before — the year of the reserve's inception — a sixty-five-year-old man named Phal Chea bid 150 million riel, about $37,500, on the lot. After some wrangling with the government and additional money paid, the lot was his.

Most Tonle Sap fishing waters are auctioned off this way, circa 1998. But this too will change. Fishermen will protest declining catches and the unfair advantage of rich lot owners. In 2000, a reform will begin, freeing up more than half the country's fishing lots to communities for public use. The government eventually will declare that Prek Toal shall become a fish sanctuary (someday), and all fishing within the core area will be prohibited.

But for now, Phal Chea is in charge.

He is a lifelong Prek Toal resident and he has owned the same lot several times—in 1968, 1971, 1972, and again under the Vietnamese. Owning the lot gives him freedom to do what he sees fit to prosper. In dry times, that means he can, and does, construct bamboo fences across the river and its tributaries to pool the fish in one place. The barricades keep the fish in and everything else out, including visitors and research center employees. They need his permission to enter. "It's a very unusual situation for a biosphere reserve," Young notes.

At first, Phal Chea does not want to let us into the reserve. "If the boat goes through, it will kill more fish or frighten the fish," he says. That means birdwatching is nearly impossible during the height of the season for tourists and biologists alike. But that is not his concern. He shrugs apologetically. "I cannot allow," he says, sitting in his floating home, the village's biggest building, a sprawling, open-air compound. A handful of his 130 workers mill about, dressed in nothing but *kramas*. A roasted pig's head sits beside a bubbling pot of pork in this village sustained by fish.

A gunshot sounds behind the home, then another and another. After the fifth one, Phal Chea sends a worker to find the cause.

Phal Chea sometimes fires his own guns into the horizon as a scare tactic. He enjoys seeing the avian creatures take flight; he doesn't enjoy them eating his fish. Since the European Commission has launched its campaign, birds have returned in full force, he says. "They are increasing very fast. It means that they eat fish a lot." Between the birds and the Vietnamese, blamed for all the "overfishing," Phal Chea worries about a shrinking livelihood. Fish populations have dropped 20 percent since the 1970s, he insists.

But he won't say how much he earns. He merely says this year will net small profits because he has had to buy new equipment. Phal Chea contracts his workers and pays them according to their experience. Those wages stay the same, regardless of his own profits.

In the end, we cajole Phal Chea into letting us visit the fishing lot by rowboat. There we find Chin Phan, a gritty forty-four-year-old lifelong fisherman. He makes daily wages of 8,000 to 10,000 *riel*, $2 to $2.50. Sometimes he spends his whole salary on food, he says while perched on the edge of his wooden boat, surrounded by other fishermen and their hulls full of thousands upon thousands of silvery flopping fish destined for someone else's dinner table. "It's very difficult for me to feed ten children. Just hand-to-mouth. Sometimes I spend the whole day in the lake," literally, wet to his waist in a sea of victuals. He can't eat the fish, though. "The fishing lot owner is rich, so we are poor."

Given that, he sees creatures from the point of appetite. "It's good to have the birds here, but sometimes I have no food so I have to catch one or two of them to eat. Some kinds of birds are very delicious, especially the pelicans." He makes traps by dangling hooks with pieces of fish from a line stretched across the riverbank's bushes. The birds impale their mouths on the hooks. Chin Phan catches one, two, maybe three birds a month. It's not enough to make a big difference in the greater scheme of things, he says.

Others are afraid to hunt birds. Twenty-five-year-old Lim Kong wouldn't know how to make a trap if she wanted to, she says as she severs fish heads with a cleaver in her small hut fifty meters from one of Phal Chea's bamboo fences. Her family recently left Battambang in search of work in Prek Toal. She now makes and sells fish paste, and that's the only work she can imagine. "I have no idea what I will do. I have no capital to open a business, to sell beer or food," she says. "It will be good if tourists come to see the birds." Perhaps birdwatchers will rent her rowboat.

Some villagers appreciate the aesthetic qualities of a bird haven. San Sith, twenty-five, comes from a family of ten that buys fish from the fishermen and sells them to Battambang markets and restaurants. He lives in Kompong Prahok (Fish Paste Village) a tiny settlement just a few bends in the river from Prek Toal. "The birds can beautify the area with the river and the forest." But he didn't learn about conservation from an NGO. "I only understand through myself," he says. "It is very good to conserve the birds around here because it is good for the tourists to come." That thought is new to many villagers, but it settles in their minds and eventually draws a wide smile.

And that's precisely what Young and Baijot hope to see. Tourism could inflate the local coffers and quash the drive to catch birds. "What's important is to find an alternative income." They're willing to dangle money on the line. "If we can organize environmental tourism up there, we're willing to pay the fishing lot owner something," Young says. "They can earn hard cash…. We have to show the people they can make more money by keeping the birds alive. They can make money for generations."

It's just after 4 P.M. on a Saturday in April. The heat lifts in the tranquil hours of daylight. It's prime feeding time for the birds. Ly Youleng, the center's boat pilot, approaches fishing lot 2. Ahead lies a fence of bamboo and chicken wire, a barrier that spans the waterway. Phal Chea has nodded his OK for us to enter his citadel of water this evening, slowly.

Ly Youleng wedges the boat's nose into the nooks of the barricade and fiddles with a latch. The fence top curls under the pressure of his hands. Small bloated fish cling to the wire, bobbing in murky water. He meets success with the latch, rolls back wire and forges the boat through. Smooth sailing now, he skims across the placid waters, leaving behind the rhythmic chop-chop of village women cutting fish. He steers along at a speed that could lull a baby to sleep.

At 4:20 P.M., Ly Youleng finds a dead bird hooked on a trap strung between two low-lying bushes. He calls this a "sky trap." Birds impale themselves in mid-flight. In years past, these were common, he says.

At 4:27 P.M., the boat passes a line dangling from a bush — no hook, no bird.

At 4:35 P.M., another trap intact.

At 4:43 P.M., Ly Youleng spots a vegetation trap. People pile fresh greens atop a fish on the riverbank. Then they wait for a bird to perch so they can catch it by hand.

At 4:49 P.M., an avian skeleton and a few frazzled wing feathers dangle from another line.

At 4:55 P.M., gunshots sound.

*Everywhere were felled trees — as if an army of indiscriminate lumberjacks
had simply waded through, chopping down everything in sight.*
                                      — Anthony Bourdain, *A Cook's Tour*,
                                                  in Western Cambodia.

Wood is a Cambodian staple. Logging is a Cambodian natural. In the smallest towns, in the grottiest villages, all throughout the country, you'll find hardwood tables and chairs, desks and benches, thick solid stools, king-sized beds, all made from a panoply of Cambodian hardwoods. On the streets of Phnom Penh, near the national museum, young men sandblast monstrous hunks of wood into elephants and Buddha heads. The poorest peasants don't know it, but their pool tables could fetch them a hearty sum in America. Furniture worth thousands of dollars sells for a hundred, maybe two in Cambodia.

Wood helped fuel the Khmer Rouge war. It maintains a lively, illegal cross-border trade with the Vietnamese and Thais. It makes Cambodian generals rich, and it gives impoverished rural villagers an option. Wood is the gatekeeper to many Cambodian economies.

And yet when conservationists and social scientists scrutinize logging, they tend to examine the politics, the social ramifications, the environmental degradation and destruction of ecosystems. "What hadn't been discussed too much were the economics of it," says Bruce McKenney of CDRI. So when I ask him about logging, he gives me an economist's perspective. "Sustainability" is the buzzword these days, but the key questions are: Can a company make a profit doing this? And if so, what are the incentives for them to stop at this profit level? McKenney outlines a scenario:

I run a logging company. I own a stand of trees, and I face two options. I can cut all the trees now. Or, I can cut some trees now, leave some trees to grow, and return in twenty-five years to cut some more. Which do I choose? Most likely, the option that will make me more money.

If I cut the trees today, I can put money in the bank today. I can loan out that money and expect a return of 15 percent to 25 percent. But there is always risk with loaning money. The borrower might default. So I can opt to buy no-risk bonds for a 3-percent or 4-percent return. Thus, if I cut the trees today, I can expect a risky 25-percent return at best or a no-risk 3-percent return at minimum.

Or, I can wait twenty-five years to cut the trees, thereby investing in the trees' growth and any price appreciation in that time. Wood prices fluctuate, but over the long-term, let's say I get a 1-percent increase per year. That would be a very risky investment in the trees' future. The trees could burn in a fire. Someone else could cut them (common in Cambodia). Politics could change (also common in Cambodia). At best, after twenty-five very risky years of waiting, my return may be no better than if I had cut the trees from the start.

"If you're a company, why on earth wouldn't you cut the tree today?" McKenney asks.

Meanwhile, several things happen in Cambodia. The government raises logging taxes nearly four-fold. In 2002, it imposes a moratorium on logging nationwide. That doesn't mean logging ceases—witness accounts still attest to the widespread destruction of Cambodia's forests. Illegal log trucks are spotted across the country. Forests are found with fresh stumps.

Even before all this, logging companies said they weren't making a profit. Throw in the idea of sustainability, which means fewer logs cut at a time, which means less money for both the companies and the government.

So how to address that problem? That's McKenney's dilemma, and he admits a grim outlook. This is not unique to Cambodia. "In forestry, everywhere in the world looks bleak."

If it were up to him, McKenney says he would put his protection money into sensitive areas, saving key pockets of land, doing so in a way that brings money back to the people who live in and around those lands. The idea that money handed to the government will trickle to the local level is a "falsehood," he says.

But donors — international groups that give money to countries like Cambodia, to help them solve their social, environmental and economic woes — are losing patience. "There's a level of fatigue," he says. They're tired of notorious corruption, government inertia and the absence of law enforcement. These complaints appear again and again in reports and political statements the world over, not just in reference to logging but also most every sector of Cambodia that garners aid — which is just about everything. These complaints have continued unabated for more than a decade.

McKenney mentions a recent announcement by Prime Minister Hun Sen that Cambodia's forest cover has increased to 61.1 percent, up from 58.6 percent in previous years. It's a report that flummoxes many a foreign observer. "How on earth did that happen?" he says with a hint of cynicism in his mild-mannered voice.

Much of Cambodia's forest destruction is illegal. "Officials pretend it doesn't happen, but I have seen huge trucks loaded with illegal timber trundling along Cambodian roads," Peter Leuprecht, Cambodia's UN human rights representative, tells Reuters in 2003. "Local officials just shrugged when I asked them about it." It's crippling the country. "If it is not stopped, Cambodia will face a human and ecological tragedy."

The group Global Witness is Cambodia's official forest watchdog. Representative Eva Galabru decries what's happening in the woods. She is not shy, she makes her observations well known. She links logging violations to Cambodian officials. Then one night in May 2002, she is beaten up and threatened. The next year, Global Witness is fired by the government. Prime Minister Hun Sen accuses the group of biased reporting.

Still, McKenney is not entirely pessimistic. He doesn't think the forest will disappear. Cambodia has acres of trees with little economic value, and those will stay. "The forest is not going to be gone. The commercial forest areas might be gone."

Whether the logger is a multinational corporation, a Cambodian general, a Thai businessman or a Khmer villager, the money factor remains consistent. And when McKenney explains his logging scenario, it doesn't look much different from what most Cambodians think every day. Fishing, farming, logging, selling noodles in the market — Cambodians have no history of long-term investment. But they do have potent memories of struggling to survive day to day. Millions of Cambodians still wade through life, eking their way. Their biggest worry is what to eat for dinner. That means their biggest thought on money is: How do I get it now?

Fifty-three-year-old Va has recently retired from driving a logging truck. He did this in the forests around Anlong Veng, when the Khmer Rouge controlled that land. And because the Khmer Rouge controlled that land, he could earn a pleasing sum of cash. "Now cutting the trees is difficult because there is no war," he says. It was much easier before. Va hoots, "I saw Pol Pot. He was fat and white."

Va used to transport logs between Anlong Veng and a factory in this village north of Siem Reap, not far from Banteay Srei temple. The owner of the factory was a Cambodian army general, and in this way trade between enemy soldiers flourished, making war between them something of a façade. Economics trumped politics. They did business in U.S. dollars or Thai *baht*. Everyone came out ahead.

This was not a carefree job. The jungle was dangerous. Va always traveled with four our five soldiers in case there was trouble with Pol Pot's men. "I was afraid, but there were many soldiers in the truck." Va trekked through dense jungles, thick with mosquitoes, rife with snakes. "Many times I got malaria," he says. "I used to see tigers in the forest. I saw one running from the truck. I never see them now. Before, during Ta Mok time, there were many." His truck hit a mine once. "Many people were on the truck. I sat on the back," he says, "but the mine was in front of the truck. The people were OK." That truck still rests in his yard, dilapidated, its scars the emblem of a rough-and-tumble job.

Was it worth the risks? "I regret very much," Va says. "But now I stop." Still, the job earned his family a comfortable living, up to $1,000 a month, forty-six times the nation's per-capita income.

But everything began to change when the last Khmer Rouge soldiers defected in 1998. The government has since banned logging, and, he says, only military generals and other privileged elite can circumvent the regulations now. You have to know the right people and pay the right price. "Now I cannot work because there is no war."

But Va's son still partakes of the trade. The young man does it on the sly, a risk that troubles Va. "Yes, I worry." But he knows the business, and he knows what compels his son. Va grew up as a farmer, constantly chased by war. His family moved several times, and he tired of it. His father worked in a woodworking factory, and in 1993, Va slipped into the trade. Logging was, ironically, more stable than farming his fields and far more lucrative. Today, Va's daughter and son-in-law still run a furniture factory nearby.

I ask what Va thinks about the Khmer Rouge who governed these forests. He says the people weren't so bad, one on one, but anything could happen anytime. "I could earn money easily, but we were very, very nervous."

I ask what he thinks of the wood itself. Does he know it is the envy of countries like mine?

"I understand," he says, "but now the government does not allow us to cut."

How much does a typical dining set cost?

"I don't know in the United States," he says, "but here they cost $400 for one set, a table and six chairs." The table alone has a top sliced from one slab of hardwood, four to six inches thick, stacked atop a carved pedestal five feet around, the whole thing weighing several hundred pounds.

Just up the path, around a few houses and through the weeds, is the furniture shop run by Va's daughter. She buys wood from local villagers and sells the finished goods to people from Phnom Penh or Siem Reap. It ends up in guesthouses, restaurants and private homes. The solid stool I sit on — like a smooth, round pedestal, too heavy for me to lift — costs $15. A traditional Khmer-style bed — solid, one piece of wood, like a dining table but wide as a queen-size and low to the ground — costs $270. There are vases, planters, lounge chairs, tables, all made from luscious hardwoods. But lately, she says business is bad. And whether she knows it or not, it will only worsen.

"This wood," says her astute younger brother, "we don't have so much anymore, in Cambodia."

> *Destroying wildlife means destroying our next generation's knowledge.*
> — Conservation banner in Phnom Penh, 2001.

"Cambodia is one of the last strongholds," says Joe Walston of WCS over drinks one evening in Phnom Penh. He speaks not of war or armies or men wielding weapons. He speaks of a dying species, one suddenly and brutally devastated, disappearing from the Earth. "The crash has been absolutely monumental."

He speaks of vultures.

Vulture populations are disappearing worldwide. Trials suggest that in most areas they are succumbing to one of the antiinflammatory drugs injected into the domestic cattle they eat. The chemicals build in their bodies until they can sustain no more. "If that's the case, we have a lot of hope" because here in Cambodia, those drugs aren't used. Here the problem is thought to be mainly a shortage of food, brought on by overhunting of large wild mammals.

So WCS is trying a technique they call the "vulture restaurant." A scrupulous team of researchers treks to a remote part of Preah Vihear Province, through miles and miles of hot grassland, where they place a dead cow in the field and wait for the vultures to arrive. It takes days; the researchers camp in blinds. They sit and wait, steaming in the heat. They must position themselves carefully so as not to divulge their presence. The method seems to work, so far.

There's only one problem:

"Nobody's really interested in terms of conservation because it's not a super sexy species," Walston says. "Certainly there's a real drop-off in interest for things like vultures." It's a sad realization of the dedicated conservationist, that kindhearted soul who values all living creatures and recognizes the role of every living thing in this planetary system: Not all creatures are as cute as pandas. And there is more money in cute than there is in slimy, slithery, beastly or scavenging. But that does not deter people like Joe Walston.

"We're here for the unsexy species."

Sexy species make their homes in Cambodia as well. Tigers, elephants, bears, monkeys—Cambodia has it all, supersexy and undersexy, vultures, crocodiles, gaurs, gibbons, the giant ibis, the greater adjutant. Cambodia is a haven for rare and endangered species. But sadly it is also, as the *San Francisco Chronicle* notes, "a poacher's paradise."

Endangered animals are found in markets countrywide. Their parts fetch big money. Tiger bones sell for $400 a kilogram. The skin, the penis, the claws, the teeth: all for sale between $10 and $900, depending on the piece. Spin through a traditional medicine shop in Phnom Penh. Visit the local market in Kratie. Buy noodles on the street from a pushcart. You'll find tiger pelts, snake skins, dried monkeys and flying squirrels, bear gall, elephant ivory—a veritable array of butchery, common through much of Asia.

And some species, even sexy ones, pirouette on the brink of extinction, even without a price tag on their heads.

We tether to a tree amid the river and wait. All is silent until the dolphins dance for us. They swish and swoosh, circling and spinning around our boat. They show only their fins, their noses for a flash, a bit of back, nothing more—coy, flirting, shy. They tease. They swim perfect arcs in unison. Then they disappear for several minutes, no sound, no breath. Then up again over there.

The Irrawaddy dolphin, an oceanic creature that can live in freshwater, is a rare and endangered mammal. This small, snub-nosed cetacean once populated Southeast Asian waters by the thousands. "Here, shoals of porpoises sail along with their noses to the wind, frequently bounding out of the water," Mouhot writes of dolphins scuttling through Phnom Penh's waters a century and a half ago.

But now, only a meager few remain. In recent decades, dolphin populations have dwindled. They plummeted under the Khmer Rouge regime, when the animals were killed for oil used in lighting. In later years, they were slaughtered for meat. Pollution, dams, boats and fishing with dynamite and grenades have all contributed to the animal's decline.

But the small town of Kratie offers rare glimpses of these animals' obscure lives, and conservationists hope tourists will be lured to these tranquil creatures. The Cambodian government has joined with Japanese and Australian groups to start a dolphin campaign and an educational center in Kratie.

Every day, a handful of visitors hobble off the speedboat from Phnom Penh, walk one block to central Kratie, to this small river town of crumbling colonial architecture, resplendent sunsets and throbbing karaoke bars. They come mostly for the dolphins, which congregate in nine pools in the Mekong throughout the province. Kampi is the largest home, sometimes with twenty to thirty animals. In the dry season, from November to June, viewers can sometimes stand on a platform beneath shady trees and watch dolphins swimming offshore. In the rainy season, the river swells, swallowing land all around, and the dolphins migrate. Then, admirers can hire a fisherman to motor north several miles and tether his longboat to a treetop poking above water. If lucky, dolphins will peek from below.

Jerry and I come to Kratie in August 2001. We stroll down the town's main street, skirting along the Mekong under steel skies and a frisky wind. An open gate leads to a neat new building with dark glass windows, the fisheries department and dolphin project. Sam Kim Lorn, head of the provincial fisheries department, motors through the gate. Our interest in the dolphins delights him. If we are so inclined and we hire the boat, he will take us the next morning — a Sunday, no less — to see them. We eagerly agree to meet at 8.

This town could be beautiful. It is, in a wistful way. Dim, filtered light spreads across old French walls. A sidewalk traces the river the length of the town, lined by dipterocarps, with wooden labels written in Latin. It is quiet and laid-back. But any riverside experience is tainted by whiffs of excrement. Garbage bobs on shore. Sludge pools around the market. Dust, crap, bones, shells, rambutan peels, plastic bottles — where does it all go? The river, the street, the little ponds where a man wades with his buffalo, and into the waters where the dolphins swim.

We meet the next morning, along with a researcher named Em Huy. We pile into a fiberglass speedboat and head swiftly upriver toward a dock, where we switch to a wooden longboat, then motor toward a dolphin pool. Along the way, we pass huge bamboo pontoons strung together. Em Huy tells us they are used to float wood down river. In the dry season five or six massive pontoons pass through each day, scaring the bejesus out of the dolphins. Sam Kim Lorn tells the logging companies to quit startling the dolphins, but "they never listen to me."

But locals don't intend the dolphins harm. Cambodian fishermen have long respected, even worshiped, them. "They think if they catch dolphins, they can't fish," says Em Huy. "It's very bad luck for them." The dolphin is the subject of colloquial legend. The story takes different forms depending on the teller, but Em Huy's goes like this: A family's beautiful daughter was once swallowed by a snake. The family killed the snake, and the daughter emerged. But she didn't want that fate again, so she jumped into the river and killed herself. The next year, a dolphin swam up to the family boat, and they determined it was their daughter, reincarnate. It's a curious tale, befitting a curious country. "In Cambodia, people always tell this tale to the generations," Em Huy says.

We head downstream a ways and find fifty-two-year-old Tuon Som Ol. He has lived here since pre–Khmer Rouge times and has fished since 1979, working the waters between Kratie and the dolphin pools. "In the dry season, I used to see dolphins here. There are fewer every year," he says. "Unfortunately the dolphins run into nets."

We see evidence later in the day, back at Sam Kim Lorn's office. He and Em Huy show us the darker side of the dolphin world. They open the door to a dank barn-like building, full of roofing tiles, scrap wood and tubs of formaldehyde with bones. They display the skeleton of a fifteen-year-old female dolphin caught in a net in nearby Stung Treng Province. The skeleton will be assembled and used for education.

That year three dolphins have been caught and killed in gill nets, and the number only gets worse. "No doubt more dolphins have died," says Isabel Beasley, a dolphin expert who conducts research in Kratie. "It's impossible to say the population is increasing," she later tells me. "It is such a small population, and in such a restricted range, that even one or two human-induced deaths a year are going to prevent any population increase." Beasley says Kampi's allure is key to the dolphin's fate. "If managed well, tourism will probably be the main conservation tool for the future of the population."

But the dolphins' luck is running slim. Every year, more die. They're caught in nets, and researchers suspect there might be poison in the water. In the first three months of 2004, eight dolphins are found dead in the Mekong, and Beasley wonders whether any will survive.

It would be the loss of a stunning creature. These animals lead placid lives. They seemingly wear smiles on humanlike faces. It's no wonder they enchant their fellow fishermen. "They like to live in peaceful places," Em Huy says. "They are like people."

If conservation efforts are to succeed in Cambodia, they must work in tandem with the people. "How do we both conserve an area and help the people who live in that area have a better life?" That's the critical question, says Bruce McKenney of CDRI.

Take this: 55 percent of Cambodia's population is under the age of 19. "You've got a lot of people coming into the workforce," he says. "So how do you address this problem? What are the skills of the people? Most are in rural areas." And most have little education. What does that mean?

It means a rice farm that once fed five cannot easily feed two or three or four more. People move when the status quo cannot sustain them. They creep deeper into forests, they clear new land for planting, spreading their roots. They move to Thailand; they move to Phnom Penh. They find jobs in factories; they drive *motos* around town, or they don't work at all. They erect makeshift shanties; they sleep on the streets; they return to their villages when they can. And in their villages, they find even more people with even less to eat, living on land that's ever more taxed to its limits. "I don't see any reason for these trends to reverse themselves," McKenney says.

And so, if a conservation program can offer viable options to the people, it just might work. "Communities will often choose a different lifestyle than they've had previously," says Joe Walston of WCS. "A lot of these communities have had shitty lifestyles." Most Cambodians would like nothing better than something better.

Through the right programs, things could change, he says. "I have every reason to be optimistic."

Long ago, a large terrapin swam Cambodia's estuaries in royal ease. Its olive gray carapace blended with the murky waters it loved. This turtle was legend. The species belonged to his majesty the king. So loved, so revered was it that the king hired special guards to protect it, and all but the royal family were forbidden to eat its tasty eggs.

Over time, *Batagur baska* as it is known by its Latin name, disappeared from Cambodia. People hunted them, despite the king's decree. Villagers say they recall seeing the turtles, some as recently as the 1950s, but scientists presumed the mangrove terrapin extinct in this land. Only its legacy remained.

Then, in 2001, a small colony of the terrapins is found on the banks of southern Cambodia's Sre Ambel River, in former Khmer Rouge territory. They aren't extinct after all. They've just been hiding through a very long war. This discovery is a fantastic surprise to scientists.

And then: There are more. Adult *Batagur baska* turtles start to surface in fishermen's nets and wildlife trading rings. These findings spur conservationists to action. The Wildlife Conservation Society initiates a year-round program to guard new nests, keep poachers at bay and teach villagers about the animal's precarious presence in Cambodia.

But this program does something equally remarkable for humans: It gives former Khmer Rouge soldiers the safest, most lucrative jobs they've ever had and good reason to save the turtle that pays their salaries.

Ninety miles south of Phnom Penh is a scorching, dusty smuggling and fishing port off the main road to the South China Sea. Things move through Sre Ambel town — logs, guns, drugs, illegal fishing boats, and now prized turtles. Jerry and I go there with WCS researcher Heng Sovannara in May 2002. We drink iced coffee from plastic bags and wait for a boat at a wooden dock, where trash bobs in smelly sludge. Sovannara can't wait to get out of town.

The river terrapin once lived in India and Bangladesh, extending east through Vietnam and south through Indonesia. Today, only small populations remain in Malaysia, India, Bangladesh — and here, again, in Cambodia.

The animals face many threats: hungry humans, monitor lizards, logging, dynamite fishing and weak law enforcement. They are prized throughout Asia, and every year they end up among thousands of endangered turtles in Chinese food markets. In December 2001, 10,000 live turtles were seized from a ship stopped in Hong Kong. The animals were caught in the wild, and many became sick or injured during shipment. The lot contained eleven species, including *Batagur baska*. The shipment was worth more than $400,000.

As we head up the Sre Ambel River, Sovannara shouts over the engine, "Before, this area was Khmer Rouge." He never came here then, it was much too dangerous. The rangers now guarding the terrapins fought for the Khmer Rouge. "Now they have a better job," he says.

We veer right, up the Kaong River. The water sits in stillness, like green glass. Empty beaches, small islands, no people, sylvan mountains ahead. We've reached Sovannara's beloved wilds.

We arrive at the thatch home of Osmang, former soldier-turned-ranger. He lives at the base of a small mountain, purple in afternoon radiance. A Panasonic radio hangs from a wooden post, burbling old American love songs. We learn fishermen have caught a sixty-four-pound female *Batagur baska* this week. WCS bought it for 50,000 *riel*, about $12.50, the price its meat would fetch in the market. She wallows in a small shelter, in mud, behind Osmang's home. She awaits a trip to town until the king or a suitable representative sets her free.

We sit on the hard slat floor of Osmang's house on stilts, talking with him, his wife and a visiting friend. Their possessions consist of the Panasonic purchased in the last year, a radio for WCS work, a fishing net, cooking utensils, and numerous young cassava, chili and papaya plants surrounding the home. They have five kids, three girls and two boys, aged five to nineteen.

Osmang is forty-one. Until the 1993 elections, he was a Khmer Rouge soldier. When I ask Osmang what he thinks of that former life, his wife, Kaow, is quick to answer: "Didn't like it! Didn't like it!"

Osmang agrees. "This job is better.... I didn't like to work with the Khmer Rouge soldiers, but there was no way to choose because the government was Khmer Rouge and the Khmer Rouge were the government." Like many, he was forced to fight. Osmang readily admits he used to eat turtles. "Every year I hunted to bring food to my children." But now he wants to save the terrapins. "I have a contract with WCS for conservation."

Salayman, the friend, wears nothing but a checkered *krama* cloth around his waist, as many country men do. In 1959, he tells us, turtles thrived around here, and the king hired rangers just as WCS does today "so people didn't kill the wildlife." Kaow's grandfather was one of those royal rangers, though she never saw the turtles while growing up.

We step outside into air so humid it hangs like smoke. Dragonflies swarm the sky. We climb into a small, wobbly wooden boat and head upriver toward the nests. A parakeet swoops low; a cluster of butterflies flanks a small beach, their wings clasped and erect. We pass several dead fish, and Osmang says someone might have been fishing with explosives, a ubiquitous problem.

We stop at a small sand hill with four bamboo cages. These nests inside were transported from a low spot upriver, where high water could have washed them away. "They cannot hatch in the water," Sovannara says. It's a meticulous process to move turtle nests because each egg must be recorded and placed into the new nest precisely as it was laid, same side up.

In the trees are three small huts where the rangers stay. They report no activity around the nests. It's been more than three months since the first egg was laid. Three men disassemble a cage top, and Sovannara clambers inside. He paws through hot sand, flinging golden grains, digging a hole six inches down to check on the eggs.

"Yes!" he yelps. "Hatch already!"

There, at the bottom of the hole, is a little *Batagur baska*, legs flailing, carapace flipping — boom, on its back — then upright again, skittering about, trying to escape the hole. The audience breathes a collective, joyous, "Ahhhhhhh."

The little terrapin is about three inches long with a yellowish shell. Sovannara holds it in the air, and it squirms. Its white eggshell is shed on the sand. This nest had eight eggs, and Sovannara digs for the others, plucking them one by one. He finds six live turtles and two dead. "I'm very, very happy because I started this project by myself," he beams. "It's successful."

The rangers place the critters into a metal pot for safekeeping, and they *skritch-skritchskritchskritch* in an instinctive search for water. They do this all day; they will do it all night and all morning until they meet their new home in the Sre Ambel River. They have tiny little noses with two perfectly round nostrils. They clamber over each other, scratching, clawing, pushing. "We'll put the fish in for them and slice it up," Sovannara says. And that's dinner.

"I feel very happy when I see the *Batagur* hatch like this," says team leader Yen That. He also works for the Sre Ambel Fisheries Unit, and he's the only one who wasn't Khmer Rouge. Every day he watches over the nests, making sure no one tampers with them. No one has, but if he had to he would arrest the troublemakers and scold them. He carries no gun, only the heft of his words and the weight of his government office. So far, that's enough.

Each cage has a sign with a picture of two female turtles thinking in bubbles: "People collect our eggs. They kill us. They kill our children." The back of each sign explains the terrapin's royal history and its recent comeback. "Please protect together," the sign implores in Khmer.

We check two more nests upriver, and the tally is complete: thirty-one live *Batagur baska*. The rangers rip a fish net and tie it over each pot, keeping the turtles inside. Sovannara pays his employees $40 each, and they sign receipts by thumbprint. Ranger Sok Seng immediately hands his two crisp $20 bills to his wife.

We return to Osmang's house amid monkeys swinging through trees and hornbills flying overhead. We sleep that night under mosquito nets, with the moon rising large, yellow and misty over far-off trees. The turtles scratch the entire night, their clattering claws like soft rain.

Early the next morning, Sovannara and Yen That carry the adult female to the boat. The two men flip her on her back, and she squirms like the babies. Her thick body spills from her shell.

The river is glass again, like a faintly warbled window, the air sweet with jasmine. We motor slowly, passing families fishing. An otter swims across our path. Five years ago, this trip would have been impossible, this land lost to bandits and soldiers and fear.

The female terrapin is frightened, and she cranks her head to look around. Yen That cools her with buckets of water. As we approach Sre Ambel, we disembark at a grassy path that leads to the highway. We lug all belongings up to the road, turtles too, then hitch a ride to town in a cramped, overweight minivan. But first: Everyone waits while Sovannara tells a local council leader about the turtles so he can spread word: Let them live.

In Sre Ambel town, Sovannara dangles each baby in a heavy Ziploc bag clipped to a hand-held scale. He measures height from shoulder to foot. He measures width across the belly. When that's done, we're back on a boat and heading upriver.

We stop at a cluster of thatch huts called Kring Chek where about forty villagers jostle for a view of the terrapins. They say they have seen soft-shelled turtles before, but nothing like these.

It's time to release them, and everyone wants a part. The river lies a quarter mile away, and most of the village files down the path to a mucky perch at water's edge. We're covered in mud up to ankles, calves, thighs. A woman digs into the basin, grabs each turtle and — plop — drops it into the water. Then we're all digging in and plopping turtles. They sink then rise up and around and swim into the rapids. The crowd squeals with delight.

In a minute, it's over. All are gone, seeking a new life. Some turtles return toward land as though confused, but villagers spin them in the proper direction. Tiny heads bob in straight lines through the water. "I am very happy, the baby can swim across the river," Sovannara says. "I think in the future the population will increase."

Back in the boat, en route to Sre Ambel, we see a man in the river up to his chest, net in hand, swirling it about the water. A woman riding with us yells at him in Khmer. Words burn through her mouth in amazing pitch, volume and speed for several minutes, while the man silently nods his head, yes, yes, yes.

What did she say? we ask Sovannara.

"She said: 'Don't catch.'"

17. The Fringe: People on the Edge

Cambodia is the most homogeneous society in Southeast Asia. Ninety-five percent of the population is ethnic Khmer, although many people will tell you this isn't true, that the country is overrun with Vietnamese. Nevertheless, not only do the people share the same blood, they share customs and beliefs. It is a country of farmers and fishermen. It is a country that speaks the same language, Khmer, same as the ethnic group's name. And it is a country of Buddhists.

But there is diversity. There are small pockets of people who are not Khmer, not Buddhist, not part of the mainstream. There are tribal people living in the farthest stretches of eastern Cambodia — the *chunchiet*, some 70,000 hill-tribe villagers from a dozen different ethnic groups, each with its own language, culture and history. Collectively, they are called Khmer Loeu or the "Upper Khmer."

There are, too, some 200,000 Cham Muslims, with ancient roots in this land. Their rulers contended with Angkor kings and fought vicious battles over territory. Kampuchea Krom, that land around Saigon in southern Vietnam which Cambodians claim as their own, belonged to the Chams before the Khmers. Today, the Chams live in small pockets scattered around Cambodia, many in rural enclaves. Their roots are firmly planted in Cambodian soil.

Through history, these remote populations have suffered persecution, derision, and discrimination. The hill tribes were hunted and sold during Angkor times. "The ancestors of the dark-skinned Khmer Loeu were among the slaves named 'dog,' 'cat,' and 'detestable,'" writes journalist Elizabeth Becker. During Pol Pot times, both Muslim Chams and Khmer Loeu were targeted and swiftly expunged. The Khmer Rouge viewed the Chams as foreigners, as enemies to quash. Many Chams supported the Khmer Rouge revolution in its early stages but soon changed their minds. The Khmer Rouge turned against them. They destroyed Cham schools and copies of the Koran. They turned mosques into granaries and pigsties. Becker writes that in four years of Khmer Rouge rule, up to half of the Cham population died.

Today these minorities form just a small slice of Cambodia. Less than 2 percent of the population is Cham, less than 1 percent Khmer Loeu. But their cultures, their lifestyles, have endured centuries of hardship. They have always lived on the Cambodian fringe.

Every morning when Ply Ch'hroeut goes to work in the Phnong forests of eastern Cambodia he dons the local workman's attire of rubber flip-flops, long-sleeved shirt, blue shorts and a stinky stogie, with the curved bamboo handle of an axe slung over his shoulder. Some days he chops wood, hunts lizards or readies a field for rice planting. But once a week, he pays homage to an array of evergreens and sets off to tap their worth.

The trees, six different types of dipterocarps, grow tall and wide through eastern Cambodia's jungles. Their resin is used to light homes, waterproof boats and produce lacquers, paints, varnishes and perfumes. From that resin, Ply Ch'hroeut and his neighbors can earn up to $32 a month, depending on the season. It's the best income he's ever known.

Ply Ch'hroeut demonstrates his trade for us. Each of his tree trunks has a gouge, about ten inches by six inches, where resin collects. He takes a homemade scoop made of a bamboo handle and a tin can to loosen the resin, scraping the wood, funneling black syrupy goo into a jug on his shoulder. When finished, he lights a small fire in the hole. Sweet-smelling flames engulf the trunk. Heat pours from the source, like an open oven door. Resin sizzles and drizzles inside the tree until he snuffs the fire with green leaves, and smoke billows from the hole. An oily scent lingers in its wake.

Each tapped tree yields up to a quart of liquid resin, or *chor tuk*, per week. Villagers also collect resin in solid form, *jor chong*, which falls in amber chunks from treetops like manna from heaven.

Ply Ch'hroeut has lived his entire life in these forests, as remote as it gets in this country. He is Phnong, the largest hill-tribe group of Mondulkiri, a province of 38,000 people and vast amounts of space. He resides in a village called *Dam Swai*, meaning "mango tree," named for a massive fruit-laden lode that has fed generations. "This mango tree is very old already, planted when I was not yet born," he says.

Ply Ch'hroeut has practical knowledge of his landscape: He knows the jungle harbors more wild pigs than before because there are fewer tigers to hunt them. He knows where wild elephants tromp during the rainy season. He knows which plants are edible and which aren't. He says, while looking at a clump of tasty-looking yellow tomato-like bulbs, "You can eat, but you can die."

Ply Ch'hroeut's work, his trees, his village and his lifestyle are helping to save one of Cambodia's last great, biologically diverse forests. If the forest survives, so will the wildlife within. Hence the Wildlife Conservation Society has sent a team here to learn everything it can about the Phnong, to create a sustainable plan for resin tapping that will preserve the forest, its wildlife and the Phnong population.

So here we are, knee-deep in bramble and bamboo, mosquitoes wafting about, gibbons hooting in the background. Jerry and I have followed Ply Ch'hroeut into the forest with WCS researcher Phet Phaktra. The full WCS ensemble consists of our guide; British researcher Tom Evans, who earned his PhD in tropical rattans at Oxford; Hout Piseth, a researcher from Phnom Penh; and Hang Mary, a Phnong woman who cooks and talks with the womenfolk, gathering crucial information while the men trundle through the Cambodian outback. Throughout our excursion, Phet Phaktra is called "Tra," and Hout Piseth goes by "Piseth."

Our troupe of six noticeably enlarges Dam Swai, which numbers seven huts on a rutted oxcart "road" three hours by foot from another Phnong village called Raka Thmei, which is two hours by four-wheel-drive pickup from the main road, which is half an hour from the WCS camp headquarters, which is five hours from the nearest fully paved road, then another two hours to the capital of Phnom Penh.

The conservationists' mission entails a number of sometimes grueling, often mundane, occasionally thrilling activities: counting, measuring and plotting the locations of resin trees; interviewing villagers about hunting, fishing and farming patterns; waiting endlessly in ceaseless heat for villagers to return from the forest; dining on dried fish and rice three meals a day; swatting mosquitoes; plucking leeches; dodging monsoons; and, as we learn, avoiding angry illegal loggers and border cops armed with assault rifles.

For all our disruption, the Phnong seemingly carry on as though we're nothing noteworthy. And they show no astonishment at the high-tech gizmos, little hand-held global positioning system units, that WCS researchers use to note their position in the world.

After all, Ply Ch'hroeut is a man who has never been in a car. He's seen airplanes but says, "I've never driven one." He has no desire to visit the famed Angkor Wat or even Sen Monorom, the provincial capital. Ply Ch'hroeut has only seen neighboring villages, and those are too large for him. Too large, in fact, for all the residents of Dam Swai. "I came back to my homeland," Ply Ch'hroeut says, after years of absence. Like most Cambodians, his is a history of moving.

In pre-war times, Dam Swai's families harvested resin from a few trees for personal use, mainly to light their homes at night. There was no resin trade, and villagers subsisted on farming. "It was different then," Ply Ch'hroeut says. "More people and more land cleared."

Then, in the 1970s, the entire area was evacuated during the Khmer Rouge attempt to create an agrarian utopia. Dam Swai's forty families, and those of numerous other villages, were removed to another place in Mondulkiri called Koh Nyek, or "island of people," for "collectivized paddy agriculture," the Khmer Rouge euphemism for slave labor camp. Jungle swallowed thatch homes. The provincial capital, Puoy Plok, was abandoned. Nothing remains today but chunks of a French colonial airstrip, heavily bombed by the Americans. "When I was young, the French came here on airplanes," Ply Ch'hroeut says. Now, it's all grass.

When war ended, many Phnong families resettled in Memong, a nearby village where land is good for growing but swollen with people. So Ply Ch'hroeut and a handful of others sought another trade. They learned they could make money in the forest. Thus, the old mango tree flanks a village once again.

But Dam Swai, like many villages around here, exists within a logging concession, and although Cambodia's logging system is under reform, the bottom line remains: at least 19 percent of the Phnong's resin trees have been felled in the past few years, and not by them. If these trees are gone, so is the resin, so is the money, so is the Phnong life as they know it.

To the Phnong, the forest is sustenance. "It's a job," Ply Ch'hroeut says. Yet if work changes, if the resin stops flowing for any reason, the Phnong will find other means—hunting, farming, cutting trees, whatever. The villagers know this. The Phnong need no computers, GPS units, scientific data points or PhD analyses to tell them this. It's what every culture does when old lifelines break.

Conservationists also know this. Thus the need for a sustainable resin-tapping plan if they want to save the forest. To create one, WCS does need computers, GPS units, scientific data points and PhD-grade analyses. They must count, measure and plot each resin tree with scientific certainty. They must define the forest based on resin tapping and wildlife habitat with scholarly acumen. They must tirelessly ask: How and where do villagers tap resin? Where and how do they hunt? Do resin trees grow where wildlife roams? What happens when someone steals fish? What happens when a young couple marries? Where do they go? What will they eat?

Ergo, they make an ironic but practical pairing, the Phnong and WCS. Two groups with vital interest in some monstrous evergreen trees for vastly different reasons from different worlds and different eras. The Phnong don't quite fathom the WCS mentality — why it does what it does the way it does it — but WCS knows it must understand perfectly the Phnong thinking — why they do what they do the way they do it — or else this unique coupling will never work. And then the forest could perish.

Jerry and I begin our first day of this journey in May 2002 on the smog-choked streets of Phnom Penh. But in two hours we've left traffic behind, as well as paved roads. It's a different world, a dusty world with earth, people and buffalo all of the same red hue. When a truck passes, we glide for a minute, unable to see through the thick billow of crimson dust.

The Samling Logging Camp sits several hours into this lonely land, amid cracked and rotting logs, all with neat Mylar tags, bar coded for international sale. There are hundreds, piled higher than buildings. The camp has been nearly abandoned since commercial logging stopped in Cambodia. WCS now occupies one end of the grounds with a bunkhouse, mess hall, guard room and storage room. Tom is out foraging when we arrive, but he's left us a note: "Welcome to WCS-Samling Holiday village. We hope your stay here is a pleasant one!" He soon returns, covered in sweat and blood, toting a trunk of mystery rattan and absolutely giddy with his discovery, which he asks Jerry to photograph for his records.

That evening, as the orchestral growling of the Samling generator lulls the WCS crew to sleep, Tom stays up awhile, reading an interesting selection: P. J. O'Rourke's *Holidays in Hell.*

Early the next day, we leave Samling in a WCS 4x4 pickup, with an armed guard who sits in the bed as we bounce along roads and paths and trails that fan through the forest. Tom rather enjoys these jaunts. "It's a really great way of life," he says. "I'm trying to wean myself of it because it's not really compatible with a family." He's been doing it on and off for a couple of years. While he treks through primordial malarial jungles, his wife and young son remain in England. (In time, his family grows, and his wife and two sons will move to Phnom Penh.)

Tom says much of the land we drive through was scrub brush in 1967. He knows this because "the Americans, when they were mucking around here, made some really good maps. And now it's all grown back into good forest already."

We rise high upon rolling green hills with tufts of stubbly grass, small trees and vast vistas. Tom says the area has potential for spectacular wildlife viewing. Years ago, big beasts roamed Mondulkiri savannahs as they do in Africa today. And eventually, the World Wide Fund for Nature will propose turning a mosaic of Mondulkiri into a protected safari park, like those in Africa.

Meanwhile, a guy in the front seat hangs his phone out the window, searching for a signal. "Have! Don't have! Have! Don't have!" he shouts as we travel along, and a guy in the pickup bed bangs on the truck to Stop here! No, there! No, here! They want to call home, and the only cell phone tower is dozens of miles away in Sen Monorom, the provincial capital. "Here!" They jump out, and we're atop a gorgeous clearing with views of rolling blue-green hills all round, reminiscent of Oregon in wintertime but much, much, *much* hotter. We leave four of them alone on the road with their phone, miles from nowhere, and the only clear connection to the cell tower. The truck will return at some unknown time in the future to pick them up. They'll just have to wait. Meanwhile, we head toward forest, where bamboo slaps us through the windows.

The road quickly degenerates to trail, and slick at that. We snake and slide, pausing once to rebuild our path, piling rocks atop a trench that inhibits our journey, until we finally reach the Phnong village of Raka Thmei, a stopping point before we head to Dam Swai.

Raka Thmei was settled in 1998. Tra, Piseth and Hang Mary have been stationed here for some time, conducting interviews, staying in a thatch hut with a tin roof. There are no toilets in this village and nothing of a garbage service. "I suppose they just toss it through the floor," Tom says after eating a lunch of bread and mango with leftover peels he scrunches through the bamboo slats, as the others do. Dogs and chickens lap it up below.

The house overlooks a hillside of stumps chopped, charred and baked silver by sunlight. Villagers are busy clearing lands for planting. Men with arm muscles like coiled snakes heave axes and set scrap wood afire. Flames rise fifteen feet high as more clearings are made down the road.

Washing takes place downhill, at a small spring full of jumping water spiders and dead wasps. It's the only accessible bathing spot around. Buff village women haul eight-gallon jugs of water up from this hole in the staggering heat of afternoon. There is a well in the village, but this is the dry season and the well nearly is, too.

Jerry and I take an uninhibited stroll that afternoon, a pleasure Cambodians rarely know. No land mines here, no reeking city garbage, no noise, no thieves, no work to do. Just a walk through the forest, with no purpose greater than exploration.

A gibbon *whwhooot-whoot-whooots* at us, and a hidden deer offers a solitary bark. We find a snake, a slender, three-foot yellowish-tan creature that cranes its kite-shaped head toward Jerry's foot as he's about to step through the reptile's range. We back off, and it makes an *S* curve up a tree. Tom later tells us it's a twig snake; he sees one just like it and declares it gorgeous.

Tom is raring to work, ready to investigate a stand of trees several miles away before the day ends. "We're trying to piece together, based on people's descriptions in the interviews, where these trees are," he says. We round up two *motos* and set off at a breakneck speed. After fifty feet, after I'm flung off the cargo rack of the *moto* for the second time, I quit. Enough — I'll go perch on a log and write. Tom and Jerry proceed without me, racing oncoming darkness over slippery trails to plot a pair of far-flung resin trees. Jerry sits behind a one-handed driver who picks his nose while flying through forest. Hmm. If he has one hand and he's picking his nose with his fingers, then that must mean ... better not think about the driving method.

Jerry returns at the brink of dark, but Tom does not. We wait; the night bugs sing; we wait; finally he comes on foot. The *moto* has run out of gas, and he is giddy again. He proclaims it an "Exciting!" ride. "It's not usually this dangerous," Tom says of his research. He maintains a perpetual optimism. His motto: "If something goes wrong, you just redefine the goals and then nothing really has gone wrong at all."

Starlight and candlelight illuminate the village at night. Not a single home has a generator or a karaoke machine. Not a single home — despite one radio, a man hammering and two dogs fighting — has sound to outdo the forest chorus of crickets and critters.

Tom, a steadfast vegetarian (unless the animal is already dead and the meat will surely rot), cooks his dinner every night. That night, he is not pleased with the Raka Thmei kitchen after Hang Mary has her way with a chicken. "The whole place is splattered with little bits of flesh and blood." But he manages to prepare his vegetables unsullied.

After dinner, the villagers invite us to drink jar wine, an ancient brew. Damp rice, sprinkled with yeast, sits for days or weeks in a huge jar, historically sold for the price of an elephant. When drinking time comes, water is poured over the top and alcohol is sucked from the bottom through curved straws several feet long. We ask whether *barangs* have drunk wine with them before. After much animated discussion and translation, Tra rolls his eyes and translates in a long, drawn-out drawl: "Every year."

"Every year?"

"They come 2000, 2001, 2002."

"Tourists?"

More chatter and gesticulations.

"No," he says. "Mostly researchers." Scientists who come to study the Phnong land and the forest animals. Cambodians are used to foreigners poking about their business since the country sustained a UN infusion of more than 20,000 foreigners in the early 1990s and subsequent waves of international aid groups and their thousands of expatriate residents. But the boisterous streets of Phnom Penh are a long way from Raka Thmei.

They're just happy we're here because our presence offers an excuse to slug some back. Soon enough, they carry on as though we're not even here. The party grows raucous, lit by candles and little bamboo cups of flaming resin. And in proof that some humor is universal, the men start telling fart jokes. They howl and hop about. It all goes pleasantly downhill when one man bends over and sticks a lighter beside his rear and lights one.

The next morning, Jerry talks with a woman who runs a small shop, one of three in Raka Thmei. She tells him a neighbor has been robbed, and she's terrified to take the oxcart road to the main road, and she's also terrified of the route to Sen Monorom because she thinks it's crawling with cops. And these aren't your friendly neighborhood cops. These cops have a reputation for being as bad as the criminals.

Then we learn of a murder the previous month. A man was killed, but the villagers say all is now OK because the assailant was caught. This is the story Tom hears. But now this morning Piseth tells him they "didn't catch all.... They caught one of him."

"One of him?" Tom asks.

We have planned to hike the four miles to Dam Swai along jungle paths while an oxcart transports our bags down a rough, isolated six-mile road. But now, there is much more animated discussion of bandits, robberies on the road, the questionable safety of the oxcart, the odds of arriving in Dam Swai unscathed. "I'm slightly horrified by this news," Tom asserts. We persist with the day, nonetheless.

While we wait for the oxcart, Tom and Piseth soon engage in an involved conversation about electric fishing in the village. Piseth has, through earlier interviews, found there aren't enough fish for the village because some fishermen use electrical prods or explosions. These methods are illegal and kill more than one's fair share. Tom wants to know why the villagers don't stand up to their neighbors. He explains to Piseth that in England, people don't help bad neighbors. "I need to understand their thinking," Tom prods Piseth. "If one family does something bad, what can the others do to stop?"

"You cannot stop. Only to *say* stop," Piseth answers. Then he thinks for a moment and decides, "Maybe they can complain to the head of the village."

"And what can the head of the village do?" Tom asks.

Piseth translates this and discusses the question with Hang Mary, the bona fide source of local wisdom. Eventually Piseth answers. Such a scenario has only happened when one man's cows have eaten another man's corn. The third such complaint elicited the village head to arrange a meeting.

And what happened?

"If the cows don't stop..." Piseth starts, carefully phrasing his answer.

"The cows will be killed?" Tom inserts.

"*Not killed*," Piseth exclaims, mortified. Certainly not killed. "Hit. The cows will be *hit*."

After further discussion, Piseth tells Tom, "If you really want to stop this, you have to make the law." The two continue on, discussing possible ways WCS can help bring the rule of law to the rural Phnong world.

And with that, the oxcart arrives, soon leaving with our bags and Hang Mary riding shotgun without a shotgun, aiming for Dam Swai. Meanwhile, we hike through a forest of wild orchids, blooming ginger, laughingthrushes, volcanic rock grottos, giant millipedes and chunks of *jor chong*. Three hours of no vehicles, roads or people, except a few surprised Raka Thmei fishermen at a crystal-clear stream gurgling over boulders.

We arrive in Dam Swai, where Ply Ch'hroeut greets us. The villagers offer us

Deep in the forests of eastern Cambodia, the Phnong people live hours from roads and other towns, and far from the lifestyles of the rest of the world. Here, children crowd around a typical thatch hut in the evening. The Phnong usually live in homes like this. Dam Swai, Mondulkiri, 2002.

sleeping quarters in a thatch hut on stilts, no walls, open to the elements. Behind us, through a small copse, is a river, a gift to human skin on a scorching afternoon. The oxcart arrives forty-five minutes later, fully intact. Piseth and Tra tell us there are no motorbikes today, so no tree plotting to be done; we must remain in the village for the afternoon. But in fact, we later learn, there are no motorbikes at all, just the shell of one that rusts beneath a hut.

It's 2 P.M., which seems to be the time when women pound rice. Up and down the village path is the thud-thud-thud of a huge stick against grain in a wooden mortar. I steal from Paul Theroux: "That rhythmic thud of the pestle and mortar was like a heartbeat on the river." The work sculpts the sort of upper-body muscles Westerners envy. Sweat runs down the women's faces and necks, soaking shirts and sarongs. Meanwhile, Ply Ch'hroeut chops bamboo poles, driving the axe down the center, jiggling the tool until the wood splits. Presto: bamboo flooring. Order this stuff online through FastFloors.com, and pay $27 a square meter, on sale.

I watch from amid a passel of kids, and I ask how many Ply Ch'hroeut has. He looks at the seven around him and answers, "a lot."

Next door, I find a leopard cat pelt drying against a log, which immediately piques Tom's interest. He sends Piseth to determine how it was killed, where it was killed and whether this occurs regularly. That evening, when he and Tra fail to find informative answers, they do as usual: They ask Hang Mary to dig around for an answer.

Tom plans his hunt for the morning. He estimates a four-hour hike to the trees he hopes to count and measure, a four-hour return, and six hours between, traipsing through sweltering thickets with a GPS. "But it's worth it. I'll get my data point. It's what I live for."

After dinner, several village elders gather at our hut, huddled beside a giant map illuminated by the yellow flicker of a resin torch. They light cigars by the flame, while women sit on nearby ladders smoking their own cigarettes and watching the conversation unfolding on our floor. The elders say the largest Phnong villages are not on the map and no longer exist. They were all erased during the great Khmer Rouge evacuation.

The next morning we go with Tra and seventy-year-old Pouey P'sheu to look at his resin trees. He tells Tra it's a short walk, about fifteen minutes. He says he has ten trees. We pass piles of elephant dung, and Pouey P'sheu says, "In the rainy season, the elephants travel through here."

Well beyond fifteen minutes or any visible trail, we find two old trenches, buried in a tangle of greens, which our guides say date to 1979, when the Vietnamese fought the Khmer Rouge. Shortly thereafter, the first two resin trees appear, near each other, an hour into our hike. They are black with fire, sticky with resin. Tra unpacks a tape measure and a GPS unit to record girth and position.

We move up and down the banks of a dry, pebbly streambed that fills in the rainy season. We scramble through scrub and thorns, scratching our flesh to see more trees. A hornbill's wings swoosh above, chased by a caterwauling pair of greater racket-tailed drongo, whose shrieks shatter the forest sky.

By survey's end, we conclude Pouey P'sheu has seventeen trees, three of which no longer produce, all of which stand within a three-hour loop walk. This is remarkable news to Pouey P'sheu, who never before measured trees or his time on the job. His eyes grow wide by the numbers.

A short while later, we accompany Ply Ch'hroeut on a similar trek. We follow the pungent trail of his cigar smoke into the forest. He guesses he has a hundred trees, but nobody has counted them before.

Ply Ch'hroeut and Pouey P'sheu never counted their trees for the same reason few people in Dam Swai have watches. They live by land, sun and stars; numbers, time and math are superfluous. They have as many trees as they have; they collect as much resin as they do; that earns them as much money as it does, and it all happens when it happens.

Similarly, my questions about life ambitions and happiness fall flat here. Does Ply Ch'hroeut like the forest? He looks confused. Does he like his life? Are there things he doesn't like about the forest? These questions don't translate well. Life, for the Phnong, simply is the way it is, and if it changes, well, then life is what it becomes.

The trees belong to whom they belong; first come, first served. When a man finds a tree and marks it, it's his. That's protocol. No stealing, no fighting, Tra says. Yet the WCS researchers know what Ply Ch'hroeut does not: From an aerial view, the forest around them is shrinking, that outsiders increasingly tread on the Phnong way of life, and that forest attenuation is likely to continue. I ask Ply Ch'hroeut if he's afraid the forest will disappear. The idea has never really occurred to him.

As we talk, a monitor lizard kicks branches and leaves upon us from its perch in the trees above. "This is the top food of the minority people," Tra says. "Very good to eat." But of course, as a wildlife conservationist, he speaks from hearsay, not experience.

Soon enough we return to our starting point, where Ply Ch'hroeut retrieves a can, and we head in another direction over the top of an empty waterfall, that will surge when the monsoons arrive. A bit farther uphill, he scrapes a tree, collects the resin, lights the fire, snuffs the flames. It's what Ply Ch'hroeut and Pouey P'sheu and all their male neighbors do every week to make nearly all the money they have, which isn't a lot. It's also to some extent what keeps this forest intact and gives it hope for the future.

When we return to Dam Swai, Ply Ch'hroeut learns he has seventy-five trees in all. And if he wants to know precisely where in the world they are, Tra could read him the longitude and latitude plots from his little GPS unit.

Our group awakens the next morning just after 6 — hours after the chickens, the dogs, the entire village. Life starts early. We take note of the Phnong routines:

A woman named Koot, who has a soft mellifluous voice, cleans and weeds her cassava garden surrounding our hut. Three little boys play a game that resembles hopscotch, running and singing through chalky boxes outlined in dirt. A hen guards her eggs inside a rattan barrel that sits beside our sleeping area in the hut. Two enormous trays of fresh rice dry in the sun, amid charred stumps in a nearby field. And a young muscular man (one of many potential underwear models in the vicinity) digs six perfectly round holes about eighteen inches deep, making the foundation for a new hut. A wedding will take place in four days. The new couple needs a home, right beside the in-laws.

Out of pure curiosity, I take inventory of the contents in one of the huts: a woven mat, a mosquito net, a can of Raid, clothes in a heap, a plastic jar of cassette tapes, a Sony boom box, a blackened tea kettle. That's all it has. The boom box and cassette tapes are remarkably extravagant for this neck of the woods.

It's a bit hazy which Dam Swai house belongs to whom. They blend. The people are fluid, as are their lives. Some families seem to spill into two or three huts, and some are never around. Tom jokes that it's an "upwardly mobile" sort of place; locals have a house in Dam Swai and a cottage in the countryside for fishing on the weekends.

At lunchtime, Pouey P'sheu invites me up to his hut while he eats. His ladder is a foot from ours. I ascend.

"Delicious?" I ask.

"No," he shakes his head with certainty, still grinning. "Not delicious."

"Soup?"

"No. Water."

Then he shows me the salt bag, and there's his lunch — rice and salt water. I see the difficulty in persuading people to preserve lizards, cats and birds in the interests of global ecological sustainability when they have little else to eat.

Up the path thirty yards, forty-year-old Ran chops wood while his wife, Moo Saroeun, thirty-four, sits inside with a month-old baby named Samnang — another child in Cambodia named Luck. She shoves a large brown nipple into his mouth, and he suckles happily. This is her seventh child.

She invites me to her floor, about four feet off the ground. I show her pictures in the *Lonely Planet* guidebook. The name Angkor Wat sounds familiar to her, but Bayon, another famous Khmer temple, does not. She calls in Ran, who examines the photos. "I saw Angkor Wat, in 1982," he says. Ran has not been to Phnom Penh, Battambang, Kratie or any other Cambodian city. Moo Saroeun has never seen a monk and doesn't recognize a picture of one with bald head and saffron robe. When I explain that monks stay in a *wat*, she understands. She knows what a *wat* is, but she's never seen one.

I ask whether Moo Saroeun would like to visit Phnom Penh.

"No, I don't want to."

Angkor Wat?

"No, I don't want to."

Sen Monorom?

"No, I don't want to." She explains: "We don't want to go because we are poor people. We have no money."

I display a Cambodia map, and they look with disinterest. I point to the Tonle Sap, the great lake, which feeds 70 percent of the nation. Ran repeats the name, as though it's new to him. I point to cities and towns, and they stare blankly. The map means nothing to them.

Later that afternoon, there's a noise. A faint metallic grinding in the distance. It gets louder, it draws closer. Five minutes later a *moto* appears, and everyone runs to see the matter. It's the mobile grocer with goods from Sen Monorom. The grocer is a pertly dressed Khmer woman with clean clothes, gold jewelry, a made-up face and a voice like a carnival barker. One of the village's strapping young men runs off for an air pump to inflate the *moto's* sagging tires.

Ms. Moto Merchant brings chilies, tomatoes, garlic, shallots, carrots, a plastic bag of beef, onions, limes, salt, neon fruit drinks, white gourd juice, Red Bull, candy wafer bars, MSG, puffed rice snacks, vegetable oil, cabbage, greens, noodles, crackers, jelly, milk, chili sauce and soap. "We buy with resin money," Moo Saroeun says, although no one buys much. They simply gather around the woman and chat. The next day, the seller will go on to another jungle village.

Later that afternoon, rain batters the earth, and the village turns to a big puddle. We tie a tarp to the side of our hut as water breezes in. "The rain is my favorite part," Tom says. "No nagging guilt for not being in the field." He spends the fading daylight reading reports from previous tree-plotting expeditions while Piseth fills us in on the upcoming wedding, between a seventeen-year-old woman named Dee and a young man from Memong. Dee trots by later, and I tell her good luck. Piseth translates and adds to my wishes the usual, "May you have a child in a year."

That evening, Piseth reports that the villagers have informed Hang Mary the "leopard cat" drying against a log is, in fact, an otter. It was, after all, found in a fishing net. Tom balks at this news. I do too, for we have both seen some otters in our lives, we've seen some leopard cats as well, and this was no otter. Nonetheless, the villagers insist: No cat. Dead otter.

After three days in Dam Swai, we pack up the oxcart with the same driver, who wears a black T-shirt with white letters saying "Interesting Holiday," and we set out on our return hike to Raka Thmei.

The excursion delights with many sights: goldenback woodpeckers, earth-toned men, an eagle, fabulous green damselflies whose wings close at rest. We snack at a beautiful stream, clear, bubbling over boulders. And along the road, not far from Raka Thmei, Tom finds a different tree, with whitish resin, which villagers say is relatively rare.

The owners of our resting spot in Raka Thmei are here. They keep a dead lizard drying on the kitchen ceiling, chopped in many pieces, its claws splayed and evil looking. The woman of the house, P'nam, has short curly hair bobbed at the nape of her neck, and she smokes an indigenous cigarette. She wears a tattered sarong and no shirt. A relative, Bou Koh, is mute and communicates with his hands.

We watch them in their work. Bou Koh rethreads an old rattan rice tray. He shaves fine curls of ribbon from each green strip, cutting to size. Then he pries a slot in the weave and pushes the new fiber through, making a mottled mix of old brown and new green rattan. He wheezes as he works. A radio murmurs in the background, playing a fuzzy language lesson in Australian English, with today's emphasis on prepositional phrases. "The television is *in* the corner." "*Behind* the sofa … *in* the cabinet … *between* the bed…." The owners of this house, and all the residents of Raka Thmei, for that matter, understand not a word of this lesson. Nor do they have TVs, sofas, cabinets or beds.

The oxcart arrives with our bags. Piseth pays the driver 35,000 *riel* for the trip, about $9, and then we wait for the WCS truck to take us back to the Samling camp.

We wait.

Tom hikes up the road, expecting to watch birds until the truck arrives. The sun fades as an underlayer of gray moves swiftly beneath fleecy cirrus clouds. The air smells of the word "tropical." A rainbow, half an arch, appears momentarily behind us.

We wait and wait until 1:30, when a *moto* driver arrives with a note:

"Tom — Car is broken — accident with illegal loggers & some shooting: lots of action. You will have to try and get motorcycle back here." It is signed by another WCS researcher who also happens to be named Tom.

Normally, the WCS troupe would relish an extra few days in the jungle. But this time, Tom has a plane to catch. He's scheduled to jet off to London to meet his wife and son in two days. He does *not* want to miss the flight.

We discuss our options and contemplate taking an oxcart to the main road, eighteen miles, but Piseth and Tra say the cows couldn't do it. Not in one day, not today after the hot hike from Dam Swai. So Tom leaves on the *moto* with his daypack and a few essentials. He will head to the big WCS camp and arrange for a car from Sen Monorom to Phnom Penh the following morning.

Jerry and I wander some more. We inspect the village well, sixty feet deep. A young woman turns and turns the wheel, reeling in a bucket with a few inches of murky beige water. What does Raka Thmei do in the dry season, when all the land is parched and the wells dry? This is not enough to sustain a village. The three local shops—little huts with bags of salt, garlic, chili, rice, candy and palm sugar—have no more drinks. No more goods until a new supply arrives from town, whenever that is.

The next morning, we're awake, again, in Raka Thmei. A brilliant breeze sifts through the house. A chicken has been slaughtered and boiled and picked and digested. Hang Mary slurps on the leftovers for breakfast. Later, Tra jokes that he eats a whole chicken in three meals: dinner, breakfast, lunch. Feathers and innards rest below the hut, awaiting dogs and flies and other hungry scavengers.

We watch two men strap two eight-gallon jugs of resin to a red SunZuki motorbike with half a front fender, no front brake and a plastic soda bottle half-full of gasoline hanging from the rear seat. The first jug barely fits between driver and handlebars; the second is tied with rubber straps to the back seat. The load lifts the front wheel off the ground and nearly topples the *moto*. The driver struggles to kick start it. Pump—grgrgrgrgr. PUMP—grgrgrgrgrgrgrgrgrgr. Pump—grgrgrgrgrgr. This continues ten times, twenty times, more. Eventually the engine catches, and the driver heads hours into rough terrain toward Sen Monorom and the prospect of money.

We wait some more. Sometimes the wind sounds like a motor.

At 4 P.M., it's the real thing. A WCS truck arrives, bouncing toward us, this time with two armed soldiers. We are promised the full story when we arrive at the main camp. Everyone scurries like mice in a maze. We say our goodbyes, procure seats amid sacks in the truck bed with no view ahead, and race back to the WCS camp, sprinting against dusk. Branches slap back over the truck, thrashing heads and brushing faces. We slide through mud, slipping backward, hitting a wall of dirt. When we finally reach the blue-green hills on the horizon, the sun sinks. Rain starts. We meet the main road in darkness, barreling ahead. Camp appears at 6:45 beneath a black sky with no starlight. Tom is here, worried. Finally, we learn of the week's events.

It goes like this: A logging patrol jointly run by WCS and the Department of Forestry and Wildlife, driving a 4x4 truck like the one we were in, crashed into illegal Vietnamese loggers on a massively reinforced pushbike used to transport logs. The truck rolled; the Vietnamese were badly injured. The patrol righted the truck, arrested the loggers and detained them at the Samling camp. One remained unconscious through the night.

Upon this news, the loggers' friends—members of the Cambodian Border Patrol, with whom they're in cahoots—became outraged. They went on a rampage, firing guns in the air to threaten a WCS group they found conducting unrelated bird surveys in the jungle, and they threatened to kill the other Tom if they met him on the road. The bird team scattered in the forest, at night, in their underwear. One team researcher, scared and nearly naked, found the road the next morning and stumbled into camp headquarters. WCS sent out a search party for the other two team members. When Tom Evans returned to camp, a "high-ranking" meeting of officials from Sen Monorom was taking place right there. The illegal loggers were taken to the provincial capital for further legal action.

All of this has Tom and the other WCS researchers extremely worried. Tom also shares rumors that another conservation project across the country has suffered some recent rocket attacks. While the researchers know the risks of their work, the stakes are high: the future of Cambodia's wildlife and wildlands. Tom feels lucky to know such committed conservationists who aren't deterred. Dipping into some gallows humor, he says, dryly, "If they're shooting at you, it means you're doing something right."

We ride back to Phnom Penh the next day on a road of lumps and bumps and bathtub holes, a middle-quality road for Cambodia. I am reminded of what WCS bird researcher Tan Setha told me our first night: "When there are good roads, the wildlife is destroyed. When bad roads, the wildlife can survive. This is always the conflict with conservation and development."

Tom discusses the economics of resin collecting and possible scenarios for the future. Cambodia's population is growing. This area of Mondulkiri, he says, has essentially hit carrying capacity. If the population grows, the forest must sustain more people. Eventually that won't work, so the people will do something else.

Perhaps they will leave and find other work. Or perhaps they will grow more crops and clear more land and cut deeper into the forest WCS hopes to save. The same will result if more people move to Dam Swai from surrounding villages, as those villages grow too. Perhaps the cost of resin will rise, enabling the trees to sustain more people. But then what? Will villagers divide that money among more people, or will some villagers hoard profits? Will people buy as much resin at a higher price? Will villagers turn to hunting for profit? And what if new roads go through? Will the people start to cut and sell bamboo? Will they start to trade in wildlife?

Such questions swallow our thoughts for hours; no easy answers arise. Only the endless stretch of pockmarked road with rocks and ruts, a road that, as birder Tan Setha says, is both bane and boon to the area's future.

It's an empty road that gradually fills with cars, trucks and oxcarts brimming with plastics, food and people. It passes through dust-choked towns ringing with horns, engines and karaoke bars. It's a road leading to real pavement, congestion swelling like a snowball, with more noise, more people, more vehicles until it hits the outskirts of Phnom Penh where traffic halts in a stifling jam. It's a road that resin travels in syrupy jugs stacked on rickety motorbikes from the hill-tribe world to the outside world, from a small hole in a living tree to wads of *riel* in a Phnong man's hands. It's a road that Ply Ch'hroeut has never seen, never traveled, never imagined. Yet it sustains his life and his forest.

For now.

Many miles from the Phnong, another group struggles on the Cambodian fringe: The Chams, Cambodia's Muslim minorities who have lived here for centuries.

In late May 2003, Cambodian authorities arrest one Cham and three foreign Islamic teachers. They deport twenty-eight others and close the private Om Al Qura Institute, one of the largest schools in Cambodia. Until this happens, the school houses, feeds and teaches some 700 students from across the country. Its funding comes from Saudi Arabia. The children learn Islamic studies, Arabic, English, Khmer, math, science. It's a better and more rounded education than they could get in a Cambodian public school, all free. Many of the students return to rural villages and poor families that can't afford to send their kids to school at all.

The authorities close Om Al Qura based on tips from the U.S. government that the school and its teachers have ties to Jemaah Islamiyah, a Muslim extremist group in Southeast Asia with alleged links to al-Qaeda. These arrests come shortly before then–U.S. Secretary of State Colin Powell arrives in Phnom Penh for a regional meeting of the Association of Southeast Asian Nations.

A few months later, prime terror suspect Hambali, the alleged al-Qaeda leader of Southeast Asia, is arrested in Thailand. And the world learns, shortly thereafter, he recently spent six months at a Phnom Penh guesthouse.

In a matter of months, the Chams turn suspect. Fingers are pointed, rumors spread; the U.S. speculates Muslim terrorists are trying to dig roots in Cham society, and Cambodian officials refuse to discuss the situation. "It's very difficult to talk about the Chams," says Khon Dara, an administrator at the Ministry of Cults and Religion. "This incident is not connected to this ministry; it is dependent on the Ministry of Interior," he says. "This ministry doesn't know anything about the arrests of the Muslims." But when I ask at the Interior Ministry, I am avoided. I am sent from office to office, then upstairs. I am told only one man can answer my questions: Chhay Sinarith, director of Information. I sit in his waiting room, and his secretary tells me he is a busy man. I wait a long time, and finally he comes out, tells his secretary he does not have time to talk, and he leaves. He never returns my calls.

The Chams are befuddled. They have no idea why this has happened. They live in poor, rural villages with few newspapers and little contact with the outside world. "I never know about the news; I never listen to the radio; I never watch TV," says Abdul Rozat bin Abusamas, an Islamic teacher I interview in a small rural Cham village. Most Chams say they hate war, terrorism and violence, which they know too well, as the Chams were targets for extermination by the Khmer Rouge.

All they want is to live, farm, fish and pray, unhampered and unpestered.

When the arrests and the furor occur, I contact an old colleague from the *Daily*. Her name is Anou, and she is Cham. She and her friend, Ramlee, offer to help. They arrange meetings with Cham leaders in Kompong Ch'hnang Province, which is home to many Cham villages, a long distance from city life.

Early one Friday, the day Muslims go to their mosques, the four of us pile into a *tuk-tuk* and putter through the sea of traffic heading north toward Kompong Ch'hnang. We pass Svay Pak, the infamous brothel zone on the outskirts of Phnom Penh. We pass factories and restaurants and the Stung Treng port and *moto* repair shops, schools, brothels, dogs, women, kids, trucks, *cyclos*, *motos*, Land Cruisers, NGOs, government offices, fish farms, filthy markets, mosques, Vietnamese *pho* shops and very little greenery. It's a loud and polluted rumble through the city's outskirts.

Anou wears long sleeves even though it is broiling. I notice my bare arms and ask if it's OK. She says yes, "because you are not Cham but I am, so I must." She never goes to the village with her arms bared.

Along the ride, Ramlee tells us he used to work for a Cham human rights group, but funding ran out. He worked on economic development, a big issue for the Chams because so few have jobs and so few options exist. Most are farmers and fishermen, and many don't know how to start a business. "If they have some goods, they don't know where to sell," he says. The Chams don't have their own markets as Khmer people do. "I need to help the Chams, but I don't know how to do it."

We pass old army stations. "Before, this place was dangerous," Anou says. "There was fighting between Hun Sen's Army and the Khmer Rouge Army" in the late 1990s. But all that is past. "Now, everywhere it is safe."

After two hours of a bumpy ride, we reach Chrok Romet Village, a green settlement right on the main highway but quiet and clean with cats skittering around, the yards bountiful with bananas, papayas and squash. In this village, women wear knit hats, and men don nothing more than a *krama* around the waist. The people are casual and open, and there's nothing about them to suggest they are Muslim except the plain white mosque around which all homes are situated. We meet imam Ali bin Ibrahim, who is happy to talk. He, of course, covers his head but says attire is a personal choice for women and men.

This village has three imams, but Ali bin Ibrahim is the first, the most revered. "The people in this village chose me. I don't like it very much, but the people want me to do it," he says. "This position is difficult because we don't have much time for earning a living." Guiding a village, answering their questions and fulfilling their needs is not easy. "When we lead them, sometimes they don't want to listen to us."

We sit with him on plastic chairs in the entryway of the mosque, surrounded by stark white tile the color of Ali bin Ibrahim's teeth. He has a scraggly beard, little curly gray hairs in a small tuft on his chin. When I ask about the incident at Om Al Qura, he says, "I'm not involved with this problem. Some people know the information from TV, but they don't know the reason why they were arrested. They still don't know because the people don't follow the news." They are too busy trying to make a living. This is a blacksmithing village, and most men work long hours. When they aren't toiling under a bamboo roof by a fire, soiling their hands and bodies, they're farming their fields.

"I'm a blacksmith and a teacher," he says. His school, funded by the Malaysian government, is inside this building. There are 272 students, ages 12 through 20, both girls and boys. Here, they study the Koran, the Malaysian language and Arabic. They study other subjects at public school. All five teachers here are Cham.

Ali bin Ibrahim says he knows only enough Arabic to read the Koran, which is typical — except for those who grew up during Pol Pot time and can't read at all. "I teach students from 1 to 4 P.M., and I'm a blacksmith from 3 A.M. to 6 or 7 A.M." That early-morning job earns him about a dollar a day. His fingers and toenails are rimmed with black stains that don't wash away.

Ali bin Ibrahim has lived here since 1979, the end of the Khmer Rouge regime. He has a wife and six grown children. He terms this village "medium to poor." There is a market up the road, and the people are not as poor as some Chams. They also get along with their Khmer neighbors. "We talk to Khmer people and do business with them. We never have problems. We live together, and we are friends."

So what are his worries? "The biggest problem is earning a living. This is the only problem," he says. "My wife helps me." If they relied on his salary, they couldn't survive, so she sells porridge in the market.

I ask if he knows about the stories of Cham people in Cambodia, about the carvings on Angkor temples that depict his ancestors. He says, "I don't know about history.... Nobody tells me about history." He focuses on the immediate needs of his village.

We wander through the village and find L Lymas, a woman making a fish net. This is her work. She wears a pink knit cap atop her head and keeps her seven-month-old baby, Rooma Saki, by her side. She makes nets every day, each one selling for 170 *baht* in Thailand. That's about $4.25, but she earns only $1 on each net. She gives them to a middleman who sells them and later returns with her money.

L Lymas says she has heard about the recent hubbub, and some of the villagers fear they will be next on the government's list. A local noodle vendor ran away two weeks earlier. "He was afraid of being arrested because he was a teacher." People don't think he is necessarily guilty of any crime, just scared of what the government might do.

Three blacksmiths work just a few yards behind her house, in an open-sided hut. The constant clunking makes the ears ring. They are all covered in black. The leader, Math Sart, is streaming with sweat. He has worked as a blacksmith since 1979. "I like this job because I know how to do this and I don't know how to do anything else."

Math Sart has seven kids, almost all adults now. One is a blacksmith, another has gone to Malaysia to work in a factory. "It's not easy." And now, that son lives in hiding because he overstayed his visa. Like many Chams, he hopes to make a better life abroad than he can at home.

When I ask about the recent arrests, Math Sart says, "I don't know about this story. None of my children study there." But he wants me to know this: "I believe strongly in Islam." His whole family is Muslim; they always have been, and no one has ever questioned that. It has never occurred to anyone around here to leave the religion. But Math Sart's Islam is not like other types, not the sort that makes women cover their faces. Anou and I discuss the word "fundamentalist," and after several translations back and forth, Math Sart concludes that is not him, not the type of Islam he enjoys.

Just up the road a few miles is another village called Prey Pes, and here we meet a teacher named Abdul Rozat bin Abusamas. He sits on the wooden floor of his house on stilts, wearing a green-and-blue plaid sarong, no shirt and a red checkered *krama* slung over his shoulder. He keeps a bag of tobacco and a green lighter by his feet and a thermos of tea by his side. His white hat sits across the room. "I teach the Koran and Malaysian language just for religion," he says, blowing smoke that hangs in the window light in airy swirls.

He came here twenty years ago from another village. "There was no teacher here, so the people requested me to teach." His take on Islam is similar to Math Sart's. "It's up to your beliefs," he says. "Some teachers in Battambang, they follow a vision of fundamentalism." That's not his style.

I ask what a person does to be a good Muslim. "It's easy, we're normal just like you," he says. This is what he tells his students: Don't do bad things. Don't steal; don't drink; don't take drugs; respect your mother and father; study hard; work hard. "Some people follow; some people do not." If they don't follow the rules, "I still try to teach them."

But he never talks politics. He focuses only on his teachings. "Every day, I go to the mosque." When he's not in the mosque and not in his school, he's in the field. "Most people here work on the farm, and several people earn a living by selling meat in the market." And with that, it's time to go, time for prayers at the mosque.

It's up the road a smidgen. The men come, one by one, by *moto* and bike. Before entering the holy building, they gather at a PVC pipe outside, tapped with ten spigots for washing hands, face and feet. Only men come here; women pray at home. If a mosque has a second floor, women are allowed. But this one doesn't. "Men and women are equal, but for prayers, women cannot come," says Haji Adam bin Ali, the *ha-kem*, or community leader.

The mosque has lime green walls inside, with green and yellow tiles on the floor. Outside, cows graze through the yard; butterflies flitter about, and pillowy white clouds hang over palms and eucalyptus trees. The men come in mixed attire, some wearing sarongs and long overcoats, others in T-shirts. They spread their rugs in rows on the floor, while young boys play on the porch outside. At 12:15 soft mumbled prayers waft through the grounds; this is a quiet mosque. Anou and I watch through a side door. The men inside fidget, pick at their rugs, look at us, look all around. Some seem to doze.

When the service is over, we meet Haji Adam bin Ali outside again. When we first arrived, he was off on a CPP campaign, though he insists he supports no single party. He helps them all — that's his job. "I'm responsible for this village." What he really wants is for the top three parties to govern equally and for the government to care about the Chams. "I want the government to build a road and school." The village sits on a dirt track about a mile from the main highway. "The road is the biggest issue for the village. All the people in this village pooled together to build a road, but there is not enough money. We want the government to finish it." The people gathered $1,500, and they need about $2,000 more. "I requested the government to do it, but the government said this road is very short." In Cambodian government logic, it's not long enough for them to bother with. So the government said: Find an NGO to build it.

Haji Adam bin Ali is one of the few people around here to keep up on the doings of George W. Bush. "I know because I watch TV." He knows Bush started a war in Iraq, and he has heard allegations of Iraq's hidden weapons of mass destruction. If those stories are true, then he thinks the war is good "because the weapons are dangerous to everyone." But war in general is not good. "When the U.S. makes a war," he says, "civilians die."

Everyone we ask agrees, terrorism is no good. Many Muslim cultures have people who make war, Haji Adam bin Ali says, and that's bad behavior. "Because of war I have no sister or brother. My sister and brother died in war in the Lon Nol regime…. That's why I hate war." His people agree on this. "We all have the same feeling," he says. "Our hearts will tear if we hear about war."

The third village we visit is Ramlee's homeland. Everyone knows him, and they greet him warmly. But this village is different. It is stricter. *Ha-kem* Ismael bin Haro tells us the people follow the edicts of a former imam who died long ago. Women should cover their heads entirely. "Even one hair cannot show." It matters not if women from other villages or other countries don't follow suit, but the women in this village should obey. As he talks, about twenty women gather on the other side of the mosque, all lined up in rows, covered in black chadors from head to toe and cinched tightly around their chins. They do not come near the men.

Both Ismael bin Haro and the village officer Abdullah bin Tavert say this is a poor village, and visibly so. It sits several miles from the highway, and many homes have no modern conveniences, only the tools they make from the land. The nearest clinic is several miles down the highway. The people here say they like their village life; no one leaves. But they would also like a paved road and a place nearby to treat their sick kids. "I want to have electricity and a school," Abdullah bin Tavert says.

I ask if I can speak with the women, and the two men decide I may, but they are in a hurry. It is almost time for the women's Friday teachings with the *ha-kem*, who instructs them in health and hygiene. We shift to the other side of the porch where the women are seated like elves in black. They are shy; these women have seen little beyond this village.

Sun Sy Phas, seventy-two, has lived here since 1977. "My husband died," and she lives with two widowed daughters. She knows this village, and the plain black chador that covers all but her face differs from what's found in other Cham communities. "I know it's different, but I can't explain." To her, the attire feels natural. It's the same for Sophiyas binti Abdullah, a seventeen-year-old girl who has worn her chador since she was eight, and she wouldn't trade it for another outfit. "I like these clothes."

But we soon discover not all women in this village adhere to the dress code. Several don't cover their heads at all, and many aren't particular about concealing their hair. As we walk through the village toward the house of Ramlee's uncle, we pass through shady, clean paths among thatch houses. There are ducks, cats, Egyptian geese, birds tweeting in the trees and a radio playing softly in the background. Big palms bend in the breeze, and hammocks sway beneath homes. Anou says the *ha-kem* thinks this village is poor "but in my opinion I think this looks better than some in Phnom Penh." Not for the wealth, but the serenity.

We meet Ramlee's sister and her young child. We are their first foreign visitors, ever, and they are excited to greet us. We sip tea on their slat floor and chat a bit, and just before we leave they offer a gift: a plump, succulent bunch of homegrown bananas.

Far from there, on the highway northeast of Phnom Penh, the Om Al Qura School stands barren and quiet. Everything is gone. Within days of its closure, looters took all they could: papers, desks, doors, windows, screens, lights, the spigots from water tanks. The lovely grounds of palms and flowers seem wasted.

"All the students were transferred to the provinces," says administrator Abass bin Yousoh. He is not happy about this. "We ask the government to open this school

Sophiyas binti Abdullah, age seventeen, sits on the veranda of the al Husainiah Mosque with her friends. Cambodia's small Cham Muslim population came under scrutiny in 2003 when several teachers at an Islamic school were arrested for links to terrorist groups. Also, Southeast Asian terrorist leader Hambali was found to have spent several months living in a Phnom Penh guesthouse. Kagu Jury village, Kampong Chhnang 2003.

again because this school does not have relations with Osama bin Laden." The Cham people didn't know anything about the foreign teachers sent to them, he says, because Saudi Arabia handled all the recruiting. Their job was teaching Arabic, math, science; things the students wouldn't learn in a public school. He doesn't know what happened or whether the accusations cast against individuals are right or wrong. But this school had no ties to terrorists. "It is related to individual problems, but it is not related to the school," he says. "All the Cham Muslims in Cambodia don't like terrorists."

School officials were not informed of the arrests, he says. The police had a list of names, and they invited those people to the police station. "Then they never came back." The next day, the government closed the school. "No questions," he says. The students went home, and these buildings have stood empty since then.

We sit for a while with him and a guard named Kob. I ask both men how they feel about the war on terrorism. "We are full of war, with the Pol Pot regime," Abass says.

Kob agrees. "I don't like the war."

Then the two men escort us through looted grounds. The blackboard inside one classroom still notes the last day of class: Wednesday 28th May 2003. A fine film of cobwebs covers the desks, and cat prints form a pattern through the dust. One classroom has Arabic writing on the board; another shows lessons in geometry. All the doors are now locked for fear of more thieves.

The dorm rooms look like a war zone. About 300 students slept here; now, cupboards are torn open, empty bottles strewn across the floor, screens broken, mats crumpled, old shirts tossed about. Windows and doors are open or missing, the floor is wet from rain. "Two to three days after the school closed, thieves stole all the windows and shutters," Kob says. The hallways are full of empty cabinets. The day it happened, school officials were busy with paperwork. "We were in the office taking care of things, so we don't know what happened out here."

But it's hard to believe. The school sits in a rural stretch of rice paddies, surrounded by other small villages. Who could do this? Neither man ventures a guess, but Ramlee does. He thinks villagers and police shared in the pillaging, as they would have known the school was closed for business but open for the taking. "In Cambodia, it's not like your country."

On the other end of these grounds sits the high school. The grass is overgrown in the courtyard, and frogs croak in nearby puddles. One classroom still has soup bowls stacked on the floor, another with economics lessons printed on the board. Exam results are posted on the office door, with student numbers running down the side. They were tested in English, history, math, biology, chemistry, morality, geography, physics and Khmer.

And then: the school mosque, with its dusty and gritty floor. This building hasn't been used in a while. Mats are heaped in the corner, and dust bunnies float across the tile. This is all a waste to Ramlee. This is sad, when he sees so many Cham people struggling for a mosque of their own or a school or the money to get by. The Om Al Qura offered these things to 700 youngsters. Now it sits useless and abandoned.

The families we meet with Anou and Ramlee are poor. But the Chams we meet just across the river from Phnom Penh are poorer still. They have nothing but the water they ply, the dirt upon which they tie their boats, and those boats—their lifelines.

About twenty Cham families live on what's called the Chruoy Changvar Peninsula, a jut of land between the Tonle Sap and Mekong rivers, just across from the Royal Palace. Most families have lived here since 1979, since they were free of Pol Pot. Fishing has never been an easy income—but never before as hard as it is now. Locals say an influx of Vietnamese has taxed the fish populations. That, and the water is low. "Before it was easy to find fish, but this year it's very difficult. There are many

Vietnamese people living here now. We can only find very small fish," says Aysah, a fifty-five-year-old woman who lives here with her husband and six kids. "We live all together on our boat." She points to the water, a small floating house about eight feet wide and twenty-five feet long with a metal outhouse hanging off the back. She stays on that boat, rain or dry, season after season, even in the monsoons when storms pitch them against the water. "Twice our boat tipped over," she says. "My grandson fell into the river." But he's OK.

A few of these families live on land in one-room huts on stilts on the banks that will disappear when rain returns. Say Nup does just that, with her son. Her husband died the year before, but she continues to eke out a living here beneath her frond roof, pitched in the rumpled humps of the worn riverbank. She and her neighbors sell their fish in the Kandal market, in town across the river. They earn 5,000 to 10,000 *riel*, about $1.25 to $2.50, a day.

Late this afternoon, a man named Khin returns from a day on water. He wears no shirt and a blue plaid sarong, and he has a basket of fifty small fish. "Not a good catch," he sighs. He fishes every day, starting around 4 A.M., quitting ten hours later. On Fridays he stops early, dons his hat and walks to the mosque a mile up the street.

Khin says he fought for the Americans in 1972, meaning he fought during the Lon Nol regime. "I volunteered to be a soldier," he says, but then denied that history during the Pol Pot time. He buried his military ID card. "Pol Pot asked me, are you a soldier? I said I was a fisherman. If they knew I was a soldier, they would have killed me." Those days still haunt him. "I think a lot about Pol Pot time because they killed my parents."

The curly hairs of Khin's beard fold over and under his chin. His tiger eyes sparkle in the sunlight. He fishes on a narrow, coverless longboat belonging to his son-in-law. He lives with his wife and three kids on another boat, where we talk. It's about thirty feet long and seven feet wide. "Before we had eight people living here." His other children have since married and moved to their own boats.

When I ask Khin about the war on terrorism, he says he supports American foreign policy. "America is the first country in the world. The U.S. always wants to help people around the world, to bring democracy. I'm very happy to hear about America." He thinks terrorists will meet their fate in due time. "You know, in the Buddhist religion and in Islam, when people do bad things, they always receive bad things. When people do good things, they receive good things. God knows." God knows who is good and who helps the poor. "God will bless them."

As we talk, his wife and neighbors chop fish in the other boat, stringing some on loops to sell. The fish flop around in baskets as the people work with their cleavers.

When I ask about the September 11 terrorist attacks, Khin says he only knows what he has seen on TV. "I was very sorry about that." When I ask about Hambali, who lived just a few miles away, he says he never thinks about the man. "I only think about 4 A.M., when I will leave here to hunt for fish, and then I try to sell them." He reiterates Aysah's words: The fish are dwindling. "When there are a lot of fish, I like fishing. But now it's very difficult." People are breaking the law. With more people catching fish eggs and small fish, there are fewer adults to be found.

This is all Khin knows. If the fish disappear, so will his life. Khin has never gone to school. "I don't know how to read or write." He cannot read the Koran, although he can speak Khmer and Cham. "Some children go to school over there," he says, pointing toward land. But some still don't. They learn to work the waters at an early age.

When the women finish stringing his catch, they say goodbye and push off, heading toward market. We're soon on our way as well, and as we are leaving, a big teak tourist boat motors by. Its name is *La Reine du Mekong*. The late afternoon sun casts pleasant shadows, and we can see foreigners taking pictures of this little grouping of fishermen. Then, when they spot Jerry and me on shore, they stop abruptly. This happens again, a few days later, when Jerry accompanies Khin fishing in the morning. Another tourist boat arrives; the people snap photos, and when they spot a six-foot-tall Caucasian man aboard Khin's boat, they stop their cameras. The tourist boat motors upriver a ways, then anchors. The Khmer captain skips to the front, peels off his shirt, flings a net overboard and acts the part of a fisherman so the tourists can snap his picture instead.

Perhaps it is not fair to suspect the tourists simply want quaint photos of fishermen on their shimmering waters. Maybe they want to document the flagrant poverty here, twenty boats jostling each other, side by side, families with no privacy, living five or more people to a boat, existing on a few dollars a day from a catch that gets smaller each month.

I wonder if the tourists know these families are Cham. I wonder if they know some people worry they will be arrested for no more reason than being Cham, on the suspicion they have terrorist ties. Khin's wife tells us this. Her husband talks openly, but she is afraid when we ask so many questions. Sometimes, in this country, the police appear and take people away for no apparent reason.

Perhaps it is unfair; perhaps the tourists do know the hardships these families endure. Perhaps they realize what life is like out here on Cambodia's fringe.

PART III

LOOKING AHEAD

18. The Crossroads:
Tugged in Two Directions

It's a Saturday afternoon, and the Casa thumps. Hundreds of young Khmers jigging to dance music, lights flashing, whiskey pouring, fashion flaunting. Every week, this club just north of Wat Phnom thrives with techno and rap, hip hop and R&B. This is a new generation. This is not a Khmer Rouge generation. This is not an impoverished crowd. Entrance costs $3 for men, $1.50 for women, and the place is packed with them squeezing past bouncers in a smoky lobby with psychedelic walls. "Maybe 600 people, maybe 1,000. It's all full. We have upstairs and downstairs," says DJ Lux, a protégé of the hip and locally famous DJ Cake. "I think Casa is the big club in Cambodia."

I guess there are maybe 300 people but it's trendy, no doubt. There is no comparison to the flooded streets and snack vendors and garbage pickers just outside the door. This is a cavernous discothèque where the sons and daughters of Cambodia's elite release. "This is the rich class," says Cake. It's for "the beautiful people," a place where youngsters can be happy. "The boys, they can meet all the beautiful young girls."

It's like a club anywhere else, but that's just it: This isn't anywhere else. This is Cambodia, where the gathering of a few hundred wealthy young kids to do nothing but let loose and spend wads of money is not a typical sight.

We watch Cake work. We follow him, his bodyguard close behind us, into the vibrating bowels of the dance room, to the way back, in a tiny dark alcove, a cage where he spins his tunes. Red lights, disco lights, neon, blue. Tight white women's shirts aglow.

Outside the cage: tables full of cigarettes, ashtrays, beer mugs, ice buckets, beer cans, lighters. Upstairs: men and women, whiskey and soda, a man pouring a drink down a woman's throat. Bodies caught in strobe lights, their movements stopped in time. Faces of wildness, happiness, drunkenness, oblivion. People lost completely to music and drink. Up another floor: all private party rooms with TVs and couches, and a guy running up and down, up and down, making deliveries, carrying trays of whiskey and bouquets of flowers, lots of flowers.

Jerry is not allowed to photograph the dance floor outside the DJ's cage. This is clear. The armed bodyguards at the door threaten to confiscate his cameras if he does. There are kids, powerful and dangerous kids, in this crowd who do not want their pictures taken. This is an imperious bunch of youths.

Everyone loves Cake and Lux; everyone knows their voices from their radio shows, and many come here just to see them. Lux tells me this. "Everybody, they heard my voice." We pause our conversation a moment as a young man pours Johnny Walker down Lux's throat. He gulps, then resumes talking.

This is not traditional Khmer music they're playing. Lux learned about foreign tunes through MTV. He says Cake taught him the way to speak on air, like a buddy. "DJs make everybody happy; they don't make everybody so sad," he says. "One thousand people, they listen to me, so I say something to make them happy."

Cake honed his skills in the United States, where he spent a lot of time in hip-hop clubs. He studied at Western Kentucky University, where he learned media management, how to run a radio station, how to be a DJ. His teacher, a French DJ, taught Cake about playing the music people like and finding advertising to fund the job. Cake returned to Cambodia hoping to follow his mentor's heels.

Cake is twenty-four, born on the cusp of the Khmer Rouge. He is of a new regime.

Cambodia has hit a cultural crossroads. Half the population is under eighteen. An older generation of Khmer Rouge survivors lives among a new crop of youngsters who understand little about their country's past or their parents' plight. "I don't really know what really happened to the old generation except that they told us there was a lot of killings, hardships," a twenty-one-year-old student tells The Associated Press on the twenty-fifth anniversary of the Khmer Rouge fall. Some people just don't talk about the past.

Look around, and you'll see it: a collision of worlds. Streets of gilt *stupas*, robed monks and *cyclos*; of *motos*, cell phones, Internet shops and karaoke. Phnom Penh is a city where market vendors can earn $300 to $400 a day selling T-shirts and accessories of the hot Taiwanese pop band F4. It's also a city where the prime minister bans mini skirts on TV as too risqué, and the mayor wants all new architecture to reflect traditional Khmer style, not French colonial. It's a city of muddy signals.

The young today don't know how to interpret their place in country and culture. They don't know what's expected of them in a modernizing world. "The population is moving, is changing," says Mu Sochua, minister of Women's and Veterans' Affairs. The war changed society. Today's youngsters aren't raised with the mores she learned in pre-war times—family, trust, religion, tradition. It's especially rough on women, a tug between the ancient ideals of village wife and mother and the modern reality of city worker. War destroyed the bedrock of Cambodian culture, and now messages of affluence, new technology and modern life abound. "We cannot deny the fact that Cambodian women are getting a lot of information regarding more material life rather than spiritual values," she says. And they aren't finding people to point them in a clear direction. "Young people have a harder time these days to find role models, especially women."

Her words are illustrated on TV, in songs, in movies, in ads. "I cannot see what

DJ Cake, center, brings the house down at the Casa nightclub. He is one of the country's first hip-hop DJs. Phnom Penh, 2003.

is Cambodian," she says. "What are we selling to the youth, especially to the women? We're selling foreign objects, foreign culture." And this broadens the gap between young and old. At home, a young Khmer woman hears from the elders: Stay home, be modest, raise a family. But out in the world she learns to admire fashion, men, beer, dancing, drugs. She's bombarded with images of women from China, Thailand and the West but few from her own heritage. "As soon as she walks out of the village, she is exposed to other things," Mu Sochua says.

She grows up without role models. "It's confusing inside," and it's difficult to navigate through life. Mu Sochua sees this as a threat to the nation's future. "I feel the young people have less and less hope, and therefore they rebel." They have no hope in their country's leadership, so they fight back. But to what end, they don't know. "They rebel without a cause," she says. "And I'm sorry I'm one of the leaders. We're not offering enough."

To survive in Cambodia today, it takes a determined strength. "You need a much more solid person to make the right kind of decisions," Mu Sochua says.

On our last evening in Phnom Penh in 2002, Jerry and I take two of the most solid young people we know to the Raffles Elephant Bar for drinks and appetizers. It is a thank you to our translator, Sok Chea, and his friend. The two young men are smart and motivated, and they epitomize the struggles of a young, educated class of Cambodians. This bar is arguably the swankest in town, plus it has a fantastic happy hour. To step inside the Raffles is to set foot outside Cambodia.

The trip is a surprise. We tell them to follow our *motodop*. When we arrive at the hotel gate, their eyes wide, the friend hesitates on his sputtering two-stroke. "I don't know if this hotel takes the *moto*," Sok Chea says. After some confusion with the guard, a prim and proper Khmer man in a uniform red beret, he parks the *moto* in a secluded gravel lot.

We enter. I go first, and Jerry holds the door so they are assured entrance without hassle. I choose a cozy little corner divided from the rest, with sofa, two chairs, two stools and coffee table. It's cold and quiet inside. I forget how chilled the Raffles air is, like melting ice against Asian skin.

Then we learn they do not drink alcohol. Never? "Never." They are afraid. They fear getting drunk, getting into trouble, letting go. So they order fruit juices instead. I get a Brass Monkey; Jerry gets a Singapore Sling. We offer sips, but they refuse even those. "If I take one now, next time I will have two," Sok Chea says. He worries it will become habit. We tell them they cannot get drunk or addicted from one sip, but they stand firm in their decision.

The waitress brings a tray of taro chips and red salsa. "New food," Sok Chea says. His friend thinks they're like potatoes, which his family grows in Takeo. They dip their chips only marginally, capturing just a speck of red flavor with each one. They like it and continue to nibble. We ask, and they tell us they are not hungry. I order a Mediterranean plate anyway, more "new food." I want them to try new things. Marinated chicken kabob, hummus, tabouli, green and black olives, shrimp, a layer of cilantro and pita bread. They are quite curious.

What's the couscous? It's like rice, they determine after a taste. "I think if I eat this every day, I get fat," Sok Chea laughs. His friend says that's OK, because now he is skinny. He wants to be fatter.

Neither has been inside the Raffles before. They've only gazed from the street. Once, Sok Chea says, he walked up the front driveway, but that was it. "It is very comfortable in here," the friend says. Plush would be the word. He later tells me, "I think this is very romantic."

An American friend of ours arrives. We all say hello, then our two guests sit quietly and politely through too much *barang* chitchat. We try to include them, but I feel bad. Our American friend is a teacher, and he relays a story of a class trip to Siem Reap, an emergency appendectomy, and a town surgeon who arrives well-lubricated, straight from a wedding party.

I recall that Sok Chea has never been to Siem Reap, never seen the Angkor temples. His companion went the year before with his father—first time for both. He doesn't know the English words to describe it, and the Khmer words he uses mean indescribable. It was the most profound experience of his life.

After a couple of beers, our friend leaves for another engagement. He bids goodbye, and our friends regain their pluck. We talk of marriage. They are both in their early twenties, but neither knows if he will ever marry because neither has money. The friend says if he gets married, then he feels he must get a job to support his wife. Too many Cambodians marry very young, seventeen or eighteen in the city, even younger in the countryside. In the first year of marriage, they will have a baby — that's the way it is. It buoys them. All effort goes toward surviving with family intact.

Jerry and I tell them people are shocked to hear we have no kids, especially after five years of marriage. But kids are expensive, and if we had them, we wouldn't have money to travel (and work). Sok Chea's eyes twinkle. "Oh, this is a new idea," he says. Tonight he samples new ideas and new food, and this makes him happy.

Both young men hope to become teachers, but that doesn't offer much money. I ask what a professor's salary is. "I heard my father makes 100,000 *riel*," Sok Chea says. That's about $25 a month. He teaches psychology to Cambodian university students. But like most professors, he has taken on other jobs. Professor Om also teaches Khmer to foreigners. If he were to work a full week charging the $5 an hour he charged us for Khmer lessons in 1998, he would earn thirty-two times his university salary.

Sok Chea says his university's sociology department now has only one teacher because the others are young and have gone elsewhere to study, with hopes of better prospects. Many teachers abandon their public-school salaries to work for NGOs that need sociological expertise.

We finish our drinks and talk politics. They don't know what the following year's elections will bring. They voted in 1998 but not in the 2002 commune elections. Sok Chea, like many young Cambodians, doesn't trust the outcome to reflect the wishes of the people. The two young men think change will come to Cambodia slowly, and when they graduate, Cambodia will be a little bit different — but not much.

This conversation takes us through our drinks and through all the "new food." Jerry and I leave with our heads feeling pleasantly calm. We exit with the two young men, who leave with new ideas in their heads and stomachs, but utterly sober and perpetually concerned about their own and their country's future.

In an era of uncertainty, many elder Cambodians hope to put the younger generation in touch with their ancestral roots.

Deep inside a compound, set far behind a gate opening onto a choking, honking street in central Phnom Penh, is a scene that epitomizes Cambodian tradition. There are two dozen girls dressed in sarongs of royal blue, purple and burgundy. They wear silky shirts tight across their breast, accessorized in gold. About twenty girls wait on mats on the floor while others stand in formation as a teacher bellows instructions.

Their teacher is a princess, Bopha Devi. Her full name and proper title is Her Royal Excellency Samdech Rech Bottrei Preah Ream Norodom Bopha Devi. And today, she is instructing the class in the ways of their ancestors. It is said she was the country's best and most beautiful traditional Khmer dancer forty years ago when she was a young woman.

They practice in a grotty, dilapidated hall. The entryway is full of discarded shoes, shed by habit but for what? The floor is sandy and filthy, a thick layer exposed in the window light. This exercise is not about the place here and now, it's not about this poor old building or the turmoil outside in the streets of Phnom Penh. It's about memory, about reviving the past, recalling history, about something so tangibly Khmer, something to see and feel and wrap your fingers around. It's about cultural identity.

There is immeasurable grace in the bends and shuffles of these girls, the way their bodies carry sound and light. Their movements are 180 degrees opposite, a striking clash, to the dusty, oily, blaring street outside and to the thrusting, jumping maneuvers found at the Casa on a Saturday afternoon. These girls' fingers curl, their necks crane, their torsos stand upright in almost magical ways.

The dance is meticulous. The girls snake back and forth, each movement precise. They act out a story about fetching water in jugs. They frolic. They transform, through curved fingertips and flexible bodies, into the *apsaras* of Angkor made human.

Bopha Devi holds a lit cigarette in her left hand and a lighter in the right as she guides girls' bodies through movements, smoke drifting among them. She takes a puff. She bellows more instructions.

I am here with Sok Chea, my upstanding translator. He knows from his childhood this story the girls perform, and he explains their steps along the way. The girls go together to fetch water from a pond, and they play until it's time to go. They go round and round with hands held. Then they say goodbye and take their jars home, but one girl can't carry hers; it's too heavy. So they call someone to help, and a man comes to the rescue. But the man is played by a woman. I find it ironically appropriate: Just as in real life, women do the heavy work but men get the credit.

When the girls are finished practicing, they gather around Bopha Devi, kneeling at her feet. She gives each one a handful of *riel*, a token of encouragement. This, too, is tradition. The royal family has always revered dance and encouraged poor, young talented girls with a bit of money. The dancers graciously accept, then scamper off in leaps and gallops, clasping their *riel*.

When the last girl has gone, Sok Chea and I approach the princess for a few words. Sok Chea is nervous; he has never talked to royalty before.

"I rarely come here," she says. "This is a special time. I come to teach all the students how to improve. I come to revive our art and culture, which has disappeared." Since the Khmer Rouge regime, she and her colleagues have researched the lost art of ancient Khmer dance. "Technically we have revived it all," she says, but now they must develop the actual art of it by teaching youngsters who will remember for future generations.

The princess is the minister of Culture and Fine Arts, and this class is run through the Royal University of Fine Arts. They train about 300 dance students, 200 of whom study the classical variety. "They would like to preserve the legacy of our ancestors," the princess says. She fidgets as we talk; she has an appointment and must leave soon.

I ask her about the money, and she says, "It's the tradition of my grandmother." She was the director of classical dance, and she, too, gave money to poor students. Most of the students here are from Phnom Penh. She would like to bring students from all provinces, but most are too poor to make the trip and remain here for study. "You know well the living of our artists: They are still poor."

And then the princess is on her way. She leaves behind an ashtray with five stubbed-out cigarettes. She hops into a silver Land Cruiser waiting outside. The driver sits up front, the princess in back with five little dogs. They head into the hectic world.

Sok Chea breathes. "When I speak to her, my language is always wrong," he sighs. The Khmer language has a separate lexicon for addressing royalty. Many Khmers have never fully learned it because few ever have the chance to use it.

Princess Bopha Devi has an aura about her, a charisma associated with aristocracy. Sok Chea says, as we gaze upon her Land Cruiser's tracks in the dirt, he has heard she is not nice. "But actually, she is not nasty. She is friendly." He goes home that day, proud to tell his family he mingled with a princess.

There are other ways, and other places for Khmers to renew their connections to the past. Cambodia is, despite decades of war and destruction, still a country of festivals that have survived the ages. Each April, the entire nation takes a week of rest, a week of play, time with their families to celebrate the Khmer New Year. They clean house, wash their Buddhas, cook and feast, douse neighbors with water guns, paint their faces, and issue prayers for those who have passed. The new year always falls at the height of the hot season, just before the rains begin. It is a celebration of seasons, of rituals that bring forth life. It is a prayer for good harvests and a plentiful year to come.

It does not rain for the first three and a half months of 1998. It is blisteringly hot by mid–April. Jerry and I take a ferry that week across the Mekong with our friend and fellow photographer, Sinith. He takes us home to family, and we are welcomed like royal guests. We drink beer, eat fish and rice and share an honorable afternoon among relatives. It is not a safe or happy time in Cambodia, yet this week passes untarnished. Cambodia comes together in peace.

And an amazing thing happens.

On April 15, Pol Pot dies. He is poetically cremated in a pile of garbage and old tires.

On that New Year's day, rain falls and drenches the city.

On that New Year's day, people dance in the sopping streets, and Cambodia changes, by a stroke of history.

Something else happens each year, each November on the Tonle Sap, when the river reverses its flow.

Around this time, the banks of the Tonle Sap in Phnom Penh swell with humanity. For centuries, Khmer people have praised the moon and reveled in the river's turn. Both are symbols of prosperity to come. It's said the king can stand at the riverbank and, with the flick of his hand, propel this phenomenon into course.

And then the parties ensue. For three days and then some, Phnom Penh doubles in size. A million people choke the riverside streets in a fanciful carnival of rides and games and grilled bananas and roasted chickens and fireworks. And just as their ancestors did 700 years ago, villagers travel for days to flood the river with hand-crafted longboats—gilt dragons and tigers and snakes on water, ninety feet long, thirty men full, racing 1,850 yards from the Japanese Bridge to the Royal Palace. Teams in yellow shirts, red turbans, green pantaloons, white ballcaps, fanciful emblems, silk sashes. It is more than a sporting competition, it is a time, one of few, when fathers and sons and neighbors unite in purpose. For this week, the river roils with color and life and innocent fun.

And then, as quickly as festivities begin, the city empties, the trash remains, the violence returns, the foul waters flow. And the people search again for another good omen, another reason to carry on.

When a country's roots are dug up and tossed aside, as they were in Cambodia, the people do need to find reasons for carrying on. In this country, all was lost. Temples were destroyed and monks killed. But more than that. People lost their faith in each other and in religion. "I found that we even lost faith in Buddhism," says Youk Chhang of the Documentation Center. "It's a problem. It's a big problem."

He is urging our friend Sinith, the photographer, to do a project on the changing nature of Cambodian Buddhism, to reveal monks who aren't really monks and believers who don't know what they really believe.

Sinith is at the riot in 1998, when police rail upon a procession of monks, when I fall under a stampede of holy men. He has a photo from that riot, of monks fleeing in terror as police bludgeon them in the street. That, Youk Chhang says, is proof of something lost, something wrong. In past times, Cambodians would not have lashed out at a holy man. "It's disgraceful. It shows we have lost our faith in Buddhism. I have never seen that before. Never."

The religion is changing, inside and out.

"During the Pol Pot regime, Buddhism was destroyed, but now it is revived little by little," says Som Tok La, the daughter of seventy-five-year-old artist Som Bon. He paints giant, bigger-than-life pictures of Buddhist stories. His pieces end up in *wats*, in funeral processions and celebrations, all over the city. He paints in blazing oranges and crisp blues, colors that jump at the eyes and beg to be stared at. Many people talk of Cambodia's "dark days," yet this country is anything but dark. It is replete with color, everywhere, all the time. The color is mesmerizing in a place of bleak realities.

"My father learned to paint when he was young," she says. I would talk to the artist himself, though he is napping, a bit under the weather. But his daughter knows all about his life and much about the changes her country has endured. Ancient teachings died with the monks who perished in the Khmer Rouge regime. It all needed rebuilding. Monks came from Sri Lanka to teach Cambodians what they once knew about their own religion. For years books were scarce, and young monks had no foundation in their own beliefs. That is slowly changing. "Buddhism now is improving," she says, perhaps more so in the countryside because city monks tend to study English and modern subjects. Country monks study the religion of their past.

And the Cambodian people understand the simple precepts of Buddhism, the tenets that help a person get through the day. "If you do good, you will get good," she says.

She is forty-six years old, and, as an adult during the Khmer Rouge time, she didn't stop praying. "I worked for Pol Pot, making a farm. I also prayed to God to help me. I believe in God. I never forgot Buddhism." But she did it silently, alone. "I prayed in my mind only. If I showed that I believe in God, they would take me to be killed."

She lives, and has lived for years, surrounded by Buddhist stories; her life is engulfed in the religion.

But the religion is not always what it appears.

It was once a mark of honor, and an obligation, for a young man to become a monk for a time. He did it for faith, for his family, for tradition. He did it for sanctity. But today, the *wat* is often a path to learn English, to get a job, to eat regular meals, to sleep in a bed, to live more comfortably than perhaps at home, wherever home may be. It is not something people like to discuss, but a few brave ones do.

The Venerable Muny Van Saveth at Wat Norea, in Battambang, is a visionary. I go to see his orphanage and his many projects helping villagers with AIDS. He is wise and articulate, so I ask him questions about Buddhism that I've been curious about for some time.

I ask him about monks who smoke and drink, about rumors of monks hiring prostitutes, about monks who don't behave as monks are supposed to. He tells me some young men "become a monk, and they don't understand about the law

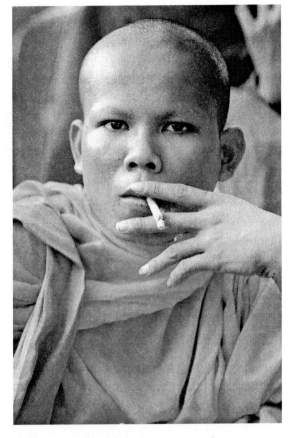

A novice Buddhist monk smokes while attending a pre-election political rally for opposition party leader Sam Rainsy. Phnom Penh, 1998.

of Buddhism." Some enter the *wat* with ulterior motives. "He wants to find money; he wants to buy something…. So he shaves his head; he wears the robes, and he goes to the people to ask the people for money." This is not a true monk. "He doesn't believe, but he wears the robes and goes to ask for money. But when he gets the money, he loses the robes, and he goes to drink wine."

To become a real monk, it takes perseverance and dedication. A man must ask the commune leader, ask the district leader, and then study for three months to a year. He becomes a novice first. When he understands and he believes, he can follow the law, then he can become a monk. The others, Muny Van Saveth calls the "not true monks."

When The Venerable sees this, he tries to tell the young men they are not real. "I'm not angry, but I try to explain to them. I'm sorrowful. I am sorrowful for their spirits."

The "untrue" monks create another problem. Monks should be the moral staff of a village. People should trust them and go to them with their troubles. But how can a false holy man cater to the moral needs of a community? Since Khmer Rouge time, he says, Cambodian people have "many, many problems because they lost their morality." People don't trust the government; they often don't trust each other, and if they can't trust their monks, where do they turn? "If the Buddhist religion is broken, the people cannot depend on them.... There is no one to educate them about the good way."

And then Muny Van Saveth says something even more revealing about his culture. He thanks me for asking him these things. "It's very good for me, your question.... I hope I have the time to go to a workshop with high Buddhist people, and I try to ask your question because they believe you more than me." That's because I'm a foreign reporter. If he asked on his own, he says, they wouldn't answer him. He is not of a high enough rank. "So I hope I have the time to talk about your questions."

In Phnom Penh, I ask Sok Chea to help me speak with a government official about Buddhism. I want to ask about Buddhism in society, about the ways in which the religion has changed in the years since the Khmer Rouge. I tell him the questions I'm trying to get at, and he understands immediately what I'm saying. "Since I was young I always see the monk smoking." He's not even sure whether they are supposed to or not. (There's no law against it, but it's often frowned upon.) And he says monks are not supposed to wear shoes and, "now almost all the monks wear shoes."

Several times we try to find someone at the Ministry of Cults and Religions. We are sent upstairs. We are told to speak to one particular woman; when that woman arrives, she says we must speak to a certain man. She can't talk to me "because I only know a little bit." We must speak with her director.

Her director is at the Buddhist Institute library, in a meeting. We go there; he will be out at 1 P.M. That afternoon we return to the ministry. He has not yet come to his office. We wait half an hour, and the woman we met earlier calls him. He's not coming in, she says, and I cannot make an appointment to see him because she does not know his schedule.

Can I speak to someone else?

No, only him, she says. "If I say something and you put it in the paper and someone else reads, they will be angry with me." He is the expert. His name is Seng Nath, and he knows all about Buddhism.

I leave my card, and she gives me his number. She says she'll have him call me. But she tells Sok Chea, "Please, I don't want her to think Khmer people don't know how to work. I am very sorry."

Later in the week, after not hearing from Seng Nath, I have Sok Chea call. He reaches him! But he is busy. He has no time to meet. He doesn't know when he will. And: "I don't know very much about Buddhism in society. I know only a little."

Sok Chea asks if we can meet the next morning. He doesn't know. He's busy. And then suddenly, mysteriously, the phone cuts off and the connection dies.

Cambodia is at a cultural crossroads, and no one is sure how the meeting of old and new will proceed.

One morning in early 1999, Jerry and I attend a ceremony at an orphanage on the outskirts of Phnom Penh, run by Bernie Krisher, my publisher at the *Daily*. He is a do-gooder around the world. He gathers rice for starving North Koreans. He sets up fundraising web sites for needy people around Asia. He runs a hospital here as well.

And on this day, it is the opening of a computer project at the orphanage. He has hooked up the place up to the Internet and provided, through generous donations from the United States, more than thirty computers for 250 poor, mother- and father-less children who now live in a beautiful group home in the boondocks of Cambodia. Today's guest speaker is a well-known American technology visionary, Nicholas Negroponte. He has written a series of fascinating columns for *Wired* magazine about the future of the Internet and computing. Many of those back issues are scattered throughout the house where we live, and Jerry and I are eager to hear him speak.

The event begins with a message from the kids, to the Negropontes. "Five years ago, we had nothing to eat, we were not healthy." The opening remarks waft through the windy, dusty, hot air. Then, Negroponte steps to the front and begins a speech praising the future of developing nations that seize their opportunities with computers while many developed nations take it all for granted. These developing countries will someday lead the world in the digital arena, he says, presciently describing today's India.

We, as foreign guests, sit on cushy upholstered banquet chairs in the center of an open-air shelter. The Cambodians, official and otherwise, sit on plastic lawn chairs surrounding us. The orphanage workers sit outside, under umbrellas. The kids go round and round a merry-go-round, chatting among themselves, playing footsie and other typical kid games while the speech continues in English, immediately translated into Khmer. Negroponte speaks directly to the kids, telling them of their fortunes.

Then we all stand for a tour. Inside an exquisitely clean air-conditioned room with cool tile flooring, children sit on high wooden chairs, dangling feet, maneuvering a mouse, drawing welcome signs for their guest while reading his name from crumpled cheat sheets they hold in their hands. Thirty different delightful attempts at "Welcome Professor Negroponte." My favorite: "We Prof. Negro."

Many kids smile and draw pictures on their computers—scenes of rice fields and palm trees and buffalo; red skies, green grounds, trees with swaying leaves and mountains in the distance. But they all shudder with fright when spoken to, English or Khmer, it doesn't matter. Do you speak English? Do you like computers? How old are you? What's your name? Only the meekest little voices emerge.

After the tour, the guests sit to a traditional dance performance while men in white suits with gold buttons serve finger pizzas, fried chicken, caviar on bread, glasses of wine and soda. The kids eat after the crowd disperses, when two women haul out an army-sized pot of French bread sandwiches filled with meatloaf and cucumbers.

Soon thereafter, the guests leave. Jerry and I remain awhile with Bernie and the Negropontes. We tour the orphanage baby room, where six or seven little newborn bundles sleep in cradles, waiting for Americans to take them to new homes. They've all been tested for HIV; they're all negative. This is 1999, when adoption is not yet a scandalous affair.

I ask what happens to the HIV-positive babies.

"A horrible thought," the Negropontes say in unison. And it is a horrible thought, but no one answers my question. We continue the tour in the next room.

A while later, Jerry and I catch a ride back into town with a man who teaches computers to the kids. He also holds a prominent government job and previously worked overseas. I ask him how the children are doing. Do they learn computers well?

"It is very difficult because they do not know English and they don't understand how computers work," he says. But they're all excited about the prospects, and they know most Cambodian kids don't have computers. They know because they go to school with villagers surrounding the orphanage. What they don't understand, he says, is that computers cost money. And when they leave the orphanage, they won't have any money to buy a computer.

"But I don't tell them that. It would break their heart," he says. "I just tell them they can use computers in the future."

19. Development:
Building on Quicksand

We're riding through the Cardamom Mountains in a minibus, on a ruddy new road heading toward Sihanoukville. It is June 2003. A handful of tourists travel with us—an Israeli, a Korean, an American, an Irishwoman—and at one of our stops, the American woman, learning that we are journalists, asks me why Cambodia is still developing. She researches race and ethnicity for a university and says she would like to read, to know, more about the Khmer people before the Khmer Rouge. She has been traveling for six months through the United States, the Pacific and Southeast Asia. And everything she has seen makes her wonder: Why are some countries like this? People talk of the "new millennium," but what does that mean here?

We talk for five minutes, but this is not the stuff of a five-minute conversation. Her questions have me thinking for nearly a year and beyond.

And I come to a circle, a web. I come up with no single, simple answers but a tangle of causes, a whole plexus of effects, all bound together. And then I examine this web and see it is still not finished, I find another strand, then another and another. And I see it could be shaped in many ways, pulled taut in one direction or another, it's all a matter of perspective. But the web itself doesn't change. Its appearance might, from time to time, but the overall form remains the same.

And you will see, it ends right where it starts, which means it really has no end at all:

Cambodia is a country of poor farmers. The average income is $280 a year, and 80 percent of the population lives in the countryside. Its farmers cultivate some of the world's best rice, and Cambodia's neighbors know this country has good growing land. But Cambodia's rice production lags behind its neighbors. It doesn't have the irrigation systems necessary to increase yields. Almost 90 percent of Cambodia's cultivable land is covered in rice. But only 16 percent of that land is irrigated. And if there isn't too little water, there's too much. When a flood comes, farmers lose everything. They're stuck. So what do they do? They try to increase yields. Maybe they spray their fields. They buy pesticides banned in the rest of the world but dumped in places like this, where law enforcement is nil. Farmers spray their fields with no

291

gloves, no shoes, not knowing the dangers. They don't know because they can't read, and no one tells them. They get sick and go to the hospital. They can't afford to pay their hospital bills, so they borrow from rich land owners. They go into debt and perhaps lose their land. They don't eat well. They're malnourished, as are their kids. Brains don't develop properly; people become listless. They aren't as productive when they're listless, so they lose more money. They can't afford to send their kids to school. Even if they could, the kids wouldn't go to school. There might not be a school in their village. The school might be several miles away. It might require a long walk. The walk might be flooded in the rainy season, or the bridge might be out. Or parents might want their kids to stay and work in the fields. If kids don't go to school, they'll never get off the farm. If they do go to school, particularly a rural school, they might not learn much. The teachers themselves have poor educations. When the Khmer Rouge era ended, the government took anyone as a teacher. Hiring had nothing to do with skills or quality or ability — just bodies to fill the empty slots. Their textbooks, too, are outdated and poorly written. Cambodians who go to school learn to memorize but don't learn critical thinking. They don't learn to see the connections in the world around them, which is such a critical skill when trying to fix a broken country. Economy, health, education, infrastructure, technology, psychology are all related, but students don't learn to think that way in a Cambodian school. The ones who do, learn it somewhere else. And those people go on to work in other countries. Or they leave the government and work for high-paying NGOs. They don't go back to teach in public schools; there's no incentive. Teachers are paid an appallingly low salary, sometimes $15 or $20 a month. So teachers are forced to demand money from their students. Teachers have to, just to survive. This is true of most all civil servants. Cops, too. They make the same pay as teachers. So they demand money from people on the street. They tell vendors: Pay me, and I won't make you move. They tell motorists: Pay me, and I won't take your *moto*. Lower-ranking cops must pay their bosses just to keep their turf. The authorities take money from everybody. Example: A CDRI study follows one shipment of fish from Chhnouk Trou village to the Thai border, nearly 200 miles. Along the way, the fishermen are stopped for payments twenty-seven times to fifteen different institutions in sixteen locations. Eighty percent of those institutions have nothing to do with fish at all. Many payments are made to military police, customs officers, traffic police and immigration officers. The Cambodian government collects next to nothing in income taxes, but it takes money in other ways. Perhaps most troubling of all: Cops take bribes from criminals, money that criminals willingly offer. Criminals bribe judges, too. There is no working judicial system in Cambodia. No "transparency," as people like to say. So people take the law into their own hands. There is street justice. "People's courts." A thief on the street? Yell "thief," and the people come, from homes and shops and alleys. They pounce and pummel and attack the culprit — sometimes until he dies. Still, the robberies continue because there is no true rule of law, and the people want more. Plus, you can get away with it. Many criminals aren't poor, they're rich. They're greedy. They are the sons of politicians. They can afford guns. They hire kids and form gangs. Kids are easy to sway, and the kids on the street have no choice, so they comply. They are young, sometimes four or five years old. They are orphans or their families send them out begging. They go to the city to shine shoes or peddle newspapers or flowers. They get lured into these gangs, and then their master, the *bong thom*, takes all their money. They are trapped. They have little hope for the future. They don't think of tomorrow, they think only of surviving today. This, in part, is a legacy of the Khmer Rouge. Today's youngsters grow up in families with mental illness, post-traumatic stress disorder, depression resulting from having survived genocide. Parents don't recognize these problems, and they don't know they're passing them on to their kids. But the kids pick it up from parents and friends and neighbors. And they proceed in life, malnourished, with confused heads and violent hearts and a serious lack of trust. Whether a street child or son of a politician, they want to feel better. They take drugs. They sell drugs. They sell their bodies. They get HIV. HIV — now that's a big problem, that's a problem on the international Richter scale of need. Donors pour money into problems like those. They send foreigners to work in Cambodia, fighting AIDS and drugs and prostitution. The foreigners mean well, but they often arrive with little concept of the culture. They live in nice houses, they have cars and guards and maids. They seem to ooze money. And the money keeps coming, every year. The more problems Cambodia has, the more NGOs show up, the more money that comes. The people see this. The government surely sees this. Why should the government solve its own problems when foreigners can? Or will? And Cambodia becomes a dependent nation. A "beggar nation" some call it. The government begs the world; the world gives, and the powerful take what comes. More and more money to line officials' pockets. It is, after all, tradition. The rich are rich; the poor are poor, and if you're rich, you must be doing something right to have that power, that good karma. Buddhism tells us that, so it must be OK. Or at least, that's what many derive from the tenets of Buddhism. Buddhism says to accept what comes. Buddhism does not spark rebellion. It does not inspire the masses to fight the system. The lowest and weakest in society have, for centuries, accepted their lot. They don't like it, but they don't know what else to do. Only now, only after years of foreign influence and the presence of NGOs and the UN, are people learning about something called human rights. This is a new concept in Cambodia — rights for all. This is not consistent with Asian thinking. But it's a good idea, many Cambodians are realizing. Why not fight for our rights (whatever those rights might be)? Why not, if I work in a garment factory, demand overtime pay? Why not strike for better working conditions? Yes! We will. We will form a union and fight. Until our leader is shot. He is shot and killed one morning, 9 A.M., on a central street of Phnom Penh, while reading the newspaper next to a *wat*. Now, this is the reality Cambodians live with. The violence, the danger, the "culture of impunity." None of it looks good to the outside world, to the watchdogs. Especially not when Cambodia has just joined the World Trade Organization. Many international observers wonder whether Cambodia will benefit from the WTO. They wonder whether the country is ready, whether it's competitive enough. Some say the decision to enter the WTO was rash. No one really thought about the possible outcomes. One of those outcomes will be a set of rules. Accountability. The WTO does not look kindly upon the sort of corruption, nepotism, backroom deals, budget-skimming and bribery that define Cambodia's work code. Cambodia's economic practices have never been up to international standards. Perhaps that's why so few long-term investors are here now. No long-term investment and a big national debt — that's the economy. That debt is a burden. There are no definite numbers (And we might ask, Why are there no precise numbers? Shouldn't there be?), but estimates range from $2.7 billion to more than $3 billion. One Cambodian economist predicts 20 percent of the annual national budget eventually will have to go toward debt payments. Where will that money come from? Some optimists hope it comes from new industry. From trade. Perhaps the garment industry will continue on an upward swing. The garment industry accounts for 90 percent of Cambodia's light industry, and it has expanded substantially since 1999. That's largely because in 1999, Cambodia signed an agreement with the United States, which essentially caps China's market share of the industry and assures Cambodia a certain number of garment orders. Plus, this agreement is based on behavior. If Cambodia's factory managers behave themselves — paying overtime, allowing bathroom breaks, refraining from abuse — Cambodia gets more work. But it all stops at the end of 2004. The agreement expires. And people worry the garment industry will collapse. Why? China. China is cheaper, and it has the ability to mass produce. Operational costs in Cambodia are higher than in neighboring countries. Gas is more expensive. Electricity costs more. Transportation is inefficient. Supplies must be imported. So China's a big threat, come January 2005. Still, people hope the WTO will open new doors, giving Cambodia full access to American and European markets. But there's at least one problem. Eight months after the 2003 election, the National Assembly still has not ratified the country's membership in the WTO because the National Assembly cannot do anything until a new government is formed. For months, there is no government. That's because Hun Sen won, but with not enough votes to rule alone. He needs a coalition, and his opponents don't like him. They don't want to cooperate with a bully. So there's a stalemate. Eight months now and still no government, no new laws. Eventually, there will be a new government, but what will change? Cambodia's government has never before been swift or competent in its doings. How will that change, if Hun Sen still controls the country? And how will that change, if someone new with less experience and less money and less clout controls the country? Regardless, for a long time now there is no functional government, and this is a problem, too, for a proposed Khmer Rouge tribunal. It took years for the UN and the Cambodian government — the old government, still a Hun Sen government — to agree on this, and it's supposed to happen soon, but when? And how? And will it really ease the pains of a victimized nation? These are questions the people ask every day. Yet many economists and analysts say cheer up, there are some good things ahead. They point to an economy growing at 5 percent a year, bustling markets and new life in a once war-torn nation. But: Cambodia still takes in more than $600 million a year in foreign aid. And despite all that, all the international aid, all the donors, all the attention, Cambodia has had for a decade, more than a third of the population still lives below the poverty line, which is about 46 cents a day. There are many reasons for that. There are many reasons why *Cambodia is a country of poor farmers. The average salary is $280 a year and 80 percent of the population lives in the countryside.*

And there we are, right back where we started.

This skein of reality has existed a long time, and that impotence, that stasis is itself a huge factor in "why Cambodia is still developing." Certainly, yes, life has changed in recent decades. Cell phones, Internet shops, disposable income, new *motos*, a greater connection to the world, all have arrived. But in other areas, little has changed in centuries. Let us examine a few observations on Cambodia, then and now. Who said what, when?

a.) On customs officers: *"Here they gain by begging; they are licensed beggars.... The more you give, the less strict the search will be."*

b.) Cambodia, as a nation, has become an *"international beggar."*

c.) *"The poverty of the inhabitants of these miserable villages engenders a repulsive dirtiness: a strip of matting or an old filthy cushion thrown on the ground, and full of vermin, some basins of coarse Chinese porcelain, a sort of hatchet, and a piece of cotton ... are the usual contents of a Cambodian hut."*

d.) *"I hadn't seen a single house, not a single building with what could be called walls, not a TV aerial, not a power or phone line in hours. We could have been traveling up the same body of water a thousand years ago, with no discernible difference."*

e.) *"Waste-disposal education is practically non-existent in Phnom Penh.... Cambodia currently has no Ministry or Government Department of Housing, no housing policy document, and no substantial housing developer."*

f.) *"Here are millions of unhappy creatures in great poverty in the midst of the richest and most fertile region imaginable; bowing shamefully under a servile yoke made viler by despotism and the most barbarous customs."*

g.) *"Today's Cambodia is a basket case.... In large measure its workers are exploited, its women ill-used, its children unprotected, its soil studded with treacherous land mines primed to kill. No equitable rule of law or impartial justice shelters Cambodians against a mean-spirited establishment of political and economic power, a cabal that is blind and deaf to the crying needs of an abused people."*

h.) *"Functionally literate people make up only 37 percent of Cambodia's adult population."*

Answers:

a.) Henri Mouhot, in his diaries, in the 1860s. Corruption, extortion, bribery — the stuff of old-time Cambodia.

b.) King Norodom Sihanouk, August 28, 2003, blasting the current government for its reliance on foreign aid.

c.) Mouhot again. On page 181 of his book is a sketch of a thatch and bamboo house on stilts, with a longboat in front on a riverbank. It could be a portrait right now. Add a *moto*, maybe a TV antenna, little plastic wrappers scattered below the hut, and that would be today.

d.) Anthony Bourdain, in his global quest for the ideal meal, *A Cook's Tour*, 2001. One hundred forty years later, he describes what Mouhot saw.

e.) The UNFPA (United Nations Population Fund) in a 1998 report on the develop-ment of Phnom Penh and the "unique" characteristics of this capital, where pri-vate ownership was abolished during the Khmer Rouge and land rights have never been sorted out. Thousands of squatters come from country villages, where they have never lived among so many people, never dealt with sanitation, never thought about garbage.

f.) Let's hear it again for Mouhot.

g.) Henry Kamm, the Pulitzer-Prize winning former Southeast Asia correspondent for *The New York Times* in his 1998 book, *Cambodia: Report from a Stricken Land.*

h.) The UNDP (United Nations Development Programme) in its plan for Cambo-dia, 2001–2005. If a nation can't read, it's hard-pressed to develop.

In early 2004, I meet Dr. Sorn Samnang, president of the Royal Academy of Cambodia. I meet him at his school, on the far western edge of the city. The build-ing sits in a crackled dry yard with stray dogs plodding about and weeds growing through the walkways.

The president sits in an air-conditioned room, in a comfortable leather seat with a laptop on the coffee table. He is one of the country's top scholars, having earned a doctorate in France with a dissertation on "The Evolution of Cambodian Society between the Two World Wars." He has studied in Japan and visited Califor-nia. He is well-versed in the history of Cambodian education, and he frets about the future. It is, he says, "my deep concern."

There was a time when Cambodian kids learned as the French did. He calls this "education for elite." In a primary-school class of 100 students, only one would even-tually graduate with a secondary-degree. Only one was deemed good enough to go on. But that one received an education that would put him (and it was classically a "he") in a league with any other kid graduating from a school anywhere else in the French empire. Samnang graduated in 1970, just before war ravaged his country.

And then things changed drastically, brutally, with the Khmer Rouge, when edu-cation was abolished. "After 1979, our schools were reopened one after another," he says. "But as you know, most of our teachers were exterminated during the Khmer Rouge regime, so in order to reply to the urgent need in Cambodia, after the national rebirth in January 1979, we had to recruit the teachers among the survivors of the Khmer Rouge regime."

Under the UN in 1993, UNESCO urged a different education philosophy from the one the French instilled. "They said to provide education for all Cambodian chil-dren." That's an honorable idea, Samnang says, but troublesome when the pool of educated teachers remains slim. How does Cambodia educate everyone with so lit-tle money and so few educators?

Today, schooling is compulsory for nine years: six years in primary school and three at a lower secondary school. Beyond that, students can take another three years in secondary school before going on to college. "We are trying to put this policy into practice. But it is not easy, you know, because of a shortage of funding, a shortage of qualified human resources."

Thousands of children never go to school at all. Less than 5 percent of fifteen-year-olds stay in school, and less than 2 percent graduate from high school, according to a study by *Mith Samlanh*, the NGO that works with street kids. In the northwestern province of Preah Vihear, some 100 children attend school in Laos because the nearest Cambodian schools are up to 90 miles from their village.

As most every teacher knows primary and secondary schools are the foundation for higher education. If there is no solid foundation, how can Cambodians pursue and attain a quality college education? So providing education for all is a problem. "It is easy for the U.S., for Japan, for France," he thinks. "But it is not easy for Cambodia."

Since they earn barely enough to get by, teachers rarely have time or energy to focus on teaching. "Their concern is for everyday life." Samnang has a plan: "One of the best ways of improving the quality of education is improving the quality of textbooks." He hopes foreign scholars will help him on this by donating time and writing books for both students and teachers in their areas of expertise because, "We have no financial means to provide the retraining."

As it is, twelfth-graders in Cambodia have no history books. Officials haven't decided how best to discuss key facets of the recent past. A new text has been written, but it is returned to the government in 2003 because of "political sensitivities" since 1979. So graduates today go without. The people on the textbook committee "have no experience," Samnang says.

He thinks Cambodia can't change without foreign aid. He envisions a sort of "Marshall Plan" as Western Europe had to usher it through post–World War II recovery. That is the only way, he says. "We need international support because we have become a war-torn country."

He says poverty continues to cripple education and all facets of society. He calls the decade from 1970 to 1979 "the period of lost education, the period of lost opportunity." From 1979 through the Paris Peace Agreements signed in 1991, "Cambodia was partly in peace, partly in war." At the same time, the international community placed a trade embargo on the country while it was under Vietnam's tutelage. That embargo unfairly hurt the poor, he says. "During that time we were punished. We did not receive assistance." The effects still hamper this society.

And this should be noted: While many may argue it is not the international community's responsibility to rebuild Cambodia, the international community is in many ways responsible for the appalling state of Cambodia today. Cambodia suffered for ninety years under its French colonial "protectors" who favored the people next door, installing Vietnamese bureaucrats in Phnom Penh. And the United States: The United States entangled Cambodia in its war with Vietnam, for years bombing Cambodia to rid the country of Viet Cong. The United States dumped 257,465 tons of explosives on this country in a carpet-bombing campaign that lasted seven straight months in 1973. Those bombs killed scores of people, demolished thousands of homes, made travel through the country nearly impossible. The bombing sent hundreds of thousands of people to Phnom Penh, cramming the city. People camped where they could. Diseases spread. It was no longer safe to work the fields. People starved. While there is no single explanation for what followed, the Khmer Rouge rise to power, the seeds of that regime were undeniably scattered through the seared fields of American bombs. And then, the United States and other Western powers determined the Vietnamese ouster of the Khmer Rouge amounted to an illegal invasion, a move that needed punishing. They stopped international lenders and donors from giving to either Vietnam or Cambodia. Just when Cambodia needed it most, help was denied. The Vietnamese economy nearly suffocated, and Cambodia's couldn't begin to breathe after years of genocide and war. Moreover, the United Nations accorded Cambodia's seat to the overturned Khmer Rouge leadership. It was a roundabout slap in Vietnam's face, which still stings Cambodians today. And then: More than a decade later the United Nations arrived in Cambodia, offering to bring peace and democracy through the elections it sponsored in 1993. But it brought neither. Fighting continued another five years and the victor — the candidate the people chose — was forced to share power with Cambodia's long-term strongman, who rules to this day. And now: Cambodians don't trust elections.

Samnang doesn't say these things, but they must be considered.

Meanwhile, today, Cambodians are frothing at the prospect of new wealth, new money, the tiniest cell phones, the shiniest *motos*, the fastest Internet connections. They see changes in the world, and, finally, their chance to jump aboard the shuttle. All around Phnom Penh these days, new institutions advertise the way to attaining dreams. Samnang says a French professor visited him recently. "One day, I took him in my car." They drove through the center of the city, past parks and monuments and *wats*. "My friend said, 'I saw a university on every street!'" Build Bright University, Western University, the American University of Hawaii. Options are everywhere.

On one hand, he says this is good. State-run universities cannot handle all 30,000 high-school graduates each year, and those youngsters need something. If the nation's graduates are given no further opportunities, no appropriate places to use their skills, "those people may cause some problem to the society." On the other hand, he wonders what these institutions are teaching and who ensures their quality.

He reiterates the general lack of qualified teachers and textbooks, which leads to an overwhelming lack of qualified professionals, anywhere in the country, in any field. "A working democracy, I think, depends on qualified human resources."

And how do you get those, when you have none to teach the next generation?

It is a question neither he nor anyone else can answer.

One day in 2002, I visit Chuch Phoeurn, an archaeologist, in his office at the Ministry of Culture and Fine Arts. He is the deputy secretary of state for the ministry, as well as the deputy secretary general for the National Commission for UNESCO. I am here to talk with him about bats.

Bats, because a huge colony of them, two million or so, used to live in the rafters of the national museum until just a few months before when their rooftop homes were blocked. These bats were well loved and well known through Phnom Penh, for their nightly excursion through the sky, a sunset parade from the museum as they went on their evening sortie in search of dinner.

For years conservationists tried to find a solution for the bats because, despite their endearing nature, they pooped on the artifacts and caused great havoc among the antiquities. Some of the workers, however, profited from the bats' excretion, as they collected tons of guano each year and sold it in the market.

There was talk of plans for a new roof that would allow the bats to roost without hurting Cambodia's archaeological treasures. The roof needed, still needs, rebuilding anyway; it's falling to pieces. But this plan involved $700,000 and too much time, so the head of the museum arranged for the bats to be evicted.

I've come to chat with Chuch Phoeurn about the bats.

He tells me all about the effects of bats on archaeological wonders. And he tells me his job is a balancing act. He would like to save both bats and relics, but he must be realistic. There is not enough money in the coffers. So he weighs the options and determines the bats can live elsewhere, but the museum artifacts can never be replaced.

And then he tells me about his struggles to find foreign funding for any of his work. He wants to build museums in three provinces, where ancient archaeological finds pile up in provincial offices, in corners, on desks, anywhere they fit. But he hasn't the money.

Take this example: The national museum charges visitors a $2 entrance fee. In the peak tourist season, he says, that brings in $25,000 to $30,000 over a few months. But the government gives only 10 percent of that money back to the museum. Where does the other 90 percent go? "I don't know. I can't say." But he doesn't want to raise entrance fees (although they eventually do go up to $3). He equates it to a noodle shop. If you want a lot of customers, "it should be cheap."

Chuch Phoeurn is one of the country's highest-ranking officials, and his office is moderate. "I have no stationery," he says. "I buy my pens myself. All the things behind me, I bought myself." His computer, his printer, Internet access, he buys. The government bought his office furniture, but only once in four years, same as paper.

He does, occasionally, get the government to pay his auto-repair costs. "If one of my tires are broken, I can ask." He tells the ministry: "If you don't provide one, I don't go to the ministry for work. If you can't pay, I stay home."

I ask how much his office expenses are. "It's a lot. It's a lot. At least $100 monthly." His salary is $200. When he travels abroad for work, he gets $120 a day for food, $200 for accommodation and $40 pocket money. The cost is very high in other countries, he says. But he stretches that money. "If I have three or four missions a year; I save my money. I keep for my own family."

And this is how one of the country's elite does business in a government on the path of development.

Interlude: Cops and Dogs

Warning: Some readers, particularly those who love dogs, may not appreciate this bizarre account of culinary habits among Cambodia's impecunious police force.

It is August 2003 and we're living in a third-floor apartment near the riverfront in central Phnom Penh. Behind us is an old colonial mansion, as ramshackle today as it surely was exquisite in its time. For years now, a contingent of cops have occupied that house with their families. These cops are not rich, nor do they hold the clout to make them powerful. They live the grotty lives that millions of Cambodians do.

Our kitchen window overlooks their courtyard. Children play and screech; women cook; men kickbox; cats chase rats; laundry dries in the sun. It stinks. It's full of garbage. Toddlers run amok with no guidance. Men and children pee on an open concrete ledge, visible to all the buildings around. For three months, Jerry and I have an eagle's eye over their lives laid bare.

One night, around 11 as I get ready for bed, I notice a fire in the courtyard. Our kitchen clouds with smoke as orange flames billow beneath a blackened pot down below. Our neighbors seem to neglect the fire, which grows and shrinks with the wind. So I check it once more before going to sleep. And then, my body stretched over the counter, I can see through the bars of our window half a dozen men around a mammal with women squatting nearby on a stoop. The animal is black and white, it's certainly not a pig. They're about to butcher it, cook it or dismember it. I'm not sure what it is.

I call Jerry to bring his camera, and he also fetches the binoculars. We confirm: It's a dog, with a short white coat and black patches throughout, fatter than most on the street. Its muzzle is black, its feet black. The body is limp, not yet stiff.

For the next hour, the men take a razor to its coat, shaving it meticulously, a section at a time, working beneath the light of a single bulb. They dip the animal, part by part, into a pot of boiling water. The body is too big for the pot, so one must hold the animal while dipping.

We grow weary around midnight, but just as I'm about to leave my window perch, a cop hauls out another dog, same routine. Jerry and I have seen enough. We sleep.

By morning, the two carcasses hang from the metal roof below us. A crowd gathers and women squat around the meat while a man brings a scale. They weigh each section and women exchange *riel*. The cops make money off this work.

I look back periodically through the morning, and by 11, the carcasses are dismantled and tossed in a black garbage bag. A man plucks the bits, section by section, from the bag and cleans them in a plastic pail of water. He chops the meat into bite-sized cubes while other pieces turn to jerky in the sun, drying in a red colander on their roof. Later, the men and women join in making stew. It simmers most the day, emitting a brash, smoky scent.

This is not the only incident, we watch this scene again a few weeks later. In Cambodia, many people would never admit they eat dog. Many view it as taboo at best, evil at worst — an abhorrent practice of the Vietnamese, but not the Khmers. Yet some find it a delicacy, and the meat is eaten in cooler months to keep warm. For the poor, dog is an option when other victuals run out.

In the next month, the governor of Phnom Penh gets on a kick to rid the streets of stray dogs. He defends dog meat as practical for the poor. "Come on, dog meat is so delicious," he tells *The Cambodia Daily*. "Poor people can enjoy their dog meat with palm juice wine."

We see no wine among the cops behind our apartment that night, but we see many smiles huddled around the steaming poorman's stew.

When Jerry returns to Phnom Penh seven months later, he sees lots of cops, lots of beggars, the same number of people trudging through life. But not a single stray dog.

20. Heroes: Doing It Their Way

As I write this book, I dig through an Angkor beer box full of Jerry's slides and negatives. I paw through plastic bags full of prints. I find more questions than answers. What has become of Hui and his clovers? Of the man shot in the arm? Of Mai at the dump and Cheth with his foot? And I wonder each time we return, will we see Sovann selling his papers on the street corner? Will Monin be there to take us anywhere we want on his *moto*? And when we return, and the people we know aren't there, I wonder: Is he dead? Has she gone to her village? Are they at home planting rice in a field far away? Because one never knows what will happen here.

And yet, over the years, amid all the uncertainty, all the dreams turned upside down, we also find more stories of hope, fewer accounts of harrowing ends. We find a man who de-mines his homeland by hand. A reporter who builds a school for his village; another who builds a library. A monk helping the orphans of AIDS. A woman leading against the ruling party. A blind man finding jobs for the disabled. Two young girls facing life bravely after rape and injustice.

Somehow, these people have found the strength and zeal to change their world when no one else will. These are not powerful politicians, nor their sons and daughters. They are not rich or famous or always educated. They are ordinary Cambodians who have taken life by the reins, slowly steering it into a future they are determining—for themselves, for their country.

The eight people featured here are not alone; they are a few of many. But their stories exemplify a certain drive that will, in the end, define the Cambodia that lies ahead. They are heroes of the boldest kind.

Rith and LC

I remember Rith's tousled hair, his round body flung over a worn couch with loose springs. I see him napping, eating, laughing, lounging, doing everything but work as his expatriate editors wished he would. The stories about him were newsroom legend. The excuses he had for not coming in, for not being on time, distant relatives forever tugging on his shirttails.

And that's about all I retain of Rith early on because the image I see now clouds

Saing Soenthrith, a reporter at *The Cambodia Daily*, runs himself ragged between his journalism job in Phnom Penh and this school he built with his own hands and money in his village. Takeo, 2002.

most other recollection. I later learn the excuses, the relatives— they're all true; his is a heart of immense proportions. And now, perhaps he's changed; perhaps I have, or maybe we've both evolved. No matter: Rith is now a teacher, a volunteer, a builder. And a hero to a new generation.

We worked together at the *Daily*, where foreign editors are hired to train Cambodians in writing, reporting and ethics. After all Cambodia's troubles, Bernie, the publisher, wanted to help rebuild. But years later, it is Rith who teaches me about that.

Saing Soenthrith — his name in full — started a school in his village outside Phnom Penh. He saved his money, raised some more, collected books and chairs and desks, bought wood to nail and trees to plant. He built by hand. Every weekend now, he motors forty miles over a partially paved road to the Volunteer English School, known as VES. He can't stop the deluge of students at his door.

Rith is not alone in this sort of grassroots succor.

Another *Daily* reporter, Lor Chandara, known as LC, built a library in his home in a village just beyond Rith's. He too saved money, found donors and posted his cause online. "I just want to encourage the people," he says.

The ground floor of his house brims with books and shelves and a classroom where kids gather for English lessons. When LC works in Phnom Penh, his family and neighbors keep the library alive, checking out books, issuing cards, guiding patrons to purveyors of wisdom in the stacks.

"I am a farm boy," LC says. But he went to school, moved to Phnom Penh and found work at the *Daily*. Now village elders tell their kids about "long-nose" foreigners who come to work with LC. Study hard, the elders say, and you, too, may succeed like LC.

When the library opened in Takeo, the governor gave a speech. He stressed the importance of reading and doing good deeds. "I am not proud," says LC, "but I think I am like a role model."

Jerry and I return to Cambodia in 2001. Rith shows us pictures of his school. He spent $2,000 of his own money and garnered $100 and books from his boss, desks from the Phnom Penh mayor, $10 toward a teacher's salary paid monthly by a *Daily* reporter. He wrote to an uncle in California, imploring, simply, "Please help Cambodian people." He got a $600 check in return.

Rith hired two teachers, but he still helps on his days off. That means less time with his family at home, but his wife supports him. "She says, 'Good! You help your country.'" He has piles of student applications, all awaiting Rith's official red stamp. Everyone around here knows about VES.

We meet Rith there one afternoon, amid monsoons. We skid through Phnom Penh on motorbikes, with mud and rain slapping our skin. We zip in and out of traffic, around potholes, past garment factories spilling workers fresh off their shifts. Our vision is blinded by exhaust and needling rain.

But the city ends, commotion fades and greenery burgeons beneath pink streaks igniting the sky. We find the school amid puddles and bugling frogs. Rith teaches twenty-six pupils sitting at simple desks on a concrete floor, their umbrellas hanging on lattice windows to dry. It's a small wooden room, about ten feet by fifteen feet, full of flip-flops, sarongs and the glowing robes of Buddhist monks. Rith teaches introductions in English. The monks sit in back and ask me perfectly annunciated questions:

"Do you have children? What is your job? How do you think about it here? I would like to be your friend."

I answer their questions, but they don't understand my replies. For now, they only know how to ask — and laugh a healthy lot.

Rith spent thirteen years living at a temple in Phnom Penh that takes in the homeless, the orphans, the people with nowhere to go. For so long, so many Cambodians had nowhere to go. Rith was a refugee, like all the others. "I understand the suffering of Cambodian people," he says. That's why he teaches.

He expected the school to grow little by little, like the bananas, papayas and chilies around it. When VES opened, he expected ten students. He now has eighty-six, of all ages.

English can carry Rith's students far. Cambodians who can't speak English, he points out, have a rough time finding decent, steady work. But many farming families don't understand his mission. He says they don't read Khmer, and they don't know why their children should either, much less learn a foreign language. So he provides a spot where kids can study, away from home, no explanations needed.

For Rith, as for many Cambodians, education is privilege. It was rare under the

French; there was none during the Khmer Rouge, and the subsequent Vietnamese government didn't allow Cambodians to study Western languages for another decade. "But some people," Rith says, "they studied, they talked very quietly, huddled in a room."

He writes on the board, his words flowing from English to Khmer. Rain tinkles on the roof, and insects sing in the pond next door. Class ends when clouds part and the sky bursts into an orchestra of triumphant light. Everywhere, rice glows in a prism of color. We ride through it, back to Phnom Penh, bathed in an array of rainbows.

It's 2002, we've returned again to Cambodia, and LC shows us his library. We wake early and pile into a van with two *Daily* editors named Dave and Jody, LC and his family, a box of books, two bookcases, and a rattan couch strapped to the roof. We jounce about, past Rith's school, on a bit farther down a dirt road. We stop at an ordinary two-story house with a sign in front and a lower level of books. LC's relatives live upstairs and behind, but it's the front of the house that's famous.

It's bigger, Jody says. She's been here before. The library swells as living space shrinks. Everywhere, there are books: English, Khmer, Japanese, literature, geology, technology, physics, history. LC thinks he has 1,000, maybe 1,500 — he hasn't counted. About twenty kids perch on long wooden benches. They come most every day for English lessons.

Dave and Jody have brought an old Pentium laptop, a donation from Bernie. They speak about how computers can change lives. "I was twenty-six the first time I saw a computer," Dave says. It's never too late to learn; it's impossible to break the machine. He exhorts: Play around! See what comes!

A twenty-one-year-old library intern named So Phann examines the computer and says, "I am afraid of mistake." We talk briefly, I exit momentarily, then return to find So Phann at the keyboard, fingers flicking with pep. He's typed me a message:

"I want to meet you every day Because I want to talk with you. I miss you so much/from Mr. Sophann."

I respond: "You type very well. I think you are quite smart."

He writes: "I thank you foryou that say good for me."

We continue our chat:

"You are welcome. If you practice, you will understand computers very well."

"I want to talk with so much for my practice EngLish for my job."

"If you speak English and use the computer, you will learn quickly."

"Thank you for advice. I will to try for to study for my futur"

"Good luck in your studies," I tell him.

"I wish you lucky all the time," he replies.

When we're through, LC introduces sixteen-year-old Mouy Heak as an accomplished English student. Her mother works at a factory in Philadelphia, so we move to a colorful U.S. map on the wall. I point to Oregon, my home at the time. I show her Philadelphia, the Wisconsin of my youth, and the home of Jerry's parents in California. Two things surprise her immensely: the great distances dividing these places and the fact that our families don't live close by.

Then she asks about computers. "I have never used because I am poor.... How much is this computer?"

"I don't know," I say. "This one is not new, *thmei thmei*, so maybe it is about $500." But *thmei thmei* computers cost more, I tell her.

"I want to put my paper for school on the computer," she says. "But how can I do?"

I explain the concept of a printer, and when we find the word in a dictionary, she understands immediately.

Then LC calls us to lunch, and we indulge in bitter fish soup, fried beef, onion and tomato doused in lime, fried chicken over greens, and a dessert of fresh lychees and succulent mangosteens. Afterward, he takes us to his new family *stupa*, a memorial to his ancestors. A young man wanders nearby, through the village cemetery. Although the man doesn't know LC, he knows of the library. He is a teacher from a village up a dirt path toward a small mountain in the distance.

"My students tell me you have a computer," he says. "I want to use, but I have no money."

Portrait of *Cambodia Daily* reporter Lor Chandara over lunch in Phnom Penh. He has begun a library in his rural hometown to promote reading in the countryside. Phnom Penh, 2003.

LC says there is much demand, but he hopes to find a second computer soon — and don't worry, it will be free.

Then we head to the village where LC's wife grew up. It's a rare picture of countrified Cambodian prosperity, a quaint spread of homes on stilts with weaving looms and silk tapestries below. People live in quiet harmony, surrounded by mangos, hibiscus and green hills. Our hosts pluck palm fruit from the trees, and LC tells us to pitch the hard shells in the bushes when we're through. They will decompose.

When we see LC a few nights later, at a boisterous party in Phnom Penh, he tells us he wants to teach environmental values to villagers in Takeo. "You probably didn't notice," he says, but he's divided garbage into two bins at his library — one for plastic, one for paper. In addition to husband, father, reporter, editor and entrepreneur, LC deems himself the environmental guru of his village. "I am not proud," he says, "but I am kind of famous in Takeo."

After visiting LC's library and his wife's village, we head briefly to Rith's school. It has changed. In seven months, he has built another room with a bookcase, a small reading nook. He has cleared the field behind him, digging a pit for a fish pond. He'll plant forty mango trees, with milk-fruit between, and in two or three years he'll have fruit to sell. In the rainy season, the adjacent canal will flood, and his pond with teem with fish. He'll have more than a school, he'll have a sustainable system where students can eat and learn and plant their own papayas and examine big toads in the trees.

His bananas and chilies are growing strong amid night-blooming jasmine and bamboo. When the bamboo grows tall, he says, the house will be prosperous. To him, that means happiness with plenty of food, enough books to read and vibrant students to teach.

He's well on his way.

We talk some more, then Rith pulls a small green mango from a sapling in his yard. It's the tree's first fruit, and he feeds it to us with chili and salt. We sit on his stoop, admiring the sigh of a hot afternoon as it slips away. This is special, Rith tells us. It's a virgin mango for good luck.

Aki Ra

At five years old, Aki Ra was orphaned by murder, mother and father both victims to the Khmer Rouge. At ten years old, he got his first gun, an AK-47, and in the years between, his parents' killers taught him to lay mines, fire rockets and make bombs. They offered him a banquet of weapons: M16s, M60s, mortars, bazookas. By eighteen, he had fought for three armies— the Khmer Rouge, the Vietnamese and the Cambodian government—all enemies, all killing each other, each pitting Aki Ra against former neighbors, friends and relatives. He did what he was told to stay alive. His whole life was steeped in war, and every day was the same: "Go to fight, lay mines, kill."

After his fighting days, before the 1993 elections, the UN asked Aki Ra to help de-mine the country. He knew where the mines were; he knew the language, and he knew the culture of war. The UN offered Aki Ra a chance at peace, and he took it.

For the first time, he saw life outside his ravaged existence. He saw Siem Reap town with its brick and concrete homes, which he touched with great curiosity, so different from the thatch and bamboo he and his comrades had known. He was dazzled by paved streets, cars, lights, toilets, movies on big screens and people of all kinds. "We were happy to see people like that," he says. "No war. We had good food." He realized life could be good, too.

When the elections were through, Aki Ra kept on. He was determined to disarm Cambodia step by step, mine by mine, bomb by bomb, digging alone. "I now work solely for the people of Cambodia," he writes in his autobiography, neatly typed and copied on twenty-three pages, which he sells for $3 to help fund his work. He runs a museum; he raises orphans; he educates the world about land mines, and he risks his life every time he walks into Cambodia's fields.

Aki Ra now feels compelled to undo the doings of his past. No one else is de-mining fast enough, the workload is simply too great. "We live daily with the legacy of the land mine and also unexploded bombs," Aki Ra writes. "For us, the horror is not yet over."

After the UN left, Aki Ra bought a thatch hut on stilts, down a dirt track off the main road leading to Angkor Wat. "My museum took a long time to make because I had to build a place to exhibit everything, and this required money," he writes. He slowly saved enough and filled his home with munitions unearthed by his work. He landscaped a mini minefield, safe and defused, where visitors walk among snares, booby-traps, spikes and anti-tank mines. In the beginning, he greased the poles of his hut at night and pulled the ladder inside, protecting himself from thieves and enemies. Not everyone likes his work.

Jerry and I meet Aki Ra during the Khmer New Year, in the hot month of April. He has recently completed a de-mining mission to Anlong Veng, returning home with malaria. He spent several feverish days in the hospital, and now he rests.

He offers a weak handshake and talks about his work, tugging at a rice sack of evidence. About ten square feet of land near Anlong Veng contained ten mines, he says. "I clear in thirty minutes." He uses only rudimentary tools, no metal detectors, no blast-proof trucks, no safety gear. Some mines are old, some are newer. He pulls one from the bag. "Vietnamese mine. They lay in 1987." He points to another. "Very new. They lay in 1998."

Day by day, his stash grows: American Claymore mines, Chinese MBV78A1 mines, Bulgarian POMZ-2s, Russian POMZ 2Ms, North Vietnamese MBV78A2s, Vietnamese P-40 TNT mines, Russian TM-62M tank mines. Bouncing Bettys, named for the way they bounce five feet in the air and burst into fragments, killing most everything within a ten- to twenty-yard radius. Most of these mines have the look of a discus, the kind thrown at a track meet. Some look like little green pineapples, others like masses of sharp, welded spikes, made of plastic and metal, brown and green.

He calls his place a land mine museum, established in 1999. But it's not open to the public, not officially, not when we visit. The Cambodian military has its own museum, the official War Museum across town. There, visitors pay $3 to enter, and inside they see a tank, a plane, a motley mix of war paraphernalia and a vast array of Aki Ra's artifacts, confiscated from his place over the years. The local authorities are clear: Aki Ra's museum detracts from their own. So they show up at Aki Ra's door with a host of demands. First they pilfer any new ordnance he's uncovered. Then they command a little more. "I pay the cigarette, the food, everything, you know what I mean?" Aki Ra explains. "Sometimes they say, 'My telephone card, put $20 in my card.'" He gives what they ask so they leave him alone — until next time.

Ten minutes before we arrive, the police visited Aki Ra and demanded he buy beer for their New Year's party. "I say I don't have money, but they don't believe." The officers saw a motorbike parked in Aki Ra's yard and concluded it belonged to a tourist. Tourists always have money, they reasoned, so Aki Ra must as well. But the motorbike belonged to a friend who has no money. In fact, that friend has just left on the troublesome motorbike, on a fundraising mission to Siem Reap where he'll knock on a few rich doors, hoping to drum up $200 to pay for Aki Ra's next de-mining trip — and beer for the cops' shindig.

Solo de-miner Aki Ra displays a rice bag of mines, booby-traps and UXO he uncovered on a de-mining trip two days previous. Under his finger he tips a spike. Siem Reap, 2002.

De-mining costs money. There are basic expenses, such as transportation and food. But Aki Ra also hopes to teach villagers to de-mine on their own, and they insist on being paid. So he does, a few dollars for their time. He also pays Army soldiers to tell him where the mines are hidden, though they don't always tell him all the spots. And he pays to raise the orphaned children of land mine victims when they have no other guardians.

Aki Ra does all this on donations, rarely more than a few dollars a day. "It's enough for me, but it's not enough for many children," he says. "They have no leg, no arm, or no eye with the land mines. They want to come and stay with me and go to school, but I have no money." He used to garner more donations when more tourists came. But then the military removed his sign from the road leading to Angkor Wat. People stopped coming because they didn't know he was there.

As a technicality, given Aki Ra's trouble with authorities, a sign on his wall notes that visitors are not in fact visiting a museum. Rather, they are "guests" of his family.

Another sign notes his mission:

> At this museum, we're doing these three: 1. We take care of the children who lost their arms or legs and help them to live by themselves. We also gather children around the area and send them to school. 2. We clear mines/UXO. 3. Through this demonstration, we want you to know about the war in Cambodia and its mines/UXO. Helping here is more useful than helping from the distance. Any kind of help, for example, cleaning the museum, leaving your towel here, would be considered a great donation.

There are people, young and old, hovering about. One of them is an orphan he rescued in 1995, whose story is featured in Aki Ra's autobiography. The young boy, then a baby, was riding with his mother and father in an oxcart piled high with rice, returning from a day in the fields. The cart's heavy weight tripped an anti-tank mine. Mom, dad and two cows were killed instantly, their bodies flung into a minefield. The baby survived, suckling his dead mother's breast for three days. Villagers couldn't, wouldn't, go near the field, but Aki Ra did when he heard the story. He cleared the mines and took the boy home to live.

When Aki Ra heads to the fields, he consults the Army near Anlong Veng. They're former Khmer Rouge soldiers, men he fought with and against at various times. For a fee, they tell him where to look for old mines, but they don't tell him about the new ones they've laid to guard their buildings. So Aki Ra tromps about in the forest, looking for certain mines, not sure about others. He has a preternatural faith in his abilities to spot and clear any mine, anywhere. He doesn't believe he'll ever err. He is not afraid.

His missions require long days of work. He drives a land mine flanked road to Anlong Veng, hikes to a mountaintop, consults the Army, hikes some more to a minefield. That leaves him just an hour or two before nightfall to clear the mines. Then, he takes his AK-47 and hunts for dinner. He tells us he saw a tiger on his latest trip, but he left it alone. He shoots only small mammals. After dinner, he spends the night wrapped in a hammock, strung between trees, until hitting the fields again in early morning, reaping mines.

He hauls his findings back to the museum and adds them to the piles. There are tons, literally, heaped in corners, stacked on shelves, hanging on walls. They're categorized by type, and each one has a little card describing its use, its origin and the way it kills. He has mines and bombs made in Bulgaria, China, Poland, Russia, Vietnam and the United States. He has others used not only in Cambodia but also in Afghanistan, Eritrea, Ethiopia, Angola, Iraq, Korea, Kuwait, Mozambique, Namibia, Nicaragua, Rwanda, Somalia, Vietnam, Zambia and Zimbabwe. A blatant display of humanity's most abysmal proclivities.

Aki Ra knows now that the world of his youth was not normal, not good and should never endure. "I thought that the whole world existed like we did," he writes in his history. "And the brutality and hardship, the starvation and all the guns, became my normal world."

The horror is in the details. His father's death: a starved and ailing man who went to the hospital. They gave him rabbit feces and told him it was medicine. They fed him soup, which made him stronger. And then they accused him of faking his illness, so they took him away.

His mother's death: She told an old man to be careful, not to spill his food. The Khmer Rouge didn't like her talking to the man and took her away to "school," for re-education. "If you went to school," Aki Ra writes, "You never came back."

The young boy learned to evade death. He ate insects and, once, an elephant's trunk. He peed on his rice when he didn't have water to soften it. He watched other soldiers eat dead men's flesh. He learned to do anything his superiors asked. "They had my innocence in their hands and were able to warp it any way they chose."

The Khmer Rouge stole the innocence of everyone. Aki Ra gives examples: All food belonged to the *Angka*, the organization. To take anything not given was a crime. One hungry boy stole pig scraps to eat, but the leaders found out. The Khmer Rouge regularly checked people's feces to see that they had not eaten anything unauthorized. The boy's shit looked different, so they killed him. Another man, he writes, stole a banana from a tree. The soldiers disemboweled him and made his family clap.

This was the world of Aki Ra's youth. He shot and killed entire units of soldiers, then switched allegiance when necessary to survive. And he somehow came through it all, perfectly capable of understanding right from wrong when offered an alternative life.

He tells us these stories as we tour his minefield. He tells us how he's changed and how he wants to redeem his country. We paw our way through dusty, rusty, cobwebbed heaps of metal. He demonstrates his de-mining maneuvers, shuffling his toes, zigzagging his steps, prancing his feet, still weak with malaria.

"I know how to walk in the minefield," he says. "You cannot see, but I can see."

Aki Ra believes he is special, that he has a talent others don't share. Some say he's brave and fearless; some think him an enigma; some call him crazy. Or heroic. Or all of that entwined.

A tourist beside us, who has been silent until now, deeply entranced by the weight of Aki Ra's objects, asks him: But do you know exactly where they've laid the mines? Do they tell you?

"No," Aki Ra says bluntly. He knows generally where they are. Sometimes. But not always. He thinks he can safely feel his way.

We look at Aki Ra and the tourist says with astonished eyes:

"You must be an angel."

Boun Mao

The start of Boun Mao's life story mimics many in Cambodia. He chuckles when asked to tell it, he has been asked many times. "I was born in a poor family. I'm an orphan. My parents and brothers and sisters were killed during the war. After the Pol Pot regime, I came back to Phnom Penh." He lived with his godsister in 1993, when the UN was here. The streets were chaotic and crime was brutal.

One day a thief yanked Boun Mao's *moto* from his grasp, threw battery acid in his face and blinded him for life. "I was hopeless, so hopeless," he says now. "Sometimes you feel you died already.... You lost everything." For months, a German doctor soothed the injuries that scarred his head, his hands, his inner spirit. He didn't want to face life as a blind Cambodian. "I told the German doctor, 'Please kill me.'"

Boun Mao, director of the Association of the Blind in Cambodia, signs monthly accounting sheets and pay slips with help from a coworker at the association's office in Phnom Penh. A thief stealing his *moto* threw acid in his face several years ago, leaving him scarred and blinded. Phnom Penh, 2002.

But the doctor wouldn't allow his defeat, and neither did his girlfriend of the time. "They energized me," Boun Mao says. The man hung on.

Today he is a different man. He's a happy, confident human being. He's strong and positive and secure in his job as head of the Association of the Blind in Cambodia. He knows the depths of tragedy, and he knows a decent job can restore hope to the hopeless. So he's helping to turn blind Cambodians into self-sufficient masseurs and masseuses.

"This is an easy job the blind can do," he says. He is not belittling or patronizing, he is practical about the plight of the blind. There are an estimated 132,000 blind Cambodians. The causes are many: land mine accidents, traffic accidents, vitamin deficiencies, scarlet fever, glaucoma, cataracts. The results are the same. Jobs are hard to find. Stigma is a barrier. Begging is not an uncommon fate. The blind are "one of the most socially and economically marginalized groups in Cambodia," according to a report by his group. "This marginalization is due largely to the belief that they cannot play a productive role because of their disabilities."

Boun Mao knows this well. "In Cambodia, they put the blind in second class."

Cambodians sometimes think a blind child is bad karma, perhaps punishment for sins of a past life. They keep blind kids inside, and the youngsters grow up thinking they can do nothing in life. But massage simply works. "The blind can see by hand," Boun Mao says.

Just a few miles outside the ancient Angkor temples, down a quiet alley in Siem Reap town is Seeing Hands 4, Massage by Blind. It is, as the name connotes, Cambodia's fourth such venture. Sunlight dribbles through windows and doors, the room's only light, as the workers need no more. Foam mats, white sheets, white towels and cotton pillows are set on hardwood tables. The floor is spotless; the air imbued with soft flute on tape. A standing fan breaks the stifling heat. Visitors change into cotton scrubs behind a blue curtain in the corner.

Masseuse Wan Som starts with a client's head, face down, with cloth between hair and hands. Her fingers travel down the body, slowly pressing on meridian points. Then she slaps her hands, up and around. She leans into her work, climbing upon the table, lifting legs, stretching muscles.

Wan Som was blinded by fever at the age of one. She says her new skills will keep her employed. "If I didn't know how to do massage, I would ... just stay at home."

Now, home is here at Seeing Hands, where work and family merge. Employees are friends, colleagues and roommates alike.

Sam San, the twenty-four-year-old Seeing Hands 4 proprietor, went blind as a child. "It just happened," he says. His parents hoped doctors in Battambang city, several hours away, could cure him. But they couldn't. He was determined to work somehow. "I did not want to be a beggar," he says. "It's very hard to look for a job. Before, I lived in the countryside. I did nothing—just played music. But that wasn't a job."

Now he runs a business. On good days, he averages thirty-five customers. Over a month, that's enough to pay his $300 rent and $50 to $100 for each employee. But not always. "This month ... only enough for rent."

Still, a fluctuating income is better than none, a threat Boun Mao understands.

After his accident, after his recovery, Boun Mao studied massage through Mary-knoll, a Catholic aid group. He also studied English and went to Thailand on a scholarship to learn computers. He later returned to Cambodia, and around that same time Maryknoll closed its training centers. The money ran out, and there was no one to help the blind. There were groups for children, but no one to help the adults. So Boun Mao knew he had to do something. "October 25, 2000, we established the Association of the Blind in Cambodia," he announces proudly.

Since then, Boun Mao's work has gained notoriety. He's been featured in magazines and newspaper stories around the world, and he says the publicity helps the blind. When the blind appear on TV or in the news, people think: Oh, the blind can work and live and interact just like anyone else. "Some people release the discrimination from their mind." When people see him on TV tinkering with computers, parents ask their kids, "Why can't you do like the blind man on TV?"

A smiling Sarah Knight, a tourist from San Francisco, exits the Seeing Hands 4 office in Siem Reap. "It was wonderful," she says, after an hour-long massage. It helped her lower-back problems, and the foot massage was one of the best she'd ever had. "I was happy I could help … so that they're actually working and making money for themselves."

A spin through the Seeing Hands 4 schedule book finds similar sentiments. There isn't a bad comment in the book, just repetitions of "excellent," "best ever," and "brilliant." All written by foreigners. All inked in a script that the recipients of these compliments will never see.

Knight exits into bright sunlight, leaving a tip. Her massage artists can't understand her kind words, nor can they see the amount of money she's left. But one thing is certain: They know the feel of crisp dollars between their fingers, earned in an office they call their own.

Ly Chheng Ky

Every morning, Ly Chheng Ky climbs the stairs to a bare office with no electricity, no water, no phone. The drapes and rods are gone, light switches missing, air-conditioner removed. Her couch has no pillows, her staff no income. The empty offering tray of a Buddhist spirit house hangs on the wall. "Now nothing remains," she says.

Ly Chheng Ky, whom everyone calls Mrs. Ping Say, the name of her husband, is an elected leader of the Sam Rainsy Party, Cambodia's loudest party fighting against the ruling regime. She is a commune leader, the equivalent of a city councilor or alderman, except she's not a man. She's a woman, and she is the only woman elected in the 2002 commune elections on this opposition party ticket. "It's only me," she says.

Ly Chheng Ky is also a teacher, and that life in education led her here.

She attended Cambodia's college of arts and literature and became a professor of pedagogy before Pol Pot came to power. Those years still evoke pain. "Unfortunately, one of my sons, my oldest son, died in the Pol Pot regime.... I don't know how he died, but we assume he died because we didn't hear anything from him."

After the terror, she moved to Phnom Penh and taught high school. She retired from that in 1991 and went to work for a Japanese aid group, teaching disabled students. At sixty-seven, she still runs private classrooms, under the name of Phnom Nokor English School, out of her Phnom Penh home. She squeezes those duties in before and after her hours at the office.

There, she sits behind a metal desk with nothing more than the pens, pencil, highlighters, Post-It notes, calendar, message sheets and map of Phnom Penh, which she supplies. She employs eleven people, but no one has been paid. "Now we keep patient," she says. "According to law, the government will pay to the commune one million *riel*." That's about $250 a month for utilities, salaries and all work expenses. "But so far, nothing." This is late April 2002, almost three months after the commune elections that gave her this job. "I don't know what the government is thinking. How can we survive not paying people?"

Ly Cheng Ky, also known as Mrs. Ping Say, is the country's only female commune leader of the opposition Sam Rainsy Party. Her office was stripped bare by the previous commune head, a CPP member, leaving her the desk here and one chair. She has had to supply everything else herself. Phnom Penh, 2002.

Still, Ly Chheng Ky holds a remarkable place in this office, in this country, where fifteen opposition candidates and activists, including two women, were killed in political violence before the vote. The political season, according to Human Rights Watch, fared better than most, but it was still marred by 200 reported cases of intimidation and harassment against the opposition, 24 death threats, 23 arbitrary arrests and detentions of opposition supporters, 50 cases of property violations against the opposition and restricted media access for the opposition, which severely hampered the vote.

But Ly Chheng Ky displays little fear; she thinks the CPP wouldn't "dare" hurt her. "I'm not personally afraid," she says. "Well, not a lot, because the foreign press knows me."

She is a woman of change, and she effects change through her teaching. But the classroom alone is not enough in Cambodia, so she uses this office to teach as well. People are beginning to understand democracy, but illiteracy, ignorance, weak skills and corruption still stymie the nation. She hopes to change that in her own small way.

She was drawn to the Sam Rainsy Party after the 1998 election resulted in riots that splintered the city. "I read their party policy, and it fit with my mind," she says. So four years later, when Cambodia held its first-ever commune elections, she ran on the SRP ticket. Before that, commune leaders were appointed by the government. Even so in 2002, of 1,621 communes around the country, the Sam Rainsy Party won only 13. It was a strong-willed constituency of former students who loved, trusted and elected their teacher in this corner of Phnom Penh.

Ly Chheng Ky wears a gold silk shirt, brown skirt, gold rimmed glasses, diamond stud earrings and a brown leather watch with a gold face. We meet in her office, surrounded by eager underlings with lots to do but few resources to do it with.

She tells me about her life, her background, born in Kompong Cham Province. She married in 1957 and had six kids. They are adults now and several live nearby. Her daughter and son-in-law are doctors, another daughter keeps a small restaurant and shop in the same building where she lives and teaches.

The commune office is in an old building with a police unit below. When Ly Chheng Ky first arrived, she found the former CPP leader had wiped it clean. "On the opening day, they gave me only one sheet of document." She pulls out an inventory sheet for the office listing the address, House #14 Eo on Plot #14, Rd. #259, with 4,519 square feet of space. That was it, all the information she was allotted upon her new vocation.

She faces an arduous five years presiding over, she thinks, 20,000 people. "I say about, I say approximately, because the previous commune chief took the documents." She admits reservations about this job. "Since I came to this office, I have seen many problems." Nothing will change quickly, she knows, but her spirit remains intact. "We have to think critically.... We have to look at our capacity."

Her capacity draws enormous strength from her steadfast record. People know her. People like her. When she campaigned, she walked the boisterous alleys and scorched streets of tin-roofed homes, stating her case. "When I went door-to-door, they always welcomed me," but her neighbors know well the CPP grip. "The people asked me, 'Teacher'—they called me teacher—'how could you win?'" She told them it depended on their confidence in her, and she wowed them with her forthright intentions.

Ly Chheng Ky conducts her business unlike other politicians. She takes no currency under the table. Money doesn't make her work faster. "The main point I'm interested in is eliminating corruption," she says. "The country cannot develop because of corruption."

She sees a steady stream of constituents with problems. There are snafus with family identity cards, housing papers, electricity hook-ups and bill payments. One man enters and explains he wants the water turned on at his home. He tries to slip her a thick wad of 500 *riel* notes, worth about 12 cents each. Ly Chheng Ky is appalled. "No, no, keep your money." And she shoves it back at him.

The man tries to stuff it in her notepad.

"No, no, I do not want your money."

The man is shocked — and grateful.

On an average day, Ly Chheng Ky rises early with the heat, conducting her business at home, preparing the school for the day. She reaches the commune office by 7:30, works, breaks for lunch and returns to the school, then back again to the office, then home again to her classrooms.

She tells me what she sees as Cambodia's toughest challenges: corruption, poverty, illiteracy, human rights abuses, all related. She tackles first the issues relating to women. They need job training. They need education, and they need to understand a husband has no moral right to hit his wife. Women must know the law, and police must obey it. Some of Cambodia's worst sex crimes are condoned and carried out by the police themselves. It's hard to get a man to understand a woman, she says. So women must fight, they must help rebuild society. "We try to push ourselves ahead."

Her cell phone rings, and a man enters the office to give her a receipt. But her streamlined thoughts resume where they left off.

"Women must struggle, and they will struggle, and they will understand gradually about participation in society's building."

We talk some more, then she leads us to another room on the same floor where Jerry can take her picture. In that room, is a wooden desk and a rattan couch with no pillows. A faded and torn red curtain hangs through metal slats on an open window, which has no glass. The door has no knob, only the hole. A pulley and wires on the ceiling indicate where a chandelier should go. Ly Chheng Ky works for the Interior Ministry, which controls the communes, but she has never been invited to a meeting at the stately new offices across town.

She says she is proud to live independently, without fear of the ruling class. This is something she instilled in her children, "so they can live in a good condition."

She invites us to her home to see her school. We hop on motorbikes and rumble through the neighborhood, turning onto a dirt road with garbage heaps and bricks and construction refuse piled around newly built villas.

At her home, a large schedule board is posted on the wall: She has a meeting to attend, a ceremony, an interview with *The Cambodia Daily*, another with Radio Free Asia. A car is parked in the living room, which is not unusual for a house of this size in this city. But, then, most of this house is not a house.

We head to the kindergarten, behind a sandbox and a garden filled with banana trees and epiphytes growing in potted air. Laundry hangs in the noontime sun. There's a slide, a teeter-totter and a dragon-shaped swing. The blackboards inside show English lessons in a room replete with tiny chairs, stuffed animals, paper birds on the walls, a boom box and a world map.

Upstairs, chemistry, biology, math and English are taught to older students in concrete rooms with wooden tables. The morning's geometry lesson remains in Khmer and English on the board.

And this is it — a humble house hemmed in by classrooms, where the seeds of intellect have sprouted in a thousand little minds, and where one woman nurtured a yen to do more for her country.

Ly Chheng Ky points out she'll be seventy-two by the end of her term as commune leader, and she's not sure she'll make it. "I find myself now facing many obstacles, many difficulties." The old system of a ruling party, bribery, extortion, corruption — so much inertia to overcome. She calls these things "blocks to leadership" and believes the commune elections never would have occurred had foreign governments and agencies not pressed for them. "This could not happen. This could not take place." Democracy is "only on our mouth," she says. "It does not exist."

What, then, propels her? It's the faith her students have entrusted in her. It's the faith she has in the people who elected her. It's the fragile hope in the next generation and the belief that one day, Cambodia will evolve. Perhaps she'll have a hand in the lessons that shape a nation. But progress takes time, and she'll wait.

"Now, we keep patient."

Muny Van Saveth

The Venerable Muny Van Saveth runs the Wat Norea Peaceful Children's Home on the outskirts of Battambang town. During the years of Cambodia's armed conflict, he took in the region's war orphans. Now a new killing force sweeps Cambodia, and The Venerable, as he is known, is housing a growing population of children orphaned by AIDs. Battambang, 2003.

In the early 1990s, the children of war appeared at Muny Van Saveth's door. He took them in, all orphans whose parents were lost in battle. He housed dozens at a time at his home in Battambang. Since 1992, he has fostered 368 children.

Muny Van Saveth is the head monk at Wat Norea, and the new home he gave those orphans is known as the Peaceful Children's Center. He fed them, clothed them, schooled them and showed them a better life. By the late 1990s, Cambodia's war was yawning to a close, but the orphans did not stop coming. The Venerable realized he had another problem at hand: "We worry about children orphaned by AIDS."

Many people call AIDS Cambodia's new war, one that will take a devastating toll. The UN predicts the disease will leave behind 140,000 orphans in the following few years. Again, Battambang sits on the front lines. This is Cambodia's second-largest city, situated on a highway linking Bangkok to Phnom Penh and Saigon. People travel through here, and AIDS spreads with them.

In response, Muny Van Saveth has decided to be radical. He started teaching his monks about AIDS a few years ago, when most people thought monks had no place talking about such a stigmatized disease. He confronted stigma. He told people they shouldn't shun a person who has the disease. He told patients not to fear, that he would always support them. He sent Wat Norea's monks to the villages to teach other monks about AIDS. And now, he's telling Cambodians that some of their ancient beliefs just aren't right.

The Venerable says a 2,000-year-old Buddhist women's law, called *ch'hbat srey*, holds some dangerous ideas that become deadly in the age of AIDS. The law outlines the purportedly proper way for women to act, dress, speak, to be. The teachings emphasize a woman's duty to act politely, dress conservatively and obey her husband, "but they never say anything about human rights," he says. It is common for Cambodian men to beat their wives and visit brothels; it is common for Cambodian women to remain silent, following the interpretations of *ch'hbat srey*. "They are afraid of their husbands, so they never say anything," Muny Van Saveth tells us. In this way, "It is easy to transmit HIV."

And that, The Venerable says, is wrong. He wants to stop this. He wants women to know they have rights, he wants men to know their wives are equals. He wants everyone to know that some points of *ch'hbat srey* are not healthy. Ultimately, he wants to vanquish AIDS from his country.

Jerry and I visit Wat Norea several times in 2002 and 2003. The Venerable invites us into the orphanage, where dozens of children laugh and jump and scamper through a wide room with a red-and-white tiled floor. We sit adjacent a play area with the chief monk and Sor Samnang, his deputy director, financier and translator. Together, they brief us on the details of Wat Norea.

There are always forty-seven or forty-eight kids here. In our first visit, workers at Wat Norea suspect forty-four of the children might be infected with HIV. But the children don't always know it, and they don't always know how their parents died. They may know their mother had a disease or their father had malaria, but they know little about AIDS.

Muny Van Saveth wants people to help each other. "Home is hospital in the community," he says. When a parent dies of AIDS and the children are left with no relatives, Muny Van Saveth first tries to find a home in the village. He goes door-to-door, looking for sponsors. After he arranges a new home, he visits several times in the following months. "The community is responsible for them," he says. He estimates each village in Battambang Province has about 10 orphans, and perhaps 300 families. One child may be too much for one family to feed and house, but 10 children among 300 families should be no problem. "We try to use the resources in the community." When there is no option, the child can stay at Wat Norea.

A while back, he realized many patrons readily donate to the *wat*, to spruce it up for festivals and holidays. But the *wat* is already beautiful, he says, so why not give money to the children who need it? Now, when Wat Norea's monks travel the morning streets with their offering bowls in hand, they collect food and money for the orphanage.

The Venerable is a networker, and his work slinks through the province. His AIDS program, started in 2001, involves 240 monks at 120 pagodas, as well as 47 commune officials and four nuns. They study at Wat Norea about AIDS and HIV transmission, then share that knowledge among their neighbors. "We want them to train all the monks in their pagoda to know about AIDS," he says. And now his training includes teachings on domestic violence and human rights.

Administrator Lim Sophat joins our discussion and tells us about *ch'hbat srey*, repeating what Muny Van Saveth has told us about the interpretations of women's decorum. "We want to change our people's conduct," Lim Sophat says. Traditionally men view women as "slaves in sex." This is very wrong. Wat Norea emphasizes that "a few points" of *ch'hbat srey* are not good. That drinking, going to bars, meeting girls and visiting brothels are not behaviors consistent with the Buddha's teachings.

This is bold work in a mostly rural country that lives on the rhythms of its past. The rain, the heat, the Earth, the ancient Cambodian customs—pounding rice, driving an oxcart, weaving *kramas* by hand: Change is slow to come in Cambodia. While many Buddhist teachings were lost during Khmer Rouge times, tenets such as *ch'hbat srey* have long been embedded in the culture. They are more than religious teachings; they are a way of life. And that didn't change through Cambodia's genocide and war.

But The Venerable is not deterred. His vision is much too important. "I think they will listen to us," he says of his villagers. "When they know clearly about human rights, they can choose the best way."

He takes us to see a session next door.

It's a dimly lit room with a concrete floor and wooden walls, and twelve people gather around a large center table. On the walls are pictures of people with AIDS and photos of The Venerable sitting beside spindly patients. The six men and six women gathered around the table listen to a woman in front who talks of all the things the chief monk has mentioned. Namely: women's rights.

It is soon time for The Venerable's lunch. He eats alone on a cot in his bedroom, with small dogs below him. He has fish and fried egg, lime, rice and salt. He eats first, then the kids follow, as is customary. Their meal is served in a back room on a slat floor over a lotus pond. They gather in circles. A girl scoops rice with a bowl from a monstrous wok built into an oven. Another girl ladles soup from a huge pot. The dining area is breezy and pleasant; the kids sit on colorful mats, and cats prowl around them. Before they eat, they bow their heads in prayer.

When the children have finished and left for an afternoon nap, I sit and talk with the monk. He tells me his personal history. "I am thirty-three years old but I am in twelfth grade," he says. "I was born in the war so I never went to school." This saddens him because he is clever enough to know how much he doesn't know. He only started his studies at eighteen years old, when he became a monk. He keeps apologizing for his lack of English. "I study by myself," he says. "I try to listen to the radio to learn about other countries' policies." He thinks developed nations can teach him valuable ideas. "I can make world peace around my society." Democracy, equality and human rights brought home to Battambang.

During the Khmer Rouge regime, Muny Van Saveth lived in Prey Veng, a province across the country. He was put to work in a group with other boys, but he survived with little problem because he befriended a Khmer Rouge soldier in charge. "Some children were not as lucky as me," he says. "Some children the Khmer Rouge killed with their parents. But I was very lucky." Yet the war still torments him today. "I saw the shooting; I saw the fighting." He doesn't know how to say it in English, but "my head is full."

And he worries about his kids—he does call them his own. He thinks the government could do more. He thinks too many kids lack basic human rights. "Maybe in Phnom Penh you can see them sleeping in the streets." They don't go to school; many take drugs. "Fourteen years old, they smoke heroin." Then he asks the English word to explain how one person gives HIV to another. I tell him: "transmit." AIDS, too, is spreading among the young generations, he says. But he hopes if everyone works hard, Wat Norea can show Battambang's kids "this is the way for them to live."

One afternoon in 2003, Jerry and I hop on *motos* and accompany The Venerable up a red-dirt road to the home of a woman named Mot Van. She is 23, and she has HIV. She learned this in 2000, as her husband lay dying of the disease. She has one son, a four-year-old named Bun Ya, whose name means "Wisdom." He has never been tested for HIV.

"After her husband died, she wanted to die the same," Muny Van Saveth says. But he helped her through depression and suggested she open a small shop to make a living. She did, and through the monk's words, she learned that people care. "I'm very happy because before she didn't want to live. But now she changes her mind," he says.

When we arrive, she sits on the floor of her doorway while The Venerable and another monk sit in plastic chairs outside, the monks seated higher, as is customary with the holy. It's a small house over a small gully, with a mismatch of corrugated cardboard and thatch making the walls. Her eyes fill with tears of happiness to see the monks. She tells us, "Now I don't feel sick," not like her husband did before he died. "I didn't know my husband's story," she says. "I don't understand, but I think maybe he went to sex workers before we married." Mot Van is no longer scared, she is not angry; she just hopes to do the best she can.

Her mother, Sok Neth, is here too, having come to visit from a village far away. "Before, I was afraid and sorry," she says. But no longer "because she has the monks, and she has the people supporting her." She knows many people with AIDS and many others who have already died. She knows she is not alone.

Still, Mot Van frets about her future because hers is a sparse village where people grow rice and vegetables and do little else. Her neighbors have no jobs, no money, and they buy from her on credit. She doesn't know how her shop will support her. She wants to move, and The Venerable says he will help her.

As we talk, Muny Van Saveth notices a child standing nearby who looks quite sick. He asks whose child he is and asks the people here to tell the child's father, "Come to my pagoda, and I will take him to the hospital." Many people don't seek medical care because they don't have the money. But as a monk, he can take the child for free.

We talk a bit more; it begins to mist, and we soon leave on our *motos*. We visit one more villager in another neighborhood a few miles away. The people Muny Van Saveth visits are all around here. They're living in and among the communities surrounding his *wat*. They are the people next door.

This man's name is Lom Om; he is forty. He, too, has AIDS. The Venerable greets him behind his house beneath a large palm tree and hands him a sack with a shirt, a notebook, a jar of vitamins and money. The man wears no shirt, only a red-and-black *krama*. All up and down his legs are little black splotches. Scabies, Muny Van Saveth says. But now, he's feeling better.

Lom Om learned he had HIV in 2001. He was a primary school teacher, but he has since quit his job. His health is inconsistent. "Now he's better than before, but this man, he feels feeble," The Venerable says. He opens the vitamin jar and hands several to the man's young daughter.

Lom Om has three children, two sons ages twelve and nine, and the daughter age three. When the monk learns the daughter's age, he says, "that is the same as me, as my child," meaning the youngest child in his care.

Lom Om's first wife died, and his second wife left him for Phnom Penh. The Venerable tells me he knows this story well. When Lom Om tested positive for HIV, he was afraid to tell his second wife. The Venerable went to talk to her, but she had already left. "The first wife, I supported her" while she was dying a year ago.

Lom Om suspects he got HIV during UN times. "When UNTAC came to Cambodia, he had a lot of money. In the day he worked as a teacher, and at night he was a mototaxi driver," Muny Van Saveth says. "He thinks maybe he transmitted HIV from sex workers." (He uses the word "transmitted," as we discussed earlier, though in this case he means "contracted.") After Lom Om learned of his disease, he wanted to stop teaching. He went to the monk for advice, and he suggested raising chickens and pigs.

Lom Om's two boys are OK, but the girl has not been tested. "Now he thinks about his children, but I told him please don't worry," The Venerable says. He will take care of the kids.

When I ask Lom Om if he is afraid, he says no, "But I try to find medicine." There are no antiretroviral drugs in Battambang, and in Phnom Penh they are expensive and sometimes hard to find. "I want to live with my children a long time," he says. "I want to tell the companies that make AIDS drugs, please reduce your price."

Lom Om says he didn't know much about HIV when he first learned he had it. He didn't know about the disease or how it's spread; he didn't think going to brothels was wrong, it's a part of Cambodian culture. I ask The Venerable whether he thinks that will ever change, whether Cambodian men will stop visiting prostitutes. "The man has more freedom, so he can get money, and he can go to sex workers," he says. "It depends on *ch'hbat srey*."

And it depends, perhaps, on the new teachings of The Venerable Muny Van Saveth.

Two Girls

They are small. They are shy. They are quiet, but they are strong. They are two girls, two teenagers, I meet one hot summer day at the Cambodian Women's Crisis Center in Phnom Penh, a refuge for women in trouble.

I have arranged interviews with three victims of abuse and sexual misconduct. I see three females in the lobby while I wait. One is older, but two are small. And one is so young, so petite, my stomach lurches, and I groan. I hope: She can't possibly be one of my interviews.

But she is.

Her name is Sok Ly.

She is seventeen, though to me she looks twelve. She wears a pink shirt and purple pants and the most inviting smile I've seen in a long time. Her eyes are jet black and dancing with life. She is about four feet tall.

She comes from Kandal Province, and she tells me her story in whispers and coy grins as she fidgets in her chair. "My father wanted to sell me, so when I got that information, I left home." Her first stop: "I went to the police station."

She continues: "The police went to arrest my father." But he wasn't there, so they couldn't get him. "Now he went to live with his second wife." The "second wife" is, technically, her father's third. Her birth mother died five years ago, and her father remarried. Then he took another wife at the same time. The "first" second wife is kind, she says, but the other one told her father to sell her. Sok Ly has a ten-year-old sister; she fears for her as well. But now her neighbors have adopted the sister, so she should be safe.

Sok Ly doesn't know why her father tried to sell her. She doesn't know the buyer, "but my father knows him." She doesn't know how much the man was going to pay. How does she feel about her father now? "I hate him," she says. "I feel hurt, so much." Her father is a thief and has spent time in jail for robbery. Before this incident, she says, "He never did a bad thing to me, but he always goes to cheat people."

Sok Ly came to the shelter a month before our interview. She plans to stay for six. "I will get a job after I leave here," she says. "My auntie will help me." Here, at the shelter, she's learning to cut clothes so that one day she may work in a garment factory.

Sok Ly has not gone to high school; she has finished only grade seven. But she thinks the skills she's learning here will help her get a job. "I think the future will be good."

I ask whether she has told her story to many people, and she has not. "I didn't say anything to my friends. I was afraid, but they will know the story about me because they will hear." Word like that travels fast on the street.

About the status of women in Cambodia, she says simply, "It will not change." About her father, she says, "I am angry." But she doesn't think all men are bad, she doesn't think all men are like her father. And she has hope that tomorrow will be a better day.

The second girl is Som Tith Minea. She is sixteen. She, too, is from Kandal Province.

She came here six months ago. She is here, as she says, because "someone raped me." Her home has no bathroom, so she went to the field in the middle of the night. A man came up beside her. "I didn't know him," she says. "The man came after me and took off all my clothes." He beat her, then he took a lighter to her body to see if she would move, to see if she was dead. He burned her on her wrists and neck, touching the lighter to her skin. She was alive but dared not move. "Then he carried me and threw me in a lake." She was conscious but dared not swim. The man stood and watched her still body for several minutes, then finally rode Som Tith Minea's bicycle away, into the night.

When she was certain he had left, she went home. "I walked by myself." This happened 100 yards from her house. She told her family what happened, and they went to the police. "The police went to arrest that man," and now he's serving fifteen years in prison — one successful rape prosecution in a country with few. He had come from another village to live with relatives in hers. "I hate him very much," she says. "I lost my happiness," and my translator explains it's a common way to describe a virgin's social shame. "My parents are very sorry," she says.

Som Tith Minea has stayed here at the shelter for so long because she thinks it will help her future. "I will not stay here forever, but when I have the skills, I will go to find a job." She doesn't know what that will be, but she insists it will be legal.

"I don't know why I was raped." She has lost her sense of trust. "I'm afraid of men, even you," she says to my very mild-mannered translator. An employee at the center, a man, tries to console her, to tell her she can trust the people in this room, that things will be OK.

And she agrees: Maybe things will be better in the future.

These two girls are but children, still growing up. They do not run an orphanage or an organization; they have not built a school; they do not de-mine the countryside by hand, and they are not elected leaders fighting the ruling elite. They are ordinary girls facing tragedies that no one deserves. But they have kept their wits, they have shown their smarts, they have acknowledged their fears and thrust themselves back into the world. They are facing their own youth, headstrong. They went to the police (who miraculously did the right thing) and left home for their own good. Those things alone are enough to make them heroes. If they succeed, if they defy the odds and beat the dirty hand dealt by life, they will be more than heroes. They will be the heart and guts of a new Cambodia.

21. Prospects: No Easy Peace

The present state of Cambodia is deplorable, and its future menacing.
— Henri Mouhot, 1860

People ask me, What's the answer for Cambodia? My response is: There is no answer. There is no simple solution to fit the constraints of a page or a chapter in a book. "Nothing would be straightforward about the Cambodian war or revolution," writes Elizabeth Becker. And nothing about Cambodia's peace is crystal, either. Reality is much too complicated, and the consequences of any action much too unpredictable. Solutions are like drops of water, causing waves and ripples, dependent on the pools they enter. Pour a drop into a choppy sea, you'll never notice the difference. Dump a bucket onto calmer waters, the eddies will reach far beyond our sight, into little nooks where we may never even think to look.

Some Cambodians say their country could use another colonizer or at least a custodian to evoke change. And a few Western thinkers are inclined to agree. Henry Kamm concludes his book *Cambodia: Report from a Stricken Land* by saying the country's leaders are not equipped to run the nation. "Cambodia, I fear, is past helping itself," he writes in 1998, and little changes in the six years after. "Its future, if it is to have one, cannot be entrusted to the hands of its present leaders, most of their opposition, and the class that they represent." He suggests entrusting the country to an outside, impartial caretaker for an entire generation until all the bad juju is driven from the societal fabric and a new legion of Cambodians is ready to take control. That, he knows, is an unrealistic scenario, though not impossible.

But even so, what then? How do you make a colony in the twenty-first century in a society that has already tasted the first morsels of democracy? Who makes the decisions? Who rules the village? What happens to the strongman when his power is eclipsed? Is such a takeover ethical?

Some say Cambodia needs a regime change, a new and democratic leader. But what then? A new leader will have no experience. He will not have the money currently secured in the hands of a seemingly tenured regime. Money here is power, democracy or no. How does a new leader win legitimate support? How do the current leaders gracefully bow down without losing face? What keeps them from expelling their enemies, as Khmers historically have? Or forming their own armies? Or starting a war?

Some Cambodians wish the United States would bomb Hun Sen. They see the American government waging war on other enemies, on leaders it doesn't like, so why not Hun Sen? A rumor to this effect spreads in 1998, during post-election riots, when former U.S. President Bill Clinton is in office. It spreads again in 2003, after the United States says it will tie foreign aid to the outcome of Cambodia's national elections. President George W. Bush is at the helm; he has just ousted Saddam Hussein. Who's next? Why not Hun Sen? And what if such a preposterous scenario came true? Then what? Who rebuilds a post–Hun Sen Cambodia? Who pays for that? How often does the United States successfully oust a foreign leader and successfully implement a new government without eliciting rebellions, terrorist attacks and ruptures to the country's social system? In this age of war and terror, the world is seeing — not for the first time — how treacherous it is to break a country down and build it up again. It does not go smoothly, cleanly or peacefully. The answers don't fit in a box. People die brutally, shamefully, along the way. Post-war reconstruction is a horrid mess. Everyone should know this already. This is not news. Cambodians know this very well. For all that's missing in their lives, Cambodians possess this one astonishingly prescient, critical insight: Life is not black-and-white, and it never will be. There's a bloody middle ground between war and peace.

And time is the only staid solution.

Time: It causes no great splashes but gradually wipes the stones of history clean. It requires no outside force to do the pouring. Time flows on its own. It is often imperceptible when viewed up close; it requires a vantage, several steps back. It is slow; it is painstaking, and for many it is too much or too little. But it moves.

"Time is passing. The wounds are less raw," says *New York Times* correspondent Seth Mydans. "New generations are being born. Even though the Cambodians have done almost nothing to heal themselves, time itself does eventually heal." Normality is returning step by step. Kids (some kids, more than before) are going to school; they're growing up; society is cultivating new generations. It is springtime after a winter of the most wretched kind, one not of dormant hope but of death and abandon, pure and raw. Those days still blight the memory of most adults. But now — now the youngest are prepared to breathe, to taste, only a future they trust will be better than the past.

Time is a hope in all fractured countries. "That suffering would flower into purity, out of the anguish of history…. A new world must be born." Colin Thubron encounters these thoughts among the people in post-communist Siberia. "It made sense of sorrow, of tedium. It made suffering dangerously embraceable. It seemed to heal. Time."

In January 2004, Jerry and I return again to Phnom Penh. Just a few days before we arrive, a child heads in the opposite direction. A three-year-old girl named Pisey crosses the ocean on a plane with her new dad, Chuck. They are heading home to Judy, the woman from Wisconsin, for whom I wrote an essay many months ago. Finally their adoption proceeds.

And more than that, it succeeds.

"We can say this about the adoption: Although malnourished and covered with bug bites and skin infections, Pisey is an extremely bright and energetic child. She is very independent and headstrong, obviously traits that are important when surviving amongst so many other children," Judy emails me after Pisey settles into her new home.

When I ask her how things are going, Judy replies with a turn of the tables. "How do you condense a three-year process into a couple of paragraphs?" She is hooked. She is immersed now in Cambodia. She knows what I have felt for many years.

They don't know much about Pisey's short history. "We received only basic information on her, such as date of birth, general health, and what little background information they had. Pisey's mother died when she was nine months old (from what, we have no idea), then lived with her aunt and uncle who finally gave her to the orphanage because they couldn't feed her anymore. Her biography stated that her aunt and uncle still visited her regularly at the orphanage."

But Judy knows this, too: "What most stands out about her is that she is very affectionate and loving. If you lie next to her, she wraps her entire body around you; she's always sharing hugs and kisses and she is very protective of her baby sister. She showed this trait from day one, so it was not a latent development."

For that, Judy credits the orphanage. "For whatever difficulties the Cambodian orphanages had in feeding the children and in providing adequate hygiene and health care, they more than make up for it by providing the children with a solid base of trust and love." Pisey's experience was nothing of the horror stories found in some places. "She surely didn't spend her days stuck in a crib. She knows how to cut fruit, fold clothes, do somersaults, throw and catch a ball." Pisey's character aptly reflects the Cambodian society Judy sees. "I think her development is a testimony to the integrity of the Cambodian people."

Judy has one last comment about the adoption process, an uplifting note: "Our surprise gift was that in the end the Cambodian government only asked for $150. I thought they made a mistake and left out a few zeroes. Go figure." She and her husband paid the orphanage extra.

Just as Pisey is bracing herself through snowstorms and sub-zero chills, Jerry and I meet again with Phnom Penh's unfailing heat. The capital is thriving with tourists as we've never seen — still not quite a million, but perhaps soon. All over the city, up and down the riverfront, in the parks, at the palace, visitors with blond hair, blue eyes, tanned skin, a dozen European and North American accents. They hoist their packs upon their backs, gazing up toward temple spires. They sit happily in *cyclos*, guidebooks in hand, an air of discovery all about them.

We return, this time, to open a photo exhibit displaying Jerry's images of Cambodia spanning six years. We meet tourists and journalists new to town; we meet people passing through. And many are shocked, curious and mystified because the images they see on the walls are not the pictures they see in tour guides nor are they the smiling faces they meet on the streets. We spend significant time discussing the deeper layers of Cambodian society.

It is something Cambodians, of course, already know. And the Cambodians who come to this exhibit are equally shocked, curious and mystified — not because they see things they didn't know but because someone has bothered to remember, bothered to point them out to an unsuspecting crowd. They mill around the photos from 1998 — riots, violence, a body dug from a shallow grave. Several Cambodians thank Jerry for showing reality.

A few days after we arrive in Phnom Penh, I see our friend and *moto* driver, Monin. He tells me we didn't see him the day before because he took his wife to the hospital. They checked her stomach, he says.

"Is she OK? What's wrong?" I ask.

"Yes, she's OK. She's going to have another baby."

"Congratulations!" I am excited for him.

Monin is not happy. This means he will have someone else to feed and house. His landlady has told him she doesn't want a baby in the room. He still stays at the same place, but now maybe he'll have to find a new home. Maybe a new job. He has no idea what.

I don't know what to say.

A few days later, the afternoon before the exhibit opens, I race around the city with Monin, dropping off invitations. Jerry has told Monin about this show, and I give him an invitation, but he is antsy. I'm not sure why.

The next invitation goes to Sovann, our paper boy. I see him on the street. He reads the card, looks confused, and I explain. He can't come at 6:30 P.M., he says, he has class, the English class he pays for with his own earnings. But 7 is OK, he says. I tell him to invite his family. He grins a deep-down grin, muffled by his cool exterior. I can tell he's tickled.

A moment later, after I've left, he races after me. "Is this the ticket? Is this the ticket to get in? If I have this, no problem?" He is worried about getting in the door, past the guard. I tell him not to worry, he can get in.

Monin frets about this, too. "I think maybe the guard does not let me in." I assure him we will talk to the guard because we want all our friends to come.

It happens again when I drop an invitation at *The Cambodia Daily*. I leave the invitation with the guard at the gate, and I tell him everyone is invited.

"Everyone?"

"Yes! Everyone! *Moto* drivers, too. Please tell them."

"*Moto* drivers can go, too? No problem?"

"No problem," I say.

In the end, Monin is the only one of these friends to come. There are no explanations spoken, no questions, no hard feelings. Perhaps Sovann's parents didn't want him to go, perhaps the *moto* drivers felt uncomfortable. Some things are the way they are in Cambodia, and it doesn't really matter why.

But our friendships continue. Within two months, Sovann will have an email address, and he will write to us in Thailand. We will exchange news of our distant lives, little typed snippets of information about nothing critical but everything important. Technology and language will transcend borders and human barriers. "How are you today?" he will ask. "I am good boy."

The opening night of Jerry's exhibit, we return to our room around 10 P.M. The photos hang in a popular riverfront restaurant, and our hotel is right around the corner. Through our windows, we hear a skirmish outside. We step to the balcony, and the street is full of kids, teenagers, racing toward the museum across the street, then back again toward the river. They're brandishing beer bottles, 2x4s, lengths of steel pipe. They're breaking glass on the sidewalk and yelling back and forth. The shouts are followed by flip-flops slapping against pavement. They chase each other in a rage.

The restaurant, during this, is still bright and full of people, so is the bar across the street. The people at that bar are seated facing inside, with their backs to the mayhem below. Everything beyond our block is black with night. There are no cops, no streetlights, only the kids looking to fight. Eventually they charge up the road, up the river, rudimentary weapons in hand.

We learn the next day from the guesthouse desk clerk that it's a *bong thom* battle, an ongoing fight between kids on the riverfront and kids near the museum. Jerry teaches him the English words "gang" and "turf war," and he agrees these are precisely the right descriptions.

The *bong thom* of the museum is the son of a woman who maintains the bathroom in the park. She has had that job for years. Her son shows up occasionally and fights her for money to buy his drugs. These turf wars happen all the time and they make trouble for the hotel. The desk clerk warns us to be careful. Many tourists like to stroll the riverfront, but these kids will pull a knife. Last night, he says, some of the kids had guns. They were looking to kill.

This conversation springs from a short stop in the lobby to watch the TV news as we're heading out the door. There on screen is a policewoman talking and talking, and a sullen young man standing with head drooped. He has killed his younger brother. He came home and found his brother beating their sister for drug money, not the first incident. So he killed his brother. Problem solved. New problem begun.

The following week, Jerry and I leave town for the day. We're heading to Veal Thom to check up on Bun Na, the former beggar, and Poeun, his wife, to see how their new lives are faring four months after they left the city.

We drive south with two men from Veterans International. We head toward the coast, on Cambodia's best highway. It is the middle of Chinese New Year, and all vehicles point south. We are constantly passed by young men racing on *motos* with their girlfriends seated behind them and by vans packed with Khmers and a foreigner or two. I stare out the back window and see both lanes full of traffic speeding in one direction. No one goes north to Phnom Penh. Everyone goes to the sea.

Rith, our companion, tells us this has changed. In years past, rich people in the countryside went to Phnom Penh for the Chinese New Year. But now it's the reverse. The countryside is poor, but the city is richer. It's good to see people celebrating the holiday, but he doesn't approve of this traffic. Kids today act insane, he says. He shakes his head and says he disciplines his son. He doesn't want him to act this way, foolishly.

Back in Phnom Penh that afternoon, I go for a run. The city beams for the holiday. Hotels and restaurants are packed; the parks are throbbing. I run at sunset as children cheer on carnival rides and jump on a giant inflated slide. People carry balloons and toddlers trundle in squeaky shoes. There is more wealth, more entertainment. By day, shopkeepers close their gates; their owners can afford time off. This is different from the days when they had no choice, when they closed their gates in riots.

But later we learn of tragedy, this New Year's Day. At 9 A.M., just as we drove south toward the coast, a gunman approached the country's top labor union leader as he read a newspaper near a *wat*. The man shot the leader three times. Dead. The city mourns, and people speculate. Was it political? Of course it was, Sam Rainsy says, and the ruling party tells him he better have proof before making such allegations. There are rumors: More shootings, more blood will surely follow when workers gather for the man's funeral. But it doesn't happen like that; things always proceed in unpredictable ways. There are no shootings at his funeral, but the next month his pregnant wife flees to Thailand and applies for refugee status. The air in Phnom Penh remains tense.

The dead man's name was Chea Vichea. The gunman shot in the daytime. He shot from the street. He shot with witnesses all around. The assassin didn't even bother to conceal his face. Two men were arrested in connection with the crime, then freed for lack of evidence.

Will this be another trademark Cambodian murder, no justice, no closure?

Back to that morning, the morning Chea Vichea dies: Jerry and I go to Veal Thom with photos and donations in hand, the gifts of family and friends in the United States. The truck pulls up to a small house on the edge of the village. We hop out, and in a minute there is yelling and chattering and a man running — running! — toward us on one leg and a crutch. It is Bun Na, with Poeun at his heels. He is spewing words in Khmer so quickly we understand nothing of what he says. He wears no shirt. They both wear scratches and bruises across their bodies and big, passionate smiles.

Come, they say. Come this way! They are eager to show us their house, behind this one and up a small path. It's a grass hut on stilts, its walls erected three days before. For four months, they lived in this house with no walls. It is their house, made by their hands, with logs and grasses they cut and hauled on their own. "I climbed up the tree to cut wood for the house, but it was very difficult, and I always fell down," Bun Na says, still grinning.

They've started a small garden next to the house, growing cassava, jackfruit and papaya. "But we don't have water yet," Poeun says. For now, they use a neighbor's well until they can gather the money and cement to dig and make their own.

They want to invite us inside their house — because they can. So we remove our shoes, climb the ladder and sit upon its new slat floor. It smells of grass and wood and fresh air. It smells wonderful. They're still smiling. They have a small white cat with a bell around its neck. Its name is *Swat*, meaning Skinny. It just appeared one day, very small and bedraggled. Now it keeps them company.

"I'm busy all the time," Poeun says. "Never time to relax. First I go to cut the grass, then I go to collect the water." But she's happy. She describes how they made

Poeun and Bun Na now live in a house they built with their own hands in rural Veal Thom village. Bun Na lost a leg and part of his face to a land mine while fighting for the Cambodian Army and spent several years begging in Phnom Penh. Poeun had occasional work sweeping city streets. They now share their new life with their cat, *Swat*, or Skinny. Veal Thom, 2004.

their walls, sewing together strips of grass. They could have bought a roof in separate strips, but each strip would cost 4,000 *riel*, a dollar, which they didn't have. So they made their own.

They say they have no money, and Bun Na would like a new bike. His has broken. They borrow rice from their neighbors since they moved here too late in the season to plant their own. They are not complaining, merely filling us in. They are happier than ever before.

Bun Na went to Phnom Penh a few weeks back, for one night, to retrieve the wooden cart they had left by their old apartment. He talked with other beggars on their streetcorner, his old post, and he told them about Veal Thom. "All it took was one night for me to know I never want to go back there," he says.

He will attend vocational classes here in the village, starting next week. The course is offered through an aid group, and when he finishes, he will receive either a pig or some chickens for his efforts.

I ask about their neighbors, and Poeun says, "It's like we're family. For example, if I'm sick, the villagers come to see me. If they are sick, I go to see them to see how I can help."

Veal Thom has had a bit of trouble, and they relate the news. Some military men have come to the village and warned Touch Sour Ly, the former Khmer Rouge soldier who founded the village. The military men aimed their guns to the sky, to the ground, shooting and trying to scare Touch Sour Ly. They want their land back. They threatened to force the villagers out. But Touch Sour Ly, well-accustomed to war, was not and is not afraid of their guns. He told them to get lost, and they did—for now. He tells Rith, our companion from Veterans International, that he would rather die defending Veal Thom than by some meaningless accident. Touch Sour Ly may be a bit dismissive at times, but he's socially righteous. And he has the chutzpah to face down bullies with guns.

Bun Na and Poeun describe more of their adventures, climbing trees, hauling wood through the jungle. His arms and fingers look worn. She points to a lump on her shoulder, born of heavy loads. During harvest time, Poeun worked for a rich landowner outside the village, and he paid her in rice seed. She will plant it when the rains come.

And for that reason, they do not worry. "I presume this year is difficult," Poeun says, "but next year will be better because we will plant rice." Rice—the stanch of all wounds. "We're not worried about next year," Bun Na says.

Will they stay here a long time? I ask, and they answer in unison:

"We will stay here forever. We're not going back." Bun Na smiles, proud to announce: "We have fruit trees and vegetables planted. We cannot move." Their days are hard, but they will persist. They hit the bottom of Cambodian life and languished there for several years. Now, they have a house, a cat and compassionate neighbors. They have land and visions of their days ahead. They have that one luxury so precious, so wanted but rare in this country of grievous despair:

They finally have hope.

Afterword

It's hot and steamy, the mosquitoes biting with vigor. The Wisconsin country-side rolls past cornfields and rural churches into a subdivision of two-story homes, perfect lawns, smooth blacktop driveways and suburban quiet. Three-year-old Pisey is here in a house on a hill with vast views of flat terrain. If you squint, you can almost picture the Cambodian landscape, jade and dramatic.

But this quotidian American backdrop is nothing like the country Pisey left, nothing like the Cambodia of today.

It is July 2004 when Jerry and I return to the United States to visit our families after more than a year away. We meet Pisey in her new American home. She greets us in English; we greet her in Khmer. I ask her questions—How is she? How old is she? I know the answers, but I want her to talk. She won't respond in Khmer, only English. This has happened in the last month, Judy tells us. I try numbers: *muy, pii, bei, buon*. She stares into my eyes and studies her fingers. "One, two," she says, res-olutely. She speaks, now, like an American child.

Our encounter with Pisey takes place just as Cambodia gets a new government. After eleven months of stasis, the CPP and Funcinpec agree to form a coalition, and Hun Sen is again made prime minister. This means the National Assembly can again make law. Our friend and colleague, LC, describes the stalemate as a "chronic abscess" that maimed his country. LC is an optimist and the new coalition offers some hope. He dreams of a government that will elevate the nation, like an airplane "ready to take off."

Yet LC is not blind. The abscess has vanished, but the scars won't heal for a long time. It is the same with many Cambodian wounds.

Time passes, but news doesn't stop with the final chapter of this book. In the months following our encounter with Pisey, the National Assembly approves Cam-bodia's entry into the World Trade Organization. And it ratifies the necessary law to establish—someday—a UN-backed Khmer Rouge tribunal.

Cambodia enters the WTO—but garment quotas, which assure Cambodian factories a steady workload, are set to end in January 2005. Workers fear their fac-tories will move to countries with cheaper operating costs. A Khmer Rouge tribunal is approved—but Cambodians wonder: When? Who will pay? Will the guilty be alive by the time it comes about? Tourism hits an all-time high — but also, the UN names Cambodia a potential terrorist "breeding ground." The government is back at work — but Hun Sen creates 180 new ministerial positions, many sold for $100,000 or more a slot. Some say Cambodia now has the biggest per capita government in the world. It seems no good news shall go unpunished.

"Same same but different," Cambodians say. The phrase describes everything from the price of rice to one's route through life.

Recall Ke Monin, the Phnom Penh *moto* driver with little hope, who thinks his country is not a democracy. By January 2004, his wife is pregnant with their second child and he wonders how they will survive. Ten months later, they have a healthy baby girl — but no *moto*, on which the family income rides. Monin has sold it to pay the hospital bills, and now he must rent a vehicle for 10,000 *riel* a day, nearly all he earns. They live life day by day. Same same but different.

And the stories roll on.

In October 2004, King Norodom Sihanouk abdicates the throne, citing ill health. His son, Norodom Sihamoni, is chosen to succeed him. The new King is a 51-year-old ballet dancer, a bachelor, who has spent most his adult life abroad. For years, he was stationed in Paris as Cambodia's ambassador to UNESCO. He returns to a country that barely knows him. Yet he vows to visit the countryside each week, and to "never live apart from the beloved people." It's a bold promise, coming from the son of a King who has spent more time in Pyongyang and Beijing in recent years, than in his own ailing country.

Many think Sihamoni a kind and gentle man with a character they admire. But they doubt the new King can, or will, fight a bully government and wrest peace for the people. And technically, it wouldn't be his place to do so, for the Cambodian Constitution stipulates the monarch shall "reign but not govern" (though few would deny Sihanouk's influence on politics).

There is much speculation that Sihanouk still runs the show, his abdication a mere tactic to secure an heir while he's still alive. For this reason, and many others, Cambodians remain skeptical of Norodom Sihamoni's ability to bring real change to their land. Will he flit across the royal stage, a mere shadow of his father? Many Cambodians simply say they will wait and see.

As they always do.

That hot day in July when we meet a rambunctious Pisey in her living room, I wonder many things. What does she recall of her homeland? Does she remember the bugs that bit her legs and left them scarred? Or the red hair she had from malnutrition? Some of her traits seem instinctively Cambodian. She tells Judy she doesn't prepare rice the proper way. She suffers nightmares when she sleeps alone, never having had a bed of her own. She handles knives and scissors with precision, as do most Khmer children. She lives in America, but she is still Khmer.

"The hope is for the Cambodians not yet born," Henry Kamm writes in his book, *Cambodia: Report from a Stricken Land*, quoting Andrew Morris, head of Cambodia's health services for UNICEF, in late 1997. Pisey came along about four years later, of that generation then not yet born. She is still too young to tell us what or who she will become; she is years in the making. The answers are not yet formed, many of the questions yet to be imagined. Pisey is young, her identity nascent, like the country she left. Both need time to mature. Both have set tender feet upon a road to inner peace.

Pisey has the hope that Morris foresaw. Sadly, she had to leave Cambodia to find it. Even the richest Cambodians don't have wide, paved roads; creditable schools and universities; well-funded hospitals and life-saving medicines; a police force that protects, not oppresses; and the public trust in a system that, for all its faults, still works for the people rather than against them. Those are the marks of development and democracy. Those are the litmus tests by which Cambodians will continue to judge their government. But Cambodians are not fools. They don't expect those changes soon.

Thousands of miles from Cambodia's dramas, Pisey has adopted her older American brother's interest in dinosaurs. She devours them, she loves them, Judy says. She goes to the library — the library where Judy first met my sister-in-law, sparking our acquaintance — and Pisey looks only for books on those magnificent ancient beasts. Judy jokes about all those dinosaurs in her house, that maybe she should find a different hobby for Pisey. But I think dinosaurs are perfect. So are astronauts and presidents and ponies and anything else that makes little kids dream.

In America, Pisey is free to dream big. She can imagine whatever she wants to be — it's a hallmark of developed and democratic nations, the luxury of imaginative hope. Perhaps one day she will grow to be a paleontologist, digging in the windswept plains of Montana. Perhaps she will be a Milwaukee doctor, a Washington lawyer, a Berkeley teacher, a New Orleans chef. Or maybe, an NGO worker in Phnom Penh. It's her choice, growing up in a country like the United States, with loving parents who can provide.

It is my dream that future Piseys will have those choices in Cambodia, too. Someday.

— Karen Coates
Chiang Mai, Thailand, November 2004

Glossary

Ai-u-dom—His excellency

Amok—Dish of fish in coconut steamed in banana leaf

Angka—The organization; the term referred to the Khmer Rouge leadership in Democratic Kampuchea

Ao dai—The Vietnamese term for a woman's traditional dress of pants and a long tailored top that reaches the knees or lower

Apsara—Carvings of mythical Hindu celestial nymphs

Awt prum daign—Without borders. Also means freelance

Awt te—No

Baay—Rice

Baat—Yes, for men

Barang—Literally "French," but used to describe any white-skinned Western foreigner

Baray—A large pool used in Angkor times to irrigate the rice fields.

Bauk—Gang rape

Bong thom—Gang leader or street-kid group leader

Ch'hbat srey—An ancient Buddhist women's law

Chor tuk—Liquid resin collected from trees in remote areas

Chunchiet—Hill tribes, or ethno-linguistic minorities

Coen—Child or children

Cyclo—A bicycle taxi, common in Phnom Penh

Dantoc—The Vietnamese term for indigenous

Ha-kem—Cham community leader

Jaa—Yes, for women

Jor chong—Solid resin collected from forests

Krama—The common checkered scarf worn and used by all Cambodians

Kru Khmer—Traditional Cambodian doctor

Laksmi—Hindu goddess of beauty

Linga—A Hindu phallic symbol representing the creative powers of nature, and often made of polished stone or carved wood

Lok Chumtieu—Her excellency

Mahout—A working elephant's caretaker

Mith Samlanh—Friends

Moto—Cambodia's most popular form of transportation, a small motorcycle, usually 100 cc

Motodop—A moto taxi driver, found on most any Cambodian street corner, who will take you across town for a few *riel*

Phnom—A hill or mountain

Pho—The Vietnamese name for noodle soup

Prahok—fish paste

Praw tien—Boss

Psar—Market

Psar Thmei—New Market or Central Market, one of the most popular in Phnom Penh

Punyaha—Problem

Riel—Cambodia's currency; one U.S. dollar is worth approximately 4,000 riel

S'aht—Fresh, beautiful

Samdech— Essentially, "your highness," as in Samdech Prime Minister Hun Sen

Singha— A mythical lion creature

Slahp— Dead

Sua s'dey— Hello

Sok s'bey— How are you?

Sompiah— The Buddhist practice of clasping hands and bowing the head.

Srey— Sister or woman

Srey s'aht— Beautiful woman

Stupa— A Buddhist funerary monument, shaped like an upside-down cone

Thmei— New

Tourmada— Normal, ordinary

Trow kooen— a spinach-type vegetable that grows in water

Tuk— Water

Tuk-a-luk— Fruit juice or fruit shake, often sold by women at small stands on the street

Tuk-tuk— A three-wheeled, open-sided taxi popular in Thailand but has shown up in Phnom Penh in the past few years

Vishnu— A Hindu god known as The Preserver

Wat— A Khmer temple

Yama— Amphetamines

Yuon— Controversial term that Cambodians use to describe Vietnamese people

People, Places and Names

The Cambodia Daily— English-language newspaper started in 1993 by American Bernie Krisher

CARE— Cooperative for Assistance and Relief Everywhere, Inc.

CCHR— Cambodian Center for Human Rights

CDRI— Cambodia Development Resource Institute

CPP— Cambodian People's Party, the ruling party

CWCC— Cambodian Women's Crisis Center

DCCam— Documentation Center of Cambodia

Democratic Kampuchea— Name of Cambodia under the Khmer Rouge

Funcinpec— National United Front for an Independent, Peaceful, Neutral and Cooperative Cambodia; the Royalist opposition party

Hun Sen— Current prime minister

Ieng Sary— Former foreign minister of Democratic Kampuchea; brokered a deal with Hun Sen in 1996, currently living freely in Phnom Penh

IRI— International Republican Institute

Khieu Samphan— Former Khmer Rouge head of state, currently living freely

MSF— Medecins Sans Frontieres

NGO— Nongovernmental organization

Norodom Ranariddh— Son of King Sihanouk, a prince, former second prime minister

Norodom Sihanouk— Former Cambodian king; abdicated in 2004

Nuon Chea— Brother Number Two behind Pol Pot, currently living freely

Pali— The ancient language of Theravada Buddhism

Pol Pot— Brother Number One, supreme leader of the Khmer Rouge; died in 1998

RCAF— Royal Cambodian Armed Forces

Sam Rainsy— Opposition leader and democracy advocate; former finance minister and Funcinpec member before forming his own party

Sanskrit— The ancient language of Mahayana Buddhism

SAMU— French acronym for Emergency Medical Aid Service

SRP— Sam Rainsy Party

TPO— Transcultural Psychosocial Organization, a Dutch NGO that deals with mental health

UNCHR— United Nations Commission for Human Rights

UNDP— United Nations Development Programme

UNESCO— United Nations Educational, Scientific and Cultural Organization

UNFPA— United Nations Population Fund

UNHCR— United Nations High Commissioner for Refugees

UNICEF— United Nations Children's Fund

UNTAC— United Nations Transitional Authority in Cambodia

USAID— United States Agency for International Development

WCS— Wildlife Conservation Society

WHO— World Health Organization

WMF— World Monuments Fund

WTO— World Trade Organization

Organizations

There are hundreds of worthy organizations and people doing good deeds in Cambodia. Here are just a few, which appear in this book. Please keep in mind that contact information frequently changes in Cambodia.

The Pookai Book Project, an organization established to help Lor Chandara's Angsoeng Library in Takeo, Cambodia. Contact: The Pookai Book Project, P.O. Box 6421, Rockford, IL 61125-1421. Tel. 815-397-7032. pookaibooks@pookaibooks.org, www.pookaibooks.org.

Volunteer English School, a rural school established by *Cambodia Daily* reporter Saing Soenthrith. Contact: villageveschool@hotmail.com.

Angkor Hospital for Children, in Siem Reap. Contact: Friends Without a Border, P.O. Box 50, Siem Reap, Cambodia. Tel. 855-063-96-3490. admin@angkorhospital.org or www.fwab.org or fwab@fwab.org.

Aki Ra, founder of the Land Mine Museum in Siem Reap. www.landmine-museum.com, thailandisfreedom@yahoo.com.

Mith Samlanh/Friends, an organization helping street children. Contact: #215 Street 13, P.O. Box 588, Phnom Penh, Cambodia. Tel./Fax: 855-23-426-748. friends@everyday.com.kh, www.streetfriends.org.

Wildlife Conservation Society Cambodia Program, #21 Street 21, Tonle Bassac, P.O. Box 1620, Phnom Penh, Cambodia. Tel./Fax: 855-23-217-205. Cambodia@wcs.org, www.wcs.org.

Veterans International, a program of the Vietnam Veterans of America Foundation, which runs the Kien Khleang Physical Rehabilitation Center. www.vvaf.org/programs/cambodia. In Washington, D.C., call 202-557-7524.

Transcultural Psychosocial Organization, #209, Street 63, Sangkat Boeung Keng Kang I, Khand Chamcamorn, P.O. Box 1124, Phnom Penh, Cambodia. Tel./Fax: 855-23-219-182. tpo@forum.org.kh, www.camnet.com.kh/tpo.

Association of the Blind in Cambodia, #3, Street 55, Sangkat Chak Tomuk, Khan Duan Penh, P.O. Box 175, Phnom Penh, Cambodia. 855-23-213-882. abc@bigpond.com.kh.

Cambodian Women's Crisis Center, Phnom Penh. Tel./Fax: 855-23-982-158. cwccct@forum.org.kh.

Wat Norea Peaceful Children's Center, P.O. Box 362, Norea Village, Norea Commune, Sangke District, Battambang Province, Cambodia. 012754505@mobitel.com.kh.

Cambodian Time Line

The majority of this time line stems from Becker, Chanda, Kamm, Rooney, Shawcross, and the Mehtas.

802 Angkor era begins. Jayavarman II declares himself a godking, marking the beginning of the grand Angkor empire. Six centuries of Cambodian kings follow, ruling much of modern-day Southeast Asia.

1431–1432 Angkor era ends. Thailand topples the city of Angkor. In the following years, while villagers continue to live in and around the temples, the buildings fall to ruins; the jungle takes over, and the temples remain mostly unknown to outsiders.

1858–1861 French explorer Henri Mouhot visits Cambodia and surrounding countries. He finds the ruins of ancient Angkor and informs the Western world.

1864 Cambodia established as a French protectorate. France signs a series of treaties with King Norodom. Cambodia becomes part of French Indochina.

1925 Saloth Sar born in Kompong Thom. He will later change his name to Pol Pot.

1941 Japan occupies Cambodia during World War II. They ask Vichy French rulers to continue running the country. Then-Prince Sihanouk is first crowned king. Thailand attacks and seizes western provinces of Battambang and Siem Reap. The Japanese force the French to cede the lands to keep peace with Thailand.

1945 France regains control of its Indochina territories from Japan.

1946 First Indochinese war begins. Ho Chi Minh and his Vietminh begin their fight for independence from France.

France secures return of Battambang and Siem Reap to Cambodia. The provinces are given back so Thailand can join the UN.

1949 Saloth Sar studies in France.

1952 Future prime minister Hun Sen is born in Kompong Cham. There is some discrepancy over the exact date of his birth.

1953 King Sihanouk claims Cambodian independence from France. Saloth Sar returns to Cambodia in 1953 with a communist ideology learned in Paris.

1954 French defeated at Dien Bien Phu. This marks the end of French colonialism in Vietnam.

Cambodia's independence is recognized.

1955 Sihanouk gains political power. After abdicating and installing his father as king, now-Prince Sihanouk starts his own political party, which sweeps national elections.

Late 1950s Sihanouk begins long pogrom against political opponents and communists in Cambodia. He anoints the communists "Khmer Rouge," or "Red Cambodians."

1963 Saloth Sar becomes head of Workers Party of Kampuchea, the future Communist Party of Kampuchea (commonly known as the Khmer Rouge). Many communists take shelter in the countryside where they build their movement against Sihanouk's government.

1965   **The United States sends first ground troops to Vietnam.** Sihanouk breaks ties with the United States.

1966   **Sihanouk allows North Vietnamese forces into Cambodia.** They set up bases along the Vietnamese border and transport war *matériel* along the Ho Chi Minh Trail through Cambodia.

1967   **Cambodian communists begin armed struggle against Sihanouk's government.**

1969   **The United States begins secret, illegal bombing campaign against Vietnamese targets in Cambodia.**

1970   **General Lon Nol ousts Sihanouk, with U.S. backing.** Sihanouk flees to Beijing, where China, Vietnam and the Khmer Rouge offer support. Sihanouk agrees to form a united government in exile to overthrow Lon Nol. He becomes head of resistance groups fighting the Phnom Penh government. The Khmer Rouge gain support in their fight against Lon Nol by their new alliance with Sihanouk.

    U.S. and South Vietnamese soldiers invade Cambodia. They search for North Vietnamese forces.

1972   **Lon Nol elected president of the Khmer Republic.**

1973   **August 7: U.S. B-52 accidentally bombs Neak Luong on the Mekong.** The attack kills 137.

    August 15: U.S. bombing campaign in Cambodia ends.

1975   **January 1: Start of Khmer Rouge final offensive against Phnom Penh.**

    April 1: Lon Nol flees to the United States after being forced from office.

    April 17: Khmer Rouge enter Phnom Penh, ending the war in Cambodia. This is the start of the Khmer Rouge era under the name "Democratic Kampuchea." They begin evacuating the city and declare Cambodia has entered "Year Zero." Borders are closed and phone lines are cut as the country seals itself off from the rest of the world.

    April 30: North Vietnamese troops roll into Saigon, ending the war in Vietnam.

1976   **April: The Prime Minister of Democratic Kampuchea is announced as Pol Pot.** This is the first time the public is informed about the regime's leadership. Sihanouk is put under house arrest at the Royal Palace.

    S-21 interrogation and torture center opens at Tuol Sleng school in Phnom Penh. Nearly 14,000 people are tortured and interrogated here; many are eventually sent to Choeung Ek, the Killing Fields, outside Phnom Penh.

1977   **Hun Sen escapes to Vietnam.** He leaves his post as a deputy regimental commander with the Khmer Rouge to avoid being killed in a political purge. With the help of the Vietnamese, Hun Sen forms a force of 20,000 soldiers to overthrow the Khmer Rouge.

1978   **December 22: Vietnam launches offensive against Cambodia.** This follows years of Khmer Rouge attacks against Vietnamese border villages, which kill thousands.

1979   **January 7: Vietnamese soldiers capture Phnom Penh.** Khmer Rouge and Pol Pot flee to western Cambodia. Vietnamese forces discover Tuol Sleng torture center, where they find corpses still chained to beds. Vietnam sets up client government. Hun Sen becomes foreign minister of the new People's Republic of Kampuchea. Khmer Rouge and groups allied to Sihanouk begin vicious civil war against the Vietnamese-backed government. Hundreds of thousands of Cambodians flee the fighting and end up in refugee camps just inside the Thai border. The UN continues to recognize the Khmer Rouge as the official government of Cambodia. It is an effort led by the United States and China to punish the Vietnamese invasion of Cambodia.

1985   **Hun Sen becomes Prime Minister of People's Republic of Kampuchea.** Cambodia remains a client state of Vietnam, which has thousands of troops still fighting the Khmer Rouge around the country.

1989   **Vietnam begins pullout from Cambodia.** Thousands of Vietnamese soldiers have been killed and maimed in the ten-year quagmire. During this time the Khmer Rouge are supported by the Chinese and Thai governments.

1991   **Paris Peace Accords signed.** Nineteen UN member nations agree to help end Cambodia's civil war. Yet fighting continues for several more years.

1992 The United Nations Transitional Authority in Cambodia arrives. UNTAC is the largest UN peacekeeping operation to that date. It deploys 22,000 people and costs $1.6 billion. Its many-fold mission is to resettle 350,000 refugees from Thailand, disarm the various armies, prepare for national elections, supervise the transitional government until the new government is elected and begin rebuilding the country in the two years between the 1991 Paris Peace Accords and the 1993 election. The goals are, to say the least, ambitious.

1993 UN-sponsored elections held. The Khmer Rouge back out and return to their jungle lairs. The disarmament process collapses. The election season is marred by widespread violence, intimidation, murder and irregularities. The election is won by Prince Norodom Ranariddh, son of Prince Sihanouk, on the Funcinpec Party (National United Front for an Independent, Peaceful, Neutral, and Cooperative Cambodia) ticket. After losing the election, Hun Sen of the CPP (Cambodian People's Party, the renamed ruling communist party set up by the Vietnamese) says he is the only person who can keep Cambodia together after another faction threatens to break away with several eastern provinces. Ranariddh agrees to a power-sharing arrangement with Ranariddh as first prime minister and Hun Sen as second prime minister.

September: Sihanouk crowned king again, and a new Constitution is ratified. Fighting continues against Khmer Rouge.

1994 Khmer Rouge attack a train, killing numerous Cambodians and three Western tourists. Nuon Paet, Sam Bith and Chhouk Rin are all eventually convicted in the foreigners' deaths and become the first senior Khmer Rouge leaders to face trial — but not for crimes against Cambodians.

1996 Khmer Rouge leader Ieng Sary defects to the government. He makes a deal with Hun Sen, to Prince Ranariddh's approval, which allows him to rule over his soldiers in Pailin.

1997 March 30: Grenade attack against opposition candidate Sam Rainsy. At least sixteen people are killed and more than 100 injured during a political rally in a park across from the National Assembly building. No one is arrested.

July: Hun Sen stages military putsch. Second Prime Minister Hun Sen's personal army attacks and scatters military forces loyal to First Prime Minister Prince Ranariddh. Ranariddh previously fled the country and remains in exile for many months. The move is widely seen as a *coup d'etat*, but Hun Sen claims Ranariddh had been secretly — and illegally — dealing with the Khmer Rouge to oust Hun Sen. He is later proven correct.

August: Khmer Rouge place Pol Pot on a show trial to prove to the world he is no longer in power.

1998 April 15: Pol Pot dies near the Khmer Rouge stronghold of Anlong Veng, in northwest area of the country.

July: National elections held. They are marred again by widespread intimidation and pre-election violence. Hun Sen's CPP wins 64 of 122 seats in the National Assembly. Opposition protesters set up "Democracy Square" in the park across from the National Assembly building, halting government. Government troops are sent in to break up protests in September. A coalition government is formed with Hun Sen as prime minister and Prince Ranariddh as National Assembly president.

Late 1998: Khmer Rouge collapse and last soldiers defect to the government, effectively ending the civil war. Khieu Samphan and Nuon Chea, two architects of the Khmer Rouge reign of terror, retire. They hold a press conference in Phnom Penh, stay at a fine hotel and eventually move to Pailin in the country's west.

2001 Failed coup in Phnom Penh. A group calling itself the Cambodian Freedom Fighters, with leadership in the United States, jumps off a train in Phnom Penh, crosses the street and attacks the Ministry of Defense in a short-lived attempt at overthrowing the government. Their leader vows to try again.

2002 Local commune elections are held for the first time. Hun Sen's CPP wins 61 percent of the vote, Funcinpec wins 22 percent and the Sam Rainsy Party 17 percent.

2003 January 29: Anti-Thai riots flare in Phnom Penh. Mobs burn the Thai Embassy and raze Thai businesses, causing $50 million in damage.

March: UN and Cambodian government agree to establish tribunal for former Khmer Rouge leaders. This comes after years of negotiations.

July: National elections held. Polls go smoothly, though pre-election season sees regular killings and intimidation. Hun Sen and his CPP win but lack two-thirds majority needed to rule alone. Opposition leaders Prince Ranariddh and Sam Rainsy form an alliance and refuse to form coalition government with Hun Sen.

2004   April: Government remains in limbo; no coalition.

July: After a nearly year-long stalemate, a new government is formed with Hun Sen as Prime Minister and Prince Norodom Ranariddh as National Assembly president.

August: Parliament ratifies Cambodia's entry into the World Trade Organization.

October: The National Assembly ratifies a law allowing a U.N.-backed tribunal for former Khmer Rouge leaders. King Norodom Sihanouk abdicates the throne. Norodom Sihamoni, Sihanouk's son, is crowned the new King.

Notes

Preface

It was not an election so much as a "celebration." From: Elizabeth Becker. *When the War Was Over: Cambodia and the Khmer Rouge Revolution.* New York: PublicAffairs, 1998, p. 514.

"This was a delightful surprise to the foreign experts watching." From: Henry Kamm. *"Cambodia: Report from a Stricken Land."* New York: Arcade, 1998, pp. 222–228.

"In the West almost no writers..." From: John Pilger. *Distant Voices.* London: Vintage, 1992, pp. 15–16.

Ek Madra, "U.N. to Call for Khmer Rouge Trial Funds Soon," Reuters. Dec. 10, 2004.

Introduction

"Nobody sees a flower, really, it is so small." From: Georgia O'Keeffe as quoted in the exhibit, "O'Keeffe's O'Keeffe's: The Artist's Collection, Milwaukee Art Museum, 2001.

"They ignored Africans or else made them insubstantial figures in a landscape." From: Paul Theroux. *Fresh Air Fiend: Travel Writings 1985–2000.* New York: Houghton Mifflin, 2000, pp. 27–28.

"Fascination, beauty, stimulation, empathy, compassion." From: author email interview with Seth Mydans, Sept. 2003.

I: RECONCILING THE PAST

Chapter 1: War Remnants

(I would like to thank Sok Chea, Kim Samon, Hing Channarith for their help in translating for this chapter.)

The country has shed its wartime past for "the everyday misery of a land of poverty, injustice and continuing brutality." From: Seth Mydans. "Fragile Stability Slowly Emerges in Cambodia." *The New York Times.* June 25, 2000, International, pp. 1, 6.

Khmer Rouge regime of 1975–1979 when 1.7 million people died — a quarter of the Cambodian population. From: numerous sources. There will never be an exact tally, but 1.7 million is the estimate used by many scholars.

It is impossible to know how many land mines. From: the London-based group, Adopt-A-Minefield, the International Campaign to Ban Landmines. See: "Landmine Monitor Report." Cambodia, International Campaign to Ban Landmines. 2002.

At the rate of current technology, it will take half a century to vanquish the world's land mines, responsible for 15,000 to 20,000 casualties a year in 90 countries. From: Claudia Deane and Richard Morin. "Rand Urges World Focus on Land Mines." *Washington Post.* Feb. 18, 2003, p. A23.

In Cambodia, land mines and UXO still kill and disfigure more than sixty Cambodians every month. From: The Cambodia Campaign to Ban Landmines, as quoted in *The Cambodia Daily* "Group Releases Report Detailing Land Mines." Sept. 12, 2003, p. 11.

In July 2003, a primary school cook in Kompong Thom Province finds an unexploded 81-mm mortar shell while cleaning the school's kitchen. From: *The Cambodia Daily* "Buried Mortar Shell Found in School Kitchen." July 10, 2003, p. 11.

Two months later, four young brothers and a friend retrieve an old shell. From: *The Cambodia Daily* "Shell Blast Kills Five." Sept. 9, 2003, p. 17.

In January 2004, again: four brothers find an old bomb. From: "Wartime Bomb Kills Four Cambodian Boys." ABC Radio Australia News. Feb. 1, 2004.

Two months later, two brothers and a friend find a war-era mortar. From: The Associated Press. "Three Killed in Cambodia Mortar Accident." Mar. 12, 2004.

Jerry and I first meet Bun Na camped in a cart. From: author interview, April 2002.

Samnang, Phon Pheap, Sok Chamran, Nhat Pon. From author interviews, April–May 2002.

In late August 2003, about forty hospitalized soldiers from the Royal Cambodian Armed Forces ... march to the Ministry of Defense to complain. From: *The Cambodia Daily* "Hospitalized Soldiers Ask Gov't for Relief." Aug. 27, 2003, p. 16.

"And a person who is physically disabled become a burden." From: AsiaWatch, Physicians for Human Rights. Land Mines in Cambodia: The Coward's War. September 1991. Quoted in John Pilger. "A Faustian Pact." *Distant Voices*. London: Vintage, 1992, p. 239.

Kien Khleang Physical Rehabilitation Center. From: author interviews, 2002.

The Cambodia Daily reports that government schools refuse to employ disabled teachers. From: William Shaw and Phann Ana. "School for Disabled Bypasses Government Ban," *The Cambodia Daily*. Sept. 11, 2003, p. 1.

In May 2003, *The New York Times* runs a story about a place called Veal Thom. From: Seth Mydans. "What War Wrought, Cambodians Can't Stand to See." May 20, 2003, p. A4.

Kin briefs us on Veal Thom. From: author interviews, 2003.

Chapter 2: Leaving Cambodia

(Parts of this chapter originally appeared in *The Cambodia Daily* in February 1999, the *San Jose Mercury News* in April 2000, and *The Chattahoochee Review* in Summer 2002.)

We're at a place called the Nutrition Center orphanage. From: author interviews and observations, Jan. 1999.

I head to the Transcultural Psychosocial Organization, Kann Kall, Kang San. From: author interviews, Jan. 1999.

The conversation takes place shortly after Khieu Samphan ... and Nuon Chea ... defect to the government. From: author observations and numerous sources. See Youk Chhang, Dith Pran, and Ben Kiernan. "Bloody Tourists in a Land of Skulls." *The Guardian* (London). Jan. 2, 1999.

Officials estimate 200,000 people have HIV, and up to 100 new people are infected each day. From: numerous sources. See Agence France-Presse. "Cambodia AIDS: Activists, officials in Cambodia urge reduced AIDS discrimination." Dec. 1, 2003.

Chapter 3: Genocide

"When we meet an affable, smiling Cambodian." From: Youk Chhang, "Genocide Justice in 2002?" From the Documentation Center of Cambodia.

In December 2003, Khieu Samphan ... admits the regime committed genocide, but he denies any involvement in the killings. From: Seth Mydans, "A Top Khmer Rouge Leader, Going Public, Pleads Ignorance," *The New York Times*, Jan. 3, 2004, p. A4, and Ker Munthit, "Ex-Khmer Rouge Chief Acknowledges Genocide," *Washington Post*, Dec. 31, 2003, p. A20.

Less than a month later, Nuon Chea ... admits he made "mistakes" during the Khmer Rouge regime. From: The Associated Press. "Khmer Rouge's Brother No. 2 Says He Will Face Tribunal." Jan. 18, 2004.

Pailin: ... the fiefdom of Ieng Sary. From: numerous sources. Becker, 515.

The stalwart comrades of his past celebrate [his daughter's wedding]. From: numerous sources. *The Straits Times* (Singapore). "Wedding reunites Khmer Rouge leaders." Mar. 17, 2002.

Hun Sen "has sabotaged the trial at every opportunity." From: *The Asian Wall Street Journal*. "Cambodia's Quest for Justice." Review & Outlook (editorial), Feb. 14, 2002.

In February 2002, in a low point of negotiations, the UN pulls out. From: Colum Lynch. "UN Ends Negotiations on Khmer Rouge Trials." *Washington Post*. Feb. 9, 2002.

The Cambodian cabinet and the UN sign a draft agreement for a tribunal. From: numerous sources. See statement by UN Under-Secretary-General Hans Corell, Mar. 17, 2003; Reuters, "U.N. Team in Cambodia to Prepare Genocide Trial," Dec. 7, 2003; Samantha Brown, "Khmer Rouge Tribunal to Cost Around 50 Million Dollars: UN," Agence France-Presse, Mar. 18, 2004.

"There was not a single child, not one living creature." François Bizot. *The Gate*. New York: Alfred A. Knopf, 2003, p. 181.

"Everyone I met had a different explanation

for how the Khmer Rouge could have happened." From: Andrew Solomon. *The Noonday Demon: An Atlas of Depression.* New York, London, Toronto, Sydney, Singapore: Simon & Schuster, 2001, p. 33.

The Khmer Rouge recruited young, unmarried men, easily malleable and lacking attachments. From: David Chandler. *Voices from S-21: Terror and History in Pol Pot's Secret Prison.* Berkeley, Los Angeles and London: University of California Press, 1999, p. 33.

"This culture of exploitation, protection, obedience, and dependency had deep roots in Cambodian social practice." *Ibid.*, 148.

"Most of us ... could become accustomed." *Ibid.*, 155.

Ke Pauk dies. From: numerous sources. Ben Kiernan. "Ke Pauk: One of Pol Pot's Leading Military Commanders, He Was Responsible for the Murders of Many Thousands of Cambodians, but Escaped Justice." *The Guardian.* Feb. 21, 2002.

The Killing Fields, Tuol Sleng. From: author interviews and observations, 1998, 2001; Chandler, *Voices from S-21*; Becker.

It is not unusual for survivors to mourn their losses and celebrate their lives through art. From: Svay Ken exhibit, Reyum, Phnom Penh, 2001.

In 1998, Vann Nath published his memoirs. Vann Nath. *A Cambodian Prison Portrait: One Year in the Khmer Rouge's S-21.* Bangkok: White Lotus, 1998.

"As a survivor, I want to be worthy of the suffering that I survived as a child." Chanrithy Him. *When Broken Glass Floats: Growing Up Under the Khmer Rouge.* New York: W.W. Norton, 2000.

"I'm doing this for my mother." Youk Chhang. From: author interview, Aug. 2003.

For additional reading on genocide, see The Associated Press, "Cambodia Skull Map Dismantled," Mar. 10, 2002; Mark Baker, "Calling to Account: William Barnes, "UN Says Khmer Rouge Leaders to Stand Trial Soon"; Human Rights Watch, "Cambodia: Tribunal Must Meet International Standards"; Reuters, "UN Team in Cambodia to Prepare Genocide Trial"; and *The Nation* (Bangkok), "Cambodia Still in Shadow of KR."

Chapter 4: Angkor

(Parts of this chapter originally appeared in *Archaeology* magazine in May 2004. I would like to thank Morn Sor for his help in translating.)

"It contains a moat ... battles." From: Dawn Rooney. *A Guide to Angkor: An Introduction to the Temples.* Hong Kong: The Guidebook Company Ltd., 1994, pp. 84–108.

The Angkor complex extends deep into the Cambodian countryside. From: Robert Philpotts. *Reporting Angkor: Chou Ta-Kuan in Cambodia 1296–1297.* London: Blackwater Books, 1996; and Rooney.

The mere sight ... a traveler, "making him forget all the fatigues of the journey ... light." From: Henri Mouhot. *Travels in Siam, Cambodia, Laos, and Annam.* Bangkok: White Lotus, 2000, p. 221.

"Greatness flows in our veins." From: the website vimean-akas.khmerconnection.com.

The month ... Khmer Rouge rebels kidnapped three aid workers. From: Marc Levy and Van Roeun. "Trio Released on 8th Day of Captivity." *The Cambodia Daily.* Dec. 16, 1998, p. 1.

That same week, more rebels took forty villagers hostage. Lor Chandara. "Police Say KR Bandits Seized Villagers for $2,000 Ransom." *The Cambodia Daily.* Dec. 10, 1998, p. 11.

History and downfall of the Angkor empire. From: numerous sources. Becker, Philpotts, Rooney. Stephen O. Murray. *Angkor Life: Pre-Cambodian Life 800 Years Ago in the Society That Created the Stupendous Monuments of Angkor Wat and Angkor Thom.* San Francisco: Bua Luang Books, 1996.

"There have been so many hiatuses in the history of this poor country that one can no longer find any trace of conscious memory," Bizot, 106.

The first wave of tourists arrived in 1907. From: www.unesco.org/courier/2000_05/UK/signe.htm.

In 2000, the Cambodian government announces a $3 million plan to upgrade the temples for tourism. From: Deutsche Presse-Agentur. "Cambodia Announces 3-Million-Dollar Upgrade for Temple Tourism." May 4, 2000.

Between 2000 and 2003, the number of guesthouses in Siem Reap skyrockets 60 percent. From: Brett M. Ballard. "Employment and Trade in Angkor Park: Some Preliminary Observations on the Impact of Tourism." *Cambodia Development Review.* Jan.–Mar. 2003, Vol. 7, Issue 1, pp. 5–7, 16.

In April 2004, more than 2,000 luxury hotel workers go on strike.... From: Yun Samean and Daniel Ten Kate. "Workers at 6 Top Hotels Go on Strike." *The Cambodia Daily.* Apr. 6, 2004, p. 1.

During one of our visits to Siem Reap, former

Sofitel employee complains he made only $30 a month. From: author interview, 2002.

"It became unpleasant" ... butterfly garden instead. From: author interviews, 2002.

A few miles away is Choun Nhiem. From: author interview August 2003 and author observations 1998, 1999, 2001, 2002, 2003.

He is famous because *Lonely Planet* has put his picture on the cover. Oct. 2002 edition.

Our mission ... the elite paraded beneath golden parasols. From: Philpotts, 26.

Today, the Angkor Archaeological Park management is equally striated. From: author interview at UNESCO headquarters, Phnom Penh, 2003.

"It is the hearer's responsibility to understand what is being said." From: Richard E. Nisbett. *The Geography of Thought: How Asians and Westerners Think Differently ... and Why.* New York: The Free Press, 2003, pp. 60–61.

Power is a precious commodity in Cambodia. From: numerous sources. Philpotts, Mouhot, Becker, Seanglim Bit. *The Warrior Heritage: A Psychological Perspective of Cambodian Trauma.* El Cerrito, Cal.: Seanglim Bit, 1991.

We arrive at the Preah Khan entrance. From: author interviews and observations, overnight Aug. 2003; day trips 1999, 2001, 2002.

"You cannot be too much on your guard; going to bed or getting up, you are ever in peril of putting hand or foot on some venomous snake." From: Mouhot, 184.

All these Angkor ruins recall a brutal and violent past. From: numerous sources, author interviews.

Even since ... the ruins still face threats from a deluge of tourists and from thieves plundering the last riches. From: numerous sources, author observation 2001.

The Apsara Authority works from a large, hulking pink building with little inside. From: author interview attempt, Aug., Sept. 2003.

My answer comes a few months later. From: Van Roeun. "Police Launch Sweep for Angkor Thom Looters." *The Cambodia Daily.* Jan. 16, 2004, p. 14.

Interlude: Siem Reap to Phnom Penh

In this case, point A is Siem Reap ... National Route 6 by minivan. This piece is based on a trip taken in April 2002. Since then, road conditions have improved a bit, although the rainy season makes them worse again. However, several companies now offer regular service between the two cities on large, air-conditioned buses, making the trip much more comfortable — and cheaper.

"The play was simply a phantasmagoria tolerably well managed." From: Mouhot, 157.

Chapter 5: Neighbors and Borders

(Parts of this chapter originally appeared in *The Cambodia Daily* in June 1998, and in a series of stories in the *Daily* in September 1998, detailing the poisonings and beating deaths. I would like to thank Lor Chandara, Van Roeun, Kimsan Chantara, and Heng Sinith for their help.)

The epigraph to Chapter 5 is drawn from Ryszard Kapuscinski. *Imperium.* New York: Vintage International, 1994, pp. 20–21.

They douse them with gasoline ... the Vietnam-Cambodia Liberation Monument ... ousted the Khmer Rouge. From: author observations and several *Cambodia Daily* articles, Sept. 1998.

This is Democracy Square. From: numerous sources and author observations, 1998.

"*Yuon,*" that word of fierce debate. See the *Phnom Penh Post,* June–Aug. 2003 for an ongoing discussion in print.

Ho Chi Minh City, or Saigon, was then called "Prey Nokor," and it was a small Cambodian fishing village. From: numerous sources. See Nayan Chanda, *Brother Enemy: The War After the War,* New York: Macmillan, 1986; see also the Vietnam History Museum in Saigon.

"The French had decided that the Vietnamese were the industrious race of the future and the Khmer a lazy doomed people." From: Becker, 36, 121.

When Lon Nol presided over Cambodia in the 1970s, he thought himself a holy man commissioned to wage war against the infidels next door. From: Becker, 118–122.

In April 1970, the Cambodian Army attacked a large ethnic Vietnamese settlement on the Chruoy Changvar peninsula, in the river across from Phnom Penh. From: Becker, 125.

The Khmer Rouge enacted likewise pogroms against the Vietnamese. From: numerous sources. See Becker, 134, 137, 228, 242, 245–246.

In 1994, Vietnamese were attacked at Piem So ... fishing village of Chhnouk Trou villages in the night. From: Statement by Thomas

Hammarberg, Special Representative of the UN Secretary-General for Human Rights in Cambodia, May 4, 1998.

Many Cambodians think the current government *is* Vietnamese because they see no difference from the 1980s. From: numerous author interviews, 1998–2004.

Prime Minister Hun Sen fled to Vietnam when he escaped the Khmer Rouge and organized forces to overthrow that brutal regime. From: Harish C. Mehta and Julie B. Mehta. *Hun Sen: Strongman of Cambodia.* Singapore: Graham Brash. 1999, p. 19.

Such incendiary rhetoric colors the campaigns of opposition candidates in 1998 and again in 2003. From: numerous sources and author observations. See an Agence France-Presse report on the Virtual Information Center website, July 25, 2003; "Vietnamese Flee Cambodia's Racist Jibes," Agence France-Presse, July 23, 2003. Also, Richard S. Ehrlich. "Hun Sen Favored, But Security on Voters' Minds." *The Washington Times,* July 22, 2003.

"The extravagant building program and foreign policy of the God-kings led to the destruction of Angkor.... In 1431 the country "became a vassal of Siam." From: William Shawcross. *Sideshow: Kissinger, Nixon and the Destruction of Cambodia.* London: The Hogarth Press, 1993, p. 40.

It's in the meat ... the talk of the town goes. From: numerous sources, author interviews, and observations at Calmette Hospital in Sept. 1998, as reported in *The Cambodia Daily.*

"A rumor startles Phnom Penh. Food is being poisoned!" From Peter T. White. "Kampuchea Wakens from a Nightmare." *National Geographic,* May 1982, p. 622.

In the next four days, the furor continues. Based on translations by Khmer staff at *The Cambodia Daily.*

Just over the Monivong Bridge, in a place the locals don't call Phnom Penh, ethnic Vietnamese lead a tight-knit life between two worlds. From: author interviews, Sept. 1998.

"The entire camp was surrounded by barbed wire." From: Sarah Streed. *Leaving the House of Ghosts: Cambodian Refugees in the American Midwest.* Jefferson, N.C.: McFarland & Co., 2002, p. 88.

What's more, Thailand acted as a conduit for Chinese guns heading to the Khmer Rouge. From: numerous sources. See Becker, 508–509 and Kamm, 150–169.

And so ... storm the new Thai embassy building. From: numerous sources, covered widely in the *Bangkok Post, The Cambodia Daily,* the *Phnom Penh Post, The New York Times, The Nation,* the *Straits Times* (Singapore) and many other newspapers and wires.

The U.S. government calls the Cambodian government "irresponsible," "incompetent" and guilty of "nationalistic rhetoric." From: Agence France-Presse. "US Probe Castigates Cambodia Over Thai Riots." May 12, 2003.

Fifty-eight suspects are arrested.... King Sihanouk questions their involvement, and eventually all fifty-eight are freed. From: "Cambodia Frees Two Students Jailed After Anti–Thai Riots." ABC Radio Australia. Sept. 25, 2003. And Reach Sambath. "Cambodian Court Frees 56 Charged Over Anti-Thai Riots." Agence France-Presse. Sept. 15, 2003.

"Many Cambodians feel that Thailand has looked down on them for too long." From: "Cambodian, and Proud of It." *Far Eastern Economic Review.* May 22, 2003.

Koh Kong Casino information. From: numerous sources, author interviews in May1998 and June 2003.

Reports from Koh Kong are based on author trips through there in May 1998 and June 2003. Reports from Poipet are based on author trips through there Apr. and June 2003 and Jan. 2004.

"The border is quiet." From: author trip in June 2003.

A seven-mile stretch of disputed rice paddies. From: numerous sources and author interviews, 1998–2004. Phann Ana and Kevin Doyle. "Border Is Burning Issue for Svay Rieng Voters." *The Cambodia Daily,* July 16, 2003, p. 1.

Chapter 6: Kampuchea Krom

(Much of this chapter originally appeared in *The Cambodia Daily* in October 1998 and in the *South China Morning Post* in December 1998.)

It's an ironic twist of history. From: Chanda, 96, 224.

This chapter is based on an author trip through Kampuchea Krom in September 1998. For further reading on Kampuchea Krom and the history of Khmers in modern-day southern Vietnam, see: Chanda; Becker.

Chapter 7: Anlong Veng

(Parts of this chapter originally appeared in *NurseWeek* magazine in December 2001 and in the Drexel Online Journal, December 2003. I would like to thank Morn Sor for his help in translating.)

This chapter is based on author trips to Anlong Veng Aug. 2001 and July 2003. For further reading on Anlong Veng, see: Puy Kea, "Anlong Veng Sees a Future in Pol Pot's Ashes," Kyodo News Service, April 13, 2000; Seth Mydans. "Prayers for the Lottery at Pol Pot's Grave Site," *The New York Times*, June 25, 2001; Barry Wain, "Cambodians Promote Killing Fields to Tourists," *The Wall Street Journal*, Feb. 20, 2002; and Thomas Crampton, "Cambodia to Restore Khmer Rouge Sites," *International Herald Tribune*, Aug. 20, 2003.

[Anlong Veng] is "where the losers live." From: Craig Etcheson, quoted in Wain.

[Ta Mok's] men helped Pol Pot and Brigadier General Ke Pauk slaughter more than 100,000 people in the east, in the largest mass murder in Cambodian history. From: Kiernan.

"Expressionless faces imprint themselves on your mind and it did not matter what bad news you had, these people took it as though they were not surprised." From: "Remembering Rwanda," by Lyndall Moore, *Australian Nursing Journal*. May 1997, Vol. 4, Issue 10, p. 19.

II: LIVING NOW

Chapter 8: Democracy

(Parts of this chapter originally appeared in *The Cambodia Daily* in July and September 1998. I would like to thank Kay Kimsong and Kimsan Chantara for their help in reporting.)

Quotes from Cambodians talking about democracy are based on author interviews, July–September 1998, except where noted otherwise.

The UN failed, and "it did not acknowledge ... Paris agreement." Harry Kamm, p. 215.

Twenty-one killed before the 1998 vote, fifteen before commune elections in 2002, thirty-one killed before the vote in 2003. From: numerous sources. See "The 2003 National Assembly Elections," a report by the UN special representative of the secretary general for human rights in Cambodia, July 8, 2003.

"Many Cambodians have been made acutely aware that active involvement in politics, particularly on behalf of the opposition, could result in death." From: Human Rights Watch "Don't Bite the Hand that Feeds You: Coercion, Threats, and Vote-Buying in Cambodia's National Elections. July 2003.

In November 2001, five men are paid $10 each to kill a Sam Rainsy Party candidate in the commune election campaign. From: Reuters. "Cambodians Paid $10 Each for Killing Politician." Feb. 8, 2002.

In January 2002, three female opposition candidates are shot to death. From: numerous sources. See Seth Meixner. "Women Candidates Killed in Pre-Election Violence." *South China Morning Post*. Hong Kong. Jan. 8, 2002.

In February 2003, prominent democracy supporter and member of the Royalist Funcinpec Party, Om Radsady, is shot to death after eating lunch at a restaurant. From: numerous sources. See The Associated Press. "Adviser to Cambodia's Royalist Party Shot to Death." Feb. 18, 2003.

In October 2003 ... journalist Chou Chetharith, of the Funcinpec Party radio station is shot to death in front of his office. From: Reuters. "Pro-Royal Cambodian Radio Journalist Shot Dead." Oct. 18, 2003.

Singer Touch Srey Nich, "the voice of Funcinpec," is shot and her mother killed while leaving a flower shop in mid-morning. From: Amy Kazmin. "Cambodian Pop Star in Critical Condition." *Financial Times*, Oct. 23, 2003.

In January 2004, Chea Vichea, leader of the country's largest trade union, is shot to death while reading a newspaper near Wat Langka in Phnom Penh. From: numerous sources. See Bronwyn Sloan. "Killing Shame. *Far Eastern Economic Review*. Feb. 5, 2004.

Democracy definition. From: *Pocket Oxford English Dictionary*. Oxford University Press. 2002 edition.

1998, 2002 and 2003 election results compiled from author observations, *The Cambodia Daily* and *Phnom Penh Post* reports, wire reports and UN reports.

Two grenades mysteriously explode in Hun Sen's house. From: numerous sources. There is some inconsistency in the reports, whether one or two grenades exploded. The author was at the scene, *The Cambodia Daily* reports two explosions, and the author witnessed a third dud on the ground.

"I think it's pretty fair to say the rest of the world doesn't give a damn." From: author interview, July 1998.

For a variety of reactions to the election, see: Glenys Kinnock. "Lessons from the 1998 National Election," *Phnom Penh Post*, Vol. 11, Issue 3." The European Union; United Nations Commission on Human Rights. "Commune Council Elections 2002." Jan. 2002.

"Cambodia teetered between democracy and

authoritarianism and the international community showed little interest." From: Kinnock, the European Union's special representative to the elections, statement, p. 2.

Democracy Square reports. From: author interviews and observations, *Cambodia Daily* articles 1998.

"It is not a crackdown." From: Kay Johnson. "Sit-In Crumbles After Early-Morning Crackdown." *The Cambodia Daily.* Sept. 9, 1998, p. 1.

It starts at 7:30 P.M. From: author interviews and observations; regular reports from *The Cambodia Daily*, the *Phnom Penh Post*, AP, Reuters, Deutsche Presse-Agentur and Agence France-Presse.

"Westerners seem inclined to believe there is only one kind of relation between the individual and the state that is appropriate." From: Nisbett, p. 198.

"I will say, the UN did leave one very positive legacy that offers hope for change ... the concept, at least, of human rights." From: author email interview with Mydans, Sept. 2003.

"The 2002 election was anything but free and fair." From: Sam Rainsy Party. "Analysis of Election Results." Feb. 12, 2002.

The election is "free and fair enough." From: Reuters. "Cambodian PM Says Historic Elections Were Fair Enough." Feb. 7, 2002.

"Cambodian elections neither free nor fair." From: Agence France-Presse. "Cambodian Elections Neither Free Nor Fair: US Monitor." Feb. 6, 2002.

"A little democracy is better than no democracy at all." From: Leo Dobbs. "Better Than No Polls at All." *Far Eastern Economic Review.* Feb. 7, 2002. Vol. 165, No. 5, pp. 24–26.

Cambodia is a land "steeped in blood." From: John Pancake. "A Ballot for the Future of a Land Steeped in Blood." *Washington Post.* Mar. 15, 2002.

It is ruled by a "culture of impunity." From: numerous sources. See: Irene V. Langren. "Cambodia in 2000: New Hopes Are Challenged." Asian Survey: A Bimonthly *Review of Contemporary Asian Affairs.* University of California Press. Vol. XLI, No. 1, Jan./Feb. 2001, pp. 156–163.

It is a "lawless country with the thin veneer of democracy." From: Mitch McConnell. "Elections in Cambodia." Statement, July 24, 2003.

The 2003 elections were true, acceptable, transparent and conducted in a meticulous manner "that one would like to see everywere." From: Michelle Vachon. "Observer Groups Praise Election Process." *The Cambodia Daily.* Aug. 1, 2003, p. 13.

The 2003 elections were so successful that Cambodia "could easily shame most of its regional neighbors." From: Marwaan Macan-Markar. "Analysis: Democracy Elusive in Southeast Asia." Inter Press Service. July 29, 2003.

The elections were "well conducted," but there is "still some way to go to full democracy." From: The European Union Statement on the 2003 Elections. http://europa.eu.int/comm/external_relations/human_rights/eu_election_ass_observ/cambodia03/ July 30, 2003.

"If the conduct of these 2003 national elections provides a safe environment for all participants to compete..." From: Philip T. Reeker. "Credible Elections in Cambodia." U.S. State Department Press Statement. Washington, D.C. May 30, 2003.

But the biggest accusations of over-stepping the lines come against the International Republican Institute. From: Andrew Wells-Dang. "Republican Group Meddles in Cambodia." *Asia Times Online.* Apr. 16, 2004.

Reports from Anlong Veng. From: author interviews and observations, July 2003.

"The prime minister grew up a poor farm boy in a Kompong Cham village that had no high school." From: Mehta and Mehta, p. 19.

Dr. Sorn Samnang. From: author interview, Jan. 2004.

For additional readings on Democracy, *see* Bjornlund; Chachavalpongpun; Perrin and Unmacht; Santoli, ed., "Escalating Corruption & Violence in Cambodia's Faux Democracy"; and Schmetzer.

Interlude: Sam and Vic

(Parts of this piece originally appeared in *The Cambodia Daily*.)

Chapter 9: Violence and Crime:

(Parts of this chapter originally appeared in the *Montana Journalism Review*, Summer 2000.)

The epigraph to chapter 5 is drawn from Kapuscinski, *Imperium*, on Tbilisi, Georgia, 124.

March 30, 1997, grenade attack. From: numerous sources. The casualty toll varies; the most conservative estimate is used. See Wayne Crenshaw. "Cochran Man Seeks Justice for 1997 Grenade Attack in Cambodia." *Khemara Jat*, posted on Camnews. Mar. 30, 2004.

Cambodia is "plagued by four basic evils— poverty, violence, corruption and lawlessness." From: United Nations Third Committee. "Promotion of Human Rights, Poverty Eradication and Development." GA/SHC/3762. Nov. 10, 2003.

"This country" … "has fallen into a vicious circle." From: author interview with Kann Kall, Jan. 1999 and subsequently, Aug. 2001.

"The kids have nothing to look forward to." From: author interview with Sebastien Marot of *Mith Samlanh*, or Friends, 2003.

Examples of violence. From: author observations, experiences and interviews, 1998–2004.

"Obviously a culture that produces such stories is not as single-mindedly gentle as its reputation." From: Becker, 67.

"Criminals were sometimes punished by having their toes cut off." From: Philpotts, 29–30.

"Some are being pounded in mortars." From: Mouhot, 230–231.

"Visitors are often struck by the apparent normality of Phnom Penh." From: Pilger. "Return to Year Zero," 175.

"Danger … is like a wind that blows." From: Bizot, 271.

Examples of crimes and arrests. From: *Phnom Penh Post* police blotters, 2003.

In 2000, … a chess player who clubs opponent. From: *San Jose Mercury News*. "Insufficient Reasons to Kill Someone." News of the Weird. Jan. 29, 2000.

In February 2004, The Associated Press reports on a "monk's war." From: AP. "Monks Turn Nasty as Temple Feud Erupts." Feb. 29, 2004.

The *Times* of London reports that the Cambodian government has banned water pistols. From: James Pringle "Water Pistol Ban." The *Times*. Apr. 15, 2000.

"In fact, the police and military are often involved in crimes and human rights violations." From: UN Commission on Human Rights, "E/CN.4/2001/NGO/68." Fifty-seventh session. Item 11(d) of the provisional agenda, Jan. 30, 2001.

"People are regularly and routinely beaten." From: *Phnom Penh Post*. "Torture now as ever Cambodia's curse." July 7–20, 2000.

People have expanded their minds. From: author conversation with Kay Kimsong, 2003.

We see it one day from our balcony. From: author observations, September 2003.

Sixty-five cases of mob assaults and killings. From: "Cambodia Country Reports on Human Rights Practices 2002." U.S. State Department, Bureau of Democracy, Human Rights and Labor. Mar. 31, 2003.

Villagers in Battambang pulled an accused rapist from his police cell. From: Agence France-Presse. "Cambodian women cut off rapist's penis." Aug. 25, 2000.

"A legal system that has proved itself incapable of dispensing justice objectively." From: numerous sources. See UN Commission on Human Rights, "E/CN.4/2001/NGO/66." Fifty-seventh session. Item 11(b) of the provisional agenda. Jan. 30, 2001.

UN General Assembly again urges the Cambodian government to make legal and judicial reform a priority. From: United Nations. "Human Rights Questions." Draft Resolution. Fifty-eighth session, third committee, agenda item 117 (b). Nov. 18, 2003.

Ouch Borith … informs the UN General Assembly that mob killings have ceased. From: United Nations Press Release. "GA/SHC/3762." Nov. 10, 2003.

Three thieves are caught stealing a motorbike. This continues to happen frequently over the next year. See *Phnom Penh Post* police blotters, 2003–2004.

Chapter 10: Psychology

(I would like to thank Kimsan Chantara for his help with some of the information in this chapter.)

Po Kith Ly and Ouk Yom. From: author interviews, July 2003.

Descriptions of the Sihanouk Hospital psychiatric ward stem from author observations and interviews the same day.

There are only twenty psychiatrists in Cambodia. From: author interview with Ang Sody, July 2003.

Beneath is a "tone of melancholy." Seanglim Bit, p. 105.

The Ministry of Health outlines a twenty-year plan for dealing with mental illness across Cambodia. From: Alex Halperin. "Gov't Outlines 20-Year Plan for Mentally Ill." *The Cambodia Daily*. July 11, 2003, p. 12.

The amount the Pentagon spent in a single minute. From: numerous sources. See: George C. Wilson, "Tilting at the Pentagon," *National Journal*, May 27, 2003; Halford H. Fairchild, "A Wake-up Call for Peace," http://pzacad.pitzer.edu/~hfairchi/essays/WakeUpCall.html; and Dick Meyer, "Pigs at the Taxpayer Trough," CBSNews.com. Dec. 11, 2003.

"The people of Cambodia live in the compass of immemorial tragedy." From: Solomon, 32.

"Testimony psychotherapy." From: Stevan M. Weine, codirector of the Project on Genocide, Psychiatry, and Witnessing at the University of Illinois, Chicago. "Bosnian Refugees: Memories, Witnessing, and History After Dayton." www.refugees.org/world/articles/bosnians_wrs96.htm.

"We feel they are all victims." From: author interview with Sotheara Chhim, July 2003.

[Kang Om] agrees that war is a major factor. From: author interview with Kang Om, Aug. 2003.

Many young Cambodians are wrapped in a continuous cycle of worry. From: a 2002 study of college, university and technical-school students. Leakhena Nou. "What Motivates Khmer Youth to Gang-Rape? A Sociological Interpretation of the Bouk Phenomenon." *Phnom Penh Post.* July 18–31, p. 13.

"The problem in Battambang is worse than in other provinces." From: author interviews and observations, Aug. 2001 and June 2002.

"Theravada Buddhism offers rational explanations for previous life and any future lives, but is largely silent on how to resolve the dilemmas of this existence." From: Bit, p. 97.

In 1998 villagers in Sihanoukville take to drinking urine of two oxen. From: www.trowbridgeplanetearth.com/P_ARKA/v1/bu/v1.n10.p1.html.

In 2003, it's the ... "Python boy. From: Reuters. "Cambodians flock to see Python Boy." May 22, 2003.

Cambodians find hope on a small island. From: author interviews and observations, Oct. 1998.

"No single traumatic episode, not even the barbaric extremes of the most recent period, fully account for the state of anomie which characterizes Cambodian society today." From: Bit, p. 92.

Kann Kall hears the news from afar. From: author interview, Jan. 1999.

Chapter 11: The Wanderers

(I would like to thank Sok Chea, Saing Soenthrith, Morn Sor and Hat Saman for their help with the information and translations for parts of this chapter.)

Epigraph from chapter 11. From: Leo Tolstoy. *Writings on Civil Disobedience and Nonviolence.* 1886. As quoted in http://dwadmac.pitzer.edu/Anarchist_Archives/bright/tolstoy/tolstoy.com

Cambodia is a land largely populated by "wanderers." From: Mydans. "Pushed from the Land, and the Trees." *The New York Times.* April 6, 2000.

Land ownership was destroyed during the Khmer Rouge, all titles and deeds abolished, and in 1979, it became a free-for-all. Some people chose new plots and stayed for decades and secured rights to that land. Many others never found a place to settle — or a place where they were allowed to stay. From: Michael Coren. "The Poor Still Battle for Land Rights." *Phnom Penh Post.* Aug. 29–Sept. 11, 2003, p. 5.

This outrageous plunder found general acceptance." Kamm. p. 209.

Military police armed with AK-47s force hundreds of scavengers from the Stung Meanchey dump outside Phnom Penh. From: ABC Radio Australia News. "Hundreds of Illegal Settlers Evicted from Cambodian Dump Site." Aug. 7, 2003.

A few days later, 1,506 country folk appear at Sam Rainsy's stoop. From: Sam Rainsy. "SOS Hungry Farmers: More Than 1,500 Internal Refugees Presently at SRP Headquarters." National Assembly of the Kingdom of Cambodia. Sept. 8, 2001.

"Most of these destitute people are women, babies, and children." From: Sam Rainsy. "Another Wave of Hungry Farmers Arrive in Phnom Penh." National Assembly of the Kingdom of Cambodia. Sept. 7, 2001.

Thai police arrest Cambodians ... at dump. From: *Bangkok Post.* "Khmer Scavengers Nabbed." June 20, 2003.

Vietnam deports 206 Cambodians. From: *The Cambodia Daily.* "Vietnam Deports More Than 200 Cambodians." Aug. 26, 2003, p. 13.

Two fires roar through a squatter camp on the Bassac River. From: numerous sources. See Kazmin. "Phnom Penh slum dwellers feel the heat." *Financial Times.* Jan. 8, 2002.

Anlong Kong Thmei sits in flooded rice fields. From: author interviews and observations, July 2003. See also Saing Soenthrith and Wency Leung. "Storms Wreak Havoc on Relocated Squatters." *The Cambodia Daily*, July 7, 2003, p. 1. And *Cambodge Soir.* "Anlong Kong vide de ses habitants." July 29, 2003, p. 12.

Kim Sophornn ... doesn't croon about the splendors. From: author interview, June 2002.

"Everything you see ... it's not by the government." From: author interview, 2003.

Those who visit ... are missing a significant lot. From: author interviews and observations, 2002 and 2003.

Sixty-four families evicted from ... Angkor

Wat. From: Yun Samean. "64 Families Evicted from Angkor Wat." *The Cambodia Daily*. Sept. 8, 2003, p. 1.

"The days of begging children at Angkor are over." From: Donald Richie. "The Other Treasures of Angkor." *The Japan Times*. Feb. 26, 2002.

Cambodia exports more than $730 million worth of garments to the U.S. each year, and another $220 million to Europe. From: Media Business Networks and Promo-Khmer, *Who's Who in Cambodia Business Reference Book 2003–2004*. Phnom Penh: 2003, p. 44.

"Solid progress" in improved working conditions problem of forced overtime. From: The Associated Press. "U.N.: Conditions Better at Cambodia Plants." Apr. 9, 2004.

Sar Rann (and other) garment worker reports. From: author interviews, Sept. 2003. For additional garment-factory information, see James Brooke. "A Year of Worry for Cambodia's Garment Makers." *The New York Times*, Jan. 24, 2004.

"Other people, if they have money, they have hope." From: author interview, Aug. 2003.

Chapter 12: Women

(I would like to thank Sok Chea for his help in translating for parts of this chapter.)

I see the portrait of a fourteen-year-old girl. From: archive of Jerry Redfern.

There is Ny [and other examples of rape, crimes against women]. From: *Phnom Penh Post* police blotters, 1998–2004. And: "Girl, 10, Is Raped, Killed." *The Cambodia Daily*. Feb. 24, 2004, p. 13. And: Thet Sambath. "2 Men Accused of Raping Girls to Cure AIDS." *The Cambodia Daily*. Apr. 5, 2004, p. 15.

The ... tendency of "viewing humans of possessions." From: Jason Barber. "Torture in Cambodia: A Licadho Project Against Torture Report." June 2000.

"There is *joie de vivre* again. Nightclubs have reopened with taxi dancers. I am sure soon there will be massage parlours. It is our way of life: it is a good life." From Norodom Sihanouk, quoted in Pilger, "A Faustian Pact," p. 231.

Twenty-two percent of all tourists. From: *Straits Times*. "Sex draws nearly a quarter of tourists to Cambodia." Oct. 6, 2001.

"Shy boys on motorbikes will ferry you from bar to bar, waiting outside while you drink yourself into a stupor." From: Anthony Bourdain. *A Cook's Tour: Global Adventures in Ex-treme Cuisines*. New York: HarperCollins, 2001, p. 162.

"Cambodia's women thought they were at the start of an equal future in 1958. From: *Phnom Pehn Post*, June 20–July 23, 2003.

I met a photographer, Nicolas Lainez. From: author conversation, June 2002.

Muny Van Saveth. From: author interviews, June 2002 and Sept. 2003.

Nop Sarin Srey Roth, monitoring coordinator of the Cambodians Women's Crisis Center. From: author interview, July 2003.

"It was believed if he did not go, trouble would befall his kingdom." From: Philpotts, 70.

"A hundred little cottages with walls of clay and thatched roofs." From: Mouhot, 156.

It is now "one of the most popular after-dark pastimes among the affluent, unmarried twenty to thirty something males of the country's larger towns." From: *The Observer*. "Sex Workers Helpless as Young Men 'Bond' in Gang Rape Outings." July 27, 2003.

Bauk is symptomatic of the country's larger mental-health crisis. From: Leakhena Nou.

When numbers go up, Srey Roth says, it means more people are seeking help. From: author interview. July 2003.

Nanda Pok, head of Women for Prosperity. From: author interview, Apr. 2002.

A woman turns herself in after accidentally killing her husband. From: The Associated Press. "Dies After Attack on Testicles." Aug. 29, 2003.

Without education, there is little chance ... says Koy Veth of Khmer Women's Voice Centre. From: author interview, May 2002.

"Every day is a battle." From: author interview, August 2003.

I return to CWCC to interview three women from the shelter. From: author interview, July 2003.

Chapter 13: Children: Born Against Odds

(I would like to thank Sok Chea, Ke Monin and Sachak and Samnang of *Mith Samlanh* for their help in translating for parts of this chapter.)

"We have an increase of about 20 percent..." says Friends Coordinator Sebastien Marot. From: author interview, July 2003.

A child born in Cambodia is born against odds. From: numerous sources. The Angkor Hospital for Children brochure; Population

Reference Bureau, www.prb.org, December 2002; Cambodia at a Glance, www.world-bank.org, Aug. 20, 2003; *Mith Samlanh*, "Drug Use and HIV Vulnerability," Phnom Penh.

But how, then, do we have American women facing federal charges. From: numerous sources. See Shukovsky, Paul, "Feds Claim Adopted 'Orphans' Had Parents, *Seattle Post-Intelligencer*, Dec. 17, 2003; Shukovsky, "Second Woman Is Charged in Cambodian Adoptions." *Seattle Post-Intelligencer*, Jan. 9, 2004.

"A cruel interruption of the journey to parenthood." From: *Boston Globe*. "Babies on Hold." Feb. 19, 2002, p. A 10.

"Key people ... child to die in Cambodia." John Ringo, *New York Post*, Jan. 4, 2002.

"We were strongly encouraged." From: emails to author, Apr. 2004.

Most of the money Westerners pay in adoption fees is unaccounted for. From: Bill Bainbridge. "International Adoptions to be 'a Last Resort.'" *Phnom Penh Post*. July 4–17, 2003.

Lauryn Galindo sentencing. From: "Woman Sentenced to 18 Months in Adoption Conspiracy," The Associated Press, Nov. 20, 2004.

Jerry and I first visit the Chea Sim Orphanage. From: author interviews and observations, May 2002 and Aug. 2003.

Cheth has no shoes. From: author interviews and observations, Aug. 2001 and May 2002.

Cambodian children must be saved. From: Laurence Gray. "Letting Children Live." *Bangkok Post*. Dec. 21, 2000.

Cambodia ... has 80,000 to 100,000 sex slaves. From: The Future Group. "The Future of Southeast Asia Challenges of Child Sex Slavery and Trafficking in Cambodia." Executive Summary. Aug. 22, 2001.

A new law allows Americans charged with sexually molesting children overseas to face trial in U.S. federal court. The first person ever charged under this law is a Seattle resident deported from Cambodia in September 2003 for alleged illegal sexual conduct with young boys. Two months later: another Seattle man deported, more accusations of illegal sex with boys. From: numerous sources. See Brooke, "Cambodia Battles Pedophiles by Deporting Them," *The New York Times*, Jan. 18, 2004; and *CNN.com*, "Guilty Plea in International Sex Abuse Case," Mar. 19, 2004.

"How can we turn away?" From: U.S. Secretary of State Colin Powell to NBC *Dateline* reporter Chris Hansen. From: *NBC Dateline*. "Children for Sale: Dateline Goes Undercover with a Human Rights Group to Expose Sex Trafficking in Cambodia." Jan. 23, 2004.

The U.S. State Department is giving World Vision $500,000 to fight these crimes in Thailand, Costa Rica and Cambodia. From: The Associated Press. "U.S. Tries to Combat Sexual Abuse of Kids." Dec. 17, 2003.

We meet a boy in 1998 named Cheth ... in Phnom Penh.... Hong Vicheth.... Sovann.... Pros. From: author interviews, 1998, 2003. Also from author observations, 2001–2003.

Almost 48 percent of Phnom Penh's street kids. From: *Mith Samlanh*.

Don't feed the street kids.... "There will be 140,000 orphans by 2005." From: author interview with Marot.

"If they are smoking or injecting, we don't disturb them." From: author interviews and observations, Sept. 2003.

[Cambodia] is ... "the perfect hunting ground for child traffickers." From: *BBC World*. "New Prosperity Threatens Children, UNICEF Warns. Dec. 5, 2001.

Thai authorities round up 142 Cambodian beggars. From: *Bangkok Post*. "Police to Deport 142 Cambodian Beggars." Aug. 7, 2001.

The Thai government transports more than 600 beggars ... to Cambodia. From: Tom Vater. "Winning Face with a Facelift." *Far Eastern Economic Review*. Oct. 16, 2003.

A baby sells for about $25; an older child $50. From: *Bangkok Post*. "Police Intercept Bus Load of Beggars." Feb. 12, 2004.

Director Mao Lang says this place opened in 1997. From: author interviews, Sept. 2003.

Chapter 14: Health

(Parts of this chapter originally appeared in *NurseWeek* magazine in 2001 and 2002.)

Cambodia is inflicted with "a growing burden of disease." From: Medecins Sans Frontieres. "Cambodia: A Growing Burden of Disease." MSF 2000 International Activity Report.

It always enumerated crushing raw facts such as these. From: numerous sources. See MSF, the World Bank, WHO, UN Commission on Human Rights, The Angkor Hospital for Children brochure, Population Reference Bureau, Cambodia at a Glance, *Mith Samlanh*.

There are 0.3 physicians for every 1,000 people. From: The World Bank Group Health and Nutrition Indicators, 2001. www.worldbank.org.

The beggar in that scene is ... San Dara.... Look again, and see Kiev Vin. From: author interviews, 2002.

"The health situation in Cambodia is still a catastrophe," says Dr. Beat Richner. From: the Kantha Bopha Hospital brochure and Dr. Richner's public performance, Aug. 2, 2003.

Many countries have banned ... chloramphenicol. From: several sources. See www. wws.princeton.edu, "Appendix A: Major Studies of Pharmaceutical Labeling in Developing Countries." And the WHO Model List of Essential Medicines, updated April 2003.

Angkor Hospital for Children. From: author interviews and observations, May–June 2002.

Dr. Puth Yeang practices medicine. From: author interviews, 1998.

Dengue fever ... infects more than 10,000 Cambodians a year. From: National Malaria Center. "Annual Progress Report 2002." Cambodian Ministry of Health. Jan.–Dec. 2002.

Malaria is even worse.... Dr. Nong Sao Kry ... has come to a sobering conclusion. From: author interview at the National Malaria Center, Aug. 2003.

The funds are in the budget.... But the money isn't in his hands. From: author interview with Nong Sao Kry and Halperin. "Health System Criticized for Fund Delays." *The Cambodia Daily.* July 29, 2003, p. 13.

By January 2004, there are 22 percent more vehicles on the road. From: Kay Kimsong and Daniel Ten Kate. "Bribes, Bad Driving Help Make Roads Deadly." *The Cambodia Daily.* Jan. 12, 2004, p. 1.

Dr. Svay Kamol estimates Phnom Penh alone needs five or six stations. From: a series of author interviews, observations and ride-alongs, Aug.–Sept. 2003 and follow-up, after service has ended, Jan. 2004.

AIDS has killed about 90,000 Cambodians since 1991. From: numerous sources. See Mukdawan Sakboon, "Between the Lines: Bitter Pill for Cambodian HIV/AIDS Patients." *The Nation*, Sept. 20, 2003; Meixner, Seth and Khieu Kola, "Falling AIDS Rate Offers Little Hope in AIDS Epidemic," *South China Morning Post*. Sept. 19, 2002; Lawrence K. Altman, "Spread of AIDS Fast Outpacing Response," *The New York Times*, Nov. 2, 2003; and Dominic Faulder, Webfiles: Cambodia's Next Killing Fields: AIDS Is Carrying Out the Work of Pol Pot, Nov. 28, 2001.

Dr. Sutthep Mak arrives at out hotel. From: author interview, Sept. 2003.

"In April 1975, when Pol Pot came to power, Battambang Hospital was abandoned, its equipment and research files destroyed and most of its staff murdered." From: Pilger, "A Faustian Pact," 243–44.

Chapter 15: Pollution

(Much of this chapter originally appeared in *The Cambodia Daily* in December 1998. Parts also appeared in the *San Jose Mercury News*, *Fresno Bee* and *The* (Roseburg, Oregon) *News-Review* in 1999. I would like to thank Kimsan Chantara, Sok Chea and Ke Monin for their help in translating.)

A woman rifles through pig fat. From: author observations of Stung Meanchey and interviews, Nov. 1998.

And pollution, in the broadest sense of the word — that which makes our environment unclean or impure — lurks as a fatal danger in Cambodia more than land mines or AIDS. From: numerous sources but largely from health statistics in United Nations Children's Fund (UNICEF), "Towards a Better Future: An Analysis of the Situation of Children and Women in Cambodia," Bangkok, 1996; and United Nations Population Fund (UNFPA), "The Environment and Development in Phnom Penh Literature Review," Phnom Penh, Nov. 1998. More recent numbers on respiratory diseases and other pollution-related illnesses have not decreased, while those for land mines and AIDS have (AIDS, because of the increasing death rate).

The problem is another lasting legacy of the Khmer Rouge. From: numerous sources. See UNFPA and Coren.

"In their overwhelming majority the rural settlers in Phnom Penh never became urbanized." From: Kamm, 6.

Every year, 13,000 Cambodians die of tuberculosis. From: UNICEF, 88.

Joel Vanderburg ... rattles off a wealth of information. From: author interview at the World Health Organization offices, 1998.

Dr. Phoeng Chhy Leang ... answers questions formally in his office. From: author interview at the Municipal Hospital, 1998.

Says Dr. Kaing Sor ... "The patients don't know about dirt, feces." From: author interview at Preah Bath Norodom Sihanouk Hospital, 1998.

Just 31 percent of Cambodians have access to clean water. From: numerous sources. See UNICEF; UNFPA; UN Commission on Human Rights, "E/CN.4/2001/NGO/63," Fifty-seventh session, Item 11(b) of the provisional agenda, "Health Care in Cambodia," Jan. 30, 2001.

"Ordinary toilets in Angkor were simple pits used until they were full and then covered over." From: Philpotts, 32.

Al Zanoni. From: author email interview, 1998.

PSBK. From: author interview and company report, 1998.

Thanksgiving morning 1998. From: author ride-along, observations and interviews 1998.

Beneath that bridge bubbles a dark brew of raw sewage. From: author interviews, 1998 and follow-up, 2003.

The ... mother sits on a bed at the National Pediatric Hospital. From: author interviews, 1998.

"The household environment is a dangerous environment." From: author interview with Jamie Meiklejohn, 1998.

"Peelings, stalks and skins were thrown back into the warter." From: Philpotts, 33.

Sanitation study in Pursat Province found "a near-total lack of awareness of the relationship between human waste disposal and excreta-related diseases." From: UNICEF, 73.

People appreciate the chance to live clean lives. From: author interview — at the World Health Organization offices, 1998.

Cambodians' thoughts on sanitation "were closely associated with tidiness." From UNICEF, 71.

"Health, Environment and Livelihood Project." From: CARE documents and author interviews, 1998.

Room T.09 in Preah Bath Norodom Sihanouk Hospital's tuberculosis ward. From: author interviews and observations, 1998.

Chapter 16: Environment

(Parts of this chapter originally appeared in *The Cambodia Daily*, May 1998; *BBC Wildlife*, May 2002; *National Wildlife*, March/April 2004; *Overseas Radio and Television*, 2002–2004; *Archaeology*, September/October 2002. I would like to thank Van Roeun, Kimsan Chantara, Lor Chandara, Morn Sor, Heng Sovannara, Sam Kim Lorn and Em Huy for their help.)

Epigraph for chapter 16 taken from: Mouhot, 183.

Reports start to trickle out of the Cardamom Mountains. From: numerous sources. See Fauna and Flora International, "A Lost World of Wildlife," Sept. 11, 2000; Kay Johnson, "The Mountains That Time Forgot," *Time*, Sept. 11, 2000, Vol. 156, No. 10; Brian Mockenhaupt, "Into the Mist: Journey Into the Primeval," *The Cambodia Daily*, Mar. 25–26, 2000. Also, author interviews with Joe Walston, 2001.

"One has to expect that on the whole the overall conditions are going to get worse." From: author interview with Joe Walston, Sept. 2003.

"The entrance to the great lake of Cambodia is grand and beautiful." From: Mouhot, 211.

Cambodia's great Tonle Sap is its lifeblood. From: numerous sources. See Yim Chea and Bruce McKenney, "Great Lake Fish Exports: An Analysis of the Fee System," *Cambodia Development Review*, July–Sept. 2003, Vol. 7, Issue 3; Oxfam America, "Keeping Community Fisheries Afloat in Cambodia," www.oxfamamerica.org/advocacy/art6783.html, Feb. 3, 2004; and the Alliance of Democrats, "Fisheries and Food Security: Corruption and Anarchy Kill the Nation in Slow Motion," Dec. 22, 2003.

Cambodians capture the world's fourth-highest number of freshwater fish each year, at 300,000 to 400,000 tons. From: Yim Chea and Bruce McKenney.

"Certainly a riverside city at this position could never have reached the size and splendour that the Cambodian capital had." From: Philpotts, 21–22.

China already has built two dams on the Mekong. From: numerous sources. See: Mydans, "Where a Lake Is Life Itself, Dam Is a Dire Word," *The New York Times*, April 28, 2003, p. A4; and Poona Antaseeda, "Mekong Yielding Diminishing Returns," *Bangkok Post*, Perspective, Jan. 26, 2003; and Lor Chandara. "Drought Leaves Rice Fields, Farmers Thirsty." *The Cambodia Daily*. April 1, 2004, p. 11.

The four countries ... plan to blast through ... Mekong rapids. From: several sources. See *Bangkok Post*. "Mekong River Project: Experts from Four Nations to Review Rapids Blasting Plan." June 9, 2003.

The population of the lower Mekong. From: numerous sources. See Joern Kristensen. "The Mekong Can Become Many Rivers in One." *International Herald Tribune*. July 31, 2001.

"The pressure on natural resources will increase dramatically, as will the demand for additional food, water and energy." From: Kristensen.

"But except from the fishermen and a few environmentalists, there is no cry of alarm along the Mekong about the decline of fish in the river." From: Poona Antaseeda.

It's a political issue. From: McKenney.

Prek Toal. From: author trip, interviews and observations, 1998. Further information on Prek Toal and fishing: Yim Chea and Bruce McKenney; Oxfam America; and Ministry of Agriculture, Forestry and Fisheries. "The major activities and action plan of good governance in fisheries sector." www.maff.gov.kh/e-library/ camfishGAP.PDF. Jan. 11, 2002.

"Everywhere were felled trees." From: Bourdain, 183.

Economics of logging. From: author interview with Bruce McKenney at The Cambodia Development Resource Institute, August 2003, and: McKenney. "Questioning Sustainable Concession Forestry in Cambodia." *Cambodia Development Review*. Jan.–Mar. 2002, Vol. 6, Issue 1.

Much of Cambodia's forest destruction is illegal. From: Robert Evans. "Illegal Timber Trade Undermines Cambodia-UN Aide." Reuters. Apr. 7, 2003.

Global Witness is Cambodia's official forest watchdog. From: numerous sources. See BBC News *World Edition*. "Cambodia Ditches Logging Watchdog." Jan. 29, 2003.

Va has recently retired from driving a logging truck. From: author interview, Aug. 2003.

"Cambodia is one of the last strongholds," says Joe Walston. From: author interviews, July 2003.

"A preacher's paradise." From: numerous sources. See: Susan Postlewaite. "A Poacher's Paradise in Cambodia." *San Francisco Chronicle*. Jan. 31, 2001.

"Here, shoals of porpoises sail along with their noses to the wind, frequently bounding out of the water." From: Mouhot, 173.

The fisheries department and dolphin project. From: author trip, interviews and observations, Aug. 2001 and follow-up email interviews in 2002.

In the first three months of 2004, eight dolphins are found dead. From: Solana Pyne and Van Roeun. "Eight Rare Dolphins Die In Mekong." *The Cambodia Daily*. Apr. 5, 2004, p. 1.

"How do we both conserve ... and help the people." From: author interview, Aug. 2003.

"Communities will often choose a different lifestyle than they've had previously." From: author interview with Walston, Aug. 2003.

Batagur baska disappeared from Cambodia.... [A] small colony is found. From: author trip and interviews, May 2002, follow-up email interviews early 2003, in-person interview with Heng Sovannara, Aug. 2003.

Chapter 17: The Fringe

(Parts of the following chapter appear in *Wildlife Conservation* in May 2004, as well as in Overseas Radio & Television publications in Taiwan. The author would like to thank Ma Anou, Ramlee, Sok Chea, Ke Monin, Tom Evans, Phet Phaktra, Hout Piseth and Hang Mary for their help as well as the other WCS team members in Mondulkiri.)

Cambodia is the most homogeneous society in Southeast Asia. Ninety-five percent of the population is ethnic Khmer. From: *Who's Who*, 29.

The *chun chiet*.... Some Cham Muslims. From: numerous sources. See *Who's Who*, Becker, Shawcross.

"The ancestors of the dark-skinned Khmer Loeu were among the slaves named 'dog,' 'cat,' and 'detestable,'" From: Becker, 108.

During Pol Pot times, both Muslim Chams and Khmer Loeu were targeted and swiftly expunged. From: numerous sources. See Becker, 153, 251, 243.

The trees, six different types ... grow tall and wide. From: a week-long author trip, with a team from the Wildlife Conservation Society. This section is based on that week's experiences, observations and interviews. For further information on the Phnong or resin-tapping, see: Tom D. Evans, Hout Piseth, Phet Phaktra, and Hang Mary, "A Study of Resin-Tapping and Livelihoods in Southern Mondulkiri, Cambodia, with Implications for Conservation and Forest Management," A Wildlife Conservation Society Report, 2003; Ian G. Baird and Philip Dearden, "Biodiversity Conservation and Resource Tenure Regimes— A Case Study from Northeast Cambodia," Submitted to *Environmental Management*, Aug. 2002; and Baird and Somphong Bounphasy, "Non-Timber Forest Product Use, Management and Tenure in Pathoumphone District, Champasak Province, Southern Laos," Remote Village Education Support Project, Global Association for People and the Environment, Pakse, Lar, Jan. 2003.

"That rhythmic thud of the pestle and mortar was like a heartbeat on the river." From: Theroux, p. 146.

They ... close the private Om Al Qura Institute. From: many sources, including author interviews. See: Reuters. "Cambodia Shuts Muslim School, Thais Watch Militants." May 29, 2003.

Hambali ... arrested in Thailand. From: many sources. See: Kevin Doyle and Phann Ana. "Hambali Left Gentle Impression on Phnom Penh." *The Cambodia Daily*. Aug. 22, 2003, p. 1.

Cambodian officials refuse to discuss the situation. From: author attempted interviews at the Ministry of Cults and Religion and the Interior Ministry, Sept. 2003.

They arrange meetings … in Kompong Ch'hnang Province. From: author excursion and interviews, July 2003.

Om Al Qura School stands barren and quiet. From: author excursion and interviews, Aug. 2003.

About twenty Cham families live on … Chruoy Changvar Peninsula. From: author interviews, Jan. 2004.

III: LOOKING AHEAD

Chapter 18: The Crossroads

(I would like to thank Sok Chea for his help in translating.)

DJ Lux, a protégé of … DJ Cake. From: author interviews and observations, Aug. 2003.

Half the population is under eighteen. From: numerous sources. See *Who's Who*, 25.

"I don't really know what really happened to the old generation except that they told us there was a lot of killings, hardships." From: Miranda Leitsinger. "Cambodia's Younger Generation Cares Little for the Khmer Rouge, Looks to the Future." The Associated Press. Jan. 4, 2004.

"The population is … changing," says Mu Sochua. From: author interview, Aug. 2003.

Their teacher is a princess, Bopha Devi. From: author interview and observations, Aug. 2003.

"We even lost faith in Buddhism," Youk Chhang. From: author interview, Aug. 2003.

Som Tok La, the daughter of … artist Som Bon. From: author interview, Sept. 2003.

The Venerable Muny Van Saveth … is a visionary. From: author interview, Sept. 2003.

Several times we try to find someone at the Ministry of Cults and Religion. From: several author attempted interviews and phone calls, Sept. 2003.

A ceremony at an orphanage … run by Bernie Krisher. From: public ceremony and author observations, Jan. 1999.

Chapter 19: Development

(A portion of this chapter originally appeared in *Archaeology* in 2002.)

The average income is $280 a year, and 80 percent of the population lives in the country-

side. From: numerous sources. See Cambodia at a Glance, www.worldbank.org.

Cambodia's rice production lags behind its neighbors. From: numerous sources. See Halperin. "Future Farmers: Can Cambodian Rice Ever Make It in the World?" *The Cambodia Daily*. Sept. 6–7, 2003, p. 6. And *Who's Who*, Economic Environment.

They buy pesticides banned in the rest of the world but dumped in places like this, where law enforcement is nil. From: numerous sources. See Cynthia Phoel. "Pesticides in Cambodia: A Growing Problem." *Oxfam Exchange*, May 2003.

They don't know because they can't read. From: numerous sources on literacy rate. See Media Business Networks, 56.

They can't afford to pay their hospital bills, so they borrow from rich land owners. From: numerous sources and author interviews. See Biddulph, Robin. "Landlessness: A Growing Problem." *Cambodia Development Review*. Sept. 2000, Vol. 4, Issue 3.

They're malnourished, as are their kids. From: numerous sources and author interviews, including several at the Angkor Hospital for Children in and the Transcultural Psychosocial Organization in Battambang in 2002.

Even if they could, the kids wouldn't go to school. From: numerous sources and author interviews, including with Koy Veth of the Khmer Women's Voice Centre. See also: William Shaw and Kuch Naren. "In Preah Vihear, Some Prefer Schools in Laos." *The Cambodia Daily*. Aug. 18, 2003, p. 1.

The teachers themselves have poor educations. From: numerous sources, including author interview with Dr. Sorn Samnang at the Royal Academy of Cambodia, Jan. 2004.

Cambodians who go to school learn to memorize but don't learn critical thinking. They don't learn to see the connections in the world around them, which is such a critical skill when trying to fix a broken country. From: numerous author interviews, including one with a Khmer American artist, 2003.

Or they leave the government and work for high-paying NGOs. From: numerous author interviews and sources, including from university student Sok Chea.

Teachers are paid an appallingly low salary, sometimes $15 or $20 a month. From: numerous sources and author interviews with dozens of teachers.

A CDRI study follows one shipment of fish. From: numerous author interviews, observations and experiences. See Yim Chea and McKenney.

The Cambodian government collects next to

nothing in income taxes. From: numerous sources. See *Who's Who* on Economics.

There is no working judicial system.... There is street justice. From: numerous sources. See sources in violence chapter.

The kids on the street have no choice. From: numerous sources and author interviews, including Marot and the Friends Outreach Team.

Youngsters grow up in families with mental illness. From: numerous sources, including author interviews with TPO, Kang Om, Ang Sody.

They take drugs.... They get HIV. From: numerous sources. See *Mith Samlanh*.

Why should the government solve its own problems when foreigners can? From: numerous sources, observations and author interviews, including with Marot, McKenney and Haji Adam bin Ali.

Or at least, that's what many derive from the tenets of Buddhism. From: numerous author interviews and observations. See Seanglim Bit; Mont Redmond, *Wondering Into Thai Culture*. Bangkok: Redmondian Insight Enterprises Co., Ltd., 1998.

Only now ... are people learning about ... human rights. From: several sources, including author email interview with Mydans.

Cambodia has just joined the World Trade Organization. From: many sources. See: *The Cambodia Daily*, Sept. 6–7, Weekend Edition on the WTO; James Brooke, "Cambodia Is Working to Escape its Past," *The New York Times*, Feb. 25, 2004; Phelim Kyne. "WTO May Deliver Justice Denied at Ballot Box." *The Asian Wall Street Journal*. July 24, 2003, p. A7.

A big national debt. From: www.mekong-capital.com and Patrick Falby, "Questions Over Repaying Cambodia's Debt," *Phnom Penh Post*, Aug. 29–Sept. 11, 2003, p. 7.

The garment industry accounts for 90 percent of Cambodia's light industry. From: *Who's Who*, on Economics and *The Cambodia Daily* WTO edition.

They point to an economy growing at 5 percent a year. From: *Who's Who* on Economy.

Cambodia still takes in ... foreign aid. From: Brooke. "Cambodia Is Working to Escape Its Past."

And despite all that, all the international aid, all the donors, all the attention, Cambodia has had for a decade, more than a third of the population still lives below the poverty line. From: numerous sources. See: Alliance of Democrats letter to World Bank President James Wolfensohn. Feb. 11, 2004; *Who's Who* on Household Income; Kyne.

Poverty line ... is about 46 cents a day. From:

Asian Development Bank, "Poverty Consultants for ADB Cambodia Resident Mission." www.adb.org/documents/PRF/cam/poverty-con sultants.asp.

"Here they gain by begging; they are licensed beggars.... The more you give, the less strict the search will be." From: Mouhot, 129.

Cambodia, as a nation, has become an "international beggar." From: King Norodom Sihanouk, "Cambodia Is an International Beggar." *Koh Santepheap Daily*. Aug. 28, 2003.

"The poverty of the inhabitants of these miserable villages engenders a repulsive dirtiness: a strip of matting or an old filthy cushion thrown on the ground, and full of vermin, some basins of coarse Chinese porcelain, a sort of hatchet, and a piece of cotton ... are the usual contents of a Cambodian hut." From: Mouhot, 179.

"I hadn't seen a single house, not a single building with what could be called walls, not a TV aerial, not a power or phone line in hours. We could have been traveling up the same body of water a thousand years ago, with no discernible difference." From Bourdain, 175.

"Waste-disposal education is practically non-existent in Phnom Penh.... Cambodia currently has no Ministry or Government Department of Housing, no housing policy document, and no substantial housing developer." From United Nations Population Fund (UNFPA).

"Here are millions of unhappy creatures in great poverty in the midst of the richest and most fertile region imaginable; bowing shamefully under a servile yoke made viler by despotism and the most barbarous customs." From: Mouhot, 121.

"Today's Cambodia is a basket case." From: Kamm, 248.

"Functionally literate people make up only 37 percent of Cambodia's adult population." From: United Nations Development Programme (UNDP). "Second Country Cooperation Framework for Cambodia, 2001–2005."

In early 2004, I meet Dr. Sorn Samnang. From: author interview, Jan. 2004.

Less than 5 percent of fifteen-year-olds stay in school. From: *Mith Samlanh*, p. 11.

The United States entangled Cambodia in its war with Vietnam. From: numerous sources. See Becker, 16–17, 437, 446–447; Shawcross, the whole book, but especially p. 19–35.

I visit Chuch Phoeurn. From: author interview, May 2002.

Additional reading on Cambodia's transitional state: Macan-Markar. "UN's Cambodian 'Success' in Question." Inter Press Service. Feb. 7, 2004.

Interlude: Cops and Dogs

"Dog meat is delicious." From: *The Cambodia Daily*, Sept. 11, 2003, p. 11.

Chapter 20: Heroes

Rith and LC. From: author interviews and observations, 2001–2003.
Aki Ra. From: author interviews, Apr. 2002.
Boun Mao. From: author interviews, 2002.
Ly Chheng Ky. From: author interviews, Apr. 2002.
Muny Van Saveth. From: author interviews, May 2002, Sept. 2003.
Two girls. From: author interviews at Cambodian Women's Crisis Center, July 2003.

Chapter 21. Prospects

Epigraph for chapter 21 taken from: Mouhot, 211.
"Nothing would be straightforward about the Cambodian war or revolution." From: Becker, 118.

"Cambodia, I fear, is past helping itself." From: Kamm, 251.
"Time is passing. The wounds are less raw." From: author email interview with Mydans, Sept. 2003.
"That suffering would flower into purity, out of the anguish of history.... A new world must be born." From: Colin Thubron. *In Siberia*. London: Chatto & Windus, 1999, p. 11.
A gunman approached the country's top labor union leader. From: numerous sources. See Jim Lobe. "Cambodian Unionist's Killing Stirs Up Hornets' Nest." *Asia Times OnLine*. Jan. 26, 2004.

Timeline

1992. Its many-fold mission is to resettle 350,000 refugees.... From: Becker, 506.
1993. After losing the election, Hun Sen.... From: Becker, 514.
1997. The move is widely seen as a *coup d'état*,.... From: Mehtas, 118, taken from a 1998 *Phnom Penh Post* article.

Selected Bibliography

A note on author names: Many Asians use their family name first and given name second. I have left that name order intact, except where the author is commonly identified in bibliographies in the Western style.

Books

Anderson, Liz. *Red Lights and Green Lizards: A Cambodian Adventure*. Bangkok: White Lotus, 1999.

Becker, Elizabeth. *When the War Was Over: Cambodia and the Khmer Rouge Revolution*. New York: PublicAffairs, 1998.

Bekaert, Jacques. *Cambodian Diary Vol. 2: A Long Road to Peace, 1987–1993*. Bangkok: White Lotus, 1998.

Bingham, Robert. *Lightning on the Sun*. New York: Doubleday, 2000.

Bit, Seanglim. *The Warrior Heritage: A Psychological Perspective of Cambodian Trauma*. El Cerrito, Cal.: Seanglim Bit, 1991.

Bizot, François. *The Gate*. New York: Alfred A. Knopf, 2003.

Bourdain, Anthony. *A Cook's Tour: Global Adventures in Extreme Cuisines*. New York: HarperCollins, 2001.

Chanda, Nayan. *Brother Enemy: The War After the War*. New York: Macmillan, 1986.

Chandler, David. *Brother Number One: A Political Biography of Pol Pot*, Rev. Ed. Chiang Mai, Thailand: Silkworm Books, 2000.

_____. *Voices from S-21: Terror and History in Pol Pot's Secret Prison*. Berkeley, Los Angeles and London: University of California Press, 1999.

_____. *Facing the Cambodian Past*. Chiang Mai, Thailand: Silkworm Books, 1996.

Dagens, Bruno. *Angkor: Heart of an Asian Empire*. New York: Harry N. Abrams, 1995.

Fifield, Adam. *A Blessing Over Ashes: The Remarkable Odyssey of My Unlikely Brother*. New York: William Morrow, 2000.

Gourevitch, Philip. *We Wish to Inform You That Tomorrow We Will Be Killed with Our Families: Stories from Rwanda*. New York: Picador, 1998.

Him, Chanrithy. *When Broken Glass Floats: Growing Up Under the Khmer Rouge*. New York: W.W. Norton, 2000.

Hitchens, Christopher. *The Trial of Henry Kissinger*. New York: Verso Books, 2002.

Hogg, Ian. *Jane's Guns Recognition Guide*. Glasgow: HarperCollins, 2002.

Jacobson, Matt, and Frank Visakay. *Adventure Cambodia: An Explorer's Travel Guide*. Bangkok: Silkworm Books, 2001.

Kamm, Henry. *Cambodia: Report from a Stricken Land*. New York: Arcade, 1998.

Kapuscinski, Ryszard. *Imperium*. New York: Vintage International, 1994.

Kundera, Milan. *Life Is Elsewhere*. London: Faber and Faber, 1986.

Lafreniere, Bree. *Music Through the Dark: A Tale of Survival in Cambodia*. Honolulu: University of Hawaii Press, 2000.

Media Business Networks and Promo-Khmer.

Who's Who in Cambodia Business Reference Book 2003–2004. Men S. Narong, Editor. Phnom Penh: 2003.

Mehta, Harish C., and Julie B. Mehta. *Hun Sen: Strongman of Cambodia.* Singapore: Graham Brash, 1999.

Mouhot, Henri. *Travels in Siam, Cambodia, Laos, and Annam.* Bangkok: White Lotus, 2000.

Murray, Stephen O. *Angkor Life: Pre-Cambodian Life 800 Years Ago in the Society That Created the Stupendous Monuments of Angkor Wat and Angkor Thom.* San Francisco: Bua Luang Books, 1996.

Nath, Vann. *A Cambodian Prison Portrait: One Year in the Khmer Rouge's S-21.* Bangkok: White Lotus, 1998.

Nisbett, Richard E. *The Geography of Thought: How Asians and Westerners Think Differently ... and Why.* New York: The Free Press, 2003.

Osborne, Milton. *The Mekong: Turbulent Past, Uncertain Future.* New York: Atlantic Monthly Press, 2000.

Philpotts, Robert. *Reporting Angkor: Chou Ta-Kuan in Cambodia 1296–1297.* London: Blackwater Books, 1996.

Pilger, John. *Distant Voices.* London: Vintage, 1992.

Pran, Dith, and Kim DePaul. *The Children of Cambodia's Killing Fields: Memoirs of Survivors.* New Haven, Conn.: Yale University Press, 1999.

Ray, Nick. *Cambodia.* Melbourne, Oakland, London, Paris: Lonely Planet, 2000.

Redmond, Mont. *Wondering Into Thai Culture.* Bangkok: Redmondian Insight Enterprises, 1998.

Robbins, Christopher. *The Ravens: The Men Who Flew in America's Secret War in Laos.* New York: Crown, 1987.

Rooney, Dawn. *A Guide to Angkor: An Introduction to the Temples.* Hong Kong: The Guidebook Company, 1994.

Schanberg, Sydney H. *The Death and Life of Dith Pran.* New York: Penguin Books, 1985.

Shawcross, William. *Sideshow: Kissinger, Nixon and the Destruction of Cambodia.* London: The Hogarth Press, 1993.

Solomon, Andrew. *The Noonday Demon: An Atlas of Depression.* New York, London, Toronto, Sydney, Singapore: Simon & Schuster, 2001.

Streed, Sarah. *Leaving the House of Ghosts: Cambodian Refugees in the American Midwest.* Jefferson, N.C.: McFarland, 2002.

Stuart, Bryan L., Peter Paul van Dijk, and Douglas B. Hendrie. *Photographic Guide to the Turtles of Thailand, Laos, Vietnam and Cambodia.* Phnom Penh: Wildlife Conservation Society, 2001.

Theroux, Paul. *Fresh Air Fiend: Travel Writings 1985–2000.* New York: Houghton Mifflin, 2000.

Thubron, Colin. *In Siberia.* London: Chatto & Windus, 1999.

Ung, Loung. *First They Killed My Father: A Daughter of Cambodia Remembers.* New York: HarperCollins, 2000.

Articles and Reports

ABC Radio Australia News. "Hundreds of Illegal Settlers Evicted from Cambodian Dump Site." Aug. 7, 2003.

Agence France-Presse. "Limousines and Poverty: Hun Sen Goes on Electioneering." June 5, 2003.

_____. "US Probe Castigates Cambodia Over Thai riots." May 12, 2003.

_____. "Cambodian Elections Neither Free Nor Fair: US Monitor." Feb. 6, 2002.

_____. "Cambodian Women Cut Off Rapist's Penis." Aug. 25, 2000.

Aglionby, John. "Pol Pot's Soldiers Escape Justice for Genocide." *The Guardian.* London. Aug. 5, 2003.

_____. "Cambodia's Forgotten Temples Fall Prey to Looters." *The Guardian.* London. July 31, 2003.

_____. "Sex Workers Helpless as Young Men 'Bond' in Gang Rape Outings." *The Observer.* London. July 27, 2003.

_____. "Broken Silence: Sick of the Devastation Caused by Illegal Logging, Local Communities in Southeast Asia Are Beginning to Fight back." *The Guardian.* Oct. 3, 2001.

Alliance of Democrats. "Open Letter to World Bank President James Wolfensohn." Feb. 11, 2004.

_____. "Fisheries and Food Security: Corruption and Anarchy Kill the Nation in Slow Motion." Dec. 22, 2003.

Altman, Lawrence K. "Spread of AIDS Fast Outpacing Response." *The New York Times.* Nov. 26, 2003.

Amat, Frederic. "Artifact Repatriation: Whose Culture, Whose Treasure?" *Global Heritage Fund in the News.* Apr. 6, 2001.

Arthurs, Clare. "Violence Haunts Cambodian Polls." BBC News. Mar. 6, 2003.

Asia Watch, Physicians for Human Rights. "Land Mines in Cambodia: The Coward's War." Sept. 1991.

The Asian Wall Street Journal. "Cambodia's Quest for Justice." Review & Outlook (editorial). Feb. 14, 2002.

_____. "Cambodia's Third Flawed Election." Review & Outlook. Feb. 4, 2002.

The Associated Press. "U.N.: Conditions Better at Cambodia Plaints." Apr. 9, 2004.

_____. "Three Killed in Cambodia Mortar Accident." *The Cambodia Daily.* Mar. 12, 2004.

_____. "Khmer Rouge's Brother No. 2 Says He Will Face Tribunal." Jan. 18, 2004.

_____. "U.S. Tries to Combat Sexual Abuse of Kids." Dec. 17, 2003.

_____. "Dies After Attack on Testicles." Aug. 29, 2003.

_____. "Pol Pot's First Wife Cremated in Ritual." July 3, 2003.

_____. "Christie Whitman to Lead Observers Monitoring Cambodian Elections." June 23, 2003.

_____. "Judge in Khmer Rouge Chief's Trial Shot Dead." Apr. 24, 2003.

_____. "Fourth Cambodian Politician Attacked in a Week." Feb. 23, 2003.

_____. Advisor to Cambodia's Royalist Party Shot to Death." Feb. 18, 2003.

_____. "Cambodia Skull Map Dismantled." Mar. 10, 2002.

_____. "Cambodian General Ke Pauk Dies; Led Khmer Rouge Mass Killings." *Washington Post,* Feb. 16, 2002, p. B06.

_____. "Cambodian Monitors Site Vote-Buying." Feb. 13, 2002.

_____. "Ruling Party Sweeps Vote in Cambodia." Feb. 5, 2002.

_____. "Visas for Adopted Cambodian Children." Dec. 29, 2001.

_____. "Baby-selling Fear Puts Adoptions on Hold." Dec. 24, 2001.

_____. "Bomb Blasts in Cambodia Hotels." July 4, 2001.

Baird, Ian G., and Philip Dearden. "Biodiversity Conservation and Resource Tenure Regimes—A Case Study from Northeast Cambodia." Submitted to *Environmental Management.* Aug. 2002.

_____, and Somphong Bounphasy. "Non-Timber Forest Product Use, Management and Tenure in Pathoumphone District, Champasak Province, Southern Laos." Remote Village Education Support Project, Global Association for People and the Environment, Pakse, Lao.

Baker, Mark. "Calling to Account: Khmer Rouge Prosecutions May Deal with Cambodia's Past But Will Not Solve Its Problems Today." *The Age* (Melbourne). Jan. 10, 2004.

Ballard, Brett M. "Employment and Trade in Angkor Park: Some Preliminary Observations on the Impact of Tourism." *Cambodia Development Review.* Jan.–Mar. 2003, Vol. 7, Issue 1, pp. 5–7, 16.

Bangkok Post. "Police Intercept Bus Load of Beggars." Feb. 12, 2004.

_____. "Khmer Border: Youngsters on Drug Treks." July 5, 2003.

_____. "Khmer Scavengers Nabbed." June 20, 2003.

_____. "Mekong River Project: Experts from Four Nations to Review Rapids Blasting Plan." June 9, 2003.

_____. "Human Trafficking Takes Horrific Toll." May 9, 2003.

_____. "Acid Becomes the Weapon of Choice." Feb. 19, 2003.

_____. "Borderless Tourist Spot Will Be Rich in Beauty, Khmer Culture." Feb. 27, 2002.

_____. "Police to Deport 142 Cambodian Beggars." Aug. 7, 2001.

Barber, Jason. "Torture in Cambodia: A Licadho Project against Torture Report." Licadho. June 2000.

Barboza, David. "Children Scavenge a Life, of Sorts, at Asian Dump." *The New York Times.* Aug. 25, 2003, p. A4.

_____. "Cambodian Ire Hurts Thai Interests." *The New York Times.* Apr. 19, 2003.

Barnes, William. "UN Says Khmer Rouge Leaders to Stand Trial Soon." *Financial Times.* Dec. 19, 2003.

BBC Monitoring Service. "Cambodia Wants National Court to Try Khmer Rouge — Official." United Kingdom. Feb. 14, 2002.

BBC World. "New Prosperity Threatens Children, UNICEF Warns. Dec. 5, 2001.

Beard, Matthew. "Banned Pesticides Poisoning Millions." *The Independent.* London. Feb. 27, 2003.

Becker, Elizabeth. "Khieu Ponnary, 83, First Wife of Pol Pot, Cambodian Despot, Dies." *The New York Times.* July 3, 2003, p. A20.

Beech, Hannah. "Stealing Beauty." *Time.* Oct. 20, 2003.

Biddulph, Robin. "Landlessness: A Growing Problem." *Cambodia Development Review.* Sept. 2000, Vol. 4, Issue 3.

Bjornlund, Eric. "Democracy Inc." *The Wilson Quarterly.* Woodrow Wilson International Center for Scholars. Summer 2001.

Boggan, Steve. "Nike Admits to Mistakes Over Child Labor." *The Independent.* London. Oct. 20, 2001.

Borton, James. "Fund Banks on Mekong Region's Success." *Asia Times OnLine.* July 1, 2003.

Boston Globe. "Babies on Hold." Feb. 19, 2002, p. A 10.

Boyd, Alan. "The Heavy Price of WTO Membership." *Asia Times OnLine.* Sept. 29, 2003.

Brooke, James. "Cambodia is Working to Escape Its Past." *The New York Times.* Feb. 25, 2004.

_____. "A Year of Worry for Cambodia's Garment Makers." *The New York Times.* Jan. 24, 2004.

_____. "Cambodia Battles Pedophiles by Deporting Them." *The New York Times.* Jan. 18, 2004.

Brown, Samantha. "Khmer Rouge Tribunal to Cost Around 50 Million Dollars: UN." Agence France-Presse. Mar. 18, 2004.

Calingaert, Daniel. "Prospects for a Democratic Election in Cambodia." Statement to the Subcommittee on East Asia and the Pacific House International Relations Committee. June 10, 2003.

Cambodge Soir. "Anlong Kong vide de ses habitants." July 29, 2003, p. 12.

The Cambodia Daily. "Girl, 10, Is Raped, Killed." Feb. 24, 2004, p. 13.

_____. "Group Releases Report Detailing Land Mines." Sept. 12, 2003, p. 11.

_____. "Shell Blast Kills Five." Sept. 9, 2003, p. 17.

_____. "Hospitalized Soldiers Ask Gov't for Relief." Aug. 27, 2003, p. 16.

_____. "Vietnam Deports More Than 200 Cambodians." Aug. 26, 2003, p. 13.

_____. "Buried Mortar Shell Found in School Kitchen." July 10, 2003, p. 11.

Chachavalpongpun, Pavin. "Khmers Still Enslaved by Their Misfortunes." *The Nation* (Bangkok). Nov. 26, 2003, p. 5A.

Chinvarakorn, Vasana. "Cambodia Faces New Enemy." *Bangkok Post.* Dec. 12, 2000.

Chhay Sophal. "Cambodian Monitors Issue Warning for 2003 Vote." Reuters. Feb. 12, 2002.

Clover, Charles. "Creatures of a Lost World Found in Valley." *Daily Telegraph.* London. Sept. 28, 2000.

CNN.com. "Guilty Plea in International Sex Abuse Case." Mar. 19, 2004.

Coren, Michael. "The Poor Still Battle for Land Rights." *Phnom Penh Post.* Aug. 29–Sept. 11, 2003, p. 5.

Crampton, Thomas. "Cambodia to Restore Khmer Rouge Sites." *International Herald Tribune.* Aug. 20, 2003.

Dalpino, Catharin E. "Democracy Gains a Foothold in Cambodia." *The Japan Times.* Mar. 23, 2002.

Deane, Claudia, and Richard Morin. "Rand Urges World Focus on Land Mines." *The Washington Post.* Feb. 18, 2003, p. A23.

Decherd, Chris. "Wild Elephant Catchers Are a Dying Breed in Cambodia." The Associated Press. Aug. 17, 2003.

_____. "US Ambassador to Cambodia Ridicules Government Denial of Political Killings in Election Campaign." The Associated Press. Feb. 7, 2002.

_____. "1st Ever Electoral Debate in Cambodia." The Associated Press. Jan. 21, 2002.

_____. "Starving Cambodians Sell Babies." The Associated Press. Feb. 10, 2001.

Deutsche Presse-Agentur. "Four Men Open Fire on Cambodian Premier's Nephew." Dec. 18, 2001.

_____. "Cambodia Announces 3-Million-Dollar Upgrade for Temple Tourism." May 4, 2000.

Dobbs, Leo. "Better Than No Polls at All." *Far Eastern Economic Review*. Feb. 7, 2002. Vol. 165, No. 5, pp. 24–26.

Documentation Center of Cambodia. "Report in Brief." Oct. 2001–Mar. 2002.

Doyle, Kevin, and Phann Ana. "Hambali Left Gentle Impression on Phnom Penh." *The Cambodia Daily*. Aug. 22, 2003, p. 1.

Drillbits & Tailings. "Ruby Fever Engulfs Cambodia's Old Killing Fields." Feb. 7, 1999, p. 4.

The Economist. "Pol Pot's Deputy in Court." Dec. 19, 2002.

Ehrlich, Richard S. "Hun Sen Favored, But Security on Voters' Minds." *The Washington Times*. July 22, 2003.

Evans, Robert. "Illegal Timber Trade Undermines Cambodia-UN Aide." Reuters. Apr. 7, 2003.

Evans, Tom D., Hout Piseth, Phet Phaktra, and Hang Mary. "A Study of Resin-Tapping and Livelihoods in Southern Mondulkiri, Cambodia, with Implications for Conservation and Forest Management." A Wildlife Conservation Society report.

Falby, Patrick. "Cambodia Cashes in on Grim Past." BBC News. Sept. 12, 2003.

_____. "Questions Over Repaying Cambodia's Debt." *Phnom Penh Post*. Aug. 29–Sept. 11, 2003, p. 7.

Far Eastern Economic Review. "No-Show: What's Hampering Governance in Cambodia." Oct. 9, 2003, editorial.

_____. "Cambodian, and Proud of It." May 22, 2003, Vol. 166, No. 20, p. 9.

Faulder, Dominic. Webfiles: Cambodia's Next Killing Fields: AIDS Is Carrying Out the Work of Pol Pot. Nov. 28, 2001.

Fauna & Flora International. "A Lost World of Wildlife." Sept. 11, 2000.

Fawthrop, Tom. "The Country Goes to the Polls July 27. The Real Test of Democracy Comes When the Results Are In." *Far Eastern Economic Review*. July 24, 2003.

_____. "Anger in Phnom Penh over Governor's Sacking." *The Straits Times*. Singapore. Feb. 12, 2003.

_____. "Angkor Strains: Cambodian Temples Creaking Under Weight of Tourist Invasion." *The Straits Times*. Singapore. Mar. 11, 2002.

_____. "The Khmer Rouge Tour." *The Straits Times*. Singapore. Mar. 5, 2002.

Frankel, Rafael D. "For Cambodia, It's Time to Look Ahead — and Back." *Chicago Tribune*. July 7, 2003.

The Future Group. "The Future of Southeast Asia Challenges of Child Sex Slavery and Trafficking in Cambodia." Executive Summary. Aug. 22, 2001.

Gagliardi, Jason. "The Roads to Ruins: Will Improved Access Despoil Angkor's Monuments?" *Time Asia*. May 19, 2003, Vol. 161, No. 19.

Ganjanakhundee, Supalak. "Washington Frowns on Cambodians' Repatriation." *The Nation*. Bangkok. Oct. 7, 2003.

Gittings, John. "Living with the Buddhas of Angkor." *The Guardian*. London. Aug. 7, 2001.

Global Witness. "Global Witness Investigators Could Face Two-Year Prison Sentence." Press release. Jan. 27, 2001.

_____. "Malaysian Loggers in Cambodia Threaten Proposed Cardamom Mountain Reserve." Press release. June 8, 2000.

Goodspeed, Peter. "Cambodia Can't Escape Violent Past." *National Post*. Quebec. Oct. 23, 2003.

Gray, Denis D. "Many Work to Save Mekong Dolphins." The Associated Press. June 15, 1998.

Gray, Laurence. "Letting Children Live." *Bangkok Post*. Dec. 21, 2000.

Halperin, Alex. "Future Farmers: Can Cambodian Rice Ever Make It in the World?" *The Cambodia Daily*. Sept. 6–7, 2003, p. 6.

_____. "Health System Criticized for Fund Delays." *The Cambodia Daily*. July 29, 2003, p. 13.

_____. "Gov't Outlines 20-Year Plan for Mentally Ill." *The Cambodia Daily*. July 11, 2003, p. 12.

Human Rights Watch. "Don't Bite the Hand That Feeds You: Coercion, Threats, and Vote-Buying in Cambodia's National Elections." A Human Rights Watch Briefing Paper. July 2003.

"The Run-Up to Cambodia's 2003 National Assembly Election Background Briefing."

http://hrw.org/backgrounder/asia/cambodia/index.htm. June 13, 2003.

_____. "Cambodia's Commune Elections: Setting the Stage for the 2003 National Elections." Report. April 2002.

_____. "Cambodia: Tribunal Must Meet International Standards." Feb. 12, 2002.

International Republican Institute. "Election Process Falls Short of International Standards." Preliminary Report. July 29, 2003.

Jeldres, Julio A. "Cambodia's Monarchy 10 Years On." *Asia Times OnLine*. Sept. 2003.

Johnson, Kay. "Cambodia's Samaritans: On a Night of Savagery, They Risked Death to Save Life." *Time Asia*. Apr. 28, 2003, Vol. 161, No. 16.

_____. "PM Pulls Plug on Angkor Karaoke Club." *South China Morning Post*. Hong Kong. Dec. 12, 2000.

_____. "The Mountains That Time Forgot." *Time*. Sept. 11, 2000, Vol. 156, No. 10.

"Sit-In Crumbles After Early-Morning Crackdown." *The Cambodia Daily*. Sept. 9, 1998, p. 1.

_____. "Cradle of Khmer Civilization Emerges from K Thom Forest." *The Cambodia Daily*. June 17, 1997.

Kazmin, Amy. "Cambodian Pop Star in Critical Condition." *Financial Times Online*. Oct. 22, 2003.

_____. "Cambodian Parties Boycott Parliament Over Resignation Call." *Financial Times*. Sept. 29, 2003.

_____. "Phnom Penh Slum Dwellers Feel the Heat." *Financial Times*. Jan. 8, 2002.

Kay Kimsong and Daniel Ten Kate. "Bribes, Bad Driving Help Make Roads Deadly." *The Cambodia Daily*. Jan. 12, 2004, p. 1.

Khmer connection. "The Legacy of the Warriors and the Builders." http://vimean-akas.khmerconnection.com/. June 10, 2000.

Kiernan, Ben. "Ke Pauk: One of Pol Pot's Leading Military Commanders, He Was Responsible for the Murders of Many Thousands of Cambodians, But Escaped Justice." *The Guardian*. Feb. 21, 2002.

Kinnock, Glenys. "Lessons from the 1998 National Election." *Phnom Penh Post*, Vol. 11, Issue 3.

Kulthida Samabuddhi and Nauvarat Suksamran. "Study Panel Divided on Golf Course." *Bangkok Post*. Feb. 27, 2002.

Kyne, Phelim. "WTO May Deliver Justice Denied at Ballot Box." *The Asian Wall Street Journal*. July 24, 2003, p. A7.

"Landmine Monitor Report." Cambodia, International Campaign to Ban Landmines. 2002.

Langren, Irene V. "Cambodia in 2000: New Hopes Are Challenged." *Asian Survey: A Bimonthly Review of Contemporary Asian Affairs*, University of California Press. Vol. XLI, No. 1, Jan./Feb. 2001, pp. 156–163.

Leakhena Nou. "What Motivates Khmer Youth to Gang-Rape? A Sociological Interpretation of the Bouk Phenomenon." *Phnom Penh Post*. July 18–31, p. 13.

Leitsinger, Miranda. "Cambodia's Younger Generation Cares Little for the Khmer Rouge, Looks to the Future." The Associated Press. Jan. 4, 2004.

Lobe, Jim. "Cambodian Unionist's Killing Stirs Up Hornets' Nest." *Asia Times On-Line*, Jan. 26, 2004.

Lynch, Colum. "UN Ends Negotiations on Khmer Rouge Trials." *Washington Post*. Feb. 9, 2002.

Macan-Markar, Marwaan. "UN's Cambodian 'Success' in Question." Inter Press Service, Feb. 7, 2004.

_____. "Analysis: Democracy Elusive in Southeast Asia." Inter Press Service. July 29, 2003.

Madra, Ek. "Explosion, Grenades Mar Cambodia's General Election." Reuters. July 27, 2003.

Maejima, Susumu. "Dolphins Charm Ex-Banker to a New Life." *The Asahi Shimbun*. May 14, 2001.

Martin, Steven. "A River Lost in Time but Open for Travel." *Time*. April 23, 2001, Vol. 157, No. 16.

Marukatat, Saritdet. "Shantytown Neighbours Sprang to Rescue of Fleeing Diplomats." *Bangkok Post*. Feb. 7, 2003.

_____, and Bhanravee Tansubhapol. "Analysis/Thai-Khmer Ties: Ministers Hope to Put Relations Back on Track." *Bangkok Post*. March 21, 2003.

McConnell, Mitch. "Elections in Cambodia." Statement, July 24, 2003.

_____. "Cambodia's New Political Reality." *Boston Globe*. Feb. 11, 2002, p. A15.

McGivering, Jill. "Cambodia's Ambitious Youth." BBC News. Aug. 7, 2003.

McKenney, Bruce. "Questioning Sustainable Concession Forestry in Cambodia." *Cambodia Development Review*. Jan.-Mar. 2002, Vol. 6, Issue 1.

McManus, Joanne. "Health on the Mend." *Far Eastern Economic Review*. Feb. 22, 2001, Vol. 164, No. 7.

Medecins Sans Frontieres. "Cambodia: A Growing Burden of Disease." MSF 2000 International Activity Report.

Meixner, Seth. "Women Candidates Killed in Pre-Election Violence." *South China Morning Post*. Hong Kong. Jan. 8, 2002.

_____, and Khieu Kola. "Falling AIDS Rate Offers Little Hope in AIDS Epidemic." *South China Morning Post*. Sept. 19, 2002.

Men Soriyun, Keo Omasliss, and Chak Sokhavicheaboth. "Mammals of Cambodia." Phnom Penh: The Department of Forestry and Wildlife, The Department of Nature Conservation and Protection and the Wildlife Conservation Society Cambodia Program, 2000.

Mith Samlanh. "Drug Use and HIV Vulnerability." Phnom Penh, 2002.

Mockenhaupt, Brian. "Running Out of Lives." *Far Eastern Economic Review*. June 21, 2001.

_____. "Into the Mist: Journey Into the Primeval." *The Cambodia Daily*. Mar. 25–26, 2000.

Montlake, Simon. "Cambodia Goes Online." BBC News. March 3, 2003.

Munthit, Ker. "Ex-Khmer Rouge Chief Acknowledges Genocide." *Washington Post*, Dec. 31, 2003, p. A20.

_____. "Cambodian Police Open Fire on Demonstrating Factory Workers, Killing One." The Associated Press. June 13, 2003.

_____. "Cambodians Mark Downfall of Khmer Rouge." The Associated Press. April 18, 2003.

_____. "Researcher: Pol Pot Planned Escape." The Associated Press. March 2, 2002.

_____. "Cambodia's Genocide Museum Is Crumbling for Lack of Money." The Associated Press. Feb. 24, 2002.

Mydans, Seth. "A Top Khmer Rouge Leader, Going Public, Pleads Ignorance." *The New York Times*. Jan. 3, 2004, p. A4.

_____. "Inching toward Democracy, Cambodia Again Visits Polls." *The New York Times*. July 26, 2003.

_____. "What War Wrought, Cambodia Can't Stand to See." *The New York Times*. May 20, 2003, p. A4.

_____. "Spirits Get the Blame in Cambodian Illness." *The New York Times*. May 11, 2003, p. A6.

_____. "Where a Lake Is Life Itself, Dam Is a Dire Word." *The New York Times*. April 28, 2003, p. A4.

_____. "Flawed Khmer Rouge Trial Better Than None." *The New York Times*. April 16, 2003.

_____. "A Stooped Icon of Angkor, Forever Sweeping." *The New York Times*. March 22, 2003.

_____. "Face That Stirred Cambodian Chaos." *The New York Times*. Feb. 1, 2003, p. A8.

_____. "Cambodian Leader Rules as if from the Throne." *The New York Times*. March 19, 2002, p. A3.

_____. "For a Cambodian, a Life Transformed by Dance." *The New York Times*. March 9, 2002.

_____. "Trees Bind Angkor Temples in Perilous Grip." *The New York Times*. Aug. 19, 2001, pp. A1, 16.

_____. "Unexpected Toll: Animal Victims of Land Mines Mount." *The New York Times*. Mar. 7, 2001.

_____. "Fragile Stability Slowly Emerges in Cambodia." *The New York Times*. June 25, 2000, International, pp. 1, 6.

_____. "Cambodia's Latest Plague: Lynch Law." *The New York Times*. April 13, 2000.

_____. "Pushed from the Land, and the Trees." *The New York Times*. April 6, 2000.

Nanuam, Wassana. "Brutal KR Chief Poisoned Surayud Says Autopsy Revealed Chemical Traces in His System." *Bangkok Post*. Mar. 19, 2002.

The Nation (Bangkok). "Cambodia Still in Shadow of KR." Editorial. Jan. 10, 2004.

_____. "Cambodian Casinos 'an Outlet for Thai Drug Users.'" Bangkok. July 5, 2003.

_____. "Cambodian Casinos Reopen." Bangkok. Mar. 24, 2003.

_____. "Cambodian Killing Bodes Ill for Future." Bangkok. Editorial. Feb. 20, 2003.

_____. "Army Officer Killed at Poi Pet Casino." Bangkok. Feb. 21, 2002.

_____. "Brothels on Increase at Borders." Bangkok. May 15, 2001.

National Malaria Center. "Annual Progress Report 2002." Cambodian Ministry of Health. Jan.–Dec. 2002.

NBC Dateline. "Children for Sale: Dateline Goes Undercover with a Human Rights Group to Expose Sex Trafficking in Cambodia." Jan. 23, 2004.

O'Connell, Alex. "Britons Find 'Lost' Crocodile in Cambodia." The Times. London. Sept. 28, 2000.

Opdyke, Jeff D. "Changes in Global Adoption Rules Toughen Process." The Wall Street Journal. Oct. 14, 2003.

Oxfam America. "Keeping Community Fisheries Afloat in Cambodia." www.oxfam america.org/advocacy/art6783.html. Feb. 3, 2004.

Pancake, John. "A Ballot for the Future of a Land Steeped in Blood." The Washington Post. Mar. 15, 2002, p. C01.

Perrin, Andrew, and Matt McKinney. "Blast from the Past: The Roots of Last Week's Eruption of Anti-Thai Violence in Phnom Penh Date Back Centuries." Time Asia. Feb. 10, 2003, Vol. 161, No. 5.

_____, and Eric Unmacht. "Ballots and Bullets: A Series of Politically Motivated Assassinations Sweeps Cambodia." Time Asia, Nov. 3, 2003, Vol. 162, No. 17.

Phann Ana, and Kevin Doyle. "Border Is Burning Issue for Svay Rieng Voters." The Cambodia Daily, July 16, 2003, p. 1.

Phnom Penh Post. "Torture Now as Ever Cambodia's Curse." July 7–20, 2000.

Phoel, Cynthia. "Pesticides in Cambodia: A Growing Problem." Oxfam Exchange. 2002.

Poona Antaseeda. "Mekong Yielding Diminishing Returns." Bangkok Post. Perspective. Jan. 26, 2003.

Postlewaite, Susan. "A Poacher's Paradise in Cambodia." San Francisco Chronicle. Jan. 31, 2001.

Prusher, Ilene R. "The Language of Change in Cambodia. The Christian Science Monitor. Aug. 28, 2001.

Reeker, Philip T. "Credible Elections in Cambodia." U.S. State Department Press Statement. Washington, D.C. May 30, 2003.

Reeves, Phil. "Hopes of Genocide Trial Fade with Deaths of Khmer Rouge Leaders." The Independent, London. July 4, 2003.

Reuters. "UN Team in Cambodia to Prepare Genocide Trial." Dec. 7, 2003.

_____. "Pro-Royal Cambodian Radio Journalist Shot Dead. Oct. 18, 2003.

_____. "Cambodian Rioters May Face Elephants." July 23, 2003.

_____. "Cambodia Shuts Muslim School, Thais Watch Militants." May 29, 2003.

_____. "Cambodians Recall Killing Fields on 'Day of Anger.'" May 20, 2003.

_____. "Senior Cambodian Judge Shot Dead in Capital." Apr. 23, 2003.

_____. "General Ke Pauk, Former Khmer Rouge Military Chief, Dies at 68." Feb. 16, 2002.

_____. "Cambodians Paid $10 Each for Killing Politician." Feb. 8, 2002.

_____. "Cambodian PM Says Historic Elections Were Fair Enough." Feb. 7, 2002.

_____. "Hunters Take a Toll on Cambodian Wildlife." Dec. 13, 2001.

Richardson, Michael. "Phnom Penh: Coming Back to Life." International Herald Tribune. Mar. 2, 2001.

Richie, Donald. "The Other Treasures of Angkor." The Japan Times. Feb. 26, 2002.

Romero, Simon. "Cambodia Re-Emerges." The New York Times. Oct. 19, 2003, pp. 8, 9.

Saengpassa, Chularat. "Another Bump in Route 48 Upgrade." The Nation. Bangkok. Mar. 11, 2003.

Saing Soenthrith, and Wency Leung. "Storms Wreak Havoc on Relocated Squatters." The Cambodia Daily, July 7, 2003, p. 1.

Sakboon, Mukdawan. "Between the Lines: Bitter Pill for Cambodian HIV/AIDS Patients." The Nation. Bangkok. Sept. 20, 2003.

Sam Rainsy Party. "Another Fine Example of a Police State." National Assembly of the Kingdom of Cambodia. May 21, 2003.

_____. "Analysis of Election Results." Feb. 12, 2002.

_____. "Taking Stock of the Ten Years Following the Signing of the Paris Peace Agreements." Oct. 24, 2001.

_____. "SOS Hungry Farmers: More Than 1,500 Internal Refugees Presently at SRP Headquarters." National Assembly of the Kingdom of Cambodia. Sept. 8, 2001.

_____. "Another Wave of Hungry Farmers Arrive in Phnom Penh." National Assembly of the Kingdom of Cambodia. Sept. 7, 2001.

_____. "The Cambodian Government Shows Inconsistency and Bad Faith in the Case of the Murder of Three Foreign Hostages in 1994." National Assembly of the Kingdom of Cambodia, July 22, 2000.

_____. "New Appeal to Stop Vigilante Justice and Extrajudicial Executions." National Assembly of the Kingdom of Cambodia. June 30, 2000.

San Jose Mercury News. "Insufficient Reasons to Kill Someone." News of the Weird. Jan. 29, 2000.

Santoli, Al, ed. "Escalating Corruption & Violence in Cambodia's Faux Democracy." *Asia Security Monitor.* American Foreign Policy Council, Jan. 12–Feb. 4, 2004.

_____. "Challenges to Democracy Across SE Asia: Pre-Election Violence in Cambodia." American Foreign Policy Council. *Asia Security Monitor.* July 2, 2003, No. 3.

Schmetzer, Uli. "Anarchy Reigns as Cambodia Avoids Its Past." *Chicago Tribune.* Feb. 6, 2004.

Shanks, Leslie, and Michael J. Schull. "Rape in War: The Humanitarian Response." *Canadian Medical Association Journal.* Oct. 31, 2000, Vol. 163, Issue 9, pp. 1152, 5p.

Shaw, William, and Phann Ana. "School for Disabled Bypasses Government Ban," *The Cambodia Daily*, Sept. 11, 2003, p. 1.

_____, and Kuch Naren. "In Preah Vihear, Some Prefer Schools in Laos." *The Cambodia Daily.* Aug. 18, 2003, p. 1.

Shukovsky, Paul. "Second Woman Is Charged in Cambodian Adoptions." *Seattle Post-Intelligencer*, Jan. 9, 2004.

_____. "Feds Claim Adopted 'Orphans' Had Parents. *Seattle Post-Intelligencer*, Dec. 17, 2003.

Sihanouk, King Norodom. "Cambodia Is an International Beggar." *Koh Santepheap Daily.* Aug. 28, 2003.

Sipress, Alan. "For Torture Camp Survivor, Time Is Scarce." *The Washington Post.* Feb. 18, 2003, p. A20.

_____. "Illegal Logging Rife in Cambodia." *The Washington Post.* Feb. 16, 2003, p. A28.

Sloan, Bronwyn. "Killing Shame: The Assassination of a Top Union Official Threatens to Exacerbate the Current Political Crisis and Erode Confidence in the Country." *Far Eastern Economic Review*, Feb. 5, 2004.

_____. "Khmer Rouge Officials Finger Regime's Top Leaders." Reuters. March 19, 2002.

South China Morning Post. "Cambodia on Way to Losing Next Generation." Hong Kong. Dec. 1, 2001.

Special Representative of the Secretary General for Human Rights in Cambodia. "The 2003 National Assembly Elections." July 8, 2003.

The Straits Times. "Wedding Reunites Khmer Rouge Leaders." Singapore. Mar. 17, 2002.

_____. "Pol Pot Man Accepts Responsibility." Singapore. Mar. 15, 2002.

_____. "Fire-Hit Squatters Move to Tent City." Singapore. Dec. 5, 2001.

_____. "Sex Draws Nearly a Quarter of Tourists to Cambodia." Singapore. Oct. 6, 2001.

The Sunday Times. "From Pol Pot to Leith." London. Sept. 7, 2003.

Sumitra Pooltong. "Under Siege in Phnom Penh." *Bangkok Post.* Perspective. Feb. 9, 2003.

Thaitawat, Nusara. "From Strength to Strength." *Bangkok Post.* May 31, 2001.

Tobacco Control Online. "Smoking Among Buddhist Monks in Phnom Penh, Cambodia." http://tc.bmjjournals.com/cgi/content/full/9/1/111. Spring 2000.

_____. "Relations with Cambodia: New Border Posts Planned, Hours Extended to Boost Trade." *Bangkok Post.* Jan. 17, 2003.

Turnbull, Robert. "Cutting Through Angkor's Wats, Politics and Banyans." *The New York Times.* March 30, 2003.

United Nations. "Human Rights Questions." Draft Resolution. Fifty-eighth session, third committee. Agenda item 117 (b). Nov. 18, 2003.

_____. "Situation of Human Rights in Cambodia: Report of the Special Representative of the Secretary-General for Human Rights in Cambodia, Peter Leuprecht." Fifty-eighth session. Item 19. Dec. 28, 2001.

United Nations Children's Fund (UNICEF) "Human Rights for Children and Woman: How UNICEF Helps Make Them a Reality." UNICEF New York. June 1999.

_____. "Towards a Better Future: An Analysis of the Situation of Children and Women in Cambodia." Bangkok, 1996.

United Nations Commission on Human Rights. "Commune Council Elections 2002." January 2001–Jan. 10, 2002.

_____. "Evidence of Summary Executions, Torture and Missing Persons." United Nations Report. July 2001.

_____. "E/CN.4/2002/117." Fifty-eighth session. Item 19 of the provisional agenda. Dec. 27, 2001.

_____. "E/CN.4/2001/NGO/68." Fifty-seventh session. Item 11(d) of the provisional agenda. Jan. 30, 2001.

_____. "E/CN.4/2001/NGO/66." Fifty-seventh session. Item 11(b) of the provisional agenda. Jan. 30, 2001.

_____. "E/CN.4/2001/NGO/63." Fifty-seventh session. Item 11(b) of the provisional agenda. "Health Care in Cambodia." Jan. 30, 2001.

_____. "Civil and Political Rights, the Question of Disappearances and Summary Executions." Fifty-seventh session. Jan. 30, 2001.

_____. "Situation of Human Rights in Cambodia." Commission on Human Rights resolution 2001/82.

United Nations Development Programme (UNDP), "Second Country Cooperation Framework for Cambodia, 2001–2005."

United Nations Foundation. "Cambodia: New Prosperity Threatens Children, UNICEF Warns." *UNWire.* Dec. 5, 2001.

United Nations General Assembly. "A/58/268." Fifty-eighth session Item 119 (b) of the provisional agenda. Aug. 8, 2003.

_____. "A/56/230." Fifty-sixth session. Item 131 (b) of the provisional agenda human rights questions. July 31, 2001.

_____. "GA?9720." Twenty-third Special Session "Women 2000." June 7, 2000.

_____. "Cambodia: Country Reports on Human Rights Practices, 2001." Bureau of Democracy, Human Rights, and Labor. Mar. 4, 2002.

_____. "Cambodia: Country Reports on Human Rights Practices, 2000." Bureau of Democracy, Human Rights, and Labor. Feb. 2001.

United Nations Population Fund (UNFPA). "The Environment and Development in Phnom Penh Literature Review." Phnom Penh. Nov. 1998.

United Nations Third Committee. "Promotion of Human Rights, Poverty Eradication and Development." GA/SHC/3762, Nov. 10, 2003.

Unmacht, Eric. "Cambodia's Pesticide Gamblers." BBC. July 9, 2003.

Vachon, Michelle. "Observer Groups Praise Election Process." *The Cambodia Daily.* Aug. 1, 2003, p. 13.

Van Roeun. "Police Launch Sweep for Angkor Thom Looters." *The Cambodia Daily.* Jan. 16, 2004, p. 14.

Vater, Tom. "Winning Face with a Facelift." *Far Eastern Economic Review.* Oct. 16, 2003.

Waewkhlaihong, Chakkrit. "New Routes to Link Trat with Cambodia." *Bangkok Post.* Feb. 27, 2002.

Wain, Barry. "Cambodians Promote Killing Fields to Tourists." *The Wall Street Journal.* Feb. 20, 2002.

_____. "Understanding Hun Sen." *The Asian Wall Street Journal.* The Region. July 9, 1999.

Walston, Joe, and Olivia Walter. "Initiating Bat Conservation in the Royal Kingdom of Cambodia." Wildlife Conservation Society. Jan. 2001.

Weine, Stevan M. "Bosnian Refugees: Memories, Witnessing, and History After Dayton." www.refugees.org/world/articles/ bosnians_wrs96.htm.

Wells-Dang, Andrew. "Republican Group Meddles in Cambodia." *Asia Times Online.* Apr. 16, 2004.

White, Peter T. "Kampuchea Wakens from a Nightmare." *National Geographic.* May 1982, p. 622.

Whitman, Christine Todd. "The Election Cambodia Deserves." *Washington Post.* Aug. 8, 2003, p. A17.

Yim Chea, and Bruce McKenney. "Great

Lake Fish Exports: An Analysis of the Fee System." *Cambodia Development Review.* July-Sept. 2003, Vol. 7, Issue 3.

Yun Samean. "64 Families Evicted from Angkor Wat." *The Cambodia Daily.* Sept. 8, 2003, p. 1.

Yuwadee Tunyasiri. "Cambodian Beggars to Be Flown Home." *Bangkok Post.* Sept. 21, 2003.

Index

adoption 4, 8, 34, 35, 40, 177, 178, 181, 182, 290, 323, 326–327, 335; scandals 8, 34, 176–179

Aedes aegypti 206; *see also* malaria

Agence France-Presse *see* newspapers and news organizations

aid workers 24, 52, 88, 106, 130, 167, 193, 203, 228, 230, 231, 258, 314

AIDS/HIV 6, 21, 33, 38, 40, 79, 98, 99, 165, 167, 189, 194, 196, 197, 199, 202, 212–214, 218, 221, 286, 292, 293, 318–323; anti-retroviral drugs 212, 322; HIV testing 35, 38, 289–290; orphans 8, 35, 39, 194, 196, 212–214, 290, 318–319

Aki Ra 307–312, 341

Alliance of Democrats 121, 126

Al-Qaeda *see* terrorism

ambulance service 208–212

amok 128, 129, 337

amphetamines see *yama*

Ang Snoul 73, 76

Angka 43, 311, 337

Angkor 50, 67, 84, 99, 102, 134, 158; Angkor Archaeological Park 60, 61; Angkor Conservation Authority 53; Angkor era 71, 72, 73, 91, 124, 168, 222, 229, 234, 252; Angkor Wat 51, 52, 53, 57, 78, 94, 107, 159, 263, 306, 310; children 50, 56, 159–160; history 51, 53–54, 64, 65, 66, 70, 169, 222, 235, 252, 343; police 60–66; statues 50, 53, 54, 59, 64, 65, 299; temples 8, 51, 52, 97, 107, 158, 160, 202, 269, 282; tourism 54, 57, 65, 158–159; vendors 50; in war 62, 63, 64

Angkor Hospital for Children *see* hospitals

Anlong Kong Thmei 155–158

Anlong Veng 97–108, 122–126, 244–245, 308, 310–311

Anlong Veng Health Center *see* hospitals

Anlong Veng Pagoda 104–105

Anopholes 206; *see also* dengue fever

anti–Thai riots *see* Thailand

Apsara Authority 60, 61, 65–66

apsaras 50, 63, 94, 284, 337

Asia-Pacific Economic Cooperation 196

Asian communication 61

AsiaWatch 20

The Associated Press *see* newspapers and news organizations

Association of the Blind in Cambodia 312, 313, 314, 341

Baht 4, 81, 82, 83, 166, 196, 244, 268

Bangkok 81, 158, 178, 196, 197, 213, 216, 319

Bangkok Post see newspapers and news organizations

barangs 24, 167, 235, 258, 282

Bassac River 77, 149, 155, 156, 157, 221

Battambang 1, 20, 45, 74, 92, 136, 138, 146, 152, 154, 158, 196, 208, 212, 213, 215, 216, 219, 230, 236, 239, 263, 269, 287, 313, 318, 319, 321, 322

Battambang Provincial Hospital *see* hospitals

bauk 169, 337

Bayon 52, 158, 263; *see also* Angkor

Becker, Elizabeth 71, 134, 253, 325

beggars 16, 17, 18, 20, 23, 24, 28, 32, 78, 130, 153, 159, 175, 187–188, 196, 199–200, 292, 293, 295, 301, 313, 331

birds: black-headed ibis 238; cormorants 236; greater adjutant 238, 246; laughingthrush 259; oriental darter 238; painted stork 238; spot-billed pelicans 238; vultures 238, 245

Bizot, François 43, 53, 59, 135

bong thom 124, 175, 190, 293, 329, 337

Bopha Devi, Princess 283–285

boxing 32, 187, 210

bribery 61, 66, 170, 209, 292

Brother Number One *see* Pol Pot

Brother Number Two *see* Nuon Chea

Buddhism 71, 92, 94, 105, 134, 148, 286–288, 292; Mahayana Buddhism 92; Theravada 92, 148; under the Khmer Rouge 104–105, 286, 320

Bush, George W. 270, 326

The Butcher *see* Ta Mok

butterfly garden 55–56

Calmette Hospital *see* hospitals

Cambodia Academy of Business Studies 117

The Cambodia Daily see newspapers and news organizations

Cambodia Development Resource Institute (CDRI) 166, 236, 242, 248, 292, 339

Cambodian Center for Human Rights 122, 339

Cambodian Freedom Fighters 345

Cambodian Institute for Cooperation and Peace 119

Cambodian Navy *see* military

Cambodian People's Party (CPP)
  1, 72, 106, 111, 112, 117, 121, 122,
  123, 124, 126, 158, 163, 168,
  270, 315, 316, 333, 339
Cambodian Red Cross 209, 210,
  212
Cambodian Royal turtle see
  Wildlife, *Batagur baska*
Cambodian Traditional Medicine Association 205
Cambodian Women's Crisis
  Center (CWCC) 169, 170,
  172, 323–324, 339, 341
Cambodiana Hotel 114, 118, 210
capitalism 37
Cardamom Mountains 80, 233,
  291
CARE 52, 230–231, 339
casinos 155
Chams 71, 72, 252, 253,
  266–275; *see also* Islam;
  Khmer Rouge; terrorism and
  terror suspects
Chandler, David 43
Chanrithy Him 47
charcoal 31
Chea Sim Orphanage 179–182
ch'hbat srey 319–321, 337
Chhnouk Trou 72, 292
children 8, 175–198; abuse
  197–198; street children 8, 54,
  132, 175, 176, 182–188,
  190–196, 292, 297
China 42, 70, 92, 100, 104, 166,
  234, 281, 294, 311
Chinese New Year 329
Choeung Ek *see* Killing Fields
cholera *see* illness
chor tuk 254, 337
Choun Nhiem 57–60
Christianity 156–158
Chrok Romet 268–269
Chruoy Changvar 71, 273–275
Chua Ang 93
Chua Phuong 91–93
Chuch Phoeurn 298–299
Clinton, Bill 326
communism 78, 85, 127, 159,
  163, 201
condoms 82, 99, 185, 199, 214
conscription 18, 26, 145
corruption 2, 7, 35, 48, 66, 81,
  92, 104, 108, 110, 123, 131, 136,
  170, 201, 222, 243, 292, 293,
  295, 316, 317, 318
CPP *see* Cambodian People's
  Party
crime 104, 128, 130–136, 151,
  259, 312
cryptosporidiosis *see* illness
cupping 205

Dam Swai 254–266

DanChurch Aid 157
DCCam *see* Documentation
  Center of Cambodia
death, reactions to 202
debt: national 294; personal
  170, 196, 290
de-mining 16, 302, 307–312
democracy 1, 5, 37, 78, 102,
  111–129, 158, 163, 164, 274,
  298, 316, 318, 321, 325, 334,
  335; definition 119
Democracy Square 70, 78, 112,
  113, 114, 140
Democratic Kampuchea 339,
  344; *see also* Khmer Rouge
dengue fever *see* illness
depression *see* psychology
development 108, 147, 232, 234,
  235, 236, 237, 266, 268,
  291–299, 335
diarrhea *see* illness
diphtheria *see* illness
disabilities 56–57, 153–154,
  190–191, 199–200, 312–314
Disability Action Services 28
DJ Cake 279–280
DJ Lux 279–280
Documentation Center of Cambodia (DCCam) 41, 47–48,
  145, 286, 339
dogs 214–217, 300–301
domestic violence 169–170,
  172–173, 320
Dong 86, 224
drugs 131, 145, 150, 151, 175, 191,
  194, 195, 197, 249, 270, 281,
  291, 293, 321, 328
Duch 42
Dutch aid workers and scientists
  35, 53, 99, 106
dysentery *see* illness

l'Ecole Française d'Extreme Orient 53
economy 94, 147, 292, 293–294,
  298
education 32, 51, 101–102, 104,
  146–147, 170–171, 176, 191,
  271–273, 292, 296–297,
  304–306, 317–318
elections: 1993 1, 40, 111, 114,
  127, 152, 298, 345; 1998 2, 7,
  44, 95, 111, 112–114, 283, 345;
  1998 post-election riots 2, 6,
  70, 90, 114–118, 141, 316, 326,
  345; 2002 commune elections
  112, 121, 171, 283, 314, 316,
  318, 345; 2003 24, 82, 84, 87,
  102, 104, 105, 112, 121–127, 135,
  149, 151, 157, 168, 194, 207,
  283, 294; 2003 post-election
  stalemate 112, 121, 126, 127,
  178, 194, 294, 333, 346

Emergency Hospital for War
  Victims *see* hospitals
encephalitis *see* illness
environment 145, 218, 221, 222,
  228, 230, 233–252, 306
European Commission Support
  Program to the Environmental Sector 236
European Union 114, 121, 123

famine, hunger, starvation 152,
  192, 297, 311
farming 20, 23, 25, 28, 59, 65,
  87, 89, 111, 119, 124, 152, 156,
  157, 191, 232, 235, 237, 239,
  243, 244, 248, 253, 255, 256,
  267, 268, 270, 286, 291, 292,
  294, 304
FCC 18, 24, 28
The Fighter (Neak Prayuth) see
  newspapers and news organizations
fish and fishing 235, 236–241,
  243, 249, 273, 292; lots
  239–240, 273–275; paste 235,
  241
Fisheries Department 239
floods 152, 220, 291, 292
foreign aid 294, 295, 297, 326
forests and jungles 25, 28, 60, 62,
  63, 65, 80, 100, 101, 142, 205,
  233, 234, 236, 238, 241, 243,
  244, 245, 248, 252–266, 310
French colonialism 70, 71, 73,
  127, 140, 163, 212, 255, 280,
  296, 297, 325, 343
French Red Cross 209, 212
Friends *see Mith Samlanh*
Friends Without a Border 202;
  see also Angkor Hospital for
  Children
Funcinpec 74, 111, 112, 121, 126,
  171, 333, 339
The Future Group 189

gambling 80, 83, 134, 151, 172,
  191, 192
gangrene *see* illness
gangs 29, 132, 152, 175, 190,
  292, 293, 329
garbage 223–226
garment factories 161–162, 208,
  293, 294, 330, 333
genocide 2, 6, 40–49
ghosts 61–62
giardiasis *see* illness
Global Fund 207
Global Witness 243
glue sniffing 54, 144, 192–193
grenades 132–133, 135, 203;
  1997 attack against Sam
  Rainsy 130–131, 345; 1998
  attack on Hun Sen house 114

Gulf of Thailand 79, 128
guns 35, 37, 43, 62, 131,
132–134, 208, 236, 239, 241,
248, 292, 328

Hambali *see* terrorism and terrorism suspects
Hat Lek 79, 80
health care 99–101, 183–186,
199–217, 221–222, 292; *see also*
ambulance services; illness;
psychology
HELP 230–231
hepatitis *see* illness
hill tribes 207, 253
HIV *see* AIDS/HIV
Ho Chi Minh 71, 93
Hok Lundy 126
Homeland Shelter 196–197
homeless 17, 54, 79, 155, 183,
185, 191, 196, 224, 234, 304
hookworm *see* illness
hospitals: Angkor Hospital for
Children 201–204, 341;
Anlong Veng Health Center
99–101, 105–106; Battambang
Provincial Hospital 212–214;
Calmette Hospital 73–76,
209; Emergency Hospital for
War Victims 215–217;
Jayavarman VII hospital
200–201; Kantha Bopha
200–201; Municipal Hospital
221, 229; National Pediatric
Hospital 229; Preah Bath
Norodom Sihanouk Hospital
142–145, 149, 222, 231–232;
Ta Cheng hospital 117
human rights 37, 111, 119–121,
131, 136, 162, 174, 266, 293,
316, 319, 320, 321
Human Rights Watch 112, 315
Hun Sen 16, 18, 21, 41, 42, 70,
72, 79, 89, 102, 106, 111, 112,
114, 121, 122, 126, 128, 243,
268, 294, 326, 333, 334, 339,
343, 344; childhood 124; and
Vietnam 42, 72
Hun Sen Park 140
hunting 237, 238, 239, 240–241,
245, 248, 250, 254, 255, 256,
266, 310
hysteria 73–75; *see also* psychology

Ieng Sary 41, 45, 98, 339
illiteracy 29, 33, 34, 158, 207,
275, 292, 295, 314, 315
illness, infectious disease:
cholera 221, 229; cryp-
tosporidiosis 229; dengue
fever 99, 201, 203, 206, 207,
216, 226, 229; diarrhea 38, 40,

76, 182, 202, 214, 221, 229;
diphtheria 176; dysentery 221,
229; encephalitis 39, 201; gangrene 23, 215; giardiasis 229;
hepatitis 216, 229; hookworm
100; malaria 25, 65, 80, 99,
101, 105, 119, 128, 161, 201,
203, 206–8, 216, 244, 256,
308, 311, 319; measles 176;
meningitis 203; pneumonia
203; polio 23, 176, 200; rabies
203, 216; respiratory infections 38, 99, 212, 220;
rheumatic fever 203; STDs
99; stomach ailments 74, 181,
205, 211, 226, 229, 231; tuberculosis 39, 99, 201, 203, 213,
221, 231–232; typhoid 99,
203, 216, 221, 229; typhus 201;
worms 23, 203
impunity 36, 121, 131, 136, 293
Indochinese Communist Party
163
infant mortality 176, 199
International Campaign to Ban
Landmines 16
International Republication
Institute 121, 122, 339
Iraq war 142, 270
Islam 71, 72, 253, 266–275

Japan, occupation of Cambodia
343
jar wine 258
Jayavarman VII 60, 62, 65
Jayavarman VII hospital *see*
hospitals
Jemaah Islamiyah *see* terrorism
and terrorism suspects
job discrimination 22
jor chong 254, 259, 337
journalists 43, 70, 72, 85, 88,
96, 111, 112, 118, 130, 133, 134,
152, 164, 217, 253; *see also*
newspapers and news organizations
justice and rule of law 15, 36,
41, 42, 48, 112, 119, 130, 135,
136, 137, 148, 201, 292, 295,
330

Kamm, Henry 111, 112, 152, 219,
296, 325, 334
Kampi 246–248
Kampot 20
Kampuchea Krom 90–96, 253
Kandal 72, 142, 144, 195, 323,
324
Kantha Bopha *see* hospitals
Kao Kim Hourn 119
Kapuscinski, Ryszard 70, 130
Ke Pauk 42, 98; *see also* Khmer
Rouge

Kenro Izu 202; *see also* Angkor
Hospital for Children
Khieu Samphan 36, 41, 339
Khlong Yai 81
Khmer dance 283–284
Khmer language 285, 333
Khmer New Year 136, 285
Khmer People's National Liberation Front 74
Khmer People's Revolutionary
Party 163
Khmer Rouge 21, 34, 36, 40, 41,
64, 78, 80, 97, 100, 103–104,
244–245, 343–345; attacks
against Chams 253; bandits
52, 72; defections 6, 15, 41, 64,
102, 131, 233, 345; emptying
Phnom Penh 6, 43, 219; and
environment 244–245, 246;
explanations for 43; family
separation 10, 36; former
leaders 41, 42, 45, 48, 97, 98,
144–145; former soldiers 24,
25, 248, 249–252, 307–312;
health care 47, 100, 200–201,
206; and hill tribes 253, 255,
261; line between victims and
persecutors 44, 145–146;
memoirs 47; mentality, 21, 43;
number of dead 6, 15, 41, 42,
44, 48; records 46; recruit-
ment 43; and societal
upheaval 9, 152, 200, 218–219,
296–297; survivors 47, 142,
144, 149, 280, 293; and Thailand 78, 81; tribunal 3, 42, 47,
48, 145–146, 294, 333, 346;
tribunal negotiations 6, 42,
294; and Vietnamese 43, 71,
72, 90
Khmer Women's Voice Centre
171
Kien Khleang Physical Rehabilitation Center 21, 22
Killing Fields (Choeung Ek) 9,
41, 44, 45, 155, 228
Kissinger, Henry 200
Kob 78
Koh Keo 72
Koh Kong 79–84
Koh Kong International Casino
80, 83
Kompong Cham 85, 102, 124,
162, 190, 316
Kompong Ch'hnang 267
Kompong Speu 20, 111, 145, 191
Kompong Thom 16, 158
Koy Veth 170
Kratie 182–188, 246–248, 263
kru Khmer 150, 204, 206; *see
also* traditional medicine

land mines 6, 15, 16, 18, 20, 21,

22, 27, 53, 68, 90, 94, 99, 100, 106, 142, 149, 183, 203, 215, 218, 221, 295, 307–312, 313, 331; *see also* de-mining
Laos 90, 198, 232, 235, 297
legal system 138, 292
Licadho 165
Light of Angkor (Rasmei Angkor) see newspapers and news organizations
linga 63, 94, 337
logging 81, 234, 237, 242–245, 249, 255, 256, 264–266
Lon Nol 71, 270, 274, 344
Lonely Planet 57, 263
looting 99, 118, 271–273; Angkor temples 53, 54, 60, 64, 67
low birth weight 39, 199
Ly Chheng Ky 314–318

malaria *see* illness
Malaysia 202, 249, 268, 269
malnutrition 39, 147, 176, 202, 203, 204, 292, 293, 326
Maryknoll 314
mass graves 8, 44, 45
maternal mortality 199
McConnell, U.S. Senator Mitch 121, 122
measles *see* illness
Médecins Sans Frontières 99–101, 199, 339
Mekong River 85, 91, 92, 140, 149, 182, 221, 234–235, 246, 247, 248, 273, 285
Mekong River Commission 235
Mekong River Delta 43, 71
meningitis *see* illness
mental health *see* psychology
migration 101, 141, 152–164, 196
military: Cambodian Navy 88; Hun Sen's personal army 41, 268, 345; Khmer Rouge Army 26, 64, 249, 268, 307; Lon Nol forces 274; military hospitals (*see also* hospitals) 16, 23; Norodom Ranariddh forces 345; Royal Cambodian Armed Forces (RCAF) and Cambodian Army 42, 53, 64, 71, 83, 102, 307, 310, 331, 339, 350; Vietnamese forces 26, 307, 344
Ministry of Cults and Religion 267, 288
Ministry of Culture and Fine Arts 298–299
Ministry of Education 22
Ministry of Environment 222
Ministry of Health 73, 100, 142, 201, 207, 212
Ministry of Interior 80, 150, 267, 317

Ministry of Women's and Veteran's Affairs 171–172, 280–281
Mith Samlanh (Friends) 132, 175–176, 190, 191, 193, 194, 195, 297, 341; shelter 190, 195
Mondulkiri 254–266
monks 8, 46, 52, 68, 90, 92, 93, 94, 98, 104–105, 136, 141, 148, 287–288, 319, 320, 321; violence against 114–117, 286
monsoons 141, 149, 155, 160, 184, 211, 220, 235, 255, 262, 274, 302
Mouhot, Henri 52, 53, 62, 68, 134, 233, 234, 246, 295–296, 325, 343
Mu Sochua 170–172, 280–281
Municipal Hospital *see* hospitals
Muny Van Saveth 287–288, 318–323
murder 9, 44, 46, 98, 112, 131, 133, 135–136, 143, 213, 259, 330
Museum of Indigenous Khmer 93
Muslim *see* Islam
Mydans, Seth 11, 120, 152, 326

Nanda Pok 170, 171
National Assembly 70, 113, 115, 117, 127, 130, 167, 294, 333, 346
National Malaria Center 206–207
National Museum 16, 52, 242, 298–299
National Pediatric Hospital *see* hospitals
national reconciliation 35, 36
National Reconstruction (Stabna Cheat) see newspapers and news organizations
Neak Luong 85, 87, 91
The New York Times see newspapers and news organizations
newspapers and news organizations: Agence France-Presse 36, 114, 161; The Associated Press 136, 280; *Bangkok Post* 168, 235; *The Cambodia Daily* vii, viii, 2, 5, 22, 66, 87, 114, 154, 190, 206, 208, 301, 302, 306, 328; *The Fighter (Neak Prayuth)* 36; *Light of Angkor (Rasmei Angkor)* 36; *National Reconstruction (Stabna Cheat)* 36; *The New York Times* 11, 15, 24, 26, 57, 120, 152, 296, 326; *Phnom Penh Post* 26, 135, 136, 167, 169; Reuters 243; *see also* journalists

NGOs 22, 52, 121, 139, 144, 156, 162, 167, 170, 231, 241, 267, 270, 283, 292, 293, 297, 339; *see also* individual group headings
1997 political fighting (coup, putsch) 127–129, 205
Nuon Chea (Brother Number Two) 36, 40, 41, 42; *see also* Khmer Rouge
Nutrition Center 34, 36, 40

Olympic Stadium 93, 195, 223
Om Al Qura Institute *see* terrorism and terrorism suspects
orchids 56, 259
orphanages 8, 179, 289–290
orphans 8, 37–39, 177–178, 183–188, 289–290, 292, 304, 318–321
Osama bin Laden 272
Overseas Development Administration 230

Pailin 16, 18, 41, 98, 116, 151
Pali 150, 206, 339
Paris of the Orient 43, 218
Paris Peace Accords 1, 111, 297, 344
peace 1, 2, 15, 36, 37, 77, 93, 95, 102, 111, 118, 119, 149, 153, 201, 285, 298, 321, 325, 326, 334, 335
Peaceful Children's Center *see* Wat Norea
Pedophilia 189; *see also* prostitution
per capita income 6, 291, 294
The Perfect Woman 65; *see also* Angkor
Perry, former U.S. Defense Secretary William 89
pesticides 291–292
Phnom Bakheng 57; *see also* Angkor
Phnom Penh Post see newspapers and news organizations
Phnong 253–266
Piem So 70
Pilger, John 134, 166, 211
pneumonia *see* illness
poaching 233, 239, 246, 249
Poipet 79, 155, 167, 194, 197
Pol Pot (Saloth Sar, Brother Number One) 2, 6, 41, 42, 47, 58, 72, 74, 90, 95, 97, 98, 102, 210, 244, 284, 339, 343, 345; *see also* Khmer Rouge
polio *see* illness
political parties *see* CPP, Funcinpec, Sam Rainsy Party
political violence 111, 112, 114, 115–118, 315

pollution 147, 218–232, 246
Pookai Book Project 303–307, 341
Post-traumatic stress disorder 144, 293
poverty 8–9, 147, 158, 171, 254–266, 268–275, 284, 294, 295, 296, 300–301, 330–332
Powell, Colin 188, 267
power 43, 53, 60, 61, 66–67, 119, 121, 123, 124, 293
Preah Bath Norodom Sihanouk Hospital *see* hospitals
Preah Khan 52, 60–66; *see also* Angkor
Prek Toal 234, 236–241
Prey Nokor 71, 94
Prey Pes 269; *see also* Chams
Prey Veng 34, 156, 321
Project on Genocide, Psychiatry and Witnessing, University of Illinois, Chicago 144
prostheses 21, 22, 23, 159
prostitution 79, 165, 166, 167, 170, 188, 194, 214, 287, 293; child 165, 166, 188–189
Psar Chas 210, 225
PSBK 223, 226; *see also* garbage; pollution
psychology 35–37, 131, 142–151; depression 43, 142, 143, 150–151, 164, 174; psychosomatic illness 37, 99

rabies *see* illness
Raffles 160, 281–282
Rainsy, Sam 72, 112, 114, 120, 121, 122, 126, 130, 131, 132, 153, 287, 314, 315, 316, 330, 339
Raka Thmei 255, 257, 264–265
Ranariddh, Norodom 111, 112, 128, 339, 345
rape 120, 135, 136, 165, 167, 169–170, 323–324
RCAF *see* military
Reagan, Ronald 122
resin tapping 254–266
respiratory infections *see* illness
Reuters *see* newspapers and news organizations
rheumatic fever *see* illness
rice 21, 24, 26, 39, 47, 51, 53, 58, 71, 87, 94, 95, 104, 111, 119, 152, 174, 204, 222, 233, 234, 235, 248, 289, 291, 305, 322
rice wine poisonings 73–76
Richner, Beat 200–201 *see also* Jayavarman VII hospital; Kantha Bopha
Riel 4, 9, 16, 18, 21, 27, 28, 29, 50, 68, 81, 83, 87, 98, 106, 124,

145, 153, 156, 160, 162, 175, 183, 186, 188, 190, 193, 200, 213, 224, 239, 240, 249, 264, 274, 283, 284, 300, 315, 331
roads 67–69
Royal Academy of Cambodia 127, 296
Royal Palace 115, 130, 140, 152, 191, 210, 273, 285
Rwanda 101, 311

Saigon (Ho Chi Minh City) 71, 90, 93–96, 213, 253, 319
Saloth Sar *see* Pol Pot
Sam Rainsy Party *see* Rainsy, Sam
Samling Logging Camp 256
Samnang, Dr. Sorn 127
Samroang Group 57
SAMU 208–212, 339
sanitation 21, 35, 199, 219, 222, 229, 230, 231, 294
Sanskrit 150, 339
scavengers 152, 153, 225–226
scorpions 65, 144
Seeing Hands Massage 313–314
Sen Monorom 255, 257, 259, 263, 264, 265
sewage 82, 98, 139, 218–221, 222, 226–228
sex tourism 164, 166, 176, 189; *see also* prostitution
sex workers *see* prostitution
shanties, descriptions of 30, 186–187, 227, 295
Siem Reap 45, 51, 52, 54, 55, 66, 69, 79, 84, 97, 106, 107, 158, 159, 160, 179, 190, 191, 180, 192, 200, 208, 216, 219, 236, 244, 245, 282, 307, 308, 309, 313, 314
Sihamoni, King Norodom 334, 346
Sihanouk, Norodom 26, 74, 79, 93, 166, 295, 334, 339, 343, 344, 345, 346
Sihanouk Center of Hope 221
Sihanoukville 127–129
Sisophon 194
skull map 46
skulls 44, 45
snakes 50, 56, 61, 63, 149, 233, 244, 246, 247, 257
social class, hierarchy 21, 119–120, 124, 152, 156–158, 253, 293, 328
South China Sea 91, 249
squatters 54, 55, 138, 141, 152, 154, 156, 157, 160, 185, 219, 296
Sre Ambel 249–252
STDs *see* AIDS/HIV; illness
stomach ailments *see* illness
street kids *see* children

Stung Meanchey 152, 218, 221, 225, 226
superstition 52, 148–149, 150, 204, 205, 230
Svay Ken 47

Ta Cheng hospital 117
Ta Mok (the Butcher) 42, 96–100, 102–106, 123, 244; house 99, 102; *see also* Khmer Rouge
Ta Prohm 52, 56–60, 63; *see also* Angkor
Takeo 16, 23, 83, 84, 207, 282, 303, 304, 306
terrorism and terrorism suspects 267, 270, 272, 274, 334; al-Qaeda 267; Hambali 267; Jemaah Islamiyah 267; Om Al Qura Institute 266–267, 268, 271–273
Thailand 92, 128, 153, 166, 196, 232, 234, 248, 267, 280, 314, 330; anti–Thai riots 73, 78–79, 85, 345; border 23, 25, 27, 79–84, 97, 154, 196, 200, 292; border camps 78; embassy 78–80; and Khmer Rouge 100, 104; relations 72–73, 78–79, 83; and trafficking 176, 188, 196–198; *see also baht*
Tolstoy, Leo 152
Tonle Sap Biosphere Reserve 236–241
Tonle Sap Lake 234, 235, 236–241
Tonle Sap River 140, 141, 149, 221, 231, 235, 262, 272, 285
torture 136, 197; under the Khmer Rouge 34, 45, 46, 47, 93, 134, 142, 144, 149–150
tourism 54, 56, 67, 127–129, 158, 328, 334; ecotourism 240, 248
tourists 17, 50, 51, 52, 53, 54, 56, 57–58, 61, 64, 78, 81, 82, 84, 85, 102, 106, 126, 129, 133, 158, 166, 240, 275, 298, 308, 314, 327
TPO 35–37, 130, 131, 145, 147–148, 158, 215, 339, 341
Tra Vinh 91–93
traditional medicine 204–206; *see also kru Khmer*
traffic 68–69; accidents 69, 208
trafficking 79, 153, 169–170, 196–198
train 142, 144, 153–155
transportation 67–69, 107–108
Trat 81
trauma 35, 36, 37, 143, 147, 150, 149, 201

tuberculosis *see* illness
Tuol Kok 229
Tuol Sleng Genocide Museum
  (S-21) 36, 42, 45, 46, 48
typhoid *see* illness
typhus *see* illness

UN 1, 15, 42, 110, 114, 117, 118,
  120, 138, 162, 293, 294, 298,
  307–308, 319, 333, 334, 345
UNCHR 131, 136, 138, 199, 243
UNDP 295–296, 339
unemployment 33, 35, 104, 107,
  119, 156, 186, 212, 234, 248,
  321
UNESCO 60, 236, 296, 297,
  298, 334, 339
UNFPA 295–296, 339
UNHCR 339
UNICEF 101–102, 178, 229, 334,
  339
United States 88, 92, 95, 211,
  274, 333–335, 344; bombing
  of Cambodia 85, 200–201,
  255, 297–298, 344; embassy
  117, 118; relations with 121,
  122, 161, 177, 180, 182, 188,
  294, 326; State Department
  122, 189
universities 298
University of Cambodia 169
UNTAC 40, 110, 111, 127, 258,
  296, 307–308, 312, 322, 339,
  345
USAID 122, 339
UXO 15, 16, 99, 307, 308, 309,
  310

Vann Nath 47
Veal Thom 24–29, 31, 33, 329,
  330, 331, 332
veterans 17, 24, 25, 26, 28, 30,
  52, 54, 56–57, 192
Veterans International 21, 24,
  26, 329, 332, 341

Victory Beach 127
Victory Monument 140
Viet Cong 64, 297
Vietnam 71, 89–96; border
  84–87, 242; history 71; invasion and occupation 6, 45, 46,
  47, 53, 70, 93, 201, 238, 240,
  261, 297, 298, 344; relations
  70–72, 74–75, 83, 87, 90–96
Vietnam-Cambodia Liberation
  Monument 93, 140
Vietnam Veterans of America
  Foundation 21
Vietnamese: attacks against 71,
  72, 74–76, 78; treatment of
  and attitude toward 39,
  70–75, 163, 253, 272, 274; villages 70, 77
vigilante attacks 136–138, 292
village life 219, 249–250,
  254–266, 268–275, 330–331
violence 28, 130–138, 151, 329;
  Angkor-era 134; *see also*
  domestic violence; rape; vigilante attacks; women
volleyball 23
Volunteer English School
  302–307, 341
voting 122–126

Wat Angkorechaborei 93
Wat Langka 19, 112
Wat Norea 287, 318–321, 341
Wat Ounalom 18, 20
Wat Phnom 7, 279
water festival 285
wats 17, 19, 20, 90, 92, 93, 95,
  96, 104, 105, 136, 149, 156, 194,
  195, 263, 285, 287, 293, 298,
  318, 322
WHO Model List of Essential
  Medicines 201
wildlife 233, 234, 245–252, 260;
  Batagur baska (Cambodian
  royal turtle) 248–252; bats

298–299; bears 244, 246;
  crocodiles 175, 176, 178, 233,
  244; elephants 7, 50, 56, 69,
  126, 148, 181, 233, 244, 254,
  260, 311; gaurs 244; Irrawaddy
  dolphins 246–248; monitor
  lizards 248, 262; primates 50,
  181, 185, 236, 246, 251, 254,
  257; tigers 61, 181, 233, 236,
  244, 246, 254, 310
Wildlife Conservation Society
  (WCS) 234, 245, 248–252,
  254–266, 339, 341
women 165–174; in Angkor
  times 169; attitude toward
  165–166, 168–169, 171, 172,
  270, 271, 280, 281, 295, 319,
  320, 323; in politics 167, 171,
  317; violence against 165, 167,
  169, 315, 317, 319; and work
  168; *see also* domestic violence; rape
Women for Prosperity 170–171
World Bank 199, 207
World Health Organization
  (WHO) 199, 201, 207, 221,
  222, 229–230, 339
World Monuments Fund 60,
  62, 339
World Trade Organization
  (WTO) 293, 294, 333, 339
World Vision 188–189
worms *see* illness

Yakuntur Island 149; *see also*
  Buddhism
yama (Amphetamines) 54, 193,
  194
Youk Chhang 41, 47–48, 145,
  286; *see also* Documentation
  Center of Cambodia
young generation 37, 106–108,
  171–172, 194, 248, 279–285,
  289–290, 324, 326
yuon 39, 71, 72, 151, 76, 338